MUSICAL VOICES OF EARLY MODERN WOMEN

Women and Gender in the Early Modern World

Series Editors: Allyson Poska and Abby Zanger

In the past decade, the study of women and gender has offered some of the most vital and innovative challenges to scholarship on the early modern period. Ashgate's new series of interdisciplinary and comparative studies, 'Women and Gender in the Early Modern World', takes up this challenge, reaching beyond geographical limitations to explore the experiences of early modern women and the nature of gender in Europe, the Americas, Asia, and Africa. Submissions of single-author studies and edited collections will be considered.

Titles in the series include:

Queenship and Political Power in Medieval and Early Modern Spain
Edited by Theresa Earenfight

The Bawdy Politic in Stuart England, 1660–1714
Political Pornography and Prostitution
Melissa M. Mowry

Widowhood and Visual Culture in Early Modern Europe
Edited by Allison Levy

Architecture and the Politics of Gender in Early Modern Europe
Edited by Helen Hills

Publishing Women's Life Stories in France, 1647–1720
From Voice to Print
Elizabeth C. Goldsmith

Maternal Measures
Figuring Caregiving in the Early Modern Period
Edited by Naomi J. Miller and Naomi Yavneh

Musical Voices
of Early Modern Women

Many-Headed Melodies

Edited by
THOMASIN LAMAY
Goucher College, USA

ASHGATE

Published by
Ashgate Publishing Limited
Gower House
Croft Road
Aldershot
Hants GU11 3HR
England

Ashgate Publishing Company
Suite 420
101 Cherry Street
Burlington, VT 05401-4405
USA

Ashgate website: http://www.ashgate.com

British Library Cataloguing in Publication Data
Musical voices of early modern women : many headed Melodies. — (Women and
     gender in the early modern world)
     1.Women musicians—Europe—History—17th century 2.Women musicians—
     Europe—History—16th century 3.Women in Music
     I.LaMay, Thomasin K.
     780.8'2'09032

Library of Congress Cataloging-in-Publication Data
Musical voices of early modern women : many headed melodies / edited by
Thomasin LaMay.
     p. cm. — (Women and gender in the early modern world)
 Includes bibliographical references and index.
 ISBN 0-7546-3742-5 (alk. paper)
1. Women musicians—Europe. 2. Music—Europe—16th century—History and
criticism. 3. Music—Europe—17th century—History and criticism.
I.Title. II. Series.

 ML82.M798 2004
 780'.82--dc22

2004008709

ISBN 0 7546 3742 5

Printed and bound in Great Britain by MPG Books Ltd, Bodmin, Cornwall

To all the many-headed contributors who went on this journey with me and with BOOK, as she has affectionately been called during her maturation

I thank you
This book is for you all.

Contents

List of Illustrations

List of Music Examples

List of Contributors

Enrique Alberto Arias is Associate Professor at the School for New Learning, DePaul University, and president of Ars Musica Chicago. He specializes in music of the Spanish Renaissance, but has also written about music in New Spain during the colonial period. He has published articles on these subjects in such periodicals as *Heterofonìa, Anuario Musical,* and *Latin American Music Review.* He also has done much work with resources at the Newberry Library, Chicago that relate to Spain and New Spain during the early modern period. Ars Musica Chicago has performed some of these works, as well as music from the Basilica of the Virgin of Guadalupe.

Linda Phyllis Austern is Associate Professor of Musicology at Northwestern University. Her numerous articles have appeared in such journals as the *Journal of the American Musicological Society, Modern Philology, Music and Letters* and *Renaissance Quarterly*, and in collections of essays on topics ranging from the history of music theory to gender studies to the history of medicine. She has published books with Gordon and Breach and with Routledge, and has written on a wide range of themes covering Western music from intellectual and cultural perspectives from the later Middle Ages through the era of rock and roll.

Colleen Baade is adjunct professor of Spanish at Concordia University in Seward, Nebraska. Her dissertation on the musical activity of female religious in early modern Castille (Duke University, 2001) represents her varied interests: she holds graduate degrees in Performance Practice, Musicology, Organ Performance and Spanish Language and Literatures. In fall, 2003, she continued her research into nuns' music-making with the assistance of a grant from the Spanish Ministry of Foreign Affairs.

Jeanice Brooks is currently Senior Lecturer in Music at the University of Southampton, United Kingdon. Previously she studied singing and music education in the United States and France, completing the Ph.D. at the Catholic University of America. Her interests include music and gender, patronage studies, modal theory, performance practice, source studies and text-music relations. She has written for *Journal of the American Musicological Society, Early Music History, Early Music, Revue de musicology, Journal of the Royal Musical Association* and *Revue belge de musicologie*, and is co-editor of *Music and Letters*. She has published a number of critical editions and received the Noah Greenberg award from the American Musicological Society for the best project combining performance practice and scholarship. Her book *Courtly Song in Late Sixteenth-Century France* was published in 2000 (University of Chicago Press).

Suzanne G. Cusick teaches music history and criticism at New York University. She has published widely on questions of gender and sexuality in relation to music-making, with special emphasis on early modern Italy and twentieth century North America. Her monograph on Francesca Caccini, tentatively titled *A Romanesca of Ones Own: womanhood, vocality and power in Francesca Caccini's World* is forthcoming by University of Chicago Press.

Beth L. Glixon is an instructor in music at the University of Kentucky. She specializes in seventeenth century Venetian opera, with a focus on opera production and the lives of opera singers. Her work has recently appeared in *Early Music* and *Musical Quarterly*, and includes significant new information on the composer and singer Barbara Strozzi. She and her husband Jonathan Glixon are currently writing a book on opera production in seventeenth century Venice.

Catherine E. Gordon-Seifert is Associate Professor of Music at Providence College, Rhode Island. Her work on religious and erotic parodies, airs as seductive dialogues, and the allemandes of Louis Couperin has appeared in various books and journals, and she is currently writing a book, *Music and the Language of Love in Late Seventeenth Century French Airs*. She is also a professional harpsichordist.

Shawn Marie Keener is a graduate student in Italian musical culture of the late middle ages and early modern eras at the University of Chicago. In fall, 2003, she served as visiting instructor at the Colorado College, where she received both the Cowperthwaite Prize for Excellence and Music and her B.A. in 1993.

Thomasin LaMay teaches jointly in the music, dance and women's studies departments at Goucher College, Baltimore, and she also designs and teaches interdisciplinary first year seminars on issues of popular culture, gender, and race. Her interests range from early modern to popular musics, especially those somehow informed by women. She has published editions of music by several early modern women (*Women Composers: Music Through the Ages, G.K. Hall*), and her performative story of Casulana's life recently appeared in *Music and Sexuality in Early Modern Music* (Routledge, 2002). Other publications on Monteverdi, French opera, and women in popular music appear in various places.

Pilar Ramos López is Professor of Music History at the University of Girona, Spain. She has published articles on Spanish sacred and theatrical music of the sixteenth and seventeenth centuries, and on problems of musical historiography. She is author of the books *La musica en la Catedral de Granada en la primera mitad del siglo XVII: Diego de Pontac* (Granada, 1994), *Feminismo y Música. Introducción crítica* (Madrid: 2003), and co-author of the introduction to the facsimile edition of an *Officium* by Hernando de Talavera, 1492 (Granada, 2003).

Inna Naroditskaya, native of the former Soviet Union, is currently an Assistant Professor at Northwestern University. She earned her Ph.D. and M.A. in ethnomusicology at the University of Michigan, and degrees in piano performance and musicology from the Azerbaijanian State Conservatory in Baku. Her areas of specialization include Russian musical culture, Eastern and Azerbaijanian music, and gender study. Her current work on women in Russian musical theater of the seventeenth and eighteenth centuries integrates a traditional historical approach with current methodology, allowing for investigation into underrepresented areas of women's scholarship.

Janet Pollack is Assistant Professor of music history and theory at the University of Puget Sound, Washington. She is also a keyboard performer and her research reflects both performance and historical components. She has written on topics ranging from the early English *Parthenia* to Thelonius Monk, and has taught English literature at Duke University, where she also received an International Travel Dissertation Fellowship.

Colleen Reardon is Associate Professor of Music and Director of Undergraduate Studies at Binghamton University (SUNY). Her interests center on musical culture in seventeenth century Siena. Her publications include *Holy Concord within Sacred Walls: Nuns and Music in Siena, 1575-1700* (Oxford University Press, 2002), and *Agostino Agazzari and Music at Siena Cathedral* (Oxford, 1993). She also served as editor for *Music Observed: Studies in Memory of William C. Holmes* (Harmonie Park Press, forthcoming) and *Musica Franca: Essays in Honor of Frank A. D'Accone* (Pendragon, 1996).

Raphael Seligmann is a businessman, freelance writer and independent scholar in Richmond, Virginia. He has a Ph.D. in English Literature from Brandeis University and is also working on a book titled *Roaring Girls*.

Jennifer Thomas is Assistant Professor of Music at University of Florida's School of Music, Gainesville. She specializes in music prior to 1750. She recently earned her Ph.D. from the University of Cincinnati's College-Conservatory, where she was awarded the University's Distinguished dissertation Award for *The Sixteenth-Century Motet: A Comprehensive Survey of the Repertory and Case Studies of the Core Texts, Composers, and Repertory*. She created the most comprehensive catalogue to date of the Renaissance motet, available in database form at http://www.arts.ufl.edu/motet/. The Renaissance motet remains at the center of her research, which also extends to biography, repertory formation, patterns of dissemination, and relationship between musical sources. Current research focuses on retrieving the repertory of the French royal court in the late 15th and early 16th centuries.

Amanda Eubanks Winkler is an Assistant Professor in the Department of Fine Arts, Syracuse University, specializing in English theater music of the seventeenth century. She has published on diverse subjects, including music and gender and political allegory. Her critical edition, *Music for Macbeth*, is forthcoming with A-

R Editions (2003). In 2001 she was awarded a fellowship funded by NEH to pursue research at the Folger Shakespeare Library. She is currently completing her book *Disorderly Subjects*, a study of the music for witches, melancholics and the mad on the seventeenth century English stage.

INTRODUCTION TO THE MANY-HEADED ONES

Chapter 1

Preliminaries

Thomasin LaMay

Many-headed melodies looks to address early modern women's musical activities across a broad spectrum of cultural events and settings. It takes as its premise the notion that while women may have been pushed to participate in music through narrower doors than their male peers, they nevertheless did so with enthusiasm, diligence, and success. They were there in many ways, but as women's lives were fundamentally different and more private than men's were, their strategies, tools, and appearances were sometimes also different and thus often unstudied in an historical discipline that primarily evaluated men's productivity. Countless writers have concurred that the most important *virtù* an early modern woman could embrace was that of silence. Silence protected her chastity, and the latter was a requisite commodity for her and her family.[1] Whether they were silent or not, however, the historical canon has placed these women's musical lives, and also the feminine presence in musical thought, representation, and creativity, behind the assumption that she was not allowed to be there on her own terms. The remarkable careers of a few, such as Francesca Caccini and Barbara Strozzi, have filtered through history as exceptional. Yet I suspect that they were initially permitted the nod of historical acknowledgement primarily because they seized the pen and behaved like men (historians could measure their output), and not because they may have been part of a larger musical culture which included women.[2]

---

[1] The importance of these themes during the period is reflected in a wide body of literature dealing with female behavior. Too numerous to cite here, the pervasiveness of these "virtues" for women can perhaps readily be summed up in Suzanne Hull's book, *Chaste, Silent and Obedient: English Books for Women 1475-1640* (San Marino, CA: Huntington Library, 1982). For further discussion on the "commodification" of women's chastity, and the paradox between her required virginity and a public culture which constantly bombarded women with sexual demands, see Elizabeth S. Cohen, "No Longer Virgins: Self-Presentation by Young Women in Late Renaissance Rome," in: *Refiguring Women. Perspectives on Gender and the Italian Renaissance*, ed. Marilyn Migiel and Juliana Schiesari (Ithaca: Cornell University Press, 1991), 169-191. Cohen stresses that chastity was literally a commodity for her father/brother/husband, something of intrinsic financial value.

[2] Important new studies on both these women reveal just how very inter-connected these women were. At the time of this writing we await a full biography on Francesca Caccini by Suzanne Cusick; also useful is her article "Thinking from Women's Lives:

"BOOK," as she has affectionately come to be called by her creators, explores the possibility of such a culture by examining early modern women in "many-headed ways" through the lens of musical production. We want to see how women composed, assuming that compositional gender strategies may have been used differently when applied through her vision; to know how women *were* composed, or represented and interpreted through music in a larger cultural context, and how her presence in that dialog situated her in social space; to trace how women found music as a means for communicating, for establishing intellectual power, for generating musical tastes, and for enhancing the quality of their lives. Some women performed publicly, and we want to see how it impacted on their lives and families. We inquire about the economics of music and women, and how in different situations some women may have been financially empowered or even in control of their own money-making. Some of our women were brash and barrier-defying, while many were simply trying to make the best lives they could in the context of what was possible. We glimpse at women from home, stage, work, and convent, from many classes and from culturally diverse cities and countries, and imagine a musical history centered in the realities of those lives.

This would seem a very useful, but also a quite possible and exciting way to re-visit our musical history. Recent scholarship has offered a veritable landslide of studies about early modern women, illuminating them as writers, thinkers, midwives, mothers, in convents, at home, as rulers.[3] The pioneer women's historian Margaret King observed that what is evident from this array of inter-disciplinary perspectives is "the clear articulation, for the first time in history and anywhere on the globe, of women's voices, the female voice."[4] She further suggested that this was not merely a transitional phase, but a movement, something tangible where women in many languages and from many social positions claimed that they could participate in their intellectual culture, male-dominated as it was, and they began to define themselves by speaking. "It is the age of the emergence of

---

Francesca Caccini after 1627, in: *Rediscovering the Muses. Women's Musical Traditions*, ed. Kimberly Marshall (Boston: Northeastern University Press, 1993), 206-226. Beth Glixon added significantly to our knowledge of Barbara Strozzi in her articles "New Light on the life and career of Barbara Strozzi," *Musical Quarterly* 81 (1997): 311-336, and "More on the life and death of Barbara Strozzi" *Musical Quarterly* 83 (1999): 134-142. This complements the considerable research by Ellen Rosand, "Barbara Strozzi, *virtuosissima cantatrice:* The Composer's Voice," *Journal of the American Musicological Society* 31 (1978): 241-281, reprinted in slightly revised form in *Women Making Music: The Western Art Tradition, 1150-1950*, ed. Jane Bowers and Judith Tick (Urbana: University of Illinois Press, 1986), 168-190.

[3] In this Ashgate series alone, *Women and Gender in the Early Modern World*, there are several important volumes on a wide variety of topics. They can be found under the Series Listings at http://www.ashgate.com. I am happy to report that a list of studies on early modern women is completely beyond the scope of this introduction.

[4] Margaret L. King, "Women's voices, the early modern, and the civilization of the west," *Shakespeare Studies* 25 (1997): 21.

the female voice – previously unheard, and not since, as some lament, silenced."[5] Despite copious recommendations for their silence, and the extraordinary punishments women could legally incur, they were going about the business of thinking, producing, and strategizing their lives. Our work adds to the mix of early modern studies a volume that correlates women's musical endeavors to *their* lives, which means that many of these stories will not necessarily embrace a standard musical repertoire, even as they seek to expand canonical borders.

The book is organized around certain kinds of musical participation rather than by geographic or chronological perspective, though the group headings are broadly interpreted through the individual essays, which can easily be read in any order. These groupings appeal to me because they offer comparative looks at different women who attempt or effect similar kinds of musical production in separate cultural settings. To that end, Linda Austern's opening piece serves as a larger introduction to this study because she examines the complex social and cultural factors that positioned music among the other arts and sciences for early modern women throughout Europe. What did it connote to be musical, or musically literate? How did such ability situate women among their male and female peers, and how could a musical self-presentation suggest a much broader sense of intellectual power? Using a rich array of visual iconography, Austern looks at how women represent, or "perform" themselves as highly accomplished through their associations with music. To be seen as musical might also imply that they were well educated across multiple disciplines. She especially looks at how women artists who portrayed themselves as musical had a much deeper understanding of music's position in the cultural framework then previously thought.

The first section, *Women En-Voiced*, counter-poses four essays which in various ways attempt to watch women as they are given voice or are silenced through musical convention, but also how they speak for themselves or even parody their own silencing through performance. These women come to us anonymously, yet their voices were clearly articulated in the popular music of their respective situations. Jeanice Brooks examines this en-voicing through the French *air de cour* during the late sixteenth century. While the vast majority of these strophic songs set courtly love poems narrated by men, a significant subgroup are told by women. Brooks focuses on texts spoken by aristocratic court women which purport to reflect their experiences in love relationships. She particularly looks at songs dealing with silence and secrecy, since these pieces occupy a paradoxical position in that they quite literally sing out about the need for women to be silent. Especially when performed by women, these airs offered fascinating possibilities for female musical agency.

In a different sense, Pilar Ramos López challenges notions of female silencing in Spanish musical culture. Spanish music theorists and educational treatises alike strongly prohibited musical learning for women. Cerone was so concerned that women would make music more effeminate (just beneath the surface was his even

[5] *Ibid.*

greater fear of being perceived as homosexual, or at the very least castrated) that he felt especial need to silence them. However, López notes that despite the strictures which were assumed to be in force, women were a palpable musical presence, especially in court comedies where they even sometimes cross-dressed and assumed male roles. It was their visible and audible presence on the musical stage that most likely provoked contemporary writings that would silence them. Those treatises subsequently led to a Spanish historiography that failed to consider women's musical contributions despite a popular literature that suggested otherwise. López also offers for English readers a vast amount of Spanish source documentation and evaluation not hitherto available to us.

Shawn Marie Keener looks at the role of the courtesan in re-voicing the *giustiniana*, a popular fifteenth-century Venetian song cultivated by the elite in northern Italian courts. While we have long known of the courtesan's presence in Italian cultural centers,[6] Keener suggests that the mythology surrounding these women, and the dismissal and silencing of their arts as mere "delights," has served to obscure their very real artistic contributions. It was in fact the courtesan's art of illusion, her ability to elude definition and at the same time sell her elite clientele a construction of an aristocratic self which was itself an illusion, that allowed her to move fluidly among gender and class boundaries. *Cortegiane oneste* and other marginal women flourished in the notationless universe of improvisatory song. Not simply unwritten, their music defied transcription. The legacy of their mastery of illusion was the creation of new conceptual space for women in the public sphere.

Catherine Gordon-Seifert's essay closes this section and brings us back to the French air a century further along from Brooks' observations. She points to an extraordinary stylistic transformation that happened alongside changing concepts of musical-gender relationships. Mid-century airs allowed *galant* males who lamented the loss of a beloved an "effeminate" display of emotion, while women were depicted as *honnête femmes* who boldly shunned male advances. Near the end of the seventeenth century, however, an increasingly masculinized public sphere identified with the reign of Louis XIV coerced Parisian society to project men as bellicose and untouched by a gentler emotion. This was overtly reflected in a new musical style which also quieted and over-sentimentalized women. In this scenario, women clearly began to lose the range of expression previously afforded them, their musical voices conflated into a sentimental "old" melodic style, or that voice which, perhaps, men *used* to be. Masculine musical tones became a "new" style, a voice men needed to sound out in an improved world order where they were no longer affected by the passionate expressions of an earlier melodic language now designated and debased as merely effeminate.

Our second section, *Women on Stage*, focuses directly on public musical performances by women and attempts to position them within their cultural

---

[6] In this light I am grateful for a fascinating conference, The Courtesan's Arts, presented 5-7 April 2002, by the Franke Institute for the Humanities of the University of Chicago, and the Center for Renaissance Studies at the Newberry Library.

settings. In various ways, the writers try to assess what it meant for these women to be on stage, how public exposure impacted on their personal lives and musical conventions, and how their musical personae were seen in their communities. Amanda Eubanks Winkler describes not a specific performer, but the musical settings for the erotic character Venus, goddess of love, as she appeared on the English stage during the late sixteenth and seventeenth centuries. Her character was manipulated to suit the needs of current political figures, and she evolved over the century from a lustful, seductive and destructive character who needed to be curbed to a positive symbol for the Stuart "court of love." During the late seventeenth century composers endowed Venus with extremely persuasive musical conventions, making her one of the most compelling and powerful characters on the Restoration stage. By looking at these musical entertainments through the lens of this female character, Eubanks Winkler is also able to trace many societal reconfigurations that Venus both reflected and enacted.

Raphael Seligmann writes about the musical performances of the notorious Mary Frith, whose stage name was Moll Cutpurse. One of the most overtly rebellious female characters to appear on any stage, in 1611 she sang at the Fortune playhouse wearing boots and breeches and carrying a sword. She entertained the audience with stories about sex, and accompanied her singing with a lute. Among her many gestures of defiance, Seligmann describes how the musical aspects of her performance would have struck audiences as particularly disturbing. She threw standard positions about identity and musical artifice into confusion, wearing men's clothes but not pretending to be male, and playing the lute before men on stage without trying to seduce them. She refused to be the seductress, the stereotype of a woman musician, and for a period of time she actively enjoyed the cooperation of the theater establishment. Seligmann especially looks at the comedy *The Roaring Girl*, where Mary's character uses song to offer her private thoughts in order to gain sympathy for a woman who might otherwise be dismissed as freakish.

Beth Glixon focuses, through several kinds of documentation, on the life and performing career of Caterina Porri, who sang primarily on the Venetian stage from 1654-1684. In a venue where most women remained popular for only a decade or less, Porri was highly acclaimed for at least thirty years. A native of Rome, she – like many Roman women singers – traveled north to Venice to make her living in an atmosphere which was more encouraging for women. Glixon examines this particular phenomenon, and also the remarkable burgeoning of women who learned singing in Rome, and then either re-located to Venice or traveled back and forth in order to participate in the vigorous competition for female singing roles. Using letters and previously unseen archival testimony, Glixon traces not only Porri's singing career, but her two marriages, an accusation of murder, her acquisition of extraordinary wealth, her childbearing, and the impact of her singing career on her private life and that of her children and husbands.

Inna Naroditskaya then takes us to the remarkable territory of the tsarinas' Russia during the late seventeenth and early eighteenth centuries. This somewhat later date reflects a difference in Russian history and perhaps also enlightens us as to what determined an "early modern period." For this era, marked by a dramatic reformation of Russian society and culture, was largely defined by several women tsarinas who governed – gained power and voice – in a male-dominated empire. If the historic designator "early modern" connotes a time, it also, as recognized earlier by Margaret King, suggests an eruption of the female voice, and this happened somewhat later in Russia. Naroditskaya describes how a chain of female rulers enacted major political and social reforms, transformed court etiquette, engineered the concept of a Russian nation, and encouraged the development of arts and sciences. Passionate supporters and patrons of theater, they wrote plays, and staged and acted in productions. On the other end of the social spectrum were the serf actress-singers, seldom known by name, and separated out from the masses by their beauty and talent. They were owned by noblemen, and became publicly exposed body-performer-objects. Virtually ignored in Russian historical accounts, women's substantial involvement in staged musical theater leads Naroditskaya to a significant reassessment of the traditional history of early modern Russia.

Women from the Convents forms a third set of essays. Recent and thoughtful scholarly attention to specific convent settings, especially by Robert Kendrick, Craig Monson, and Colleen Reardon, has already offered important insights to this subject.[7] But convents were such an important place in women's lives – not only for musical opportunities, but in a more profound sense as a second or only home for many women – that we could not fail to include them in this study. We have tried instead to visit them in somewhat different ways and in places that have not been previously considered. Colleen Reardon's essay details a warmly personal life story about one family's struggles to find a happy solution for their daughters, since convent life was a necessity for them. The custom of forcing young women to enter convents against their will was both denounced and widely practiced throughout early modern Italy. However, letters found by Reardon and written by Sienese women who belonged to the prominent Chigi family reveal that the decision to consign daughters to the cloister was not always made heartlessly. Reardon focuses specifically on Olimpia Chigi Gori, whose choice of the unusual Sienese institution *Il Refugio* for her daughters revealed much about the kind of life she wished them to experience. This convent in fact insisted that its members periodically leave the cloister for outside events, a highly unusual practice in a time when complete enclosure was the norm, so Olimpia took her daughters to musical events. Reardon speculates that it was the love of music, passed on from

---

[7] See especially Robert L. Kendrick, *Celestial Sirens: Nuns and their Music in early modern Milan* (Oxford: Clarendon Press, 1996); Craig Monson, *Disembodied Voices: Music and Culture in an early modern Italian Convent* (Berkeley: University of California Press, 1995); *The Crannied Wall: Women, Religion, and the Arts in Early Modern Europe*, ed. Craig Monson (Ann Arbor: University of Michigan Press, 1992); and Colleen Reardon, *Holy Concord within Sacred Walls: Nuns and Music in Siena, 1575-1700* (Oxford: Oxford University Press, 2002).

mother to daughter, that persuaded her once unhappily enclosed child Laura to enjoy an environment which nurtured her musical talent.

Colleen Baade opens up for us the scarcely studied situation of nun musicians in early modern Castile. Her primary sources include contracts for reception and profession of nuns who were given dowry waivers in exchange for musical service, and monastery account books which recorded regular stipends paid to nun musicians. She considers questions about the economic and social background of nun musicians, why they were offered financial compensation, and what that money was actually worth to these women. She describes how girls were prepared from a young age to become nun musicians because their families had no other means of paying a nun's dowry. Once "hired," these women were expected to serve their monasteries for life, and were required to pay off their dowry if they reneged on musical duties, or were found not to have sufficient musical talent. While allowed a musical career that may have been rewarding for them, socially they were similar in status to nuns who performed domestic chores. Yet Baade also details the remarkable resilience and self-sufficiency of some musical nuns as they gained positions of authority and were able to circumvent those who would lessen their payments in fiscally difficult times.

Enrique Alberto Arias' subsequent discussion of Sor Juana Inèz de la Cruz allows us to draw fascinating comparisons between the situation for Spanish nuns and what seems to have been a far more culturally liberated life for cloistered women in Neuva España at the end of the seventeenth century. Sor Juana was one of Mexico's most prodigious intellects during the early modern period, and Arias looks at her remarkable career through the lens of her musical background and interests. She spent most of her life in the S. Jerónimo convent in Mexico City, where she enjoyed considerable freedom to write poetry, conduct scientific experiments, and converse with Mexico's intellectual leadership. Music was perhaps her most powerful stimulus. She had a profound grasp of its theoretic principles, and read and commented on Pedro Cerone's *El Melopeo y Maestro* and Kircher's *Musurgia Universalis*. Arias examines the reasons for her selection of these authors and re-evaluates her resonance to their approaches in the context of the vibrant (and largely unstudied) musical life in Mexico during this era. He also looks at the place of music in her poetry, and further inquires as to why music was for her a dominating image of conflict, harmony, and resolution. He concludes with a look at the present-day annual Sor Juana Festival held at the Chicago Mexican Fine Arts Museum, providing a fascinating juxtaposition of the "early" and the "modern."

The final section of our book, *Women, Collections, and Publishing*, is perhaps the most wide-ranging in content, though all the articles deal in some way with women's visions for musical collections. Their individual trajectories towards this end are all quite different and it seemed fitting to put them last in our volume only because their stories keenly reflect the many-headedness of women's musical participation in early modern culture. Firstly, Jennifer Thomas comes to a powerful new interpretation of a long-vexing musicological mystery surrounding the manuscript denoted as London Royal 8.G.vii. This collection was produced at the

Netherlands court, and given as a gift to the English monarchs Henry VIII and Katherine of Aragon by Marguerite of Austria. Scholars have long puzzled about why the collection included five settings of the classical text *Dulces exuviae*, which details the suicidal thoughts of a queen, since the consecutive repetition of a single text of this nature is unprecedented in early musical sources. But Thomas traces this text to Marguerite's own personal *chansonnier* (now designated as BrusBR 228), of which she was both author and patron, where it in fact appeared twice. This led her to re-examine the significant personal links between Katherine and Marguerite, who had established a close friendship at the Spanish court after the latter's marriage to Katherine's brother Juan. Both women subsequently endured parallel tragedies: the deaths of their young husbands, stillborn children, and the burdens uniquely borne by women in the powerful ruling houses of Europe. By asking what might have prompted the outpouring of five settings of this sorrowful text, Thomas convincingly argues that these pieces convey Marguerite's compassion for Katherine over her five unfulfilled pregnancies. She offers a poignant re-interpretation of its purpose as a gift of understanding from one woman to another in difficult circumstances, and through a medium usually associated with formal diplomacy.

My own article details the musical and textual choices of the Italian composer and singer, Madalena Casulana, who published three known collections of madrigals in 1568, 1570, and 1583, and also had individual pieces published in anthologies. This essay looks especially at her first published collection, *Il primo libro de madrigali a Quattro voci*, printed in 1568 by Scotto. Casulana wrote in her dedication that she insisted on publishing her music in order to show the world the "vain error of men" who believed that women could not achieve such goals, and she was the first woman to publish collections. She was also a highly acclaimed singer, and I elected to look at her compositions through the particular vocal technique for early modern women, which included and exploited a visibly undulating throat. Poems about her singing help describe the kind of mouth and flapping flesh that were prized by those who watched women singers in close proximity. Casulana's texts often seem to speak from a male subjectivity, and while there are notable exceptions I wanted to know, in light of Margaret King's declaration that women were asserting their right to speak as women, what it was that Casulana hoped for us to hear from her. What emerges is a woman who was clearly aware of the meaning behind traditional madrigal texts and the musical gestures which informed them. By her very refusal to ignore these ideologies, she in effect re-wrote them, not only to show the world that women could claim intellectual space, but also to help re-create the image of her patron, Isabella Medici-Orsini, whose extra-marital affair and public music making had rendered her whorish in the eyes of her family.

Janet Pollack's essay recognizes how a woman's musical tastes and talents fashioned an important musical collection. She proposes that princess Elizabeth Stuart (1596-1662), the only daughter of King James I of England and VI of Scotland, participated directly in musical creation by directing composers' artistic choices in ways previously unconsidered. Her musical preferences, concerns (political and personal), and performing ability directly contributed to the creation of the *Parthenia*, one of the most celebrated English musical collections and the only published book of keyboard music in England before the Restoration. The collection was a wedding present for her, and intended for her personal practice. Pollack examines Elizabeth's personal letters, official documents concerning her musical education, newly uncovered contemporary descriptions of her musical abilities, and the technical demands of *Parthenia*. Together these sources paint for us an accomplished musician who empowered as muse, rather than as patron or composer, but who had formidable impact on the newly-developing English keyboard style, an influence which has been critically overlooked in favor of the composers who actually penned the music.

As BOOK comes full circle, we close with an epilogue by Suzanne Cusick, who not only brings together various woman-centered threads that permeate our stories but then locates them in a '600 Gynecentric View of Francesca Caccini as she moved among women. The material here comes from Cristoforo Bronzini's *Della dignita e l'eccellenza delle donne*, commissioned by the two women who ruled Florence as Regents in the 1620s, Archduchess Maria Maddalena d'Austria and her mother-in-law Granduchess Christine de Lorraine. It formed part of an intensive cultural program to justify female rule. Ranging over many topics, it also locates Francesca in a conception of musicality that is made entirely of women and women's musical practices. The musical world this source projects avoids all the arguments for new styles, words as governing musical choices in madrigals, or the emergence of opera – the canonized view of music history reported to us in books. Instead it is all about chamber music, private performances sponsored by women to praise the Virgin, and convent music. All the music-makers are women, and the praises constitute a composite portrait of the woman musician in which most of what we think we know about Francesca Caccini turns out to be not exceptional, but a particularly high level of achievement from inside a completely normal category of existence: the erudite musical woman.

The title for this book derives from the complex "many-headed melodies" sung by Medusa and her two gorgon sisters. These melodies were first described in Pindar's Twelfth *Pythion Ode*. As observed by Charles Segal, Pindar's *Ode* exemplifies the process for mythologizing and mystifying the female voice in western culture.[8] It was written in 490 B.C.E. to celebrate the victory of Midas in the flute contest at Delphi and signifies as one of the founding myths about the female voice. Medusa is one of three gorgon sisters born to sea creatures. Her name designates power, meaning "she who commands," and the word gorgon derives from the Indo-European root *garj*, describing a fearful shriek, roar, or shout. These women were in a very corporeal sense women heard, women with powerful voices who sang a wide range of feelings. Medusa had the misfortune to

---

[8] Charles Segal, "The Gorgon and the nightingale: the voice of female lament and Pindar's Twelfth *Pythian Ode*" in: *Embodied Voices. Representing Female Vocality in Western Culture*, ed. Leslie C. Dunn and Nancy A. Jones (Cambridge: Cambridge University Press, 1994), 17.

be raped in Athena's sacred space. So the angry goddess, who kept her virginal eyes averted during the scene, took revenge on Medusa for "allowing" her sanctuary to be defiled and sent Perseus to kill her.

Medusa was be-headed – an ultimate silencing of the female voice and a veritable isolation of the source of its production – and at her death she was mourned by her sister gorgons with plangent wails and dirge-cries described as "many-headed melodies." These sounds were appropriated by Athena, who wove them into only once voice, their power and diversity folded into a single theme deemed fit for the most masculine of all gods, Apollo. The passionate emotion of the gorgons and their gaping mouths was transformed into submissiveness, a sound emerging from the constricted passage of a single flute that now "produces the many-headed melody at all-male contests of art and athletics."[9] This was a formidable cultural appropriation as it captured their lament – an expression generally sanctioned for women – and re-fashioned it into a musical artifice that fit the model for civic propriety. The many-headed became one, behind the frame of Medusa's violently enforced silence.

Medusa was largely obliterated from view during the medieval era, but came back to life during the early modern period as an evocative image that had special resonance in the popular mind.[10] It seemed to me both curious and highly signifying that this Medusa, with her connotations both of female impropriety and power, should surface again just as women were also emerging as a voice, asserting a right to be heard. The early modern Medusa derived her identity largely from Book 4 of Ovid's *Metamorphosis*. It is in his story that we hear how Medusa could turn to stone any who looked at her; how Perseus engaged his shield, in the form of a mirror, to deflect the danger of the Gorgon's gaze so he could slay her; and how he appropriated the power of her gaze by then impressing the image of her dead face upon his shield so he might then turn others to stone. We also learn that originally Medusa was beautiful, with resplendent hair, but she was rendered a fearful monster after being raped:

> Medusa was astonishingly fair;
> she was desired and contended for –
> so many jealous suitors hoped to win her.

---

[9] *Ibid.*, 23. Segal argues further that Athena's musical-vocal appropriation and transformation also recognizes the cultural shift happening in Greece at the time, whereby the male sky gods replaced female goddess figures who still had much popularity among the population. Athena's musical re-creation of the gorgons' voices banishes the "radical otherness" of their wail to a world of pain and suffering, far from the city's music, rituals, athletics and sacred space. Brought within the city as a well-healed flute tune, the dirge has become the "imitation of the wail" through an instrumental, rather than living, female voice. The flute song in effect neutralizes its corporeal origins.

[10] For a fascinating discussion of the history of Medusa and the gorgons throughout western culture, see Stephen R. Wilk, *Medusa, Solving the Mystery of the Gorgon* (Oxford: Oxford University Press, 2000); this particular early modern phenomenon appears on p. 92.

Her form was graced by many splendors, yet
there was no other beauty she possessed
that could surpass the splendor of her hair –
and this I learned from one who said he'd seen her.
Her beauty led the Ruler of the Sea
to rape her in Minerva's sanctuary
(so goes the tale). Jove's daughter turned aside
chaste eyes: the goddess hid her face behind
her aegis – but she made Medusa pay:
she changed that Gorgon's hair to horrid snakes.
And to this day, to this day, Minerva, to dismay
and terrify her foes, wears on her breast
the very snakes that she herself had set –
as punishment – upon Medusa's head."[11]

In Ovid's epic, the many-headed song of the gorgons is gone altogether, represented not even by the flute, but by a silenced, contained, framed and re-appropriated symbol of what was *once* an ultimate female musical vocality. The very fact that Medusa was re-invented and re-silenced so vigorously during the early modern period only strengthens our notion that women were indeed becoming many-voiced, taking multiple opportunities to engage not only in musical but in other vocal forms of public declamation. Why else would such effort be made to silence with such horrifying and total brutality a once beautiful and musical woman? So, with all due respect to the goddess Athena, we attempt to unravel her single tune and find again some of its many threads, some of the exuberant voices whose tones and stories have been overlooked. And we hope that Medusa might enjoy hearing, wherever she may lurk, the many-headed melodies of women making music in their own ways.

---

[11] *The Metamorphoses of Ovid*, transl. Allen Mandelbaum (New York: Harcourt Brace and Co, 1993), 141-142.

Chapter 2

Portrait of the Artist as (Female) Musician

Linda Phyllis Austern

Slanderous tongues shoot their darts as they please. They concoct satires and invectives against the female sex, singling out as their greatest accomplishments the use of the needle, distaff, and spindle. . . However, it is a fact that that unhappy sex, because of being reared within the confines of the home and kept from the exercise of various disciplines, becomes soft, and has little aptitude for noble pursuits. Nevertheless, in spite of man the female sex triumphs[.]

Carlo Ridolfi (1648)

When I went back into the studio after a period of other activity, I began working and discovered that. . .Everything you make is a self-portrait.

Peggy A. Reinecke (1992)

In spite of Man, or occasionally aided by an extraordinary one, early modern Woman triumphed again and again. Contrary to influential male conduct writers who would confine her to the home and keep her from many worthwhile pursuits, her accomplishments went well beyond the personal exercise of needle, distaff, and spindle. She did not always maintain the silence and invisibility prescribed for her. The musical and visual arts were only two of many areas in which she prospered as private and public practitioner. In the face of customs that kept her from standard paths to many occupations, the early modern woman worked not only as composer and painter, but as money-lender and shipper, butcher and brewer, miller and iron-monger, among other professions still often considered more suited to men. She also excelled as weaver, spinner, midwife, and agricultural husbander, sometimes as a member of a male-dominated guild.[1] Nonetheless, modern scholars are still in the process of re-discovering precisely who the early modern woman was, and how

---

[1] For an excellent survey of the professions practiced by working women during the middle of the early modern era, see Alice Clark, *Working Life of Women in the Seventeenth Century* (London, 1919; reprint ed. New York: Augustus M. Kelley, 1968); see also Margaret L. King, "Women of the Renaissance," in: *Renaissance Characters*, ed. Eugenio Garin, transl. Lydia Cochrane (Chicago and London: University of Chicago Press, 1991), 217-222.

diverse her many intellectual and cultural roles.[2] Within music alone, she was amateur and professional, patron and performer, composer, critical listener, and publisher. She was the highly trained darling of the stage, and the household physician whose music healed and prevented illness.[3] She taught and learned from other women, as well as men. She sang and played instruments in home, church, salon, theater, and the barn where she milked her cows. She could read and write in several languages, and she was illiterate. She was daughter, wife, and mother; nun, servant, monarch, and courtesan. She was trained to many musics, and for many purposes. Numerous words and images from the late fifteenth century through the Age of Enlightenment present such varied women musicians in satire, allegory, and in admiration. Yet how did they see themselves? Beyond the notes and texts of their music, how did they wish to be perceived?

Among the body of artifacts and information relating to early modern women musicians stands a series of self-portraits made by some of the most celebrated artists of their eras, who happened to be women who chose to represent themselves in musical roles. They not only constitute a unique and valuable source of information about the self-perception of musically trained women. They also provide insight into the changing position of music in relation to the arts and

---

[2] Even feminist scholars of the last quarter of the twentieth century still succumbed enough to previous male propaganda that Joan Kelly could conclude in a famous essay of 1977 that women did not share in the intellectual and cultural advances of the fifteenth and sixteenth centuries; see Joan Kelly Gadol, "Did Women Have a Renaissance?" in: *Becoming Visible: Women in European History*, ed. Renate Bridenthal and Claudia Koonz (Boston: Houghton Mifflin, 1977), 137-164; reprinted in Joan Kelly [Gadol], *Women, History and Theory: The Essays of Joan Kelly* (Chicago: University of Chicago Press, 1984), 19-50. The problem is not so much a lack of participation in many spheres by early modern women, or even early modern men's accounts of the exceptions to women's limited (ideal) upbringing, but nineteenth and twentieth century attitudes toward gender and achievement; in a surprisingly egalitarian point-by-point comparison of the intellectual capacities and education offered to women and to men, famous psychologist Carl E. Seashore concludes in an article of 1940 that there had been "no great women composers" because "Woman's fundamental urge is to be beautiful, loved and adored as a person; man's urge is to provide and achieve in a career," in Seashore, "Why No Great Women Composers?," *Music Educator's Journal* (1940): 21 and 88. "[T]he [early modern] texts that I discuss find a woman who has always existed, yet has not been recognized in recent times," writes Pamela Joseph Benson fifty-two years after Seashore and fifteen years after Kelly in *The Invention of the Renaissance Woman: The Challenge of Female Independence in the Literature and Thought of Italy and England* (University Park, PA: Pennsylvania State University Press, 1992), 2. Scholars of women's cultural history are still sweeping aside the myths of their own generation, and of those who trained them.

[3] For further information on the link between women's music and the capacities to heal and nurture in domestic setting, see Linda Phyllis Austern, "'My Mother Musicke': Music and Early Modern Fantasies of Embodiment," in: *Maternal Measures: Figuring Caregiving in the Early Modern Period*, ed. Naomi J. Miller and Maomi Yavneh (Aldershot, Burlington, Singapore and Sydney: Ashgate, 2000), 240-247.

sciences, to gender, and to female accomplishment over more than two centuries. Perhaps most importantly, through the manipulation of well-established visual and cultural codes concerning both music and feminine propriety, these images begin to indicate how capable, determined women succeeded in multiple male-dominated arenas between the sixteenth and eighteenth centuries.

The period of European history between the later Middle Ages and the Enlightenment was a watershed not only in music and the other arts and sciences. Understanding of the self, paths toward social status, and the categorical relations between forms of human knowledge also underwent radical revision. The woman professional artist, like her sister in the composition of secular music, was a creation of the era.[4] In fact, individual women, like their male counterparts, deliberately fashioned selves as they created representational works, and as they wrote, and lived.[5] What we now accept as Fine Arts (referred to as "Polite Arts" when the category was young), proper "finishing" for a young lady of good pedigree as well as an appropriate range of professions for certain individuals, were only linked together from among ancient liberal and mechanical arts at the end of the era.[6] The unshakeable image of "artistic genius" as tormented Man often inspired by his supernatural (and super-passive) muse came later.[7] The early

---

[4] See Francis Borzello, *A World of Our Own: Women as Artists Since the Renaissance* (New York: Watson-Guptill Publications, 2000), 20-28; Jane Bowers, "The Emergence of Women Composers in Italy, 1566-1700," in: *Women Making Music: The Western Art Tradition*, ed. Jane Bowers and Judith Tick (Urbana and Chicago: University of Illinois Press, 1987), 116-161; Germaine Greer, *The Obstacle Race: The Fortunes of Women Painters and Their Work* (New York: Farrar Straus Giroux, 1979), 169-188; Mary Lierly, "Women Painters: A Sense of Time and Place," in: *Images of the Self as Female: The Achievement of Women Artists in Re-Envisioning Feminine Identity*, ed. Kathryn N. Benzel and Lauren Pringle de la Vars (Lewiston/Queenston/Lampeter: The Edwin Mellen Press, 1992), 140-142; and Joanna Woods-Marsden, *Renaissance Self-Portraiture: The Visual Construction of Identity and the Social Status of the Artist* (New Haven and London: Yale University Press, 1998), 188-190.

[5] See Benson, *Invention of the Renaissance Woman*, 2; Stephen Greenblatt, *Renaissance Self-Fashioning From More to Shakespeare* (Chicago and London: University of Chicago Press, 1980), 1-2; and Woods-Marsden, *Self-Portraiture*, 9.

[6] See Cosmetti (pseudonym), *The Polite Arts* (London: W. Roach, 1768), dedication "To the Ladies;" Paul Oskar Kristeller, "The Modern System of the Arts," *Journal of the History of Ideas* 1 (1951):   496-527, and 13 (1952): 17-46; reprinted in Kristeller, *Renaissance Thought II: Papers on Humanism and the Arts* (New York, Evanston and London: Harper Torchbooks, 1965), 163-212; *The Polite Arts, or, a Dissertation on Poetry, Painting, Musick, Architecture, and Eloquence* (London: J. Osborn and T. Lownds, 1749), 4-7; and [Jean André] Rouquet, *The Present State of the Arts in England* [N.P.: London, 1755], 10.

[7] The modern notion of genius (and its burden of masculine gendering) has roots as old as Classical antiquity, but is primarily a product of the late eighteenth and nineteenth centuries; see Christine Battersby, *Gender and Genius: Towards a Feminist Aesthetics* (Bloomington and Indianapolis: Indiana University Press, 1989), 3-24.

modern women who presented themselves on canvas as musicians solidified their status as learned and widely accomplished persons within their cultures, exceptional but not completely impossible creatures. By so doing, they advertised their capability to live and work among their wealthy (potential) patrons in a complex economy of exchange. They also used subtle devices to empower creative, cultured, learned women in ways generally inaccessible to men. Each one demonstrated technical excellence and mastery of the subtle gradations through which physical reality and deeper meaning overlapped. The two eldest, Sophonisba Anguissola and Lavinia Fontana, perhaps in competition with each other, reflect on the relative positions of music and painting in sixteenth century thought even while commenting on women's participation in courtly culture. Marietta Robusti and Artemisia Gentileschi demonstrate understanding of allegorical practices more often related to, and by, men. The youngest, Angelica Kaufmann, positions herself into a traditionally male allegory to show a subtle distinction between the gendering of professionalism and dilettantism. All of them cleverly balance social expectations of themselves as arts professionals and as women, not always contiguous categories.

The early modern era witnessed a transformation in the relationship between objects of the senses of sight and hearing, which ultimately influenced social perception of artists and musicians of both genders. There was a growing rift between the medieval intellectual tradition of the liberal arts and the experiential aesthetic that dominates the more modern category of fine arts. Thinkers and practitioners across a wide range of disciplines continued to re-categorize art, craft, and science by reconsidering relative aims and modes of creation and production. The seven liberal arts, including music, had long stood as the pinnacle of human learning. They both required and conferred intellectual refinement. These were the disciplines of the erudite and noble, female as well as male. The mechanical arts, including painting, sculpture, and armory, were mere tradecraft, conventionally practiced by unlettered guildsmen. German philosopher Gregor Reisch's important compendium of human knowledge of 1517, for example, not only privileges the seven liberal arts above the mechanical ones. He dignifies each of the former with its own chapter, while he relegates the latter to a single sub-section of his much later discussion of moral philosophy.[8] At the end of the same century, however, the English occult philosopher John Dee conjoins the traditional liberal arts of astronomy, geometry and music with such previously unrelated fields as perspective (drawing), architecture, and navigation as "methodical arts" originating

---

[8] Gregor Reisch, *Margarita Philosophica* ([Basel: M. Furter,] 1517), sigs. K8^v-Y2 and Rr3-Rr3^v.

in mathematics.[9] By the late eighteenth century, music and painting together belonged to "the Polite Arts. . . those whose first Object is to please."[10]

The old system, and the relative status it conferred on its practitioners, was already under careful scrutiny by the late fifteenth century. Many scholars, music theorists, and traditional intellectuals like Reisch continued to reinforce the Classical hierarchy of arts and crafts well into the seventeenth century. Meanwhile, a new class of artisans had begun to argue eloquently for a more esteemed place for neglected intellectual products. In words that reflected concurrent discourse about the five senses, Leonardo da Vinci compares the liberal art of music unfavorably to painting:

> But painting excels and is superior in rank to music, because it does not perish immediately after its creation, as happens unfortunately with music. Rather painting endures. . . . It is to be more praised and exalted than music. . . [S]eeing that you have placed music amongst the liberal arts, either you should place painting there, or remove music.[11]

A generation later, Baldassar Castiglione transferred this idea into the realm of courtly conduct in his highly influential manual for the gently bred. In particular, Castiglione addressed the inferior status granted to painters, and the fact that the advantage of studying music (but not painting) was backed by an enormous Classical literature. Following a lengthy section on why the ideal courtier should be trained in music, one of the main interlocutors in the dialogue begins:

> I will talke of an other thing, whiche for that it is of importance (in my judgemente) I believe our Courtyer ought in no wise to leave it out. And y^t is ye cunning in drawyng, and the knowledge in the very arte of peincting. And wonder ye not if I wish this feat in him, whiche now a dayes perhappes is counted an handycraft and ful little to become a gentleman; for I remember I have read that the men of olde time, and especially in all *Greece* would have Gentlemens children in the schooles to apply peincting, as a matter both honest and necessary. And this was received in the first degree of liberal artes[.][12]

---

[9] Dee, preface to [Euclid], *The Elements of Geometrie*, transl. Henry Billingsley, preface by John Dee (London: John Daye), sigs. *.iiii-A.iiii.

[10] *The Polite Arts*, 7. See also Cosmetti (pseudonym), *The Polite Arts, Dedicated to the Ladies*, p. 1. For a history of the concept of the fine arts and its partial evolution from the disintegration of the older liberal arts system, see Kristeller, "The Modern System of the Arts."

[11] Martin Kemp, *Leonardo on Painting* (New Haven: Yale University Press, 1989), 35-37.

[12] Baldessare [Baldassar] Castiglione, *Il libro del cortegiano* (Venezia: Aldo, 1528), transl. as *The Courtyer of Count Baldessar Castilio*, transl. Thomas Hoby (London: Wyllyam Seres, 1561), sig. Jiiiᵛ.

Castiglione cleverly cites (or invents) unimpeachable ancient authority for adding painting and drawing to the most reputable musical studies for his ideal courtier. Furthermore, in his long section about music, he manages not only to insinuate painting, but to name even more worthy visual artists than musicians of his own era:

> Mark the musick, wherein are harmonies sometime of base soun[d]e and slow, and otherwhile very quicke and of new divises, yet do they all recreat a man. . . And no lesse doeth our *Marchetto Cara* move in his singinge; but with a more softe harmonye, that by a delectable waye and full of mourninge sweetnesse maketh tender and perceth the mind, and sweetly imprinteth in it a passion full of great delite. Sundrye thinges in lyke maner do equally please oure eyes somuche, that a man shall have muche to do to judge in which they most delite. Behould in peincting Leonardo [da Vinci], Mantegna, Raphael, Michelangelo, George of Castelfranco: they are all most excellent dooers, yet are they in working unlike, but in any of them a man wold not judge y^t there wanted ought in his kind of trade: for every one is knowen to be of most perfection after his maner.[13]

Throughout the sixteenth century and into the seventeenth, participation in the visual arts became increasingly acceptable for courtly amateurs; and exceptional ability as painter, sculptor, or architect occasionally helped elevate those born to lesser rank to the status of courtier. However, particularly during the earlier phases of this transition, music retained its ancient cachet as highly regarded liberal art. The performer of art-musics became ennobled, or solidified high status in the most influential intellectual and cultural milieux. The visual artist was still often a mere maker of the useful and the beautiful.[14]

As Castiglione implies so eloquently, aesthetic theory during his era was dominated by a body of technical terms and forms of rhetoric designed to particularize affective parallels between the arts. Through them, the powers and privileges of one art could be rendered equal or superior to another. By the end of the sixteenth century, and throughout the next, musical and visual arts so often evoked each other as well as poetry that unification through multiple sense experience became an ideal.[15] Although there had been little agreement about the ranking of the five senses from the days of Aristotle onward, sight and hearing had

---

[13] *Ibid.*, sigs. Gii^v-Giii.

[14] See Peter Burke, "The Courtier," in: *Renaissance Characters*, ed. Eugenio Garin, transl. Lydia Cochrane (Chicago and London: University of Chicago Press, 1991), 113-118; and Chastel, "The Artist," in *Renaissance Characters*, 180-183. For further information about the social status of the Renaissance visual artist, see Woods-Marsden, *Renaissance Self-Portraiture*, 1-9.

[15] See Ernest B. Gilman, *The Curious Perspective: Literary and Pictorial Wit in the Seventeenth Century* (New Haven and London: Yale University Press, 1978), 1-15; Clarke Hulse, *The Rule of Art: Literature and Painting in the Renaissance* (Chicago and London: University of Chicago Press, 1990), 8-10; and John Rupert Martin, *Baroque* (New York: Harper and Row, 1977), 73-83.

most often been considered the two strongest, contending with each other for first place above the three lower ones. Across the span of early modern thought, eye and ear were both considered capable of elevating the inward contemplative facilities to divine truth and beauty, whereas objects that delighted taste, touch, and smell were considered mundane distractions. However, in the era that witnessed the rise of print culture and increased literacy, of exquisite commodities produced and consumed more conspicuously than ever before, and of multi-media representational works, there was increasing agreement about rank. Although hearing remained more closely allied with memory and pedagogy, vision was most often granted primacy during the sixteenth and seventeenth centuries for its particular connection to reason, spirituality, and consciousness. It was the sense through which human beings were deemed most capable of invention and discovery, key concepts in an age of materiality and global expansion. Painting was privileged by its proponents for its self-contained capacity to communicate a specific narrative, whereas music, enormously complex in other ways, required text to do the same.[16] Vision thus emerged most often as the principal sense, hearing as second. "The eye, which one may well call the window of the soul," says Leonardo:

> is the principal means by which the central sense can most completely and abundantly appreciate the infinite works of nature; and the ear is the second, which acquires dignity by hearing of the things the eye has seen... And if you, O poet, tell a story with your pen, the painter with his brush can tell it more easily, with simpler completeness, and less tedious to follow.[17]

Dee is particularly emphatic about the connection between image and light, with all of its physical and metaphysical implications:

> Among these Artes, by good reason, Perspective ought to be had. . . bycause of the prerogative of *Light*, beyng the first of *Gods Creatures*: and the eye, the light of our body, and his Sense most mighty, and his organ most Artificiall and *Geometricall* Perspective. . . concerneth all Creatures, all Actions, and passions, by Emanation of beames perfourmed. [B]y this Art. . . we may use our eyes, and the light, with greater pleasure: and perfecter Judgment[.][18]

---

[16] See Tom Conley, "The Wit of the Letter: Holbein's Lacan," in: *Vision in Context: Historical and Contemporary Perspectives on Sight* (London and New York: Routledge, 1996), 47-50; James Elkins, *On Pictures and the Words That Fail Them* (Cambridge: Cambridge University Press, 1998), 213-214; and David Summers, *The Judgement of Sense: Renaissance Naturalism and the Rise of Aesthetics* (Cambridge: Cambridge University Press, 1987), 32-41.

[17] Leonardo da Vinci, *The Literary Works*, ed. [and transl.] by Jean Paul Richter; 2nd ed., revised and enlarged by Jean Paul Richter and Irma A. Richter, (Oxford: Oxford University Press, 1939), I: 367.

[18] Dee, Preface to *The Elements of Geometrie*, sig. B.j.

The artist who could encode the musical within the visual, who could loan an implication of sound to mute imagery, could cover in one still work much of human intellectual and perceptual experience. The one who could preserve his or her own image as musician not only granted permanent status to the ephemeral, but showed the erudition and virtuosity of the true courtier while embedding the liberal within the upwardly-mobile mechanical. "Painting satisfying the sense of sight is more noble than music which only satisfies hearing," says Leonardo, "therefore painting is to be preferred to all other occupations."[19]

The meaning of imagery within any particular culture is conferred against the background of other forms of discourse, particularly those which encode knowledge and power. Like literature and music, visual art helps to shape and reinforce (or occasionally subvert) a common set of values and shared identities. Gender stands prominently among these.[20] In all Western European vernacular languages with gendered nouns, "music" is feminine. It becomes a she, and "she" had been inherited by the sixteenth century as mother, lover, seducer, virgin bride: in short, the range of male fantasies of Woman herself.[21] In the ancient world, Music had been represented by the muse Euterpe. The early Christian liberal art of Music, like her six mathematical and linguistic sisters, became embodied as a woman – a young and conventionally attractive one, who remained a fashionable beauty across many centuries of image making. By the early modern era, then, Music had already been allegorized as an attractive woman for millennia.

Lucas Cranach's woodcut "Lady Music" (Fraw Musica), published in 1545, presents a winsome young lutenist, gazing coyly at the viewer with her head turned modestly aside (see Figure 2.1). "[W]hen [a woman] commeth to daunse, or to show any kinde of musicke," recommends Castiglione's most gynophilic male courtier, "she ought to be brought to it w[ith] sufferinge her selfe somewhat to be prayed, and with a certein bashfulnes, that may declare the noble shamefastness that is contrarye to headinesse."[22] In spite of the limitations of the genre, Cranach's woodcut conveys this sweet shamefastness through the posturing of her head, and the slight turn of her legs to the opposite side. The erotically pleasurable and nutrative/reproductive aspects of her body face forward even as she turns just enough away to demonstrate her own feminine propriety. Cranach's vision serves

---

[19] *Leonardo on Painting*, 35-37.

[20] Thomas McEviley, *Art and Otherness: Crisis in Cultural Identity* (New York: Documentext, McPherson and Co., 1992), 102-120; H. Diane Russell, *Eva/Ave: Woman in Renaissance and Baroque Prints* (Washington: National Gallery of Art; New York: The Feminist Press at the City University of New York, 1990), 14; and John Walker and Sarah Chaplin, *Visual Culture: An Introduction* (Manchester and New York: Manchester University Press, 1997), 18-26; 101.

[21] See Austern, "'My Mother Musicke'," 242-254; and Austern, "The Siren, the Muse, and the God of Love: Music and Gender in Seventeenth-Century English Emblem Books," *Journal of Musicological Research* 18 (1999): 108-115.

[22] Castiglione, *The Courtyer*, sig. Cci[v].

fraw Musica.

Figure 2.1 Lucas Cranach, *Fraw Musica*, 1545
Library of Congress

as an appropriate subject for a culture in which a woman's chastity was her greatest virtue.[23] But it is also an object of desire. Fraw Musica is at once brash and bashful, typical of the paradoxical depictions of women in early modern literary discussions.[24] As if also taking her sartorial cue from Castiglione's fantasy of the ideal woman musician, Cranach's figure wears her gorgeous garments exquisitely:

> But forsomuch as it is lefull & necessary for women to sett more by their beauty then men, thys woman [musician] ought to have a judgement to know what maner garmentes set her best out, and be most fitt for the [musical] exercises that she entendeth to undertake at that instant, & with them to arraye herself."[25]

Not only is this Lady Music clad in elaborate and presumably costly garments that "set her best out." She has evidently arrayed herself perfectly, showing at once the sweet modesty of the ideal lady and the erotic enticements of the perfect beauty. The artist has draped her garments not to conceal, but to reveal, the most feminine aspects of her body. The belly of her lute emphasizes her perfectly proportioned shoulders, and almost teasingly conceals the suggested roundness of her breasts. It draws equal attention to the massive jewels that encircle her throat. Sumptuous folds of cloth pool richly between her thighs, and somehow, in spite of thick gatherings of fabric, reveal the intensely feminine curves of her buttocks. Her legs are carefully outlined in light and shadow from thigh to the top of each slim foot, even though modestly covered by her embroidered gown. Above her jaunty feathered cap and carefully bound hair, intermingled with the other tools of her craft, hang plump clusters of grapes. In the symbolic language of the time, these

---

[23] See Ruth Kelso, *Doctrine for the Lady of the Renaissance* (Urbana: University of Illinois Press, 1956), 42-49.

[24] *Distaves and Dames: Renaissance Treatises for and about Women*, ed. Diane Bornstein (Delmar, NY: Scholars's Facsimiles and Reprints, 1978); Bornstein, *The Feminist Controversy of the Renaissance* (Delmar, NY: Scholars Facsimiles and Reprints, 1980); Katherine Usher Henderson and Barbara F. MacManus, *Half Humankind: Contexts and Texts of the Controversy about Women in England, 1540-1640* (Urbana: University of Illinois Press, 1985); Kelso, *Doctrine for the Lady*; Joan Kelly, "Early Feminist Theory and the *Querelle des Femmes*, 1400-1789," in: Kelly, *Women, History and Theory*; and Ian Maclean, *The Renaissance Notion of Woman* (Cambridge: Cambridge University Press, 1980). For particular information about the place of music in this body of literature, see Austern, "Music and the English Renaissance Controversy over Women," in: *Cecilia Reclaimed: Feminist Perspectives on Gender and Music*, ed. Susan C. Cook and Judy S. Tsou (Urbana and Chicago: University of Illinois Press, 1994), 52-69.

[25] Castiglione, *The Courtyer*, sig. Cc1ᵛ. Cranach's image was published as the frontispiece to Martin Agricola [martinum agricolum], *Musica Instrumentalis Deudsch* (Wittemberg: Georg Rhaw, 1545). For further information about such images in the early modern era, see Tilman Seebass, "Lady Music and her Proteges from Musical Allegory to Musician's Portraits," *Musica Disciplina* 42 (1988): 23-61.

represent the paradox of virgin, wife, and mother in one.[26] Bashful in her own deportment, yet eroticized for the viewer's gaze, this Lady Music has become an accomplished, secular Virgin Mary as well as the perfect court lady.

Gregor Reisch gives us a less overtly sexualized, yet still magnificent, version of the same theme as part of his discussion of the liberal art of music (see Figure 2. 2). Here, deportment and arrangement of garments is not an issue, for the woman neither dances, plays, nor sings. Nor is she alone within her frame. She literally towers over six little male "types of music," larger than life from their perspective. Again, Lady Music wears exquisite, highly fashionable clothing, from her feathered hat to the hem of her elaborate gown. Even at the center of the visual composition, even facing forward, her gaze does not meet the viewer's, but turns modestly askew. To her is given the everlasting visual code for sounding music – notation – offered to viewer and male musicians alike. Without her, music would fade and die. This guardian of knowledge, allegory and embodiment of an ancient liberal art, is represented as a woman, while the men are mere mechanical producers of sound. Yet she stands passively in their midst while they actively engage in their craft. Only the viewer, outside the frame, seems aware of her physical presence. As such, this Lady Music is typical of allegorical figures introduced for symbolic affirmation into "real" space.

Such images as these stand as powerful reminders of the venerable tradition of merging music and the female body in representational work. In them, as in other works of the period, women often stand as passive objects of longing, whether to be read as individuals or additionally as types or allegories. The majority of early modern images served as objects by men for men to gaze upon, or from which to learn their relative positions in the world. The same sorts of catalogues of virtues and vices addressed by Ridolfi appear in visual form, Woman as what Man was not, Woman as whatever Man could render her, "saint, virgin, carnal temptress, lover, witch, shrew, worthy."[27] Even in female portraiture, the male artist was sometimes more concerned with idealized beauty than with particularity; not only did The Beauty emerge as a visual character type during the sixteenth century, but the painting of an attractive woman could be read as a synecdoche for art itself.[28]

The section for draftsmen in Durer's course in the art of measurement with compass and ruler is particularly revealing. This work, primarily a treatise on geometry, was not overtly intended to reinforce gender codes or attitudes toward

---

[26] For more information on this early modern signifier and its particular association with the Virgin Mary, see Edy de Jongh, "Grape Symbolism in the Paintings of the Sixteenth and Seventeenth Centuries," *Simiolus* 7 (1974): 174-177 and 185-190.

[27] See King, "The Woman of the Renaissance" 207; and Russell, Eva/Ave, 14-17.

[28] Elizabeth Cropper, "The Beauty of Woman: Problems in the Rhetoric of Renaissance Portraiture," in: *Rewriting the Renaissance: The Discourses of Sexual Difference in Early Modern Europe*, ed. Margaret W. Ferguson, Maureen Quilligan, and Nancy J. Vickers (Chicago: University of Chicago Press, 1986), 175-190; and Woods-Marsden, *Self-Portraiture*, 192.

Figure 2.2 Gregor Reisch, *Typus musicae*, from *Margarita Philosophica*, 1517
Courtesy of the John M. Wing Foundation, The Newberry Library, Chicago

subjects and objects. But the woodcuts that illustrate its instructions for building and using mechanical drawing aids do so nonetheless. The first in the series demonstrates how to draw a life-like portrait. The subject being studied and sketched by the draftsman is a mature, bearded man, seated upright and alert in an ornate chair. His right hand rests firmly atop a sphere on the chair's arm, and he looks directly at the draftsman who sites him through a geometrical device.[29] In contrast, a languorous reclining female figure illustrates the instructions for drawing a nude. Unlike the model for portraiture, her eyes are shut in chaste repose while the draftsman examines her with clinical detachment through a reticulated net that divides the image into working fragments. Her body is youthful, her right hand invisible, and her left loosely sagging across her thigh. She is laid out in such a way that it is the viewer, not the draftsman, who sees her body from the clearest and most comprehensive perspective, with breasts, belly, and suggestively draped crotch facing awkwardly to her side.[30] Her passive repose and recumbent position as an object displayed on cushions suggest the lute in another of these instructional woodcuts, rendering both into glorious commodities.[31] One is, in fact, reminded of the Guerilla Girls' famous observation almost half a millennium later that their own contemporary art presents a disproportionate percentage of eroticized female nudes, made normative by centuries of male artistic practice.[32] One is also reminded of the paradoxical early modern recommendations that (male) artists avoid the presence of women, which could make the hand unsteady.[33]

It should not be surprising that so many images empower not only the viewer/consumer, but also the artist. The increasingly noble art of painting, ranked by Castiglione as one in which the ideal courtier should gain skill, was deeply linked to manliness during his century and the next. Most early modern visual works were created by men like Durer's exemplary draftsman, for equally male patrons. In courtly circles, painting became another vehicle of masculinity

---

[29] Albrecht Durer, *Underweysung der Messung mit dem Zirckel und* Richtscheyt (Nuremberg, 1525), sig. Q2^v.

[30] Albrecht Durer, *Underweysung der Messung mit dem Zirckel und Richtscheyt*, 2nd ed. (Nuremberg, 1538), sig. Q3^v.

[31] Albrecht Durer, *Underweysung der Messung mit dem Zirckel und Richtscheyt* (1525), sig. Q3. See also Russell, *Ave/Eva*, 23; and Charles W. Talbot, *Durer in America: His Graphic Works* (Washington, DC: National Gallery of Art, 1971), 353-355.

[32] See the famous "Do Women Have to be Naked to get into the Met. Museum?" poster (1985 and 1995) by this New York-based feminist "conscience of the art world" at http://www.guerillagirls.com/posters/naked2.html, and in *Confessions of the Guerilla Girls* (New York: Harper Collins, 1995), 8. For a very witty, popular introduction to early modern women artists and their relationship to male practitioners, see *The Guerilla Girls' Bedside Companion to the History of Western Art* (Harmondsworth and New York: Penguin Books, 1998), 28-45.

[33] Patricia Simons, "Homosociality and Erotics in Italian Renaissance Portraiture," in: *Portraiture: Facing the Subject*, ed. Joanna Woodall (Manchester and New York: Manchester University Press, 1997), 44.

performed, along with literary works, musical virtuosity, and skill at arms.[34] Perhaps most fundamentally, ancient ideas about the sort of creativity necessary for the production of art (or music) were deeply linked to the male usurpation of female procreative capacities, and to a male-dominant understanding of the reproductive process. Pythagorean thought had long associated form with masculinity, substance with femininity. The intellect was gendered male, the body female. Creative products were therefore often analogized as children of the mind, born of its action on unformed, raw material.[35] Aristotelian and Galenic medicine continued to explain reproduction as a male-dominant act, even though both partners contributed some substance. These systems considered menstrual blood the source of passive matter, awaiting insemination to give it life and the impetus toward form.[36] Paint-pot was thus easily allegorized as the uterus full of cool moisture, waiting for the painter's phallic brush and seminal ideas.[37] Furthermore, as art transcended craft to join with other noble intellectual endeavors, the painter or sculptor (like the musician, the scientist, and the engineer) became a manipulator of Nature, another feminine noun translated across media into a womanly body.[38] The homo-sociality of most artists' workshops and guilds probably did little to discourage these gendered metaphors, especially in a culture in which the physical and metaphysical merged so seamlessly into each other.

On ancient authority, men had long been considered to have higher rational faculties and more fully developed intellects than women. As men's bodies were deemed more powerful and more generally capable, so were their minds. Women were conventionally held to be simpler sorts, with strong spiritual instincts but weak powers of meditation and reflection. They were less focused, easily diverted by trivialities. One English emblematist even explains that this is why "a minde distracted with much levitie" is visually figured as a woman even though men could occasionally suffer the same problem.[39] Men were encouraged toward a wide range of professions and pastimes, according to skill and social status. Women were most

---

[34] See Burke, "The Courtier," 107-113; and Woods-Marsden, *Self-Portraiture*, 188.

[35] See Linda Phyllis Austern, "'My Mother Musicke'," 239-244; Carolyn Bynum, "Why All the Fuss about the Body?," *Critical Inquiry* 22 (Autumn 1992): 16-17; Jacobs, *Renaissance Virtuosa*, pp. 27-44; Thomas Laqueur, *Making Sex: Body and Gender from the Greeks to Freud* (Cambridge, MA: Harvard University Press, 1990), 29-30; 52-62; and Gaytari C. Spivak, "Displacement and the Discourse of Women," in: *Displacement: Derrida and After*, ed. M. Krupnick (Bloomington: Indiana University press, 1987), 169.

[36] See Laqueur, *Making Sex*, 35-43; and Maclean, *The Renaissance Notion of Woman*, 36-37.

[37] See Woods-Marsden, *Self-Portraiture*, 188.

[38] See Linda Phyllis Austern, "Nature, Culture, Myth and the Musician in Early Modern England," *Journal of the American Musicological Society* 51 (1998): 7-24; and Russell, *Eva/Ave*, 22.

[39] Wither, A Collection of Emblemes, 231. See also Maclean, The Renaissance Notion of Woman, 64; and Russell, *Eva/Ave*, 16-17.

often relegated, as Ridolfi complains, to mundane domesticity, or to learning merely what was necessary.[40] However, by the mid-sixteenth century, it became increasingly acceptable in certain intellectual and cultural circles to reconsider women's innate inferiority.[41] This was particularly so among the courtly classes that provided patronage and demand for artistic products, ultimately paving a path for exceptional women to work in such male-dominant fields as painting and music composition. Henry Peacham, who revised Castiglione's ideas of courtly conduct for the seventeenth century English gentleman, names a woman (Marguerite of Navarre) among his three exemplary amateur artists of noble rank.[42] His countryman and contemporary, George Wither, emphasizes that women and men alike possess positive and negative capacities. It is mere convention, he says, by which:

> . . . Most *Vices*, heretofore.
> And *Vertues* too, our *Ancestors* did render,
> By words declined in the *female gender*.[43]

Nonetheless, programs for creating learned, accomplished women were still generally pale reflections of their manly equivalents. The full range of training for men in virtually every field was unavailable for women. Furthermore, there is still a strong sense that exceptional women were either paradoxes, wonders of nature, or deliberate creations by and for male delight. Castiglione likens the courtier's mental conception and fashioning of his female equivalent to the myth of Pygmalion, the artist who sculpted his perfect woman from a block of marble.[44] This idealized "Renaissance Woman" was to be trained in music, letters, conversation, and the techniques of visual art – but to a lesser extent than men, and to display particularly feminine virtues. She was also to retain all manner of womanly graces and modesty.[45] Even within the highest social strata, a woman's primary duties were to be a model Christian wife and mother.

This sort of cultural background makes the achievements of women artists in male-dominated fields remarkable, which fact was not unnoticed by the admiring male critics who praised them. All had in common strong support of their talent during their formative years. Parallel to the situation of women composers of the

---

[40] See Paul F. Grendler, *Schooling in Renaissance Italy: Learning and Literacy, 1300-1600* (Baltimore and London: Johns Hopkins University Press, 1989), 87-89; and King, "The Woman of the Renaissance," 207.

[41] See Maclean, The Renaissance Notion of Women, 66; and Ian Maclean, *Woman Triumphant: Feminism in French Literature 1610-1652* (Oxford: Clarendon Press, 1977), 155-232.

[42] Peacham, The Compleat Gentleman, 106.

[43] Wither, *A Collection of Emblemes*, 231.

[44] Castiglione, *The Courtyer*, sigs. Bbii^v-Bbiii.

[45] *Ibid.*, sigs. Bii^v-Ccii.

same period, the majority of female visual artists were trained in convents. The careers of the small minority of lay women were generally shaped by fathers, who nurtured their daughters' talent as mothers had nourished their infant bodies.[46] As with courtly amateurs and female composers, women artists were largely dissuaded from forms and genres considered most intellectually challenging or technically difficult. Their minds were simply not believed capable, even by some of the critics who grudgingly praised individual talents. For an era that perceived the literal, physical world as full of signs and significations of invisible truths, the highest forms of art were those that most transcended the realm of the tangible. Thus, complex allegorical narratives that led away from the natural, sensible world were particularly prestigious. Merely to replicate or transcribe the superficial characteristics of nature was considered lower status. So of course this was where women were first permitted to excel from one end of Europe to the other, especially in the categorically minor genre of portraiture.[47]

Expressive naturalistic images of individuals were a product of the early modern era, linked to the historical origin and rise of the concept of selfhood between the later fifteenth and eighteenth centuries.[48] Like other vital art forms of the modern era, portraiture was devised after classical models and ancient ideals. Simple records of likeness were considered the most rudimentary form, although the genre also embraced forms of allegory and expressions of a subject's inner essence. This superficial imitation of nature was thought to require only coordination of hand and eye – the skills of the mechanical craftsman rather than the emerging fine artist. It was thus deemed suitable to women's tender intellects. Perhaps more importantly for the gender on whom so many social and sexual limits were imposed, the making of a portrait required no impudent observation, no (necessary) revelation of sights unfit for virtuous female eyes.[49]

---

[46] See Greer, *Obstacle Race*, 161-168 and 187-188; and Lierly, "Women Painters," 140-142. For a succinct summary of conditions confronting women artists in early modern Europe, see Borzello, *A World of Our Own*, 16-77. In Italy, if not the rest of Europe, both parents had active roles in the raising of children; mothers were primarily responsible for day-to-day care and feeding, especially in early life, while fathers took an active role in education and moral guidance; see Louis Haas, *The Renaissance Man and his Children* (New York: St. Martin's Press, 1998), 134-145.

[47] See Greer, *The Obstacle Race*, 250-275; Fredrika Jacobs, *Defining the Renaissance Virtuosa: Women Artists and the Language of Art History and Criticism* (Cambridge: Cambridge University Press, 1997), 44-46; Larry Silver, "Step-Sister of the Muses: Painting as Liberal Art and Sister Art," in: *Articulate Images: The Sister Arts from Hogarth to Tennyson*, ed. Richard Wendorf (Minneapolis: Unviersity of Minnesota Press, 1983), 42-46; and Woods-Marsden, *Self-Portraiture*, 191-193.

[48] See Greenblatt, *Renaissance Self-Fashioning*, 1-9; Migiel and Schiesari, *Refiguring Woman*, 1-2; Simons, "Homosociality and Erotics," 29; Woodall, ed., *Portraiture*, 1-5; and Woods-Marsden, *Self-Portraiture*, 1-9.

[49] Jacobs, *Renaissance Virtuosa*, 45. As the genre developed, particularly in northern Italy, limitations were imposed on the physical positioning of women as portrait subjects in

The visual languages and sub-genres of naturalistic portraiture were developed during the sixteenth century, and continued to be refined over the succeeding two. Very little information has survived about the conditions under which people looked at portraits, but the genre became central to courtly and civic culture in this first age of conspicuous consumption and reflexive self-awareness.[50] Portraits became commemorative objects, and means to establish individual subjectivities and group identities. Distinctive formats and the development of visual codes particular to the genre helped to establish recognizable types and enable a wide range of purposes. Portraits ultimately served as political propaganda, and means of linking individuals across time and space. They helped to solidify or advance the social status of artists, sitters, and owners alike.[51] Musical objects and activities found their way into many sorts of portraits, where they came to encode everything from cultural refinement, to metaphors of harmony, to particular forms of individual or group identity. In fact, because portraiture shared some of its iconographies with allegorical genres, it is sometimes difficult to distinguish, for example, a St. Cecilia from a representation of Musica from a human musician – in some cases, perhaps deliberately so.[52]

Since naturalistic portraiture matured along with greater participation by women in visual art, and since music was both an activity practiced by women and one that held an astounding range of visual signification, it is not surprising to find women's portraits of female musicians from the beginning. One of the first woman painters of the early modern era, the Fleming Caterina (or Catherina) van Hemessen, not only established a reputation for her miniature portraits.[53] She was the first to show a woman making music, in a painting of her sister at the virginals in 1548 (see Figure 2.3). As we shall see, this composition is strikingly similar to the earliest woman's musical self-portrait, and may even have inspired it.

As with a number of other early modern women who established reputations in the arts, van Hemessen (1528 - after 1565) was the daughter of a man who also worked in her field. Like other women painters, she later became a court artist. In

---

order to reinforce their virtue and social status and to limit the power of their returned gazes to male viewers ; see Patricia Simons, "Women in Frames : The Gaze, the Eye, the Profile in Renaissance Portraiture," in *The Expanding Discourse : Feminism and Art History*, ed., Norma Broudy and Mary D. Garrard (New York : HarperCollins Publishers, Inc., 1992), pp. 41-52.

[50] See Lorne Campbell, *Renaissance Portraits* (New Haven and London: Yale University Press, 1990), 218; Woodall, ed., *Portraiture*, 3-5; and Woods-Marsden, *Self-Portraiture*, 9.

[51] See Campbell, *Renaissance Portraits*, 193-196 and 209; and Woodall, ed., *Portraiture*, 1-5.

[52] For the range and variety of depictions of St. Cecilia, the patron of music whose popularity increased at approximately the same time as that of portraiture, see Albert Pomme de Mirimonde, *Sainte-Cécile: Métamorphoses d'un thème musical* (Genève: Éditions Minkoff, 1974), 38-191.

[53] Greer, *The Obstacle Race*, 32.

Figure 2.3 Catherina van Hemessen, *Young Girl at the Clavichord*, ca. 1555-56
Permission of the Wallraf-Richartz-Museum, Köln

1556, two years after her marriage to the organist Christian de Morien, the two were taken to Spain in the service of Queen Mary of Hungary as an artistic double act.[54] In fact, the sixteenth-century Spanish court seems to have been especially receptive to women artists. Not only van Hemessen but all three of our musical self-portraitists from that period were invited to work there.[55] The youthful but very polished painting of her sister playing the virginals represents one of the earliest images of a woman at a keyboard in a domestic interior, later to become a distinct genre and one in which separation between literal and allegorical is virtually impossible. Van Hemessen's composition is simple, drawing full attention to its subject. No background competes with the lone human figure. The young musician is richly dressed in dark red velvet with lace at the modestly high neck and wrists, gold brocade peeking through her sleeves. Her head is covered by a fine double-layered cap, neatly tied beneath her chin. Not only is a minimum of flesh visible, but her torso is hidden in shadow. The viewer's eye is thus drawn not to her body, but to her head, which gazes slightly to the side as if listening; and particularly to her right arm, hands, and fingers as she actively plays the small table-top keyboard in its ornate gilded case. The image bespeaks wealth, taste, and sobriety.

With her clear skin and large dark eyes set off by the rich red cloth, the subject is beautiful and well displayed, but not eroticized. Everything about this image suggests accomplishment and propriety, often a paradox in the context of the early modern woman musician. Although music was a liberal art with well-established benefits to mind and body, and although Musica herself was figured as a woman, the art was also considered a dangerous inflamer of the passions and agent of erotic desire. Not only Castiglione, but conduct writers from one end of Europe to the other recommended musical training for young women of high social status. However, in most of these writings, there is an extraordinary awareness of the body in performance, the attractive female body on display to the (male) gaze in cultures that presume a heterosexual norm. Just as Castiglione emphasizes that the woman musician must demonstrate the modesty becoming to her gender, many conduct writers prohibit her from displaying her skill in front of men at all, at the risk of damaging her reputation or even her virtue. The combination of visual and auditory beauty rendered the female musician such an irresistible object of male fantasy and desire that some conduct writers warned young women for the sake of their (reputations for) chastity to play or sing only in private or in the company of other women.[56]

---

[54] Borzello, *A World of Our Own*, 32; Ferino-Pagden, *Anguissola*, 11; and *Sofonisba Anguissola e le sue sorelle* (N.P.: Leonardo Arte, 1994), 330.

[55] See Borzello, *A World of our Own*, 32; and Sylvia Ferino-Pagden and Maria Kusche, *Sofonisba Anguissola, Renaissance Woman* (Washington, DC: National Museum of Women in the Arts, 1977), 11.

[56] See Linda Phyllis Austern, "'Sing Againe Siren': The Female Musician and Sexual Enchantment in Elizabethan Life and Literature," *Renaissance Quarterly* 42 (1989): 420-448; and Kelso, *Doctrine for the Lady of the Renaissance*, 52-53 and 228.

Van Hemessen's keyboard player has no audience within the frame, nor seeks one outside of it with her eyes. She plays quietly to herself, for her benefit alone. The most gendered and sexualized parts of her body are not available to the viewer, not even suggested through the thick velvet folds of her gown. Instead, they lie in shadow, literally invisible to the probing gaze. The artist emphasizes suggestions of the auditory and tactile, and de-emphasizes the purely visual as much as the genre will permit. This musician is no passive object of erotic display, but, fingers actively moving over keys and arms firmly in playing position, she is sober and industrious in her learned pastime. Everything about her indicates the controlled concentration necessary to a good musical performance. "I will have this woman have a sight in letters, in musicke, in drawinge or peincting," writes Castiglione, "accompaniying with that discreete sober mode and with the givinge a good opinion of herselfe[.]"[57] Even her instrument is proper to a sweet, virtuous young lady whose mind is not distracted by much levity. "[T]he instrume[n]tes of musicke which she useth," writes Castiglione of the well-bred female musician:

> ought to be fitte for this purpose. Imagin with your selfe what an unsightly matter it were to see a woman play upon a tabour or drumm, or blowe in a flute or trompet, or any like instrumente: and this bicause the boisterousnesse of them doeth cover and take away that sweet mildnes which setteth so furth everie deede that a woman doeth.[58]

Not only do the virginals have a soft sound, not meant to carry over distance. The performing position permits dignified display of the body, as the technique requires no contortions or gross bodily gestures. For all of these reasons, as well as the expense they indicate, keyboard instruments of all sorts were among those most acceptable for women from the sixteenth through the eighteenth centuries and beyond. In fact, some of the best preserved and most beautiful early modern keyboard instruments still extant today originally belonged to wealthy women.[59]

The earliest known self-portrait of a woman artist as musician dates from only a few years after van Hemessen's image, and bears a number of similarities to it which may or may not be coincidental.[60] However, self-portraiture sends a rather different message than the image of another; and the artist, Sophonisba Anguissola (ca. 1535-1625), was known for her skill in music as well as in painting. Born into a family of the minor nobility of Cremona and later lady-in-waiting to the Queen of Spain, Anguissola in fact epitomized the courtly ideal of the sixteenth century.

---

[57] Castiglione, *The Courtyer*, sig. Ccii.

[58] *Ibid.*, sigs. Cci-Cci[v].

[59] See, for example, Donald H. Boalch, *Makers of the Harpsichord and Clavichord 1440-1840*, 3rd ed., edited by Charles Mould (Oxford: Oxford University Press, 1995), 85, 92, and 584.

[60] Hanna Gagel, "Sofonisba Anguissola, eine Rollenuberschreidtende Malerin," *Kritische Berichte* 14 (1986): 8; *Sofonisba Anguissola e le sue sorelle*, 202 and 330; and Woods-Marsden, *Self-Portraiture*, 210.

Beautiful, learned, multi-talented, and born to the class to which most (male) artists merely aspired, Anguissola was frequently called a "marvel" in sixteenth- and seventeenth-century sources.[61] Her ambitious father, Amilcare, decided to educate all six of his daughters as he would have educated sons. This allowed them to play prominent roles within their class, in accordance with one of their culture's ideals. Sofonisba's artistic career was his inspired idea. Not only did Amilcare provide Sofonisba with the humanist education befitting the family's rank, but sent her as a child to learn painting from a professional.[62] Thus she had a good background in music and humane letters, as well as in the field in which she gained primary fame, and seems to have had talent in all three areas. In fact, she was praised for her *suavissimo cantare* and *la sua buona letteratura* by at least one contemporary.[63] As a young adult, Anguissola was invited to the Spanish court to serve as lady-in-waiting, drawing instructor, and court painter to Queen Isabel of Valois, with whom she may have also played music in their few leisure hours.[64] She is most often accounted the first major woman artist of the early modern era, and may have been an inspiration to Italian women musicians through circulation of copies of her two musical self-portraits.[65] It is even conceivable that, late in life, she may have known Claudia Cattaneo and her husband Claudio Monteverdi.[66] Domestic portraiture predominates among her works, including many that emphasize the virtuous dignity and individuality of women. As with other women artists of the time, her self-portraits were in demand, for they advertised her professional capabilities to potential patrons even while serving as emblems of both natural and artificial beauty.[67]

---

[61] See Ilya Sandra Perlingieri, *Sofonisba Anguissola: The First Great Woman Artist of the Renaissance* (New York: Rizzoli, 1992), 77 and 190; and Woods-Marsden, *Self-Portraiture*, 191.

[62] For information about Anguissola's family background and training, see Ferino-Pagden, *Sofonisba Anguissola*, 11 and 26-35; Perlingieri, *Sofonisba Anguissola*, 21-33; Orietta Pinessi, *Sofonisbia Anguissola un 'pittore' alla corte di Filippo II* (Milano: Selene Edizioni, 1998), 11-12; *Sofonisba Anguissola e le sue sorelle*, 47-74 and 79-88; Luisa Vertova, "Lavinia versus Sofonisba," *Apollo* 140 (1995): 43-44; and Woods-Marsden, *Self-Portraiture*, 191-195.

[63] Woods-Marsden, *Self-Portraiture*, 191-192.

[64] See Campbell, *Renaissance Portraits*, 219; Perlingieri, *Sofonisba Anguissola*, 119-121 and 136-139; *Sofonisba Anguissola e le sue sorelle*, 89-116; and Vertova, "Lavinia versus Sofonisba," 43. Queen Isabel was also musically trained as befitted her rank; she ordered a new clavichord to be sent from Paris in 1564, Perlingieri, *Sofonisba Anguissola*, 139.

[65] Ferino-Pagden, *Sofonisba Anguissola*, 10-13, and Perlingieri, *Sofonisba Anguissola*, 188-190.

[66] See Perlingieri, *Sofonisba Anguissola*, 188-190.

[67] See Catherine King, "Looking a Sight: Sixteenth-Century Portraits of Woman Artists," *Zeitschrift fur Kunstgeschichte* 58 (1995): 385-386; and Katherine A. McIver, "Lavinia Fontana's *Self-Portrait Making Music*," *Women's Art Journal* 19 (1998): 5.

Anguissola painted more self-portraits than any artist between Durer and Rembrandt. Since the developing iconography of portraiture and self-representation was predominantly masculine, and since Woman emblematized so many male desires and superficial qualities of body, Anguissola was required to be carefully inventive in order to preserve her paradoxical position.[68] In accordance with her unusual status as woman, noble, and skilled (professional) painter, she particularly emphasizes the outward expression of interior virtues. She also reinforces her class status and its privileged, multi-faceted education. Her two portraits of herself at the clavichord, one from 1555-56 and the other from 1561, are no exception, for music had long been a traditional aspect of the education of a gentle person. We know from her own words and the accounts of others that she sang.[69] But yet she chose to portray herself not with the open mouth that suggested unchaste behavior to her contemporaries, nor with her body as her instrument. Instead, in both contrasting images, she reveals at once "that sweet mildnes which setteth so furth everie deede that a woman doeth" as well as inner strength and mastery over a mechanical instrument. In so doing, she retains the femininity necessary for the conservative court circles in which she operated, and to set patrons at ease about her morals. At the same time, she also communicates genuine skill over the natural (and mechanical) world at a time in which it was women *singers* – women whose music was completely of the body – who were gaining praise and prominence in her native Italy.

Like van Hemessen's portrait of her sister, Anguissola's first musical self-image shows a sober young lady in the act of playing a small, table-top keyboard in profile against a dark background (see Figure 2.4). Her simple black velvet bodice and dark brown sleeves melt into the dusky space behind her, leaving the delicate off-white lace at throat and wrists to emphasize her thinking, doing parts. We only see her upper body, in three-quarter profile. Light shines from the right, illuminating both wrists, the activity of her right hand, and the upper register of her instrument. It brightens the heart-side of her face, half-turned from darkness to meet the viewer's gaze. Her light brown hair is soberly bound to the back of her head, her back erect, her mouth chastely closed. The brightest object in the image is the vivid green of her instrument's case. The viewer has come upon another young woman playing quietly and to herself, remaining as much in chaste shadow as in light.

Her later self-portrait in the same activity, previously attributed to or thought to depict one of her sisters, is bolder.[70] But it still conveys much the same message of dignified strength, skill, and sobriety (see Figure 2.5). Here, a somewhat more mature and well-established Anguissola has literally brought more of herself and

---

[68] See King, "Looking a Sight," 385-86; and Perlingieri, *Sofonisba Anguissola*, 77-78.

[69] King, "Looking a Sight," 388; and Woods-Marsden, *Self-Portraiture*, 191-192.

[70] See *Sofonisba e le sue sorelle*, 212.

Figure 2.4 Sofonisba Anguissola, *Self-Portrait at the Clavichord*, ca. 1555-56
Museo Nazionale di Capodimonte, Naples
Permission of Alinari, Art Resource, New York

Figure 2.5 Sofonisba Anguissola, *Self-Portrait at the Spinet with Female Servant*, 1561
Permission of the Lord Spencer Collection, Althorp, Northampton, United Kingdom

her instrument to light. She is still soberly, but more finely, dressed in a gown of black velvet, embellished with embroidery and set off by a raised fur collar. The lace at her throat and wrists is finer and more voluminous, her chemise fastened with delicate tasseled cords that add brightness and texture as they cascade onto the dark fabric of her dress. Light still shines from the right, but the visage that returns the viewer's gaze is fully illuminated, full of calm confidence and self-knowledge. Her instrument is larger and more impressive, suggesting a more commanding and perhaps complex sonority. We see the complete keyboard and most of its strings this time, both hands fluttering in active performance. Perhaps more importantly, Anguissola is no longer alone. The countenance of an elderly female servant gazes toward the viewer from behind the performer as she literally blends into the background. The figure of the servant, who had also been depicted in a famous earlier painting of two of the artists' sisters playing chess *al fresco* while a third looks on, merges so thoroughly and carefully into the shadows behind Anguissola that she has been taken as a memorial portrait.[71] However, in a culture in which the wrong sort of musical performance or the wrong audience brought a woman's virtue into question, she may serve a purpose even beyond that of faithful retainer to a wealthy young woman. She is perhaps a reminder that this music is not intended for men's pleasure, not a metaphor or invitation to sexual license, but for the performer alone. At the time of the painting, Anguissola was an unmarried lady -in-waiting as well as court painter. With more of the performer quite literally on display on the miniature stage between the borders of the image, with more of her revealed from shadow into light, it is the watchful serving-woman who positions the action firmly in the world of feminine propriety. There can be no question for whom she plays, no secret lover just outside the frame. The older woman's gaze meets the viewer's from the left, turned slightly over her right shoulder, opposite of Sofonisba's. From any direction, the viewer enters a woman's domain, not simply the dark private space of one lone musician. The servant's presence guards the performer's virtue from any viewer's wandering fancy. Here is no courtesan selling more than music, no siren to entice, and no procuress staging the promise of pleasure for money. Here are harmony and moral propriety, displayed and protected. This multiply talented woman is not a courtesan, but a court lady of virtue as well as accomplishment.

Lavinia Fontana (1552-1614) infuses further detail and signification into another self-portrait making music with a maidservant, painted in 1577. Just as Anguissola may have been aware of van Hemessen's portrait, Fontana may have known of Anguissola's superficially similar composition and attempted to improve on it in the spirit of professional competition.[72] Fontana was born and raised in the

---

[71] Woods-Marsden, *Self-Portraiture*, 210. For more information about "The Chess Game," sometimes considered Sophonisba's earliest masterpiece, see *Sofonisba e le sue sorelle*, 190-191.

[72] Maria Teresa Cantaro, *Lavinia Fontana bolognese 'pittora singolare' 1552-1614* (Milan: Jandi Sapi Editori, 1989), 72-74; Vera Fortunati, *Lavinia Fontana of Bologna*

progressive city of Bologna, home to many women of vision and achievement during the early modern era. She was but the first of many Bolognese women painters of the sixteenth and seventeenth centuries, not a particularly surprising achievement in a city in which women taught and studied at the university, published scholarly texts, and composed and published music.[73] Fontana's father, Prospero, was one of the leading fresco painters and art-teachers of the city. Her mother, Antonia di Bartolomeo de Bonardis, came from a noted family of printers and publishers. The Fontana household was a cultured one, which often entertained visiting artists and intellectuals.[74] Thus Fontana came from the newly empowered educated artisan class, one which increasingly valued musical training as well as learning in letters for the status they conferred.

Fontana was not only a woman painter, but also a woman's painter. Although she took commissions from important male patrons in her native city and later in Rome, there was a specifically female dimension to much of her *oeuvre*. The leading ladies of Bologna particularly sought her out, perhaps for her attention to fine detail and use of multiple props and elaborate settings that reinforced the sitter's status. Consequently, her works reveal a great deal of information about the lives and life cycles of well-to-do early modern Italian women.[75] She even created her own distinctive formula for female sitters, which in some ways recalls Durer's stereotyped (male) portrait subject even while emphasizing the distinctive social roles of women: many are shown in dignified posture in an armchair while they caress a usually alert lap-dog, as in a portrait of an unidentified lady from the

---

1552-1614 (Milan: Electra, 1998), 52; King, "Looking a Sight," 392; and Katherine A. McIver, "Lavinia Fontana's *Self-Portrait Making Music*," 4-5.

[73] See McIver, "Lavinia Fontana's *Self-Portrait Making Music*," 3; Laura M. Ragg, *The Woman Artists of Bologna* (London: Methuen, 1907); and Eleanor M. Tufts, "Ms. Lavinia Fontana from Bologna: A Successful Sixteenth-Century Portraitist," *Art News* 73 (1974): 60. For the most in-depth study of Bologna's convent composers, see Craig A. Monson, *Disembodied Voices: Music and Culture in an Early Modern Italian Convent* (Berkeley and Los Angeles: University of California Press, 1995).

[74] Romeo Galli, *Lavinia Fontana Pittrice 1552-1614* (Imola: Cooperativa tip. edit. Paolo Galeati, 1940), 11-15; McIver, "Lavinia Fontana's *Self-Portrait Making Music*," 3; Tufts, "Ms. Lavinia Fontana of Bologna," 62-63; and Vertova, "Lavinia Versus Sofonisba," 44-45.

[75] See Caroline Murphy, "Lavinia Fontana and the Female Life-Cycle Experience in Late Sixteenth-Century Bologna," in: *Picturing Women in Renaissance and Baroque Italy*, ed. Geraldine A. Johnson and Sara F. Matthews Grieco (Cambridge: Cambridge University Press, 1997), 111-138; Tufts, "Ms. Lavinia Fontana of Bologna," 63; and Woods-Marsden, *Self-Portraits*, 216. For further information about some of the men who praised and collected her work (including papal commissions), see McIver, "Lavinia Fontana's Self-Portrait Making Music," 5. Fontana was also unusual in that, after marriage, it was her artist-husband who placed his career second to hers, and managed the majority of domestic tasks. For succinct summaries of her life and artistic achievements, see Galli, *Lavinia Fontana*, 11-51; and Tufts, "Ms. Lavinia Fontana of Bologna," 60-64.

Walters Gallery (see Figure 2.6).[76] Unlike Anguissola, nothing is known of her musical ability or training.

Her self-portrait as a musician (see Figure 2.7) both suggests and contrasts with Anguissola's second one. Perhaps most strikingly, Fontana is richly arrayed in a costume of gold and bright coral pink, lavished with lace and pearls. Two ornate coral necklaces hang about her neck, setting off her dark coloring to perfection. Here is truly a woman who "know[s] what maner [of] garmentes set her best out, and be most fitt for the [musical] exercises that she entendeth to undertake at that instant[.]" Here is a woman clearly displaying her beauty as well as skill, status – and chaste propriety. Her aged female retainer does not blend into a shadowy background, but becomes an active player on the miniature stage that further includes other vital props. Instead of dull, austere walls dissolved into shadow, the brightly lit room is exquisitely furnished. It also extends down a short corridor to an open window, before which stands an easel, symbol of Fontana's principal craft. But that is vacant now, as the painter demonstrates her ability at a higher-ranking art and another necessary skill for the learned court lady. In fact, she looks away from her empty easel, toward the viewer, speaking with her music and her eyes in a rather clever unity of arts that helps solidify both her social status and her principal talent. The busy maid-servant offers the performer a score, which is prominently displayed to the viewer; notes now faded and unreadable, it may have once held a key to Fontana's precise intentions.[77] Fontana painted the picture in 1577, the year in which she married her fellow artist and father's student, the impoverished minor nobleman Giovanni Paolo Zappi. Most scholars believe that this exquisite illustration of Fontana as accomplished female courtier was created for Zappi's father, Severo, as an introduction after the engagement. Certainly the subject's clothing shows the Petrarchan colors of love (red and white), and certainly one of the most common iconographic significances of music in early modern imagery was the true harmony of love fulfilled, giving this painting multiple layers of interpretive meaning.[78] One common function of portraiture during the early modern era was an exchange during marriage negotiations, especially of the (prospective) bride. For, as Castiglione implies, women's appearance was far more culturally important than men's.[79] However, since Fontana's career was already established, and since Zappi senior already knew who she was, the painting may have been made as an "advertisement" for prospective clients.[80]

Marietta Robusti (ca. 1555-1590), also known as Tintoretta, certainly makes use of the age-old connection between audible music and the true harmony of love

---

[76] Tufts, "Ms. Lavinia Fontana of Bologna," 63.

[77] McIver, "Lavinia Fontana's *Self-Portrait Making Music*," 6.

[78] Fortunati, ed., *Lavinia Fontana*, 52; Jacobs, *The Renaissance Virtuosa*, 158; King, "Looking a Sight," 391-392; and Woods-Marsden, *Self-Portraits*, 216-217.

[79] Campbell, Renaissance Portraits, 197.

[80] McIver, "Lavinia Fontana's *Self-Portrait Making Music*," 5.

Figure 2.6   Lavinia Fontana, *Portrait of a Lady with a Lap-Dog, (Portrait of Ginevra Aldrovandi Hercolani)*, late sixteenth century
Permission of the Walters Art Museum, Baltimore

Figure 2.7 Lavinia Fontana, *Self-Portrait at the Spinet with Female Servant*, 1577
Galleria Palatine, Pallazo Pitti
Permission of Alinari, Art Resource, New York

in her very different musical self-portrait of about 1580 (see Figure 2.8). In contrast to Fontana, little is known about her artistic career, but more about her participation in music. She was among the three of Tintoretto's (Jacopo Robusti's) eight children who became artists in their own right, the other two being her brothers Domenico and Marco. Her mother, Faustina Episcopi, came from a high-ranking if non-noble Venetian family, and, whatever her father's social origins, he, too, belonged to the culture in which artists were eager to adopt the manners and values of the elite who were their prominent patrons.[81] Carlo Ridolfi, her first biographer, claims that her father cross-dressed her and that others therefore took her for a boy. Whether true or not, this is exactly the sort of claim made in admiration or in scorn of so many women who have achieved in traditionally male fields; liberation from female garments seems to release women in traditional cultures from being treated as less able – or explains their inability to behave as "proper" ladies. Ridolfi's brief but approbatory biography begins:

> Marietta Tintoretto, then, lived in Venice, the daughter of the famous Tintoretto and the dearest delight of his soul. He trained her in design and color, whence later she painted such works that men were amazed by her lively talent. Being small of stature she dressed like a boy. Her father took her wherever he went and everyone thought she was a lad.[82]

Tintoretto is known to have had a strong interest in music. Not only did he paint musical subjects (including female performers), but his knowledge of the subject and his own performing abilities were documented by at least two contemporaries. Probably in the late 1560s, when Marietta would have been a teenager, he arranged for the organist and composer Giulio Cacchino (or Zacchino) (c. 1550-1584) to teach her to sing and play instruments.[83] A contemporary praised her ability to play the clavichord, and Ridolfi tells us in 1648 that, in addition to having a brilliant mind like her father's, she played the clavichord and sang very well.[84] "Marietta's special gift, however," says Ridolfi, "was knowing how to paint portraits well. . . . She also portrayed many noble Venetian men and women who took pleasure in meeting and associating with her because she was full of noble

---

[81] Tom Nichols, *Tintoretto: Tradition and Identity* (London: Reaktion Books, 1999), 7 and 17.

[82] Carlo Ridolfi, "The Life of Marietta Tintoretta, Painter, the Daughter of Jacopo," in: *The Life of Tintoretto and of his Children Domenico and Marietta*, transl. Catherine Enggass and Robert Enggass (University Park and London: The Pennsylvania State University Press, 1984), 98. See also E. Tietze-Conrat, "Marietta, fille du Tintoret, peintre de portraits," *Gazette des Beaux-Arts* 6th series, 12 (1934): 259.

[83] H. Colin Slim, "Tintoretto's 'Music-Making Women' at Dresden," *Imago Musicae* 4 (1987): 47; and Tietze-Conrat, "Marietta, fille du Tintoret," 259.

[84] Jacobs, *The Renaissance Virtuosa*, 158; Ridolfi, "Life of Marietta Tintoretta," 99; Slim, "Tintoretto's 'Music-Making Women'," 47; and Woods-Marsden, *Self-Portraits*, 218.

Figure 2.8 Marietta Robusti ("Tintoretta"), *Self-Portrait*, c. 1580
Galleria degli Uffizi, Florence
Permission of Alinari, Art Resource, New York

traits and entertained them with music and song."[85] Although few works can be
ascribed to her with any certainty, we therefore see Robusti as the sort of
"Renaissance woman" who could engage her clients in conversation on learned
topics and demonstrate all the virtues of the female courtier. This is evidently the
goal to which other women painters of her century aspired, at least according to the
selves they fashioned in their imagery and the accounts of those who praised them.

Robusti's musical self-portrait shows the same sort of instrument as her
predecessors in the genre, in this case a harpsichord, or the very "clavicembalo" we
know she played. However, this one does not depict her famous musical skill as
much as it invites the viewer to participate in a staged metaphor involving music.
Here, Robusti is not the courtly musical ideal, or the early modern *virtuosa* as are
Anguissola and Fontana in their musical images. She is not posed as Lady Music,
or even actively as a musician. Instead, she plays a well-established character type
of the late sixteenth and seventeenth centuries: the beloved offering harmonious
healing to the lovesick man.[86] She gazes serenely at the viewer out of the pictorial
space of the image, right hand poised over the keyboard while her left offers an
open music-book to the same viewer. The two notated pages present the Cantus
part of Philippe Verdelot's *Madonna, per voi ardo*, from his first book of
madrigals of 1533.[87] Notes and text are prominently readable as Robusti copied
them with such care: "My lady, for you I burn," a quaintly antiquated piece by
Robusti's day. Her gestures, and the spacing of the objects in the image, seem to
say that if the viewer sings of his unfulfilled longing, she will provide the harmonic
support, the parts that he is missing from that old song. Did she paint this self-
portrait around the time of her marriage, or for a particular man? We know so few
details of her biography that the circumstances surrounding the picture remain a
mystery.[88]

---

[85]   Ridolfi, "Life of Marietta Tintoretta," 98.

[86]   For more about the use of this type in early modern visual and verbal imagery, see
Linda Phyllis Austern, "'For, Love's a Good Musician: Performance, Audition and Erotic
Disorders in Early Modern Europe," *Musical Quarterly* 82 (1998): 614-653; and Linda
Phyllis Austern, "Musical Treatments of Lovesickness: The Early Modern Heritage," in:
Music as Medicine: The History of Music Therapy since Antiquity (Aldershot, Hants,
England: Ashgate, 2000), 213-245.

[87]   The madrigal was first identified by H. Colin Slim in *A Gift of Madrigals and
Motets*, (Chicago: University of Chicago Press, 1972) I: 214-215, and again in Slim,
"Tintoretto's 'Music-Making Women'," 47-49. This popular madrigal, presented in at least
one other sixteenth-century painting, was published in both editions of Verdelot's first book
(1533 and 1537), and later in editions of the volumes entitled *Tutti li madrigali* between
1540 and 1565, which also include some madrigals by Arcadelt; Slim, *Madrigals and
Motets*, I: 215.

[88]   Robusti remains the least known of the artists considered in the present study. The
only modern biography of her remains E. Tietze-Conrat, "Marietta, fille du Tintoret, peintre
de portraits," *Gazette des beaux-arts*, 6th series, 12 (1934): 258-262.

As the sixteenth century faded into memory, so gradually did the Renaissance courtly ideal and the ancient superiority of music, the mathematical liberal art, over the lesser mechanical practices of painting, sculpture, or architecture. During the seventeenth century, women artists were still rare, but images of women musicians became remarkably abundant as more and more members of the gender acquired musical skills as part of their education. Musicians male and female look down from the walls of seventeenth century art collections to this day, inviting the viewers to sin and salvation, harmony and discord, all allegorically embodied by musicians and the accoutrements of music-making. The visual vocabulary of women at the keyboard broadened to include a bewildering variety of domestic scenes with any number of meanings, from virtue to vanity to domestic tranquility. But these images were generally made by male artists, to convey old-fashioned messages involving gendered connotations of ideas or behaviors. However, allegorical portraiture of self or other subject became, if anything, more prominent. As the multi-sensory ideal of the arts became even more important across media, music became a more vital visual signifier than ever before. Artemisia Gentileschi, perhaps the best known of all early modern women artists, was not only the daughter and student of a painter who made ample use of musical imagery. She borrowed music into a number of her own works, including one self-portrait as a lute player (see Figure 2.9).

Gentileschi (1593-1652) stands among the strong-minded, productive early modern women in the arts who, at least once in their careers, produced a work to show some skeptic(s) or other "what a woman can do."[89] Trained by her no less-famous father, Orazio (1563-1639), Gentileschi was raised within a socio-artistic world that was beginning to emphasize the distinction between identity and the material body. For the lives of artists, this meant the increasing importance of non-noble elites of all sorts, for virtue and consequent social status were increasingly located less in familial blood than in such metaphysical qualities as talent and acumen. In their works, this marked greater emphasis on interior qualities and the expression of an inner, abstract subjectivity carefully encoded through physical exteriority and sensory signifiers. This trend was no less evident in portraiture than in other representative genres, from the emblem to the oratorio.[90] Nothing is known of Gentileschi's musical training or possible involvement in performance, but, given her father's famous paintings of (female) musicians and the era's extraordinary interest in encoding acoustic signifiers in visual art, she would certainly have been exposed to instruments, at least as artistic props, as a young beginner in her father's studio. In fact, she may have served as the model for Orazio's painting of a *Young Woman with a Violin* now in the Detroit Institute of

---

[89] See the summary of her correspondence with one of her noble male patrons in Keith Christiansen and Judith W. Mann, *Orazio and Artemisia Gentileschi* (New York: Metropolitan Museum of Art; and New Haven: Yale University Press, 2001), xx.

[90] See Garrard, *Artemisia Gentileschi*, 344-346; and Woodall, ed., *Portraiture*, 10-11.

Figure 2.9 Artemisia Gentileschi, *Self-Portrait as a Lute Player*, ca. 1615-17
Permission of the Curtis Galleries, Minneapolis, Minnesota

Arts.[91] This work, like so many others of its era, seamlessly blends the literal and the allegorical. It draws the viewer's mind from the evident figuration toward higher meanings of metaphysical music through light and posture, suggesting at once a human musician, divine inspiration, and even the newly important saintly patroness of the art, Cecilia, the Christianized Lady Music.

By the seventeenth century, similar figures of women, musical and otherwise, served especially as "Vices. . ./ and Vertues too/by words declined in the female gender." This was no less true in opera or oratorio than in painting or sculpture, in which such characters as Musica and Piacere were conventionally assigned female form. Cesare Ripa's highly influential *Iconologia*, which served as a source book of visual imagery throughout the seventeenth and eighteenth centuries, gives no fewer than five variants of the ancient image of Lady Music.[92] But now Musica and her almost equally venerable sister, Poesia, are joined by Arte and Pittura, although the tool-using, nature-husbanding Artificio is almost aggressively male.[93] The advantage for women artists (as well as women singers and instrumentalists) in an era of costumed role-playing on stage or on canvas was suddenly tremendous. Unlike their male colleagues, they could literally embody their own art or related forms, translating the full range of signification onto their features. The famous Lavinia Fontana was the first painter to benefit from her gender's commonality with the newly-devised image of Pittura; a commemorative medal cast in her honor in 1611 shows her on its *verso* in the same posture and guise Ripa describes for the art.[94] Gentileschi, however, created an extraordinarily vibrant *Self-Portrait as the Allegory of Painting*, modifying only slight detail from Ripa's precise recommendation.[95]

What of her self-portrait as a musician (see Figure 2.9), painted between 1615 and 1617? With only one instrument and no other symbolic objects, with no garland of flowers, no swans, or even a cicada, she fits none of Ripa's descriptions of Musica.[96] Like Fontana and Robusti in the previous century, she shows herself richly dressed; her instrument is also beautifully decorated. Her velvet gown is brilliant blue, with sparkling golden ornamentation around the neck and sleeves.

---

[91] R. Ward Bissell, "Orazio Gentileschi's Young Woman with a Violin," *Bulletin of the Detroit Institute of Arts* 46 (1967): 74-76.

[92] Ripa, *Della Novissima iconologia*, 446-447.

[93] *Ibid.*, 50-53, 96-97, 446-447, and 519-520.

[94] Garrard, *Artemisia Gentileschi*, 340-341 and 356; and Tufts, "Ms. Lavinia Fontana," 64.

[95] Garrard, *Artemisia Gentileschi*, 337-370.

[96] See Ripa, *Della Novissima Iconologia*, 446-447. For the reason for assigning these dates to Gentileschi's work, see Keith Christiansen and Judith W. Mann, *Orazio and Artemisia Gentileschi* (New Haven and London: Yale University Press, 2001), 324. This painting was unknown until it appeared at the Sotheby's London sale in July 1998 although one like it had been described in a Medici inventory in 1638; Christiansen and Mann, *Orazio and Artemisia Gentileschi*, 322.

Shown in three-quarter profile, gazing toward the viewer over the neck of her lute, she also wears a lavish head-covering and sash, both trimmed in gold. She holds the lute in playing position, though only her left hand, on the fingerboard, is completely active; her right, as far as possible from the elaborate rose, rests just above the instrument's bridge, waiting to play the next chord. Her breasts are pushed up beneath her fine chemise, revealing the *décolletage* of the full-figured seventeenth century beauty. Her cheeks are flushed. Her mouth is chastely closed, and a gold hoop shines in her left ear. Both performer and instrument are beautiful, expensive objects.

Art historians Keith Christiansen and Judith Mann suggest that the image may present the artist playing some unknown role, as she did in at least one other (non-musical) self-portrait from around the same time. They point out, quite correctly, that many images of young female lutenists from her era have strong erotic connotations, and that the inclusion of musical instruments in seventeenth century pictures has frequently been associated with lust and sexuality. Presumably, Gentileschi was no more playing into this sort of heterosexual male fantasy than her predecessors Anguissola or Fontana – especially since, by the seventeenth century, these images of bold female lutenists often suggested pleasure for purchase.[97] But this is not the only signification of a woman lutenist. Gentileschi's own *oeuvre* includes a *Woman Playing a Lute* of about 1610-12, with upturned head seeking inspiration from a higher plane in the manner of so many early seventeenth century images one short step removed from St. Cecilia (see Figure 2.10).[98] However, her self-portrait is more earth-bound than this, taking place entirely in the spatial plane of the viewer.

Even on an earthly plane, not all female lutenists are eroticized as potential possessions or sexual playthings. Giuseppe Maria Crespi presents one wearing a gown in much the same style as Gentileschi's, turned from the viewer to play and sing for herself alone (see Figure 2.11). There is a slight suggestion of voyeurism to this image, especially since the viewer approaches the lutenist from an angle of stealth. Again there is the sense of private female space, and private female action. But the image, perhaps a more mundane descendent of Lady Music, conveys neither sacred nor erotic narrative. Neither, evidently, does Gentileschi's staged self-portrait, as carefully posed as any of her female predecessors. The key to it may be as simple as the painter/subject's flushed cheeks, indicating a musical and constitutional type more often associated with men, but known to relate to female practice. Within humoral medicine, the sanguine type, identifiable by fair, ruddy skin, was the most innately musical, the most intellectual, the most energetic, most friendly to artists

---

[97] Christiansen and Mann, *Orazio and Artemisia Gentileschi*, 324. For important insights on the particular, and frequently erotic, representational relationship between women and lutes, see Julia Craig-McFeely, "The Signifying Serpent," in: *Music, Sensation and Sensuality*, ed. Linda Phyllis Austern (New York: Routledge, 2002), 299-320.

[98] This painting might well have been inspired by some of Orazio's roughly contemporaneous work; see Garrard, *Artemisia Gentileschi*, 27-28.

Figure 2.10 Artemisia Gentileschi, *Woman Playing the Lute*, ca. 1610-12
Spada Gallery, Rome
Permission of Alinari, Art Resource, New York

Figure 2.11 Giuseppe Maria Crespi, *Woman Tuning a Lute*, c. 1700
Photograph copyrighted 2003 Museum of Fine Arts, Boston

and scholars – and the most desirable to be. Music was therefore prescribed to all for its sanguinary benefits, to stir the blood of the performer of any constitution into health and vitality.[99] As is still the case, medical norms and recommendations in the early modern era were male; images of benign sanguinary lutenists (and composers such as Thomas Campion who wrote lute-songs to promote circulatory health) are virtually all male. But women were certainly encouraged to play music, quietly for themselves, to avoid melancholy and other depressive disorders. Might Gentileschi have been promoting a well-balanced, energetic, and positive artistic temperament in her image?

By the eighteenth century, not only were music and painting most often categorized together among the fine arts. Appreciation and participation in both were necessary signifiers of cultured refinement for the bourgeoisie as well as the wealthy. Just as eighteenth century musical life was marked by the dramatic expansion of public concerts and publications for amateur home use, there were vast increases in the production, display, and marketing of paintings.[100] Even well-bred young ladies were encouraged to learn artistic practices once associated with manliness displayed; music and painting were no longer categorized with feats of arms as forms of learning that made manly men. "The love of the arts softens that ferocious disposition, of which every nation partakes more or less in proportion to its more elegant improvements," writes one eighteenth century commentator.[101] Another, who dedicated a pseudonymous work on "The Polite Arts" "to the Ladies," explains that "The Heroes of the world learn now, from you [ladies], to conquer, in peace, the whole universe by mildness and courtesy."[102] Descriptions of the beneficial effects of artistic production and consumption became increasingly common throughout the century, more firmly linked to aesthetic values and civilized behavior than to particular social status. "This is the Progress of Taste," says one manual on the "polite arts," meant for wide circulation:

By little and little the Publick are caught by Examples. . . . [T]heir Manners, Discourse, and outward Appearance, all seem to be reforming, and this Reformation passes even into their Souls. They resolve that their Thoughts, when they come from them, shall appear just, natural and proper to merit the Esteem of other Men. In a word they determine that the Polite Man shall shine forth and shew himself by a lively and

---

[99] See Gretchen L. Finney, "Music, Mirth and the Galenic Tradition in England," in: *Reason and the Imagination: Studies in the History of Ideas, 1600-1800*, ed. J.A. Mazzeo (London: Routledge and Kegan Paul, 1962), 144-145; and John Henry, "Doctors and Healers in the Seventeenth Century," in: *Companion to the History of Modern Science*, ed. R.C. Olby, G.N. Cantor, J.R.R. Christopher and M.S. Hodge (London and New York: Routledge, 1990), 199-201.

[100] Peter De Bolla, "The Visibility of Visuality," in: *Vision in Context: Historical and Contemporary Perspectives on Sight* (London and New York: Routledge, 1996), 69-71.

[101] Rouquet, *The Present State of the Arts in England*, 10.

[102] Cosmetti (pseud.), *The Polite Arts, Dedicated to the Ladies*, Dedication.

graceful Expression equally remote from Rudeness and Affection: two Vices as contrary to Taste in Society, as they are in the *Polite Arts.*[103]

The gentleman had merged with the polite man as the early modern era drew to its close, participant in a civic humanism requiring skills which one could acquire through birth or through education.[104]

Against this background, naturalistic portraiture became, if anything, even more important. What Jean André Rouquet says of England, where our final woman musical self-portraitist spent much of her career, applies as much to the rest of Europe:

> Portraiture is the kind of painting the most encouraged, and consequently the most followed. . . [I]t is the polite custom, even for men, to present one another with their pictures.[105]

The culture was infused with a desire to be seen and to see oneself, notions central to this vital refinement known as politeness. Meaning was most apparent in the visual.[106] The pseudonymous "Cosmetti," describing the "Polite Arts" for "the Ladies," explains that music is "justly esteemed the greatest comfort of wise and civilized mortals," but that "[p]ainting has a divine virtue, and is a perpetual miracle."[107] As throughout the early modern era, portraits were useful tools for the solidification or even advancement of one's social position. And as we have seen, where there are portraits, there are women on both sides of the canvas, reflecting and being reflected.

Angelica Kaufmann (1741-1807) follows many of the same professional and biographical patterns as her fellow early modern women artists. Her father, Joseph Johann was a painter in the Swiss city of Bregenz. It was he who first recognized her prodigious talent, trained her, and gave her the first professional tasks as a child in his studio. Like other women in her field, she first became known as a portraitist; in fact, she produced her first competent self-portrait at the age of thirteen, and began to receive commissions very young. She also had an outstanding international career, which took her particularly to London and Rome.[108] In spite of the fact that she became one of London's leading artists and worked across media, and in spite of two previous centuries of women artists, Kaufmann still belonged to

---

[103] The Polite Arts, 4-5.

[104] De Bolla, "The Visibility of Visuality," 71.

[105] Rouquet, *The Present State of the arts in England*, 33.

[106] De Bolla, "The Visibility of Visuality," 72-73; and Silver, "Step-Sister of the Muses," 48.

[107] Cosmetti, The Polite Arts, Dedicated to the Ladies, pp. 29 and 15.

[108] Dorothy Moulton Mayer, *Angelica Kauffmann, R.A. 1741-1807* (Gerrards Cross, Buckinghamshire: Colin Smythe, 1972), 10-11; and Wendy Wassyng Roworth, *Angelica Kauffman: A Continental Artist in Georgian England* (London: Reaktion Books, 1992), 15.

a culture that generally relegated women to domestic dilettantism in the arts and promulgated medical and scientific evidence of women's inferiority and unsuitability to a life in the professions. Women arts amateurs were considered civilizing influences in the home, but avenues to professional training were still as limited as they had been two centuries earlier.[109] Like her predecessors, Kauffman evidently went out of her way to emphasize feminine propriety in her personal life, to remain beyond reproach by potential patrons and detractors alike. One of her early biographers, writing only two years after her death, particularly stresses the accoutrements of feminine domesticity:

> In her house, her garden, and her domestic establishment, all was neat, proper, and unostentatious. Her choice of books was excellent; for her judgment and taste were correct and exquisite, not only in painting but in literature. . . [A]s she was perfectly acquainted with all the principal modern languages, she could feel and enjoy the various beauties of the best productions of each of them. In music her taste was equally genuine[.][110]

This description could easily have been written for any well-bred female member of eighteenth-century Polite Society. Emphasis is placed on aesthetic taste and consumption, not on production. Here we also see for Kauffman another of the qualities emphasized in the public image and self-fashioning of many early modern women artists: intellectualism, and accomplishment across the arts. Like Anguissola and Robusti, if not others, "in music her taste was equally genuine" – trained and noted as outstanding from early on.

Kauffman was reputed to be a young prodigy in music as well as in painting, possessed of an exquisite voice. In her teens, as she later recalled, she had had to choose between the two – although selecting any public career was highly unusual for a young lady of her era. One of her first biographers tells a dramatic tale that might even have a grain of truth: being devout Catholics, she and her father sent for a local priest to help make the decision. As the story goes, the priest told the young Kauffman that early success as a musician would be easy and lucrative, but that a musical career, especially on the stage, would expose her to grave moral dangers in an unprincipled environment. In contrast, an artistic career would permit more time, said he, for proper religious devotion, even if it would require more arduous training and more intense challenge of the intellect.[111] Whether true or not, this tale represents prevailing eighteenth century attitudes toward music as an art of sensual

---

[109] See Roworth, *Angelica Kauffman*, 15; and Angela Rosenthal, "Angelica Kauffman Ma(s)king Claims," *Art History* 15 (1992): 38-41.

[110] Joseph Moser, "Memoir of the Late Angelica Kaufman, R.A." *The European Magazine and London Review* (April 1809): 254. See also Mayer, *Angelica Kauffmann*, in which she is described as "a young woman of remarkable charm. . . exceedingly graceful, and nature as well as the company she met in noble houses had taught her to bear herself with elegance," 13.

[111] Mayer, Angelica Kauffmann, 13-14; and Raworth, Angelica Kaufman, 15.

display, founded at least as much on innate natural talent as on training – qualities as easily found in women and children as in men. Painting in this little biographical fable becomes the more elite, more cerebral of the two, ultimately reversing the comparative ranking from Anguissola's, Fontana's, and Robusti's world. Both the Polite Lady and the woman who would go beyond the confines dictated for her gender would eschew the musical career.

Kaufmann's *Self Portrait: Hesitating Between the Arts of Music and Painting* of 1791 is a subtle masterpiece of gender propaganda subverted, as well as a superb representation of eighteenth-century recommendations for conjoining music, image, and narrative (see Figure 2.12). Although concerned with the sort of choice Fontana displays at a different level and for different ends, the composition could hardly contrast more. It is a product of its time, and a culture that perceived music and painting to have very different connections to each other and to the dominant consuming culture. It celebrates Kauffman's youthful decision between her two great talents by casting the entirety into the form of a famous ancient fable used by other artists of the seventeenth and eighteenth centuries: the *Choice of Hercules*, from Xenophon's *Memorabilia*. As conventionally represented, the fable shows the young hero at a crossroads, where he must choose between Vice, embodied by an eroticized, if not sexually available, woman; and Virtue, an upstanding woman clad in shining armor.[112] Like Gentileschi, Kauffman works with a subject conventionally given powerful (male hetero) sexual connotations to render it strongly feminine. All three of her female figures (for the young Kauffman takes the position ascribed to Hercules) are civilized and lovely, the sort one would invite to a costume ball or theatrical exercise at an elite girls' school. Music, replacing Vice, is no more (or less) physically "tempting" than Painting or Angelica/Hercules herself. It is through more subtle codes that Kauffman shows the "right" choice, though still showing at least the sympathy to music that Fontanagrants her easel.

The ideal painting of the eighteenth century, like the previous two, would include evocations of classical authority, as Kauffman presents. It was not unusual, but even further encouraged, to give narrative form to imagery in all genres, including portraiture, for:

> Poetry and Painting have so exact a Resemblance to one another, that to treat of them both at the same time, we should have nothing to do but to put, Poetry, Fable, and Versification, in the room of Painting, Design, and Colouring. It is the same Genius that creates in one and the other: the same taste that directs the artists.[113]

Such verses or fables particularly enabled imaginative characterization, casting modern figures into the role of time-honored heroes. Many such allegorized actors

---

[112] Raworth, *Angelica Kauffman*, 15-16, 55, and 209; and Rosenthal, "Angelica Kauffman Ma(s)king Claims," 42-44.

[113] *The Polite Arts*, 46.

Figure 2.12 Angelica Kauffman, *Self-Portrait Hesitating between the Arts of Music and Painting*, 1796
Permission of the Nostell Priory, The St. Oswald Collection (The National Trust) National Trust Photo Library/John Hammond

were female, as in Kauffman's self-representation, or indeed Musica and Pittura.[114] Even music had a place in relation to imagery as it had since Leonardo's time. Hearing was even more definitively "the second sense," making music simpler than painting to judge by sense:

> Musick should be judged in the same manner as a Picture. . . . [T]he Ear, say they, is much more delicate than the Eye. Then I am more capable to judge a Piece of Musick than of a Picture.[115]

Once again, the argument parallels Kauffman's early advisor; painting is the more subtle, more sophisticated art. The English treatise *The Polite Arts* explains that the way in which one should conjoin arts is parallel to literary or pictorial narrative, in that one should be the hero, the other(s) secondary:

> It is of the different Arts, when they join to treat of the same Subject, as it is of different Parts, which are found in a Subject treated by a single Art: there ought to be a principal one. . . When Poets and Painters represent an Action, they place a principal Actor in it, whom they call the Hero. . . It is this Hero that is placed in the most advantageous Light; he is the principal Part, and the Life and Soul of all that moves about him. . . .The Arts united ought to be th^e same as Heroes. One alone should excel[.][116]

Kauffman's classically inspired narrative not only presents her in the role of the heroic young Hercules, but gives us one art as hero, placed literally and figuratively in the most advantageous light. This is not theatre, in which Poetry plays the hero. Nor is it Music (or even Opera), with the delicate ear as principal sensory critic. Within the painted allegory, Painting becomes the principal part for the (future) life and soul of the young Angelica. The brunette Music, located to the left (or sinister) side of the composition is literally the lowest of the three figures, sitting loose-limbed in the shadow of a stone edifice. She wears red, the most provocative and sensuous of colors, crowned by a wreath of flowers, a traditional emblem of beauty that fades. Painting, in contrast, is a blonde, standing confidently upright before the bright sky in a blue gown (the traditional color of revealed truth), pointing toward a temple bathed in light. Angelica/Hercules, robed in pure white but girdled by the colors of both arts, looks backward toward Music as she clasps her hand in a gesture of friendship. Her other hand points palm up toward Painting and her palette, as her body turns away from Music and her shadowy backdrop toward Art, the sun-lit sky, and the magnificent temple on the hill. Kauffman

---

[114] See Roworth, *Angelica Kauffman*, 68-72; Silver, "Step-Sister of the Muses," 56-59; and Richard Wendorf, "*Ut Pictura biographia*: Biography and Portrait Painting as Sister Arts," in: *Articulate Images: The Sister Arts from Hogarth to Tennyson*, ed. Richard Wendorf (Minneapolis: University of Minnesota Press, 1983), 98-107.

[115] The Polite Arts, 55.

[116] The Polite Arts, 128-129.

hereby rejects Music for Painting, the art sitting before an interior space for the one who gestures the sunlit temple of everlasting fame, the one that decays for the one that lasts. Several critics have pointed out that this choice is also for the traditionally "masculine" visual position and the more "masculine" career.[117] Nonetheless, it is worth noting that Kaufmann, who succeeded in a man's profession and a man's world, retains an element of proper femininity. Her own figure in the painting is in some ways the most feminized, with its ruffled gown in the color of purity. Music, from whom she parts like a wistful friend, suggests sensuousness and frivolity, attributes a professional who is already violating gender or sexual boundaries cannot afford. By Kauffman's era, the class status implied by music in earlier eras had become less relevant. Music no longer signified the same sort of accomplishment, or understanding of the codes of courtly civility, as it had in Anguissola's, Fontana's and Robusti's day. The way to indicate that she understood how to be an acceptable professional in her own world was to leave it.

Over the two centuries of early modernity, the relative status of the arts to each other and within the most cultured circles of art production and consumption changed more than did the status of the woman artist. She remained exceptional. Nonetheless, self-representations of such artists as musicians provide valuable evidence as to how accomplished women constructed themselves and successfully negotiated their social and professional positions. Each one used music at once to reinforce her status as learned artiste and as a woman in a man's world. What Carlo Ridolfi concluded in the first biography of Marietta Robusti could speak for all of them: "This excellent lady will serve in the future as a model of womanly virtue, making known to the world that gems, gold, and precious clothing are not the true female adornments, but rather those virtues that shine in the soul and remain eternal after life."[118]

---

[117] See Raworth, *Angelica Kauffman*; and Rosenthal, "Angelica Kauffman Ma(s)king Claims," 45-49.

[118] Ridolfi, "The Life of Marietta Tintoretta," 99.

WOMEN EN-VOICED

Chapter 3

Chivalric Romance, Courtly Love and Courtly Song: Female Vocality and Feminine Desire in the World of *Amadis de Gaule*

Jeanice Brooks

First published in 1548, these verses on reading an enthralling novel will strike a chord with any modern reader who has been mesmerized by a page-turner:

> Et si quelqu'un à le lire s'espreuve,
> Pour la douceur, et soulas qu'il y treuve,
> Il en perdra le boire et le menger,
> Il laissera à son profit songer,
> Puys quand aura quelque peu de sejour,
> Y passera et la nuyt et le jour,
> Ne delaissant de lire incessament,
> Tant que iceluy ait leu entierement.
> Et peu apres s'il vient à y penser,
> Vouloir aura de le recommencer . . . [1]

> [And when someone sets himself to read it,
> The sweetness and pleasure he finds in it
> Will cause him to forget to eat and drink,
> He will leave off thinking about his business,
> Then when he has a little leisure,
> He will spend night and day over it,
> Never stopping to read incessantly
> Until he has read it completely,
> And soon after, if he happens to think upon it,

---

*My thanks to Matthew Head, Ellen Harris and Marian Rothstein for their advice and comments on an earlier draft of this essay.

[1] Michel Sévin d'Orléans, prefatory poem to *Le huitiesme livre d'Amadis de Gaule*, trans. Nicolas de Herberay des Essarts (Paris: Groulleau, Longis & Sertenas, 1548), cited after Hugues Vaganay, *Amadis en français. Essai de bibliographie* (Florence: Olschki, 1906; reprint, Geneva: Slatkine, 1970), 75.

He will want to start it all over again . . .]

Another contemporary describes how he devoured the first five volumes of the same work, each installment whetting his appetite for the next. Discovering that the sixth volume has yet to appear, he finds himself wishing he had not yet read the others so he can have the pleasure of starting the whole cycle again.[2] Both of these testimonies were printed with editions of the book itself, and might perhaps be dismissed as elements of publishing propaganda. Yet even hostile witnesses were obliged to concede the work's popularity: though he condemns the effects of reading the novel, François de La Noue admits that it was so beloved at the court of Henri II of France that people would have spit in the face of anyone foolish enough to disparage it.[3]

The novel that elicited such reactions was *Amadis de Gaule*, the sprawling chivalric romance that was the literary sensation of sixteenth-century France. The model for the French redaction was a Spanish romance so successful that François I commanded his courtier Nicolas de Herberay des Essarts to make a French translation.[4] Herberay des Essarts expanded considerably on his model, freely amplifying and rearranging material to align the novel more closely with French courtly sensibilities. At the same time, he fashioned a supple, lyrical prose style that resonated with contemporary projects of linguistic enrichment. So distinctive and appealing was the style that it became a model for courtly speech and writing, and a new verb – *amadiser*, meaning to speak in a sweetly ornate fashion – entered the French vocabulary.[5] After the publication of the first book in 1540, Herberay des Essarts produced seven further volumes before his death in 1552; a series of different writers translated subsequent volumes up to the appearance of book 24 in 1615. Re-editions of the earlier books continued throughout the century, and collections of extracts – the "thresors" of the romance – ensured the wide dissemination of its most admired speeches.[6]

---

[2] *Ibid.*, 38.

[3] François de La Noue, *Discours politiques et militaires* (1581), ed. F.E. Sutcliffe (Geneva: Droz, 1967), 162.

[4] On the background of the French version, see Yves Giraud's introduction to *Le premier livre d'Amadis de Gaule*, ed. Yves Giraud and Hugues Vaganay (Paris: Société des Textes Français Modernes, 1986), 5-6. Herberay des Essarts's biography is most thoroughly treated in Michel Simonin, "La disgrâce d'*Amadis*," *Studi Francesi* 28 (1984): 1-35.

[5] On Herberay des Essarts's style as model, see Véronique Benhaïm, "Les *Thresors d'Amadis*," in : *Les Amadis en France au XVIe siècle*, ed. Robert Aulotte (Paris: Editions rue d'Ulm, 2000), 164-180 and Mireille Huchon, "Amadis, 'Parfaicte idée de nostre langue françoise'," in: *Les Amadis en France*, ed. Aulotte, 183-200.

[6] The first four volumes in French are modeled on Garcí Rodríguez de Montalvo's Spanish romance; later volumes draw on sequels by other Spanish (and later, Italian) writers. Robert Aulotte, ed., *Les Amadis en France*, 209-211, supplies a list of early editions of volumes 1-14 of the French cycle and matches them to their Spanish originals; see also Hugues Vaganay, "Les éditions in-8° de l'*Amadis* français," *Revue hispanique* 85 (1929): 1-53. Vaganay, *Amadis en français,* and the bibliography of book 1 in Giraud and Vaganay,

If contemporary testimony can be believed, almost everyone in sixteenth century France who could read, read *Amadis de Gaule*. But the unmitigated success of the early decades yielded to more mixed reactions in the second half of the century. Though the novel was still widely read, its erotic aspects became a target for moralists, while military writers deplored the improbably fantastic quality of the combat episodes. Its polished language was linked with a courtly love of style for style's sake, regarded with distrust; *amadiser* acquired pejorative connotations, and was most frequently used to describe a kind of sweet talking used to camouflage lascivious intentions. At the same time, and perhaps as a corollary, *Amadis* became more closely identified with a female reading public, a readership explicitly targeted by printers and translators.[7] The luxurious folio format adopted for the volumes by Herberay des Essarts soon gave way to smaller re-editions; the first octavo edition of Book 1, printed in 1548, included a poem by Jean Maugin addressed "aux dames françoises" explaining that the smaller size would allow them to carry their favorite book more easily.[8] In the same year, Thomas Sébillet advised budding authors that if they wanted to be well received by women readers, they should adopt the style of *Amadis*, "le langage desquels est reçu en la bouche d'elles, comme plus doux et savoureux."[9] While Herberay des Essarts had dedicated his adaptations to male royal and military patrons, from 1552 subsequent translators addressed their books to prominent court noblewomen. Though there has been some debate over how to interpret these gestures, it seems

---

eds., *Amadis I*, 24-26. Marian Rothstein points out that the commercial success of *Amadis* was such that its editions take up ten times more space than any other work in Richard Cooper's "Outline Bibliography of Works on Chivalry Published in France Before 1600" (in *Chivalry in the Renaissance*, ed. Sydney Anglo (Rochester: Boydell, 1990)), cited in Rothstein, *Reading in the Renaissance: Amadis de Gaule and the Lessons of Memory* (Newark: University of Delaware Press, 1999), 32. On the "thresors," see Benhaïm, "Les *Thresors*," and Hugues Vaganay, "Les trésors d'*Amadis*: essai de bibliographie," *Revue hispanique* 57 (1923): 115-126.

[7] On the readership of *Amadis*, see Rothstein, *Reading in the Renaissance*, 114-124. Simonin, "La disgrâce," tracks the novel's declining reputation, though Nicole Cazauran warns against an over-facile equation of fading critical fortunes with a decline in readership Nicole Cazauran, "*Amadis de Gaule* en 1540: un nouveau 'roman de chevalerie'?," in: *Les Amadis*, ed. Aulotte, 22n. Benhaïm, "Les *Thresors*," shows that the extracts preserved in the *Thresors* extended the exemplary power of *Amadis* well after the fashion for the novel as a whole had begun to wane.

[8] The poem is edited in Vaganay, *Amadis en français*, 14. On the format of early editions, see Rothstein, *Reading in the Renaissance*, 32-34.

[9] "The language of which is received in their mouths, as the sweetest and most delicious." Thomas Sébillet, *Art poétique français*, ed. Félix Gaiffe, revised by Françis Goyet (Paris: Société des Textes Français Modernes, 1988), 61. Note Sébillet's expression, which suggests that female readers find *speaking* the words pleasurable; this notion will prove significant in my interpretation.

clear that by the second half of the sixteenth century, the *Amadis* novels had indeed begun to enjoy a substantial female readership.[10]

These shifts in the romance's reception in the second half of the century coincided with a moment when women were a conspicuous presence in prints of courtly song. In the early 1570s, the worlds of *Amadis* and of court song were especially closely enmeshed: both song books and new *Amadis* translations emanated from a Neoplatonic and Neopetrarchan salon environment inhabited by female patrons, readers and performers. Links in production and reception were matched by correspondences in content, for song texts frequently mirror moments of speech in the romance. Romance thus appears as a potentially powerful tool for interpreting the cultural role of French song at an important juncture in its history, when the popularizing strophic pieces formerly known as *voix de ville* were cultivated with increasing assiduity at court.

Romance as delineated by romantic fiction and popular song – in both historical and modern contexts – has been a topic of fierce controversy among feminist historians, sociologists and literary critics, variously regarded as opiate aimed at duping women into submission to patriarchy, or opportunity for imaginary escape from the dreary lives that patriarchy may impose.[11] The debate has underlined the importance of exploring the uses of romance in actual women's lives if we are to understand its undeniable appeal to female audiences both past and present. How precisely to go about such an investigation is less clear, however, and a range of different reader- and audience-centered approaches have been applied to romantic songs and fiction in recent decades. The application of sociological methods to collect data about consumers of romance has proved particularly fruitful for studying contemporary fiction; despite the obvious constraints on the amount of information we can assemble about historical readers, they too have become a newly important focus of study.[12] The influence of

---

[10] Helen Hackett (*Women and Romance Fiction in the English Renaissance* (Cambridge: Cambridge University Press, 2000), 4-19) observes that appeals to female readers in novels' prefatory material could function as an advertisement of the racy, emotional aspect of the books to male book buyers, and are as much a function of the feminization of romance as a genre as an indication of an actual female reading public. Elizabeth Spearing, however, on the basis of ownership marks and other evidence, argues for a large female readership for *Amadis* ("The Representation of Women and Gender in the *Amadis* Cycle," D.Phil. dissertation, University of York, 1991, 17).

[11] For an excellent overview of the issues, see Susan Ostrov Weisser's introduction to *Women and Romance: A Reader* (New York: New York University Press, 2001), 1-6.

[12] The most influential study of contemporary readers of romantic fiction has been Janice Radway, *Reading the Romance: Women, Patriarchy and Popular Literature* (Chapel Hill: University of North Carolina Press, 1984; reprint, with new introduction, 1991). Reader-oriented studies of Renaissance romance include Rothstein, *Reading in the Renaissance*; see also Helen Hackett, *Women and Romance Fiction*. For a discussion of some of the challenges inherent in attempts to recover the reactions of historical women readers, see Roberta L. Krueger, *Women Readers and the Ideology of Gender in Old French Verse Romance* (Cambridge: Cambridge University Press, 1993), 17-32.

psychoanalytic theory on recent literary criticism has ensured that readers' experience of sexuality and desire has become a central concern in post-Freudian examinations of the relationship of reader and text, though often with unacceptable results for feminist scholars. Classic psychoanalytic accounts assume that desire is an innate human urge that seeks to find expression through romance, an assumption that problematically denies the specificity of readerly activity upon which historical-sociological studies are based and the potential for change to which feminist principles are committed.[13] My own investigation thus takes as a fundamental premise that romance is one means by which desire is produced. Its constructions are historically and socially contingent: romantic songs and fiction are used by their audiences in culturally specific ways to invent their own versions of desire.[14] In what follows, I first sketch the outlines of the environment in which romance was cultivated in sixteenth-century France, to show that *Amadis de Gaule* and the court song repertory were produced for and consumed by the same interpretive community of female readers, singers and listeners. I then consider what these musical and literary romantic narratives meant for this community, and how novels and songs figured in vocal performances of feminine desire in French courtly circles of the late Renaissance.

Amadis de Gaule has much in common with the chivalric romances cultivated in France throughout the middle ages. Its structure is episodic, spawning seemingly endless numbers of characters and subplots. The narrative meanders from adventure to adventure, often leaving characters pining in towers or sailing across oceans while doubling back to rescue others who are in the clutches of malevolent giants or under a sorceress's evil spell. As the title page of the first volume declares, *Amadis* "relates many adventures of arms and love, had by several knights and ladies" ("traicte de maintes adventures d'Armes et d'Amours, qu'eurent plusieurs Chevaliers et Dames") and, as in earlier romances, a large portion of each book is devoted to descriptions of the prodigious feats of daring knights.[15]

---

[13] Such principles underlie, for example, Lawrence D. Kritzman, *The Rhetoric of Sexuality and the Literature of the French Renaissance* (Cambridge: Cambridge University Press, 1991).

[14] This is not to reject a potential role to the unconscious, or to deny the similarities that may exist between different cultures' configurations of desire, but to emphasize that the experience and understanding of desire has varied over time and across divisions of e.g. class, sexuality and gender. See Stevi Jackson, "Love and Romance as Objects of Feminist Knowledge," in: *Making Connections: Women's Studies, Women's Movements, Women's Lives*, ed. Mary Kennedy, Cathy Lubelska, and Val Walsh (Washington, D.C.: Taylor and Francis, 1993; reprinted in Weisser, ed. *Women and Romance*), 260-261.

[15] Giraud and Vaganay, eds., *Amadis I*, 9-10, characterises the structure as archaic, privileging luxuriance over coherence; see also Rothstein, *Reading in the Renaissance*, 64-70, and John J. O'Connor, *Amadis de Gaule and its Influence on Elizabethan Literature* (New Brunswick, N.J.: Rutgers University Press, 1970), 85-129.

The *Amadis* cycle differs from its medieval and Spanish forebears in its much greater emphasis on love episodes, which are strongly imbued with the Neoplatonist and Neopetrarchan ideals that shaped French court culture from the 1540s onward. Herberay des Essarts's Amadis is not only perfect warrior but perfect lover. His relationship with his adored Oriane illustrates a quest for spiritual perfection through worldly love that would have seemed familiar to readers of Ficino, Castiglione, Leone Ebreo and their French translators and adaptors. These qualities of the French *Amadis* have a special impact on the female characters of the romance. As women rarely figure in battle scenes except as pretext, the increased attention to love allows them a larger share of the novel's action than in *Amadis*'s predecessors. And the instrumental function of women in Neoplatonic love theory affords their role within these episodes a heightened significance in comparison with their earlier counterparts.[16]

Since the novel so consistently reflects Neoplatonic ideals, it is not surprising that the impetus for a new round of *Amadis* volumes in the early 1570s came from the circle around Claude-Catherine de Clermont, comtesse de Retz. Gatherings in her salon nourished a fertile creative environment whose traces have been abundantly preserved in contemporary prints and manuscripts.[17] The Retz circle is well known to literary scholars for its role in fostering a new wave of Neoplatonist and Neopetrarchan writing in the 1570s, which involved poets of the Pléiade as well as the younger generation of Jamin and Desportes. The salon also played an important part in the history of the French *Amadis*. Jacques Gohory's 1571 translation of the *Trezieme livre* is dedicated to Catherine de Clermont, and contains a preface explaining that his work on the book was undertaken at her request. Gohory, a humanist and alchemist with strong occult leanings, had translated volumes 10 and 11 of the series nearly twenty years previously; his return to the novel after such a long lapse supports his contention that the 1571

---

[16] See Rothstein, *Reading in the Renaissance*, 52-60 on the Neoplatonic conversion of *Amadis*; Catherine Mary Hampton, "Chastity: A Literary and Cultural Icon of the French Sixteenth-Century Court" (Ph.D. diss., University of Durham, 1996), 201-215, discusses the novel's illustration of the Neoplatonic icon of chastity.

[17] For biographical information on Catherine de Clermont, see Mme Michel Jullien de Pommerol [Marie-Henriette de Montéty], *Albert de Gondi, Maréchal de Retz* (Geneva: Droz, 1953), 195-218, and Christie Ellen St-John, "The *Salon vert* of the Maréchale de Retz : A Study of a Literary Salon in Sixteenth-Century France" (Ph.D. diss., Vanderbilt University, 1999). The activities of her salon are also discussed in Jacques Lavaud, *Philippe Desportes (1546-1606): un poète de cour au temps des derniers Valois* (Paris: Droz, 1936), 72-106, L. Clark Keating, *Studies on the Literary Salon in France, 1550-1615* (Cambridge: Harvard University Press, 1941), 103-125, Jeanice Brooks, "La comtesse de Retz et l'air de cour des années 1570," in : *Le concert des voix et des instruments à la Renaissance*, ed. Jean-Michel Vaccaro (Paris: Editions du CNRS, 1995) ; and Rosanna Gorris, "'Je veux chanter d'amour la tempeste et l'orage': Desportes et les *Imitations* d'Arioste," in : *Philippe Desportes (1546-1606): Un poète presque parfait entre Renaissance et Classicisme*, ed. Jean Balsamo (Paris: Klincksieck, 2000), 173-211.

translation was the result of a commission.[18] Three years later, Anthoine Tiron's translation of the *Quatorsieme livre* was published with a preface by Gohory dedicating the volume to Henriette de Cleves, duchesse de Nevers, one of Catherine de Clermont's greatest allies at court.[19]

In the same years, the countess was closely connected to seminal French music prints devoted to the nascent genre of the *air de cour*. Catherine de Clermont was a dedicatee of Guillaume Costeley's *Musique* of 1570, the first music print to employ the word *air* to describe vernacular strophic songs.[20] More significant still is Adrian Le Roy's dedication to her in the following year of his *Livre d'airs de cour miz sur le luth*, the first printed music collection to designate such songs as *airs de cour*.[21] The *Livre d'airs de cour* contains versions for voice and lute of fashionable court songs, most of which had previously been published in polyphonic arrangements in Nicolas de La Grotte's *Chansons* of 1569. In his preface, Le Roy points out that Catherine already knows their melodies and texts, and he suggests that their familiarity will contribute to her pleasure when she performs these new versions on the lute.[22] The *Livre d'airs de cour* was a sequel

---

[18] Gohory was responsible for *Le Dixiesme livre d'Amadis de Gaule* and *L'Onzieme livre d'Amadis de Gaule* (Paris: Groulleau, Longis & Sertenas, 1552 and 1553); his translation of the thirteenth book was the first new volume to appear since Guillaume Aubert's 1556 translation of book 12. On Gohory's biography, see the list of sources supplied by Rosanna Gorris, "Pour une lecture stéganographique des *Amadis* de Jacques Gohory," in: *Les Amadis en France*, ed. Aulotte, 127-156.

[19] *Le quatorzieme livre d'Amadis de Gaule*, trans. Anthoine Tiron (Chambéry: Poumar, 1575); on the friendship between Catherine de Clermont and Henriette de Clèves, see Lavaud, *Philippe Desportes* 89-90 and 93; Jeanice Brooks, *Courtly Song in Late Sixteenth-Century France* (Chicago: University of Chicago Press, 2000), 109-110.

[20] Guillaume Costeley, *Musique de Guillaume Costeley, organiste ordinaire et vallet de chambre, du treschretien et tresinvincible Roy de France* (Paris: Le Roy & Ballard, 1570), partly edited in Henry Expert, ed., *Les maîtres musiciens de la Renaissance française* (Paris: Leduc, 1894-1908; reprint, New York: Broude Brothers, n.d.), vol. 18 (1896); for pieces missing from Expert's edition see Jane Bernstein, ed., *The Sixteenth-Century Chanson*, 30 vols. (New York: Garland, 1987-95), vol. 8 (1989). Catherine's husband Albert de Gondi was another dedicatee of Costeley's *Musique*, and in the same year he received a dedicatory ode by Adrian Le Roy in Orlande de Lassus, *Mellange d'Orlande de Lassus, contenant plusieurs chansons, tant en vers latins qu'en ryme françoyse* (Paris: Le Roy & Ballard, 1570), reedited as *Meslanges d'Orlande de Lassus* (Paris: Le Roy & Ballard, 1576). See Brooks, "La comtesse de Retz;" a complete list of dedications to the Retz appears on pp. 313-314. Gondi was the *premier gentilhomme de la chambre* in the last years of the reign of Charles IX (d. 1574), a position of great power that helps to explain the rash of literary dedications to him and his wife in the early 1570s.

[21] Adrian Le Roy, *Livre d'airs de cour miz sur le luth* (Paris: Le Roy & Ballard, 1571), in Lionel de La Laurencie, Adrienne Mairy, and Geneviève Thibault, eds., *Chansons au luth et airs de cour français du XVIe siècle*, ed. Lionel de La Laurencie, Adrienne Mairy, and Geneviève Thibault (Paris: Société Française de Musicologie, 1934; reprint, 1976).

[22] For a detailed discussion of the book see Brooks, *Courtly Song*, 13-31. Its relationship with Nicolas de La Grotte, *Chansons de P. de Ronsard, Ph. Desportes et autres* (Paris: Le Roy & Ballard, 1569) is analyzed in Jonathan Le Cocq, "The Status of Le Roy's

to another book Le Roy had recently dedicated to Catherine de Clermont, a lute instruction, probably first printed in 1570, which survives only in a 1574 English translation.[23] In the preface to the *Livre d'airs de cour*, Le Roy identifies himself as a "hereditary servant" of Catherine's family. The allusion is clarified by a passage in the preface to the lute instruction, in which Le Roy evokes his service to Catherine's father, Claude de Clermont, baron de Dampierre, and recalls how he wept over Dampierre's body when he was killed in battle in 1545.[24]

This long-standing association suggests that songs from several other books by Le Roy formed part of Catherine's repertoire. Soon after Le Roy and Robert Ballard founded their music printing firm in 1551, they published a series of books devoted to music for plucked string instruments which identify Le Roy himself as the author of the tablatures. Among these was the *Second livre de guiterre, contenant plusieurs chansons en forme de voix de ville*, first printed in late 1551 or early 1552 and devoted to strophic song. It presents versions for guitar and voice of pieces that Le Roy & Ballard simultaneously printed in polyphonic arrangements in Pierre Certon's *Premier livre de chansons* of 1552.[25] As Table 1 demonstrates, Le Roy repeatedly turned to these songs as both printer and arranger over the next two decades. Shortly after dedicating the *Livre d'airs de cour* to Catherine in 1571, Le Roy produced his *Premier livre de chansons en forme de vau de ville* (1573), consisting of new polyphonic arrangements of the same strophic songs he had published in the 1550s and 1560s in both guitar and polyphonic vocal versions. The books dedicated to Catherine de Clermont in the early 1570s (whose contents even share a few concordances with the earlier prints) were the most recent manifestations of a career-long interest in music in this style. Le Roy's "hereditary service" to Catherine's family makes it seem likely she heard him perform this music when she was a child; his dedication to her of a lute instruction suggests that Le Roy may even have been her teacher on the instrument. His comments in the preface to the *Livre d'airs de cour* about Catherine's familiarity with the pieces it contains gesture toward a body of court songs well known to both and frequently played and sung in Catherine's salon. As

---

Publications for Voice and Lute or Guitar," *The Lute* 35 (1995): 4-27, and Jonathan Le Cocq, "French Lute Song, 1529-1643" (D.Phil. thesis, University of Oxford, 1997), 11-20.

[23] Le Roy's first lute tutor was probably first published in France in 1567; it survives only in a 1568 English translation. The lute instruction dedicated to Catherine probably appeared in 1570, shortly before the *Livre d'airs de cour*. Material from all three books was subsequently included in Le Roy's *A briefe and plaine Instruction to set all musicke of divers Tunes in Tableture for the Lute* (London: Rowbothome, 1574), edited as Adrian Le Roy, *Les instructions pour le luth*, ed. Jean Jacquot, Pierre-Yves Sordes, and Jean-Michel Vaccaro, 2 vols., *Corpus des Luthistes* (Paris: Editions du CNRS, 1977); an account of the bibliographical history appears in vol. 1, ix-xiv.

[24] Editions of the 1574 English translation of the preface appear in *Ibid.*, 1: 2-3, and La Laurencie, Mairy, and Thibault, eds., *Chansons*, lvi.

[25] (Paris: Le Roy & Ballard, 1555 [1556 n.s.]; this is a second edition of a lost print that was first published between the appearance of the *Premier livre de tabulature de guiterre* in September 1551 and the *Tiers livre de tabulature de guiterre* of 1552.

has long been noted, all of these prints are central to the history of the type of song once known as *voix de ville* and rebaptised *air de cour* by Le Roy in 1571.[26]

One link through the prints connected to Catherine de Clermont's salon in the early 1570s is Adrian Le Roy, printer of Costeley's volume and author/ arranger of the others. Another was Jacques Gohory, who supplied a Latin dedicatory poem to the Costeley book and a French preface for Le Roy's lost lute instruction, among a series of prefatory poems and dedications he contributed to Le Roy & Ballard prints in the years around 1570. Gohory was a long-standing acquaintance of Le Roy's as well as an habitué of the Retz salon. In the lute instruction, Gohory wrote that he was inspired by "the affection which from my youth upwards . . . I have borne, to Musicke . . . [and] the old familiaritie which it hath caused me to have with the Aucthor of this present Booke."[27] At the end of his preface Gohory mentions another current project that is almost complete: his translation of the thirteenth book of *Amadis de Gaule*. This was shameless self-publicity, but motivated at least partly by the assumption that purchasers of the lute book will also be interested in reading the romance when the translation is published.

Or at least one reader will be: Catherine de Clermont. To borrow the terminology used by Marian Rothstein in her reception-oriented study of *Amadis*, Catherine appears as one "manifest reader" of the thirteenth book of *Amadis*, Costeley's *Musique*, the lute instruction and the *Airs de cour miz sur le luth*.[28] By dedicating these books to Catherine, Le Roy and Gohory construct her as the intended reader and performer of their contents. It is more difficult to identify other readers not explicitly designated by the texts: though *Amadis* has left greater traces of its readership than most works of the sixteenth century, the music prints have left almost none. Their survival rate is poor, and in sixteenth-century inventories of libraries, notaries generally lumped all music books together under

---

[26] The songs' wide dissemination is suggested by the inclusion of most of the pieces in the collections listed in Table 1 in Jehan Chardavoine's monophonic compendium of popular *voix de ville*: *Le recueil des plus belles et excellentes chansons en forme de voix de ville*, ed. Jehan Chardavoine (Paris: Micard, 1576; reprint, facsimile, Geneva: Minkoff, 1980). The role of these collections in the history of the genre is most thoroughly treated in Jane Ozenberger Whang, "From *Voix de ville* to *Air de cour*: The Strophic Chanson, c. 1545-1575" (Ph.D. diss., University of North Carolina, 1981).

[27] Preface included in François Lesure and Geneviève Thibault, *Bibliographie des éditions d'Adrian Le Roy et Robert Ballard (1551-1598)* (Paris: Société Française de Musicologie, 1955), 33-35. Gohory also supplied dedicatory poetry to three books of Lassus motets: *Secundus liber modulorum, quinis vocibus* (Paris: Le Roy & Ballard, 1571), *Tertius liber modulorum, quinis vocibus* and *Moduli sex septem et duodecim vocum* (both Paris: Le Roy & Ballard, 1573), and to Lassus, *Mellange*, the same chanson anthology that contains Le Roy's poem to Albert de Gondi.

[28] "Manifest readers" are those to whom books are dedicated or who appear in its prefatory pages as the authors or recipients of liminary texts. Rothstein, *Reading in the Renaissance*, 114-117. For other books of the *Amadis* cycle, they include writers such as Etienne Jodelle and Etienne Pasquier, who were habitués of the Retz salon; their prefatory poems to book 9 are reproduced in Vaganay, *Amadis en français*, 89-91 and 94.

rubrics such as "un paquet de livres de musique" without supplying details of individual titles. Nevertheless, ownership marks in the rare extant copies of the song books listed in Table 1 show that their possessors frequently belonged to the same social environment of musicians, writers, court nobles and officials as Costeley, Le Roy, Gohory, Catherine de Clermont and her circle.[29] Though the information is patchy, it is consonant with what we know about the ownership of *Amadis*, and confirms that both kinds of books were consumed within as well as generated by courtly milieux.

But the relationships between the *Amadis* novels and collections of court song are more complex than simply shared readership. Many of the pieces in the song books present lyric meditations on the stereotypical situations of romance, employing the same vocabulary and language as well as position. That is, they are linked not only in a concrete economy of the book market but in the imaginative economy of expression and image. These correspondences in content combine with the strong overlap in production and reception history to suggest that romance supplied frameworks that sixteenth century Frenchwomen themselves brought to understanding song and vice versa, frameworks which we in turn can productively apply to tease out the import of song and romance to a female audience.

In one case, the link between texts is explicit: *C'est de la peine dure*, a song Le Roy included in both his 1552 guitar book and the 1573 *Premier livre en forme de vau de ville*, ends with a strophe in which the male speaker compares his loyal service to his lady to that of Amadis to Oriane:

> Vous serez Oriane,
> Je seray Amadis,
> Ou bien donc l'Eriane,
> Qui aima mieux mourir
> Que changer sa maistresse:
> Combien que par destresse

---

[29] A collection of superius partbooks in *F-Pn* Rés. Vmf. 13, which contains copies of the 1564 editions of Certon's *Premier livre* and the *Second livre de chansons*, belonged to Louis Cramoisy, a keyboard player in the household of the king's brother François d'Anjou. A set of partbooks from the Cortot collection now in *GB-LBl* k.11.e.3 belonged to one of the countesses of La Tillières early in its history; it is not clear from the ownership marks whether this was Charlotte Chabot, who married Jacques de Tillières in 1578, or Catherine de Bassompierre, who married Tanneguy de Tillières in 1608. The Veneur de Tillières were a prominent family of the court nobility; the partbooks include La Grotte's *Chansons* and the 1569 edition of the *Second livre*. Le Roy's *Livre d'airs de cour* survives in a unique example (*B-Br* Fétis 2379), which in the early seventeenth century belonged to a prominent Burgundian author and royal official, Hugues Picardet; see Laurent Guillo, "Les livres de musique de Hugues Picardet (1560-1641), procureur général au Parlement de Bourgogne," *Bulletin du Bibliophile* 1 (2001): 58-85. The poet Rémy Belleau, who dedicated a sonnet to Catherine, and, as a retainer of the Guise family, must frequently have been in contact with her, owned a lute, a cistre and a dozen music books (none individually described by title in his inventory, unfortunately; see Madeleine Jurgens, *Documents du Minutier Central des Notaires de Paris: Ronsard et ses amis* (Paris: Archives Nationales, 1985), 219 and 32.

D'amour l'aye fait mourir.

[You will be Oriane,
I will be Amadis,
or perhaps Eriane,
who preferred to die
rather than forsake his lady,
such that the torment
of love caused him to die.][30]

In another instance, a scene in Gohory's translation of Book 13 of *Amadis* intersects with the repertory of Costeley's 1570 *Musique*. Gohory frequently inserted new poems in his *Amadis* adaptations, lyric additions that represent musical interludes in the text. In Book 13, most of Gohory's songs occur as part of the wedding celebrations that make up the final episodes of the book. During the celebrations, a black female servant "garnie de sonnettes és bras et jambes et sonnant des cymbales, chanta et dança le cantique de l'antique Roine de sa region en son langage" [embellished with bells on her arms and legs and sounding cymbals, sang and danced the ancient canticle of the queen of her country in her own language]. Gohory then presents a verse adaptation of the Queen of Sheba's text from the biblical Song of Solomon, followed by a short response for Solomon himself. In Costeley's music collection, *Que de baisers de sa bouche* is a very similar French verse adaptation of the same text set as a simple strophic song.[31]

But more significant for my purposes than such explicit references or obvious parallels are instances in which song texts in the orbit of the Retz salon appear to elaborate characteristic situations of the novels and mirror moments of their characters' speech. Their resonance is clear across a range of lyric types, including songs employing feminine subject voices. The violently contested territory occupied by women's speech in this period makes these moments where feminine subjects speak or sing particularly revealing of contemporary views of female sexuality.

In the *Amadis* novels, women characters speak about their feelings in scenes that are repeated with minor variations throughout the cycle. Struck – usually at first sight – by love, they express their longing for the beloved; but, in the central relationships at least, sexual consummation almost always faces formidable obstacles. Knights errant have an unfortunate propensity for rushing off in search of adventure, and women's laments on their lovers' departures or reported deaths are common. But an even more significant impediment than separation is the

---

[30] For a modern edition of the vocal setting see Bernstein, ed., *SCC*, 15: 23-25.

[31] *Amadis XIII*, fols. 336r-337r; Bernstein, ed., *SCC*, 8: 132-34. Gohory starts with v. 5 of the Song of Solomon; the poem set by Costeley begins with v. 2 of the biblical text, reaching v. 5 in the third strophe. Though the rhyme schemes differ (that set by Costeley is *rimes plates*, while Gohory uses interlocking rhyme), both poems use quatrains of 7-syllable lines, and the opening of Gohory's text ("Filles de la cité saincte") is the same as the beginning of Costeley's strophe 3.

social constraint represented by the concept of honor. Dialogues with male characters often involve women's vigorous defense of honor against masculine pleading for its relaxation. Yet their resistance is usually in contradiction to the women's own wishes, and another topic of lament is the rigors of honor that prevent women from satisfying needs they describe as equal to those of their suitors. In the end, the woman is almost invariably conquered by the male character's unsurpassed virtues and her own passion. The lovers finally have sex, portrayed as mutually willed and mutually satisfying. Though they often exchange vows of fidelity or make marriage promises beforehand, much of the sexual activity in the novels takes place outside formal marriage structures. Even when the result is an illegitimate child, such encounters are regularly presented as virtuous; in relationships like those between Amadis and Oriane, erotic love is equated with exceptional moral and physical strength.[32]

In the standard romantic procedure, these exemplary encounters are counterbalanced by negative models, through episodes where women have chosen their lovers unwisely or yielded too quickly to libidinous impulse. Such women frequently lament their misfortune and make bitter accusations against the faithless men; in other cases, the text may allow the couple to take pleasure in sex and separate without any emotional or other consequences. And while successful or unsuccessful heterosexual relationships provide the majority of the material, *Amadis* also provides frequent glimpses of other sexualities through autoerotic or homosocial episodes, the latter usually (though not inevitably) involving cross-dressed women or Amazons who play a masculine role in relation to another woman.[33]

The range of erotic effects and potential outcomes is thus fairly wide, but feminine desire is represented in similar ways in virtually all situations. Women articulate erotic feelings only in private, to confidantes, lovers or to themselves, and in letters (whose potential interception is often an explicit cause for concern). Lovers' meetings always take place in secret, for they are aware that the society around them is likely to condemn their relationship as illicit despite its blamelessness in the divine order. Women's speeches frequently evoke the need to

---

[32] As Marian Rothstein has remarked, "Herberay's *Amadis* . . . generally considers consensual sex between nobles as a laudable activity whose results, often male offspring, were generally pleasing to God in the great scheme of things." Rothstein, *Reading in the Renaissance* 138. The attitude is common in medieval romance, and here receives a Neoplatonist spin; the physical union of faithful lovers partakes of the spiritual union that is a prerequisite for divine revelation. These attitudes are most typical of the vein of Neoplatonist erotic spirituality represented by Leone Ebreo, whose *Dialoghi d'amore* (1535) was widely disseminated in French translation.

[33] Some such encounters are discussed in Winfried Schleiner, "Laughter and Challenges to the Other in the French *Amadis de Gaule*," *Sixteenth Century Journal* 32 (2001): 91-107, and *idem*, "*Le feu caché*: Homosocial Bonds Between Women in a Renaissance Romance," *Renaissance Quarterly* 45 (1992): 293-311; a musical cross-dressing episode from Book 11 (in which two adolescent males disguise themselves as female lute-singers) is the topic of a study of my own, currently in preparation.

suffer love in silence, to conceal their passion from the outside world and often even from the beloved. Discretion is valued in male characters, but because their disclosure of the relationship will endanger the woman's reputation, not their own.

In other words, female sexuality is rhetorically figured as silence, something not to be spoken; the speaking subject allows readers to appreciate her desire only in terms of what is withheld from most or all of the other characters of the text. Well-born women that they are (and they invariably are in *Amadis*), they express their wishes to conform to contemporary feminine ideals. In conduct books of the period, silence was usually cast as a central female virtue, the restraint of a woman's mouth a corollary to restraint of her body and a sign of her unblemished chastity. Many courtly texts, in contrast, aim to rehabilitate female speech in contexts particularly relevant to women of the elite class: conversation in courtly gatherings, displays of verbal proficiency by women rulers. Yet such texts were also obliged to confront the persistent conflation of female speech and sexual activity in contemporary culture, and are careful to circumscribe women's verbal activity in ways that preserve sexual reputation.[34] The interdiction on speaking of desire resonates too with the Neoplatonic aim of rational control of the body as an ideal for both sexes, and with the socialization of Neoplatonic theory projected by Castiglione and later imitators, with its emphasis on dissimulation as part of a quintessentially courtly aesthetic. In lamenting the constraints of honor and in speaking about silence, women's voices in *Amadis* simultaneously invoke and disrupt these controls on their own utterance.

When we turn to books of *airs*, we find that feminine musical voices often echo instances of speech in the novels. Women's laments on abandonment, separation or the death of a lover appear in several of the song collections; a good example is *Mon coeur ma chere vie*, a poem possibly by Catherine de Clermont herself, included in musical setting in Le Roy's *Livre d'airs de cour*. Laments such as this participated in a much wider culture of female mourning: the topos of lament could be manipulated as a tool of female agency in a variety of social and political contexts.[35] And lament could also be a mode of articulating desire, a role it frequently serves in both novel and song. For example, the singer of *O la mal assignée*, included in Le Roy's 1552 guitar book and 1573 *Premier livre de chansons en forme de vau de ville* as well as all the editions of Certon's *Premier livre*, mourns a lover who has been killed by a jealous rival in an ambush of their tryst. As in other laments, she predicts her own imminent demise from grief; but

---

[34] For a more detailed discussion of these issues and their impact on women's speech and song at court, see Brooks, *Courtly Song*, 191-254.

[35] See the 1999 special issue of *Early Music* devoted to women's laments in the sixteenth and early seventeenth centuries. Jeanice Brooks, "Catherine de Médicis, *nouvelle Artémise*: Women's Laments and the Virtue of Grief," *Early Music* 27 (1999) in that issue and Brooks, *Courtly Song*, 209-227, deal in detail with *Mon coeur ma chere vie* in the context of Catherine de Médici's political agenda. Further on the political uses of lament see Kate van Orden, "Female *Complaintes*: Laments of Venus, Queens, and City Women in Late Sixteenth-Century France," *Renaissance Quarterly* 54 (2001): 801-845.

here she weeps not only for the loss of her lover but for the disappearance of her hopes of sexual pleasure. In the final strophe of the poem she says that the kisses she lavishes on the corpse cannot replace the sex she had expected from their meeting:

> Bouche que je te baise
> Cent foys la baiseray,
> Ce baiser ne m'appaise
> J'attendoye plus grand' aise
> Que jamais je n'auray.
>
> [Mouth, let me kiss you,
> I will kiss you a hundred times,
> this kiss does not appease me,
> I awaited a greater pleasure
> that I will never have.]

Women's laments as a mode of expressing longing and describing the effects of desire abound in the *Amadis* novels; these are among the lengthiest and most emotionally vivid speeches of the female characters, and were also frequently among those extracted for the collections of *Thresors*. Examples include Oriane's lament in Book 2, in which she compares the desolation of her waking life without Amadis to the joy of his nocturnal visits in her dreams; or Lucelle's in Book 8, in which she contrasts her current bitterness over her lover's deceit with the pleasures they enjoyed before. A telling example of sung lament as vehicle of desire, one with close parallels in *Amadis*, is *Est-ce pas mort*. The song first appeared in Adrian Le Roy's polyphonic arrangement in the revised edition of the *Second livre de chansons*, published in 1564 and reedited in 1569 and 1577 (see Appendix 1). The poem was widely distributed in text-only chansonniers in the 1570s and 1580s under the rubric "Complainte de l'amoureuse craintive mourant d'amours" [lament of the fearful amorous woman dying of love]. [36] Here the lament turns on the conflicts between desire and honor, between the urge to speak and the inability to do so. These tensions have brought the singer to the erotically charged state of near-death evoked in the refrain, "Amour pense que je dors et je me meurs." Her depiction of the physical consequences of thwarted desire echoes Marfire's situation in Book 13 of *Amadis* (see Appendix 2); her description in strophes 11-12 of masturbation as substitute for the imagined caresses of a lover is similar to a passage in Book 1 (see Appendix 3). But perhaps the most striking resemblance is to Sidere's lament in Book 13 (see Appendix 4), for Sidere too has been prevented from yielding to passion by her fear of loss of reputation, and regrets her lack of courage in not speaking to her suitor Rogel to arrange an assignation. Like the

---

[36] For example, in the *Sommaire de tous le recueils de chansons, tant amoureuses, rustiques que musicales* (Lyon: Rigaud, 1579), fols. 61r-62r. For earlier appearances of the text in such chansonniers, see Kate van Orden, "Vernacular Culture and the Chanson in Paris, 1570-1580" (Ph.D. diss., University of Chicago, 1996), 248.

singer of *Est-ce pas mort*, Sidere rails against honor, which she characterizes as the "executioner and murderer" of love-sick women.[37]

Other laments emphasize the masochistic pleasures to be derived from the tensions between desire and honor. The most venerable was probably the musical setting of Mellin de Saint-Gelais's *O combien est heureuse*, which like *O la mal assignée*, figured in Le Roy's and Certon's books of *voix de ville* from 1552 through 1573. Saint-Gelais was a friend of Herberay des Essarts and contributed liminary poetry in his honor to *Amadis*; when assuming a feminine subject voice (a gender ventriloquism the poet often adopted in his lyrics), Saint-Gelais created characters who might easily have stepped from the pages of the novel. The speaker of *O combien est heureuse* is a good example. Frustrated by the imperative of concealment, she asks her lover to show her that his ardor is as great as hers, which she describes as "violent," "hot," and the cause of unending jealous torment when, out of discretion, her lover speaks with other women and not with her. Yet as she declares from the outset, these tortures are pleasing as a variety of amorous foreplay:

> O combien est heureuse
> La peine de celer
> Une flamme amoureuse
> Qui deux coeurs fait brusler,
> Quand chacun d'eux s'attend
> D'estre bien tost content.

> [O how delightful is
> the pain of concealing
> an amorous flame
> that makes two hearts burn
> when each of them expects
> very soon to be content.]

O combien est heureuse was one of Saint-Gelais's most famous poems (it even came in for specific condemnation from the poets of the Pléiade, whose antipathy for this sort of lyric was notorious) and in its musical setting it was extremely widely disseminated; already well-known when Le Roy began publishing it in 1552, by the heyday of Catherine de Clermont's salon in the early 1570s, it surely counted as an old chestnut. A similar, but more up-to-date case was Philippe Desporte's poem *Ah Dieu que c'est un estrange martyre*, printed in polyphonic setting for the first time in Nicolas de La Grotte's 1569 *Chansons* and

---

[37] Texts such as this appear to contradict van Orden's assertion that "essentially, [sixteenth century] lyric assigns erotic longing to men and mourning to women" (van Orden, "Female *Complaintes*," 801). As these examples show, the categories of lament and erotics were not mutually exclusive. Pamela Coren points to similar cases in English lute song, where "grief is being used as a vehicle for the ardour of love complaint" ("Singing and Silence: Female Personae in the English Ayre," *Renaissance Studies* 16 (2002), 538).

then included in lute arrangement in Le Roy's *Livre d'airs de cour*. Desportes was closely involved with Catherine de Clermont's circle, and would distinguish himself in the 1570s and 1580s as the poet most often set to music in collections of strophic song. [38] *Ah Dieu que c'est un estrange martyre* is a Neoplatonic dialogue in which the woman speaker's strophes alternate with those of her lover. Both chafe at the restrictions that prevent them from speaking with each other in public, but as in *O combien est heureuse*, the interdiction on speech is a stimulant rather than a damper to desire. As the female interlocutor exclaims in her first strophe:

> Le feu couvert a plus de violence
> Que n'a celuy qui ses flammes eslance
> L'eau qu'on arreste en est plus irritée
> Et bruit plus fort plus elle est arrestée.
>
> [The smothered fire is more violent
> than one that throws out its flames,
> water that is dammed up is more furious as a result
> and the more it is stopped the more it clamors.]

In Book 12 of *Amadis*, Diane uses the same metaphor in a lament addressed to her absent lover Agesilan. Honor prevents her from declaring her love publicly in such a way that the news of it will reach him while he is gone; but the act of concealment only increases her passion: "les [mes douleurs] tenans cachées de jour en jour je sens accroistre leur felonnie dans mon courage, en la façon que le feu estroictement reserré dans la fournaise redouble continuellement ses forces" [keeping my sufferings hidden, from day to day I feel their crime against my courage increase, in the way that the fire tightly closed up in the furnace continually redoubles its strength].[39]

The link between all these expressions of female erotic longing is the consistent dialectic with the regulatory notion of honor and its demands. In one song, *L'amour avec l'honneur*, the combat between love and honor is thematized; the battle the speaker describes as taking place in her heart happily ends in a truce brought about by Nature, and the lyric functions as a mode of reconciling desire and honor as well as a site for dramatizing their conflict.[40] In Book 9 of *Amadis* this metaphorical battle for the woman's body is translated into an actual war

---

[38] On Desportes's association with Catherine, see Lavaud, *Philippe Desportes*, 100-101; for an index of his poetry set to music, see André Verchaly, "Desportes et la musique," *Annales musicologiques* 2 (1954): 271-345.

[39] I cite the text here as it appears in *Tresor de tous les livres d'Amadis de Gaule . . . pour instruire la jeune noblesse Françoise à l'eloquence, grace, vertu et generosité* (Lyon: Hugueton, 1582), fol. 218v. The image of the banked fire is a *lieu commun* in this literature, but that is precisely the point; the repetition of a limited range of metaphors in songs and novels reinforces their similarities in language and register.

[40] *L'amour avec l'honneur* appears in Le Roy's collections of 1552 and 1573, and all editions of Certon's *Premier livre*.

between two armies, though here the battle is so inclusive and the casualties so numerous that the result is somewhat less satisfactory.

Motives for the obsessive repetition and elaboration of the theme of love versus honor in romance and related lyric genres are not difficult to find. Female characters' resistance to masculine assaults on their honor allow the love episodes to be constructed as quest plots parallel to those of the battle narrative; the more vigorous and prolonged a woman's defense, the more praiseworthy is the hero's eventual victory over her scruples. Yet there are also distinct advantages for women in this formulation; in a narrative when most women – with the exception of the Amazons and warrior maidens – are barred from participation in the real business of war, the tensions between love and honor allow them to become the heroines of an interior battle with emotion and will, metaphorically exercising the same courage and determination as the male characters in armed combat. Similarly, the mode of lament allows women to adopt the Petrarchan positions of unfulfilled longing usually occupied by masculine subjects.[41] Yet the concomittant imperative of concealment that invariably accompanies women's articulation of erotic wishes marks their experience of desire as radically different from men's. As Cormelie exclaims to Esplandian in Book 5 of *Amadis*:

> Par mon ame je congnois bien maintenant que l'affection et amour des hommes est bien differente aux passions que nous autres simples femmelettes endurons quand nous tombons en ceste extremité: et sçavez vous en quoy? Vous hommes prenez communement plaisir à manifester ce que vous aymez, soit par parolles ou par contenance: ... qui est bien le contraire du naturel des femmes (j'entens celles qui se peuvent nommer sages et prudentes) car tant plus elles sont hautement apparentées, et plus ont de craincte que l'on apperçoive leurs passions amoureuses, de sorte qu'elles nient ordinairement de paroles, de gestes, et de contenance, ce qu'elles ont plus imprimé en leur coeur et esprit.[42]

> [By my soul I now know well that that the affection and love of men is very different from the passions that we poor simple little women suffer when we fall into that extremity: and do you know in what way? You men all take pleasure in showing, whether in words or in your countenance, that you love: . . . which is the opposite of the natural disposition of women (I mean those who can call themselves well-behaved and prudent) for the more they are highly born, the more they fear that their amorous passions will be detected, so that they regularly deny, with words, gestures and looks, that which they have most deeply imprinted in their hearts and souls.]

Honor, that is, is so constant an accompaniment to the desires of noblewomen as to effectively become part of them; women's erotic feelings are so inevitably marked

---

[41] In one case, Sidonie's *complainte* in Book 11 of *Amadis*, the female character even laments in the form of a sonnet modelled on Petrarch, although the poem's structure is camouflaged by the layout of the text as prose (rather than the indented italics used for other lyric insertions in the romance). See *L'onziesme livre d'Amadis de Gaule* (Paris: Groulleau, 1560), fol. IIv.

[42] Text cited from the *Tresor de tous les livres d'Amadis*, fols. 105r-105v.

by fear that Cormelie can essentialize these emotions as a product of women's "natural disposition."

These relationships between musical texts and chivalric romance can be construed in several complementary ways. The volumes of "treasures" of *Amadis* – collections of favorite extracts that allowed speeches of the book to survive independently of their framing narrative – suggest one possibility; we might think of song books as kind of lyrical *Thresor*, a mode of crystalizing characteristic romantic moments in a different form. Another productive comparison involves the tradition of lyric insertions in romances, a practice with a pedigree stretching back into the middle ages. Different manuscripts of medieval romances have different insertions, or none at all; lyric, with or without musical notation, was never an essential component of romance, but a common embellishment to it. We might understand some pieces in sixteenth century song books as providing a lyric embroidery to romance separated by print medium, and we might think of romance as providing a narrative scaffold within which such songs make sense. That is, for sixteenth century audiences, chivalric romance could supply motives and stories for the emotional situations in which women singers find themselves, stories that licensed the vocal representation of female sexuality in particular modes and styles. In both these interpretive scenarios, the function of song is to distill romance into its emotional essence, rendering its impact more forceful through the expressive power of music. In this, sixteenth century *airs* prefigure the role Crystal Kile has outlined for modern popular love songs: "In the typical pop love song, the prescribed brevity of the form combines with the intense affectiveness of music and the constructed emotional ultimacy of romantic love to create an almost orgasmic, ecstatic 'perfect love moment' or a moment of 'perfect romantic despair' over love."[43] And while creating these "perfect romantic moments," *airs* evoked the narratives of romance that gave rise to the emotional states exemplified in the songs.

Such relationships may seem obvious when we consider the closest sixteenth century Italian parallel, Ariosto's *Orlando furioso*, and its musical manifestations. (It is worth noting here that the Retz salon was a prime site for the translation and adaptation of Ariosto at the same time it was filling that role for *Amadis*.[44]) But scholars have been much slower to look to romance as a tool for understanding the place of song in early modern France, perhaps partly because the relationship between prose romance and sung poetry is less easy to grasp than the direct setting in music of sections of a verse romance such as *Orlando furioso*. The traffic between prose and sung poetry required contexts that encouraged the circulation of

---

[43] Crystal Kile, "Endless Love Will Keep Us Together: The Myth of Romantic Love and Contemporary Popular Movie Love Themes," in: *Popular Culture: An Introductory Text*, ed. Jack Nachbar (Bowling Green, OH: Bowling Green State University Popular Press, 1992; reprinted in Weisser, ed., *Women and Romance*), 419.

[44] See Lavaud, *Philippe Desportes*, 101, and Gorris, "Je veux chanter;" Rothstein, *Reading in the Renaissance*, 37 and 110-114, compares narrative procedures in Ariosto and *Amadis*.

image and style between genres.   It seems clear that Catherine de Clermont's circle provided one such environment.   And the salon also acted as a frame in which female audiences (conceived broadly in terms of women readers, singers and listeners) interacted with the images of noblewomen populating this nexus of musical and literary texts.   That men wrote the novels, and most (though probably not all) of the poetry and music – with masculine needs and goals as the principal motor – has perhaps obscured their potential use by real women as a mode of creating and enriching their own erotic lives, in contexts where performance could serve as a vehicle for agency.[45]

As a starting point, we might consider how women read the *Amadis* novels. In an acute analysis of the reading strategies built into the text itself, Marian Rothstein has observed that the romance pushed readerly participation in the realization of the text to hitherto unknown limits.   These tactics are especially apparent in the sexual encounters, where explicit description is replaced by appeals for readers to furnish whole scenes from the resources of their own experience and imagination.   Herberay des Essarts employed this technique from the outset, and subsequent translators, including Gohory, followed his lead.[46]   In some instances women are the only readers competent to fill in the textual gaps; for example, female experience is expressly solicited in the account of the night Agraies and Olinde spend together in Book 1:

> Adonc furent embrassemens et baisers par milliers: adonc caresses et tous bons traictemens que deux amans (en liberté) se peuvent faire, furent en saison, et tant que l'execution de l'amour s'en ensuiyvit la nuict mesmes, dont il advint que la gentille

---

[45] Susanne Rupp's work with English song and poetry has been influential in developing my ideas on this topic; see Rupp, "Silencing und Empowerment: Stimme, 'performance' und *gender* bei Sir Philip Sidney und Thomas Campion," in: *Sister Arts: Englische Literatur im Grenzland der Kunstgebiete*, ed. Joachim Möller (Marburg: Jonas, 2001), 29-37. Coren, "Singing and silence," argues that the female personae of English ayres were largely reductive fantasies aimed at the male readers who were the primary audiences for the repertory, but remarks (p.546) that they nevertheless offered multiple opportunities for appropriation or resistance by women, to whom they might suggest "ways out of silence."

[46] A typical example from the *Trezieme livre*: "Et pour clorre et sceeler ce bon appointement [Sidere and Rogel] s'entredonnerent maints autres gracieux baisers jusques à ce qu'ils apperceurent les tenebres faillir qui les contraignoient de se retirer chacun en sa chambre, jusques à la nuit ensuivant qu'ils s'y trouverent encore et par deux autres semblablement *en tel plaisir et soulas que tous amoureux peuvent imaginer par leur experience*." [And to close and seal this agreement, Sidere and Rogel gave each other many other gracious kisses until they perceived the darkness fading, which obliged them to return each to their own rooms, until the following night and two other nights afterward when they found each other again *in such pleasure and relief that all lovers can imagine from their own experience* (emphasis added). *Amadis XIII*, fol. 312v. See Rothstein, *Reading in the Renaissance*, 107-110, for an analysis of the technique and a series of similar examples taken from the *Premier livre*.

damoyselle en perdit le nom de pucelle, *avec tel contentement que celles qui semblable ont essayé, et non aultres, peuvent estimer.*[47]

[Then embraces and kisses by the thousands: then caresses and all the good treatment that two lovers in freedom can give each other, were in season, and so much that the act of love followed from it that same night, and the noble maiden lost the name of virgin from it, *with such pleasure as only those women who have tried the same, and no others, can guess* (emphasis added).]

In addition to the novel's calls for women to create sections of the narrative by introducing their own experience into its frame, contemporary reading habits encouraged them to perform the text in sound by reading aloud. This was a common aristocratic leisure practice in the period, and there are several extant accounts of people reading passages of *Amadis* out loud to others. It seems unlikely that Gohory's translation of Book 13 in particular was not read in this way in the chambers of the woman to whom it was dedicated. Both Marfire's and Sidere's laments from Book 13 referred to above in comparison to *Est-ce pas mort* were considered striking enough to be included in editions of the *Thresors*, so if any passages were read aloud in the Retz salon and elsewhere, these were.[48]

If *Amadis* solicited female readers in ways that encouraged, even demanded their participation in the novels' textual and sonic realization, music prints called for even greater engagement as scripts for performance. As sets of partbooks or arrangements in the gestural notation of tablature, the music the books contain is unintelligible, inaccessible as music without the intervention of a performer to realize it in sound. Adrian Le Roy testifies in his dedication of the *Livre d'airs de cour* that Catherine herself could perform the pieces. The princess Marguerite de Valois, who with Henriette de Clèves figured among Catherine's closest friends, was also apparently an accomplished performer. Brantôme (who was Catherine's cousin, and the brother of one of Marguerite's ladies-in-waiting) described Marguerite's talents as singer and lute player, and further testified that she wrote her own poetry and set it to music as song.[49] The musical style of these songs – as in the Musical Example 3.1, *Est-ce pas mort* – was especially well-adapted to the musical skills of aristocratic women. Relatively simple, often dance-based, and particularly suitable for performances with lute or keyboard (instruments heavily favored for female executants), *airs* were especially good at creating the

---

[47] Giraud and Vaganay, eds., *Amadis I*, 194.

[48] For evidence that reading aloud was a feature of aristocratic leisure, see Keating, *Studies*, and several of the essays in Olivia Rosenthal, ed., *A haute voix: diction et prononciation aux XVIe et XVIIe siècles* (Paris: Klincksieck, 1998). For specific instances of the reading aloud of *Amadis* see Rothstein, *Reading in the Renaissance*, and Simonin, "La disgrâce"; Gohory's preface to *Amadis XIII* reports that François I frequently had the book read aloud to his gentlemen-in-waiting.

[49] Pierre de Bourdeille, seigneur de Brantôme, *Oeuvres*, ed. Ludovic Lalanne (Paris: Renouard, 1864-82), 7:82.

atmosphere of feminine grace so highly recommended in courtly manuals.[50] While there is no documentary confirmation that the female members of the Retz salon performed the songs in feminine subject voices that appear in song books arranged by Adrian Le Roy, the circumstantial evidence – of their own performing skills and their familiarity with the poets and musicians who brought the repertory into print – is again so strong as to make it seem very likely that they did.

And when they spoke romances and sang courtly airs, how was their relationship to these texts construed? The open-ended nature of the *Amadis* novels – the most participatory and closure-resistant literature of the period – encouraged readers to identify with its principal characters. Female readers of *Amadis* could position themselves in ways similar to those Stevi Jackson sees as characteristic of consumers of modern-day mass market romance, who rely upon the narratives of romance in constructing their own narratives of self.[51] The sixteenth-century version of this phenomenon was particularly strong, however, and much more overtly acknowledged than in today's culture. There is ample evidence that aristocratic Frenchwomen regularly assumed or were cast in the roles of romantic heroines. Marguerite de Valois was repeatedly likened to Niquée, a central character of the *Amadis* novels.[52] Gohory compared Catherine de Clermont to Pentasilée, one of the heroines of Book 13, in his preface to his translation, and as Rosanna Gorris has shown, in several places Gohory figures the real Catherine as Pentasilée in the same way that he writes himself into the book as the tutor of the hero Sylves de la Selve.[53] That Catherine and other female members of the Retz circle embraced such roles seems confirmed by their adoption of romantic pseudonyms, employed by the women themselves in correspondence and in poetry written in their honor by writers of both sexes. Catherine herself went by the names Dictynne or more frequently, Pasithée; the latter is especially similar to names in *Amadis* such as Pentasilée.[54] This process of "becoming" a romantic heroine had particularly strong implications for female vocality, because the central role of *Amadis* as model for speech encouraged female readers to create new utterances in the style of the novel, using its vocabulary and images as tools for their own expressive needs and blurring the boundaries between the worlds of the novel and of its courtly performative milieux.[55]

---

[50] For a more detailed discussion, see Brooks, *Courtly Song*, 198-201.

[51] Jackson, "Love and Romance," 260.

[52] Rothstein, *Reading in the Renaissance*, 121.

[53] Rosanna Gorris, "Pour une lecture stéganographique," 151-154; in his translation of Book 11, Gohory had similarly conflated his dedicatee Diane de Poitiers with the heroine Diane de Guindaye (*Ibid.*, 132-150).

[54] Lavaud, *Philippe Desportes* 88-93 provides a list of pseudonyms from the salon and identifies the women to whom they were applied. Catherine frequently used these pseudonyms to refer to herself in correspondence with Henriette de Clèves (for an example, see Jullien de Pommerol, *Albert de Gondi*, 204).

[55] On the term "vocality," see the introduction to Leslie C. Dunn and Nancy A. Jones, eds., *Embodied Voices: Representing Female Vocality in Western Culture* (Cambridge: Cambridge University Press, 1994). Paul Zumthor has argued for its use in medieval studies

Similarly, contemporary ideals of musical performance encouraged women singers to inhabit the roles created by the texts and to convince listeners of their own investment in its emotional content. The Orphic image of the listener carried away, completely at one with the passions of the text and music as presented by the supremely inspired singer, is the most widely employed descriptor of successful musical performance in this period. Catherine herself figures as female Orpheus in contemporary poems. Describing the musical powers of "Pasithée," Pontus de Tyard claims that the sound of her lute could render beasts humane and restore joy to the most anguished souls.[56] Le Roy's *Livre d'airs de cour* begins with a setting of *Le ciel qui fut grand donneur*, a song whose prominent position suggests it is addressed to Catherine, the book's dedicatee. The poem, by Jacques de La Chastre, seigneur de Sillac, includes a strophe comparing the lady's voice to the harp of Orpheus, capable of moving the poet's heart, body and soul wherever it chooses.[57] And there is one fascinating account of a musical performance by Catherine in which her audience understood her to use a lament to express her own yearning for an absent lover. This is an anonymous text in Catherine's poetry album, a manuscript copied for her during the years 1573-75, just after the publication of the song and lute books dedicated to her by Adrian Le Roy.[58] The poet describes how she played the lute, her "secret sighs" translating her longing into audible musical performance:

> Encor n'est ce tout l'heur que j'eus aupres de vous,
> Oyant pinser le luth en ces acors si doux,
> Quand de soupirs secrets, les yeux levez en haut,
> La teste mi-baissée, et l'ame en son defaut,
> Vous sembliez regreter une absence lointaine.[59]

> [And this is not all the joy I had in your presence,
> hearing [you] strum the lute in those chords so sweet,
> when with secret sighs, your eyes lifted up,
> your head half-drooping, and your soul faltering,
> you seemed to regret a faraway absence.]

Paradoxically – and I will return to this point below – the silence and secrecy this text and others repeatedly emphasize as a central component of noblewomen's experience of desire here takes a sounding form that others may hear and interpret.

---

to draw attention to the role of the human voice in the composition, production and reception of texts. Here I concentrate particularly on the last two elements.

[56] Pontus de Tyard, *Oeuvres poétiques complètes*, ed. John C. Lapp (Paris: Société des Textes Français Modernes, 1966), 224-226; see also Brooks, "La comtesse de Retz," 308.

[57] See Brooks, *Courtly Song*, 37-38, for the text.

[58] On the dating and content fr. 25455, see Lavaud, *Philippe Desportes*, 82-93, Keating, *Studies*, 107-123, and Brooks, "La comtesse de Retz." St-John, "The *Salon vert*," contains extensive transcriptions from the manuscript.

[59] *F-Pn* fr. 25455, fol. 66r.

The relationship of song prints to musical practice was considerably looser than for more complex Masses, motets and polyphonic chansons, allowing for solo instrumental or vocal adaptation and rendition as accompanied or self-accompanied song as well as polyphonic performance, and inviting embellishment of vocal lines and accompaniments. The flexibility of performance practice (a feature of virtually all Renaissance music, but taken to extremes in this repertory) and the strong encouragement to improvisatory addition suggests a relationship between text and performer akin to the participatory strategies so prominent in the *Amadis* novels. And in the same way that *Amadis* provided templates for female speech, the kind of piece associated with the Retz salon furnished models for women's song. Several of the *airs* discussed above – including *Est-ce pas mort, O combien est heureuse*, and *Ah dieu que c'est un estrange martyre* – appeared in the text-only chansonniers published in large numbers in the last third of the century, where their tunes were designated as *timbres* for newly-written texts in feminine voices.[60] The economy of singing formulae permitted the creation of new utterance on the model as well as the reiterative performance of the model itself. This was an open-ended vocality in the same way as the notion of *amadiser*, gesturing toward a larger, do-it-yourself mode of musical expression in a way that a carefully crafted piece of counterpoint never could.

This flexibility of performance practice is echoed in the fluid musical form of strophic *airs*, which replicates the episodic construction of the *Amadis* novels. Performance of such pieces can easily involve transposition, repetition or elimination of strophes as well as the improvisatory addition of new strophes using the same music. That such procedures were regularly employed seems confirmed by the many variations found in printed manifestations of the repertory. Just as the additive construction of the *Amadis* novels helped to forestall closure and prolong the pleasure of reading, the varied repeat form of strophic song allowed performances of indeterminate length: add a strophe, repeat a strophe as you wish, the basic identity of the song is largely unaffected. In executing the pieces and assuming the guise of musical romantic heroines, female performers sang a version of desire similarly characterized by its resistance to definitive resolution, its quality of agonized yet pleasurable yearning toward an object unobtainable or interminably deferred. Such emotions – alluded to by the speaker of *Ah Dieu que c'est un estrange martyre* – are central to the libidinal economy constructed by these texts. Here we can understand "honor" as the concept that forces the postponement or denial of gratification, playing a crucial role in this configuration of feminine desire.

These observations prompt reflection on the ways that novels and song could serve not only as scripts for the vocal performance of a particular version of desire

---

[60] For example, *Le plaisant jardin des belles chansons* . . . (Lyon: n.p. 1580) contains a song, *Las quel malheur*, to be sung to the tune of *Est-ce pas mort*; it is labelled "complainte d'une dame, sur le chant, Amour pense que je dors, Mais je me meurs" (p.98). For other instances, e.g. *O combien est heureuse* (an extremely popular timbre) see van Orden, "Female *Complaintes*."

Musical Example 3.1 – Adrian Le Roy, *Est-ce pas mort*, from *Second livre de chansons composé à quatre parties de plusieurs autheurs* (Paris: Le Roy & Ballard, 1564; R/1569 and 1577)

but as sexual objects in their own right.   Jean Maugin's 1548 poem to female readers, pointing out that the new octavo editions would permit women to carry the books more easily, suggests that women in particular wished to keep copies of the book close to their bodies; that is, that their appetite for the narratives of the novel could translate into craving for the book as physical entity. A similar implication arises from Jacques Gohory's defense of the novel in the preface to his translation of Book 13. Gohory denounces women who in public condemn *Amadis* as dissolute, while in private they confess to their lovers that, as young girls, they delighted in reading the book by the nightlight's glow after their governesses ordered them to bed.[61] Here Gohory presents a striking image of girls in bed with a book that teaches them desire, rehearsing with the novel the sexual experiences they will later share with male lovers. Performance of the narrative here becomes a simulacrum of heterosexual practice, interestingly short-circuited by the fetishistic and autoerotic character of the situation. An even more effective effacement of the male body occurs in a contemporary poem in which music-making with a lute becomes the substitute for heterosexual sex. The sonnet, which circulated at court in the early 1570s (it is preserved in a manuscript emanating from the salon of Madeleine de l'Aubespine, wife of the secretary of state Nicolas de Neufville, sieur de Villeroy, and has been attributed to Madeleine herself or to Héliette de Vivonne), is an *énigme* or riddle poem. The answer to the riddle is "a lute," but the poem's wit lies in misleading the reader into thinking that the speaker is using a phallus as her instrument:

> Pour le plus doulx esbat qui je puisse choisir
> Souvent apres disner craignant qu'il ne m'ennuye
> Je prends le manche en main je le touche et manye
> Tant qu'il soit en estat de me donner plaisir
> Sur mon lict je me jecte, et sans m'en desaisir
> Je l'estrains de mes bras sur mon sain je l'appuye
> Et remuant bien fort d'aise toute ravie
> Entre mille douceurs j'accompliz mon desir
> S'il advient par malheur quelquefois qu'il se lasche
> De la main je le dresse et derechef je tasche
> A joyr de plaisir d'un si doux maniment
> Ainsi mon bien aymñ tant que le nerf luy tire
> Me contente et me plaist puis de moy doucement
> Lasse et non assouvye enfin je la retire.
> D'un Luc.

[For the sweetest recreation I could choose,
often, after dinner, fearing that he/it misses me,
I take his/its neck in hand, I touch and manipulate it,
until it/he is in a state to give me pleasure.
I throw myself on my bed, and without letting go of it/him,
I clasp it/him in my arms, I lean it/him against my breast,
and moving forcefully, with pleasure all delighted,
among a thousand sweetnesses I accomplish my desire.
If it happens, unhappily, that he/it slackens,

---

[61] *Amadis XIII*, unfoliated prefatory material.

I train it/him up with my hand, and once more I try
to enjoy the pleasure of such sweet handling.
Thus my well-beloved, as long as the string pulls him/it,
contents and pleases me. Then from me, gently,
exhausted but not sated, I withdraw him/it. Of a Lute.][62]

Catherine de Clermont's own luxuriously copied poetry album contains two quatrains that ring changes on the idea of music-making with the lute as both metaphor and substitute for sex. In the first, love without sex is described as vain, like trying to play the lute with one hand:

Comme sans jouir de deux mains
Le luct ne produict nulle accordz
Ainsi tous les Amours sont vains
Qui ne joint ensemble deux Corps.

[As without playing with two hands,
the lute creates no harmonies,
thus all love is in vain
that does not join together two bodies.][63]

In the second, the lute plays a role of the confidante whose harmonies "relieve the passions" of the suffering poet; its juxtaposition to the preceding quatrain suggests that the anguish may be physical:

Luct qui respond à mes affections
Qui participe aux disdains de ma vie
Faitz je te prie que ta douce armonye
Puissent allegée [sic] toutes mes passions.

[Lute who responds to my emotions,
who takes part in the distresses of my life,
I pray you, make it so your sweet harmony
will relieve all my passions.][64]

The poems appear in a section of the album where the hand of the principal scribe (a professional copyist) has given way to a series of different hands which seem to belong to Catherine, her friends and familiars, who added texts to the album after the main bulk of the copying was complete. Though the gender of the narrative

---

[62] *F-Pn* fr. 1718, fol. 57r. On the provenance of the manuscript and attribution of the poem, see Lavaud, *Philippe Desportes*. The linguistically masculine gender of "un luth" in French allows for the ambiguity, as the pronoun "le" may be read as either "it" (referring to the lute) or "him" (a male lover). For a detailed discussion of the poem, see Carla Zecher, "The Gendering of the Lute in Sixteenth-Century French Poetry," *Renaissance Quarterly* 53 (2000): 787-789.

[63] *F-Pn* fr. 25455, fol. 145r.

[64] *Ibid.*

voice for these quatrains is not clear, the poems immediately preceding them adopt a feminine subject position, raising the possibility that the lute quatrains are the work of a woman, possibly Catherine herself.

Evidence such as this suggests that for female audiences, self pleasure was a major attraction of reading novels and making music. The opening of Book 1 of *Amadis* in fact sends strong cues in this direction, through the episode in which Dariolette masturbates at the thought of the pleasure her mistress will enjoy (as readers were meant to do when imagining the subsequent sex scene between Elisene and Perion?). It could be argued that such images are primarily voyeuristic: that their principal intention was to titillate male readers and listeners by appearing to offer them entry into an eroticised, private feminine physical and cultural space. However, as Helen Hackett has observed, the patriarchal fictions of romance must have offered some attraction to the female readers who embraced them with such enthusiasm; the appeal of sexual images to male readers need not have precluded their appropriation by women for their own affective purposes.[65] Thus despite the role of their narratives in upholding patriarchal codes, books and songs may also have helped construct environments of desire in which female sexuality could effectively elude some forms of masculine control.

Here the expectation that romance would furnish a model for women's lives could cause particular anxiety, perhaps partly out of fear that female sexual desires, once so stimulated, would prove impossible to regulate. The idea that novels and songs encouraged women in unchaste behavior was fairly widespread in the late sixteenth century, as the actions of romantic heroines came to seem increasingly out of tune with the prevailing moral climate in the era of the religious wars.[66] François de La Noue's 1581 essay "Que la lecture des livres d'Amadis n'est moins pernicieuse aux jeunes gens, que celle des livres de Machiavel aux vieux" [That the reading of *Amadis* books is no less pernicious for young people than the reading of Machiavelli's books for the old] furnishes the most detailed contemporary dissection of the novel's potential to lead women astray. In his treatment of the "poison de volupté" with which the novel corrupts its readers, he is particularly concerned with its ability to do so through sound. The French translators of the book have rendered the language so appealing that it reaches the passions through the ears: "Et l'ayant rendu fluide et affetté, il ne faut point demander si son murmure est doux aux oreilles, où apres avoir passé, il va chatouiller les plus tendres affections du coeur, lesquelles il esmeut, plus ou moins, selon que les personnes sont preparees."[67] He goes on to condemn the effect on young women in particular before citing the incipit of a popular song, "Tant vous

---

[65] Hackett, *Women and Romance Fiction*, 11-12 and 68-75.

[66] For a detailed examination of the growing divergence, see Rothstein, *Reading in the Renaissance*, 125-144.

[67] "And having rendered the language flowing and ornate, we need not ask if its murmuring is sweet to the ears, after passing through which it goes to tickle the most tender feelings of the heart, which it moves, more or less, depending on the degree to which the individual is prepared." La Noue, *Discours*, 169.

allez tost Guillemette," to illustrate how rashly young women behave when under the influence of *Amadis*. Though the song is a rather rough-and-ready *chanson rustique*, it circulated at court and was published by the royal printer in 1565;[68] its distribution overlaps with that of the *voix de ville* and *airs de cour* I have been discussing. La Noue frequently cites psalms in support of his arguments, but this is the only instance in his *Discours politiques et militaires* in which he refers to a specific piece of secular music. Clearly, for La Noue, novels and songs inhabited the same world – a perilous world for women. His fears were perhaps not unfounded: Catherine de Clermont had a long liaison with the courtier Charles de Balsac d'Entragues, and was rumored to have had his child;[69] Henriette de Clèves and Marguerite de Valois lived sentimental lives of such notoriety and romantic dimensions that they later furnished the plot of one of the most famous romances of the nineteenth century, Alexandre Dumas's *La Reine Margot*.

While sixteenth-century actors were principally concerned with whether or how romance encouraged illicit sexual activity, feminist historians today ask different questions. Were songs and romance opiate or opportunity? Can they be considered a repressive or liberatory force in noblewomen's lives? Perhaps the best answer is both. Romance and related lyric types furnished valuable affective latitude for some aristocratic women by offering imaginative contexts for the articulation of feminine desire. As inscriptions of and scripts for female vocality, romance and song offered a range of possibilities for the active participation of female readers and singers in emotional expression through performance. These observations have a particular piquancy when applied to songs and speeches about suffering desire in silence and indulging it in secret. Female sexuality rhetorically figured as silence – already problematic in textual terms – becomes an even more profound paradox when real women give voice to that silence in the world. The articulation of silence as sound invested women with the power to shape and manifest their desires through identification with the longing subject of novel or song. At the same time, the constant evocation of honor as foil to desire reassured their audiences and themselves that the social structures that controlled their actions were still firmly in place. While songs and novels allowed women to give audible form to emotions that would, in other contexts, be impossible to reveal, they also helped to ensure that female sexual activity remained highly controlled and that trespasses against honor could legitimately exact heavy tolls. Treading a precarious path through interdictions simultaneously flouted and reinforced, romances and songs provided opportunities for women to voice their passions, yet supported the discourse that upheld their silence as ideal.

---

[68] The song appears as "Tant vous allés doux Guillemette," in a polyphonic arrangement attributed to Abran, in *Quinsieme livre de chansons á quatre cinq et six parties* (Paris: Le Roy & Ballard, 1565), fols. 11r-12r.

[69] Jullien de Pommerol, *Albert de Gondi*, 199-201.

Appendix 1

1 Est-ce pas mort quand un corps froid et palle,
Aveugle et sourd, transi et plus ne parle
De qui le coeur et l'ame vit ailleurs:
    Amour pense que je dors et je me meurs.

[Is it not death, when a cold and pale body,
blind and deaf, rigid, no longer speaks,
of whom the heart and soul live elsewhere?
    Love thinks I sleep, but I die.

2 Est-ce pas mort quand un autre a sa vie
Qui fuit son bien et force son envye
Qui veut et n'ose appaiser ses douleurs.
    Amour.

Is it not death when another has one's life,
to flee one's own good and force one's will,
to wish but not dare to appease one's pains?
    Love ...

3 Est-ce dormir quand sans cesse je veille,
Et que l'amour en dormant me reveille,
Pour me transir en regretz et en pleurs.
    Amour.

Is it sleep, when without cease I wake
and when love in sleeping awakens me
to transfix me in regrets and tears?
    Love ...

4 Est-ce dormir quand un desir me ronge
Toute la nuit et que tousjours je songe
Que je te baise, helas songes menteurs.
    Amour.

Is it sleep, when a desire gnaws me
all night, and I always dream
that I kiss you? alas, lying dreams!
    Love ...

5 Certes c'est mort ou plus cruel martire
Puis que les mortz ne souffrent rien de pire
Que de finir par la mort leurs malheurs.
    Amour.

Surely this is death, or an even crueller torture,
for even the dead suffer nothing worse
than to finish their misfortunes through death.
    Love ...

6 Mais moy je meurs et si vis tout ensemble
Et sans mourir tousjours morte je tremble
Pour ne jouir des biens qui me sont seurs.
    Amour.

But I, I live and yet die at once
and without dying, still dead I tremble
from not enjoying the joys sure to me.
    Love ...

7 O vie, ô mort, o mon peu d'hardiesse
Quand folle n'ose employer ma jeunesse
Et que j'yverne mon printemps, et mes fleurs.
    Amour.

O life, o death, o my own lack of courage,
since foolishly I dare not use my youth,
and cast winter on my springtime and my flowers.
    Love ...

8 Donques pour vivre, il faut que je jouisse
Mais cest honneur ne veult que j'acomplisse
Heur plus heureux du plus grand de mes heurs.
    Amour.

Thus to live, I must take pleasure
but this honor does not wish me to achieve
that happiness which is the greatest of my joys.
    Love ...

9 Mortel honneur helas la patience
De me veoir morte en fuiant jouissance
Me fait souffrir mil' autres deshonneurs.
    Amour.

Deadly honor, alas, the patience
to see myself dead in fleeing enjoyment
makes me suffer a thousand other dishonors.
    Love ...

10 Las! qui me veoit plus mourante que vive
Juge fort bien ma volunté craintive
Et que la peur refroidit mes challeurs.
    Amour.

Alas! whoever sees me more dying than alive,
can well judge my frightened will,
and that fear cools my heat.
    Love ...

11 O bras trompez, qui durant les nuitz sombres
Allez au lit n'accollans que les umbres
Voz doitz me soyent fidelles serviteurs.
    Amour.

O cheated arms, who during the dark nights
go to bed embracing only shadows,
let your fingers be faithful servants to me.
    Love ...

12 Las que celuy qui fait que je palice
Me feroit bien plus que vous de service

Alas, he who makes me grow pale
would do me far greater service than you,

Mais las je n'ose approcher ses grandeurs.
Amour.

13 Il m'est advis si tost que j'en approche
Las que desja un chacun me reproche
Que j'ay reçeu le bien de ses doulceurs.
Amour.

14 Mais par despit la peur et l'amour forte
M'endormiront bien tost de telle sorte
Qu'un autre mort finira mes douleurs
Amour.

15 Dont finiront cent mille mortz pour une
En triumphant par mort de ma fortune
Et du malheur de mes mortelles pleurs.
Amour.

But alas, I dare not approach his greatness.
Love . . .

I think each time that I approach him,
alas, that already everyone reproaches me
thinking that I have received the joy of his caresses.
Love . . .

But out of spite, fear and powerful love
will soon send me to sleep in such a way,
that another death will finish my pain.
Love . . .

So a hundred thousand deaths will finish for one
and I will triumph through death over my fortune
and the unhappiness of my mortal tears.
Love . . .]

Appendix 2 :   *Le trezieme livre d'Amadis de Gaule*, trans. Jacques Gohory (Paris: Breyer, 1571), fols. 22r-22v: . . . la gente Marfire demeura en si grand desplaisir . . . qu'elle desiroit mourir de dueil tellement que quasi plus ne mangeoit, plus ne reposoit jour ne nuict en aucune maniere: dont sa beauté alloit fort decheant et amoindrissant.   Elle en cheut au lit malade, où de jour à autre sa maladie augmentoit, jusques à ce que se voiant pres du riquet de la mort, print Cardonie sa damoiselle par la main et avecques grands sanglots luy commença à dire: Cardonie m'amie, vous sçavez bien que jamais je ne vous ay rien celé de ce que j'ay eu sus mon cueur, et moins ores le ferai-je.   Pourtant vous devez sçavoir, m'amie, que la raison de mon honneur, ne la grandeur de ma beauté, ne la rigueur dont j'ay usé à l'endroit du vaillant Prince Filisel, n'ont peu avoir tant de pouvoir, que l'excellence de sa beauté n'ait tout mis soubs le pied, et moy reduitte au piteux estant que me voiez, Auquel je ne sens en moy force ne vertu de pouvoir plus gueres prolonger ma vie . . .

[. . . the lovely Marfire remained in such discontent . . . that she wished to die of grief so that she hardly ate, and night or day did not rest at all: from which her beauty was greatly fallen and diminished. She fell sick to her bed, where from day to day her illness increased, until seeing herself at death's door, she took her maidservant Cardonie by the hand and with great sobs began to say to her: "Cardonie my friend, you know well that I have never concealed from you what I hold in my heart, and even less will I do so now. Yet you must know, my friend, that neither the cause of my honor, nor the greatness of my beauty, nor the rigor that I have exercised against the valiant prince Filisel, have had enough power to prevent the excellence of his beauty from crushing all underfoot, and reducing me to the pitiful state in which you see me, in which I no longer feel in myself the strength or virtue to be able to prolong my life much longer . . ."]

Appendix 3: *Le premier livre d'Amadis de Gaule*, trans. Nicolas de Herberay des Essarts, ed. Yves Giraud and Hugues Vaganay (Paris: Société des Textes Français Modernes, 1986), 1: 10-11: Le temps estoit lors gracieux et serein, la lune belle et luysante, qui donnoit clarté aux deux damoyselles. Mais certes l'une avoit plus d'occasion d'estre contente que l'aultre, qui eust tresvoluntiers pris ce bien, ou ung semblable pour elle mesme, si elle en eust eu moyen, et tant en donnoit de cognoissance, que Elisene voyoit bien, qu'il n'y avoit faulte que de executeur pour y satisfaire, car ceste Dariolette, sentant en son esperit l'ayse prochain, que debvoit recevoit celle, qu'elle conduisoit, ne se povoit tenir de luy manier, puis les tetins, puis les cuysses et quelque chose d'advaintaige, et de trop vehemente ardeur souspiroit souvent, tout ainsi que si elle eust deu participer à ce bien futur de la princesse Elisene, à laquelle elle disoit: Helas madame, que heureulx est le prince, par lequel vous recevrez ceste nuict tant de plaisir.

[Then the weather was pleasant and serene, the moon beautiful and gleaming, which provided light for the two maidens. But one certainly had greater cause to be happy than the other, who would very willingly have taken that good, or a similar one, for herself if she had had the means, and she showed this so much, that Elisene saw clearly that only an executor was needed to satisfy her, for that Dariolette, feeling in herself the pleasure that the woman she was accompanying was about to receive, could not refrain from touching herself on the breasts, thighs and something else as well, and from her over-fervent ardor, sighed frequently, just as if she had been participating in the future delight of princess Elisene, to whom she said: "Alas, my lady, happy is the prince from whom tonight you will receive such pleasure."]

Appendix 4: *Le trezieme livre d'Amadis de Gaule*, fols. 96v-97v:

Specialement Sidere vivoit en grieve desplaisance de ne luy [Rogel de Grece] avoir plustost ottroyé son amoureuse requeste, se plaignant en ses regrets de l'honneur, comme de bourreau, comme de meurdrier des miserables amantes, principalement de celles de son estat royal qui s'y estimoient plus obligées pour servir d'exemple aux autres. Ha (disoit elle à par soy) que ne luy avois je tranché le mot à notre arrivée de trouver le lieu de commodité, dont tant il m'importunait que avec l'obligation de ma delivrance, je pouvois estre trop excusée de le consentir: Las (discouroit elle) . . . je devois plustost sans attendre tant de dangers, tant de regards et conterolles . . . le recompenser de ses bienfaits en la commodité du long voyage que nous faisions ensemble. Puis recommencoit, ha faux honneur, garde de la chasteté des Dames, il ne fut oncques de plus cruel tiran que toy qui les gesnes, tourmentes et fais mourir à petit feu, O que je luy en escrirois volontiers ce que ne n'ay osé luy dire de bouche: la main estant plus hardie qui ne rougit point que la langue si prochaine de la face honteuse, mais la lettre escritte demeure, en danger d'estre veue et descouverte, portant suffisante preuve en soy de la condemnation de l'honnesteté.

[Above all Sidere lived in grievous unhappiness that she had not rather acceded to the amorous appeal of Rogel de Grece, in her laments complaining of honor, as an executioner, a murderer of miserable [female] lovers, especially those of her royal standing who thought themselves more obliged by it to serve as an example for others. "Ah," she said to herself, "why did I not interrupt him as soon as we arrived here to find a convenient meeting-place, for which he begged me so, that with the debt I owe him for having rescued me, I could easily have been excused for consenting. Alas," she continued, "instead of awaiting such dangers, so many gazes and checks . . . I should have rewarded him under the more opportune circumstances of the long voyage we made together." Then she started again, "Ah, treacherous honor, guardian of women's chastity, there was never a crueller tyrant than you, who restrain and torment them, and slowly torture them to death! Oh, I would willingly write to him all I have not dared tell him aloud, for the hand does not blush and is braver than the tongue, which is so close to the abashed face, but the written letter remains, in danger of being seen and discovered, in itself providing sufficient proof for the loss of reputation."]

Table 1
Music prints associated with Catherine de Clermont, Adrian Le Roy
and the early history of the *air de cour*

1) *Premier livre de chansons, en quatre volumes, nouvellement composées en musique à quatre parties, par M. Pierre Certon* (Paris: Le Roy & Ballard, 1552). Strophic songs in polyphonic arrangement.

2) *Second livre de guiterre, contenant plusieurs chansons en forme de voix de ville: nouvellement remises en tabulature, par Adrian Le Roy* (Paris: Le Roy & Ballard, 1555 [1556 n.s.]). 2nd ed. of a lost print published between the appearance of the *Premier livre de tabulature de guiterre* on 12 September 1551 and the *Tiers livre de tabulature de guiterre* of 1552; may have been printed before (1). Contains texted monophonic melodies in white mensural notation with facing guitar arrangements in tablature of strophic songs, mainly from (1).

3) *Second livre de chansons, nouvellement mises en musique à quatre parties, par bons et sçavans musiciens* (Paris: Le Roy & Ballard, 1554). Predominantly strophic songs in polyphonic arrangement, attributed to Le Roy, Certon, Maillard, Arcadelt, Mithou and Entraigues.

4) *Premier livre de chansons composé en musique à quatre parties par M. Pierre Certon* (Paris: Le Roy & Ballard, 1564). Revised ed. of (1) replacing four songs with four others by Certon from (3).

5) *Second livre de chansons composé à quatre parties de plusieurs autheurs* (Paris: Le Roy & Ballard, 1564; R/ 1569 and 1577). Heavily revised ed. of (3), contains 3 strophic songs by Le Roy amid songs by Nicolas.

[6) *Breve et facile instruction pour apprendre la tablature* . . . (Paris: Le Roy & Ballard, 1567; no copy extant).]

7) *A briefe and easye instru*[c]*tion to learn the tableture* . . . *englished* (London: Rowbothome, 1568). English translation of (6)

8) *Chansons de P. de Ronsard, Ph. Desportes, et autres, mises en musique par N. de la Grotte* (Paris: Le Roy & Ballard, 1569; R/ 1570, 1572, 1573, 1575, and 1580). Strophic songs in polyphonic arrangement.

9) *Musique de Guillaume Costeley, organiste ordinaire et vallet de chambre, du treschretien et tresinvincible roy de France* (Paris: Le Roy & Ballard, 1570). Contains dedicatory sonnets by Costeley to Albert de Gondi and Catherine de Clermont; Latin poem by Jacques Gohory. Includes a section of strophic songs labelled "meslange de chansons en façon d'airs."

[10] *Instruction de partir toute musique des huit divers tons en tablature de luth*. . . (Paris: Le Roy & Ballard, 1570; no copy extant). Dedicated to Catherine de Clermont, preface by Jacques Gohory. Possibly included a re-edition of (6).]

11) *Livre d'airs de cour miz sur le luth, par Adrian Le Roy* (Paris: Le Roy & Ballard, 1571). Dedicated to Catherine de Clermont. Contains texted monophonic melodies in white mensural notation with facing lute arrangements in tablature of strophic songs, mainly from (8); shares 1 piece each with (5) and (12).

12) *Premier livre de chansons en forme de vau de ville composé à quatre parties, par Adrian Le Roy* (Paris: Le Roy & Ballard, 1573). New polyphonic arrangements of songs from (1), (2), (3), (4) and (11) plus three new pieces.

13) *A briefe and plaine Instruction to set all musicke of divers Tunes in Tableture for the Lute* . . . *with a brief Instruction how to play on the Lute by Tablature* . . . *also a third Booke containing divers new excellent tunes. All first written in french by Adrian Le Roy* (London: Rowbothome, 1574). English translation of material from (6), (10) and (11), including dedication to Catherine de Clermont and preface by Jacques Gohory from (10).

Chapter 4

Music and Women in Early Modern Spain: Some Discrepancies between Educational Theory and Musical Practice[1]

Pilar Ramos López

Introduction

The image of the Renaissance as projected in *Il Cortegiano* by Baldassare Castiglione (1528) is so strong that we tend to associate it with the whole of Europe. In the case of Spain, musicologists have focused on sources linked with composers, theorists, patrons or performers in which music appears as an honest and erudite activity, consistent with the image depicted in *Il Cortegiano*. Spanish historiography has connected this supposedly high view of music with the artistic quality and international fame of composers of the time (Cristóbal de Morales, Antonio Cabezón, Francisco Guerrero, Tomás Luis de Victoria), so that the Spanish Musical Renaissance is presented as a Golden Age, a lost paradise. This approach informs us about notions held by professionals, but it says little about the vision for musical activity in other social circles. Non-musical literature such as novels, theatrical plays, poetry, essays, and treatises on education, medicine, theology, science and art are all valuable sources of information about music in the sixteenth and seventeenth centuries. The idea for this paper originated when I realized that these types of texts referred to music in very different terms from the ones used in our books on the history of Spanish music. They reveal a richer and more heterogeneous background, although a less golden and pleasant one. It was surprising to find that the most negative documents written about music were the educational treatises addressed to women. Yet despite this fact, women sang in their homes and convents and took part in musical plays at the courts as well as in popular public theaters and monasteries. It was perhaps the very clear presence of women in musical events that elicited such strong reactions against them.

[1] I wish to thank the Dirección General de Enseñanza Superior e Investigación Científica for the grant that supported my time as a visiting research fellow at Oxford University in 1998, where I began this research.

This study examines ideas on music in sixteenth- and seventeenth-century Spain in non-professional circles, using sources seldom considered by musicologists.[2] I will focus on how different concepts of music (music as an art, craft, science, or entertainment) related to differing social contexts, and on how those various concepts – particularly regarding education – affected women's musical practice. I will also examine how music was perceived in early modern Spanish culture, with particular emphasis on the sociological and aesthetic implications of the different musical genres as they pertained to women.

Does music educate or does it corrupt?

To answer that question, it is first necessary to determine whose education we are talking about. Writers in the fifteenth and sixteenth centuries were very interested in the education of the "prince" and the "courtier." Indeed, as many as 400 educational treatises for gentlemen and 800 for ladies have been counted during the Renaissance in Europe.[3] Except for the utopias, or descriptions of ideal worlds by such writers as Tomasso Campanella, Thomas More or Francis Bacon, very little is said about education in other social environments. It is also necessary to specify what music we are speaking about since during the Renaissance clear distinctions were made between music as a speculative discipline, liturgical vocal music, instrumental music for the organ, theatrical music, and the popular songs and dances.

Hispanic education treatises addressed to princes, gentlemen and noblemen recommended the inclusion of music in their formative program of men. In contrast, the treatises addressed to women (written sometimes by the same authors) rejected any musical activity. This apparent paradox is not only due to the known double moral code (women were submitted to a much stricter one), but also to the fact that different kinds of music are discussed. The prince is advised to know music as a mathematical science and also as a healthy entertainment. For women, the learning of a science is not even mentioned, because it was outside the limits regarded as suitable for the feminine mind. What is questioned instead is the access of women to the daily practice of music, to the popular airs performed in the court as well as in the streets.

---

[2] Luis Robledo has presented a documented background on music in the writings of the Spanish humanists. However, he continues to insist on the golden aspects (especially the neo-platonic ones) of humanism with regard to music. See Luis Robledo, "La música en el pensamiento humanista español," *Revista de Musicologia* XXI, 2: (1998).

[3] P. Burke, "El Cortesano," in: *El hombre del Renacimiento*, ed. P. Burke (Madrid: Alianza, 1993), 135.

Music in the treatises on masculine education

Among the many treatises directed to princes and gentlemen, I will highlight those of Juan de Mariana and Juan Luis Vives, both prestigious humanist authors who also wrote on the relationship between music and women. Juan de Mariana defends music in the king's education in chapter VII of his treatise *De rege et regi institutione* (1598).[4] After the traditional praises of music and the references to Orpheus, Amphion, Alexander and David, Mariana affirms the superiority of music to painting in its ability to excite the spirits and to express the affections. He advises music not only as a distraction, but also as a way of achieving moderation and the classical idea of harmony.[5] He also recommends that the prince learn traditional dances as physical exercise.[6] His insistence that the prince should only dance in private[7] reflects the ignoble connotations dancing had at that time. But Mariana also notices the "capital vices" that should be avoided in the teaching of

---

[4]Padre Juan de Mariana, "Del Rey y la Institución Real, traducido nuevamente. Tratado contra los juegos públicos." *Obras. Biblioteca de Autores Españoles, XXXI* (Madrid: Atlas, 1950).

[5]"No solo pues ha de cultivar el rey la música para distraer el ánimo, templar la violencia de su carácter y armonizar sus afectos, sino también para que con la música comprenda que el estado feliz de una república consiste en la moderación y la debida proporción y acuerdo de sus partes." Mariana, "Del Rey," 510.

[6]Mariana knew the importance given to music in the education of the Ancient Greeks. And so, in chapter V, "On the exercise of the body," he recommends gymnastics, hunting, the ball games and the "Spanish dances." In this same sense dancing is recommended by Diego Saavedra Fajardo, *Idea de un principe político-cristiano representada en cien empresas*, ed. Vicente García de Diego (Madrid: Espasa Calpe, Clásicos Castellanos, 1958, 76 y 87), 233-234. Similarly it is also recommended by the dance commentator Bartolomé Ferriol y Boxeraus, *Reglas útiles para los aficionados a danzar* (Capoa: Joseph Testore, 1745), 18-19.

[7]"En público no debería tampoco el príncipe tomar parte en el baile ni aun con máscara, pues los hechos de los reyes no pueden nunca estar ocultos. ¿Cómo ha de convenir que mueva y agite sus miembros a manera de bacante? Mucho menos le ha de convenir aun salir a la escena, representar farsas, tocar el laud ni tomarse ninguna de las libertades que tanto fueron acusadas en Domicio Neron, cuya ruina apresuraron indudablemente, por creer sus pueblos inepto desde luego para el mando al que habia degenerado en comediante. No debe tampoco asistir a representaciones ejecutadas por cómicos asalariados." Mariana, "Del rey," 506. In his *Tratado de los Juegos Públicos* (Treatise on Public Plays, 1609) after a furious attack on the saraband (chapter XII) and all the theatrical music of his time (chapter XI), Mariana defends as entertainment for the gentlemen "jousts and tournaments on foot and on horseback" and games of *cañas*, as well as "games of shooting at the target with crossbows and *arcabuces*." For the common people he recommends traditional dances "Añádanse las danzas a la manera de España, los bailes con los movimientos de los pies, siguiendo el son de la flauta o instrumento que se tañe." Mariana, *Tratado de los Juegos Públicos*, 458.

music: listening to lewd and obscene music,[8] spending too much time on it,[9] and singing or playing wind instruments.

Mariana insists on views already set out by humanists such as Rodrigo Sánchez de Arévalo (1456-57) and perpetuated by Juan de Torres (1602), Diego Saavedra Fajardo (1640) and others. He discusses the analogy between musical harmony and good government, music as an honest pastime, the rejection of lascivious music, and excessive dedication to music.[10] He also frequently defended the honest old Spanish dances against the corrupt modern foreign ones. This has been a recurrent phenomenon in the history of the expansion of some dances as, for example, the tango or rock and roll. In the words of Peter Burke

---

[8] For the Jesuit the lewd or obscene in music lay not only in the text but also in the sounds themselves: "lascivas y obscenas, ya la letra de los cantares que la acompañan, ya la misma combinacion de los sonidos, como acontecen en nuestros tiempos" [...] "La música lasciva y disoluta debe pues ser desterrada, no solo del palacio de los príncipes, sino tambien del reino, si queremos que se conserven puras las costumbres y no mengüen la fortaleza ni la constancia en el pecho de los ciudadanos." Mariana, "Del Rey," 510.

[9] "No debe, por otra parte, poner el príncipe tanto cuidado en la música, que parezca olvidar las demás artes con que debe ser gobernada la república" [....] "Hay, en cambio, otras artes, a que deberá consagrar todas sus facultades, y son las que sirven para defender la nación y colmarlas de los más pingües beneficios. La música no es un arte vil, sino liberal y noble, mas no tampoco tan importante que en ella pueda ponerse la salud y la dignidad de los imperios. Creo muy oportuno seguir la costumbre de los medos y de los persas, cuyos reyes se deleitaban con oir tocar o cantar, sin hacerlo nunca ellos mismos ni manifestar en este arte su pericia. Entre los dioses de la gentilidad no se ha pintado nunca a Júpiter cantando ni tocando la cítara con plectro, aun cuando se le haya supuesto rodeado de las nueve musas, hecho que se dirige a probar que el príncipe no debe ejercer nunca el arte por sí mismo. No doy yo a la verdad grande importancia a que se piense del uno o del otro modo; mas no podre nunca convenir en que el principe se dedique a tocar ciertos instrumentos, que son para un hombre de su clase poco decorosos y dignos. No tocará nunca, por ejemplo, la flauta [..] y a mi modo de ver, no ha de tocar nunca instrumento alguno de viento. No debe tampoco cantar, principalmente delante de otros, cosa que apenas puede tener lugar sin que su majestad se mengüe; concederé cuando mas que se satisfagan en este punto sus inclinaciones cuando no haya jueces ni esté sino delante de unos pocos criados de su casa y corte. No creo tampoco que desdiga de un príncipe tocar instrumentos de cuerda, tales como la cítara o el laúd, ya con la mano, ya con el plectro, con tal que no se invierta en este ejercicio mucho tiempo ni se jacte de tener en él mucha destreza." Mariana, "Del Rey," 510.

[10] About the *Verjel de los Príncipes* (1456-57) and the *Spejo de la vida humana*, by Rodrigo Sánchez de Arévalo, see Robledo, "La música," 392. Juan de Torres collects all the myths and classical references to music, including a curious Orpheus whose music was able to separate men from women. Nevertheless he is against music for non-gifted princes and he advises against the dangers of excessive dedication to it and against lewd music. See Juan de Torres, *Philosophia Moral de Principes, para su buena criança y gobierno y para personas de todos los estados* (Burgos: Iuan Baptista Varesio, 1602), 310. Saavedra presents the harp as the image of good government in Saavedra, 119 and ff., and he recommends the moderate learning of music, 64-66 and 233.

"like the 'Americanization' of our days, "Italianization" was the favorite subject of many ethnocentric moralists."[11]

Works by Juan Luis Vives which are not dedicated to the education of kings, as was Mariana's treatise, but to that of noblemen and scholars, offer a different perspective. In *De Disciplinis* (1531) Vives recommends that boys learn both musical theory and practice.[12] His Dialogues or *Linguae Latinae Exercitatio* (1538) – widely circulated all over Europe as manuals of Latin language – speak of music as a learned pastime. Vives presents songs accompanied by the lute, some composed by him, and sung in evening moments of relaxation.[13]

Music in the treatises on female education

The question of girls' education is usually settled in the treatises on general education (or the men's treatises) with several paragraphs on honesty and housework, recommending especially spinning and knitting. The most controversial point is whether women should learn to read or not. The issue arose, among other reasons, because the Lutherans were favorable to feminine literacy.[14] The treatises directed to women in the sixteenth and seventeenth centuries are manuals of behavior more than treatises on education. In her study on these works, Mariló Vigil has already pointed out the constant rejection of music and dancing for women,[15] a rejection, however, which has been overlooked by musicologists. The reasons given by the authors to exclude music from girls' education can be summarized in the following points:

- Music is leisure and leisure is the main enemy of virtue. This is the point where all moralists converge.[16]

---

[11] Burke, "El Cortesano," 159.

[12] Vives states that the loss of hearing is the reason for the reduced effectiveness of music of his time with regard to that of the ancients. Luis Vives, "Las disciplinas." *Obras Completas II* (Madrid: Aguilar, 1992), 633.

[13] Dialogue 14 "The room and the evening" and Dialogue 21 "The game of cards," in Luis Vives, *Diálogos sobre la educación*, traducción, introducción y notas Pedro Rodriguez Sandrián (Madrid: Alianza Editorial, 1987, [1538]), 118, 176-177.

[14] Fray Luis de León and Luis Vives were in favor of women learning to read. Others were against it and there even were those who, like Juan de la Cerda, recommended that women should learn how to read but never to write. See Juan de la Cerda, *Libro intitulado Vida politica de todos los estados de mugeres: en el qual se dan muy provechosos y christianos documentos y avisos, para criarse y conservarse devidamente las Mugeres en sus estados* (Alcalá de Henares: Juan Gracián, 1599): Book 1: 12v.

[15] Mariló Vigil, *La vida de las mujeres en los siglos XVI y XVII* (Madrid: Siglo XXI, 1994), 57.

[16] See Vigil, 105 and ff. The author starts from the debatable hypothesis that the obsession of seeing leisure as the origin of all bad habits originated in a real idleness on the part of rich urban women.

- Music is contrary to silence. Silence is one of the virtues most praised in the treatises on feminine education for the four states of women: maiden, married, widow or nun.[17]
- Musical activity, especially its learning, requires a certain social activity. In other words, musical learning is contrary to feminine enclosure, so much praised in the educational treatises.[18]
- Music supposes pleasure in the body itself, a sensual enjoyment, and as such is blameworthy. This is a much stricter point, but one underlined explicitly by Vives.[19]
- The rejection of dancing. It would also be necessary to distinguish here among dances considered immodest and dances whose exhibition of the social hierarchy puts those dances into a higher category. In the sixteenth and seventeenth centuries, however, even the dances of the court were forbidden by many moralists.[20]
- Female singing poses a threat to masculine virtue.

We can classify the treatises in order of their increased rejection of musical activities. First we have those that condemn only dances, like Juan de Soto (1619)[21] and Hernando de Talavera (ca. 1485), who even advised listening to

---

[17] Besides Vives, see Fray Luis de León, *La perfecta casada*, ed. Javier San José Lera (Madrid: Espasa Calpe, 1992); Pedro de Luxán, *Coloquios matrimoniales* [1550] (Madrid: Atlas, 1949); Vicente Mexía, *Saludable instrucción del estado del matrimonio.* (Córdoba: Juan Baptista Escudero, 1566), quoted in Vigil, 93 and 19; and Juan de la Cerda, Book I f. 9 v., Book III f. 313 r.

[18] Besides Vives and Fray Luis de León, see Alonso de Andrade, *Libro de la guía de la virtud y de la imitación de Nuestra Señora*, (Madrid: Francisco Maroto, 1642), quoted in Vigil, 20.

[19] María Vela (1561-1617), a nun organist at a convent in Avila liked to look at her hands when playing. Her confessor wrote that she used to punish herself for that. See Alfonso de Vicente, *La Música en el Monasterio de Santa Ana de Avila (siglos XVI-XVIII) Catálogo* (Madrid: Sociedad Española de Musicologia, 1989), 17.

[20] "Las ocasiones de este vicio [carnal], son, ociosidad, comer y beber demasiado, malas compañías, oyr palabras deshonestas, ver el hombre mugeres compuestas y adereçadas, ver las danças y baylar: oyrlas cantar, y dezir donayres y amores; y lo mismo la muger, ver y oyr cosas semejantes a hombres." Cerda, 546 v.
"Avisanos la Escriptura sagrada, que la vista de la muger compuesta, escandaliza y mata los coraçones de muchos. Que su plática blanda es como fuego, que enciende los coraçones en amor deshonesto: y es como cuchillo de dos filos, que hiere y mata el alma con muerte de culpa, y de pena eterna. Por lo qual dixo San Agustín (D. Aug. li. de singula clericorum) que es cosa mas tolerable, oyr silvar a un basilisco, que no oyr cantar a una muger: porque el basilisco con su vista mata el cuerpo, y la muger con sus cantos suaves y lascivos, haziendo consentir en malos desseos mata el alma." Cerda, 460 r.

[21] Juan de Soto, *Obligaciones de todos los estados y oficios, con los remedios, y consejos más eficaces para la salud espiritual, y general reformación de costumbres* (Alcalá: Andrés Sánchez de Ezpeleta, 1619), quoted in Vigil, 57. He underlines that what is

music.[22] Next are those that allow women neither to sing, play instruments, nor dance, such as Gaspar de Astete (1603)[23] and Francisco Escrivá (1613).[24] A third category includes those who not only exclude women from dancing, playing an instrument or singing, but also from listening to any kind of music. Some make their recommendation briefly in passing, like Juan de Pineda (1589),[25] but others argue it at length, as we will see in Juan Luis Vives (1523) and in Juan de la Cerda (1599). Lastly, there are writers such as Francesc Eiximenis (1396) who feel a woman should behave in the way that satisfies her husband most. According to Eiximenis gentlemen preferred wives who could dance whereas the citizens (that is to say, the plebeians) liked more serious ones who avoided such entertainment.[26]

The treatises that expound more on women's education are clearly against teaching them music. The most notorious is that by Juan Luis Vives, *De institutione Feminae christianae* (1523), perhaps the most influential sixteenth century treatise on female education, as it was translated into English (1525), Spanish (1528), French (1542), German (1544) and Italian (1546). Vives (Valencia

---

bad is not playing instruments and singing, but rather the maidens' use of these abilities "to attract young men and make them fall in love." Mentioned in Vigil, 84.

[22] However Talavera considered dances as sinful for men and women as well as some songs and pieces of music: (Treatise on the sixth commandment, article "Sins of curiosity." Confessional or Advises in all the ways in which we can sin against the Ten Commandments (ca. 1485) Quoted in J. B. Gallardo, *Ensayo para una biblioteca española de libros raros y curiosos* (Madrid: Gredos, facsimile edition from 1911, 1968), IV, 102. As confessor of Isabel the Catholic, he reprehended the queen because she had danced at a party. See Francisco Bermúdez de Pedraza, *Historia eclesiástica de Granada* (Granada: Universidad de Granada, facsimile edtion from 1638, 1989), 191 r. This archbishop wrote the text and the plainsong of the *Oficio de la dedición de Granada*, a study and facsimile of this can be seen in F. J. Martinez Medina, P. Ramos López, y Elisa Varela, *Fray Hernando de Talavera Oficio de la dedición de Granada [1493?]* (Granada: Diputación Provincial, 2003).

[23] Gaspar de Astete, *Tratado del gobierno de la familia y estado de las viudas y doncellas* (Burgos: Felipe Iunta, 1603): "No sepa qué cosa son palabras torpes, o canciones profanas, sea sorda a las músicas de la vihuela, y de la cítara, o de cualquier instrumento músico. No se cure de ver mozuelos gentilhombres, compuestos y bien ataviados [...] No salga a ver las mujeres de la tierra, no sea danzadora, ni juege juegos de burla, no vaya a públicos convites, no beba vino [...] ni salga fuera de casa." Quoted in Vigil, 57-58.

[24] Francisco Escrivá, *Discursos de los estados, de las obligaciones particulares del estado, y oficio, según las cuales ha de ser cada uno particularmente juzgado* (Valencia, 1613). He also rejects singing and dancing because they are used to attract men. Quoted in Vigil, 84.

[25] Juan de Pineda, *Los treinta y cinco diálogos familiares de la agricultura cristiana.* Salamanca: Pedro Adurza y Diego López, 1589): "no se vea a la viuda en representaciones de comedias, ni dé oídos a músicas livianas, ni de chocarreros, ni admita conversaciones de galanes," fol. 27 v. Quoted in Vigil, 204.

[26] Francesc Eiximenis, *Lo Libre de les dones*, ed. crítica a cura de Frank Naccarato (Barcelona: Curial Edicions Catalanes, 1981), 133.

1493-Bruges 1540) rejects any musical activity at all for women.[27] His logic is implacable, and the three following premises suppose that music can only be harmful for women:

1. Women's main virtue is chastity.[28]
2. Leisure is the great enemy of chastity.[29]
3. Music is leisure.[30]

Although Vives condemns almost every female musical practice, he especially dwells on dancing as characteristic of "bad women."[31] The entire chapter 25 of Book I, entitled "De las danzas y bailes," deals with this topic. Vives compares the dances in fashion in France and England with the honest and slow ancient ones of the heathens.[32] Vives says that "the most serious and landed

---

[27] He insists on this point in the three books of his treatise: Book I on virgins, chapter 15, Book II on married women, and Book III, on widows. See Juan Luis Vives, *Instrucción de la mujer cristiana*, traducción, introducción, revisión y anotación de Elizabeth Teresa Howe (Madrid: Fundación Universitaria Española, 1995), 242 y 379.

[28] "Lo primero y principal quiero que sepa la mujer cristiana, que su principal virtud es castidad." Vives, *Instrucción*, 123.

[29] "...nunca jamás entra tan fácilmente el engaño del demonio en el pensamiento de la mujer como cuando la halla ociosa." *Ibid.*, 87.

[30] "Y no solamente el entendimiento dado a la sabiduría aborrecerá al vicio, es a saber, la blancura al hollín y la limpieza a la suciedad, pero se desapegará de todo vano deseo de deleite donde se arriman a su bordón los livianos ánimos de las doncellas como son bailes cantares, y otras cosas de esta calidad vanas, ineptas y sin fruto. Plutarco, filósofo muy señalado, dice: 'La mujer inclinada a las letras nunca se deleitará de bailar.'" *Ibid.*, 55.

[31] *Ibid.*, 196 and 242.

[32] Heathens "aunque alguna vez por milagro danzaban, no obstante, era su danzar tan honesto y reposado y cortés...." Dances in fashion are the contrary: "O si no, dime, ¿a cuál hombre cuerdo, a cuál mujer honesta, a cuál cristiana pueden parecer bien estas danzas tan dañosas que ahora se usan? Dejemos ahora a nuestra España con sus castañetas (aunque a veces son más duras de romperlas a los dientes de buena fama que cuencos de dátiles) y digamos algo de Francia y de Inglaterra.

Dime, ¿quién aprobará estas danzas francesas llenas de cien mil deshonestidades muy feas y fealdades muy deshonestas?. ¿De qué sirve (veamos) tanto besar? [...] Como si de otra manera no se pudiese conservar la caridad con las mujeres sino besándolas, si ya con todo no se hace por despertar a naturaleza en aquellas tierras frías. Para esto mismo deben ser (creo yo) los saltos de las doncellas, ayudándoles los hombres con la mano sobre el brazo, para que se levanten más alto. También, ¿a qué propósito estar danzando toda la santa noche sin jamás cansarse, ni hartarse, y si les decís que vayan diez pasos a pie hasta la iglesia, hablad en al[to]. Porque no lleva medio poder ir ni un sólo paso la señora sino cabalgando o en carreta, o (si a Dios le place) llevada a cuestas de hombres. Mas ¿qué honestidad ni señal de buen seso puede haber en aquel ir adelante, volver atrás, hacer represas a una mano, y a otra, saltar en alto, hacer continencias, dar la vuelta sobre el pie, y andar en rededor como peonza? Decidme ahora (si os vaga con todo hablar en una cosa como ésta) ¿no es todo esto dar voces al cielo que han perdido de todo el seso?" *Ibid.*, 158-159.

matrons of today" do not know how to dance, and they go with displeasure to meetings where there is dancing, although he recognizes that girls are usually taught to dance.[33] According to Vives dancing is immodest because it is a corporal pleasure, it heats the body[34] (for this reason the faster the dance the more reprehensible it is) and importantly, it means leaving the home, when women should go out as little as possible.[35] He finishes the chapter with a long quotation from San Ambrose, who spoke against dancing with an allusion to the biblical dance of Salome. Vives favors a greater censorship of frivolous books *(Amadís, Tirant* or *La Celestina)* and songs, an opinion that he continued to hold some years later in *De Disciplinis* (1531), when the Inquisition had already affected him in such a painful way.[36] Although he explains that "God brought the woman to the man" Vives is against girls learning to dance and sing to find a husband faster, a habit mentioned by several commentators.[37] The point is not only that women should not learn music or practice it. Vives' position is more radical: they should not even listen to it in their own home. According to Vives, the performances of secular music in his time had little to do with the austere and purist performances of this same music nowadays.[38] However, following his logic, it is difficult to explain why a girl who was not a nun could not play sacred music at home, although he advised her to read the Bible and the lives of the saints.

---

[33] *Ibid.,* 160.

[34] "Lo que he dicho de los manjares que a natura son calientes, digo de todo ejercicicio que escalienta y altera los cuerpos, como son danzas, olores, perfumes, pláticas, y vistas de hombres, porque todas estas cosas son dañosas y fácilmente pueden prejudicar a la limpieza del ánimo." *Ibid.,* 86.

[35] *Ibid.,* 137.

[36] See Luis Vives, *Las disciplinas.,* 61. In 1524 Vives's father was tried and burnt by the Santo Oficio as a *Judaizer* (a Christian who practises Judaism). In 1528 his mother, who was already dead, was tried for the same crime and her bones were exhumed and burned. It was supposed that this would contribute to keeping Vives far from Spain. Kamen, Henry *La inquisición española.* (Barcelona: Crítica, 1985), 137.

[37] *Instrucción,* 207, 191-192.

[38] "Otrosí, ¿qué diremos de las músicas y cantares llenos de brebajos emponzoñados para matar el mundo todo? Alléganse a esto los suspiros fingidos, y los visajes sobrepuestos y contrahechos de los cantantes, y oyentes, y los otros embaimientos y trampantojos con que se enviscan las simples doncellas, como las inocentes avecicas se toman en la rama adonde menos se temen de ser presas. Y aun por eso yo no permito, ni es de mi voto, que las doncellas aprendan de música, ni menos que se huelguen de oírla en ninguna parte, ni en casa, ni fuera, ni a puerta, ni a ventana, ni de día, ni de noche, y esto no lo digo sin causa. Pues que no sin causa San Atanasio disputó con hartas razones probables y argumentos, que ni aún en la iglesia no hubiese de haber música ni sones muy delicados, sino cuanto era necesario a alabar a Dios. Y esto no porque a Dios no se le debe toda alabanza y gloria, antes todo lo que le podemos dar es muy falto, y muy poco para su inefable Majestad; sino por los desconciertos y mollez y poca devoción en que muchos se solían divertir con la música.

Con todo yo otorgaré que la virgen cristiana, si quisiere aprender algo de órgano para monja, que aprenda mucho de enhorabuena." *Ibid.,* 155.

Unfortunately Vives does not say much about the only women allowed by him to come closer to music: prospective nuns. He does, however, specify what can be learned by nuns: "something of the organ," but not at a virtuoso or a professional level. And it is significant also because he does not mention singing, which was one of the main activities of the nuns. But Vives did mention his fear of the voice's sensuality.[39] The study of singing implies an enjoyment of the body itself. And warnings against any corporal pleasure occupy all of chapter 8 of Book I "Of the care that the virgin must have of her body."[40] As he says later speaking of dancing "no tyrant is crueler than corporal pleasure."[41]   Vives' exaggerated stoicism, pessimism and melancholy were already noted by the historian Américo Castro as symptoms of his "converted character," before documentation demonstrated his Jewish origin. In this way, Vives has been one of the key pieces in the interesting historiographical debate on the influence of the Jews in the Iberian culture of the Renaissance.[42]

Juan Luis Vives dedicated his treatise to Queen Catherine of Aragon, the wife of Henry VIII of England. He was their daughter Mary Tudor's tutor, and prepared the book for her.[43]   When he wrote it, Vives was just beginning his professorship at Corpus Christi College in Oxford. He had previously studied in Valencia and Paris, resided in Bruges, and worked as professor at the University of Leuven. None of those European centers were so hostile to music for women. For this reason Vives' statements must have created a certain amount of surprise for those to whom they were addressed, because music was very much practiced by the women at the court of Henry VIII, although in a private way. According to the English behavior manuals, the sermons and diaries of noblemen from the time of Elizabeth I to Charles I suggested that noble and respectable women should reserve their musical performances for private moments and those who did not became morally suspicious.[44]   Even though women from upper-class families learned

---

[39] "Tampoco no haga [la doncella] la voz muy delgada, ni requebrada, ni se escuche ella misma cuando hablare, ni le parezca que lo que ella dice es todo muy bueno, y que parece bien a los que la oyen. Porque a veces en eso se recibe mucho engaño." *Ibid.*, 148.

[40] So he recommends maidens to drink only water, perhaps with a little wine, and to abstain from delicacies and especially "naturally hot food". Of course, "the virgin's bed is neither soft nor delicate. It is enough that is clean. The same thing is said of her dressing." *Ibid.*, 82, 83 and 86.

[41] *Ibid.*, 161.

[42] José Antonio Maravall responded to Americo Castro and to his follower, Gilman, that anthropology and ethnology were questioning biological and cultural determination and that it also supposed excluding social and economic conditions. On this controversy, see Antonio Márquez, *Literatura e Inquisición en España 1478-1834* (Madrid: Taurus, 1980), 201 and ff.

[43] Vives also dedicated to Catherine *De Ratione Studii Puerilis* (1523), a brief program of studies for her daughter Mary.

[44] See Linda Phyllis Austern, "'No women are indeed': the boy actor as vocal seductress in late sixteenth and early seventeenth century English drama," in: *Embodied*

music, they had fewer possibilities than those from other European countries for performing music in public or for composing, given the English puritan concepts about sensuality and the moral dangers of music.[45] Vives' objection to women practicing music was not in keeping with the practice of the Castilian court. He mentions as exemplary women of their time the four daughters of Isabel the Catholic, among others,[46] and at least Juana was known to have a great liking for music. Vives himself is inconsistent when he praises Pliny's wife, who put her husband's lines to the "vihuela."[47]

Vives' ideas on music had a profound effect on the treatise of Juan de la Cerda, who quotes him as well Erasmus of Rotterdam.[48] The Franciscan de la Cerda goes so far as to justify the deaths of Anne Boleyn and Catherine "Eguart" since according to him both of them became adulterous because they danced.[49] Erasmus had also dedicated his treatise *Institutio christiani matrimonii* (1525) to Catherine of Aragon, and was also against dances and licentious songs.

In reality, Vives was not "openly hostile to modern music," as it has recently been said.[50] In fact, he advised boys to learn practical music and he composed songs accompanied by the vihuela. He *was* hostile to women performing or listening to music and this is only in keeping with some other commentators of the time. The Venetian Giovanni Bruto set forth the double moral code in the same treatise (1555): music is beneficial in the hands of men and destructive in those of women. Its beneficial rational side belongs to men, while its sensual and destructive face belongs to women.[51]

Another treatise dedicated to proposing a model for women, *La perfecta casada* ("The perfect married woman," 1583) by Fray Luis de León, does not mention music among the activities advisable for women. In fact, he does not make explicit references to music. However, his program implies a rejection of feminine musical activity since his only allusion to music unites songs with leisure. Leisure was the cause of "the feminization of women," which lowered them even more in cultural status.[52] His obsessive insistence that women should always remain at

---

Voices. Representing Female Vocality in Western Culture, ed. by Leslie C. Dunn and Nancy A. Jones, (Cambridge: Cambridge University Press, 1994), 90.

[45] See Linda Phyllis Austern, "Music and the English Renaissance Controversy over Women," in: *Cecilia Reclaimed. Feminist Perspectives on Gender in Music,* ed. Susan Cook and Judy Tsou (Urbana: University of Illinois Press, 1994), 54.

[46] Vives, *Instrucción,* 54.

[47] *Ibid.,* 252.

[48] Cerda, 18v. and 416r.

[49] *Ibid.,* 470r.

[50] Robledo, La música, 405.

[51] For further discussion see Austern, Music and the English Renaissance, 58.

[52] "Así que, traten las duquesas y las reynas el lino, y labren la seda, y den tarea a sus damas, y pruévense con ellas en estos oficios, y pongan en estado y honra aquesta virtud; que yo me hago valiente de alçancar del mundo que las loe, y de sus maridos, los duques y reyes, que las precien por ello y que las estimen; y aún acabaré con ellos que, en pago deste cuydado, las absuelvan de otros mil importunos y memorables trabajos con que atormentan

home made the learning and practice of music impossible.[53] Fray Luis' position with regard to music does not come from contempt for physical activity, because he was against the prevailing general scorn for manual work common at the time. He even stated that farmers were better than noblemen or merchants.[54] His position originates rather from his fear of the dangers produced by leisure, thus opposing the sonnets and songs in fashion. It is shocking that Fray Luis, the author of the *Oda a Salinas*,[55] the most beautiful poem of his time in praise of instrumental music, does not recommend music in his manual of women's behavior.

Before finishing with the educational treatises for women I want to clarify a point that may already have surprised the reader. Was the association of dancing with prostitution, discussed by so many commentators, an extended opinion at that time outside moralist circles? In the Castilian misogynist literature the topic is as frequent as it was in English writings.[56] We can take for example the *Diálogo de mujeres* (1544) by Cristóbal de Castillejo, which was very popular.[57] Another case is that of Juan Pérez de Moya (1513-1596). As a mathematician he had been interested enough in music to dedicate two brief treatises to it,[58] but in his *Philosofía secreta* (1585), a work that explains classical mythology on a historical and moral basis, music is almost always "carnal delight" or "Venus's bait."[59] An example that shows to what extent dancing and music were associated with prostitution is the regulation of the *Casas de Galeras* (Houses of Galleys, where all homeless women were confined), which prohibits dances and songs.[60] Other prohibitions of dances and very interesting texts on them can be seen in Maurice

---

sus cuerpos y rostros, y que las escusen y libren del leer en los libros de cavallerías, y del traer el soneto y la canción en el seno, y del villete y del donayre de los recaudos, y del terrero y del sarao, y de otras cient cosas de este jaez, aunque nunca las hagan." León, 46.

[53] "Y pues [a las mujeres] no las dotó Dios ni del ingenio que piden los negocios mayores, ni de fuerças las que son menester para la guerra y el campo, mídanse con lo que son y conténtense con lo que es de su suerte, y entiendan en su casa y anden en ella, pues las hizo Dios para ella sola." *Ibid.*, 181.

[54] *Ibid.*, 106.

[55] On the concepts of music in Fray Luis' work, see Francisco Rico, *El pequeño mundo del hombre. Varia fortuna de una idea en las letras españolas* (Madrid: Castalia, 1970), 178-189.

[56] Austern, Music and the English Renaissance, 57-58.

[57] "porque essas sus cantilenas/y músicas yo las llamo/los cantares del reclamo/o cantos de las serenas." Cristóbal de Castillejo, *Diálogo de mujeres*, ed. Rogelio Reyes Cano (Madrid: Alianza, 1986), 152-154.

[58] Both works are in arithmetical treatises. An edition and study of them can be seen in Luis Robledo, "Del pitagorismo a la justa entonación: los tratados musicales de Juan Pérez de Moya y de Juan Segura," *Revista de Musicología* XIX (1996).

[59] See his passage on the sirens in Juan Pérez de Moya, *Philosofía secreta*, ed. Carlos Claveria (Madrid: Cátedra 1995), 212-218; the carriage of Venus, 382; the history of Mercury and Argus, 419; and Pollux and Castor, 510.

[60] Madalena de San Jerónimo (1608) in Manuel Serrano y Sanz, *Apuntes para una biblioteca de escritoras españoles* (Madrid: Sucesores de Rivadeneyra, 1975), II: 307 and 311.

Esses.[61] Finally, during the sixteenth and seventeenth centuries in the Basque country, popular dances were associated not only with the instinctive and sensual but also with the satanic.[62] In this context we cannot be surprised that a theorist of music such as Juan Bermudo includes in his treatise a chapter about the honesty of music.[63]

Is music an art, a science or an entertainment?

We have seen that for Juan de Mariana "Music is not a vile art, but a liberal and noble one" (mentioned above). This categorization of music as an art comes from the medieval division of the seven liberal arts in *trivium* (grammar, rhetoric and logic) and *quadrivium* (arithmetic, music, geometry and astronomy), a distinction that many humanists, like León Hebreo in his *Diálogos de amor*, [64] continued to maintain. At the same time, and in keeping with neo-platonic thought, music is for Hebreo something spiritual that can have the grace of beauty and – as beauty – it is of divine origin. The most interesting contribution by Hebreo is his belief in the virtue of music as a way to loving beauty.[65]

One of the characteristics of the Renaissance is a moving from the concept of music as a liberal art, according to the above-mentioned medieval outline of *trivium* and *quadrivium*, to the concept of music as a *studia humanitatis*, or a discipline linked to oratory.[66] Several authors in the Iberian Peninsula such as Cristóbal de Villalón align music with the arts of the word.[67] However this did not provide any stimulus for female musical activity in Spain. A special case is Vives, who on the one hand regards music as belonging to mathematics and to the old *quadrivium*, but on the other hand recognizes that poetry "is concomitant with musical art."[68]

The physician Juan Huarte de San Juan (1529-1588) in his *Examen de ingenios para las ciencias* (*Exam of ingenuities for the sciences*, 1575), widely read in the

---

[61] Maurice Esses, *Dance and Instrumental Diferencias in Spain During the 17th and Early 18th Centuries* (New York: Pendragon Press, 1992), I: 517-543.

[62] Carlos Sánchez Equiza, *Txuntxunneroak. Narrativas, identidades e ideologías en la historia de un instrumento tradicional vasco: el txistu*. Tesis doctoral. Universitat Autònoma de Barcelona (1999-2000), 140.

[63] Fray Juan Bermudo, *Declaración de instrumentos musicales*. Ed. facsimile (Kassel und Bassel: Bärenreiter, 1957), x, r and ff.

[64] León Hebreo, *Garcilaso Inca de la Vega Traducción de los diáogos de amor de León Hebreo*, Edición y prólogo de Andrés Soria Olmedo (Madrid: Fundación José Antonio de Castro, 1996), 69.

[65] *Ibid.*, 297-298.

[66] For further discussion see Reinhardt Strohm, "The Humanist Idea of a Common Revival of the Arts, and its Implications for Music History." *Interdisciplinary Studies in Musicology*, ed. M. Jablonski and Jan Steszewski (Poznan: Poznan Society for the Advancement of Arts and Sciences, 1997).

[67] Robledo, La música, 408-410.

[68] Vives, Las disciplinas, 543 and 592.

time, makes a classification of the arts and sciences according to the type of "ingenuity" [69] that they require, a position removed from the earlier medieval division of the arts.[70] Huarte de San Juan aligns music with poetry and eloquence and also with what we now call art, or painting. Of the old *quadrivium* only astrology (if we assimilate it to astronomy, although Huarte differentiates in his system between astrology and cosmography) and mathematics (without arithmetic) remain with music. What Huarte did make explicit is that poetry and music (including instrumental) are both far from the understanding and the memory.[71]

All these reflections on music as a mathematical matter or as poetry cannot make us forget that there are also authors that seem to consider music only as entertainment, for example the vihuelist and courtier Luis de Milan in his *Libro de motes* (1535).

Is music characteristic of women or men?

Although he does not say explicitly, it can be deduced from Huarte de San Juan's classification that women do not have any "temperament" (talent) for music, as according to this author the faculty of imagination depended on heat. For Huarte, as for many writers of the time, a woman was characterized by her coldness and humidity.[72] This widespread belief at the time had been endorsed among others by Aristotle and Galen. For Huarte the coldness did not make any difference in "ingenuity" (that is to say, any intelligence or ability). On the contrary the imagination, the understanding and the memory, or the three rational abilities or ways of having ingenuity, depended on heat, dryness and humidity respectively.[73] Consequently, those who were castrated, or *capones,* were inapt for music, although this was, according to Huarte, their usual profession.[74] This is an early confirmation that music was the habitual profession of the *castrati.*

The authors who insist most vigorously that music is a virile activity are the musical theorists: Pietro Cerone (*El Melopeo y Maestro,* Naples, 1613), Francisco Correa de Araujo *(Facultad Orgánica,* Alcalá, 1626) and Fray Pablo Nassarre *(Escuela Música,* Zaragoza, 1723-1724).[75] Hispanic theorists from the sixteenth

---

[69] On the concept of "ingenuity" of Huarte de San Juan, see Noam Chomsky, *El lenguaje y el entendimiento* (Barcelona: Seix-Barall, 1974), 28-31; and the discussion in Esteban Torre, *Ideas lingüística literarias del doctor Huarte de San Juan* (Sevilla: Universidad de Sevilla, 1977), 85-87.

[70] Juan Huarte de San Juan, *Examen de ingenios para las ciencias,* ed. Felisa Fresco Otero (Madrid: Espaca Calpe, Colección Austral, 1991), 150.

[71] *Ibid.,* 156.

[72] *Ibid.,* 300.

[73] *Ibid.,* 110-114.

[74] *Ibid.,* 308.

[75] A selection of texts on women by these theorists can be seen in Zaldívar Gracia, A., "Unos dicen y otra hacen: de la misógina teoría histórica española renacentista y barroca, a la relevante práctica de las compositores dieciochescas." *La otra Historia de la Música. Ponencias presentadas en el '8° Congreso Internacional de Mujeres en la Música', Bilbao*

and seventeenth centuries are centered fundamentally in liturgical vocal music (with the exception of the few commentators on instrumental music). The theorists do not speak of dance music or of the songs sung in the comedies, the musical genres closest to women.[76] So they were dealing with a musical genre that, with the exception of women's convents, was then a masculine monopoly. It seems this monopoly was not sufficient for them, so Cerone even proposed that women should be forbidden to learn music.[77] Cerone's complaint that in Spain music was believed to be a woman's thing and effeminate has been overlooked by historians. However it is a key to understanding the ill will of the theorists toward any woman that wanted to learn music.[78]

> There are many gentlemen and illustrious persons who not only do not want to learn about music, but not even hear its name. Some say that singing is an occupation of vergers and friars, not of gentlemen or of noblemen. Others assert that it is a harmful recreation for vigorous males. There are others who say that it is a craft of women and effeminate and idle persons.[79]

Only a widespread popular association between music and women can justify so many texts by theorists against women learning music, and so many allusions to music as a male activity. Desiring to masculinize a profession that they felt was threatened by the popular association between women and music, the Iberian theorists ignored the muses as "inventors" of music, substituting them with an exclusively male genealogy.[80]

The musical practice of women

Although the main objective of my study is to examine the ideas about music in the non-professional circles of early modern Spain, this paper would be incomplete if I

18-22 de marzo de 1992. (Bilbao: Real Sociedad Bascongada de los Amigos del País, 1994) and Lorenzo Arribas, Josemi, *Una relación disonante. Las mujeres y la música en la Edad Media Hispana siglos IV al XVI*. (Alcalá de Henares: Ayuntamiento, 1998) 140-146. The text by Nassarre was written at the end of the seventeenth century.

[76] Pilar Ramos López, "Mujeres, teatro y música en el Siglo de Oro," in: *Música y mujeres. Género y poder*, ed. M. Manchado (Madrid: Cuadernos inacabados, 1998).

[77] "Mas de ninguna manera se ha de sufrir que las mugeres hagan esta profesion [de músicos], si acasso no ouiessen de servir a Dios haziendose Monjas." Pietro Cerone, *El melopeo y Maestro* (Bolonia: Forli 1969, facsimile edition from Naples, 1613), 539.

[78] See for example the texts of *Escuela Música*, by Fray Pablo Nassarre, which deal with girls' training. Fray Pablo Nassare, *Escuela música según la practica moderna* (Zaragoza: Institución Fernando el Católico, 1980), II, 483-484.

[79] Cerone, 153.

[80] Francisco de Salinas derived the word "music" from "muses," but the successive Hispanic theorists ignored Salinas in this respect (in any case evident). See Pilar Ramos López, "Los estudios de género y la música ibérica del siglo XVII," *Revista de Musicologia* XX (1997), 236. By the way, Salinas, in the foreword to his *De musica libri septem* (1577), did not deny the fact that it was a nun who began to give him Latin lessons in exchange for the music lessons with which he paid her.

omitted examining the simultaneous musical activity of women.[81] If we only take into account the moral treatises against women's singing and dancing, the legal prohibitions of women's dances and songs in the theater, or the literary associations between music and prostitution, we would have a one-sided and idealized vision of musical practice in early modern Spain: ideal because it would reflect the situation *desired* by the commentators and censors. It would offer a vision perhaps as distant from the daily reality as the image of the courts of Charles V or Philip II in the books by Higinio Anglés: a cultivated and learned court where everybody understood music and valued it to the utmost and where the kings were loving husbands, Christian parents and judicious rulers. I do not try to present here an extensive discussion about the musical activity of women in early modern Spain, but I will try to offer a general outline that helps to focus on the questions regarding their practice despite the proscriptions against them.

Women at the courts

We will probably never know the proportion of young ladies of higher birth who cultivated music. But we can evaluate some significant data. Music was a pastime in the courts shared by men and women as performers and as audience. The *Libro de Motes* by Luis Milan (1535) gives proof for how in the Valencian court of the Duke of Calabria both the ladies and the gentlemen included music among their amusements. Although we do not have reliable percentages on the literacy level either in Spain or in Europe in the Modern Age,[82] some books were directed specifically to women (for example Luis Milan's *Libro de Motes*) and some allusions included by him make us think that at least an important minority was literate.[83]

The private theatrical representations in the court carried out by queens, *infantas, meninas*, and the young women at the courts were so habitual during the sixteenth and seventeenth centuries that one historian considers them a female exhibition that worked as counterpart to the male games of bullfighting and *cañas*.[84] These plays included singing.[85] In addition, the Spanish *infantas* had music and dancing teachers, and music books.

---

[81] The differences between what is prescribed by the treatises and the daily life of women, (even those of the higher stratum to whom the treatises were addressed) are not restricted, of course, to musical activity, but concern almost all the activities. This is precisely the subject of the study by Mariló Vigil, *op.cit.*

[82] On this problem see P. Burke, *Los usos de la educación. La cultura popular en la Europa Moderna* (Barcelona: Altaya, 1997). Some writers consider that ignorance dominated Spanish nobility and they laughed openly at that; see Vives's Diálogos, 83 and 85.

[83] "¿Qué ha de hacer la doncellita que apenas sabe andar, y ya trae una *Diana* en su faldriquera?" (Chaide, Malón de *La Conversión de la Magdalena*. Clásicos Castellanos, Madrid: Espasa Calpe, 1957-I [1588]) 25.

[84] Pablo Jauralde Pou, "La actriz en el teatro de Tirso de Molina," in: *Images de la femme en Espagne aux XVIe et XVIIe siècles. Des Traditions aux renouvellements et à*

The information about schools for ladies does not speak of any musical instruction. What we call teaching today did not greatly concern these schools whose aim was to guard the chastity of the maidens, and to offer them as a gift or dowry for marriage or the convent.[86] Some noble girls or *hidalgas* received musical education and it is registered in their biographies as something praiseworthy, next to their fluency in Latin, for example.[87] However, no noble girl is said to dance very well, as far as we know.[88] We receive information on the ladies outstanding in dancing from another type of source that describes the court spectacles,[89] but not from the biographies of women collected by Serrano y Sanz. It may be significant that in the paintings of the sixteenth and seventeenth centuries neither the queens, the *infantas*, nor the ladies of the Spanish court are represented singing, dancing or playing instruments (neither do the kings, princes or noblemen appear this way). But they appear doing so sporadically in the eighteenth century. Some theorists of the theater even considered it unbecoming that a king should appear singing on stage and let us remember that Mariana prohibited the prince from singing in public so as not to reduce "his majesty." In the literature, however, knowing dancing and playing instruments are sometimes presented as characteristic of ladies "of quality."[90] However, among the few literary academies of the sixteenth and seventeenth centuries in which female participation is registered only one was related to music.[91] Finally, though, in some accounts of

---

l'émergence d'images nouvelles, ed. Agustin Redondo (Paris: Publications de la Sorbonne, 1994), 240.

[85] Pilar Ramos López, "Dafne, una fábula en la corte de Felipe II," *Anuario Musical* 50-51(1995-1996): 23-46 y 300.

[86] Maria del Mar Graña Cid, "Mujeres y educación en la prerreforma castellana: los colegios de doncellas," in: *Las sabias mujeres: educación, saber y autoria (siglos III-XVII)* (Madrid: Asociación Cultural Al-Mudayna, colección Laya, 1994).

[87] For example, Lorenza Méndez de Zurita († ca. 1603) praised by Pérez de Moya in his *Varia historia de sanctas e Illustres mugeres en todo género de virtudes* (Madrid: Francisco Sánchez 1583), fol. 130 (the quotation can be seen in Serrano, II: 48 and in Nicolás Antonio, *Biblioteca Hispania Nova sive hispanorum scriptorum qui ab anno md ad mdclxxxiv floruere.* Facsimile from Madrid, Viuda y herederos de Joachim de Ibarra 1788 (Madrid: Visor, 1996), 3500.

[88] The only case quoted by Serrano y Sanz about a girl who danced well is a story of her joyful youth, before she began her life as a nun, see below.

[89] For example, in a description by Gabriel de Bocángel of a masque performed at the Salón Dorado of the Palacio Real of Madrid the 21 December, 1648, all the ladies participating are registered, the *infanta* danced *la alemana* and *el pie gibao*, and doña Antonia de Mendoza and doña Ana María de Velasco each danced a *gallarda* (quoted by Jauralde Pou, " La actriz," 242).

[90] For example in the novels by María de Zayas and Mariana de Carbajal, from the seventeenth century, quoted in Vigil, 50.

[91] So Agustina de Torres presided over an academy dedicated to musical subjects in later sixteenth-century Salamanca, according to Vicente Espinel (quoted by Etienvre, Jean Pierre "Visages et profils féminins dans les *academias* littéraires du XVIIe siècle" in: *Images de la femme en Espagne aux XVIe. et XVIIe. siècles. Des traditions aux*

"illustrious" males, such as Francisco Pacheco (1599), playing the vihuela, the harp or the organ are mentioned among praiseworthy activities, whereas these abilities are pointed out in very few accounts of "illustrious" women.[92]

Women in convents

The music of the women's convents in Spain is still quite unknown, especially in comparison with our knowledge of contemporary Italian convents.[93] The cataloguing in progress of the convents' archives will throw light on their repertoires and instrumental and vocal scores. I will not deal with the activities and earnings of the nuns who were *maestras de capilla* or instrumentalists, the subject of the study by Colleen Baade in this volume. What is interesting to highlight here is that in the sixteenth and seventeenth centuries very few biographies of Spanish nuns point out any musical activity, while they usually do mention literary abilities. In Manuel Serrano y Sanz's anthology (1903-1905), our biggest collection of nuns' biographies, the allusions to musical activity fall in the following categories: it is a practice they learned prior to convent life;[94] it is explained that it is not an idle activity;[95] it deals with a *maestra de capilla*;[96] only occasionally an activity of composition or performance is mentioned.[97]

---

renouvellements et à l'émergence d'images nouvelles. Agustín Redondo, ed. (Paris: Publications de la Sorbonne, 1994), 353. Etienvre attributes the rare female participation in academic discussions to the Muslim tradition, 357.

[92] For example, in his *Gynaeceum Hispanae minervae*, Nicolás Antonio refers to 51 women, and among them are mentioned the musical abilities of Angela Sigea, Cecilia de Morillas o Henríquez (†1631), Isabel Coello (see also Ramos, "Dafne,") and Laurencia [Méndez] de Zurita, 343 and ff.

[93] Two interesting studies are the general survey on music in Spanish convents during the Middle Ages and Renaissance are J. Lorenzo Arribas, *Una relación disonante*, 75-146; and the study and catalogue by Vicente of the Convent of Santa Ana of Avila, *op. cit.*

[94] Mariana Francisca de los Angeles († 1697). Her friar biographer compares her vain youth (She played instruments, danced, played chess and fenced etc.) with her religious life at the convent; Serrano I: 40; see also Sor Margarita del Espíritu Santo, born in 1647, in Serrano, I: 400.

[95] Ana Francisca Abarca de Bolea (born ca. 1623) She completed all her training in the Cistercian convent since she entered there when she was three "descansando de la lectura en las tareas de ocupaciones de manos, en que adquirió suma destreza, como en todo género de música, assi de instrumentos como de voz, ya permitida en decentes recreos de Religion, ya encaminada a sagrados cultos, no permitiéndose un instante al ocio." Serrano, I: 2.

[96] Constanza Ossorio (Sevilla 1565-1637) who became abbess of the Cistercian Convent of Santa Maria de las Dueñas quoted by Serrano, II: 90.

[97] María de Barahona (seventeenth century) "De ella escribe Montalván (Para todos, 537): Monja profesa y correctora en el Real Convento de la Concepción Geronima, la mayor música que oy se conoce, assi por lo perfecto de la voz, como por el magisterio del canto pues tal vez canta las letras que ella misma escrive y compone, haziendo los versos y poniendo los tonos con gran ingenio, facilidad y destreza" (quoted by Serrano, I: 148). See

However, the extraordinary musical abilities of some nuns probably gave rise to public concerts. Otherwise it is difficult to understand descriptions of the prodigious virtuosity of certain nuns who were singers and instrumentalists.[98] In some feminine monasteries comedies and musical representations were quite habitual. This is the case of the Descalzas Reales of Madrid, at least in the years when it was the residence of the sisters of King Philip II, Juana of Austria and the Empress María.[99] In communal monasteries, an especially favorable feast for music was that of Saint John the Baptist or the Evangelist. Given the rivalries among the devout nuns concerning which saint was holier, each group competed in its respective celebrations. For those occasions neither work nor expense was spared, so that the best singers and musicians were hired.[100] Josemi Lorenzo has also collected information about nuns' dances in the seventeenth century.[101]

Women in the homes and theaters

Dances by men and women were habitual in the processions, pilgrimages and popular festivals. I mentioned earlier how some moralists even defended the honesty of these traditional dances by contrasting them with the lewd character of the modern or foreign dances (as with Padre Juan de Mariana). The dances of countrymen and women are part of the idyllic descriptions of Antonio de Guevara.[102] But any description of urban celebrations or processions also included women, or women and men dancing, particularly at the feast of Corpus Christi.[103]

---

also Sor Francisca de San José (seventeenth century, Serrano, II: 331) and María de San Alberto "notable música que falleció con fama de santidad el año 1640" (Serrano, II: 473).

[98] Two letters exchanged between professional musicians in 1632 praised two nuns from two different convents in Seville, and praised other women from Castilia and from the court of the Duke of Braganza as well. See Ramos López, *La música en la Catedral de Granada en la primera mitad del siglo XVII: Diego de Pontac.* (Granada: Diputación Provincial, 1994) I, 325-328. These nuns are also praised in a document sent to the King Philip IV ca. 1632; see Jules Picus, "El Memorial al Rey Don Felipe IV de D. Juan de Espina," *Anuario Musical* XLI (1986): 216.

[99] Serrano says of Juana de Austria (1535-1573), the widow of prince John from Portugal: "En aquel retiro dedicóse a piadosos ejercicios, distrayendo sus ratos de ocio con la música" so "mandaba venir a los mejores cantores de la Capilla Real, y otros muy diestros que ella tenia, con muchas vigüelas de arco, y otros muy concertados instrumentos." (Serrano, I: 78). A study of a courtly play in the nunnery of las Descalzas Reales in 1585-1593 can be seen in Ramos, "Dafne."

[100] Vigil, 251.

[101] Lorenzo, 137-138.

[102] Antonio Guevara, *Menosprecio de corte y alabanza de aldea* (Madrid: Melchor Alegre, 1673). The first edition dates from 1539. Quoted by Vigil, 27.

[103] Ramos, *La música en la Catedral,* I: 25-27, 38-39, 52, 57 and Ramos López, "Música y autorrepresentación en las procesiones del Corpus en la España Moderna," in : *Música y cultura urbana en la Edad Moderna.* Ed. Carreras, J. J., Bombi, A. and Marín M. A. (Valencia: Universidad, forthcoming).

The extant popular poetry from the sixteenth and seventeenth centuries is plentiful in allusions to the songs of women in their homes or in the fields. The plays and novels also present domestic scenes where women sing or dance. For example, Dorotea, a rich farmer's daughter, when explaining to Don Quixote how innocently and honestly she lived in her parents' house, affirms that she practiced the "exercises [...] that are for the maidens as licit as necessary: the sewing, the reading of devout books and the playing of the harp, because the experience showed me that music composes decomposed spirits and alleviates the works born of the spirit."[104] They are similar activities to those carried out by Laurela, a rich noblemen's daughter, in a novel by María de Zayas.[105]

Women, music and theater were intricately inter-related in the seventeenth century Spanish collective imagination. But significantly, this relationship is mostly overlooked by musicological studies. Women then performed most of the male and female roles which included singing or dancing. As the songs and theatrical dances were considered characteristic of women, the theaters did not take advantage of the *castrati* active in churches until the eighteenth century. This prominence of women was due to the pervasive idea that music was an effeminizing element, low, ignoble and suitable to them, and in its turn, this strong feminine presence actually empowered that concept. In addition, women, as part of the active public, were also influential in deciding a play's success. The female prominence in the Iberian theater had important musical consequences. The shortage and simplicity of the recitatives has been explained as a consequence of the brief musical training of the actresses. In my opinion female prominence is also the cause of the predominance of dance tunes and high melodies on Spanish stages during the seventeenth century.[106]

The music used in the Hispanic theater during the first half of that century was not much different than the collections of songs from the end of the sixteenth century. So there was not any technical reason that justified the angry attacks on music and some dances called "new." The main musical difference between the old and new comedy was not the musical style, but, fundamentally, the amount of music. The new comedy had more music, and later musical genres like *zarzuelas*, operas, etc. would have even more music. Because singing was a women's task, a larger quantity of music meant a larger feminine cast. As women were identified with dancing and lasciviousness, the critics always voiced those concerns, but the real question was a different one. In a time in which "el gran teatro del mundo" (all the world is a stage) was one of the most widely discussed topics, theater

---

[104] Miguel de Cervantes, *Don Quijote de la Mancha* (Barcelona: Juventud, 1985) [1605] I, 279.

[105] Maria de Zayas, *Parte segunda del Sarao y entretenimiento honesto. Desengaños amorosos*, ed. Alicia Yllera (Madrid: Cátedra, 1983) [1647], 295-296.

[106] Louise K Stein, *Songs of Mortals, Dialogues of the Gods. Music and theatre in Seventeenth-Century Spain.* Oxford: Clarendon Press, 1993, 256-257. For further discussions about women in Spanish theater see Ramos, "Mujeres."

opponents and legislators knew very well that comedy was not only "the mirror of life" as repeated by the theorists. They realized also that, like in *Las Meninas*, the famous painting by Diego de Velazquez, the mirror's game could be inverted. A musical theater where women were almost exclusively the only performers could be too dangerous.

Conclusions

Although the reality for female musical activity in Spain is not as somber as the one desired by moralists and musical theorists, this panorama is far from being comparable to the flourishing musical activity of the Italian women of the same time. Spain was not the scene for *Il Cortegiano*. It is true that female prominence was enormous in the field of Spanish theatrical music. But the musical activity of women was more restricted in the Church, in the courts and in the houses of the Castilian and Aragonese urban centers. Would women have practiced more music if the commentators had not been so strict? Was the attack of the moralists the main obstacle to the greater development of music on the part of women? These are questions difficult to answer in a categorical way. The moralists did not condemn all secular music made by men. However it is evident that, with the exception of the vihuelists and theater musicians, the chamber musicians dedicated to secular music were not a buoyant institution in the Spain of the sixteenth and seventeenth centuries. On the other hand, based on testimonies previous to the Renaissance (such as the already mentioned Francesc Eiximenis), we can think that, among the Renaissance Spanish humanists, many of whom were of bourgeois extraction, stricter morals were being imposed with regard to music than during the Late Middle Ages.[107]

We can think that if the moralists had not been so adverse to music a greater female patronage would have facilitated the conditions of those chamber musicians (men and women). In any case, it does seem quite clear that the concept of the practice of music as a humble or low activity became widespread. This concept had probably even more influence than the moral condemnation of music of the time in keeping girls from the profession or seeking possible patronage of men and women.

Music as theoretical speculation or a mathematical branch was considered a respectable and masculine science. As long as it was entertainment it was considered honest by most masculine education commentators and immodest by most of those who wrote on female education. Dancing was popularly considered a

---

[107] Surprisingly, Eiximenis' work links the songs and dances more to paradise than to lasciviousness. In his long treatise he only once speaks of lascivious songs, when advising against singing them in liturgical services. Although he speaks at length about lasciviousness and adultery, the long discourses against unchaste songs and dances are not to be found as they are in moralists from sixteenth and seventeenth centuries. Once he refers to songs "trencats" and "françesos" as examples of vanity, but not of lasciviousness. Eiximenis, 501 y 236. See his description of the songs and dances of paradise, 567 and 568.

low-brow and female activity. Although the dances were a minority in the vihuelists' repertoire, many other sources lead us to think that the dances made up most of the secular repertoire performed in Spain in the sixteenth and seventeenth centuries. Perhaps the very low prestige of the dance genre was the reason for its rare presence in the vihuelists' printed books. As far as vocal and/or instrumental music, the question of femininity or masculinity was not so sharply defined, but some intellectuals considered it a respectable activity in masculine hands and a reproachable one in feminine hands (Juan Luis Vives, Juan de Mariana).

I conclude, as Linda Austern did when studying English Renaissance,[108] that in Spain the controversy surrounding music had many points in common with the controversy about women, because the underlying attitudes about women and music were both part of wider cultural conversations and disagreements about sensuality, morality, control and love.

---

[108] Austern, "Music and the English Renaissance," 54.

Chapter 5

Virtue, Illusion, *Venezianità*: Vocal Bravura and the Early *Cortigiana Onesta*

Shawn Marie Keener

The Virtue of illusion

Illusion was perhaps the *cortigiana onesta*'s most powerful tool. But the skill with which she constructed, presented, and camouflaged herself poses a challenge to those trying to make sense of the arts she cultivated. Her "illusion," until recently, was considered a barrier to understanding her art, or rather, was taken to negate *a priori* its quality and authenticity. Margaret Rosenthal, in her study of Veronica Franco's writings, notes the "cause-and-effect relation" that early twentieth century scholars have drawn between Franco's art and her profession as courtesan. These critics either romanticize her work as exceptional or vilify it (and her) for her sexual exploits, because they "have fallen prey precisely to the persuasive force of the Venetian cultural myth and the anecdotal lore surrounding the courtesan."[1] The same cause-and-effect relation contributes to the strong distinction drawn by Anthony Newcomb between courtesan-musicians and professionals:

> Although musical proficiency was an important and often cited part of the arsenal of delights manipulated by these women, they were not professional musicians. They were, rather, imitations of the ideal *donna di palazzo*.[2]

Impugned as a mere imitator, the courtesan's musicianship is reduced to a parlor trick, and her mastery of illusion used as a moral injunction against her.

Yet well-concealed, artful imitation and appropriation were sixteenth century ideals. This is why Aretino, however sarcastically, could hold up illusion as the

---

[1]Margaret Rosenthal, *The Honest Courtesan: Veronica Franco, Citizen and Writer in Sixteenth-Century Venice* (Chicago and London: University of Chicago Press, 1992), 4.

[2]Anthony Newcomb, "Courtesans, Muses, or Musicians? Professional Women Musicians in Sixteenth-Century Italy," in: *Women Making Music: The Western Art Tradition*, ed. Jane Bowers and Judith Tick (Urbana and Chicago: University of Illinois Press, 1986), 102.

courtesan's chief virtue. As Guido Ruggiero reports, *cortigiane* were *oneste* in Aretino's view because:

> they sold exactly what they claimed to sell, sex *and* illusion: the illusion of men being elite, refined lovers; the illusion of men being discriminating in their choice of mistresses; the illusion of men being mannered and intellectual. In sum, they sold to the upper classes the very illusion the upper classes had created of themselves.[3]

Courtesans were perhaps "imitation" *donne*, as Newcomb says, but what they were imitating was itself an illusion. Latter-day scholars may be forgiven for their difficulty in defining courtesans, since even contemporaries had a difficult time doing so. Sixteenth century Venetian lawmakers struggled mightily to define these women, who were neither "common whores" nor true ladies. The pronouncements by twentieth century critics glibly identifying certain women as courtesans and thereby dismissing their arts as mere "delights" thus do a disservice to history. The danger in excising the courtesan from the realm of "real" artists is especially acute early on when the character of the *cortigiana onesta* was still fluid and easily confounded with other types of women, from prostitutes, actresses, and singers, to courtiers and noblewomen.

  By taking the arts of the elite *donna di palazzo* to the public sphere, courtesans exploited the tensions of Venice's complex social networks and made explicit description nearly impossible. The search for courtesans of the early sixteenth century is a process of broadening and mixing categories rather than narrowing them. The musical training of noblewomen, issues of professional women performers, and the broad outlines of courtesanry's Renaissance origins come together to form a composite portrait of an early sixteenth century *cortigiana onesta*. Vocal bravura became a key element of the courtesan's illusion – the perfect analogue to her elusive social role. The *aria veneziana* or *giustiniana* may serve not only as a model for this courtesan's distinctive singing style or aria, but also as an index of the courtesan's place in the collective imagination of early modern Venice. The figures of the virtuoso singer and the *cortigiana onesta* – which would eventually crystallize in the public imagination – emerge and intersect at the cusp of the *cinquecento*.

Towards a prehistory of the *cortigiana onesta*

For all the prominence of the *cortigiane oneste* from the mid-sixteenth century onward, their origins are unclear. Reminiscent of ancient Greek *haeterae*, the courtesan held special appeal for those with humanistic aspirations.[4] A more

---

[3] Guido Ruggiero, *Binding Passions: Tales of Magic, Marriage, and Power at the End of the Renaissance* (New York and Oxford: Oxford University Press, 1993), 42. Rosenthal reads Aretino's appraisal differently, taking it as misogynistic invective rather than telling social commentary and near-praise.

[4] Ruggiero, 38.

concrete impetus is to be found in the sexual economy of the fifteenth century. Courtesan culture first emerged in *quattrocento* Rome around the increasingly princely courts of the popes and cardinals; they filled the need for graceful, charming female companionship in an all-male society.[5] According to Guido Ruggiero, courtesanry flourished because of the "newly perceived necessities in an environment of unusual wealth, power, and culture."[6] The fashion for this "elite form of prostitute" quickly spread throughout Italy, a dispersal hastened by the sack of Rome in 1527 which brought that city's golden age of courtesanry to a close.[7] The center of gravity of Italian courtesan culture then shifted north to Venice.

Though the full blossoming of Venetian courtesan culture comes mid-century, it commenced unofficially in 1498. Until that year, prostitutes had been restricted to the Castelletto area, near the Rialto.[8] Lifting the ban was a watershed, giving Venice's *meretrici* greater control of their lifestyle and clientele. The anonymous comedy *La Bulesca*, of 1514, testifies to the power independence held for ambitious *meretrici*; in the play, the young Marcolina explains to her sister how much better off she is having left the bordello to be out on her own.[9] Such fictional accounts are supported by the frequent mention of courtesans by diarist Marin Sanudo in the first decades of the century.[10] The many efforts to "bind" prostitution and socially disruptive courtesans show growing public concern as well as just how little control civic powers had over the practice.[11] The many political initiatives are paralleled by the burgeoning genre of invectives against courtesans and women generally. If *La Bulesca* is a product of upper-class fascination with the underworld, then the legal measures, invective, and defamation indicate the growing unease with which the elite viewed social change. Within two decades of closing the Castelletto, the figure of the *cortigiana* had crystallized and courtesanry had become an integral part of Venice's social networks.

That the courtesan's role transcended the duties of a sex worker is not surprising when seen in context. The complexities of the sexual and marital economies of sixteenth century Venice left many women and men with needs that

---

[5] *Ibid.*

[6] *Ibid.*

[7] Monica Kurzel-Runtscheiner, *Töchter der Venus: die Kurtisanen Roms im 16. Jahrhundert*, (München: C.H. Beck, 1995), 20.

[8] Rita Casagrande di Villaviera, *Le cortigiane veneziane nel Cinquecento* (Milan: Longanesi & C., 1968), 19-20.

[9] The so-called "*letteratura alla bulesca*," a kind of pastoral comedy adapting the rustic characters and situations to an urban setting, attests to the urban underworld and how it was changing in the early cinquecento. Bianca Maria da Rif, *La Letteratura "alla Bulesca": Testi Rinascimentali Veneti* (Padua: Editrice Antenore, 1984). See also Ruggiero, 36.

[10] Marin Sanudo, *I Diarii di Marino Sanuto* (MCCCCXCVI-MDXXXIIII), ed. Federico Stefani, Guglielmo Berchet, Nicolò Barozzi (Venezia: Stab. Visentini, 1887).

[11] Ruggiero, 48-52.

could only be met outside the confines of licit relationships. Life as a *cortigiana onesta* offered financial betterment (though not security) and a measure of freedom and self-expression, not only for former *puttane* of the Castelletto, but also for women of middling status with insufficient dowry for marriage or the convent. The consolidation of family wealth in sixteenth century Venice also left many young men unable to make appropriate marriage arrangements. In the sophisticated but transgressive institution of courtesanry, the relationship between men and women was symbiotic: courtesans vied for the attention and patronage of society's most elite, and men, in turn, vied for the attention and favor of the most exclusive *cortigiane*. While the precise genealogy of Italian courtesanry may remain obscure, it is clear, as Ruggiero writes, that the fashion for courtesanry:

> caught on quickly because it satisfied new social imperatives. In the increasingly aristocratic world of the Renaissance, upper-class males found in the courtesan, as they found in expanding interests in display and manners, yet another area of life where they could fashion themselves as a Renaissance elite.[12]

In Venice, much of this self-fashioning took place in salons or *ridotti*: loose gatherings of musicians, writers, artists, and dilettantes. These diffuse versions of the hierarchic courtly settings were an all-male world but welcomed women of the demimonde.[13] Courtesans were always an essential component of Venice's accommodation of old, courtly values to new, urban circumstances.[14]

Fame and the illusion of virtue

The courtesan's public profile was anathema to chaste *donne* who at least feigned modesty. Reputation outweighed fact in matters of fame, making the illusion of virtue tantamount to virtue itself. Mario Equicola says as much in his advice on avoiding defamation by rejected suitors:

> Though many know her virtue and the cowardice of her suitor, and will not believe the lies that he tells about her, there are others who will believe and she will be wrongly defamed. She must remember that honor or blame do not rest principally in doing some one thing, or not doing it, but in being believed or not believed to do it, honor lying in nothing but the opinion of men. Therefore every art is necessary not only to do the right thing, but to give no occasion for tales of her affairs.[15]

---

[12] Ruggiero, 38.

[13] Martha Feldman, "Enacting Gender, Revising Class: The Courtesan's Voice in Renaissance Venice" (paper read at University of Nevada at Reno, February 2002; expanded version of paper given at the American Musicological Society/Society for Music Theory joint meeting, Toronto, Canada, November 2000), 8.

[14] Martha Feldman, *City Culture and the Madrigal at Venice* (Berkeley: University of California Press, 1995), xxii.

[15] Mario Equicola, *Di natura d'amore*. Lib. V. (Vinegia, Francesco di Alessandro Bindoni & Mapheo Pasini, 1531), ff. 166-168. Quoted in Ruth Kelso, *Doctrine for the Lady of the Renaissance* (Urbana: University of Illinois Press, 1956), 191.

This equivocal environment encouraged the sequestering of noblewomen, and set the stage for those women capable of mustering "every art" in support of a persona at once public and noble.

More than other women, courtesans depended on their ability to create an illusion of virtue. The success of their efforts is evinced by the impossibility of fully defining them. The Venetian senate in the 1540s struggled to distinguish legally the *cortigiana onesta* from a *meretrice* on the one hand and a noblewoman on the other.[16] "Common whores" were easily defined in the law books, but the honest courtesan was never explicitly categorized. She could only be defined by what she was not.[17]

Capitalizing on the porous boundaries of the "public sphere," *cortigiane* deftly aligned themselves with the nobility while distancing themselves from the *puttane*. The successful courtesan, according to Rosenthal, cultivated a paradoxical mixture of noble attributes and a public persona:

> Unlike a patrician woman, whose life revolved exclusively around the private, domestic concerns of her family, the *cortigiana onesta* projected a highly sophisticated public image which she used to move beyond the domestic space of the family into the public spheres of Venetian life. Mimicking the graces and donning the costumes of the noblewoman, she was able to differentiate herself from the... *meretrice* [prostitute]. Because courtesans' increasing wealth gave them access to extravagant costumes, they were visually indistinguishable from married women of the upper classes.[18]

The melding of impossibly incompatible elements lies at the heart of the courtesan's illusion. Lavish trappings were necessary, of course, but credible performance cannot be bought. Courtesans, as Martha Feldman has argued, were deeply rhetorical beings.[19] Discomfort with their true profession may have colored the opinions of some contemporaries and scholars, but, as Stephanie Hodgson-Wright has shown, "the categorization of women as exclusively sexual traders is inevitably challenged at the very moment of performance, which testifies to [their] accomplishments...."[20]

The ambiguity of the public sphere means that we must consider any woman in the public eye – writer, scholar, singer, actress, or courtesan – in the same category, especially early on when the lines of demarcation are hazier. The limits of propriety were so narrowly drawn that the boundaries for what was improper

---

[16] Rosenthal, 67.

[17] *Ibid.*

[18] *Ibid.*, 68.

[19] Feldman, "Enacting Gender, Revising Class," *passim.*

[20] Stephanie Hodgson-Wright, "Undress, Cross-Dress, Redress: Aphra Behn and the Manipulation of Genre," in: *Women and Dramatic Production 1550-1700* (New York: Longman, 2000), 165.

were, of necessity, much wider.[21] Several classes of women were paid for their musical abilities in the fifteenth century. Itinerant musicians were at the lower end of the spectrum, and at the higher end, "it is seldom possible to differentiate between women from quite modest families who were hired by courts specifically for their musical talent and women of the lesser nobility who were tolerated at great courts because they sang well."[22] Anxiety over moral ambiguity among these professional entertainers seems to emerge in the late *quattrocento*, along with courtesanry. The professional status of singer Giovanna Moreschi, for instance, cast doubt on her reputation – doubt that was put to rest by her marriage to composer Marchetto Cara. Not much later, in 1514, Sanudo mentions in passing the funeral of Angela Trevixani – the first identifiable courtesan in his diary – who was a singer of renown. She sang well enough, apparently, to have substantially impressed the musicians of St. Mark's who sang a solemn mass on her death.[23] Vittoria Piisimi, famous actress of the eponymous "companghia della Vittoria," seems to have had no male protectors of any kind, making her status an open question. This ambiguity, for Newcomb, is problematic, since we cannot determine her social prestige even though we are certain of her fame and talent:

> Because she was unmarried (if she was unmarried), was she considered no better than a courtesan – a remarkable renegade to be looked at, applauded, but not included in polite society?[24]

An interesting question, but a search for "professional" women performers that excludes courtesans simply on principle does more than negate their talents and contributions. It also closes off an important avenue of the ambiguity that marked not only courtesans but all women who courted public opinion.[25]

The effects of that ambiguity (and the courtesan's success in exploiting it) were not limited to women. All those who had to seek patronage struggled with the need to "sell themselves" and were uneasy with the implications of self-

---

[21] Sheila Schonbrun, "Ambiguous Artists: Music-Making among Italian Renaissance Courtesans (With Particular Reference to Tullia of Aragon, Gaspara Stampa, and Veronica Franco)," D.M.A. diss. (City University of New York, 1998), 18.

[22] Howard Mayer Brown, "Women Singers and Women's Songs in Fifteenth-Century Italy," in: *Women Making Music: The Western Art Tradition, 1150-1950*, ed. Jane Bowers and Judith Tick (Urbana and Chicago: University of Illinois Press, 1986), 57-58.

[23] Casagrande di Villaviera, 190. From Marin Sanudo's chronicle, October 16, 1514 (tome XIX, column 138): "In questa matina fo sepulta a Santa Catarina Lucia Trevixana, qual cantava per excellentia. Era dona di tempo tuta cortesana e molto nominata appresso musici, dove a caxa sua se reduceva tutte le virtù. Et morite eri di note, et ozi 8 zorni si farà per li musici una solenne messa a Santa Caterina, funebre, et altri officii per l'anima sua."

[24] Newcomb, 103.

[25] For an extended critique of Newcomb and the problematic designation of "professional," see Nina Treadwell, "Restaging the siren: Musical Women in the Performance of Sixteenth-Century Italian Theater," Ph.D. diss, University of Southern California, 2000.

promotion. The ambitions of male poets, musicians, writers, and artists overlapped with those of the women of the demimonde who, like them, were plying the waters of patronage. [26] Peter Burke writes of the courtly context that noblemen could become artists, and artists were welcomed into courts by dint of their talent, but that the social status of those artists remained ambiguous, as did that of the literati. [27] The fluid conditions of an urban metropolis like Venice, where the "court" consisted of loosely structured salons and academies, could only heighten these tensions. The presence of courtesans on the same professional territory as writers, musicians, artists, and intellectuals – and their superb performance there – reveals the ironic self-satire latent in parody and invective literature leveled against courtesans. Their success offered "a paradigm for how the city, with its pliable and equivocal social structures, could become an extraordinary resource for inhabitants not born into a full measure of its benefits." [28]

An "excuse for the public display of beauty and skill"

Nothing embodied the courtesan's adaptation of elite manners to a public forum more than solo song. Musical ability, particularly the ability to sing, was expected of the elite and emulated by those who wished to ennoble themselves. The children of Ercole Primo d'Este, for instance, learned to sing and to play, performing both written and unwritten musical genres. [29] The traditional importance of music as a marker of sophistication in young ladies is shown by Alessandra Macinghi negli Strozzi's question about one of her son's prospective brides: whether this girl – Gostanza di Pandolfo – "was uncultivated (*zotico*) and was told that the girl knew how to read fairly well, was agile, and knew how to dance as well as sing." [30] Though a necessary social grace, music was considered a dangerously ambiguous activity, threatening both modesty and chastity, as Ruth Kelso notes in this precis:

> Music...fell under the disapproval of most as another inflamer of passions [along with dance] and excuse for public display of beauty and skill. Under the name of virtue, they said, it carries grave and important evils, especially at banquets, where rich food has already loosened the mind. Some would not allow the girl to be trained to play or sing at all, even though they granted that most people thought it an ornament and grace to a girl of gentle birth to master both arts. Others would have her taught but only for

---

[26] Janet L. Smarr, "Gaspara Stampa's Poetry for Performance," *JRMMRA* 12 (1991): 79.

[27] Peter Burke, "The Courtier," in: *Renaissance Characters*, ed. Eugenio Garin, trans. Lydia G. Cochrane (Chicago: University of Chicago Press, 1988), 115.

[28] Feldman, *City Culture*, 14.

[29] James Haar, *Essays on Italian Poetry and Music in the Renaissance, 1350-1600* (Berkeley and Los Angeles: University of California Press, 1986), 86. See also William Prizer, "Una 'Virtù Molto Conveniente A Madonne': Isabella D'Este As A Musician," *The Journal of Musicology* XVII/1 (1999): 10-49.

[30] Strozzi was a member of the Florentine patrician bourgeoisie in the fifteenth century. Brown, 66.

private use as a recreation and consolation in times of ...trouble...or as a pastime in vacant hours if she has nothing better to do. Then she will play or sing at the proper time and place, and always modestly and not to be heard. Or rarely, admitting the pressure of custom, one [of these writers] may be found to advise that when this girl of gentle birth must sing in public she will sing chaste songs in a low voice and without oblique looks, but with reverence and shame in her face.[31]

If writers were at such pains to warn girls away from the dangerous applications of music, it follows that someone was, indeed, using musical skill to questionable advantage.

The courtier and *donna di palazzo* were expected to be talented, but they had to balance display with decorum. In Castiglione's *Cortigiano* of 1528, Giuliano de' Medici warns the *donna di palazzo*, when singing or playing, to avoid what he calls "those abrupt and frequent *diminuendos* [meaning diminutions] that are ingenious but not beautiful."[32] Decades earlier, in 1456, Antonio Cornazano had described the singing of Pietrobono, the renowned lutenist and *cantore*, as "*tucta in semitoni, proportionando e sincoppando sempre, e fugiva el tenore a i suoicantoni.*"[33] Haar notes that the description, though "hard to take at face value, nevertheless informs us that Pietrobono's song was real music, with some melodic *fioritura*, either vocal or on the lute, over a supporting bass."[34] "*Tucta in semitoni, proportionando e sincoppando sempre*" seems to take as explicit the "ingenious but not beautiful." Perhaps Pietrobono's playing and singing simply transcended the usual pitfalls of virtuosity, or perhaps such virtuosity – and the concomitants of pride and fame – were considered unbecoming to a woman. The distinction is unclear.

While avoiding outlandish or unseemly display, the *cortigiana onesta* must have employed her musical abilities in precisely the ways discouraged above: using her voice to display beauty and skill, to loosen the mind, to be heard – without shame – and certainly employing oblique looks.[35] The *donna di palazzo* needed to be circumspect in the degree of virtuosity in her singing or playing, but the *cortigiana* had every reason to cultivate a highly individual, artful singing style, capitalizing on the moral ambiguity of music and using the voice as an instrument of social mobility. By the mid-sixteenth century, according to Feldman, it was no longer clear "whether *cortigiane oneste* might sing as

---

[31] Ruth Kelso, *Doctrine for the Lady of the Renaissance* (Urbana: University of Illinois Press, 1956), 53.

[32] Baldesar Castiglione, *The Book of the Courtier*, trans. George Bull (London: Penguin Books, 1967), 215.

[33] The passage from Cornazano's *La Sfortiade*, is cited and commented upon by Nino Pirrotta "Music and Cultural Tendencies in Fifteenth-Century Italy," *Journal of the American Musicological Society* 19 (1966): 139-146.

[34] Haar, *Essays*, 85-86.

[35] The iconography of sixteenth-century courtesans abounds with oblique gazes, which amount to a visual trope.

beautifully as noblewomen, or whether 'honest' women who sang turned into courtesans."[36]

As a richly multivalent art, solo song became the ultimate instrument of social mobility for women of the Venetian demimonde. The repertory consisted of *modi* or *aeri*, either read and adapted from notation or entirely extemporized. These simple formulae are plentiful in fifteenth and sixteenth century manuscripts and prints. Their simplicity reflects their mnemonic purpose as well as the genre's verbal emphasis. The *modi* and *aeri* in Petrucci's Fourth Book of Frottolas of 1505, for instance, were, according to Feldman, "entirely apt for the poet-reciter, for whom display of original verse was the main point."[37] The frottola itself is a nexus of musico-historical strands, as James Haar explains in describing its relation to the emergence of the sixteenth century madrigal:

> Singing to the "lyre," the humanists' favorite form of music, was practiced both by professionals and by their patrons, noble amateurs. These patrons, especially the rulers of Ferrara and Mantua and their relatives, supported the poets and musicians who created the repertory of the frottola; and within this repertory are many pieces suitable for solo singing, including the *arie* designed to fit any sonnet, any *capitolo*, any Latin verse (of right meter and line length). The frottola is certainly a link between the improvisatory tradition and that of written polyphony.[38]

The formulae that pepper the frottola books of the first two decades of the *cinquecento* also connect the exclusive halls of the court to the wider world of the urban marketplace in which the *cortigiana onesta* flourished. It is not difficult to imagine an ambitious courtesan like Angela Trevixana or the fictional Marcolina purchasing the Petrucci frottola books as valuable guides to musical self-improvement.

The question of poetic register is another matter. The nobility could afford to take pleasure in low-styled forms of poetry and song fashioned in sophisticated adaptations. Such invocations of the subaltern by the elite did not erase class structure but inscribed it further.[39] Gaspara Stampa, according to Janet L. Smarr, probably avoided the lighter styles that her male contemporaries could get away with: "Singing was an ambiguous social talent, for while it permitted an upward career, it was also associated with the seductions of the courtesan."[40] Pietro Bembo may have hailed the singing of the unassailable Isabella d'Este in 1505, but years later he refused his own daughter's request to study music, calling it a thing for "vain and frivolous women."[41] *Cortigiane oneste*, for whom reputation was everything, would have cultivated only the most revered and respectable styles of solo song; their situation was questionable enough without the ironic invocation of

---

[36] Feldman, "Enacting Gender, Revising Class," 3.
[37] Feldman, *City Culture*, 105.
[38] James Haar, *Essays*, 86-87.
[39] Feldman, *City Culture*, 97-102.
[40] Smarr, 78.
[41] The letter was written in 1541. Cited in Prizer, 25-26.

the rustic or lewd. In late fifteenth and early sixteenth century Venice, the local manner of declaiming verse – the *aria veneziana* or *giustiniana* – would have been the obvious choice.

"Per intendere l'aere venetiano"

In the 1470s, the chancellor to the Duke of Milan, Cicco Simonetta, asked the Venetian ambassador for a book of verse by Leonardo Giustinian along with the music "for two or three *canzone* in order to be able to hear and understand the Venetian melodic style [*per intendere l'aere venetiano*]."[42] In addition to being a patrician and statesman, Giustinian (c.1383-1446) was also a Venetian dialect poet and courtly *cantore* of immense renown, as this description by his contemporary, Petrus Parleoni, attests:

> He invented in his youth sweet and wonderful songs for voices and strings, which because of his art and the charm of the meter so soothe, please and hold the ears, minds and spirits of all, that no one takes pleasure in, nor is regarded as skilled in music who is not familiar with the modulations, turns, and varieties of strings and voices in the Justiniane, nor are there other songs in vogue, as you see, in weddings, banquets, on street corners, and everywhere.[43]

By century's end, his name was synonymous with Venetian song: "*veneziana*" and "*giustiniana*" became interchangeable. Even Bembo, in his *Prose della volgar lingua* of 1525, cites Giustinian as an exemplum of Venetian literature and mentions the fame of his singing.[44] In the popular imagination, the *giustiniana* represented *venezianità*.

The *aria veneziana* can be characterized in a general way from traces that survive in *quattrocento* repertories. Several polyphonic settings of Giustinian's verse from early in the century share traits that suggest improvisatory style: asymmetry of phrase structure, three-voice texture, florid vocal line, text repetition,

---

[42] What Simonetta meant by "music" is still an open debate; the language is ambiguous enough to encompass either an expert teacher or simply notated examples. Walter H. Rubsamen, "The Justiniane or Viniziane of the 15th Century," *Acta Musicologica* 29 (1957): 172-184. Giustinian's canzoniere went through thirteen known editions between 1472 and 1518. *Comincia el fiore de la elegantissime canzonette del nobile homo misier Lunardo Iustiniano.* David Fallows, "Leonardo Giustinian and Quattrocento Polyphonic Song," in: *Congresso Cremona 1992*, ed. Zappalà and Borghi (Cremona: 1995), 248.

[43] Quoted in Rubsamen, 172.

[44] He also notes that Giustinian was more acclaimed for his recitation than for his poetry. Since he couches the comment in a discussion of the literary shortcomings of Venetian language, the point should perhaps be treated with caution. "Uno de quali piu in pregio è stato a suoi tempi, o pure a nostri, per le maniere del canto, col quale esso mandò fuori le sue canzoni; che per quella della scrittura: le quali canzoni dal sopranome di lui sono poi state dette, et hora si dicono le Giustiniane." Pietro Bembo, *Prose della volgar lingua*, ed. Claudio Vela (Clueb, 2001), 38.

and second-to-unison cadences.[45]   Similar musical conceits characterize pieces labeled *justiniana* or *viniziana* throuthout the fifteenth century, the latest, most prominent examples being those in Petrucci's Sixth Book of Frottole, 1505. Extemporaneous declamation is the rule, not the exception, however, in a frottolistic context.   The idiosyncrasies of the *giustiana* – stammering text repetition and second-to-unison cadences – serve to "underscore the distinctiveness of Venetian culture," and the genre was included by Petrucci because, "unlike the other types of *frottole*, it was specifically and proudly Venetian."[46]

Strikingly similar arguments surround the late *giustiniana*, which first flourished in print from 1565 to 1578. Giorgio Brunello and Paolo Fabbri assert that the composers around Andrea Gabrieli consciously appropriated the venerable *aria veneziana* as a vehicle of Venetian patriotism. The occasion, according to Brunello, was the long-awaited ascendance of Venetian musicians at San Marco, celebrated musically by Gabrieli's circle of "*antifiamminghisti*." Fabbri attributes the phenomenon to a swell of patriotism surrounding the struggles with the Turks, culminating in the Venetian victory of 1571.

The late *giustiniana*, though a descendent of the traditional oral version, was an admixture of popular light polyphony and the new realm of theatrical comedy. The same conditions that incubated courtesanry also fostered the development of *commedia dell'arte* in the 1550s and 1560s. Indeed, the art of solo song, the recitation of elevated verse as practiced by courtesans, was the catalyst that transformed slapstick, all-male farce into the more nuanced *commedia dell'arte* of the late sixteenth and seventeenth centuries.

As an emblem of *venezianità*, the *giustiniana* proved a useful tool on the stage – shifting from characterization to caricature. In Angelo Beolco's *L'Anconitana* of 1533-34, Sier Tomao foreshadows the *commedia dell'arte* mask of Pantalone: a wealthy but decrepit Venetian merchant – speaking dialect and singing *giustiniane* – in pursuit of a *cortigiana*.[47]   When Sier Tomao and his Paduan servant Ruzante have a singing contest of sorts (Act II, 4), the rustic's obscenities are contrasted with the *magnifico's strambotti*, like this popular lyric by Giustinian:

---

[45]   Since Giustinian crossed paths with several composers while he was a student in Padua, these traits could very well take their inspiration from his performances.   Nino Pirrotta, "Echi di arie veneziane del primo quattrocento," in: *Interpretazioni veneziane: Studi di Storia dell'Arte in Onore di Michelangelo Muraro*, ed. David Rosand, (Venice: Arsenale Editrice, 1984), 145. Giustinian was in contact with Johannes Ciconia, Prepositus Brixiensis, Bartolomeo da Bologna, Petrus Rubeus, and Antonello da Caserta. Fallows has argued convincingly that Giustinian is the author of many un-attributed fifteenth century texts, making him the most frequently set poet of the era.

[46]   Haar, "Petrucci's *Justiniane* Revisited," 14-15.

[47]   Nancy Dersofi dates *L'Anconitana* to the years 1533-34, because the play is linked "practically and conceptually" to harmony, which fits with the philosophy behind the theaters built in Padua by Ruzante's patron, Cornaro, inauguration in those years. On architectural and dramaturgical harmony, see Nancy Dersofi, *L'Anconitana/The Woman from Ancona*, by Ruzante (Angelo Beolco), trans. Nancy Dersofi (Berkeley and Los Angeles: University of California Press, 1994), 18-25.

Quatro sospiri te voria mandare
e mi meschino fosse ambassatore:
lo primo sí te deza salutare,
l'altro te conte lo mio gran dolore;
lo terzo sí te deza assai pregare,
che tu confermi questo nostro amore;
e lo quarto te mano inamorato,
no me lassar morir desconsolato

[Four sighs would I send,
And my wretched self convey;
Let the first a greeting tend,
The next my grief relay;
The third begs you to bend
And let our love hold sway.
The fourth I send thee lovingly,
Lest disconsolate death be my destiny.[48]]

The same text is set by Francesco Bonardo in the *Primo Libro delle Giustiniane* of 1571. Musically, the later genre resembles the villanella, with frequent successions of parallel fifths between the voices and homorhythmic motion, especially in the sections in triple time.[49] The most characteristic trait of this and all other late *giustiniane* is the stammering on nasal syllables. Bonardo's first line reads: "Quattro sospiri te voria manda-na-na-na-re, e mi meschi-ni-ni-ni-ni-ni-ni-ni-ni-ni-no fosse l'imba-na-na-na-na-na-na- sado-no-no-no-no-no- re."[50] The parody of old love and the frequent mascherata trio, reveal the late *giustiniana's* theatrical pedigree. By the 1570s, the attributes of *commedia dell'arte* were beginning to take shape. The generic Magnifico became Pantalone, who embodies *venezianità*; the role, therefore, required a player fluent in Venetian dialect, proverbs, and phrases, who could portray a decrepit old man posing as a youth.[51] Andrea Calmo, one of the prominent forefathers of the *commedia dell'arte* generally and Pantalone specifically, was also, according to Materassi, the most likely author of the *giustiniane* texts.[52] The *Primo Libro* texts are laced throughout with the language and content of Calmo's letters. Not written for the

---

[48] Also cited are Giustinian's "El papa si ha concesso quindesse ani," and "Andemo, amanti, tuti in Barbaria" by Panfilo Sassi of Modena (1454?-1527). Translation from Dersofi, 82-83.

[49] Marco Materassi, *Il primo libro delle Giustiniane a tre voci*, I quaderni della Cartellina (Milan: Edizioni Suvini Zerboni, 1985), vii, xii-xiv.

[50] The reiterations of the last three stammers (*ni, na,* and *no*) are approximations, to save space (!). Francesco Bonardo, "Quatro sospiri," in Materassi, 14-15.

[51] Marco Salotti, "Dal giullare ai comici dell'arte," in: *Storia Sociale e Culturale d'Italia, vol 3. Lo Spettacolo* (Busto Arsizio: Bramante Editori, 1987), 319.

[52] Marco Materassi, *Il primo libro delle Giustiniane a tre voci*, I quaderni della Cartellina (Milan: Edizioni Suvini Zerboni, 1985), ix-xi.

stage, the letters nonetheless became theatrical commonplace books for the first generation of *commedia dell'arte* actors, in the 1570s.[53] The letters of Book Four are addressed to courtesans, and Calmo writes in the voice of his Magnifico character, ending each one with a *strambotto*.[54] Two of the *giustiniana* texts are comprised of verses extracted from two of these *strambotti*. "L'è na mala cosa il farse pregar" and "Vu se' la vita mia, la mia allegrezza" are drawn from the strambotti addressed to signora Ortensia, signora Fausta, and signora Fulgentia.[55]

The gravitational pull of the twin myths of the courtesan and of Venice are evident in scholarship on these late *giustiniane*. Scholars have struggled to reconcile the earlier, humanistic solo song with the salacious mockery of the later *canzonetta-mascherata*. Walter Rubsamen, writing in 1956, thought it a "ribald parody or burlesque," in which the rhapsodic text repetition and expository declamation of the original becomes "the salacious stutterings of three old patricians who complain of their unfortunate experiences with the courtesans of Venice."[56] Alfred Einstein, on the other hand, forcefully asserts no connection with fifteenth-century form.[57] Emphasizing what we might call the genre's subaltern quality, he describes a special kind of *mascherata* in the form of a *canzon villanesca*, with dialect verse put in the mouths of:

> three gray-beards – and not very respectable ones. Our old men are still troubled by the pangs of love, but love that is aimed at the kind of "Madonne" whose price for a night was available to the stranger at Venice in the form of a printed list. In their love-lorn serenades they relate the most unlovely experiences and warn the stranger against them.[58]

Most suggestive of all, however, is the colorful and faulty genealogy for the *giustiniana* crafted by Thomas Morley in *A plaine and easie introduction to practicall musicke* of 1597. He describes:

> a kind of songs…called Justinianas, and all are written in the Bergamasca language: a wanton and crude kind of musicke it is, and like enough to carrie the name of some noble Curtisan of the Citie of Bergama, for no man will deny that Justiniana is the name of a woman.[59]

---

[53] Guido Davico Bonino, *La commedia italiana del cinquecento e altre note su letteratura e teatro* (Torino: Tirrenia Stampatori, 1989), 62-63.

[54] Pirrotta, "Commedia and Opera," 309.

[55] Materassi, xxvii. Calmo, *Lettere*, ed. Rossi, 271, 302, 363.

[56] Rubsamen, 179. His study was on the fifteenth century genre and its connection with the Petrucci prints, and he argued that the latter were "glimpses" of the unwritten tradition. James Haar has recently revisited the Petrucci *giustiniane*, and modifies the claim.

[57] Einstein, Alfred. "The Greghesca and the Justiniana of the Sixteenth Century." *The Journal of Renaissance and Baroque Music* 1 (March 1946): 26.

[58] Einstein, 26-27.

[59] Thomas Morley, *A plaine and easie introduction to practicall musicke* (1597), 180.

His facile conflation of courtesans and an Italian city is no surprise.[60] The figure of the *cortigiana onesta* had fully crystallized by then and become an obligatory tourist attraction for visitors. Moreover, Venetian identity was an implicit part of public and private discourse, as Feldman writes:

> Whatever strains of unreality marred the layered myths that compounded the Venetian image, their sum total made for a powerful frame of reference: no one who sought success in Venice, native or foreign, could remain isolated from the insistent demands of the city's mythologies.[61]

The city was seen as an idyllic, harmonious polity and a pleasure-seeking, luxurious society, and it represented itself with a female icon strikingly consonant, according to Rosenthal, with the courtesan's own ambiguities:

> In the sixteenth century, the female icon of Venice, depicting the republic's unmatched social and political concord, joined in one civic figure a representation of Justice or Dea Roma with the Virgin Mary and Venus Anadyomene.[62]

The *giustiniana* – cultivated in Gabrieli's circle and incorporated into the character of Pantalone – shows how courtesanry in the cinquecento was woven into the fabric of *venezianità*.

The two-century trajectory of the *giustiniana* offers only indirect glimpses of the personal *aria* and mythic stature of the *cortigiana onesta*, but such ambiguity is inevitable. According to Ruth Kelso, the Renaissance treatment of earthly love, whether in treatises or love poetry, presents an ambiguous portrait of the lady:

> The beloved, the object of his adoration [...] remains most of the time a very shadowy figure. He stands out distinct and clear, she retreats as if behind veils. The general effect of this emphasis upon the lover to the obscuring of the beloved is to make the lady again dependent for significance and even existence on another creature of another sort. [63]

Read properly, however, such testimony speaks volumes. The shadows, the veils, the obscurity, even the dependence are part of the courtesan's illusion. Like the art of virtuoso solo song, she defies description and transcription. The nexus of song, myth, courtesan, and suitor is expressed most succinctly in Antonfrancesco Doni's *Dialogo della musica* of 1544. The work stages a dialogue among a group of gentlemen and one lady named "Selvaggia," punctuated with madrigals. Selvaggia's position within the social gathering, as Feldman writes, "is predicated on group portraiture among men who praise and adore her – and who finally cease

---

[60] Bergama was thought to have the crudest dialect on the peninsula at that time.

[61] Feldman, *City Culture*, xxii.

[62] According to legend, the city was founded miraculously, born from the sea, like the Venus Anadyomene of Botticelli's famous panel painting, on the day of the Annunciation (25 March). Rosenthal, 12-13.

[63] Kelso, 206.

singing polyphony to allow a single poet to serenade her with four sonnets while another interlocutor accompanies him on the lira, none of it given a note in script."[64] The fullest portrait of Selvaggia in sound – like the courtesan's fullest expression in song – transcends transcription.

Cortigiane oneste and other marginal women flourished in the notationless universe of improvisatory song. Not simply unwritten, their music defied transcription, tapping the realm of metaphysical power.[65] The legacy of their mastery of illusion was the creation of new conceptual space for women in the public sphere.

---

[64] Feldman, "Enacting Gender, Revising Class," 7, citing Antonfrancesco Doni, *Dialogo della musica* (Venice, 1544), 315-317. Selvaggia has been identified as Isabetta Guasca of Piacenza (n 16).

[65] Feldman, "Enacting Gender, Revising Class," 14.

Chapter 6

Strong Men – Weak Women: Gender Representation and the Influence of Lully's "Operatic Style" on French *Airs Sérieux* (1650-1700)

Catherine E. Gordon-Seifert

Late seventeenth-century French serious airs (*airs sérieux*) are love songs that present stereotypical images of males and females in a variety of amorous situations.[1]   Although serious airs appeared in both printed editions and in manuscripts, the most popular of these songs (according to the publishers) were published annually, between 1658 and 1694, by Robert, and later Christophe, Ballard in a collection entitled *Livres d'airs de différents autheurs*.[2]   Since this collection provides an unbroken source of the most fashionable songs published over a thirty-six year period, it is invaluable for documenting alterations in musical taste and style during these years. Over the course of four decades, this repertory

---

[1] Throughout the seventeenth century, various genres of songs included dance airs (*airs à danser, airs de danser, chansons pour dancer, chansons à danser, airs de mouvement,* or *chansonnettes*), drinking songs (*airs à boire*), devotional or spiritual airs (*airs de dévotion* or *airs spirituels*), vaudevilles (popular songs), and serious airs (*airs sérieux*). Generally speaking, airs were differentiated by function (dance or drinking), level of musical complexity, and the types of passions represented in text and music. *Vaudevilles,* for example, were simple songs and generally cheerful in nature. The serious airs from the middle of the century should not be confused with the *airs de cour*, which refer to an earlier form of air written before 1640 associated with the courts of Henry IV and Louis XIII. Serious airs were adapted to the more intimate environment of the *ruelles* or salon. The text and music of the *airs sérieux* were more sophisticated than dance or drinking airs and were most often associated with grievous or languid passions.

[2] Robert Ballard began the publication in 1658, and at his death in 1673, his son, Christophe, continued to publish the collection until 1694. At this point in time, Christophe began to publish another collection of airs entitled *Recueil d'airs sérieux et à boire*, which continued well into the eighteenth century. For more information regarding this collection and a catalog of its contents, see Anne-Madeleine Goulet, "Les Livres d'airs de différents auteurs publiés chez les Ballard de 1658 à 1694: une musique de ruelles." Doctorat d'Etat en lettres et science humaines, Université de Paris, X, Nanterre, 2002.

evidenced a stylistic transformation, one of the most obvious features being the introduction of musical devices borrowed from Lully's *tragédies en musique*.

Although Théodore Gérold, in his book *L'Art du Chant en France au XVIIe siècle*, claims that "around 1675, after the first operas of Lully, French song had momentarily attained the end of its development; for a rather long period of time it remained stationary,"[3] two scholars who have studied this repertory remark that a change in style did indeed occur after the 1670s. In *French Baroque Music*, James Anthony notes the introduction of "dramatic elements" into the air during the 1690s,[4] and Catherine Massip indicates that the airs of Michel Lambert, written roughly between 1650 and 1680, went out of fashion by the end of the century because "the familiarity of the public with opera modified its sensibility. The subtlety of expressed sentiments, to which the air gave a true equivalent in music gave way to the expression of the passions that necessitated for their translation a new musical language."[5] Massip also notes an increase in the number of "light" or *galant* airs after 1670, which she refers to as a preference for songs with a "neutral and ironic tone" and those concerning "the sweet charms of Spring."[6]

Whereas a variety of alterations in musical style occurred in the repertory after 1670, I will examine only the introduction of dramatic elements into the airs and purport that the transference of Lully's "operatic" style into this repertory involved more than just a reaction to popular musical trends.[7] In this essay, I

---

[3] "On peut dire qu'aux environs de 1675, après les premiers opéras de Lully, le chant français a atteint momentanément le terme de son développement; pour un laps de temps assez long il restera stationnaire" (Théodore Gérold, *L'Art du chant en France au XVIIe siècle* [Strasbourg: Librarie Istra, 1921], 235).

[4] James Anthony, *French Baroque Music from Beaujoyeult to Rameau* (Portland: Amadeus Press, 1997), 345-358.

[5] *"La familiarité du public avec l'opera a modifié sa sensibilité. La subtilité des sentiments exprimés, à laquelle l'air donnent un juste équivalent en musique a laissé la place à l'expression des passions qui nécessitent pour leur traduction un nouveau langage musical"* (Catherine Massip, "Michel Lambert [1610-1696]: Contribution à l'histoire de la monodie en France," 2 vols. [Doctorat d'Etat en lettres et science et science humaines, Université de Paris, IV, 1985]: I:354-55 and 210-211. See also Catherine Massip, *L'Art de Bien Chanter: Michel Lambert (1610-1696)* (Paris: Société Française du Musicologie, 1999), 123-133.

[6] Massip, "Michel Lambert," I:210-211.

[7] Several scholars address the influence of French musical genres and composers, particularly Lambert, upon Lully and the development of his operas, but no one has considered the impact of Lully's music upon the French air. Lorenzo Bianconi acknowledges that the *"tragédies lyriques* form part. . . of a particular French taste and musical style, quickly elevated to the rank of aesthetic code and handed down from one generation to the next," but does not specify the influence of the "code" on genres other than opera (Lorenzo Bianconi, *Music in the Seventeenth Century*, trans. David Bryant

propose that composers incorporated musical features borrowed from opera for a particular expressive function: to represent men and women with what I will define as "masculine" and "feminine" musical tones, respectively. I postulate as well that the incorporation of this new musical language into the serious air was linked to changing attitudes about gender representation that reflected an increasingly "masculinized" public sphere identified by many scholars with the reign of Louis XIV.[8]

The transference of musical features from Lully's opera did not occur in all airs, for composers chose a certain type of song-text over others as appropriate for this special treatment. Although most serious airs written between 1650 and 1700 are love songs, they all fall into different categories that reflect various aspects of love. In some, for example, the man compliments his beloved and only hints at his love for her; in others, he expresses his love for her outright; and in others, he laments the lover's rejection or infidelity. These and other types of song-texts relating to love correspond with descriptions by many seventeenth century authors of a man's seduction of a woman.[9] In his *Le Merite des Dames*, for example,

---

[Cambridge: Cambridge University Press, 1996], 251). Catherine Massip compares Lully and Lambert and summarizes their differences, describing the works of the two men as antithetical, but suggests that a more detailed stylistic analysis would be in order (Massip, "Michel Lambert," I:350-355).

[8] Maïté Albistur and Daniel Armogathe, *Histoire du féminisme français du moyen âge à nos jours* (Paris: Éditions des femmes, 1977), 134 – 135. Albistur and Armogathe point out that the reign of Louis XIV was extremely unfavorable for women. Politics, religion, moral and social codes developed during this period were hostile towards women and placed females in a position of subordination.

[9] Several authors writing specifically about love warn women that men are out to seduce them by recourse to a variety of ploys. Once a man succeeds, he will only leave her, her reputation soiled, and her life ruined. See, for example, Antoine Gombaud, chevalier de Méré, *Oeuvres complètes*, ed. Charles-H. Boudhors (Paris: Éditions Fernand Roches, 1930): I:21; Méré, *Lettres* (Paris, 1689), 60; and Duc de La Rochefoucauld, *La Justification de l'amour* (1660), ed. J.D. Hubert (Paris: A.G. Nizet, 1971), 75-76; Madeleine de Scudéry, "De l'amitié," *Conversations morales* (Paris: sur le quay des Augustins, à la descente du Pont-neuf, à l'image Saint-Louis, 1686), 871-1017; and "La teste-à-teste," *Entretiens galans, ou, conversations sur la mode, la musique, le jeu, les louanges*, vol. 2 (Paris: Jean Ribou, 1681), 69-95. The seduction process that emphasizes the man's seduction of the beloved and his eventual betrayal of her was especially conventionalized in seventeenth-century love letters (which were perceived as written forms of conversations) authored by both women and men (although male writers often posed as females). Many letters were arranged so that men's letters alternate with the women's, formulating a written dialogue (Katharine Ann Jenson, *Writing Love: Letters, Women, and the Novel in France, 1605-1776* [Carbondale: Southern Illinois Press, 1995], 29). See also Elizabeth Goldsmith, *Exclusive Conversations: The Art of Interaction in Seventeenth-Century France* (Philadelphia: University of Pennsylvania Press, 1988), 28-37, and Louise Horowitz, *Love and Language:*

Saint-Gabriel summarizes in a few paragraphs what he calls the "tyranny of men" (*tyrranie des hommes*) by describing their seduction of women. He writes:

> Unfortunately, what would you [men] not do to undertake the chastity of these beauties, who have no other thoughts than those which honor and virtue inspire in them. By your humility and your protestations of unfailing obedience in their service, you use presents and expense to do so. You work at weakening their courage and their constancy by your sighs and your tears, and just when you have drawn out these good-natured humors most tenderly, you impute the crime. You ask them for your liberty with your death. You pierce your vein in their presence, and by a pitiful look from [your] dying eyes, you demand from them life; and their goodness not once surprised cannot see you die for them without saving you. . . . Possession softens the intensity, and you begin from this point on to love not so ardently.[10]

Though generally described by a number of writers, seduction as a process involving particular steps is most specifically illustrated by René Bary in *L'Esprit de cour, ou les conversations galantes divisées en cent dialogues*, first published in 1662.[11] In his treatise, Bary offers the reader dialogues of seduction in which a

---

A Study of the Classical French Moralist Writers (Columbus, OH: Ohio State University Press, 1977), 125-143.

[10] *Mal-heureux que ne faites-vous [les hommes] point pour entreprendre sur la chasteté de ces beautez, qui n'ont d'autres pensées que celles dont l'honneur & la vertu les anime. Par vos humilitez & vos protestations d'une obeyssance soumise à tout pour leur service, vous y employez les presents & la despence. Vous taschez à fléchir leur courage & leur constance par vos sourpirs & vos larmes, & comme vous avez atiré ces humeurs debonnaires jusques au tendre, vous leurs imputez le crime. Vous leur demandez vostre liberté par vostre mort. Vous vous percez la veine en leur presence, & par un pitoyable objet les yeux mourans vous leur redemandez la vie; & leur bonté aucune fois surprise ne peut alors vous voir mourir pour elles sans vous secourir. . . La possession en emousse tout aussi-tost la pointe, & vous commencez deslors à ne plus aymer si ardemment* (Le Sieur de Saint-Gabriel, *Le Merite des Dames*, 3d ed. [Paris: Jacques Le Gras, 1660], 54-58).

[11] In one hundred short dialogues, in which the participants exchange words in regular alternation, Bary is primarily concerned with the moral education of young women. Many of Bary's conversations are, in fact, examples of improper social interactions, and feature a man's inappropriate behavior towards a woman. Several other authors wrote works as well that served as moral instruction manuals for women, and in these, they warned women of the seductive powers of men, showing how the cultivated female can defend herself against a male rhetoric of seduction. These include Jacques De Bosc, *L'Honnête femme* (Paris: Billaine, 1632); Marquise de Maintenon, *Conversations Inédites de Madame la Marquise de Maintenon* (Paris: J-J Blaise, Libraire-Editeur;1828); and Saint-Gabriel, *Le Merite des Dames*. Many other sources, particularly civility manuals and literary conversations, also advised women to avoid the threat of man's seduction and guard her reputation with care (See Marguerite Buffet, *Nouvelles Observation sur la Langue Françoise* [Paris: Boubon, 1668]; Antoine de Courtin, *Nouveau traité de la civilité* 2d ed. [Paris: Hellie Josset, 1672];

man attempts to seduce an *honnête fille* or proper young woman, who vigorously resists him.[12] For Bary, the seductive process included the man's improper advance, his use of flattery, the beloved's rejection, his complaint of her indifference and rejection, his perseverance, the breakdown of her resistance, their shared love, and eventually acts of infidelity. When comparing the poetic subjects represented by the vast majority of airs with Bary's seductive dialogues, we find that different airs correspond to different phases of the seduction process, making it possible to classify the airs accordingly. Appendix 1 shows different airs taken from *Livres d'airs de différents autheurs* correspond to Bary's dialogues and the various steps in the seduction process (see Appendix 1).

Sample dialogues such as this, even in the form of sung and/or recited poetic discourse, were cultivated in the mid-seventeenth century French *ruelles* and linked to the most influential "literary" model promoted by women and men who participated in salon culture: polite conversation or *conversation à la française.*[13]

Entretien galans, 2 vols. [Paris: Jean Ribou]; Nicolas Faret, *L'Honneste-Homme* [Paris: Toussaincts du Bray, 1630]; Antoine Gombauld, chevalier de Méré, *Oeuvres posthumes* [Paris: Guignard, 1700]; and François Poulain de la Barre, *De l'Égalité des deux sexes* [Paris: DuPuis, 1671]).

[12] For more information on seventeenth-century literary representations of love, see Joan DeJean, *Tender Geographies: Women and the Origin of the Novel in France* (New York: Columbia University Press, 1991) ; Alain Génetiot, *Les genres lyriques mondains (1630-1660)* (Geneva: Librarie Droz, 1990); Erica Harth, *Cartesian Women: Versions and Subversions of Rational Discourse in the Old Regime* (Ithaca: Cornell University Press, 1992); Horowitz, *Love and Language*; Patricia Howard, "Quinault, Lully, and the *Précieuses*: Images of Women in Seventeenth-Century France," in: *Cecilia Reclaimed: Feminist Perspectives on Gender and Music*, ed. Susan C. Cook and Judy S. Tsou (Chicago: University of Illinois Press, 1994), 70-89; Jensen, *Writing Love*; Lawrence D. Kritzman, *The Rhetoric of Sexuality and the Literature of the French Renaissance* (New York: Columbia University Press, 1991); Carolyn Lougee, *Le Paradis des Femmes: Women, Salons, and Social Stratification in Seventeenth-Century France* (Princeton: Princeton University Press, 1976); Jean-Michel Pelous, *Amour précieux, amour galant, 1654-1675* (Paris, Librairie Klincksieck, 1980); *Sexuality and Gender in Early Modern Europe: Institutions, Texts, and Images*, ed. James Grantham Turner (Cambridge: Cambridge University Press, 1993); Libby Timmermans, *L'accès des femmes à la culture (1578-1715)* (Paris: Edition Champion, 1993); *Writing about Sex: The Discourses of Eroticism in Seventeenth-Century France*, ed. Abby E. Zanger, in : *L'Esprit créateur* 25 (1995).

[13] The airs' function in the seventeenth-century *ruelles* is explored in full in Catherine Gordon-Seifert, "*'La Réplique galante'*: Sébastien de Brossard's Airs as Conversation," in: *Sébastien Brossard, Musicien*, ed. Jean Duron, (Versailles: Editions du Centre de Musique Baroque de Versailles, 1998-), 181-201. Madeleine Scudéry's involvement in the composition of song-texts and the air's function in her own *ruelle* is explored at length in Anne-Madeleine Goulet, "Les divertissements musicaux du Samedi," in : *Les Actes du Colloque international organisé par l'Université de Paris IV-Sorbonne à l'occasion du*

The airs and other literary genres were part of a specific kind of activity cultivated in the *ruelle*, which Marc Fumaroli describes in his *La diplomatie de l'esprit de Montaigne à La Fontaine* as *un grand jeu litteraire* or "a grand literary game that assumed not only the rules of dialogue, choreography. . ., but also scenery. . ., accessories (such as clothing, hair styles, and jewelry), [as well as] body language, expressions, and writings that bring to life the dialogue and intrigue."[14]   Thus the airs reflected the *jeux d'esprit* or "games of wit" that characterized literary conversations, themselves idealized imitations of the verbal interchange so artfully practiced in seventeenth century *ruelles*.   "Dialogues of seduction" were thus a cultivated literary genre that mirrored what writers, like Bary or Saint-Gabriel, described as a very real problem for a young woman: *la tyrranie des homes*, or man's attempt to seduce a proper young woman and compromise her good reputation.

The airs, then, were musical/literary representations of isolated moments in a man's seduction of a woman and her reaction to him. The airs not only correspond to the different phases of the process, making it possible to classify the airs accordingly, but groups of airs that belong to each stage of the seduction share similar musical features that represent particular types of sentiments or passions. This aspect of the airs – shared literary topics that represent the same passions and employ similar musical features – is an important distinction. It has direct bearing upon the types of song texts given "special" musical treatment, and in particular, the transference of Lully's musical style to the air.

Composers incorporated musical features borrowed from Lully's dramatic style in the most passionate of airs, laments: numbers three (he attempts to elicit her pity), five (he laments her rejection), and eight (reactions to the beloved's infidelity) given in Appendix 1.   These airs in the seduction process represent the greatest range of affect: airs filled with expressions of grief, desperation, anger, or languish.   What passions, how they are "expressed" and by whom (male or female) are the most important factors relating to stylistic alterations in the air at the end of the seventeenth century.

Laments also demonstrate the greatest distinction between varying representations of gender in both music and text beneath a web of common clichés, many of which constituted the essence of courtly love songs since the Middle Ages.[15]   Most airs are "gendered," meaning that there is almost always a male or

tricentenaire de la mort de Madeleine de Scudéry (1607-1701),   (Paris: Artois Presses Université, forthcoming).

[14] Marc Fumaroli, *La diplomatie de l'esprit de Montaigne à La Fontaine* (Paris: Hermann, 1994), 307.

[15] E. William Monter notes that courtly love outlived the Middle Ages, but subsequently it was "taken off horseback, out of tournaments, and endless knightly vows." The modern version of courtly love was established during the Renaissance "as the code of

female poetic voice that projects a specific image of man or woman. These representations of gender correspond to descriptions of males and females specified in many treatises from the period, particularly those written on subjects concerning protocol and those by authors arguing against or for the superiority of women.[16] Authors of these literary works identified various traits as positive or negative in reference to females and males. Appendix 2 is a list of the most common traits compiled from various treatises ascribed to females, males, and both genders[17] (see Appendix 2).

The ideal person, the *honnête* man or woman, was to be pleasant, tender, and elegant in action and word, and always in perfect control of his or her emotions and body. Le Chevelier de Méré writes: "To be wise, the mind and reason must subjugate the heart. . . . Reason distinguishes [the *honnête*] man from the animal, but passion joins man with [the animal]."[18] Certain traits, however, are applied more to one sex than the other. Men, for example, were to be courageous, ready

---

correct behavior, proper treatment of women, and elegant (if not necessarily adulterous) flirtation until the Victorians and beyond: here is the source of the modern version of the lady as romantic object on her pedestal." (E.William Monter, "The Pedestal and Stake: Courtly Love and Witchcraft," in: *Becoming Visible: Women in European History*, ed. Renate Bridenthal and Claudin Koonz [Boston: Houghton and Mifflin, 1977]: 127).

[16] Much of this literature (cited in footnote 5) belonged to a controversy over the value of women, *une querelles des femmes*, that began during the sixteenth century in France and continued into the seventeenth century and beyond (Albister and Armogathe, *Histoire du féminisme*, 80-209).

[17] This list of negative and positive a traits assigned to males and females was compiled by reference to the following treatises: Nicolas Boileau, *Oeuvres completes*, *Bibliothèque de la Pléiade* (Paris: Gallimard, 1966); Marguerite Buffet, *Nouvelles Observations*; Antoine de Courtin, *Nouveau traité de la civilité*; Du Bosc, *L'Honneste Femme*; Jacques Du Bosc, *La Femme héroïque ou les héroïnes comparées avec les héros en toute sorte de vertus* (Paris: A. de Sommaville et A. Courbé, 1645); *Entretiens galans*; Chevalier de l'Escale, *Le Champion des femmes qui soustient qu'elles sort plus nobles, plu parfaites et en tout plsu vertueuses que les hommes. . .* (Paris: Vve M. Guillemot, 1618); Nicolas Faret, *L'Honneste-Homme*; Marie de Gournay, *Egalité des hommes et des femmes* (S.I.,1622); Pierre Le Moyne, *La Galerie des femmes fortes* (Paris: A. de Sommaville, 1647); Méré, *Oeuvres posthumes*; Jacques Olivier, *Alphabet de l'imperfection et malice des femmes* (Rouen: Chez la vefve de R. Daré, 1658); François Poulain de la Barre, *De l'Égalité des deux sexes*; Abbé Michel de Pure, *La Prétieuse*, 1656-1658, ed. by Émile Magne (Paris: Droz, 1938); Saint-Gabriel, *Le Merite des Dames*; *Tableau historique des ruses et des subtilités des femmes* (Paris: Rolet Boutonne, 1623); Antoine de Baudeau le Sieur de Somaize, *Le Grand Dictionaire historique des Pretieuses* (Paris: Ribou, 1661); Capne du château de Brie-Comte-Robert Vigoureux, *Défense des femmes contre l'Alphabet de leur prétendue malice et imperfection* (Paris: P. Chevalier, 1617).

[18] "Pour être sage, il faut que l'esprit et la raison soumettent le coeur. . . . La raison distingue l'homme de l'animal, mais la passion le confond avec lui." (Méré, *Maximes, sentences et réflexions morals et politiques* [Paris: E. Du Castin, 1687], 262).

warriors, and respectful of women, while women were to be graceful and empathetic to the suffering of humankind. Above all, a woman was to guard her reputation: she must be chaste yet willing to please, amiable but not amorous.[19]

Most treatises underscore these positive traits by describing how men and women *should* behave, but authors also reveal the unfavorable nature of one sex or the other, for every virtue has its negative counterpart. Man, for example, could be courageous and clever but he could also be brutal and deceitful.[20] Man is by nature unfaithful, for after he conquers a woman's heart, he moves on to another victim.[21] Woman, by contrast, is considered to be physically weak and superficial in manner and speech.[22] While certain authors criticize woman for her animal-like, capricious, and passionate nature, others claim she is too cold and indifferent.[23]

---

[19] In his *Le Champion des femmes*, Chevalier de L'Escale describes the woman as "the glory of man, a faithful spirit, an ordinary profit, an eternal rest, agreable company, a haver of chastity, a vase of contenance. . . a perfect animal." (la gloire de l'homme, un esprit constant, un profit ordinaire, un repos éternal, une compagnie agréable, un port de chasteté, un vase de continence. . .un animal parfait." [Chevalier de L'Escale, *Le Champion*, 662). Quoted in Albistur, *Histoire du féminisme*, 124. Jacques Du Bosc devotes an entire chapter to the importance of a woman's reputation. He writes: "Reputation is a great treasure. It is the most beautiful ornament of a civil life, and without which the more glorious and illustrious actions remain stifled and without light." ("La reputation est un grand tresor. C'est le plus be ornement de la vie civile, & sans lequel les plus glorieuses & les plus illustres actions demeurent estouffées & sans lumiere." [Du Bosc, *L'Honneste femme*, 51]).

[20] François Poulain de la Barre points out that at the beginning of the world, men and women started out as equals. Because women had children, they were physically weakened and had to depend upon their physically superior husbands to take care of them and their families. As nations were formed, men needed war to conserve national boundaries; thus men became warriors, began to dominate their families as a prince dominates a kingdom. Men are, however, rude and uncouth, and they needed to learn from women how to be polite and compliant (Poulain de la Barre, *De l'Égalité*, 21-30). Saint Gabriel stresses that it is men who are unfaithful and cruel (Saint Gabriel, *Le Merite des dames*, 156, 160-161).

[21] Both Poulain de la Barre and Margarite Buffet point out that women are much more faithful than men by nature (Poulain de la Barre, *De l'Égalité*, 41; Buffet, *Nouvelles Observations*, 230).

[22] Poulain de la Barre explains that the *sçavants*, the poets, orators, historians, and philosophers, have the strongest and most negative view of women, attacking in particular their superficiality, and most people believe them. (Poulain de la Barre, *De L'Égalité*, 47-48).

[23] In her *Nouvelles Observations sur la Langue Françoise*, dedicated to Anne d'Autriche, Louis XIV's mother, Margarite Buffet defends women against those who claim females are "at the same level as irrational animals. . .comparing them to mules and goats... their capricious humors to the fires of these extravagant animals." (au rang des animaux irraisonnables...les comparent aux mules & aux chevres,. . .leurs humeurs capricieuses aux fougues de ces extravagants animaux." [Buffet, *Nouvelles Observations*, 218]).

Especially during the middle of the century, some women who led or participated in the *ruelles* – derogatorily referred to as the *précieuses* – were criticized for their indifference, or their desire to avoid love and marriage altogether.[24] Worst of all, they were accused of ruling their *ruelles* and its participants, men and women, like husbands ruled in the world.[25]

Using these character traits and descriptions of behavior to identify and interpret images of gender projected in the airs, I find that the vast majority of airs from the middle of the century – that is, the 1650s and 1660s – project an "effeminate" image of man. Over sixty percent of airs published in *Livres d'airs de différents autheurs* between 1658 and 1668 represent a man's reaction to the beloved's rejection, step five of the seduction process given in Figure 1, and in these, the men are characterized in text and music by those negative traits most

---

[24] Madeleine de Scudéry argues against marriage most strongly in *L'Histoire de Sapho*, volume ten of *Artamène, ou, Le grand Cyrus* (Madeleine de Scudéry, *The Story of Sapho*, ed. and trans. by Karen Newman [Chicago: University of Chicago Press, 2003]). Regarding the term *précieuses*, it has recently been argued by Myriam Maître that not all references to the *précieuses* were derogatory. She writes: "for some [the *précieuses*] are rude, sectarian, seditious, maybe; inflexible feminists, they reject love and marriage, favoring tender friendship indeed homosexuality . . . . For others, they are the queens of the court; their beauty, their minds, the exemplary virtue, their delicate and refined manners make them the paragon of women in the great world." ("Pour les uns, elles sont inciviles, sectaires, séditieuses peut-être; féministes intransigeantes, elles rejettent l'amour et le mariage, s'en tenant à l'amitié tendre voire à l'homosexualité. . . . Pour d'autres, elles sont les reines de la cour; leur beauté, leur esprit, leur vertu exemplaire, leurs manières délicates et raffinées en font le parangon des femmes du grand monde." Myriam Maître, *Les Précieuses Naissance des femmes de lettres en France au XVIIe siècle* (Paris: Honoré Champion Éditeur, 1999), 12.

[25] The greatest mid-to-late seventeenth-century adversaries of the *précieuses* were writers Charles de Saint-Denis Seigneur de Saint-Evremond, Charles Cotin, Antoine Baudeau Somaize, Nicolas Boileau, Antoine Arnauld, and Roger de Bussy-Rabutin. In his Maxime IX, Saint-Evremond writes: "The voluptuous ones feel less of their hearts than their appetites: the *précieuses*, in order to conserve their purity of heart, love their lovers without pleasure, and use their husbands firmly with loathing." ("Les voluptueuses sentent moins leur coeur que leurs appétits: les précieuses, pour conserver la pureté de ce coeur, aiment leurs amants sans jouissance, et jouissent de leurs maris solidement avec aversion." [quoted in Roger Lathuillière, *La Préciosité* (Paris: Droz, 1969), 50, and Albistur and Armogathe, *Histoire du féminisme*, 140]). See also Nicolas Boileau, "Satire X: Contre les femmes" (1694) in : *Oeuvres complètes*, ed. Françoise Escal (Paris: Gallimard, 1966); Antoine Arnauld, *Apologie pour les Saints Pères de l'Eglise*, in : *Oeurvres*, ed. Gabriel De Pac de Bellegarde and Jean Hautefage, 43 vols. (Paris, 1775-83); and Antoine Arnauld, "Lettre á M.P*** [Perrault], au sujet de la dixième satire de M. Despréaux," in : Boileau, *Oeuvres complètes*, ed. Jérome Vercruysse, 2 vols. (Paris, 1969).

commonly attributed to women in various seventeenth century sources. In the airs, men are portrayed as victims of love, powerless, and physically weak (they sigh, they tremble, they weep). But their emotional reaction to the beloved's rejection constitutes the most effeminate image given in the airs. In Lambert's "Pourquoy vous offenser," Musical Example 6.1, the woman is offended by the man's declaration of love; she is cruel and powerful, while he is weak, enslaved by her charms, and no longer the master of his own emotions.

In setting "Pourquoy vous offencer," Lambert underscores the man's loss of emotional control by representing different passions in succession, thereby imitating an impassioned speaker, whose discourse, according to rhetoricians, was to be interrupted by the diverse movement of the passions, unequal, and devoid of regular cadence and moderate tones of voice.[26]   In musical representations of the impassioned speaker, the shape of the melody, its placement in different registers of the piece, the quality of the harmonies and their relationships, the type of rhythmic movement, and alteration of meter appear in various combinations to imitate the tones of voice and rate of speech associated with different emotional states.   The first phrase of the air, for example, is a typically sorrowful expression, represented by the placement of the voice in a low register, a descending melody, and the C minor-G minor harmonies that accompany the descending minor second in the melody at the end of the phrase. The following phrase presents an abrupt cry of desperation on the words *Beauté pour qui je meurs*, as the melody leaps up the

---

[26] Many rhetoricians, including René Bary, Abbé de la Bretteville, Phérotée de la Croix, Jean-Léonor le Gallois de Grimarest, or Bernard Lamy describe the tones of voice and rates of speech associated with the representation of various passions. The application of rhetorical principles to seventeenth century music in France is treated by Phérotée de la Croix, *L'Art de la poësie française et latine avec une idée de la musique* (Lyon: Thomas Amaulry, 1694), 619-627,and Jean-Léonor le Gallois de Grimarest, *Traité de récitatif dans la lecture, dans l'action publique, dans la declamation, et dans le chant. Avec un traité des accens, de la qualité, et de la Ponctuation* (Paris: Jacques le Fevre et Pierre Ribou, 1701). The application of rhetorical principles to music is also addressed to some extent by Marin Mersenne, "De la musique accentuelle," "Des consonances," and "De la composition," *Harmonie universelle* (Paris: Sebastian Cramoisy, 1635-36). Michel de Saint-Lambert (*Les principes du clavecin* [1702; reprint, Geneva: Minkoff, 1974]) and Bénigne de Bacilly (*Remarques curieuses de l'at de bien chanter* [1679, reprint, Geneva: Minkoff, 1971]) also refer to the relationship between principles of rhetoric and music. For a complete application of rhetorical principles to an analysis of the serious air, see Catherine Gordon-Seifert, "The Language of Music in France: Rhetoric as a Basis for Expression in Michel Lambert's *Les Airs de Monsieur Lambert* (1669) and Bénigne de Bacilly's *Les Trois livres d'airs* (1668).

Musical Example 6.1 – Michel Lambert, "Pourquoy vous offenser," *Livres d'airs de différents autheurs*, 1660, f. 21v (also found in *Les Airs de Monsieur Lambert*, 1669, p.36)

octave, descends as it outlines the tonic harmony, then leaps back up to the D, which is repeated three times and is accompanied by strong tonic/dominant harmonies.[27]

The passions expressed in "Pourquoy vous offencer," and in airs like it, may or may not be sincere (according to the "game of love"), but by expressing his torment, the man hopes to soften the beloved's response by eliciting her pity, a

---

[27] For a detailed analysis of this piece, see Catherine Gordon-Seifert, "The Language of Music in France: Rhetoric as a Basis for Expression in Michel Lambert's *Les Airs de Monsieur Lambert* (1669) and Bénigne de Bacilly's *Les Trois livres d'airs* (1668),* Ph.D. diss., The University of Michigan, 1994, 207-209.

ploy described by René Bary in Conversation XXIV, *"Du Scrupule"*[28] and
summarized in this song-text:

> Beaux yeux, que voulez-vous me dire,
> Par vos regards charmans & doux:
> Si je me rends, si je cede à vos coups,
> Aurez-vous quelque jour pitié de mon martyre?
> [*Livre d'airs de différents autheurs*, 1667, f. 25v-26r]

> [Beautiful eyes what do you want to say to me
> By your charming and sweet glances:
> If I give in, if I surrender to your blows,
> Will you someday pity my martyrdom?]

Thus, in the majority of mid seventeenth-century airs, men are represented as
seducers who speak a feminine language and use an effeminate display of emotion
and physical weakness to manipulate the beloved and elicit her pity (that is, profit
from a woman's empathetic nature) in hopes of breaking down her resistance.

By contrast, women in airs from the middle of the century are represented as
honnête fille or proper young women. This is most dramatically demonstrated by
their silence. In his *L'Esprit de Cour*, Bary admits that the responses given by the
women in his dialogues are those a proper woman may think but never speak.[29] In
other sources as well, a woman is advised to remain silent especially if she has
nothing pleasant to say.[30] Indeed, the musical repertory confirms the observations

---

[28] Bary, *L'Esprit du Cour*, 55-58.

[29] Bary, *L'Esprit du Cour*, LXIV.

[30] In Madeleine de Scudéry's *L'Histoire de Sapho*, Sapho also suggests that women
should rarely speak their minds, especially in matters of the heart (Scudéry, *The Story of
Sapho*, 87). Much later in the seventeenth century, Françoise d'Aubigné, Mise de
Maintenon recommended that verbal restraint and silence are good; that it is best to talk as
little as possible (see Goldsmith, *Exclusive Conversations*, 68). In her *Conseils et
instructions aux demoiselles* from late in the century, Mme de Maintenon writes:
"Whoever must return to the world, show yourself as little as you can, flee more than death
the least interaction with men, and if you, by necessity, find yourself with them, . . .tremble
during this situation, be silent, be modest, do not think about showing your intelligence,
there is more in remaining silent than in speaking. . . ." ("Qui doit retourner dans le monde. .
.montrez-vous le moins que vous pourrez, fuyez plus que la mort le moindre commerce avec
les hommes, et que si vous vous y trouvez de nécessité,. . .tremblez dans cette occasion,
taisez-vous, soyez modestes, ne songez point à montrer de l'esprit; il y en a plus à se taire à
propos qu'à parler,. . . ." [Françoise d'Aubigné, Mise de Maintenon, *Mise de, Conseils et
Instruction aux Demoiselles Pour Leur Conduite dans le Monde*, ed. E. Du Chatenet

made by Bary and others, for less than two percent of the songs published in *Livres d'airs de différents autheurs* between 1658 and 1668 were written with a female poetic voice. When woman is given a voice in these airs, she expresses herself with bold and assertive tones.[31] She has control of her emotions and is in charge of her own destiny. In "Il est vray je suis rigoureuse," Musical Example 6.2, the speaker admits that she is cruel. She loves "seducing" men, but by never returning their love, she can live in peace and remain happy; thus, she controls "the game of love" by avoiding an emotional involvement altogether. She offers an image of woman promoted by the many so-called *précieuses*.

By the end of the century, however, the image of the effeminate man and the bold woman changes. This alteration in gender representation coincides with the diminishing influence in cultural matters of women after 1671 and an increasingly masculinized public sphere identified with the reign of Louis XIV.[32] In this strong and centralized French state, "hierarchies [were] exalted more than ever, morals [were] codified; . . . everywhere, patriarchy [consolidated] its position."[33] A most compelling manifestation of this patriarchal attitude is the striking reduction in the number of airs in which the male poetic voice laments the rejection or loss of the

---

[Limoges: Eugène Ardant et Cie, Éditeurs, 1894], 8]). In Maintenon's conversation on silence, the character Louise states that she believes silence must be shared by young people, especially girls. Éléonore responds by saying, add to that, girls nourished in a home where all must show piety. (Louise: Je crois que le silence doit être le partage des jeunes gens, surtout des filles; Éléonore: Ajoutez encore, des filles nourries dans une maison où tout doit marquer la piété (*Conversations inédites de Madame la Marquise de Maintenon, précédées d'une notice historique par M. de Monmerqué* [Paris: J.-J. Blaise, Libraire-Éditeur, 1828], 2-3]).

[31] The tendency to "mix opposites," particularly regarding the lack of "distinction. . . made between masculine and feminine virtues" (so that which presents effeminate images of men and masculine images of women), has been identified by several scholars as a primary feature of the "baroque." (R.A. Sayle, *The French Biblical Epic* [Oxford: Oxford University Press, 1955], 245. Quoted in Maclean, *Woman Triumphant*, 234). Maclean cites other authors who make similar observations, such as Madeleine Maurel, "Esquisse d'un anteros baroque," *XVIIe Siècle*, 84-85 (1969): 3-20, or Eugenio d'Ors, *Lo barocco* (Madrid, 1945).

[32] Gradually, the influence and importance of salon culture, particularly in artistic endeavors, began to wane under the reign of Louis XIV. For more information on the nature, function, and transformation of the seventeenth century salon, see Goldsmith, *Exclusive Conversations*.

[33] Les hiérarchies sont plus que jamais exaltées, la morale codifée;. . .le patriarcat consolide partout ses positions (Albistur and Armogathe, *Histoire du féminisme,* 134.)

Musical Example 6.2 – "Il est vray je suis rigoureuse," *Livres d'airs de différents autheurs*, 1666, p.4

beloved. The number drops from over sixty percent in the first ten years of the publication to sixteen percent during the last ten years. Thus, the desire to represent males as effeminate and powerless is greatly diminished.

The most profound indication of the need "to masculinize" certain airs during this period, however, is the transference of textual and musical features borrowed from Lully/Quinault *tragédies en musique*. Louis XIV's control of musical endeavors, particularly French opera, and his close association with Lully and Quinault are, of course, well documented by scholars.[34] Generally speaking, most images of men in Lully/Quinault *tragédies en musique*, images endorsed by the King himself, conform to Claude-François Menestrier's conception of heroic representation in French opera. In his *Des Représentations en Musique Ancienne et Moderne* of 1681, Menestrier warned against the introduction into musical

---

[34] See, for example, Robert Isherwood, *Music in the Service of the King* (Ithaca: Cornell University Press, 1973).

tragedies of "intrigues of gallanterie, where effeminate heroes play for pitiful personages of passionate lovers."[35] He is referring here to the game of love, the gallant seduction, promoted by women of the *ruelles* and others in novels, song-texts, and various different literary works. By contrast, in musical tragedies, according to Menestrier, the "great actions and generous sentiments" of heroes should "excite courage, virtue, . . . and admiration,"[36] indeed, the most important and positive traits ascribed to the *honnête* man.

As for heroines, characterizations in opera conform to those seventeenth-century writings that endorsed the traditional role of woman in society – marriage and her submission to man and husband. Throughout all the operas, women and men are encouraged to love, and in many, the union of hero and heroine is celebrated.[37] If a woman tries to take control of her own life, either by attempting to escape love and marriage (that is, remaining indifferent) or by attempting to exert her authority, she is punished or defeated. In the majority of operas, the woman, goddess or mortal, who tries to control the events of her life and others is either marginalized (as is the coquette Céphise in *Alceste*) or she is the antagonist who causes great social and personal upheaval (as is Armide in *Armide*).

The influence of Lully/Quinault *tradégies en musique* upon the late seventeenth century French airs is evident in a number of ways. Airs that correspond to important themes (or lessons) promoted in the operas proliferate during the last few decades of the century. The number of airs, for example, that promote love's pleasures and encourage men and women to love, airs belonging to step seven of the seduction process, given in Appendix 1, which correspond to Massip's description of "light" and *galant* airs, increases dramatically after 1670. But the most significant influence of opera, that which most radically altered the air's style, is the incorporation of musical devices borrowed from Lully's most "masculine" musical imagery – his representations of war and the emphatic or commanding style of recitative. This musical imagery underscores the most positive traits attributed to the *honnête* man: the powerful, courageous, and ready warrior.

---

[35] "des intrigues de galanterie, où des Heros effeminez font les pitoyables personnages d'Amans passionnez" (Claude-François Ménestrier, *Des Représentations en Musique Anciennes et Modernes* [Lyon, 1681]: 135).

[36] *Ibid.*

[37] Several scholars assert that the tragic conflict between glory and "perfect" love permeates all of Lully/Quinault opera. See Newman, *Jean-Baptiste Lully*, 67; Bianconi, *Music in the Seventeenth Century*, 250; and Buford Norman, "Ancients and Moderns, Tragedy and Opera: The Quarrel over *Alceste*," *French Musical Thought, 1600-1800*, ed. Georgia Cowart (Ann Arbor, MI: UMI Research Press), 181. For an overview of influences upon the development of French opera as well as specific topics treated therein, see Anthony, *French Baroque Music*, 27-91.

Lully consistently exploits those musical features associated with boldness and aggression in setting battle scenes, allusions to war, and references to glorious deeds and victory. In setting the "sound of war," for example, from the prologue to *Alceste*, Lully uses melodies that outline major triads (see Lully's setting of "Quel bruit de guerre m'eprouvant" which outlines a C major triad), rhythmic repetitions (groups of four eighths and an eighth followed or preceded by two sixteenths), major harmonies in root position, and dominant/tonic harmonic relations (C major and G major harmonies in root position dominate this passage), all considered to be strong musical devices by seventeenth century music theorists.[38] These same musical features are used in actual battle scenes taken from Act 3, Scene 3, in *Cadmus et Hermione*, where Cadmus fights and kills the giant who has taken Hermione, the heroine, hostage.[39] Here, the ascending melody emphasizes tonic triad (F major) with repeated dotted rhythms (the dotted quarter followed by an eighth), dominant/tonic harmonic relations (F major and C major as well as G major and C major).

Lully applies a combination of these musical devices for many a hero's recitation as well. In Act 4, Scene 2 of *Alceste*, for example, Alcide uses a commanding tone to convince Caron that he must cross the River Achéron.[40] The melody in m. 1 of Alcide's response outlines an F Major triad and incorporates melodic and rhythmic repetitions, mm. 1-2. Anyone at any time during an opera who asserts authority, including the most powerful women, sings in this commanding tone of voice. For even though female antagonists, such as Cybèle, Junon, or Medée, are ultimately defeated or forced to submit, they are powerful enough to exert an enormous influence over the events and characters during the greater part of most operas. If women, then, try to act like men, they often "sound" like men.

---

[38] Jean-Baptiste Lully, Alceste, *Oeuvres complètes de J.-B. Lully,* ed. Henry Prunières , vol. I.2 (New York: Broude Brothers, 1966): 15. For a discussion of "strong" musical devices see André Pirro, *Descartes et la musique,* (Paris: Librairie Fischbacher, 1907; reprint Geneva: Minkoff, 1973): 95 and 115; Benito Rivera, "The Seventeenth-Century Theory of the Triadic Generation and Invertibility and its Application in Contemporaneous Rules of Composition," *Music Theory Spectrum* 6 (1984): 63-78; D.P. Walker, "Joan Albert Ban and Mersenne's The Musical Competition of 1640," *Music and Letters* 57 (1976): 240-249.

[39] Lully utilizes the same musical devices in other references to battle throughout the *Cadmus*. For example, he projects agitation in his setting of *la guerre* (war), mm. 4-5, pg. 143, and *tonnere* (thunder), mm. 12-13, pg. 144, in Act III, scene 6, with great rhythmic activity and descending scale passages that cover more than an octave (Jean-Baptiste Lully, *Cadmus et Hermione, Oeuvres complètes de J.-B. Lully,* ed. Henry Prunières, vol. I.1 (New York: Broude Brothers Limited, 1966), 143-146.

[40] Lully, *Alceste,* 246.

While declarations by heroes, gods, and powerful women are often commanding, references to tender love, submission, and even melancholia are accompanied by a more lyrical recitative.[41] In Act 5, Scene 4, from *Alceste*, Alcide's strong tones of voice, in the style of the commanding recitative (beginning in m. 2 at the top of page 295), contrast with Alceste's submissive responses (beginning in m. 5), which are more lyrical on the words "Je fais ce qu'il m'est possible, Pour ne regarder que vous" ("I am doing what I can to look at no one but you"). Here, the melody descends by step and is accompanied by minor harmonies. Heroes sing as well in this lyrical-style recitative, but it most often accompanies tender expressions of love for the heroine or allusions to tender love, such as Alcide's reference to Alceste's sweet regards for Admête.[42]

A third type of recitative is reserved for representations of impassioned characters, who exhibit a loss of self-control by expressing a wide range of passions in rapid succession, from rage to languor, despair, and sorrow. To do so, Lully exploits abrupt changes in tessitura, erratic rhythmic movement, expressive intervals, particularly the tritone, and chromatic alterations and changes of mode that signal abrupt changes in affect. The harmonies are less frequently in root position and more complicated than simple triads; diminished chords, especially, augment emotional intensity. One of the best examples appears at the end of

---

[41] The more "commanding" style of recitation is identified by James Anthony as *récitatif ordinaire* and defined as musical declamation with continuo accompaniment, characterized by changing meters and generally used in short dialogues. He claims that a more lyrical style of recitative, often accompanied by orchestra and referred to as *récitatif obligé*, was used by Lully in later operas (beginning with *Bellerophon*). He claims that the Italian term *arioso* may be a more appropriate label for *récitatif obligé* (Anthony, *French Baroque Music*, 81-84). I would suggest that a form of *récitatif obligé* appeared earlier, even as early as *Cadmus et Hermione*, but not with orchestral accompaniment. Sections of lyrical recitative differ little in style from the airs of the 1660s, that is, the musical representation of tones of voice predominate; whereas, *récitatif ordinaire* is characterized by declamatory rhythms, a stationary bass line, a mixture of repeated notes and frequent leaps in the melody, particularly those that outline triads. Lully used one or the other in conveying particular ideas and affects. Ordinary recitative most often accompanies bold and other strong statements, while lyrical recitative most often supports tender utterances. Bianconi implies such a difference in Lully's approach to writing recitative. He writes: "In recitative . . . rhythm is subordinated to the tempo of the diction . . . to alternate freely in accordance with necessity." He also notes differences in Lully's recitative according to the degree of "melodic expansiveness, necessarily accompanied by increasing density and decreasing speed in the musical and dramatic tempo." While this "melodic expansiveness" is lacking, the "expression is entrusted to the declamatory emphasis of recitative" (Bianconi, *Music in the Seventeenth Century*, 246-247).

[42] Lully, *Alceste*, 295. See the end of m. 4 "vos regards les plus doux" ("your most tender looks").

Armide where she (Armide) has been abandoned by her lover Renaud, as seen in Musical Example 6.3. Heroes rarely lose control of themselves to this extent, but if they do, it is because they have been placed under a woman's evil spell (magic or otherwise); for example Atys falls under the spell of Cybèle and kills his lover Sangaride.

Of all the musical features that could have been transferred to the air, it is the commanding-style recitative that composers used to set a man's most passionate discourse: that is, those song-texts in which he laments the rejection by the beloved or her infidelity. The transference of Lully's musical representations of heroes to the anti-hero or *galant* seducer in the airs makes for fascinating commentary, for it is the music, more so than the text, that communicates and dictates that our interpretation of gender representation be altered. Used in the airs, this commanding-style of recitation allowed men to emote in a "masculine" manner – with bold and domineering tones – thus turning his lament into a condemnation of the woman's behavior, especially the unfaithful coquette. "Infidelle Bergere, ah! Ciel!" by M. Carrier, Musical Example 6.4, is one such air. In this piece, the speaker emotes, not so much with fluctuating passion, but with strong and decisive tones and rhythms in both melody and bass. The language is direct and not laden with *précieux* metaphors, and there is no reference to physical weakness. If greater affective intensity is called for, Carrier resorts to those expressive devices used by Lully in his recitative, but Carrier's use of these is limited, for the composer dare not represent the rejected lover with an effeminate display of over-sentimentality.

While men are "masculined" in the airs at the end of the century, women are "feminized," or made to conform to an image of the dependent, emotional, and weak woman.[43] This is most notably illustrated in "Le Printemps que l'on voit paraistre," Musical Example 6.5. Here, the poetic female recalls that her beloved promised to be eternally faithful; believing him, she pledged her love as well, a state of being she admits made her vulnerable. He then breaks his vow of fidelity.

The musical setting underscores the association of operatic devices (the "new" style) with masculine representations while also demonstrating an association of the "old" style with feminine characterizations. This is particularly apparent if each line, the melody and bass, is interpreted as a representation of the characters: she as melody, and he as bass. There is precedent for this sort of interpretation. Lully and Quinault include in their operas many dialogues between man and woman in which both sing simultaneously. In many airs, as well, both melody and

---

[43] It is also interest to note that while the number of texts with a female poetic voice is extremely limited during the 1660s, the number increases dramatically toward the end of the century. Women are, thus, no longer silent, and when they do express themselves in the airs, it is often with great passion.

Musical Example 6.3 – Jean-Baptiste Lully, *Armide*, Act 5, Scene 5, 2nd ed.
(Paris: H. de Baussen, 1710): 181-182

té qui me luit; L'hor - reur de l'é-ter-nel-le nuit Cé-de à l'hor-reur mon sup -

pli - ce. Le per - fi - de Renaud me fuit; Tout per -

fi - de qu'il est mon lâ - che coeur le suit.

Musical Example 6.4 – M. Carrier, "Infidelle Bergere, ah! Ciel," 1692, p.29

Musical Example 6.5 – "Le Printemps que l'on voit paraistre," 1687, p.6

Le Prin - temps que l'on voit - pa - rai - stre Ne fait, hé -

las! qu'aug - men - ter mon tour - ment, Je ne ver - ray ja -

mais ces boc - ca - ges re - nai - stre Sans son -

ger à l'a mour de mon per - fi - de A - mant;

mant, C'est   dans ce bois   si som - bre et si pai - si - ble

Qu'il m'as - seu - ra   d'u - ne é - ter - nel - le   foy   Mais le cru-

el m'a - yant ren - du   sen - si - ble,   Fait   son plus doux plai-

sir   de s'é - loig - ner   de moy.   Fait   son plus doux plai-

bass lines are texted, and in a few of these airs, which are even called dialogues, a different text is used for each line. By assigning gender to melody and bass, each character simultaneously reveals the essence attributed to his/her gender. In "Le Printemps que l'on voit paraistre," she is emotional, passive, and weak, having lost her innocence by giving in to his seduction, while he is active, bold, and domineering.

The polarization of gender images (her weakness, his strength) is accompanied by a polarization of old and new musical styles. Not only are the styles simultaneously opposed in melody and bass, but they are also juxtaposed from one section of the air to the next and used to oppose present and past events. While in the first half of the air, she laments in passionate tones of voice associated with the old style, he (the bass) "carries on" in the new style. In the earlier airs, bass lines tended to be less independent of the melody, moving in larger note values, and allowing the tones of the melody to dominate, but the bass line in this air energizes the melody, directs it, pushes it forward, and in fact, resembles those bass lines used by Lully to imitate thunder, flight, and to accompany battle scenes. When she resorts to a new style (recitative), it appears only in the section of the air where she (the melody) recalls the past and her former possession of him. But her passionate nature is maintained, as she exploits the most expressive devices associated with the Lully's recitative style. A return to her present situation and his domination begins in m. 25, and from here to the end of the piece, she sings in sorrowful tones of her fate, while he (the bass line) wanders about energetically, suggesting his flight from her and his pursuit and conquest of other women.

The reversal of gender representation in this repertory – from the suffering, emotional man and assertive woman to the bold, "heroic" man and overly sentient woman, suffering at the hands of her lover – reflects a dominant trend at the end of the century. The airs, however, communicate a change in gender representation in ways that literary genres could not, for it is predominately the music, and not the text, that purveys this meaning. The transference of musical styles borrowed from one genre and incorporated into another, moved from one specific context and transplanted to another, calls for an assessment of stylistic change based on expressive function. It is not enough to say that composers of airs at the end of the century embraced popular musical trends. In my opinion, the proliferation of certain types of airs over others, the specific choice of certain musical features, and their use in distinct categories of airs was not an arbitrary decision. In an artistic genre that was most likely considered "effeminate," composers searched for a means to redefine masculinity and represent men with strength, courage, and domination. Lully's success in this quest is underscored by the transference of his most masculine musical imagery to the late seventeenth-century French air. Interpreted in this new context, even men who defy the rules of proper behavior towards women are heroes. Women, however, are not portrayed as heroines, à la Lully/Quinault. Rather they reveal the suffering due to women who challenge the rules of propriety by daring to love outside the bonds of marriage and by breaking the code of silence expected of their gender.

APPENDIX 1 – Sample Dialogue

1. **The Improper Approach** (Bary, Conversation I, "Du Libre Abord," Conversation IV, "Des Beaux Yeux")
Vous demandez comment il est possible (Lambert, *Livres d'airs de différent autheurs*, 1665, f. 26v)
Vous demandez comment il est possible / Que vos yeux m'ayt charmé / Et que par leurs regards mon coeur soit enflammé? / Vos yeux sont doux, et mon coeur est sensible.
(You ask how it is possible / That your eyes have charmed me / And that by their glances my heart is inflamed? / Your eyes are sweet, and my heart is sensitive.)
2. **Her Reaction – Men Are Liars** (Bary, Conversation XIII, "De la Belle voix," Conversation XI, "De Luth," Conversation XIV, "De la Belle Pronunciation," Conversation XLV, "De la Tromperie")
On n'ayme plus dans ces boccages (Le Camus, *Livre d'airs de différents autheurs*, 1672, f. 1v)
On n'ayme plus dans ces boccages, / Tous les Bergers sont trompeurs et volages? / Fuyons l'Amour, Bergere, il cause trop de maux: / N'aymons que le chant des oyseaux, / La fraischeur des ombrages / Et le doux bruit de nos ruisseaux. Lorsque l'Amour veut nous surprendre, / Il nous parroist sincere et tendre; / Et nous pensons qu'il doit estre éternel, / Il est doux et flateur, lorsqu'il commence à naistre; / Mais sitost qu'il s'est fait connoistre, / Helas! qu'il est cruël.

(No one loves any longer in these fields, / All the Shepherds are deceptive and unfaithful? / Let us flee Love, Shepherdess, it causes too much pain: / Let us love only the song of the birds, / The freshness of the shadows
And the sweet sound of our brooks.)

(When Love wants to catch us off guard, / It appears to us sincere and tender; / And we think that it must be eternal / It is sweet and flattering, when it begins to grow; / But as soon as it has made itself known, / Alas! how cruel it is.)

3. He Attempts to Elicit Her Pity (Bary, Conversation IV, "Des Beaux Yeux," Conversation XXIV, "Du Scrupule")

Mon ame faisons un effort (Lambert, *Les Airs de Monsieur Lambert*, 1669, p. 4)

Mon ame faisons un effort / Puisque je brusle il se faut plaindre / Parlons il n'est plus temps de feindre / Nous sommes trop prés de la mort, / Ne vous offencez pas Silvie / Si je pers le respect je pers aussi la vie.

Permettez qu'à mon dernier Jour / Je vous descouvre mon martire / Et qu'au moins je vous oze dire / En mourant que je meurs d'Amour, / Ne vous offencez pas Silvie / Si je pers le respect je pers aussi la vie.

(My soul, let us make an effort / Since I burn I must complain / Let us speak, it is no longer time to pretend / We are too close to death, / Do not be offended, Silvie / If I lose respect I also lose my life.)

(During my last day permit me / To show you my martyrdom / And at least I dare say to you / That in dying I die of love, / Do not be offended, Silvie / If I lose respect I also lose my life.)

4. Her Rejection (Bary, Conversation I, "Du libre abord," Conversation XXIV, "Du Scrupule," Conversation XXVIII, "De la Fievre," Conversation XLV, "De la Tromperie," Conversation XLVI, "De la Fausse Recherche," Conversation XLIX, "De L'Indifference")

Il est vray je suis rigoureuse (*Livre d'airs de différents autheurs*, 1666, f. 20)

Il est vray je suis rigoureuse, / Mais ma rigueur me fera vivre en paix: / Il n'est rien tel pour estre heureuse, / Que d'estre aymable et de n'aymer jamais.

(It is true I am cruel, / But my cruelty will enable me to live in peace: / There is nothing that brings happiness more, / Than to be lovable, and never to love.)

5. He laments her rejection (Bary, Conversation XXIV, "Du Scrupule," Conversation LXXIII, "De la Colere," Conversation LXI, "De Mauvaise Chose")

Qu'un coeur souffre par la contrainte (Brossard, *Livre d'airs sérieux*, 1695, p. 30)

Qu'un coeur souffre par la contrainte / Ah! qu'il est digne de pitié! / S'il commence la moindre plainte, / Il dit trop de la moitié, / Il faut que toûjours en luy-même / Il étouffe mille soûpirs, / S'il veut borner quelques desirs, / Il craint d'allarmer ce qu'il ayme: / Helas! que faire en ce moment? / Tout n'est pour luy qu'un dur martyre: / Qu'un coeur souffre quand il soûpire, / Et qu'il ayme trop tendrement!

(How a heart suffers from the strain / Ah! how it is worthy of pity! / If it begins the slightest complaint, / It already says too much, / It must always / Suppress a thousand sighs / If it wants to limit its desires, / It fears offending the one it loves: / Alas! what to do now? / All is for it only a harsh martyrdom: / How a heart suffers when it sighs, / And how it loves too tenderly!)

6. She is reluctant, and then she gives in (Bary, Conversation XXXV, "De la Decouverture d'Amour," Conversation L, "De la Juste Rigueur," and Conversation LXXIII, "De l'Heureuse Rencontre")

Taisez-vous tendres mouvements (*Livre d'airs de différents autheurs*, 1694, p. 54)

Taisez-vous tendres mouvements, / Laissez-moy pour quelque moments / Tout mon coeur ne sçauroit / Suffire aux transports que l'Amour inspire / Pour les plus parfaits des Amants: / A quoy servent ces sentimens / Dans mes plus doux empressements, / Ma raison vient toûjours me dire; / Taisez-vous tendres mouvements, / Laissez-moy pour quelque moments / Tout mon coeur ne sçauroit / Suffire aux transports que l'Amour inspire / Pour les plus parfaits des Amants.

(Be silent tender feelings, / Leave me for awhile / My entire heart is incapable of / Holding the euphoria that Love inspires / For the most perfect of lovers: / What purpose do these emotions serve / In my sweetest eagerness, My reason always comes to tell me; / Be silent tender feelings . . .)

7.   Expressions of Mutual Love (Bary, Conversation XXXV, "De la Decouverture d'Amour" / Conversation XLII, "De la Belle Description" / Conversation XXXVI, "Des Honnestes Approches")

His:
Tircis ton amour est vainqueur (*Livre d'airs de différents* autheurs, 1688, p. 66)
Tircis ton amour est vainqueur, / Je ne puis resister à sa constance extréme: / Ah! quand on a donné son coeur / Peut-on rien refuser aux voeux de ce qu'on ayme?
(Tircis, your love is victorious, / I cannot resist its persistent constancy: / Ah! when you give your heart / Can you refuse the wishes of the one you love?)

Hers:
C'est assez languir, et se plaindre (*Livre d'airs de différents autheurs*, 1663, f. 5v)
C'est assez languir, et se plaindre, / En l'estat ou je suis je n'ay plus rien à craindre, / Iris approuve mon amour: / Et la belle à son tour, elle mesme soûpire: / Mon coeur a tout ce qu'il desire.

(Enough languishing and complaining, / In my present state, I have nothing more to fear, / Iris approves of my love: / And the beautiful one herself, she sighs as well: / My heart has all that it desires.)

8. Their Infidelity (Bary, Conversation LVII, "De la Coquetterie," Conversation LII, "De Juste Dedain," Conversation LIII, "Du Depit")

She is unfaithful; he laments

Infidelle Bergere, ah! Ciel! le puis-je croire (Carrier, *Livre d'airs de différents autheurs*, 1692, p. 29)

Infidelle Bergere, ah! Ciel! le puis-je croire / Que je sois pour toûjours sorty de ta memoire? / Ah! de quoy m'ont servy tant de soins et de voeux? / Si me voyant helas! sur le point d'estre heureux / J'esprouve ton indifference:
Est-ce le prix de ma perseverance? / Cruelle, est-il possible enfin que ton amour / N'aura plus pour mon coeur de sensible retour?

(Unfaithful Shepherdess, ah! Heavens! can I believe it / That I am forever out of your memory? / Ah! what good have so many cares and wishes done me? / If seeing myself, alas! on the point of being happy / I feel your indifference: / Is this the price of my perseverance? / Cruel one, is it really possible that your love, / Will no longer have any feelings for my heart?)

He is unfaithful; she laments

Le Printemps que l'on voit paraistre (*Livre d'airs de différents autheurs*, 1687, p. 6)

Le Printemps que l'on voit paraistre / Ne fait, helas! qu'augmenter mon tourment, / Je ne verray jamais ces boccages renaistre / Sans songer á l'amour de mon perfide Amant; / C'est dans ce bois si sombre et si paisible / Qu'il m'asseura d'une éternelle foy / Mais le cruel m'ayant rendu sensible, / Fait son plus doux plaisir de s'éloigner de moy.

(The Spring we see appearing / Alas! only intensifies my torment, / I will never see these fields come alive again / Without dreaming of the love of my treacherous lover; / It is in this woods so somber and peaceful / That he assured me of his eternal faith; / But the cruel one having made me vulnerable, / Takes his sweetest pleasure in leaving me.)

9. He Rebels Against Her (Bary, Conversation XLI, "De L'Art de se Faire Aimer," Conversation LVII, "De la Coquetterie," Conversation XLVIII, "De L'Inconstance")

Vous ne me verrez plus, ny triste, ny jaloux (Lambert, *Livre d'airs de différents autheurs*, 1672, 10v)

Vous ne me verrez plus, ny triste, ny jaloux, / Languir, ny me plaindre de vous, / Cloris change mon coeur, et le rend fidelle: / Qu'elle a d'appas, que mon Cloris est belle, / Et que j'ay de raison de vous quitter pour elle.

(You will no longer see me, neither sad, nor jealous, / Languishing, nor complaining about you, / Cloris changes my heart, and renders it faithful: / How charming she is, how beautiful is my Cloris, / And what a reason I have to leave you for her.)

APPENDIX 2 – Negative and Positive Traits Attributed to Women and Men in Seventeenth-Century Treatises

FEMALE - NEGATIVE

Timidity
Overly-Emotional
Weak
Lazy
Fearful
Superficial
Too Amorous
Unchaste
Unfaithful
(Negative traits specifically applied to *précieuses*)
Indifferent
Too Bold and Overbearing
Speaking in Riddles
Presumptuous
Indifferent

FEMALE - POSITIVE
(*Honnête Femme*)
Innocent
Pious
Devout
Chaste
Willingness to Please
Good Conversationalist
A Beautiful Ornament
Beautiful
Joyous
Constant in Love
Inclined to Silence
Inclined to Feel Pity

MALE - NEGATIVE

Brutal
Cruel
Insolent
Scheming
Deceitful
Arrogant
Proud
Ambitious
Unfaithful
Disrespectful of Women
Too Familiar
Vain
Envious
Extravagant
Jailers of Women
Prone to Anger

MALE - POSITIVE
(*Honnête Homme*)
Courageous
Ready Warrior
Respectful of Women
Genius for Serious Matters
Good Sense of Judgment
Heroic
Adroit
Controlled
Reasonable

BOTH GENDERS - POSITIVE
(Honnêteté or Honnêtes Gens)

Agreeable	Virtuous
Christian	Discreet
Courageous	Courteous
Pleasant	Delicate
Tender	Graceful
Elegant	
Modest	

In Control of One's Emotions

WOMEN ON STAGE

Chapter 7

From Whore to Stuart Ally: Musical Venuses on the Early Modern English Stage

Amanda Eubanks Winkler

I have a story. It is not about a tragic woman, singing impossible, soaring melodies with tubercular lungs. Nor is it a story of a woman driven to musical madness by indifferent or cruel lovers.[1] It is a story of a goddess, the "noblest prey," "Goddess of desire," "daughter Venus."[2] It is a story of a particular feminine voice and of those who attempted to capture and make use of her special power.

My tale begins in the year 1591 in a rather unlikely place: Elvetham, the country estate of a disgraced nobleman, the Earl of Hertford. The Earl's disastrous first marriage to a woman of royal blood had provoked the ire of Elizabeth I and had landed him and his wife in the Tower.[3] When the queen stated her intention to visit Elvetham, the Earl, perhaps hoping to mend his relationship with the monarch, decided to sponsor a lavish entertainment in Elizabeth's honor. On the first day of this elaborate spectacle, the Virgin Queen was associated with Venus, even being accompanied to her lodgings by the goddess's traditional handmaidens, the Hours and Graces.[4] One might think that the exigencies of female rule and Elizabeth's self-representation as the Virgin would ensure a non-sexual portrayal of the goddess of love in the Elvetham entertainment. But strangely, this is not the

---

[1] My opening obviously refers to Catherine Clément's landmark study, *Opera, or the Undoing of Women*, trans. Betsy Wing (Minneapolis: University of Minnesota Press, 1988).

[2] Quotations taken from John Blow, *Venus and Adonis: An Opera Perform'd before the King*, act 1, scene 1; William Congreve, *The Judgment of Paris: A Masque* (London: Printed for Jacob Tonson, 1701), 13; and Ben Jonson, *Love's Triumph Through Callipolis*, in *Ben Jonson: The Complete Masques*, ed. Stephen Orgel (New Haven: Yale University Press, 1969), 460.

[3] On the Earl's disastrous marriage see Curt Breight, "Realpolitik and Elizabethan Ceremony: The Earl of Hertford's Entertainment of Elizabeth at Elvetham, 1591," *Renaissance Quarterly* 45 (Spring 1992): 20-48.

[4] For other visual and poetic representations of Elizabeth as Venus during the Elizabethan era see Roy Strong, *The Cult of Elizabeth: Elizabethan Portraiture and Pageantry* (Hampshire: Thames and Hudson, 1977), 47-48 and Edgar Wind, *Pagan Mysteries in the Renaissance* (New York: Barnes and Noble, Inc., 1968), 77.

case. As Elizabeth's beauty engendered love, so this Elizabethan Venus inspired her subjects to acts of procreation; Elizabeth, though without heir, facilitated fecundity in others. While complimentary, the Earl's entertainment at Elvetham implies that Elizabeth provokes sexual urges: "All other creatures strive to shewe their joyes. The crooked-winding kid trips ore the lawnes; / The milkwhite heafer wantons with the bull; / The trees shew pleasure with their quivering leaves."[5] All of nature gazes upon the "perfections" of its monarch, but "Their eyes desire is never satisfied." One may look and look, yet never get one's fill.

Elizabeth's representation as the goddess of love in the Elvetham entertainment demonstrates the difficulties that arise when interpreting Venus. The Virgin Queen as Venus provokes desire in her subjects, encouraging them to sexual acts although she publicly eschews such pleasures. Her courtiers, and indeed all of nature, can only gaze upon her reflection, her representation, never possessing her, "never satisfied." Similarly, Venus, the protagonist in my story, is difficult to pin down, contain, or rationalize. As a musical goddess in numerous English early modern entertainments, her meaning is fluid, multivalent, and sometimes ambiguous.

Although the Elvetham text does not provide a detailed account of the music performed for Venus-Elizabeth, and the piece sung in the entertainment by the Hours and Graces, "With fragrant flowers," does not survive, other sources, such as Robert Greene's play, *The Comicall Historie of Alphonsus* (ca. 1587-8), provide a clear description of the music performed by or for the goddess.[6] When the chaste Venus of Greene's entertainment appears, the Muses, her handmaids, play "vpon sundrie Instruments."[7] Calliope, however, is disdained by her fellow Muses. Venus takes pity on her plight and asks her to "entertaine Dame Venus in her schoole" by playing on her pipe.[8] The connection between beautiful women and wind instruments, particularly the flute [recorder] had already been forged in the visual arts. (See Figure 7.1) This association may be classical in origin, as stringed instruments were connected with Apollonian, intellectual pursuits, and wind instruments with Dionysian, bodily pursuits.[9] Furthermore, the flute had a longstanding association with physical love and was a phallic symbol in both

---

[5] *Entertainments for Elizabeth I*, ed. Jean Wilson (Woodbridge: D.S. Brewer, 1980), 105.

[6] Several musical settings exist of variants of the "With fragrant flowers" text; see Ernest Brennecke, "The Entertainment at Elvetham," in: *Music in English Renaissance Drama*, ed. John H. Long (Lexington: University of Kentucky Press, 1968), 38-40.

[7] Robert Greene, *The Comicall Historie of Alphonsus, King of Aragon* (London: Printed by Thomas Creede, 1599), 4.

[8] *Ibid.*, 6.

[9] Robin Headlam Wells, *Elizabethan Mythologies: Studies in Poetry, Drama, and Music* (Cambridge: Cambridge University Press, 1994), 50.

Figure 7.1 Titian, *Venus and the Lute Player*
Permission of the Metropolitan Museum of Art, New York

paintings and music.[10] Thus, the flute seems an appropriate choice for music associated with the goddess of love.

Many of Venus's musical conventions, such as the use of flutes and vocal ornamentation, were not only associated with the goddess of love; they were associated with all kinds of amorous music. As Linda Austern has shown, early modern writers often gendered music female, but passionate, highly emotional music – especially amorous music – was thought to be particularly feminine. This feminine music, often equated with the songs of Homer's sirens, could lead the unwary male listener to indulge in a surfeit of pleasure, causing him to fall into a state of moral dissolution and effeminacy.[11] The puritanical William Prynne criticized amorous music (in his view music that was too chromatic or ornamented) in his notorious *Histrio-mastix.*[12] But, like Venus herself, this amorous music had a dual nature and could be used for good or ill. What Prynne found troubling, others found pleasing and useful. As theorist and composer Thomas Ravenscroft asserted, "Passionate Tunes make *Amorous Poems* both willinglier heard, and better remembered."[13]

The slippery meaning of music – the fact it can signify different things to different people – renders it potentially subversive. Like a wayward child, music might not behave as one intends. Even the music in the pageant at Elvetham and Greene's play – entertainments celebrating innocent pleasures – could have been heard as lascivious. As the political situation destabilized over the course of the seventeenth century, and the critiques of the decadence at court became more frequent and vehement, the chance increased that a musical Venus, even a Venus venerating harmony and chastity, would be heard as a wanton strumpet. Thus, the musical Venuses that appeared during the tumultuous reign of Charles I and his French Catholic queen, Henrietta Maria (a reign that ended in civil war and regicide) present significant interpretative problems.

Judging from their written descriptions of court masques, Caroline writers and artists hoped to present a virtuous goddess of love. A facilitator of harmonious relationships and an icon of perfect beauty, the portrayals of Venus were intended to flatter the queen and the supporters of the monarchy. For example, in Ben

---

[10] For a lucid discussion of the recorder's phallic connotations in Titian's *The Three Ages of Man*, see Rona Goffen, *Titian's Women* (New Haven: Yale University Press, 1997), 28. For a witty example of the phallic flute in music refer to act 2 of John Dryden and Henry Purcell's *King Arthur* (1691).

[11] See "'Alluring the Auditorie to Effeminacie': Music and the Idea of the Feminine in Early Modern England," *Music and Letters* 74 (August 1993): 343-352; "Music and the English Renaissance Controversy on Women" in: *Cecilia Reclaimed: Explorations of Gender and Music*, ed. Susan Cook and Judith Tsou (Urbana: University of Illinois Press, 1993), 52-69; and "'Sing Againe Syren': the Female Musician and Sexual Enchantment in Elizabethan Life and Literature" *Renaissance Quarterly* 42 (1989): 420-429.

[12] William Prynne, *Histrio-mastix* (London: E. A. and W. I. for Michael Sparke, 1633), 275.

[13] Thomas Ravenscroft, *A Briefe Discourse of the True (but Neglected) Use of Chract'ring the Degrees*, London: Printed by Edw: Allde for Tho. Adams, 1614), sig. A3v.

Jonson's final collaboration with Inigo Jones, *Love's Triumph Through Callipolis* (1631), Jonson equates heroic love with the queen and incorrect love with "sectaries."[14] In other words, those who loved correctly were loyal to the Stuarts. Those who loved incorrectly were religious fanatics and other enemies to the court. Music emphasized Jonson's point. While the music for Venus's song, "Here, here I present am," has been lost, the text celebrates "perfect love" (presumably the love between Charles and Henrietta Maria) and beauty (the queen's beauty). The connection between Venus and the Henrietta Maria is made visually explicit when the deity "ris[es] to go up to the queen." The throne disappears and a final chorus celebrates the perfect union of "Charles and Mary" – a model of peace and harmony, a microcosmic representation of the hoped-for peace and harmony within the kingdom. Ironically, it is precisely these sorts of lavish and extravagant entertainments that the puritan moralist, William Prynne, found so decadent and lascivious.[15]

The spectacular masque provided by the gentlemen of the Middle Temple, William Davenant's *The Triumphs of the Prince D'Amour* (1636), also inadvertently highlighted the ideological ruptures within Caroline society. Given in honor of Charles-Louis, the Prince of Palatine, and his brother Rupert, the masque was attended by Henrietta Maria and her circle.[16] Given the queen's connection with Venus in other entertainments, it is not surprising that the goddess of love plays a primary role; in this masque Venus's music reigns supreme.

After a humorous anti-masque in which lovers from various nations, including England, are mocked for their ineptitude, the scene changes, and Venus's priests appear from her temple crowned with "Coronets of Flowers," playing on their instruments, and singing "Unarme, unarme!," an interesting reversal of the cry usually associated with Mars, god of war ("To arms, to arms!"). While the music is not extant, the text extols the reconciliatory power of both physical and platonic love. The Priests advise, "when your Ladies falsly coy / Shall timorous appeare, / Believe they then would faine enjoy / What they pretend to fear." In other words, women want sex, even if they are not allowed to articulate their desire. In the fourth verse, metaphysical, platonic love is reconciled with sexual love, drawing together two conceits that are frequently oppositional during the Caroline period: "Breath then each others breath, and kisse / Your soules to union: / And whilst they

---

[14] See Martin Butler, "Reform or Reverence? The Politics of the Caroline Masque," in: *Theatre and Government under the Early Stuarts*, ed. J.R. Mulryne and Margaret Shewring (Cambridge: Cambridge University Press, 1993), 132 and Peter Walls, *Music in the English Courtly Masque 1604-1640* (Oxford: Clarendon Press, 1996), 233-234.

[15] On Prynne's objections see Erica Veevers, *Images of Love and Religion: Queen Henrietta Maria and Court Entertainments* (Cambridge: Cambridge University Press, 1989), 89.

[16] Mary Edmond, *Rare Sir William Davenant*, The Revels Plays Companion Library (Manchester: Manchester University Press, 1987), 62; Robert W. Wienpahl, *Music at the Inns of Court* (Ann Arbor: University Microfilms International, 1979), 273-275; and Murray Lefkowitz in: *Trois Masques a la Cour de Charles Ier D'Angleterre*, (Paris: Éditions du Centre National de la Recherche Scientifique, 1970), 111-123.

shall injoy this blisse, / Your bodies too, are one."[17] A union of the souls (a platonic conceit) is achieved through joining of lover's lips (physical consummation). The reconciliation of pleasure with spirituality reflects the Devout Humanist philosophy that was in vogue in Henrietta Maria's social circle. Believing that pleasure and piety were compatible, Devout Humanists celebrated love, enjoyed in moderation.[18] Davenant, using the language of Devout Humanism, suggests both Venuses are necessary; pleasure and virtue are not mutually exclusive. Indeed, this passage may have been intended to defuse criticism by those who only considered the relationship between Venus and her lovers (allegorically, the relationship between Charles and Henrietta Maria, between the monarch and his kingdom) in terms of its profligate excesses. But by acknowledging and even celebrating pleasure, Davenant inadvertently gives additional ammunition to those who condemned Charles and Henrietta Maria for their lavish self-indulgence.

The extant music magnifies the ideological slippages. After an extravagant banquet, the priests of Venus make another appearance, joining the priests of Apollo and Mars to perform the "song of Valediction." Interestingly, the symphony, by William Lawes, which is used to accompany the descent of all three sets of priests during the Valediction, incorporates the rhythms of the sarabande, [19] a dance with carnal associations that can be traced back to its Spanish roots.[20] The sarabande seems more appropriate for the followers of a lascivious Venus; however, by selecting this dance for a scene celebrating the harmonious reconciliation of love, war, and wisdom, perhaps Lawes was thinking of Devout Humanist philosophy, which reconciled licit physical pleasures with high-minded pursuits. Yet, to an unsympathetic listener, the sarabande could easily be heard as a

---

[17] William Davenant, *The Triumphs of the Prince D'Amour* (London: Printed for Richard Meighen, 1635), 12.

[18] On Devout Humanism and its connection with Platonic Love and Catholicism see Erica Veevers, *Images of Love and Religion*, 33.

[19] Murray Lefkowitz identifies this symphony as a courant; however, it seems to have more in common with the sarabande. For Lefkowitz's otherwise astute analysis, see *William Lawes* (Routledge & Kegan Paul, 1960), 224. For a lucid description of the sarabande see Richard Hudson and Meredith Ellis Little, *"Sarabande,"* in: *New Grove Dictionary of Music and Musicians*, 2nd ed., vol. 2, ed. Stanley Sadie (London: Macmillan Publishers Limited, 2001), 273-277.

[20] During the late sixteenth and early seventeenth centuries, the sarabande became notorious as a dance for courtesans. It was banned during the reign of Philip II. On the English definition of the sarabande see Robert Stevenson, "The Sarabande," *Inter-American Music Bulletin* 30 (July 1962): 6-7; and Richard Hudson, *The Saraband*, ed. Armen Carapetyan, vol. 35, Musicological Studies and Documents (Stuttgart: American Institute of Musicology, Hänssler-Verlag, 1982), xvi.

Musical Example 7.1 – William Lawes, Sinfony from the "Song of Valediction," mm. 8-20, Ob. Mus. Sch. B2

symptom of courtly dissolution rather than Devout Humanist idealism.[21] (See Musical Example 7.1).

Other musical features seduce the ears. In a duet, also composed by William Lawes, Venus's priests pray the Princes will have as much success in love as on the battlefield: "the Balmes rich sweat, the Myrrhs sweet tears / Perfume your breath when you would Passion move." Sensual words such as "perfume" and "passion" are emphasized with melismatic ornament, and their duet is full of sweet sonorities between the voices, replicating through musical harmony and consonance the hoped-for harmony between the Princes and their prospective

---

[21] While the recurrence of the symphony does seem to show the influence of Venus upon Mars and Apollo, it is also possible that the same music was used because Lawes and Davenant prepared the masque in great haste. In his preface, William Davenant notes he had only three days to prepare the masque.

lovers. Venus's priests then repeat this text in their subsequent chorus, which, like the symphonies, is suffused with sarabande rhythms.

The sarabande rhythms and a variant of the melody line from this chorus also reappear in the final chorus in which the priests for all three deities (Mars, Venus, and Apollo) participate. Judging from the music, amour has triumphed. Even though the text emphasizes the "conjoyn[ing]" of the attributes of all three gods in order to "raise the soule" of the honored guests and "rarefie [their] sense," the music seems to be more amorous than intellectual or warlike.[22] Given the success of Davenant's masque, Henrietta Maria and the two Princes only heard an entertaining compliment – the underlying ideological dissonance was missed. But if one heard the music with critical ears, *The Triumphs of the Prince D'Amour* could easily be interpreted as a celebration of lascivious excesses, the triumph of "whorish music" over rationality. Some of these slippages in Davenant's entertainment hinted at the chaos to come. The cracks in Charles's absolute rule were beginning to show.

After the devastation of civil war and the restrictive puritanism of Oliver Cromwell, Charles II, son of the deposed and decapitated Charles I, was restored to the English throne. Given the changed political situation and the radically different atmosphere at court (moderating his pleasure was not a primary concern for the libertine Charles II), the character of Venus needed serious reformulation if she was to be of propagandistic use. In entertainments like John Dryden and Louis Grabu's *Albion and Albanius* (1685), Venus, the goddess who had been emblematic of the (fictional) harmony present at the Caroline court, is used to symbolize Stuart legitimacy; the political association is retained, but the insistence on sexual virtue falls away.[23] The work, which Dryden calls an opera, is self-consciously reminiscent of the allegorical masques of the Caroline era, pitting Albion and Albanius, thinly-veiled representations of Charles II and his brother James, against their political enemies. Dryden's opera culminates with the appearance of Venus. She rises from the sea with Albanius (James II), restoring the rightful line of succession to England – a nod to the tradition that claimed Brutus, Venus's great-grandson, as the founder of Britain. After Venus's appearance, Apollo descends and Albion goes to "Jove's Imperial Court" to be welcomed as a new deity (a reference to Charles's death in 1685).[24] Rejoicing ensues, as Venus and her fellow gods proclaim that Albanius will rule.

---

[22] *Ibid.*

[23] On *Albion and Albanius* and politics see Edward Dent, *Foundations of English Opera* (Cambridge: Cambridge University Press, 1928), 160; Paul Hammond, "Dryden's *Albion and Albanius*: The Apotheosis of Charles II," in: *The Court Masque*, ed. David Lindley (Manchester: Manchester University Press, 1984), 169-183 and Curtis Price, "Political Allegory in Late-Seventeenth-Century English Opera" in: *Music and Theatre: Essays in Honour of Winton Dean*, ed. Nigel Fortune (Cambridge: Cambridge University Press, 1987), 2-3.

[24] John Dryden, *Albion and Albanius: An Opera* (London: Printed for Jacob Tonson, 1685), 28.

In Venus's music legitimate rule and pleasure are connected. Of course, from the perspective of the post-Restoration Stuarts and their libertine courtiers, such connotations were not necessarily problematic. Venus's sensuality is celebrated in the flute-filled "Concert of Venus" which precedes her entry. A close reading of her recitative, "Albion hail!," reveals how pleasure and political power are conflated. In "Albion, hail!" the stability of Stuart rule is celebrated in the same musical terms as the rich balms and sweet scents of *The Triumphs of the Prince D'Amour*. For example, an extended melisma on "Eternal" does not just give an aural representation of eternity; its jaunty dotted rhythms and undulating line also signify the pleasurable feeling fostered by the righteous Stuarts as they provide their subjects with an "Eternal" dance of "Peace and Plenty."

Although Charles II hoped to provide "Peace and Plenty" for his subjects, his reign was considerably more flawed than the allegorical idealization presented by Dryden. For some, sexual licentiousness was the king's prerogative – a welcome respite from the dour moral conservatism of Cromwell and even Charles I. On the other hand, the pursuit of sexual pleasure above all else could lead to the destruction of the kingdom.[25] The controversy over libertinism was addressed in plays and courtly masques of the period and in one such entertainment, John Blow's *Venus and Adonis*, the monarch's sexual adventures literally take center stage. First performed at court around 1682, this masque was designed to showcase the talents of Charles II's former mistress and retired stage actress, Mrs. Mary (Moll) Davis (Venus) and her daughter by Charles, Lady Mary Tudor (Cupid).[26] By casting Charles's mistress as the goddess of love, the connection between Charles, Venus, and corporeal pleasures is clearly drawn. The offspring of this union between a king and an actress is cast as Cupid, the deity whose piercing darts can make even heads of state fall in love.

The libretto by an anonymous author retains only the bare skeleton of the mythological tale from Book 10 of Ovid's *Metamorphoses*. The masque begins with a prologue directed at the courtiers. Although Cupid mocks the amorous proclivities of the court, libertinism actually seems to be celebrated, as the only courtiers who stay faithful are the "the foolish, ugly, and old." Texts like "Ev'ry swain by nature loves," "'Tis natural to love," and "To warm desires the

---

[25] For an excellent discussion of the political ramifications of Charles's sexual escapades see Rachel Weil, "Sometimes a Scepter is Only a Scepter: Pornography and Politics in Restoration England," in: *The Invention of Pornography: Obscenity and the Origins of Modernity, 1500-1800*, ed. Lynn Hunt (New York: Zone Books, 1996), 125-156.

[26] Evidence from a recently discovered printed libretto demonstrates that *Venus and Adonis* was performed at court sometime before 17 April 1684; see Richard Luckett, "A New Source for 'Venus and Adonis'," *The Musical Times* 130 (1989): 76-79. For an excellent analysis of the textual and musical sources as well as an alternative interpretation of the political allegory in *Venus and Adonis* see Andrew Walkling, "*Venus and Adonis*: The Politics of Consensus" in his dissertation "Court, Culture, and Politics in Restoration England: Charles II, James II, and the Performance of Baroque Monarchy," (Ph.D. diss., Cornell University, 1997).

women nature moves" all seek to re-inscribe and naturalize an underlying libertinism: it is altogether human to succumb to carnality.

In a vivid visual representation of the pleasures of physical love, at the beginning of act 1 Venus and Adonis are discovered together in a passionate embrace. In a deviation from mythological tradition, Venus encourages a recalcitrant Adonis to go hunting; variety is the spice of life, and she would not want Adonis to tire of her charms.[27] Reluctantly he departs, claiming that next to beauty, hunting affords him the greatest pleasure. Act 2 consists of a humorous exchange between Venus and Cupid, with many inside jokes directed at the courtiers. Cupid wants to destroy those who scorn him and Venus gives him advice, which he passes on to his little pupils. Venus then asks her son how to retain Adonis's affection, and Cupid tells her to "use him very ill." Act 3 has a more solemn tone, as Adonis, fatally wounded by a boar, dies. Venus laments his untimely demise, weeping over his body.

Blow's music presents a Venus who is both beautiful and dangerously persuasive. Recorders in the act 1 prelude impose her presence, even before her first appearance. Furthermore, this prelude is in A minor, a key frequently connected with Venus and amorous pursuits on the late seventeenth century English stage.[28] In her opening duet with Adonis, she shows herself to be a powerful musical temptress. Recorders accompany only her vocal line; Adonis is bereft of their accompaniment. She sings lengthy ornaments on words that highlight her passionate nature and paints her lover's name, "Adonis," with a melisma beginning and ending on the leading tone, giving the passage forward thrust, a sense of anticipation. Adonis's subjugation by the goddess and his devotion to pleasure is apparent: his longest melismas are on words such as the descending flourish on "soft" and a gently syncopated melisma on "bosome."

Venus's ability to influence Adonis is further demonstrated in their duet, "Adonis will not hunt today."[29] Adonis begins in the key of C major, but Venus assiduously tries to convince her lover of the virtues of variety. She sings a charming air, accompanied by her omnipresent flutes. On the word "desire" the harmony begins to modulate and as Venus sings, "I would not have my lover tire," she continues to turn the key to her advantage. When the music finally cadences in her key, A minor, the bass line wittily demonstrates the dangers of over-exertion, flaccidly sinking downwards (mm. 9-11). (See Musical Example 7.2.)

Thus, Venus musically warns Adonis of his potential emasculation – a result of his affair with her – while encouraging him to reassert his masculinity by hunting. Apparently, Venus's arguments are persuasive: when Adonis tries to reiterate his position, "Adonis will not hunt today," he is musically, if not textually

---

[27] In the mythological tale, Venus warns Adonis about the dangers of boar hunting.

[28] Curtis Price has noted that Henry Purcell frequently used this key to represent sexual ardor; see *Henry Purcell and the London Stage* (Cambridge: Cambridge University Press, 1984), 22.

[29] Venus's harmonic influence also manifests itself in her duet with Mars, "Great God of War" from Matthew Locke's *Psyche* (1675).

Musical Example 7.2 – John Blow, "Adonis will not hunt today," mm. 1-12,
Lbl. Add. MS 22100

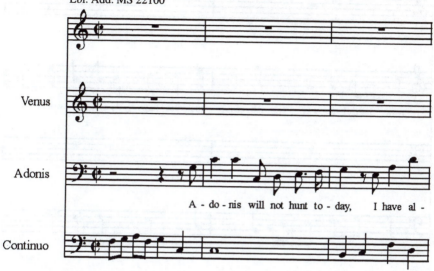

way, hast[e] a - way.   Ab-sence kin - dles new   de-sire, I would not

[Violin]

have my lov - er tire,   I   would not   have my lov - er tire.

won over to Venus's side as he sings in her key, A minor. His triadic gesture is also reminiscent of a horn call – another indication of Venus's complete victory.

While Venus seems the perfect mistress in this duet, persuading her lover that those men who "delight in heavy chains" are "fools of mighty leisure" and encouraging him in the manly pursuit of hunting, it is her success as a musical seductress, her Orphic talent, that places Adonis in harm's way, leading to his fatal wounding by the boar. The Venus presented by Blow is simultaneously a loving and understanding mistress who willingly grants "easy pleasures;" a laughing jilt who delights at Cupid's suggestion that she "use [Adonis] very ill;" and a lamenting lover, driven to distraction by her lover's death. As modern scholars have found multiple ways to interpret this masque, so it is likely that contemporary audiences also acknowledged multiple meanings in the music and text. The Venus presented for "the entertainment for the King" simultaneously celebrated the monarch's libertine prerogative and warned against its potential outcome. The royal Adonis should be allowed his libertine pleasures, but if he were to become the slave of his mistress Venus, obeying her every command, the kingdom would suffer.

While the Stuarts attempted to harness the musical power of Venus for their propagandistic purposes, the connection they forged with the goddess would later come back to haunt them. After the Glorious Revolution of 1688, old Stuart myths were rewritten in support of the new Protestant king, William III, and Venus, once celebrated (albeit problematically) as the goddess of platonic love at the court of Charles I, was now characterized as a dangerously seductive harlot. The mythological story of the judgment of Paris served as the perfect medium for promulgating this image of a destructive Venus. According to the tale, a shepherd, the exiled son of King Priam of Troy, judges a beauty contest among three goddesses, Juno, Pallas Athena, and Venus. Juno entices Paris with the promise of empire and Pallas offers him success in war, but the amorous shepherd succumbs to the charms of the goddess of love, who rewards him with Helen, the most beautiful woman in the world. Paris accepts his "gift" but his lack of judgment and discretion, his placement of love above duty leads to the devastating Trojan Wars.

Venus's potential usurpation of male power, an anxious undercurrent even in pro-Stuart entertainments, was fore-grounded by writers of the 1690s who appropriated the judgment of Paris story to critique Charles II's unwise choices made under the influence of a real-life Venus, his mistress, the Catholic Duchess of Portsmouth.[30] The mythological story was also the basis of William Congreve's *The Judgment of Paris* (1701), a libretto written for a song contest sponsored by members of the Kit-Cat Club. The Kit-Cat Club, founded by publisher Jacob Tonson, was a group of writers and noblemen, many of whom were prominent Whigs, a political party that had frequently opposed the Stuarts in Parliament and who were instrumental in the accession of William to the throne.[31]

Four composers set the libretto as part of the contest: John Eccles, a friend of Congreve, prolific theater composer, and music director at Lincoln's Inn Fields; Daniel Purcell, the younger brother of Henry, a theater composer at the Drury Lane theater; John Weldon, a relative novice who had been serving as an organist at Oxford; and Gottfried Finger, a Moravian who had been working in England from about 1685. Their music for Congreve's powerful, but morally suspect Venus was performed at the Dorset Garden theater.[32] In the three extant settings (Finger's score does not survive), Venus has no trouble communicating her merits to the amorous shepherd. She employs musical gestures marked as seductive through years of use – minor keys, recorders and transverse flutes, balanced phrases, ground basses, running eighth-note bass lines, chromaticism – to sway the heart of her "gentle Swain." Words that flatter Paris or emphasize his amorous nature are singled out for ornamentation, as are texts that highlight her pleasurable qualities. Employing this seductive and powerful musical rhetoric, she easily persuades Paris to award her the golden prize. Indeed, if the Stuart court were being critiqued for its lascivious excesses, it would have been an effective strategy to hearken back to the musical language that had enraptured the Stuarts in past entertainments. However, it was not just Paris who was seduced. The librettist Congreve was smitten by his own Venus, the actress-singer, Anne Bracegirdle. Bracegirdle performed the role in at least one of the musical settings, and, in a letter to his

---

[30] See [John Phillips], *The Secret History of the Reigns of K. Charles II and K. James II* (London, 1690*)* and *The Secret History of the Dutchess of Portsmouth* (London: Printed for Richard Baldwin, 1690). For a complete discussion of *The Judgment of Paris* see Amanda Eubanks Winkler, "'O Ravishing Delight': The Politics of Pleasure in *The Judgment of Paris*," *Cambridge Opera Journal* 15 (2003): 15-31.

[31] Curtis Price, "The Judgment of Paris," in: *The New Grove Dictionary of Opera*, vol. 2, ed. Stanley Sadie (London: Macmillan Press Ltd., 1992), 924. On the Kit-Cat Club see Kathleen M. Lynch, *Jacob Tonson: Kit-Cat Publisher* (Knoxville: The University of Tennessee Press, 1971).

[32] Stoddard Lincoln, "A Congreve Masque," *Musical Times* 113 (November 1972): 1079.

friend, Joseph Keally, an effusive Congreve described her performance as a "miracle."[33] Congreve's own capitulation to Venus further demonstrates the difficulty of channeling the goddess's voice towards specific ideological ends. His Venus, as performed by Bracegirdle, obviously possessed the power to charm even those determined to resist her harmonious lures.

Ever connected with beautiful music, Venus could represent both divine harmony and the problematic seductiveness of the feminine. While her musical conventions were fairly stable, the meanings conveyed by these conventions changed, depending on the political situation, the dramatic context, the performance circumstances, and who was listening. Consonant triple meter music with melismas may have been heard either as innocent pleasure or as dangerous allurement. What Henrietta Maria might have heard as a beautiful representation of divine harmony was for William Prynne "whorish musick crowned with flowers."[34] What Charles II might have considered a pleasurable musical celebration of his kingly prerogatives, could later represent the debauched lasciviousness of his reign. Danger was in the ear of the auditor. Whatever meanings were perceived, composers frequently lavished their most beautiful music on this infuriatingly complex goddess of love, allowing audiences to revel in her musical charms, even if it was a guilty pleasure.

---

[33] *William Congreve: Letters and Documents*, ed. John C. Hodges (New York: Harcourt, Brace, & World, Inc., 1964), 20-21.

[34] Prynne, *Histrio-mastix*, 275.

Chapter 8

With a Sword by Her Side and a Lute in Her Lap: Moll Cutpurse at the Fortune

Raphael Seligmann

The Legend and the Life

Moll Cutpurse. "She slips from one company to another like a fat eel between a Dutchman's fingers," a stage character once said.[1] *Roaring Moll.* Almost 350 years after her death in 1659, Mary Markham, née Frith, seems as protean as ever. *Mary Thrift.* Legal transcripts and literary accounts depict a consummate quick-change artist. *Mad Moll.* One moment a gang leader, the next a detective investigating the disappearance of gentlemen's valuables, now a penitent promising to behave "honestly soberly & womanly," a fortnight later "maudelin druncke" at her public shaming, she was London's most celebrated female rogue.[2] *Merry Mall of the Bankside.* From 1610 to 1612, when she was most active as a public figure, she could be seen going about town in a gallant's outfit with a sword or a staff, getting high on Virginia tobacco, performing stand-up comedy at London's second-biggest playhouse and even flashing the congregation at St. Paul's cathedral on Christmas day. Three comedies from this period feature representations of her; in two of them she is the main character.[3] She may have liked it when, in 1615, a critic referred to her as a loose cannon bombarding London with the spirit of theatricality:

> I will not particularize those…*Fortune*-fatted fooles, and Times Ideots, whose garbe is the Tooth-ache of witte, the Plague-sore of Iudgement, the Common-sewer of

---

[1] Thomas Middleton and Thomas Dekker, *The Roaring Girl*, ed. Paul Mulholland (Manchester: Manchester University Press, 1987), 2.1.206-207.

[2] On her behavior under interrogation, see Appendix E, *Officium Domini Contra Mariam Frith*, in Mulholland's edition of *The Roaring Girl*. On her penance, see John Chamberlain's letter to Dudley Carleton dated February 12, 1612 in Chamberlain, *Letters*, ed. Norman McClure, (Philadelphia: American Philological Society, 1939), 1: 334. See also Gustav Ungerer, "Mary Frith, Alias Moll Cutpurse, in Life and Literature," *Shakespeare Studies XXVIII* (Madison, N.J.: Fairleigh Dickinson Univ. Press, 2000): 42-84.

[3] They are John Day's lost *Madde Pranckes of Merry Mall of the Banckside* (1610), Middleton and Dekker's *The Roaring Girl* (1611), and Nathan Field, *Amends for Ladies* (acted 1610-11).

Figure 8.1 Title-page depiction of Moll Cutpurse from the 1611 quarto of *The Roaring Girl*
Permission of the Folger Shakespeare Library

Obscaenities, and the very Traine-powder that dischargeth the roaring *Meg* (not *Mol*) of all scurrile villainies vpon the Cities face.[4]

The figure of Moll Cutpurse has lived on for four centuries in heroic, anti-heroic and mock-heroic veins, the epitome of riotous female power. A Restoration-era satire on feminist stirrings in the Netherlands uses her as a bogey(wo)man to insinuate that if the "*Low-country* Amazons" are not stopped, a "Woman-Parliament" will cost the Dutch their preeminence in naval power: "Wou'd these be thought the *Soveraigns* of the *Seas* / Lords, thus Bear-garden'd with *Mal*-Cut-purses?"[5] Other late seventeenth century writings depict her carousing with Aeneas and dividing up stolen treasure with the god Hermes.[6] However, even as she was becoming an archetype, accounts of her life appeared purporting to reveal the true Moll. The earliest biography, from 1662, mingles historical fact, folk humor, moralizing commentary and anti-Puritan propaganda, some of it in the first person in a section labeled "Mal Cutpurse's *Diary*." In 1719, a Captain Alexander Smith plagiarized a chapbook version of this source. His third-generation knockoff has given ten generations of Anglophones access to Moll Cutpurse lore via the *Dictionary of National Biography* and the *Newgate Calendar*. In the latter, Smith's text appears beneath the rubric, "Mary Frith otherwise Moll Cutpurse / *A famous Master-Thief and an Ugly, who dressed like a Man.*"[7]

All sources of information on Mary Frith / Moll Cutpurse are fictional to a degree, even the judicial ones, which incorporate the truth shading and finger pointing of the original cases. Many accounts reflect the archetype's moralistic and humorous uses, many borrow from pre-existing genres of rogue literature and jest-books, and nearly all betray the authors' unease with the strength and mobility of their female subject. Because the Moll Cutpurse legend is a joint creation of Mary Frith, the contemporaries who wrote about her and most major institutions of her day, I have not tried to privilege any sources as pathways to an objective assessment of the once-alive

---

[4] I.H. *This Worlds Folly. or A Warning-Peece discharged vpon the Wickednesse thereof.* (London 1615), B2r. A "roaring Meg" was a large cannon used in sieges. "Fortune-fatted fooles" probably refers to the playhouse where *The Roaring Girl* premiered and Mary Frith performed.

[5] Matthew Stevenson, *The Woman's Warre; Or, the Dutch beat to Dirt by the Frowes* (1673), lines 59-60, Chadwyck-Healey English Poetry Full-Text Database, Cambridge 1992, http://collections.chadwyck.com.

[6] John Phillips, *Maronides OR Virgil Travesty* (1678), l.1534, and Robert Whitehall, *The English Rechabite* (1681), l.117, in the Chadwyck-Healey English Poetry Full-Text Database. The database lists seven seventeenth century references to *Moll Cutpurse, Mal-Cutpurse* and *Mary Frith* among its approximately 2,000 poems.

[7] The 1662 *Life and Death of Mal Cutpurse* is reprinted with footnotes in *Counterfeit Ladies*, ed. Janet Todd and Elizabeth Spearing (New York: New York University Press, 1994). On its textual afterlife see Ungerer, "Mary Frith," 44-45. An online source of the *Newgate Calendar*, www.exclassics.org/newgate/ngbibl.htm, lists 21 editions, all different in content, from 1705 to 1997. An experience from my childhood demonstrates the staying power of this work: in the mid-1960s, a friend's father used to entertain us over dinner with readings from what he called "the original rogues' gallery."

woman. Neither have I dismissed any portrayals as too distorted to reveal anything about her. In the case of the *Life*, for instance, I take a middle position between Spearing's assertion that the diary section is "by and large a 'told-to' autobiography" and Ungerer's denial that it is more than "mythmaking."[8] Frith's Royalist fervor may have been hyped by her Restoration biographers, as Ungerer claims, but it is not necessarily a fabrication. She surely knew she had less to lose from the Cavaliers, who were not as inclined to legislate morality as their Parliamentary opponents. Generic conventions, moralism or partisan rhetoric do not obliterate the subject, and events may have occurred more or less as described despite evident spin in the retelling. To avoid further entangling life and legend, this essay foregrounds the context of its source materials and sometimes asks the lawyer's question, *cui bono*? Who benefits? It also attempts to validate propositions about the biographical Frith by "triangulating" on her with mutually corroborative sources, searching for recurrent situations and behaviors that seem more personal than generic. Common threads include her desire for specific intoxicants (tobacco and wine) and her interest in the idea of women paying for sex.[9]

The accumulated evidence indicates that Frith was often successful in her ventures, thereby suggesting that bold forms of female self-fashioning were achievable in early modern London despite the well-documented "obsessive energy" invested by church, state and the neighbors in controlling unruly women.[10] Discounting the contemporary view of Frith as a creature of innate disorder, this essay considers how her provocations may have advanced a deliberate strategy for economic survival and personal expression. Taken as a whole, the record describes how she managed to make popular the categorically monstrous, suspend social hierarchies and the taboos that preserved them, and even co-opt a legal system organized to restrain unwarranted mobility. In these endeavors, she rarely acted alone; indeed, her success depended on contacts with diverse institutions, including the theater, the press, the nobility, the crown, the city and the criminal underground. This essay traces those contacts and details how Frith used her physical build, style of dress and musical skills with reference to London's institutions, sometimes inside and sometimes outside their norms.

In solo musical performance Frith found a powerful medium for self-presentation. Her projection of an individual persona from the stage using her voice and an instrument betrays a complex understanding of music's persuasive power, embracing both orthodox and progressive views. Functionally, her use of onstage music to underwrite her personal authority recalls royal spectacles such as masques. According to the aesthetics of absolute monarchy, the authority on display in court

---

[8] *Counterfeit Ladies*, xiii; "Mary Frith," 44.

[9] The latter theme is unusual in seventeenth century literature, but it occurs in the *Life* (see below), *The Roaring Girl* (in Moll's "dream" song, 4.1.102-8) and Field's, *Amends for Ladies*, 3.1, in which Moll calls the tailor's wife, "as sound a jumbler as e're paid for't."

[10] Lynda E. Boose demonstrates the obsessive quality of the many prosecutions and shaming rituals in this era in "Scolding Brides and Bridling Scolds: Taming the Woman's Unruly Member," *Shakespeare Quarterly* 43 (1991): 178-213.

spectacles devolves from the movements of heavenly bodies and flows outward to elite social bodies moving in time to "measured sound" within a providential scheme.[11] In her Fortune show, Frith did not hesitate to borrow masque imagery for political commentary, and a masque-wise reading of her performance might have identified her with such civic virtues as helpfulness, industry and patriotism, themes sounded in written sources that portray her favorably. However, viewed without allegory, her performance proceeds from a subjective, exposed position, in which the meaning of the music derives from the particular body producing it. That is a dramatic model of musical signification, a product of the focus on "inward character" and "privat'st thoughts" associated with playwrights of the sixteen-teens.[12] This model may have also had value for Frith, as it encourages the audience to suspend *a priori* judgments so the one can express her thoughts to the many. Perhaps the two models appealed to different sides of Frith, who loved courtly and civic ceremony and was a regular playgoer. In the furtherance of her self-fashioning strategy, she may have recognized the benefits of using music to promote a double image of herself as an institution providing wanted services and as a free-thinking individual following her own inclinations.

Looks

Even if Mary Frith had never adopted her mixed-gender attire, she would have stood out in a London crowd. Beholders marveled at her body and how she carried it. *The Roaring Girl*, for instance, contains allusions to Moll Cutpurse's prodigious size, including the comment "I never knew so much flesh and so much nimbleness put together," plus the epilogue's punning promise that "The Roaring Girl herself, some few days hence / Shall on this stage give larger recompense."[13] Frith's imposing build coupled with her rebellious impulses led to situations that produced her "roaring" image. As a young girl, according to the *Life*, "she would fight with boyes, and courageously beat them," and well into adulthood she "made nothing to crack any mans head with a good Battoon" (11, 40). By 1612, her pugnacity was known to Londoners of all stations. The courtier John Chamberlain refers to her as one who "challenged the field of divers gallants."[14] In *The Roaring Girl*, Moll prevails in four onstage fights and boasts twice of beating a gigantic German fencer.[15]

---

[11] The phrase is from Thomas Campion's *Lord Hayes' Masque*, ed. Walter R. Davis (New York: W.W.Norton & Co., 1967), 221. As the musicians played and sang, nine golden trees came to life, danced, and bowed to the king.

[12] Phrases from the opening scene (lines 157 and 315) of John Webster's *The Duchess of Malfi* (1614). In a typical example of music as a tool for disclosing character, *The Roaring Girl's* Moll Cutpurse uses an impromptu recital to express inner turmoil and to establish a bond of sympathy with her listener. This scene is analyzed further on in this essay.

[13] 2.1.204-5; Epilogue lines 35-36.

[14] Chamberlain, letter to Carleton, February 12, 1612.

[15] See Mulholland's note to 4.2.368. A description in the *Life* of a fight with wooden swords may refer to this encounter (41). The frontispiece woodcut of the *Roaring Girl*

Nearly all of the literary sources invest Moll's larger-than-life size and spirit with sexual overtones. In a satire on character types seen in theaters, a law student named Henry FitzGeffrey depicted the stir she created on entering Blackfriars playhouse as a spectator:

> Now Mars defend vs! seest thou who comes yonder?
> Monstrous! A *Woman* of the *masculine Gender*.
> Looke! Thou mayst well descry her by her groath,
> Yet, point not man! Lest wee be beaten both.[16]

The passage associates Moll's martial prowess with a sexuality that contemporary rhetoric deemed "monstrous" or "hermaphroditic." FitzGeffrey's horror is tongue-in-cheek, yet the figure of a woman over-endowed with masculine attributes was genuinely unnerving to many of his contemporaries. Whereas in modern usage a woman with "balls" is someone who seizes patriarchal prerogatives for herself, early modern ideology supposed that a "monster with two trinkets" would project her power outward to change the men around her and potentially upset the whole "natural" patriarchal order.[17] In the case of Frith's physical strength, the threat is perceived as direct and non-symbolic: the power to rape men. Other texts articulate that threat more explicitly than FitzGeffrey's. In *The Roaring Girl*'s dueling scene, Moll announces her ability to "prostitute a man" then beats her opponent so badly he concedes, "I yield both purse and body" (3.1.111-21). In a passage from the *Life*, the redactor proposes that only Frith's low sex drive spared the men of London from assault:

> She had a power and strength (if not the will) to command her own pleasure
> of any person of reasonable ability of body, and therefore she need not
> whine for it as long as she was able to beat a fellow to a complyance without
> the unnecessary trouble of Entreaties. (15)

The symbolic corollary of Frith's monstrous endowment is even more sensational. Early modern logic went by opposites, demanding a complement for every term: a Jack for a Jill, an Antichrist for Christ, a dry humor for a wet one. Thus, to

---

quarto shares important details with plates in a leading fencing tutor, *Vincentio Saviolo his Practise* (1595): a bare floor drawn in perspective with shadows; a rapier with an s-shaped handguard; and tall, decorated hats. Both illustrations resemble each other more than they resemble contemporary examples in their own genres.

[16] FitzGeffrey, *Notes from Black fryers* in *Satyres and Satyrical Epigrams* (London, 1617), F2r. FitzGeffrey does not name the woman, but all the details point to an individualized portrait of Mary Frith rather than a broad satire on women's mannish fashions.

[17] The "trinkets" epithet is in *The Roaring Girl*, 2.2.76. On the "hermaphroditic vision" see Linda Woodbridge, *Women and The English Renaissance* (Urbana: Illinois University Press, 1986), 145 and 315-317 and Jonathan Dollimore, *Sexual Dissidence* (Oxford: Oxford University Press, 1991), 296-297. On its applicability to Moll, see Susan E. Krantz, "The Sexual Identities of Moll Cutpurse," *Renaissance and Reformation* 19 (1995): 5-21.

imagine a woman of the masculine gender meant imagining her male counterpart. The discourse of the time regarded male hermaphrodites as "effeminate men" given to "that abominable sin of Sodomy, wherein they are both active and passive in it." [18] Such male monsters, it was thought, were once normal men who had become denatured by submission to assertive women. In a poem of advice to would-be husbands, John Davies of Hereford links female and male hermaphrodites in a process of reciprocal degeneration through which the man's lack of dominion creates a "man-kind-woman" who completes the destruction of his virility: "She is a monstrous *wo-man*, of *man*-made, / But *man* to marre; or, making, to inuade."[19] Mary Frith / Moll Cutpurse, with her masculine heft and vigor could not only overcome, and perhaps invade, the average man, she could reduce him to the status of an unmanned wretch "whose vicious actions are only to be whispered amongst us."[20]

The preeminent testing ground where early modern Londoners explored dynamics of appearance versus essence, stability versus transformation, and the natural versus the monstrous was the theater. Therefore, it is not surprising that most of the literary sources on Mary/Moll have playhouse connections. The title page of *The Roaring Girl* quarto makes reference to stage conventions of cross-dressing to imply that Moll Cutpurse acquired her hermaphroditic appearance through a self-willed sex change. A woodcut illustration shows her standing on stage-like boards wearing men's clothing associated with her at different points in the play: a short wool jacket with standing collar; baggy, knee-length pants and an Irish-style woolen wrap draped across her chest.[21] This is a composite image representing Moll in her most mannish moments. Completing the almost emblematic picture of transvestism, she smokes her pipe and holds up her sword. Her hair is cropped. Only a hint of one swelling breast indicates that all these signifiers of masculinity are (mis)laid over a female form. A slogan placed nearby seems to explain this incorrect image: "My case is altered; I must work for my living." This is a pun – *case* meaning genitalia as well as clothes as well as life situation – and it yields a typical early modern reading of the picture: Moll has altered her appearance in line with her desire to succeed like a man and in so doing has made herself functionally, if not physically, into one. Change your threads, change your nature.

This reading is cogent in a Shakespearean sort of way, like Rosalind's belief that "doublet and hose ought to show itself courageous to petticoat." Seasoned playgoers scanning the *Roaring Girl* title page would likely have deciphered the graphic and its tag line in light of their experience with Rosalind and other disguised heroines from

---

[18] *The Wandring Whore*, bk. 4, ed. Rudolph Trumbach (reprint, New York: Garland, 1986), 5. This serialized publication, appearing between 1660 and 1663, is at once a bawdy dialogue in imitation of Aretino, an exposé of vice, and a Yellow Pages-like directory of the London sex trade. Several characters described in *The Life and Death of Mal Cutpurse* are mentioned in *The Wandring Whore*.

[19] Davies, *A select second husband for Sir T. Overburies wife, now a matchlesse widow* (London, 1616), D3r.

[20] *Wandring Whore*, 4.5.

[21] These moments are respectively 2.1.174 s.d. ("frieze jerkin"), 3.3.29 (standing collar), 2.2.80 ("Dutch slop"), 2.1.202, 222 ("shag ruff").

the gender-bent world of stage make-believe.[22] Yet such a gloss would be misleading. Moll's appearance is less stable than a one-time change of case would admit. She rarely stays in one costume for long or adopts the complete suit of one gender. Mostly she blends masculine and feminine articles, as in her first appearance in "a frieze jerkin [masculine] and a black safeguard [feminine]" (2.1.174 s.d.). A mix and match approach is also seen in the only other surviving stage play with Moll Cutpurse as a character. In Nathan Field's *Amends for Ladies*, a city wife accuses Moll of looking like "a rogue and a whore vnder a hedge," i.e., man on top, woman on bottom.[23] Eye-catching collisions also characterize Frith's dress in the *Life*. There, the redactor links the doublet-petticoat dichotomy to the two most divergent religious sects he can think of: "*She was the Living Discription and Port*[r]*aiture of a Schism and Separation, her* Doublet *and* Petticoate, *understanding each other, no better than* Presbytery *and* Independency."[24] Such a flaunting of heterogeneity is the opposite of romantic gender camouflage.

Surprisingly, a feature common to all portrayals of Moll/Mary is the consistency of her self-presentation. Except in moments of duress, such as while under interrogation by the Lord Mayor, Frith comports herself as a woman claiming men's prerogatives.[25] A major point of her Fortune act seems to be that clothes do not make the man, for she is neither man, neuter nor hermaphrodite. This message evidently caused special concern among the church authorities that interrogated her, for the only remark from the stage they noted down was her assertion of an unambiguous, private identity grounded in a normal, female biology:

> she told the company there pr[e]sent [tha]t she thought many of them were of the opinion [tha]t she was a man, but if any of them would come to her lodging they should find that she is a woman & some other imodest & lascivious speaches she also vsed at [tha]t time (*Roaring* Girl, Appendix E).

Mary Frith's transgression, the passage suggests, had nothing to do with hiding her true gender and everything to do with using men's garments to tease the public – or, to make a dirty joke of her appearance, then defer the punch line into a private

---

[22] Shakespeare, *As You Like It*, ed. Stanley Wells, *William Shakespeare: The Complete Works*, compact edition, edited by Stanley Wells and Gary Taylor (Oxford: Oxford University Press, 1988), 2.4.7. Any discussion of a dramatic character's gender identity is complicated by the use of a boy actor to play the role. It is not certain whether audiences perceived female stage-characters as boys, women, or something else. Four excellent contributions to the scholarly debate reach very different conclusions about what early modern audiences thought they were watching: Lisa Jardine, *Still Harping on Daughters*, 2nd. ed. (New York: Columbia University Press, 1989), 9-36; Stephen Orgel, "Nobody's Perfect: Or Why Did the English Stage Take Boys for Women," *The South Atlantic Quarterly* 88 (Spring 1989): 7-29; Laura Levine, "Men in Women's Clothing: Anti-theatricality and Effeminization from 1579 to 1642," *Criticism* 28 (1986): 121-143 and Marjorie Garber, *Vested Interests* (New York: Routledge, 1992), 21-40.

[23] Field. *Amends for Ladies*. (London, 1618). 2.1.48.

[24] "Epistle to the Reader," 4.

[25] Arrested for vagrancy ("unseasonable and suspitious walking"), she claimed she had been on her way to assist a woman in labor. (*Life* 27).

transaction out of view of the regulating bodies. The preservation of this joke in the records of an "office case" (an inquiry by the ecclesiastical court responsible for sexual misdemeanors) suggests what the authorities imagined that obscure transaction to be.

Even without any winking from the stage, the city fathers might have wondered about the circumstances that made possible Frith's elaborate costume, for the purchase of tailored clothes by independent women raised the question of what they were doing to get the money. For the ex-soldier Barnaby Rich, the way to "distinguish between a good woman and a bad" when both are wearing sumptuous clothes is to "looke into her ability, is she able to pay for them."[26] That question was a fertile source of situations and gags for comedy writers such as Middleton and Field, whose plots confirmed or denied the inevitable suspicions of mercenary sex. Female self-fashioning, economics and sexuality are entwined in both *The Roaring Girl* and *Amends for Ladies* in scenes that show Moll Cutpurse buying men's clothes as a woman while trading insinuations of prostitution with shopkeeper wives.

For this investigation, however, the most interesting cash transaction is the one we know about: the stage act itself. Ungerer sees Frith's transvestism as a public relations ploy, "her signature as a popular entertainer."[27] It was that but also a creative riff on the symbolic value of clothes, converting that most legible of attributes into a token of private commerce and enjoyment to be negotiated in the wearer's "own lodging." Such open-ended negotiations align Frith's enterprise, whatever it was, with the commercialism thriving in London's theater and publishing industries. According to historian David Harris Sacks, the growth of these industries that sold products expressing any and every viewpoint "habituated customers, as well as producers, to a world dependent on the open clash of doctrines or of styles."[28] Viewed in this light, Moll's show of doublet and petticoat advertises not inner schism but the power of a rising consumer economy to absorb difference and spin it into capital. More than once, Frith staked her livelihood and freedom on that power.

First acts

The idea of fighting for personal liberation by challenging feminine dress codes seems to have occurred early to Frith. According to the *Life*, even repeated beatings could not compel her to abandon "Boys play" for "that sedentary life of sewing or stitching." The redactor, purporting to express her thoughts, explains why: "a Sampler was as grievous as a Winding-sheet, her Needle, Bodkin and Thimble, she could not think on quietly, wishing them changed into Sword and Dagger for a bout at Cudgels."[29] While the tone betrays the redactor's sarcasm, the passion it expresses is plausible as the young Frith's

---

[26] Rich, *My Ladies Looking Glasse* (London, 1616), 42.

[27] "Mary Frith," 61.

[28] Sacks, "London's Dominion: The Metropolis, the Market Economy, and the State" in: *Material London, ca. 1600*, ed. Lena Cowen Orlin (Philadelphia: Pennsylvania University Press, 2000), 42.

[29] *Life*, 9.

response to compulsory needlework and the ideological program behind it. Commentators anxious about the moral development of youth touted the usefulness of textile crafts to stifle girls' yearnings. A book of patterns published in 1596 advertises itself as a tool to keep young minds too occupied with minutiae to wander into fantasy: "Then prettie maidens view this prettie booke, / Marke well the works that you therein do finde / Sitting at worke cast not aside your looke, / They profit small that haue a gazing minde."[30] The author suggests that the reader's social survival depends on following his instructions: "Come then sweet gyrles and hereby learne the way, / With good report to liue another day" (lines 23-24). To imagine Frith declaring death better than a clean reputation under such constraints is to imagine the intellectual birth of a roaring girl.

Frith's refusal to submit to the discipline of stitchery set the pattern for more forthright rebellions to come. Nearly all of her public provocations over the next four decades involved clothes, and many used dress to signal a particular oppositional stance. In the first of these, her appearance at the Fortune, cross-dressing stands for a broad range of personal liberties. The actions she is said to have performed – joke telling, singing and lute playing – were all popular pastimes, as was the institution of theatergoing. Though common, these activities were also controversial. Sanctioned by English custom and classified as "things indifferent" by the Anglican Church, they nonetheless came under continual attack by religious fundamentalists. One Puritan tract lumped together "Carding and Dicing, Masking and Dauncinge; for Men to put on Woomens apparell, and women mens: Drincking to healthes; Ribald Stage-playes, &c." with an eye towards their eradication.[31] By 1611, Mary Frith was already notorious for "[resorting] to alehowses Tavernes Tobacco shops & also to play howses" dressed "vsually in the habite of a man."[32] Therefore, putting her on stage as herself reflects a decision to display a walking catalogue of what some considered "heathen debaucheries" and others considered fun.

For Frith and the Fortune management, this tactic was both clever and safe. Her act probably occurred in one of the post-play variety shows known as jigs, which routinely pushed the boundaries of taste. That these entertainments were also highly popular drove one moralist to complain, "But what voice is heard in our streetes? Nought but the squeaking out of those… obscaene and light Iigges, stuft with loathesome and vnheard-of Ribauldry, suckt from the poysonous dugs of Sin-sweld Theatres."[33] By appearing in a jig, Frith could ride the form's popularity with little risk of outrage, since the spectators who stayed for one could be counted on to accept at least some of the lifestyle she embodied. And while there was shock value in the sight of a woman onstage attired as a gallant with a sword, Frith could not have played to a more open-minded audience. An implicit compact with a public exercising its right to view adult entertainment might mitigate disapproval of her

[30] *A Booke of Curious and strange Inuentions* (London, 1596), preface, lines.31-34.

[31] William Bradshaw, *Twelve Generall Arguments*, London, 1605, C1r.

[32] *Roaring Girl*, Appendix E.

[33] I.H., *This Worlds Folly*, B1v. The author was acquainted with the Moll Cutpurse legend; see above.

cross-dressing, which would have appeared on a continuum alongside other embattled but communally indulged behaviors.[34]

The same cannot be said about Frith's next recorded provocation involving clothes, the flashing incident at St. Paul's. Once again, the *Consistory of London Correction Book* is the sole source of information: "She was since vpon Christmas day [1611] at night taken in Powles Church with her petticoate tucked vp about her in the fashion of a man w[i]th a mans cloake on her to the great scandall of diu[e]rse p[e]rsons who vnderstood the same & to the disgrace of all womanhood." This brief description provides important details. First, the incident took place in England's largest cathedral at its most crowded time. Frith apparently placed herself in one of the galleries above the nave, where she could raise her cloak to maximum effect.[35] Second, what she exposed was not her naked, female body but underclothing wrapped around her legs to give the illusion of breeches. Paradoxically, this exhibition may have packed a greater erotic charge than nakedness, for wearing breeches under a long skirt was a well-known tactic of Venetian and French prostitutes.[36] Whether or not Frith was alluding to this practice, the church authorities took her act as a sexual solicitation. This, not her stage routine, is what landed her in the episcopal jail, where she was "pressed to declare whether she had not byn dishonest of her body & hath not also drawne other women to lewdness by her p[e]rsuasions & by carrying her self lyke a bawde."[37] Frith cleared herself of these charges, yet it remains a mystery how she expected her captive audience to react to this act of clothed exhibitionism, which contains an element of blasphemy never hinted at by Middleton: disgracing "all womanhood" on the day the paragon of womanhood redeemed the sin of Eve and exposing her loins on the day another Mary's loins brought forth the savior.

Logic

With two very different public acts sharing one central feature, a woman displaying herself as a forked animal, the question arises: what logic binds these provocations? *The Roaring Girl* provides some clues. Several times, Moll Cutpurse expresses her aversion to sex and marriage. The most straightforward of these statements is her quip, "marriage is but a chopping and changing, where a maiden loses one head, and has a worse i'th' place" (2.2.44-45). More obliquely, there is her jesting disclaimer at

---

[34] On the sexual sophistication and libertarian attitudes of the majority, see Ann Jennalie Cook, "'Bargaines of Incontinencie'," *Shakespeare Studies X* (New York: Burt Franklin, Inc., 1982): 286-287.

[35] *Roaring Girl*, Appendix E. "Persons who understood" means literally those standing underneath her.

[36] Lynne Lawner, *Lives of the Courtesans* (New York: Rizzoli, 1987), 19-21. According to Lawner, they used this trick to tease customers with intimations of bisexuality. Italian courtesans were regarded as world-class professionals of vice. In *The Wandring Whore*, bk. 1, the expert Julietta the opens the dialogue wishing "to talk a little bawdery" concerning "all the profitable Venetian Customs and Curtezans actions amongst us," A2r.

[37] *Roaring Girl*, Appendix E.

the end of her performance on the viol, "all this while I was in a dream: one shall lie rudely then; but being awake, I keep my legs together" (4.1.126-27). Other, similar comments, coupled with the extraordinary set piece of Moll's duel with a would-be seducer, give the sex-aversion theme weight beyond being merely an excuse for smutty by-play. It also appears in the diary portion of the *Life* and is suggested by Frith's apparent abandonment of a husband and perhaps in the absence of syphilis from her catalogue of bodily ills.[38] In this light, cross-dressing can be seen as another of Frith's tactics for keeping control of her body.

Support for this reading comes from the flip side of the aversion theme: a mass of cultural material depicting men's uninvited access to women's bodies through the gap in their skirts. Typical situations include men walking underneath scaffolds to peer between women's legs and sly lads creeping between the thighs of sleeping girls. As Moll Cutpurse's remark about spread-legged dreaming suggests, responsibility for the ensuing seduction and/or shame attaches to the woman.[39] In the case of a wife, safeguarding personal honor was part of her responsibility to protect her husband's property, as expressed in this epigram by the courtier John Harington:

> A vertuose Lady sitting in a muse,
> As many tymes fayr vertuous Ladies vse,
> Leaned her Ellbow on one knee full harde,
> The other distaunt from it halfe a yarde.
> Her knight, to tawnt her by a privy token,
> Said, "Wife, awake, your Cabbinet stands open."
> She rose and blusht and smylld and soft doth saye,
> "Then lock it yf yow list: yow keepe the kaye."[40]

Caught in a paradigm of male opportunism and female guilt, London women, whose daily routine might involve casual contact with strangers, must have felt intense pressure to guard against compromising situations. Liza Picard, considering the open design of their clothes, suggests that "perhaps women lived in a constant state of alert."[41] Therefore, it is noteworthy that masculine fashions caught on among city women around 1610, just as female mobility was increasing and raising

---

[38] See her remarks on "insensibleness of my carnal pleasure" (*Life*, 45). On her apparently *pro forma* marriage to Lewkenor Markham, see Ungerer, "Mary Frith," 48-49, 53-54. On her illnesses, see *Life*, 70-72.

[39] On scaffold voyeurism, see the servant Sordido's comment in Middleton's *Women Beware Women*: "And you shall find me apt enough to peeping; / I have been one of them that has seen mad sights / Under your scaffolds" in *Middleton: Five Plays*, ed. Bryan Loughrey and Neil Taylor (Harmondsworth: Penguin, 1988), 3.3.105-107. On sex with sleeping girls, see Thomas Campion's air, "It fell on a sommers day," in *The Works of Thomas Campion*, ed. Walter R. Davis (New York: Norton, 1970), 31.

[40] Harington, Epigram No. 404 (ca. 1603) in David O. Frantz, *Festum Voluptatis* (Columbus: Ohio State University Press, 1989), 172.

[41] Liza Picard, *Restoration London* (New York: Post Road Press, 2000), 160.

widespread concerns about sexual misconduct.[42] Whatever people may have thought about the world-upside-down symbolism of women wearing the breeches, in a practical sense, it removed an element of feminine vulnerability and thereby some amount of culpability. Richard Brathwaite, an ex-actor who was fascinated with mannish women, jokingly suggested that the fashion began as a kind of moral prophylaxis for court ladies: "it is sayd to shun the meanes of sinnen, / Came that vse vp to weare their breekes of linen."[43] Intriguingly, Lawrence Stone describes a similar logic at work in an old Welsh courtship practice known as "bundling": the boy and girl are permitted to fondle each other in bed half-naked but are prevented from intercourse by means of a knot tied in the girl's under-petticoat.[44] Given Mary Frith's concerns about bodily integrity, a similar line of thinking may have occurred to her when she opted to start wearing pants. By putting this defensive gesture on display at the Fortune, she defies the assumption that a woman at liberty in the city is sexually open to all men (as Moll Cutpurse does in *The Roaring Girl*). By making a similar display in church during a celebration of the *supernatural* penetration of a woman, she may have defied more devoutly held beliefs about patriarchal power.

Considered in the context of national politics, the timing of Frith's drag show implies a logic that goes far beyond defensive positions. By 1611, James Stuart's honeymoon with the English people was over. Eight years into his reign, he was still regarded as a foreigner. He spoke with a thick accent, seemed to favor Scotland in his policies, and surrounded himself with an inner circle of Scottish lairds, whom he endowed with taxpayer-financed emoluments. Courtiers and commoners alike resented his conciliatory approach towards the archenemy, Spain. James' loathing of London, whose crowds he feared would literally tear him apart, compounded all these tensions. His phobia drove him to discontinue the public appearances that Elizabeth had used to link the fate of city and nation to her personal well-being. In this vacuum of public leadership, a cult of militant Protestant chivalry formed around James' heir, Prince Henry, whose independent household constituted an alternative center of power and patronage from 1610 until his death at age eighteen in 1612.[45] Fostered by Henry

---

[42] "Material Londoners" in: Orlin, ed., *Material London*, 184-187. See Linda Woodbridge's examination of the belief that "a woman's going outside was an aggressive and probably immoral act," in *Women and The English Renaissance*, 171-176; and Coppélia Kahn's discussion of the term *whore* in "Whores and Wives in Jacobean Drama" in Dorothea Kehler and Susan Baker, eds., *In Another Country* (Metuchen, N.J.: Scarecrow Press, 1991), 246-260.

[43] Brathwaite, epigram, "It's a mad world my Masters" in: *A Strappado for the Diuell. Epigrams and Satyres alluding to the time* (London, 1615), 108.

[44] Stone, *The Family, Sex and Marriage*, abridged edition (New York: Harper & Row, 1979), 384.

[45] On the ideals and symbols of Prince Henry's circle, see Roy Strong, *The Cult of Elizabeth* (London: Pimlico, 1999), 187-191. On Queen Anne's role in promoting the mythology, see Barbara Kiefer Lewalski, *Writing Women in Elizabethan England* (Cambridge: Harvard University Press, 1993), 15-43. For a general picture of the political scene, see Christopher Haigh, "Politics in an Age of Peace and War" in John Morrill, ed., *The Oxford Illustrated History of Tudor and Stuart Britain*, (Oxford: Oxford University Press, 1996), 330-360.

himself and Queen Anne, the cult was reactionary, bent on reviving an Elizabethan golden age under a young, masculine monarch. Its point of reference was "Astraea's sword," passed to Henry in the masque honoring his investiture as Prince of Wales (Samuel Daniel's *Tethys' Festival*) and symbolizing a transfer of mythological prestige bypassing James.[46] Though aristocratic in origin, the nostalgic imagery was disseminated to the masses via printed masque libretti and emblem books that packaged court arcana for city readers.

Another channel available to transmit dissent from the court was a company of players, the Prince's Men, which performed at the Fortune under Henry's patronage. It is known that Anne used her troupe, the Children of the Queen's Revels, to mount satirical plays offensive to her husband, and Henry may have followed suit. One of the two plays that can be assigned to the Prince's Men during Henry's adolescence was Dekker's *The Whore of Babylon* (1606), a piece of anti-Spanish propaganda with Queen Elizabeth as the heroine. Its purpose, according to Jean Howard, was to provide "a rallying point for political partisans."[47] The company's other known production from this period is *The Roaring Girl*. From a political standpoint, it does not seem coincidental that the main characters of both plays are sword-wielding warrior women, for the martial attributes of the late monarch were then being held up against the present one to show his shortcomings. The fact of Elizabeth's womanhood, which had posed challenges for royal image making in her lifetime, was now used to rebuke James for acting weaker than the "weaker sex." A commentator writing at the end of the century pictured James' subjects abusing him for presiding over a national sex change:

> Every Man's Tongue…could not refrain from mouthing it out, that Great Brittain *was become less than little* England; *that they had lost strength by changing Sexes; and that he was no King but a Fidlers Son, otherwise he would not have suffered so many disorders at home, and so much dishonour abroad.*[48]

With such rhetoric in the air, the stage spectacle of Moll Cutpurse knocking down foreigners and fops would parallel this line of political criticism, its topicality discreetly signaled by imagery calling to mind Elizabeth as she was remembered and as

---

[46] Astraea's sword had potent topical applications. According to Daniel's script, is it "not to be unsheathed but on just ground" (Strong 188). This recalls of Elizabeth's most famous verse "The Doubt of Future Foes," in which she warns "aspiring minds": "My rusty sword through rest / Shall first his edge employ / To pull [poll] their tops who seek such change / Or gape for future joy." *Elizabeth I: Collected Works*, eds. Leah S. Marcus, Jane Mueller and Mary Beth Rose (Chicago: University of Chicago Press, 2000), 134. The implication of Daniel's paraphrase for latter-day aspiring minds – such as the current favorite, Robert Carr – is clear and ominous.

[47] Howard, *The Stage and Social Struggle in Early Modern England* (London: Routledge, 1994), 52. On Anne's use of theater patronage to oppose her husband and his outrage at this ploy, see Lewalski, 24 and Linda Phyllis Austern, *Music in English Children's Drama of the Later Renaissance* (Philadelphia: Gordon and Breach, 1992), 9-10.

[48] D. Jones, *The Tragical History of the Stuarts* (London, 1697), 314.

resurrected in the pro-Henry allegories. The Irish mantle Moll wore and the sword she carried were both associated with the queen, who displayed them at public occasions and/or had them depicted in official portraits. They carried distinct political meanings, the mantle representing English hegemony over the Gaelic peoples and the sword designating justice. To a public grumbling about the eclipse of English prestige by upstart Scotsmen, the presentation of a plebeian Astraea by the Prince's Men would have seemed an encouraging gesture.

Mary Frith playing herself at the Fortune shortly afterwards would have been able to piggyback on this imagery, and perhaps the sword and the lute she carried onstage indicate such intent.[49] Whatever her political affiliations at this time, the chance to appear before 2000 spectators decked out in remembrances of the marriage-averse queen with "the heart and stomach of a man" would have appealed to her, not least as a means of asserting her own prestige to a hidden subset of the audience. Around 1611, Frith was in the process of establishing herself as a career criminal. Having previously operated as a purse-snatcher and burglar, she apparently moved into management roles in the London underworld sometime between 1610, the last time she was charged with theft, and 1612-14, when she set up a licensed brokerage for the recovery of stolen goods.[50] The *Life*'s redactor describes Moll in her prime as a "governesse" possessing:

> an absolute incontroleable power, more than ever the Law or Justice had over the Mercureal Tribe [thieves], they being entirely at her beck and command; submitting themselves and their stolen purchases to her onely Order, Will and Pleasure (4, 16).

This is a fantasy description from an unreliable source, yet as fantasy it is congruent with both Queen Elizabeth's role as "general, judge, and rewarder of your virtue in the field" and the fantasies of charismatic rule then circulating through court and city. [51] It would have been a serviceable fantasy for many of the parties brought together by the performance: the twenty-something Frith enjoying open command over the audience and private control over her gang; the cutpurses robbing the crowd as their leader sang; the Fortune's owners reaping revenue from the live spectacle of a woman on top; the anti-court satirist Middleton watching his model Roaring Girl perform a street version of a masquer monarch; partisans of the patron prince in whose support the imagery was invoked; and, finally, politically astute audience members who were treated to a novel manifestation of their favorite figure: the woman warrior who puts to shame her feckless antitype, the *rex pacificus*.

---

[49] The lute was another of Elizabeth's emblematic props, discussed below.

[50] Ungerer, "Mary Frith," 62-68.

[51] *Works*, 326.

Later stages

After her 1612 appearance at the bishop's court and a follow-on incarceration, Frith curtailed her public cross-dressing and explored innovative business ventures on both sides of the law: the brokerage in the sixteen-teens and a novel type of brothel in the 20s or 30s, in which women as well as men could hire a partner and couples could rent space for trysts.[52] Functionally, these businesses mark Frith's career move from actor to dramaturge. Her descriptions of both businesses in the *Life* acknowledge the importance of illusion making beyond merely deflecting suspicion about where the goods came from or what the couples were doing in the chamber. For the brokerage, she decorated her house with mirrors and encouraged her clients to believe they were magic glasses used to find their lost belongings (38). For the brothel, she made her Fleet Street house into a "Double Temple of *Priapus* and *Venus*" where she occasionally presided, as "chief Priestesse," over made-to-order chance encounters between her clients and the men or women they fancied (54).[53] It is unknown whether costumes played a part in the role-playing, such as the "Longe Gowne & a white beard" that Ben Jonson put on to deceive a lady into thinking he was an astrologer.[54] Given Frith's longstanding awareness of the reality-transforming power of clothes, some amount of dressing up would seem probable.

Later, during the English Civil War, clothing was central in Frith's most overtly defiant act, her participation in the women's peace march of 9 August, 1643. In this action, several hundred women marched on Westminster Palace to protest Parliament's passage of a new levy. The altercation that broke out took shape as a battle over clothes. The women, who wore white silk ribbons in their hats, encountered Parliamentarian soldiers wearing brown ribbons. According to a Parliamentarian newspaper, "At last ten Troopers (some of them Cornets) came to passe by the women, who had their Colours in their hats, which the women seeing, made 2 of them take their Ribbands out of their hats, not contented with that, they offered to do the like to the rest, & laid violent hands upon them."[55] The choice of

---

[52] *Life*, 52-54.

[53] Unlike the brokerage, which is referenced in court records, the brothel does not figure in any source other than the diary portion of the *Life*. Though the description sounds literary, that is not a reason to rule out the possibility of Frith operating such an enterprise. Other sources depict brothels where the sex play includes coy make-believe concerning what the people are doing there, including role-playing of nymphs and shepherds as well as less conventional scenarios. See *Wandring Whore*, 3:9 and Thomas Nashe, "The Choice of Valentines," in *The Unfortunate Traveller*, ed. J.B. Steane (Harmondsworth: Penguin, 1972), 462-467.

[54] Ben Jonson, *Conversations with William Drummond of Hawthornden* (1619), G.B. Harrison, ed. (London: The Bodley Head, 1923), 14.

[55] *The Kingdomes Weekly Intelligencer*. No. 30 (August 8-15, 1643), 229. When the guards called for backup, a troop of cavalry came and dispersed the women by slashing at them with swords. The women's unruliness and the brutality of their suppression were cited by both sides in a battle for public opinion that followed the incident. Royalists such as Simonds D'Ewes claimed that notwithstanding the "indiscreet violence" of the women, "the remedy

hat ribbons to express anti-Parliamentary sentiment was not fortuitous. Such accessories were perennially in danger of being banned as sinful vanities by hardliners in Parliament, a situation described satirically in a Cavalier song: "They'l not allow what pride [long hair] brings, not favours in hats, nor no such things, / They'l convert all ribbands to Bible strings, *which no body can deny*."[56] Additionally, white ribbons had associations with the Royalist cause. Describing an alleged plot to blow up the Thames embankments and flood the city, one writer claimed, "and for the Malignants they shal have all notice of it before; and shall be known by their white rybonds about their rists."[57]

Pro-Parliament commentators writing in the riot's aftermath were divided over whether the participants were unwitting tools of Royalist agitators from Oxford; normally docile citizens driven to "furious zeale" by the "distractions of Civill War;" or witches, such as one "most deformed Medusa or Hecuba, with an old rusty blade by her side" who was interrogated "concerning the prime contrivers of this Designe."[58] At any rate, the official inquest included a search for the source of the white ribbon: "Being asked, where they got so many hundred yards of silke Ribbin to were [*sic*] in their hats, some said at the Lady *Brunckhards* house in Westminster, others that came from the otherside of the water, had some at a Ladies house in Southwarke, and so others at other Ladies houses in other parts of the Suburbs."[59] It is not known whether Mary Frith was one of the ringleaders they sought. In the diary portion of the *Life*, she narrates her actions during the fight but does not say whether she helped in planning the march (60). Whatever her role, it stands as Frith's final act of street theater and sartorial rebellion.[60]

---

used against them…was most cruel and barbarous" (letter quoted in Samuel R. Gardiner, *History of the English Civil War*, [London: Longmans, Green, 1904], 1:187). The Parliamentarian press countered with the argument that the protestors were beneath pity, being "for the most part, Whores, Bawdes, Oyster-women, Kitchen-stuffe women, Beggar women, and the very scum of the Suburbs, besides abundance of Irish women" (*Kingdomes Weekly Intelligencer*, 229-231).

[56] "Englands Woe (to the tune of Greensleeves)" in *Rump, or an exact collection of ye choicest poems and songs relating to the late times* (1662).

[57] *A Dialogue, or Rather a Parley betweene Prince Ruperts Dogge whose name is Puddle, and Tobies Dog whose name is Pepper &c* (London, Feb. 1642), A4r.

[58] For the first position, see the *Kingdomes Weekly Intelligencer*; for the second, see *The Parliament Scout* Aug. 3-10, 1643, 55 and John Coke the Younger's letter dated August 9, 1643 in Historical Manuscripts Commission, *Twelfth Report* (London: Eyre and Spottswoode, 1888), Appendix, Pt. 2; for the third, see *Mercurius Civicus* No. 11 (August 3-11, 1643), 88.

[59] *Kingdomes Weekly Intelligencer*, 230.

[60] Ungerer cites two sources that place her as a leader in similar protests later in the war ("Mary Frith" 72).

As musician

Music appears to be another area where Mary Frith occupied a space between legitimate trade and outlawry. She was not a professional musician in any capacity her contemporaries would have recognized – for example, a member of the King's Music, the City Waits, a nobleman's household consort or the Company of Musicians (which had jurisdiction over all independent musicians in London). Her legal status was that of an unlicensed minstrel, subject to fines, if not of a vagrant perpetually vulnerable to arrest.[61] In terms of skill, she is hard to place based on the meager evidence available. In her own estimation, Frith was not much of a singer; her voice, she said, sounded like "the squeaks of a Mandrake." [62] As an instrumentalist, she was probably somewhat better, good enough at least to perform a lute solo at the Fortune (her playing is cited separately from her singing in the bishop's report). In *The Roaring Girl*, Moll Cutpurse improvises a song while accompanying herself and plausibly impersonates a viol teacher. This ability would put her at or slightly above the level of the practitioners described by the composer Thomas Whythorne as "pettifoggers of music" who set themselves up as professionals "after they have learned a little to sing pricksong [written-out music], or else have learned by hand, or by ear, or else by tablature, to play or sound on musical instruments, such music as hath been and is made by others and not by them." [63] If *The Roaring Girl*'s characterization of Moll as self-taught (4.1.82-83) applies biographically, Mary Frith was probably a consumer of a new type of cultural product: the printed musical tutor. Following the appearance of simplified notation systems, movable type for notes, and a burgeoning demand for how-to manuals of all sorts, composers such as Thomas Morley, William Barley and Thomas Robinson published instruction books for beginners. These books addressed buyers' social aspirations as much as their musical ambitions, with introductions urging them to learn the rudiments of music lest their peers and betters wonder how they were brought up.[64] Robinson's *Schoole of Musicke* would have seemed an especially good value, as it promised quick proficiency in two instruments for the price of one book: "Now, when you can play vpon the lute, I will (God willing) shew you how... you may verie easilie attaine to play vpon the Viol de Gambo, either by Tabliture or by pricksong notes."[65] Around the time, circa 1610, that Frith gave up petty thievery, learned genteel manners and "seemingly betook her self to a civiler

---

[61] On the social position of independent London musicians, see Walter L. Woodfill, *Musicians in English Society* (Princeton: Princeton University Press, 1953), 3-32. On their vulnerability to the vagrancy laws, see A. L. Beier, *Masterless Men* (London: Methuen, 1985), 96-99.

[62] *Life*, 61.

[63] Whythorne, *Autobiography* (c. 1576) quoted in David Wulstan, *Tudor Music* (Iowa City: Iowa University Press, 1986), 40.

[64] Morley, *A Plaine and Easie Introdvction to Practicall Mvsicke* (London, 1608), B2r. See Michael Chanan, *Musica Practica* (London: Verso, 1994), 111-20 on musical technology and taste in the seventeenth century.

[65] Robinson, *The Schoole Of Mvsicke*, (London, 1603). C2v.

life," she may have acquired some musical literacy through resources such as *The Schoole of Musick.*[66]

Besides being part of a general campaign for respectability, musical competency may have served as a means for Frith to achieve specific objectives as a performer. Ungerer sees her Fortune act as extending to a mass audience the "relation of interactive fellowship with the public" and the "communal spirit of indoor entertainment" she had absorbed in alehouses and tobacco shops.[67] Facility on the lute and viol would have been a tool for transmitting that atmosphere across vast differences in scale, both physical (from a dozen or so drinkers to over 2000 spectators) and social (from a purely plebeian clientele to a mixed crowd comprising the groundlings and the gallants in the boxes). Both instruments had appeal across social borderlines, and both were in the category known as "soft" or "still" music requiring proximity to the performer and creating a familiar mood. In literature, the presence of these instruments could represent intimacy itself.[68] Within the audience, the shared activity of leaning towards the stage to catch the delicate sounds would create temporary bonds with one's neighbors and with the performer. Mary Frith might have counted on these bonds to inoculate the more controversial aspects of her act from censure.

Besides striking a tone of taproom bonhomie, Frith's viols and lutes would have helped her frame issues of sex and gender. While the playing of these instruments was generally eroticized, the connotations differed according to gender presuppositions peculiar to each. By playing her lute at the Fortune, Frith made public (and thus transgressive) a feminine activity that carried a strong erotic charge.[69] Contemporary visual representations show lute-playing women as ambivalent figures. One set of images conveys ideal harmony in domestic vignettes and political portraits such as Nicholas Hilliard's miniature of Queen Elizabeth playing a lute while seated on a throne. Other images represent lust, even prostitution.[70] In written examples, a spirit-body dichotomy divides the instrument into asexual and sexual zones. One class of lute metaphors focuses on the strings, with their Pythagorean tunings and sympathetic vibrations, and averts attention from the

---

[66] *Life*, 16.

[67] "Mary Frith," 60. On the social composition of the early modern alehouse, see Peter Clark, *The English Alehouse* (London: Longman, 1983), 123-159. See also Beier, 80-82.

[68] For example, in the English *Orlando Furioso*, the witch Alcina leads her lover from a passage where trumpets, shagbot [sackbuts], cornets and flutes (i.e. "loud music") sound into a chamber where couples dally to the music of virginals, viols and lutes. Ludovico Ariosto, *Orlando Furioso*, trans. Sir John Harrington (London, 1591) edited by Rudolf Gottfried (Bloomington: Indiana University Press, 1963), canto 8, lines 144-152.

[69] See Linda Austern, "'Sing Againe Syren.'" *Renaissance Quarterly* 42 (1989): 420-448.

[70] See Marjorie E. Wiseman, "Theodoor van Thulden," in Peter C. Sutton, ed., *The Age of Rubens* (Boston: Museum of Fine Arts, 1993), 363-364, and Roy Strong and V. J. Murrell, *Artists of the Tudor Court* (London: Victoria and Albert Museum, 1983), 119. For the use of lutes by prostitutes, see H. Colin Slim's study, *The Prodigal Son at the Whores'* (Irvine, Cal.: California University at Irvine Press, 1976) and Lawner's *Lives*, 53.

body upward to the motions of the soul or inward in the conceit of plucked heartstrings. The resonant strings nearly always represent the spirit or emotions of males. In the other class, the instrument stands for the body of a woman, its roundness mirroring her thighs and breasts.[71] Alternatively, the instrument, light-colored in front with a dark hole in the center, could connote the female pubic region, as in the line "her white Belly'd *Lute* she set to his *Flute*" from a late seventeenth-century ballad.[72] Though these gender divisions were constricting to contemporary thought about women's potential, Mary Frith may have discerned an opportunity in them. The extremes of subjectivity and objectification associated with the lute and its connections to both poles of female status would have made it a versatile prop that could help her shift in and out of roles from transvestite courtesan to warrior queen.

In *The Roaring Girl*, the choice of a bass viola da gamba to accompany the dream song reinforces Moll's characterization as "a self-fashioned sexual enigma."[73] The instrument is a visual and sonic complement to her androgynous dress and reputation as a hermaphroditic "codpiece daughter" (2.2.92-93). In shape, tone and playing posture, the instrument bore attributes of both genders. Its body was thought to resemble a woman's figure, and women's heads were often carved above the peg box; however, carved male heads are found too. The viol's sound was described as soft and feminine, yet it could also be played roughly in the chordal "lyra way" suitable for depictions of hunting and battle scenes. It could be held across the lap, a mode considered decorous for women but musically ineffective, or between the legs in a style that could lead to the "indecent" shaking of the instrument.[74] In literature, when a man plays on a viol, the act can symbolize his possession of a woman, famously in *Pericles* where an incest victim is called "a fair viol played upon before your time."[75] When a woman is playing, the act marks her as mannish, sexually hungry, or both. The court lady Saviolina in Jonson's *Every Man out of His Humor* is ridiculed for her bad viol playing and her attempts to match wits with gallants. Her name, the feminine diminutive of the swordsman Saviolo, reinforces the sense that she is poaching on masculine preserves while also alluding to her instrument. An autoeroticism that

---

[71] Austern "Syren," 443-447.

[72] "The Wanton Trick" in Thomas D'Urfey, ed., *Wit and Mirth: or Pills to Purge Melancholy* (London, 1719-20), Vol. 4. (New York: Folklore Library, 1959), 93.

[73] The phrase is Susan E. Krantz's in "Sexual Identities," 8.

[74] The viol's leading English exponent, Tobias Hume, insists on its masculine credentials in his *Musicall Humors* (London, 1605), introduction. Nonetheless, his statement that the "passion" of music could be best expressed instrumentally on the viol links it to new singing styles coming out of Italy associated with actual female voices. See Annette Otterstedt, "A Sentimental Journey," *Journal of the Viola da Gamba Society of America* 19 (1982): 50. On playing positions, see Christopher Simpson's Restoration-era tutor, the *Division Viol* (London, 1667), 7.

[75] William Shakespeare and George Wilkins, *Pericles*, ed. Gary Taylor, *Oxford Shakespeare*, 1.1.124-29. On the range of sexual innuendos involving viols, see Ungerer, "The Viol da Gamba as a Sexual Metaphor," *Renaissance and Reformation* 8 (1984): 79-90.

leaves out the male was also attributed to the female gambist, as in the couplet: "Her violl da gambo is her best content / For twixt her legges she holds her instrument."[76]

The Roaring Girl imputes both gender poaching and sexual self-sufficiency to Moll via dirty musical jokes and an allusion to "close dames that will call the viol an unmannerly instrument for a woman" (4.1.96). What separates Middleton's treatment of Moll as gambist from the misogyny of most literary portrayals is that the viol in her hands is, like her sword, an equalizer that puts her on an even footing with masculine society. By providing an occasion for her and the young gallant Sebastian Wengrave to discourse on music and sex, the viol establishes an empathic bond across class and gender lines that temporarily pushes all forces of normative morality (including the female love interest who is physically present) to the sidelines. Handing Moll the instrument, Sebastian urges her to forget about her detractors, assuring her, "Thou'rt here where thou art known and loved" (4.1.94-95), and she requites him with the musical dream, whose lyrics expose the corrupt sexuality of the wives who hypocritically attack her in public. This is the comedy's most intimate moment and a rare instance of male-female friendship on the early modern stage, yet it remains un-idealized and steeped in bawdry. Modern readers attempting to understand the novelty of the Moll Cutpurse image should picture a musical performance – breeches, spread legs and all – that maximizes the viol's sexual connotations without demeaning the player. It is tempting to imagine that this treatment, conventional in content yet unprecedented in import, might have owed something to Middleton's contemporaneous experience with Mary Frith as a show business colleague.

Mysteries and connections

Besides the provocations and exhibitions discussed here, the literature provides many other instances of Mary Frith crossing boundaries, forging alliances, escaping perils, challenging prejudices, making a living and managing her image. These acts have yet to be adequately researched and interpreted, especially those for which the *Life* is the only source. The effort is clearly warranted, for some acts seem to function as Moll's dissident commentary on herself, her city and her government. They range from publicity stunts, such as a ride across London wearing a man's suit and carrying a trumpet and banner (36), to oppositional street theater, such as two political bull-baitings that allegorized Puritan and Royalist figures as dogs and bulls (50, 59). Such events could prove as rich and revealing as any of Frith's better-documented inventions of the 1610-12 period; however, they await an archive search to establish their factuality and test the diary's account. Additional detective work would also be needed to shed light on her relationships with noblemen such as the Earl of Dorset, a Royalist leader whom she seems to have served as a tax accountant (62).

Other opportunities for understanding the Moll Cutpurse phenomenon require only the imaginative comparison of printed sources, including works portraying unnamed figures. For instance, Richard Brathwaite's conduct guide, *The English Gentlewoman*, describes a brawling, masculine woman in separate accounts two

---

[76] Ungerer "Viol," 85.

pages apart, first as a "feminine myrmidon" possessed of "not onely a *virile* habit, but a *virago's* heart" and then as an English Amazon battling for the honor of womanhood in a recapitulation of the duel in *The Roaring Girl*. Is he describing Moll Cutpurse or Mary Frith, or is he conflating the figures? The question is important because the first description is negative and the second positive. Examination of Brathwaite's other works might show how he made moral distinctions within a rogue model of femininity that evidently fascinated him.[77]

An extremely suggestive deposit of hints and traces lies in writings about Prince Rupert, Charles I's field marshal. Rupert's advance on London in 1642 and his victories at Gloucester and Newark the following year terrified Parliament. The war party, fearful that his battlefield successes would spawn a mass peace movement in London, personalized the struggle by smearing the prince as an immoralist. They spread rumors that he enjoyed music, theater and bull baiting on the Sabbath, that he swore incessantly, and that he traveled with two women "in boyes apparrell who constantly attended him."[78] The possible links to Mary / Moll occur in a series of satirical pamphlets issued by the Roundhead press in 1642-44, which portray the prince's dog Boy, who rode into battle in the prince's saddlebag, as a demon or witch's familiar. In one, the dog performs a broker-like function as "a kind of a spirit that doth helpe Colledges to their loost spoons and two-eard pots, when they are lost or stolne." In another, the dog, a spirit of mischief, installs then exposes Pope Joan, an exemplary figure of cross-dressed female misrule to whom the *Life* compares Mary Frith.[79] (8). A subgroup of anti-Rupert pamphlets gives the dog a Moll-like animal companion: a she-monkey that carries a sword, takes tobacco and plays bawdy tunes through her pipe. Rupert's dog and monkey are also similar to pets shown in a well-known portrait of Moll Cutpurse.[80] Both dogs have a lion-like look, and one pamphlet describes the monkey in the same pose as the pet monkey in the engraving: "clapping her hand on

---

[77] Brathwaite, *The English Gentlewoman* (London, 1631), The English Renaissance 215 (Amsterdam: Da Capo, 1970), 123-124, 126. Brathwaite, an actor, may have seen or taken part in the play in his youth. See Raphael Seligmann, "A Probable Early Borrowing from Middleton and Dekker's *The Roaring Girl*," *Notes and Queries* 238 (1993): 229-231.

[78] Manuscript account cited in Robert Ashton, *The English Civil War* (New York: Norton, 1979), 207.

[79] The broker role appears in *A Dialogue*, A2r. The Pope Joan reference is in *A Dog's Elegy, or Rupert's Tears* (London, July 27, 1644), 5.

[80] The picture first appeared in the 1639 quarto of Field's *Amends for Ladies* and was reproduced in the *Life* and later biographies. The *Amends* frontispiece is included in Todd and Spearing's *Counterfeit Ladies* (1), and a reprint from an eighteenth century printing of the *Life* is given in Jane Baston, "Rehabilitating Moll's Subversion in *The Roaring Girl*" in: *Studies in English Literature* 37 (1997): 324. Ungerer misidentifies the parrot in the picture as an eagle and the dog as a lion ("Mary Frith" 76). The dog is actually a poodle ("water spaniel" in early modern parlance) and conforms to the time's aesthetic preferences. Frith, who owned poodles, may have known the opinion of her (probable) father-in-law, the writer Gervase Markham, on the ideal appearance for the breed: "the general features of his countenance being united together would be as lion-like as might be, for that shows fierceness and goodness." *Hungers Prevention* (London, 1621), 32.

her buttock and scratching it as if she were troubled with the lustfull itch."[81] Another monkey pamphlet alludes to the "green sickness" – a malady that was thought to induce strange oral cravings in virgins – in the same terms the *Life* uses to describe Frith's adolescence. The statement that the monkey "would eat no oatmeal nor lome of walls to cure her green infirmitie" nearly duplicates the *Life*'s comment that Frith "never eat Lime, Oatmeal, Coales or such like Trash" (14).[82] These echoes may be coincidental, there being only so many ways to impugn uppity women, but they might also indicate hitherto unknown paths through which the Moll Cutpurse legend circulated in seventeenth century English politics and culture.

Note: in citations throughout this essay, *S.T.C.* refers to A.W. Pollard and G.R. Redgrave, *A Short-Title Catalogue of Books Printed in England, Scotland, and Ireland, and of English Books Printed Abroad, 1475-1640* (London: Bibliographical Society, 1926) and later editions. Likewise, *Wing* refers to Donald Wing, *Short-Title Catalogue of Books Printed in England, Scotland, and Ireland, and of English Books Printed Abroad, 1641-1700*, 2nd ed. (New York: Modern Language Association, 1972).

---

[81] *An exact description of Prince Ruperts Malignant She-Monkey, a great Delinquent* (London, Feb. 25, 1642). A2v.

[82] *The Humerous Tricks and Conceits of Prince Robert's Malignant She-Monkey* (London, Mar. 15, 1642), A2r.

Chapter 9

La sirena antica dell'Adriatico: Caterina Porri, a Seventeenth-Century Roman Prima Donna on the Stages of Venice, Bologna, and Pavia

Beth L. Glixon

The past several decades have seen a growing interest in the lives of women in early modern Europe. It would seem, by now, that women of nearly all classes and backgrounds have been studied: nobles, middle class, the poor; wives, widows, and nuns; the typical working woman, as well as courtesans and prostitutes.[1] Indeed, the bibliography concerning women and women's issues has grown exponentially, in studies that cover most parts of Europe. Music historians have made valuable contributions to this corpus. Female composers have received special emphasis, with important studies on Francesca Caccini, Chiara Margarita Cozzolani, Barbara Strozzi, and Antonia Bembo, to name only some of the women active in *seicento* Italy.[2] At the same time that women began to gain their voices

---

[1] Portions of this research were carried out with the assistance of the Gladys Krieble Delmas Foundation, to which I am most grateful. I would also like to acknowledge the generous advice and assistance of Patricia Allerston, Nello Barbieri, Patricia Fortini Brown, Mauro Calcagno, Monica Chojnacka, Stanley Chojnacki, Tracy Cooper, Michela dal Borgo, Paola de' Piante, Jonathan Glixon, Paologiovanni Maione, Margaret Murata, Colleen Reardon, Ellen Rosand, and Helen Deborah Walberg.

[2] The bibliography for women in early modern Europe is extremely large; for a good, comprehensive listing, see the bibliography in Monica Chojnacka, *Working Women of Early Modern Venice* (Johns Hopkins University Press: Baltimore, 2001). On Cozzolani, see Robert Kendrick, "The Traditions of Milanese Convent Music and the Sacred Dialogues of Chiara Margarita Cozzolani," in: *The Crannied Wall: Women, Religion and the Arts in Early Modern Europe*, ed. Craig Monson (Ann Arbor: University of Michigan, 1992), 211-233; idem, *Celestial Sirens: Nuns and Their Music in Early Modern Milan* (Oxford: Clarendon Press, 1996). For the most recent biographical information on Francesca Caccini see Suzanne Cusick, "'Thinking from Women's Lives': Francesca Caccini after 1627," *Musical Quarterly* 77 (1993): 484-507. On Barbara Strozzi, see Ellen Rosand, "Barbara Strozzi, *virtuosissima cantatrice*: The Composer's Voice," *Journal of the American Musicological Society*, 31

as composers, however, a new and much larger class of woman musician began to emerge: that of the professional opera singer. This article will explore the life and career of one of these women, Caterina Porri, who sang on the stages of Italy for nearly three decades during the mid-seventeenth century. Porri's situation, and the choices she made, will also be brought into focus through a look at some of her female predecessors in Venice.

Women opera singers in Venice

Female singers and opera did not follow equal evolutionary paths. While the first surviving opera, Peri's *Euridice* of 1600, featured women among its cast, Monteverdi's *Orfeo* of 1607 did not.[3]   Although women had a long tradition of performing publicly as the *prime* and *seconde donne* of the *commedia dell'arte*, they were not always accepted on the operatic stage.   A papal ban preventing women from appearing on the stages of Rome continued until 1798, although exceptions to the rule occurred from time to time. Church doctrine, particularly as expressed in the seventeenth-century publications of the Jesuit Giovan Domenico Ottonelli, saw women performers as endangering both their own morality and that of their male spectators.[4] Operas mounted in other cities in Europe such as Dresden and Munich also routinely excluded women from their casts.

Some parts of Italy, however, were more receptive to the idea of women on the public stage. It was in Venice, with the institution of public opera in 1637, that women began their ascent to the status of prima donna. The first company, run by Francesco Manelli and Benedetto Ferrari, featured Manelli's Roman wife,

---

(1978): 241281; Beth L. Glixon, "New Light on the Life and Career of Barbara Strozzi" *Musical Quarterly* 81 (1997): 311-335; idem, "More on the Life and Death of Barbara Strozzi," *Musical Quarterly* 83 (1999): 134-141. The most complete account of Antonia Bembo's life will appear in Claire Fontijn-Harris, *Desperate Measures: The Life and Music of Antonia Padoani Bembo* (forthcoming, Oxford University Press).

[3] On the training of one of the female singers in the opera, see Timothy J. McGee, "Pompeo Caccini and *Euridice:* New Biographical Notes," *Renaissance and Reformation*, New Ser., 14 (1990): 82-87. See also Claude Palisca, "The First Performance of *Euridice*," in: *Studies in the History of Italian Music and Music Theory* (Oxford: Clarendon Press, 1994), 432-51. On the singers in Monteverdi's *Orfeo*, see Tim Carter, "Singing Orfeo" *Recercare* 11 (1999): 75-118.

[4] Church doctrine argued against women performers in general, but also against women singing on the stage; during the seventeenth century these views were perhaps voiced most publicly through the writings of the Jesuit Giovan Domenico Ottonelli. See Sebastiano Giacobello, "Giovan Domenico Ottonelli sulle donne cantatrici," *Studi musicali* 26 (1997): 297-311. Operas at the Teatro Tordinona in Rome featured women singers during the 1670s, but performances later in the century did not. For the all-male casts at the Tordinona and the Capranica in 1696, see Saverio Franchi, *Drammaturgia Romana. Repertorio bibliografico cronologico dei testi drammatici pubblicati a Roma e nel Lazio* (Rome: Edizioni di Storia e Letteratura, 1988), 700-702. On Ottonelli and his discussions of opera, see Lorenzo Bianconi and Thomas Walker, "Dalla *Finta pazza* alla *Veremonda*: Storie di Febiarmonici," *Rivista italiana di musicologia* 10 (1975): 379-454 (esp. 406-410).

Maddalena.[5] Several other Roman women followed in those first years: Felicita Uga, Anna de Valerio, and Giulia Saus Paolelli.[6] Indeed, for some reason during this time the best female singers were thought to come from, or to have been trained in Rome; unable to sing on the stage there, they made their way to the north. The most celebrated, at least in print, was Anna Renzi, who came from Rome in 1640, at the age of about eighteen, to star in Francesco Sacrati's *La finta pazza*.[7] She sang in at least three of Venice's theaters: the Novissimo, SS. Giovanni e Paolo, and the smaller and less aristocratic S. Aponal. Renzi, like her male counterparts, enjoyed a long career on the stage. Her last documented appearance in Venice occurred in 1657, but she very well may have sung publicly after that date. Documentary evidence concerning Renzi and to a lesser extent her predecessors, provides the earliest basis for the study of a female professional opera singer's life.

Given that the operatic world during the mid-seventeenth century was centered in Venice, each woman singing there must have arrived at a decision that would dictate the rhythm and patterns of her life: would she consider the city as a temporary stopping point, a place to live only during periods of rehearsal and performance, or would she seek to establish new roots there? Of the early singers, Maddalena Manelli falls into a special category, perhaps, as her husband – in addition to composing and performing in the first public opera in Venice – eventually found employment in the Cappella di S. Marco in 1638. The couple seems to have remained in Venice until 1645.[8] On the other hand, our knowledge of Manelli's successors, such as Anna de Valerio, Giulia Paolelli, and Felicita Uga, is too limited to allow an assessment of their professional and private lives in Venice.

Our view of mid-*seicento* opera singers, and their connection with Venetian opera, has largely been colored by impressions gathered from letters written to the impresario Marco Faustini and housed in the Archivio di Stato in Venice.[9] The

---

[5] On Maddalena Manelli, see Luisanna Stefani, *Francesco Mannelli (1595-1677)* (Tivoli: Assessorato alla Cultura, Quaderno n. 4, 1985). Manelli had also performed the previous year in Felice Sances' *Ermiona*, in Padua, seen by many scholars as a catalyst for the beginnings of public opera in Venice.

[6] All of these women are discussed briefly in Ellen Rosand, *Opera in Seventeenth-Century Venice: the Creation of a Genre* (Berkeley: University of California Press, 1991).

[7] On Renzi, see See Claudio Sartori, "La prima diva della lirica italiana: Anna Renzi," *Nuova rivista musicale italiana*, 2 (1968): 430-452; Bianconi and Walker, "Dalla *Finta pazza alla Veremonda*, especially 417-418, 442; Rosand, 228-235, 385; and Beth L. Glixon, "Private Lives of Public Women: Prima Donnas in Mid-Seventeenth-Century Venice," *Music & Letters* 76 (1995): 509-531.

[8] Francesco Manelli was hired by the Cappella di S. Marco in 1638. It would seem that Maddalena was resident in the Veneto before her husband, for she performed in *L'Ermiona* in Padua in 1636, and saw to the publication of Francesco's *Musiche varie*, op.4 (Venice, 1636). See Stefani, *Francesco Mannelli*.

[9] Three major articles have been based on the Faustini papers: Remo Giazotto, "La guerra dei palchi," *Nuova rivista musicale italiana* 1 (1967): 245-286 and 465-508; Bruno Brunelli, "L'impresario in angustie," *Rivista italiana del dramma*, 19 (1941): 311-341; and

correspondence from singers and talent scouts, dating for the most part between 1665 and 1668, shows ample evidence of Faustini's efforts to attract the best singers to his theaters in Venice. We meet performers such as Caterina Tomei, Antonia Coresi, Vincenza Giulia Masotti, and the sisters Anna Maria and Lucia Olimpia Cimini. All of these women came to Venice early in their careers to serve the impresario; in nearly every case they were living in Rome, and required reimbursement for round-trip travel between Rome and Venice.[10] As travel costs were high, impresarios may well have diminished their profits by bringing these and other Roman women to Venetian stages on a regular basis.

When I began in the early 1990s a systematic reading of the notarial documents drawn up in Venice, however, I began to see that some Roman singers were resident in Venice during parts of the year when their service would not have been required; a number of them made more-or-less permanent homes in Venice, sometimes with other members of their families. Anna Felicita Chiusi and Angelica Felice Curti, who had sung for Marco Faustini at S. Aponal during the 1650s, lived there still during the early 1660s, and both of them shared their homes with female family members including sisters, mothers, and grandmothers.[11] Perhaps these women had styled a northern-Italian existence for themselves, drawing from the examples of earlier Roman women who lived in Venice during the 1640s and 1650s, such as Anna Renzi.

Renzi lived in Venice for nineteen years, absenting herself from time to time in order to appear in operas elsewhere.[12] During those years she never married (despite having once entered into an agreement to do so), so that she made her way as an independent woman. Renzi could rely on the support in Venice of her musical mentors, Filiberto Laurenzi and Francesco Sacrati, but the singer seems to have fairly quickly established a wider network of contacts who helped her in different ways as she negotiated her way throughout the professional and financial necessities of her life. A number of the men at her side were Venetian, both nobles

---

Carl B. Schmidt, "An Episode in the History of Venetian Opera: The Tito Commission (1665-66)," *Journal of the American Musicological Society*, 31 (1978): 442-466. New documents from the archive were introduced in Beth L. Glixon and Jonathan E. Glixon, "Marco Faustini and Venetian Opera Production in the 1650s," *Journal of Musicology* 10 (1992): 48-73. See Rosand, *passim*.

[10] Coresi's first appearance for Faustini came when she was already in Venice in the entourage of the Contestabile Lorenzo Onofrio Colonna. See, for example, reports in Archivio di Stato di Firenze (henceforth ASF), Mediceo del principato (henceforth MP), filza 3033, f. 846v, 6 February 1666.

[11] Chiusi's sister died in Venice, as did Curti's mother. See Archivio Storico del Patriarcato di Venezia (henceforth ASPV), Parrocchia di S. Angelo, Morti, 1650-1672, 20 November 1658, for the death of Angela Caterina Chiusi. For the will of Vittoria Curti, see Archivio di Stato di Venezia (henceforth ASV), Testamenti Camillo Lion, b. 590, probated in August 1662. Another singer, the Bolognese Orsetta Parmine, also lived in Venice for some years after her performances in the 1650s.

[12] See the testimony in ASPV, Examinum matrimoniorum, b. 65, f. 589, 24 November 1662.

(such as Alvise Michiel) and citizens, that class just below the nobles; on the other hand, one man who formed part of her household was a Roman tailor who had crafted her confirmation dress years earlier in Rome.[13] On occasion, some male singers – specifically Giacinto Zucchi and the Roman Francesco Manetti – came to her assistance as well.[14]

I have described Renzi's supporters as men. It would be most interesting to know of her contacts with women. Unfortunately, many of the sources available to us, such as wills, notarial documents, and legal contracts, all required male witnesses, and Renzi's business transactions also happen to have concerned men. One of the greatest gaps in our understanding of female opera singers is the presence and influence of a community of women. Scholars have written about the bonds formed between early modern women, the fostering of lives in countless ways, the acts of generosity among women that helped to ease their way through life.[15] We must, then, wonder what relationships existed among the Roman women who came to live in Venice. Much documentation shows how foreigners there tended to seek the company of their countrymen and women. Many of them formed friendships, lived in the same neighborhoods, and frequented the same businesses. Unlike some other professions or ways of life, however, that of female opera singer exemplified competition since each opera had only two or three roles for women. Did this competition hinder the formation of social bonds among the singers, or could they turn to each other for assistance or support? When a young Roman woman considered making the trip to Venice, to embark on the life of an opera singer, did she seek the advice of her predecessors? Nearly all of the correspondence from and about singers is written from the male point of view: we hear from male impresarios, talent scouts, protectors, and husbands. Although the letters occasionally mention the mothers of the singers, we have little direct evidence of their influence, or of connections to other women.

Much of what we know of Anna Renzi's career comes from contemporary publications. For the most part they celebrated the early offerings of the Teatro Novissimo, where Renzi performed, but a book, *Le glorie della signora Anna Renzi romana*, was published in her honor by Giulio Strozzi in 1644; two later librettos called attention to Renzi's appearance in operas (*Argiope* in 1649 and *Le fortune di Rodope e Damira* in 1657). The variety of this documentation is extraordinary, and no other singer of the time in Venice was so honored, nor her career so well charted.[16] A number of contemporary notarial documents provide

---

[13] Giera acted as a witness for Renzi in a number of notarial documents, and he appears to have formed part of her household for a time; he most likely had moved to Venice some years before she did, however.

[14] See Glixon, "Private Lives of Public Women," 517-519.

[15] For the lives of working women in Venice in the early modern period, see Monica Chojnacka, *Working Women of Early Modern Venice*.

[16] Renzi was mentioned in a number of works published by the Accademia degli Incogniti. To some degree, the publicity concerning Renzi was part of a structure designed to promote the Teatro Novissimo, where she appeared. On this publicity and other documentation on Renzi, see Bianconi and Walker, "Dalla *Finta pazza*," 417-419; Rosand,

additional details; two of them concern contracts to sing on the stages of Venice and Florence, while others track some of her financial dealings both in Venice and in Rome. Still other sources attest to her appearance in operas in Innsbruck (and possibly Genoa) in the 1650s; the papers of the impresario Marco Faustini supply additional details concerning her later years in Venice.[17]

I turn now to Caterina Porri who, like Renzi, enjoyed a long career on the Venetian operatic stage, although it must have been much richer and more nuanced than we can judge from the skeletal sources at hand. In Porri's case, unlike that of so many other singers, we can employ several distinct filters through which to view her life: as a singer, naturally, but also as a wife, as a mother, and as a widow. Because we lack, for the most part, publications of the sort that highlighted Renzi's career, reconstructing Porri's life proves a more difficult task. Many of the details surrounding her career lie buried in the archives of Venice, Ferrara, Florence, and Mantua. Fleeting references to her in letters of diplomats and a few other singers allow us to discern the outlines of her career, while Marco Faustini's receipt book, along with several other documentary sources, allows us to track her earnings. Finally, church archives, as well as notarial and government records, illuminate the singer's life off the stage.

Caterina Porri was born in Rome around 1638, and came to Venice in 1653, at the age of fifteen, to sing in the famed Teatro SS. Giovanni e Paolo, the venue for Monteverdi's last operas a decade earlier.[18] Caterina's brother made the initial trip with her, and her sister made two visits to Venice during the next year and a half. Some time during that first season Porri made the decision to stay in Venice. Did she prefer the seasonal work in Venice to the social life in Rome, where women often performed in the homes of the nobility? Perhaps she had not, at first, even made a long-term decision. In February 1655, however, shortly after the end of her second opera season, she began the process that would soon lead to her marriage to Bortolo Caresana several weeks later. Following that union Porri would stay in Venice for another twenty-three years, before continuing her career in other cities in northern Italy.

Husbands of opera singers

Before discussing Porri's life and career subsequent to her marriage, I would like to explore briefly the issue of opera singers' husbands. To put the question simply, what sort of man would want to marry an opera singer? As in other areas regarding the lives of musicians, there are too few examples to study. If we look back to the 1630s, we find Maddalena Manelli, mentioned previously, who came to Venice already married to Francesco, the composer of the first "public" opera to be performed in Venice. This marriage, of course, represents a trend reminiscent of

---

Opera in Seventeenth-Century Venice, 228-33.

[17] See Glixon, "Private Lives of Public Women," 518.

[18] The information concerning Porri's arrival in Venice is found in testimony in the series Examinum Matrimoniorum in the Archivio Storico del Patriarcato di Venezia.

the *commedia dell'arte* troupes, such as the "Gelosi" (the troupe of the Andreini family), a company sustained by an artistic and marital partnership.[19] During the 1660s we find the Roman Antonia Coresi married to another singer, Nicola Coresi, whose talent, it would seem, was far inferior to hers (although at the time of their marriage she had apparently not yet sung on the Venetian stage).[20] This coming together of two musicians made sense both financially and socially; as we shall see later, marrying a singer could confer some degree of social stigma on the spouse's family. Certainly any such stigma perceived by the husband's family regarding marriage to a singer would be mitigated if the husband, too, were a performer. The Roman Silvia Gailarti married another Roman, Pietro Manni, who most likely facilitated and encouraged her career, as he himself became an opera impresario.[21] Like Porri, another Roman singer Virginia Rochi married a Venetian resident, a "middleman," during the early 1650s, and performed later under her married name, Virginia Camuffi.[22] This marriage, unlike Porri's, was more of a shotgun event, as she bore a daughter less than three months after the wedding. As a final example, we find in 1658 the marriage of the Venetian Elena Lorenzoni to a Riminese captain and gentleman, Galeazzo Passarelli. After her marriage Elena went on to have a successful career, performing on the stages of Venice and other cities in Italy under her married name. The marriage of Elena and Galeazzo represents that rarity where the notoriety of the husband may have exceeded that of the singer/wife, as he spent time in prison on at least two separate occasions, and was fortunate to survive a murderous attack.[23] Caterina Porri's husband seems to have been a far less flamboyant character.

Bortolo Caresana, the son of Giovanni Battista Caresana, was a man in his late twenties or early thirties at the time of his marriage, thus a little more than ten

---

[19] For a general overview of the life of Isabella Andreini, see chapter one of Anne Elizabeth MacNeil, "Music and the Life and Work of Isabella Andreini: Humanistic Attitudes toward Music, Poetry, and Theater during the Late Sixteenth and Early Seventeenth Centuries" (Ph.D. diss., University of Chicago, 1994).

[20] While Antonia Coresi was a prima donna on the Venetian stage, Nicola had to settle for minor parts. Coresi's concerns for both his and his wife's parts are conveyed in the letters he wrote to Marco Faustini.

[21] On Manni, see Glixon, "Scenes from the Life of Silvia Gailarti Manni, A Seventeenth-Century *Virtuosa*," *Early Music History* 15 (1996): 97-146.

[22] Camuffi's appearance in an opera by Giovanni Antonio Boretti was the focus of a paper delivered by Irene Alm: "A Singer Goes to Court: Virginia Camuffi and the Disaster of *Alessandro amante* (1667)" (Paper delivered at the Annual Meeting of the American Musicological Society, November 1996). The information regarding Camuffi's early history in Venice comes from church records: she had come to Venice around 1649 to perform in an opera mounted by Giovanni Faustini. ASPV, Examinum matrimoniorum, b. 55, f. 344.

[23] Passarelli was in prison by 1651, and was released in 1654 (ASV, Consiglio dei dieci, Comune, registro 103, f. 291). Three years later he was seriously wounded in his own home by a man who had "taken a dislike towards him." See ASV, Consiglio dei dieci, Criminal, filza 89, 11 January 1657. By 1676 he was once again in prison (ASV, Archivio notarile, Atti Giovanni Antonio Generini, b.6798, f.14, 7 March 1676).

years senior to his wife. The church records indicate his profession as that of a silk merchant, the same as his paternal uncle, Francesco, who also lived in Venice. How would Caterina and Bortolo have met and decided to marry? Any history of their relationship prior to marrying is lacking, but one curious note is the presence of two young musicians active in Venice precisely during this time: Andrea and Cristoforo Caresana, also the sons of someone named Giovanni Battista Caresana.[24]   Could Bortolo have been the brother of the musicians Cristoforo and Andrea, and have met Caterina through them?   Evidence suggests that the two families were not closely related.   While Bortolo is referred to as "Venetian" in a number of documents, it seems that he, along with his uncle Francesco, came from the small village of Cureglia, near Lugano (now part of Switzerland). Most likely Bortolo accompanied his uncle to Venice (or joined him) when he was still quite a young man.[25] The musicians and some members of their family, on the other hand, are referred to in a number of documents as *milanesi*. One of their sisters was born in Bergamo around 1641, and the family moved to Venice some five years later.[26] It is certainly possible that the two families were related, as Milan and its territory were not far from Lugano. Moreover, they very well may have come to know each other in Venice, precisely through the rarity of their surname: I have found no other Caresanas in the city other than Bortolo and his uncle, and the much larger family that included the musicians.

   To return to the details concerning Porri's marriage: on 23 February 1655, Porri appeared before the representatives of the Patriarch of Venice with two witnesses to "prove" her single state, and her freedom from any other promises of marriage.   Such practice was standard for foreigners marrying in Venice. Testifying on Porri's behalf were Giovanni Vertecchi, a Roman musician then resident in Venice, and Lorenzo Arciti, a native of Todi.   It was Vertecchi who spoke of Porri's recruitment for the Grimani theater: "[Porri] had always been in Rome, until a year-and-a-half ago, when she left for Venice with her brother Prospero, in order to perform in the Teatro SS. Giovanni e Paolo of the Grimanis."[27] Arciti, on the other hand, failed to mention Porri's profession, but

---

[24] On the brothers' appearance in Cavalli's *Calisto* and *Eritrea*, see Glixon and Glixon, "Marco Faustini and Opera Production," 59.   Cristoforo Caresana left Venice for Naples in 1658, and pursued an active career as a musician and composer there.

[25] The parish records of Cureglia list the baptisms of Bortolo's father, Giovanni Battista, and his uncle, Francesco, in 1600 (9 July) and 1602 (5 July) respectively. Someone named Giovanni Battista Caresana – most likely the brother of Francesco Caresana – had a son, Bortolo, who was baptized in Cureglia on 1 August 1618. I am grateful to the Church of Jesus Christ of Latter-Day Saints, who enabled me to view a microfilm of the baptisms of the parish of San Cristoforo di Cureglia (Ticino), 1595-1685.   Francesco Caresana had moved to Venice by December 1639, when he appeared as a witness to a notarial document (ASV, Archivio notarile, Atti Giovanni Piccini, b. 10801, f. 583v).   The Caresanas of Cureglia seem to have been one of the most important families of the village, with priests, a notary, and artists (including Giovanni Domenico Caresana) among their members.

[26] ASPV, Examinum matrimoniorum, b. 63, f. 214.

[27] "Continuamente la medesima è stata in Roma, sino già circa un'anno e mezo, che di

attested to the fact that she had remained in Venice since her arrival, and that as a friend of the family, he had accompanied Porri's sister to Venice two times, most recently in January.[28] Five days after the testimony the couple received the nuptial blessing during the celebration of a mass at the church of S. Giorgio Maggiore.[29] They were then married in Porri's home in the parish of S. Antonin (where the couple would live, in the Calle del Forno Vecchio) on 8 March, with Giovanni Maria Correggio and a priest, Giovanni Maria Vico, serving as witnesses.[30]

When talking about women of any era, we often try to assess how their lives were affected by the state of marriage. In this case, however, it is perhaps of interest to consider how Bortolo's life was changed by his marriage to Caterina. In making this alliance with a prima donna, he entered a new world, and almost certainly began to move in higher circles of society. As I mentioned above, opera singers tended to form alliances with Venetian noblemen. Porri's connections soon provided the means by which Bortolo rented an office in the Venetian government bureaucracy from the nobleman Ottavian Valier, that of accountant in the financial office of the "Insida." The agreement for the rental, carried out in 1656, was drawn up not at the notary's office, nor at the house of one of the principal parties, but in the palace of Giovanni Grimani, the theater owner, thus providing some indication of Bortolo's rise in status, and of the connections that were now working in his favor.[31] The contract stipulated that Caresana would execute the duties of the office himself (he could not transfer the office to another party), and henceforth he always identified himself as an accountant, rather than as a silk merchant. Bortolo's duties, however, did not prevent him from taking an interest in his wife's career. The marriage provided Porri with someone able to act in her immediate interests (although she would certainly have maintained her

---

la si partì per Venetia con il Signor Prospero suo fratello, con occasione di recitare nel Teatro de SS. Gio. e Paulo de' Signori Grimani." ASPV, Examinum matrimoniorum, b. 63, f. 214.

[28] Perhaps Porri's sister had come to Venice not only to view the opera performances, but also to bring with her items that would serve the soon-to-be bride.

[29] "Adi 28 febraro1655. Riceverono la benedition nuptial nella celebration della santa messa da me sopradetto Piovan in Chiesa di S. Giorgio Maggior giusta'l ritual Romana. Presenti il Signor P. Z. Maria Vico titolaro in S. Gio. in Bragora et il Signor Z. Marco Correggio sopradetto." Parrocchia di S. Antonin, Matrimoni, 1589-1665. I am grateful to Don Renato Volo of S. Giovanni in Bragora, who allowed me to examine the archive of S. Antonin (now housed at S. Giovanni in Bragora).

[30] "Adi 8 Marzo 1655. Fatta una solenna publicatione del contrascritto matrimonio tra la Signora Catarina del Signor Giovanni Battista Porri Romana sta nella nostra parochia et il Signor Bortolo Caresana mercante da seda sta in contrada di S. Stin.... li congionsi in matrimonio per verba de presenti in casa della sposa presenti il Signor Lucio Vico q. Signor Piero et il Signor Z. Maria Correggio compare." Ibid. The couple paid D90 in annual rent for the house in S. Antonin (owned by the nobleman Vicenzo Erizzo). ASV, Dieci Savi sopra le Decime; for the district of Castello, see registro 420, S. Antonin, Calle del Forno Vecchio, f. 472v.

[31] ASV, Archivio notarile, Atti Angelo Calzavara, b. 3807, f. 95, 15 August 1656. The Insida dealt with the taxation of goods leaving Venice.

associations among the upper classes).

Scenes from the life of a marriage: Caterina and Bortolo Caresana

Bortolo Caresana had married a young woman on her way to becoming one of the leading prima donnas in Venice. During the second year of their marriage she traveled to Bologna to perform in Aurelio Aureli and Francesco Cavalli's *Erismena*, an opera that had premiered the previous carnival in Venice (1655/56), but with two other Roman women, Curti and Chiusi, portraying the lead roles.[32] Porri's Bolognese performance was celebrated by a publication, *Applausi canori di Pindo alla Signora Caterina Porri Romana*.[33] The twenty-eight-page booklet comprises a series of seventeen poems in Porri's honor written by sixteen authors, eleven of whom are identified by name.[34] It opens with an extended poem by the Roman Giovanni Pietro Monesio[35] in which he alludes to Porri's Roman birth, and her move to Venice: "O magnificent Siren, former splendor and pride of the Latin land; rightly you left your native shores and, yearning for glory, eager only for

---

[32] On the production of *Erismena* at S. Aponal, see Glixon and Glixon, "Marco Faustini Venetian Opera Production in the 1650s."

[33] Some sixteen years earlier, the performance of *Il ritorno d'Ulisse in patria* had been commemorated by a publication that celebrated a variety of members of the cast and the production team, rather than one singer alone. See Wolfgang Osthoff, "Zur Bologneser Aufführung von Monteverdis 'Ritorno di Ulisse' im Jahre 1640," in *Oesterreichische Akademie der Wissenschaften. Anzeiger der phil-hist. Klasse 1958.* Mitteilungen der Kommission für Musikforschung, Nr. 11, 155-160.

[34] The volume, published in Bologna by Giovanni Battista Ferroni, bears the date MDCLVI, but no libretto for *Erismena* survives from that year. A libretto does exist, however, for a 1661 performance of the same opera; it is possible, then, that the date on the celebratory volume is a misprint. Poems in Porri's honor were written by Giovanni Pietro Monesio, Giacinto Onofrio, Co. Vincenzo Marescotti, Orazio Passerini, "Confuso Accademico Intrepido", "G.D.F.," Alessio Bellaria, Laysnè (sonnet in French), Agesilao Romdidei, Flaminio Gracchi, "F. C.," N.N., Giovanni Francesco Bonomi, Camillo Ravaglia, and Giovanni Bolandi. A unique copy of the booklet survives in the Biblioteca Archiginnasio in Bologna. I am grateful to Robert Kendrick, who obtained a microfilm of the print for me. Bonomi, a member of the Bolognese Accademia de' Gelati, was the author of a number of books in prose, as well as a book of poetry. On the Teatro Formagliari see Graziano Ballerini and Elvidio Surian, "Bologna," *New Grove Dictionary of Opera*, 1, 531. See also Corrado Ricci, *I teatri di Bologna nei secoli XVII e XVIII: storia aneddotica* (Bologna: 1888).

[35] Monesio wrote one of the poems for Barbara Strozzi's *Diporti di Euterpe* (1659), as well as two texts set by Emperor Leopold I in Vienna: *La simpatia nell'odio overo Le amazoni amanti* (1664) and *Il Figlio prodigo* (between 1674 and 1684). His poetry for music was published in two separate volumes, *La Musa seria* and *La musa famigliare*, by Giuseppe Corvo and Bartolomeo Lupardi in 1674. On Monesio's Roman publications, see Saverio Franchi, *Drammaturgia romana: Repertorio bibliografico cronologico dei testi drammatici pubblicati a Roma e nel Lazio. Secolo XVII* (Rome: Edizioni di Storia e Letteratura, 1988). Franchi cites Monesio as the secretary of Cardinal Francesco Maidalchini, with a death date of 1684.

honors, you turned your steps towards the city of waves because there the Adriatic is used to strolling with wandering steps: the sea is the proper abode of sirens."[36] Most of the poems in the volume celebrate her portrayal of Erismena, highlighting the most dramatic moments in the opera. Two of the poems, however, by Camillo Ravaglia and Alessio Bellaria, praise the singer's modesty, as well as her voice. Porri's performance at the Teatro Formagliari (also known as the Guastavillani or dei Casali) points to the opportunities that would have been available to the prima donnas of Venice outside of the carnival season: other cities would have sought to compete for these singers who had performed on the elite stages of Venice. Our knowledge of such performances is, for the most part, limited by a lack of supporting archival evidence and, more specifically, by an absence of cast lists in most librettos of the time.

By the end of 1656 Bortolo had settled in to his new post as an accountant, and the couple had welcomed the birth of their first daughter, Santa, born on 8 November 1656. Two more children would follow: Lucietta in December 1657, and Giovanni Battista in November 1659.[37] At the baptisms, three different Venetian noblemen appeared as godfathers for the children: Nicolò Mocenigo, Nicolò Sagredo, and Nicolò Corner, respectively.[38] If we look at the birth dates of the children, we can see that they all were born before the start of a new carnival, hence conceived after the conclusion of the previous one. Was the timing of their births a remarkable coincidence, or had Porri come up with a fail-safe plan to insure that her pregnancies would not interfere with her annual appearances on the Venetian stage? In any case, Porri's career at the Grimani theater continued during those early years of her marriage. She still led the roster there during the impresario Faustini's first three years at the theater in the early 1660s, maintaining a constant salary of 100 doble (about 451 ducats).[39]

On 25 March 1665, Porri sent a letter to the Duke of Mantua requesting his assistance with a professional matter. It provides new information about her career, as well as her husband's participation in it. Porri wrote:

> I apply to the authoritative and gracious protection of Your Highness, my supreme Prince and Lord, in a most grave matter that concerns my liberty and my life. The Signori Casali of Bologna profess to obligate me to perform in the opera *Mutio* in their theater after Easter. They consider me engaged because Bortolo, my husband, wrote

---

[36] "O fastosa Sirena/Già del Latino suol pompa, e decoro/lasciasti con ragion la patria arena,/E a le glorie anelante/Avida sol d'onori/Volgesti il piede a la Cittade ondosa,/ Che se con piè vagante/L'adriatica Dori/Suol colà passeggiare:/ De le Sirene è propria stanza il Mare." Translation by Nello Barbieri.

[37] S. Antonin, Battesimi, 1652-1664.

[38] Nicolò Sagredo, later doge, was the dedicatee of Barbara Strozzi's *Diporti di Euterpe opera settima*, published in 1659.

[39] We do not have concrete evidence for each year in the last half of the decade, but a letter from the singer Gostanzo Piccardi (25 January 1659) mentions that the opera for that carnival season had not yet begun, and that Porri was gravely ill. ASF, MP, filza 5469, f. 630.

them a letter, [saying that] when they had set my honorarium for 100 doble, he, along with me, would serve them. But in truth, I never gave my assent; rather, [Bortolo] informed me in the abstract that we should go to Bologna and I, believing him to have said it in jest – as is his usual way – declared myself ready. But then, upon hearing that he had written to them, [and in order to] give them time to find someone in my place, I immediately took up my pen to advise those gentlemen that I could not, for appropriate reasons, bring myself to serve them. Not satisfied with this, they sent someone expressly to persuade me to come, to which I answered resolutely that I could not; they state in their letters that they will see that I remain obligated by Your Highness, and I believe that [by] now that they will have carried out something (although I can hardly believe it) to command me [to go] there. Nevertheless, in order not to link the esteem I enjoyed in Your Highness's theater with that of others, and, in hope of a good outcome, I dare, humbled, as one who lives meekly under your most happy protection, to implore you not only to concede to me the grace of my own liberty, but also to let me, as one of your own, remain protected from any other such attempt that might be undertaken...[40]

The letter tells us, aside from the fact that Bortolo was prone to "joking around," that he had come to play some part in managing Porri's career, in this case with unwelcome results. We can also see that the singer was maintaining a presence on stages outside Venice after the Carnival season, appearing in Mantua at the Ducal theater, and most probably in Bologna as well; other evidence points to a possible recruitment in Torino at about this same time.[41] Moreover, Porri felt confident enough about her connection to the Duke, who had undoubtedly heard her sing numerous times in Venice – he was a frequent visitor during the carnival season

---

[40] "Serenissima Altezza: In un mio gravissimo interesse concernete la mia libertà et la mia vita, ricoro alla auttorevole et benigna prottetione dell'Altezza Vostra, mio supremo Prencipe et Signore. Professano li Signori Casali di Bologna obligarmi a recitar nel loro theatro l'opera del *Mutio* doppo Pasqua, et mi stimano impegnata, per che Bortolo mio marito gli abbi scritta una lettera, che quando resti stabilito l'honorario in doble cento, egli meco sarebbe stato a servirli. Ma la verità è che io non ho mai prestato l'assenso, solo che significatomi egli in astrato che si doveva andare a Bologna, credendo io detto per scherzo, come è suo solito, dissi esser pronta. Ma intesone poi che gli haveva scritto, immediate presa la penna avisai quelli cavallierri in tempo che facessero provisione d'a[l]tro soggetto, che io non potevo per convenienti rispetti portarmi a servirli. Non appagatisi di ciò hanno inviato persona aposta per persuadermi alla qualle ho rissolutamente risposto di non potere; motivono in loro lettere di far in modo ch'io resti obligata da Vostra Altezza, et credo sino a questa hora - s'haverano eseguito cosa, che se bene non credo, sij per comandarmela per non accomunare il preggio ch'io goduto nel Teatro di Vostra Altezza con quello d'altri. Tuttavia ad ogni buon fine ardisco humiliata supplicarla che come quella che vive rassignata sotto li suoi felicissimi auspicij, non solo mi concedi la gratia della propria liberta ma anzi come cosa sua, resti preservato da qualunqe altro attentato fossero [per] intraprendere..." Archivio di Stato di Mantova, Archivio Gonzaga, filza 1574, 24 March 1665. Punctuation has been changed in order to clarify the sense of the passage.

[41] Giovanni Antonio Cavagna, a singer at Torino, made reference to the recruitment of Porri for two operas planned in commemoration of the Duke of Savoy's marriage. ASV, Scuola grande di S. Marco (henceforth SGSM), b. 188, f. 100, 6 April 1665.

and a friend of the Grimanis – that she could ask for his help.[42] What effect did Porri's letter have on her problems with the Bolognese impresarios? Her follow-up letter to the Duke suggests that he had offered no assistance in the matter, so she probably went through with the engagement at the Teatro Formagliari.[43] The opera, Cavalli's *Mutio scevola*, had been performed just the previous month at the Teatro S. Luca in Venice, the rival theater to the Grimani, and Porri may have been one of the singers in the production, as she was certainly employed there by the subsequent season. What had caused her to move over to the competition, given her decade-long service to the Grimani theater? Did the prima donna market in Venice operate like a game of "musical chairs," with the singers shifting venue in order to garner the best wages or working conditions?

The yearly bidding for prima donnas was a constant preoccupation for impresarios, and very likely also a worry for the singers. New talents constantly entered the market, inevitably changing the *status quo*, and such was the case in Venice in 1663. That year Porri still held top billing at SS. Giovanni e Paolo, but S. Luca, for its third season as an opera theater, brought in a singer previously unheard in Venice, the Roman Giulia Masotti. Masotti created a tremendous sensation, and one listener remarked that she had stolen the "glory" from Porri, something that apparently had not happened before.[44] Giovanni Grimani had been angered and offended by Masotti's stunning success at S. Luca. Grimani's reaction, however, stemmed in part from considerations other than his quest to obtain the best singers for his theater. The situation was far more complicated, for Masotti had been brought to S. Luca by Grimani's own cousin, Vettor Grimani Calergi, who was active that year at S. Luca in competition against his own family's theater. Giovanni Grimani and his successors at SS. Giovanni e Paolo would recruit Masotti for several years running, so that Porri finally left that theater, her home base, to move on to S. Luca.[45] Evidence suggests that she sang

---

[42] Evidence of the Duke of Mantua's visits to Venice can be found in diplomatic accounts within the Venetian government (Collegio, Espositioni principi), and in the dispatches of various diplomatic representatives in Venice from Florence and Modena.

[43] The Gonzaga papers for 1665, unfortunately, lack any letters, either from the Casali brothers, or from any other principals of the theater in Bologna, that pertain to Porri's recruitment. I would like to thank Jonathan Glixon for his assistance in searching those papers for evidence of the problem between Porri and the Casali.

[44] "... Ho sentito a recitar due drami in una sera, uno al teatro di S. Gio. Paolo, e l'altro a quello di S. Luca, tutti due veramente bellissimi per le macchine, scene, et habiti, e per l'eccellenza de musici, che sono invero perfettissimi, per lo contrario non meritando gran lode queli c'hanno composto le parole. Sopra l'altre cose vi è una donna nuova venuta di Roma c'ha tolto tutto il vanto a Catterina Porri, tanto è piaciuta, e certo non si può migliorare nè in voce, nè in rappresentazione d'affetti." Archivio di Stato di Ferrara, Archivio Bentivoglio, Lettere sciolte, b. 337, ff. 86-87, Florio Tori to Sante Magnani, Venice 17 January 1663. See Sergio Monaldini, *L'Orto dell'Esperidi: Musici, attori e artisti nel patrocinio della famiglia Bentivoglio (1646-1685)*, 179. Masotti is mentioned by name in other letters in the collection. My reading varies slightly from Monaldini's.

[45] For more on the recruiting of Masotti, see Rosand, *Opera in Seventeenth-Century Venice*, 239-240 and Glixon, "Private Lives of Public Women," 524-526. Masotti's career

there for the remainder of the decade, although not always in the most favorable circumstances.

As a new opera theater, S. Luca did not, in its early years, have a reliable financial base. Apparently Porri's wages were not paid promptly for the 1665/66 season;[46] the next year rumors surfaced that the theater would not operate owing to its debts, and Porri, for a time, was considered for the lead role at SS. Giovanni e Paolo in place of Giulia Masotti.[47] Porri did evidently sing at S. Luca for the 1666/67 season, however, but made sure that her salary was guaranteed by a group of businessmen.[48] Two years later she was still at the theater, joined by Masotti, who sang the title role in Cesti's *Argia* to Porri's Dorisbe.[49] The financial problems at S. Luca had not abated, however, and Porri, along with a number of other singers in the cast (but not Masotti) saw far less than her promised wages at the end of that season.[50] One account suggests that she was to sing the following year (1669/70) at S. Moisé, a smaller theater with a spotty record of opera production.[51]

I mentioned earlier that Porri's childbearing had occurred outside the carnival season, so that those milestones of her marriage did not interfere with her career. In the final episode of her marriage, however, she was less fortunate. Bortolo died after a brief illness, on 2 March 1666, precisely one week before the end of the very long carnival season in which Porri appeared at S. Luca in Antonio Sartorio's *Seleuco* and Francesco Cavalli's *Pompeo Magno*, both to librettos by Nicolò Minato. One day before his death, Bortolo dictated his will, which was filled with numerous references to his "dearest and most beloved wife," to whom he left his worldly goods for her own use, and that of their three children. He asked her to

---

will be discussed further in Glixon and Glixon, *Marco Faustini and Opera Production in Seventeenth-Century Venice* (forthcoming).

[46] ASV, Avogaria di comun, b. 2193 /143, 5 May 1666. Porri had gone to one of the Venetian courts, apparently in efforts to see her contract fulfilled.

[47] ASV, SGSM, b. 188, f. 294, undated letter of Marco Faustini concerning the 1666/67 season.

[48] ASV, Archivio notarile, Atti Cristoforo Brombilla, b.1166, f. 277, 4 January 1667.

[49] Porri's and Masotti's roles are revealed in a collection of poems appearing in Rome, Biblioteca Apostolica Vaticana, MS Ottoboniani latini 2861. I am grateful to Margaret Murata, who provided transcriptions of the titles of the poems.

[50] An account sheet for the season surviving in the Casa Goldoni is reproduced in Rosand, 197. Nicolò Minato, one of the impresarios, apparently had not fully repaid Porri for her services even in 1674, when she authorized a businessman to collect her credit with the librettist (ASV, Notarile atti, Alvise Centoni, b.3838, f. 452v, 29 September 1674). In 1672 Minato had signed a repayment agreement with various creditors, including Porri, who was owed D600 at the time (see Venice, Casa Goldoni, Archivio Vendramin, 42F 6/2, f. 30).

[51] "Quelli da S Moisè nè ha un cane, che lo guardi, mentre è infelice la comp[agni]a. La opera poi ha questa disdetta, d'essersi amalata Catarina Porri, onde si differiscono le recite." Hannover, Staatsarchiv, Aktes-Korrespondenzen italienischer Kardinäle und anderer Personen, besonders Italiener an Herzog Johann Friedrich, Cal. Br. 22, vol. 2, no. 625, f. 407, Letter of Pietro Dolfin, 3 January 1670. I am grateful to Ellen Rosand for sharing her films of this valuable collection of letters with me.

provide for the education of their children, and also that she "live with her usual, utmost prudence."[52]

Widowhood

After Bortolo's death, Porri followed the path of so many Venetian widows before her, and initiated the process to reclaim her dowry. On 17 June 1666 she appeared before one of the Venetian courts, the "Giudici del Proprio," the governmental office responsible for the restitution of dowries either to widows themselves after the death of their husbands, or in the case of the wife's death, to her own family or descendants.[53] The text of Porri's dowry, unlike so many others, was not copied into the Proprio's registers, but a separate notation, on 9 May 1667, lists its components (in five sections) ranging from 900 ducats to six thousand, with a total value of D10500.[54] The portions correspond to various categories of property, here unspecified, such as jewelry, paintings, cash, furniture, and clothing. A dowry of this size would have been viewed as unusually large during this period for non-noble women, or for one not marrying into the nobility. Indeed, the amount surpasses that found for all other singers of the period. Lucietta Gamba, a singer of opera but also a courtesan, brought a dowry of over 8000 ducats to her marriage in 1661, but others were substantially lower.[55] Elena Passarelli's dowry in 1658 amounted only to D2100, while Silvia Manni's, in 1645, was slightly higher, at D2400.[56] Even dowries of D2000 were far larger than that offered by many women, however; the sculptor and painter Clemente Molli, for example, accepted a dowry of D700 when he married a woman named Maria Bonelli in 1640.[57]

One of the steps necessary to the restitution of dowry funds was an evaluation of the household property, and such an inventory appeared in a separate listing in the Proprio's records on 10 May 1667. It would seem to reveal the trappings of a very comfortable life, with several indications of Porri's wealth. A large portion of the value of the dowry must have derived from the value of Porri's clothing. Scholars writing about both the sixteenth and seventeenth centuries have pointed to the *"camicia"* (a thin blouse, often seen in portraits of the time) as one indicator of

---

[52] "...solo che prego la Signora Cattarina vivere con la sua solita, et soma prudenza..." ASV, Archivio notarile, Testamamenti Fabio Lio Turighello, b. 997, no. 36.

[53] For a clear synthesis of matters concerning dowries and their restitution during the mid-*seicento*, see Isabella Cecchini, "Nuovi dati su Clemente Molli," *Arte Veneta* 52 (1999): 147-151. For a comprehensive study of Venetian dowries, particularly during the Renaissance, see Stanley Chojnacki, *Women and Men in Renaissance Venice: Twelve Essays on Patrician Society* (Baltimore and London: Johns Hopkins University Press, 2000), esp. chapters 3, 4, and 6.

[54] ASV, Giudici del Proprio, Lezze e giudice delegato, b. 123. f. 88, 9 May 1667.

[55] On Gamba, see Glixon, "Private Lives of Public Women," 522-524.

[56] For Passarelli's dowry, see ASV, Archivio notarile, Atti Giovanni Antonio Generini, b. 6800, f. 309, 15 September 1678. For Manni, Ibid., Atti Beazian e Bronzini, b. 662, f.116v, 2 October 1645.

[57] Cecchini, "Nuovi dati su Clemente Molli," 147-151.

wealth. The noted costume historian, Rosita Levi Pisetzky, singled out the 1644 inventory of a Venetian noblewoman, remarking on Cecilia Contarini's forty-two *camicie*.[58]   Porri's collection would seem to have exceeded even that noblewoman's, for she possessed sixty of them, over half of them embellished with lace. Moreover, we can make a direct comparison of Porri's collection with those of the singers Manni and Passarelli who, in their dowry inventories, listed thirty-six and fifteen of them, respectively; according to the values in Passarelli's inventory of 1658, Porri's *camicie* would have been worth several hundred ducats.[59]

One striking element of the inventory is the nature of Porri's garments. In contrast to the wide range of colors evident in typical dowry lists, here we find a variety of apparel in black (and musk) – Porri's widow attire – complemented by several in more typical shades of red and scarlet. According to custom, Porri's richly colorful wardrobe would have been shed in order to don the widow's garb. Clothing in black, on the other hand, did not necessarily signify plain, humble garments; rather, paintings of seventeenth-century noblewomen often portray rich, sumptuous costumes in black. Many of Porri's dresses were executed in fabrics of velvet, silk, satin, and wool, and bore decorations of black lace.[60] Following the death of Bortolo, then, Porri's appearance on the stage – with her wardrobe of costly confections of gold or other rich colors – would have contrasted sharply with that of her everyday life.[61]

Porri's collection of jewelry, valued at around D1430, contained a variety of items. Like many of her contemporaries she owned hundreds of pearls, fashioned in necklaces, chokers, and earrings.   Diamonds were featured in bracelets, earrings, a ring, and a brooch (with twenty-five diamonds), while other pieces included amber, garnets and rubies.[62] It is very likely that at least some of this jewelry had been given as gifts from wealthy patrons and admirers, a common practice of the time.[63] Another entry in the inventory specified the weight of the

---

[58] Rosita Levi Pisetzky, *Storia del costume in Italia* (Milan: Istituto Editoriale italiano: 1966), 3:399.

[59] For Passarelli's inventory, see ASV, Archivio notarile, Atti Generini, b. 6800. f. 310-11; for Manni's, ASV, Archivio notarile, Atti Beazian and Bronzini, b. 662, ff. 117-117v.

[60] Some of the fabrics mentioned are *seda* and *cenda* (both types of silk), *veludo* (velvet), and *raso* (satin).

[61] For a fascinating look at a female artist's paintings of widows and their garb, see Caroline P. Murphy, "Livinia Fontana and Female Life Cycle Experience in Late Sixteenth-Century Bologna," in: *Picturing Women in Renaissance and Baroque Italy*, ed. Geraldine A. Johnson and Sara F. Matthews Grieco (Cambridge: Cambridge University Press, 1997), 111-138, 272-277. For an introduction to the subject of widowhood in early modern Europe – as well as a copious bibliography – see Sandra Cavallo and Lyndan Warner, eds., *Widowhood in Medieval and Early Modern Europe* (Singapore: Longman, 1999).

[62] The jewelry was valued at D1432 .   For a history of jewelry in Venice, see Piero Pazzi, *I Gioielli nella civiltà veneziana* (Treviso: Tipografia Zoppelli, 1995).

[63] On a necklace given to Monteverdi, see Denis Stevens, "Monteverdi's Necklace," *The Musical Quarterly* 59 (1973): 370-381. Various dispatches mention gifts of jewelry to

household silver, which would have included things such as serving pieces and platters; this amounted to nearly six hundred ducats, or about six times that owned by the impresario Marco Faustini at the time of his death. Also singled out were two musical instruments, a spinet inlaid with ivory and including ivory keys, and a harpsichord. While the very wealthy of Venice possessed furniture, clothing, gold, silver, and jewelry far beyond Porri's, this inventory nonetheless reflects the rewards of a successful life on the Venetian stage.

One of the most intriguing features of the inventory are the works of art that are listed intermittently among the other items, some forty-eight in all. Although none of them were attributed, some of the artists' names (as well as the paintings' values) can be obtained by a comparison with a later inventory compiled in 1678. Those mentioned there include such popular Veneto artists as Pietro Bellotti, Joseph Heintz, Johann Karl Loth, Antonio Zanchi (and the less well-known Stefano Paulucci), as well as the Florentine Carlo Dolci. One work was a picture of the Madonna executed in needlework;[64] fourteen others, *"quadri di devotion"* (devotional pictures), may have been printed devotional drawings, twelve of which, in this case, had been colored.[65] Two other groupings included six narrative paintings (*quadri d'historia*) and ten small landscapes (*paeseti*).

One group of five paintings – displayed together – appears to have constituted the most valuable part of the collection: *Mary Magdalene* by Loth, *Saint Helena* by Zanchi, *Saint Cecilia* by Dolci, an un-attributed *Saint Catherine* [of Alexandria], and, finally, *Saint Mary of Egypt* (in a carved frame, the only one so designated), also by Loth, and almost certainly a companion piece to the *Mary Magdalene*.[66] In 1678 the *Saint Cecilia* was valued at D350 (by far the single most valuable painting in the collection), and the works by Zanchi and Loth at D80 each. Saint Cecilia, of course, was the patron saint of music – most appropriate for a prima donna – and Saint Catherine, naturally, would have been Porri's name saint. Two of the other choices in the group, however, are even more intriguing. Saint Mary Magdalene, traditionally viewed as a reformed prostitute, was worshipped by all penitents. But she also retained an association with her former profession, especially in Venice, where the convent of S. Maria Maddalena (the Convertite)

---

singers. For instance, in 1673 according to a Florentine government agent, Matteo Teglia, Antonia Coresi was given some diamond jewelry worth fifty doppie (about D225). See ASF, MP, filza 1573, f. 1048v, 1 February 1673.

[64] Needlework art must have been relatively common during this time. Even the inventory of the possessions of Cardinal Leopoldo de' Medici (taken in 1675) boasts two such works: "un quadro di punto con seta di più colori entrovi al naturale il giudizio di Paride..." and "un quadro fattovi di punto o ricamo, la testa della Madonna..." Miriam Fileti Mazza, *Eredità del Cardinale Leopoldo de' Medici: 1675-1676* (Pisa: Scuola Normale Superiore, 1997), 39, 75.

[65] "Quadri di devotion numero 12; due detti senza pittura." ASV, Proprio, Mobili, b. 253, f. 9.

[66] "quadri numero cinque, cioè uno di Madalena, altro di Santa Elena; altro di Santa Cecilia, altro di Santa Cattarina, et altro di Santa Maria Eggiciacca soazze di legno intagiade" Ibid., f. 8.

housed courtesans and prostitutes "converted" from a life of sin to one of religion.[67] Saint Mary of Egypt, cited variously as a reformed actress, singer, or prostitute, was also revered by penitents and, more particularly, by reformed prostitutes. Identified images of her occur far less frequently, perhaps in part owing to a confusion between the two saints, whose stories came to resemble each other in a number of aspects.[68]

Although we will never know the specific motivations behind the acquisition and display of these five paintings, and especially the significance they held for Porri, the presence of the *Mary Magdalene/Saint Mary of Egypt* pair is certainly striking.[69] Although Magdalene paintings are extremely common in seventeenth century Venetian inventories, Saint Mary of Egypt is far less so. One famous pair still extant in Venice today is that by Tintoretto, housed in the Scuola Grande di S. Rocco. The placement of this pair of saints around the valuable Saint Cecilia would seem to suggest some special meaning for Porri, perhaps pointing both to a private association with the penitents and also to a semi-public sentiment apparent to select visitors in Porri's home.[70] Did Porri, who supported herself through a profession seen by many as less than reputable, take comfort from these fallen women who had found salvation through religion? Did she draw some special solace from the veneration of these saints? These questions lead us back to the value of Porri's dowry, and even to the nature of her marriage.

We saw earlier how the value of Porri's dowry (D10,500) was extremely high in comparison to those of other young singers (and indeed other young women) of the time. It seems unlikely that she could have accumulated that sum solely from her earnings on the stage: even if she had been singing professionally

---

[67] See Susan Haskins, *Mary Magdalen: Myth and Metaphor* (New York: Riverhead Books, 1993), 282-284. On Mary Magdalen and music, see H. Colin Slim, "Mary Magdalene, Musician and Dancer," *Early Music* 8 (1980): 460-473, and Christopher L.C.E. Witcombe, "The Chapel of the Courtesan and the Quarrel of the Magdalens," *The Art Bulletin* 84 (2002): 273-292.

[68] On Mary Magdalen (and Saint Mary of Egypt), see Haskins, *Mary Magdalen: Myth and Metaphor*. Both women were said to have lived as hermits, clothed only in their long hair. Haskins explores Mary Magdalen through religious readings, art, and music.

[69] Loth is said to have come to Venice in 1656, so that the paintings must date from that year, or later. On Loth in Venice, see Jonathan Bikker, "Drost's End and Loth's Beginnings in Venice," *The Burlington Magazine* 144 (2002): 147-156. An inventory taken at the time of Loth's death includes a Magdalene/S. Mary of Egypt pair. See Margareta Lux, "L'inventario di Johann Carl Loth" *Arte veneta* 54 (1999): 146-164. One example of the confusion that has existed amidst images of the two saints may be seen in a *Saint Mary of Egypt* by Pietro Liberi in Praglia (Padova), cited in an inventory as a "Maddalena." See Ugo Ruggieri, *Pietro e Marco Liberi: Pittori nella Venezia del Seicento* (Rimini: Stefano Patacconi Editore, 1996), 180-181. Liberi's painting features a lion, thus suggesting the image of Mary of Egypt rather than Mary Magdalene (a lion is said to have helped dig Mary of Egypt's grave).

[70] It would be interesting to know more of the painting collections of other singers, and of the types of religious and secular art they collected and exhibited. Unfortunately, no such inventories of Porri's contemporaries have as yet come to light.

for as many as four or five years when she married, the salaries of that time would not have been sufficient to gather such a figure in so short a period. Her father or mother may have contributed a good part of the dowry, but as yet we have no knowledge of the family's situation, and – unlike with the Romans Anna Renzi and Angelica Felice Curti – no surviving notarial records point to the maintenance or transferal of funds secured in Rome. Yet even if the family had contributed funds, why was the dowry so large in the first place? Had Porri been drawn to, or had she been in danger of succumbing to the ways of the courtesan? Could some wealthy patron and admirer have supplied a large portion of the dowry, easing Caterina's way into a more honorable state through the sanctity of matrimony?

Whatever the situation before her marriage, as a widow Porri found herself (as did other singers) an independent women of some means. Like several other singers before her, such as Anna Renzi and Barbara Strozzi, she began to carry out financial transactions, lending money to noblemen and *cittadini*, something neither she nor Bortolo had apparently done during his lifetime.[71] While she loaned only D300 to Antonio Cesana in early 1667, transactions in 1671 and 1672 amounted to D1000 and D1100 respectively. Several years later, in 1678, she invested D2000 – previously in an account of her dowry funds – with six brothers from the Morosini family.[72] Daniel Morosini was the godfather of Porri's grandson, baptized on 29 March 1677.[73] Porri's residence in Venice changed as well. By 1669 she had left her lodgings in S. Antonin, perhaps for the first time since 1653 or 1654, and moved across the city to a different parish, S. Martial.[74]

Porri's career continued to flourish much as it had before. The influx of new prima donnas such as Giulia Masotti, who had come to Venice only with the promise of extremely high fees, had a beneficial effect on Porri's income. For the 1666/67 season at S. Luca, appearing in *La prosperità di Elio Seiano* and *La caduta di Elio Seiano*, she earned 1000 scudi (D1500), a sum over three times what her fees had been in the earlier part of the decade, and two years later her fees rose slightly, to D1550 for her appearance in Antonio Cesti's *Argia*, also at S. Luca.[75] Earnings such as this placed her among the more privileged residents of Venice,

---

[71] On Renzi's and Strozzi's financial transactions see Glixon, "Private Lives of Public Women" and Glixon, "New Light on the Life and Career of Barbara Strozzi," *Musical Quarterly* 81 (1997): 311-335.

[72] For the loan of D300 in 1667 to Antonio Cesana (cancelled in July 1669), see ASV, Archivio notarile, Atti Francesco Simbeni, b.12059, f.157, 9 July 1669. For the loan of D1000 to the nobleman Francesco Condulmer, see ASV, Archivio notarile, Atti Generini, b. 6793, f. 92v, 26 May 1671. On 10 May 1672 Porri loaned D1100 (along with the doctor Girolamo Rota, who contributed a further D600) to Francesco Azzo; see ASV, Archivio notarile, Atti Raffaele Todeschini, b.12675, f. 71. Finally, on 3 February 1678. Porri loaned D2000 to the brothers Pollo, Daniel, Marc'Antonio, Zuanne, Giacomo, and Zaccaria Morosini, sons of Andrea Morosini (see ASV, Archivio notarile, Atti Iseppo Bellan, b. 1340 bis, f. 696v).

[73] ASPV, Parrocchia di S. Benedetto. Battesimi, 1577-1677, f. 341.

[74] ASV, Archivio notarile, Atti Francesco Simbeni, b.12059, f.157, 9 July 1669.

[75] ASV, Archivio notarile, Atti Cristoforo Brombilla, b. 1166, f. 277, 4 January 1667.

and attracted the attention of at least one suitor. In October of 1667, some nineteen months following the death of her husband, Porri appeared once more before the officials of the Church in Venice, this time along with a Venetian lawyer, Pietro Antonio Ordano.

Both Porri and Ordano wished to marry, but without the traditional public reading of the banns;[76] they had different reasons for desiring this sort of marriage. Porri sought to protect the financial well-being of her children. According to the testimony of two witnesses, it was understood that Bortolo's uncle, Francesco Caresana, would leave his fortune to Porri's children (who were apparently the last ones surviving along the male line of that branch of the Caresanas from Cureglia), but only should Porri remain a widow.[77] Ordano, too, had an elderly relative from whom he hoped to inherit money, and he feared he might lose his inheritance should his marriage to Porri become known. One of the witnesses questioned regarding their petition described the prospective husband's concerns in this way: "should Signor Ordano's relatives come to know of this marriage that he intends to contract with Signora Catterina, he would suffer greatly in his [financial] pretentions, as well as regarding his reputation, [primarily] because Signora Catterina is a singer who has always performed in public theaters."[78] Ordano, then, felt that his family – apparently unlike that of Bortolo Caresana's during the 1650s and early 1660s – would have resorted to some sort of punishment should he marry a famous performer. This was the paradox that surrounded female singers: they could be adored, adulated, and admired within the highest ranks of Venetian society, but propriety demanded that they not commingle with those admirers in any sort of marital relationship, even when the prospective husband was not of the noble class. In marrying Porri, Ordano would undoubtedly have been flouting tradition, because lawyers in Venice almost always married someone of the *cittadino* class (at the same societal level), or in some cases, a woman of the noble class. Whatever their intention, however, the couple's marriage plans never came to fruition; no further entries appear in the Church registers concerning their petition, and later documents concerning Porri speak against the possibility of the marriage.

Porri and Ordano's relationship became an issue several years later, however, in an anonymous and undated accusation placed, in 1670, in one of the "lion's mouths," boxes dedicated to the collection of secret denunciations. The document, through its heightened rhetorical stance, compellingly accuses Ordano of sinister acts worthy of punishment:

---

[76] For more on secret marriages during this time, see Alexander Cowan, "Patricians and Partners in Early Modern Venice," in: *Medieval and Renaissance Venice*, ed. Ellen E. Kittell and Thomas F. Madden (Urbana: University of Illinois Press, 1999), 276-293.

[77] Francesco Caresana had two stepchildren, but no biological children.

[78] "...e sapendosi il matrimonio da essi parenti, che detto Signor Ordano intende contraher con detta Signora Catterina, discapitarebbe molto ne' suoi interessi, et anco nella riputatione, per esser massime detta Signora Catterina Cantatrice, ch'è stata sempre a recitare ne' publici theatri." ASPV, Examinum Matrimoniorum, b. 100, 1667-1668, f. 315v, 8 October 1667.

Pietro Antonio Ordano, who was the bastard son of the late doctor of Swiss descent, holds the job of prosecutor in the Illustrious Office of the Inspector. In past months, having spent time in the house of Cattarina Pori, and having had carnal intercourse with her, he aspired, beyond the mere enjoyment of the woman herself, to gain possession of her belongings, which consisted of a considerable amount of cash, jewels, silver, and notable household goods. Bortolo Caresana, the husband of Porri, despite becoming aware of this domestic situation, and the frequent visits [of Ordano], tolerated it with patience in order to avoid further disgrace. In any case, the unhappy man could not [free himself] from death, which the wicked Ordano deemed necessary in order to establish a permanent and secure situation for his profligacy; he therefore established in his mind the intention to remove from this world the poor Caresana. Executing his diabolical resolution, he got, from a diamond worker – who will appear among the witnesses named below – a certain quantity of chips, or diamond dust. Given repeatedly to the wretched man in fresh eggs, porridge, syrups, and in other forms, the substance did its deadly work within days: his internal organs eaten away, the unhappy one rendered his soul unto God. The villain having in this manner made himself the master of this woman, tried also to gain possession of her things, flattering her with promises of marriage. Knowing his perfidious nature, however, she did not respond with complete fervor, nor did she allow him to meddle in her business affairs. She told him that when she had married him, then, as his wife, she would assign to him as her dowry that which they had agreed to. But he, who desired nothing more than to steal her belongings, was cheating her by playing a waiting game. Finally the above-mentioned Porri realized that fact with certainty, and evicted him from the house...[79]

---

[79] "Pietro Antonio Ordano, che fu figlio bastardo del quondam medico Ordano di natione Sguizzera, che essercita la carica di fiscale nel officio Illustrissimo del Sindico, praticando li mesi passati nella casa di Cattarina Pori, et havendo seca comercio carnale, aspirava oltre il godimento della dona ad'inpossessarsi di suoi haveri, che consistevano in suma considerabile di denari contanti, gioie, argentarie, e riguardevoli supeletili di casa. Bortolo Caresana, marito di detta Pori, benché s'accorgesse di questa domestica, e frequente pratica, tolerava però con pacienza, per non incorere in maggior disgratia, ad ogni modo non pottè l'infelice essimersi dalla morte, che fu riputata dall'empio Ordano necessario per stabilirsi un comodo permanente, e sicuro alla sua sfrenatezza; è però stabil[ì] nel suo animo di levar dal mondo il povero Caresana, et essequendo il sua diabolico proponimento pigliò da un diamantero (che sarà da gl'infrascritti testimonij nominato) certa quantità di scaglie, ò polvere di diamante, che replicata più volte al meschino in ovi freschi, panada, siroppi, et in altra forma, facendo la sua mortifera operatione in pochi giorni corose le viscere all'infelice rese l'anima a Dio. Fatto in questa forma il scelerato libero padrone della donna, tentò anco d'inpadronirsi della robba, lusingandola con promesse di sposarla, essa però conoscendo la natura perfida di costui, non le prestò tutta la ardenza, onde andava ristretta nel corrisponderli dinaro, ne lasciava, che s'ingerisse con quella libertà da lui pretesa, ne suoi interessi dicendole, che quando l'havesse sposata all'hora come sua moglie l'havrebbe assegnato in dotte quello si fosse tra loro stabilita, ma lui che ad'altro non aspirava che a rapirlila robba, andava temporrgiando schernendola, di che finalmente con sicurezza avedutasi la sudetta Pori li diede l'esilio di Casa..." ASV, Consiglio dei dieci, Criminal, filza 103, 11 April 1670. I would like to thank Nello Barbieri and Mauro Calcagno for their assistance with the translation.

The accusation, which we cannot automatically accept as fact, takes a firm stance on the identity of the guilty party, and casts Porri in a rather benign light (other than her apparent extramarital relations with Ordano). The accuser sees Ordano, driven by his desire for the singer's ample worldly goods, as the perpetrator of evil crimes; Porri, if not portrayed as a faithful wife or grieving widow, is granted the writer's tacit approval for turning Ordano out of her house. The writer has also refrained from drawing attention to Porri's professional life, and any negative associations that would have invoked. She appears merely as a wealthy woman inhabiting a private world, not as a public singer or cultural icon. Did the writer feel that Porri's professional persona was irrelevant to the case, or did he ignore the issue in order to avoid interference from Porri's noble friends and supporters, who most likely would have come to her assistance?

These two accounts of Porri and Ordano's relationship, one gathered from their efforts to marry in 1667, and the other from an anonymous denunciation presented in 1670, just over four years after Bortolo Caresana's death, come together in a difficult manner. When was the denunciation written? It would seem that by 1670, the romance was long over. Read in isolation, without knowledge of the marriage plans, the denunciation would seem to imply that Porri had tired of Ordano within months of her husband's death. Could its author have been unaware of the true nature and duration of the relationship? One curious factor is the timing of the denunciation. It surely can be no coincidence that Bortolo's will, which had been opened the day of his death, came to be examined (or reexamined) by the tax authorities at the Magistrato delle Acque on 10 April 1670, the day after the denunciation was collected from the box where it had been secretly deposited.[80] Whatever suspicions may have been aroused, either before the accusation or after it, Ordano seems to have escaped prosecution by the Council of Ten, the government body to whom the denunciation was forwarded. Moreover, although I have found no sources linking Porri and Ordano after 1667, Ordano remained on friendly terms with Girolamo Rota, the Roman doctor who had treated Bortolo at the time of his death, and who himself stayed close to Porri in the ensuing decade.[81] The story of Porri and Ordano, then, is open to many interpretations, none of which can be substantiated without further documentation.

Porri most likely continued to perform in Venice during the early 1670s, but sang in Naples, instead, during the carnival of 1674. One correspondent had written in the months preceding that season: "This year we will neither see nor hear the ancient siren of the Adriatic, Caterina Porri. She is going to Naples with

---

[80] The notation on the will reads " Intimata parte offitij Illustrissimi aquarum, 1666 2 marzo. Gasparo Acerbi Cancellier Ducale. Adì 10 Aprile 1670 visto all'Aque, A[vocato] F[iscale]" In normal circumstances, the Magistrato alle acque would have registered a will within days of its probation.

[81] One final irony is that the doctor Rota was murderously attacked in 1678 by someone who, apparently, cultivated a friendship with him in order to gain access to his house; coveting the doctor's jewels, the so-called friend orchestrated an assault on Rota. See ASV, Consiglio dei dieci, Criminal, filza 112, 3 July 1679.

Padre Ziani, who is the Orpheus who will take her away."[82] Was Porri's temporary transferal to Naples an indication that her status as prima donna had begun to slip? That year marked the twentieth anniversary of her debut in Venice, so by that time she had outlived the active careers of a great many of her contemporaries. Porri performed in Naples at the famous Teatro S. Bartolomeo, presumably in all three operas mounted that season.[83] The theater had the rare distinction of being run by a female impresario, the apparently infamous courtesan and singer Giulia de Carro. So far the research of Paologiovanni Maione has not shown any other performances at S. Bartolomeo by Porri or by her Venetian contemporaries.

The report of Porri's travels to Naples brings to a close what little knowledge we have of the singer's performances during the 1670s. One year after the trip her daughter Lucietta married a lawyer, Nadalin Merlo, providing him with a comfortable dowry of 2000 ducats. Porri's other daughter, Santa, had by this time become a nun in S. Marco e Andrea, a convent on the island of Murano.[84] Three years later another marriage transpired in the family: not that of her son, but, finally, the remarriage of Porri herself, some twelve years after the death of her first husband.[85]

---

[82] "Si preparano li theatri; un solo, et il Grimano per le opere; e li altri per altre compagnie de comici. Quest'anno non vederemo, e non udiremo la sirena antica dell'Adriatico, Caterina Porri. Questa è ita via a Napoli col Padre Ziani, che è il suo Orfeo conduttore; Van seco due altri musici, il castrato Mocenigo, et un altro." Hannover, Staatsarchiv, Aktes-Korrespondenzen italienischer Kardinäle und anderer Personen, besonders Italiener an Herzog Johann Friedrich, Cal. Br. 22, No. 627, f. 413, 3 November 1673. On Porri's appearance in Naples, see Paologiovanni Maione, "Giulia de Caro 'seu Ciulla' da commediante a cantarina: osservazioni sulla condizione degli "armonici" nella seconda metà del Seicento," *Rivista italiana di musicologia* 32 (1997): 61-80 (72-74). Porri was paid D50 on 10 March 1674 as a final installment. Presumably Porri was characterized as "ancient" by virtue of her nearly two decades on the Venetian stage.

[83] Maione, 65. The operas Porri would have performed in are *Marcello in Siracusa*, (Ziani/Boretti, November 1673); *Eraclio* (Ziani/Giovanni Cicinello, December 1673); and *Massenzio* (Sartorio, Carnival 1673/74).

[84] ASV, Monasterio di SS. Marco e Andrea di Murano, b. 9, Quaderno cassa, 1670-1688, entries on 14 April 1671 and 21 November 1684. I would like to thank Jonathan Glixon for sharing this data with me.

[85] Bortolo's uncle had indeed died (in 1676) before Porri married for the second time. Francesco Caresana left each of Porri's children 100 ducats plus, for Giovanni Battista, some land in his native Cureglia, or the equivalent sum of D200. This inheritance may well have been much less than the singer had hoped for when she adjusted her marriage plans with Ordano in 1667 in order to comply with the wishes of the elder Caresana. In the end, however, Francesco left the bulk of his estate to his wife, Angela Pesenti, and after her death, to her two children from her first marriage, rather than to his nephew's heirs, or other relatives in Cureglia. For Francesco Caresana's will, see ASV, Archivio notarile, Testamenti Giovanni Piccini, b. 935, no. 63.

Life after Venice:　Porri's marriage to Ercole Mezzetti and her appearances in Bologna and Pavia

On 3 September 1678 two witnesses, the priest Giovanni Maria Balbi and the ragseller Antonio Rosetti (both former neighbors from her years at S. Antonin) appeared before the church authorities, attesting to Porri's status as a widow.[86] The testimonies do not mention Ordano or any possible marriage plans with Porri. She was described merely as the wife and widow of Bortolo Caresana. Also irrelevant to the proceedings this time, apparently, was Porri's reputation as a singer on the public stage; that issue simply never arose.

Porri chose as her second husband a Bolognese gentleman named Ercole Mezzetti. Porri's dowry was entered into the acts of a Venetian notary, the value just two hundred ducats more than she had offered at the time of her first marriage: D10700. In this case we have a precise breakdown of the different sections of the dowry. The largest component was *"mobili"* (moveable items such as clothing, jewelry, and furniture), worth over 4000 ducats (included in the D4129 were the two musical instruments inventoried in 1667, a spinet worth D300, and a harpsichord appraised at D200). Gold and silver were valued at D2900, while Porri's paintings – clearly the best in her collection, those by "diverse good painters" – were appraised at D1100. These belongings undoubtedly included many of the same things that Ordano had admired in her comfortable household. Cash and investments rounded out the dowry, with a value of D2500. As part of the marriage agreement Porri's new husband agreed to house her son, Giovanni Battista, then nearly nineteen years old, and to support him should he wish to pursue a university education. The couple married at their parish church, S. Ternita, on 10 September 1678.[87]

The dowry's listing of paintings differs fundamentally from that in the 1667 inventory, for it represents only the "cream of the crop," nineteen works in all. Three of these seem to have been lacking in the earlier list: a *Saint Martin* "in the manner of Pordenone," a *Saint Barbara*, and a head by Tintoretto.[88] Thirteen of the paintings are attributed, and one thing stands out: the collection is remarkable

---

[86] ASPV, Actorum Sede vacantis, 1678, f.128, 3 September 1678. I am grateful to Jonathan Glixon for sharing this document with me. Both witnesses lived in S. Giovanni in Bragora, the parish adjacent to S. Antonin.

[87] Parrocchia di S. Ternita, Matrimoni, 1676-1687. "Adì 10 settembre 1678. La Signora Cattarina figlia del Signor Gio. Battista Porri Romano, relita in primo votto dal Signor Bortolo Carezana q. Z. Battista della mia contra ha contratto mattrimonio per verba de presenti alla presenza di me P. M. Antonio Scolari Piovan, coll'Illustrissimo Signor Ercole Mezzetti Bolognese." I would like to express my gratitude to the staff of the Archivio Storico del Patriarcato di Venezia, who facilitated my visit to the archive of S. Francesco della Vigna, where the records of the former parish of SS. Trinità (colloquially, S. Ternita) reside.

[88] The "head" by Tintoretto and the painting "in the manner of Pordenone" (un S. Martin maniera del Pordenon) represent two nods to an older style: Pordenone, a contemporary of Titian, died in 1539, Tintoretto in 1594.

(or perhaps unremarkable) for its *venezianità*.[89] As mentioned earlier, all the attributed paintings but two were the work of artists active in Venice. The two by Carlo Dolci, an artist who spent his entire career in his native Florence, stand out as exceptional and we might wonder how Porri came to have these Florentine works in her possession. Were they obtained in Venice, perhaps with the help of a knowledgeable friend or patron, or had Porri herself taken a trip to Florence to help her career? Dolci's *Saint Cecilia*, valued at D350, would have been unusual in Venice, a city where his paintings appear only very rarely in inventories. (Porri also had one of the same artist's most copied works, a *Salome with the Head of John the Baptist*).[90] Porri's second most valuable painting, at D110, was Pietro Bellotti's *Portrait of an Old Woman*, one of his specialties.[91] A number of paintings were not attributed, including, unfortunately, the portraits of Bortolo Caresana and Porri herself, valued at ten and thirty ducats respectively. Porri's collection, however, undoubtedly exceeded the nineteen works in the list; either the remaining examples fell outside the dowry (forming part of her personal property), or were included among the more general category of *"mobili."* It is also possible that some of the paintings listed in the 1667 inventory had accompanied both of Porri's daughters to their new residences.

On 26 September Porri authorized the Venetian nobleman Antonio Maria Surian to handle various aspects of her financial affairs in Venice, a sign that she and her husband had made preparations to leave the city. It would seem that Surian had become Porri's chief protector and ally, someone who supported her and her family in moments of transition. He had been the godfather to Porri's first grandchild, born in 1675, had accompanied the two witnesses who testified for Porri before the officials of the church, and he was also one of the two witnesses at Porri's second wedding.[92] Surian continued to act on Porri's behalf for some time to come. Our last account of her, in March 1685, appears in a notarial act where the nobleman made financial transactions on her behalf, having been authorized by

---

[89] Missing from the list are other popular artists in mid-*seicento* Venice such as Pietro Liberi, Pietro della Vecchia, Giovanni Battista Langetti, and Francesco Ruschi. Bernardo Strozzi had died before Porri's arrival in Venice, so it is perhaps not surprising that he is absent from the list. On Bellotti, see Luciano Anelli, *Pietro Bellotti, 1625-1700. Saggi di Alfredo Bonomi, Isabella Lechi, Jutta Rosengarten* (Brescia: La Valsabbina, 1996). As a comparison we may look to the composer Nadal Monferrato, who owned original paintings by Strozzi, Ruschi, Liberi, Zanchi, Langetti, Loth, and Heintz, and several copies of works by Luca Giordano, who had spent time in Venice during the 1660s. These paintings – which would have comprised only a part of his collection – were cited specifically in his will as legacies. See ASV, Archivio notarile, Testamenti Brachi, b.180 , no. 1013.

[90] Two different renderings of Saint Cecilia by Dolci survive, one in Dresden (Gemäldegalerie), the other in St. Petersburg (Hermitage). On Dolci, see Francesca Baldassari, *Carlo Dolci* (Torino: Artema, 1995). The Dresden *S. Cecilia*, of which there are two copies, is thought to date from the late 1640s, while the St. Petersburg *S. Cecilia* was painted around 1670 for Cosimo III de' Medici. See Baldassari, 109.

[91] Porri's friend Gerolimo Rota also had a number of Bellotti's paintings in his collection.

[92] ASPV, Parrocchia di S. Benedetto, Battesimi 1577-1677, f. 341.

her to do so the previous January, apparently in Milan.[93]

Ercole Mezzetti had married a wealthy woman in her early forties. It would seem that Porri's intention was to leave Venice, perhaps to settle in Bologna, the native city of her husband, or even another locale. In doing so, she would leave behind her daughter and her grandchildren. Did Porri choose to abandon the place of her artistic success, unwilling to remain where she could no longer reign on the stage? Did she intentionally marry a man who would prefer to live outside of Venice? Evidence shows that Porri continued to sing publicly on stage after her second marriage, although we do not know the true range of her performances at this point of her career. Her name appeared in two libretti during the 1680s, first in Bologna (1681), where she played the title character in Tomaso Stanzani and Giuseppe Felice Tosi's *Erismonda*. There she was no stranger to the stage, of course, and her performances of 1681 might well have been viewed by friends and family members of her second husband. Three years later, in 1684, she performed the title role in Domenico Freschi's *Olimpia vendicata* in Pavia, not far from Milan; in this case she herself signed the dedication of the libretto.[94]

Porri's appearance in *Erismonda* at the Teatro Formagliari, under the direction of Marchese Gaspare Malvezzi, became the occasion for a disturbance among the Bolognese nobility. Ercole Pepoli wrote to his father-in-law, Hippolito Bentivoglio, about the incident, as his brother Cornelio, Porri's protector, was one of the key players in the affair:

> Marchese Malvezzi and other parties interested in the opera wanted Porri to perform more times than had been arranged, which was ten. [Porri] would easily have agreed to do that if she had not, in the preceding performances, been maltreated by some interested parties as had, in effect, been the case. So that when the time came to perform the opera, [Porri], disgusted at being treated badly, said no, and so that this refusal would have greater force, she implored the help of my brother, who declared that he did not want [the opera to be played] if they did not make some gesture of respect to him and some gesture of satisfaction to Porri. These things were not done and therefore the opera was not performed again.[95]

---

[93] ASV, Archivio notarile, Atti Martin Corte, b. 3926, f. 36, 31 March 1685. The document legalizing Surian's authority appeared in the acts of a Milanese notary on 30 January 1685, indicating that Porri was at that time in the vicinity of Milan.

[94] I have not consulted a copy of this libretto, which survives, according to Sartori, only in one private collection, of the Sormani family. See Sartori, *I libretti italiani a stampa dalle origini al 1800* (Cuneo: Bertola e Locatelli, 1990-1994), 4: 275.

[95] "Signor Marchese Malvezzi, et altri interessati nel opera si voleva che la Porri recitasse più volte del concertato, ch'era il numero di dieci volte, a questo la medesima sarebbe facilmente condescesa, ogni volta che da signori interessati nelle passate recite non fosse stata mal trattata chome in effetto era seguito; per il che venuta l'occasione di replicare l'opera questa nauseata da mali trattamenti disse di nò, e per far che questo nò havesse maggior forza implorò l'aiuto di mio fratello, quale si dichiarò non volere, ogni volta che non prendessero qualch'atti di convenienza verso lui, e di sodisfazione verso la Porri, queste cose non ebbero effetto onde l'opera non si replichò." Monaldini, 458. I am grateful to Nello Barbieri for his assistance with the translation. Ercole Pepoli was the husband of

Pepoli's telling of the story would seem to place a good deal, if not most of the blame on Porri: she no longer wished to perform in long runs of more than ten performances, but more importantly, she also sought – or demanded – respect from her employers. Pepoli told Bentivoglio, however, that he did not know all the facts behind the events, but promised to write again when he understood the situation more fully. He did relate that rising tensions among the nobility had caused both Malvezzi and Cornelio Pepoli to leave the city.

Another account of the affair, however, as described in Corrado Ricci's *I teatri di Bologna*, shows that the difficulties arose not from the actions of Caterina Porri, but from ongoing disagreements between the directors and supporters of the two theaters in Bologna, the Formagliari and the Teatro della Sala. Ricci reports that Marchese Antonio Legnani, the protector of the "Sala," asked Pepoli to see that Porri refuse to perform at the Formagliari on a certain evening. Porri obeyed her protector's "wishes" even though, only the day before, she had declared that she would sing during the last days of Carnival.[96] The situation ended with the closure of both theaters, and the anger of many of the Bolognese.

Porri's role in the theatrical disturbance in Bologna points up the vulnerability of the operatic singer in these times. "Asked" by her protector to refuse to perform on stage, she precipitated the closure of the theater. Yet she could hardly do otherwise. Porri's troubles with the Teatro Formagliari both in 1665 and 1681 provide us with a rare glimpse into a professional singer's life in the seventeenth century, and of the perpetual adjustments and compromises that must have been necessary in order to sustain a career. One such adjustment, and a major one at that, was Porri's decision to marry Ercole Mezzetti, and to move away from the city that had been at the center of her life for more than twenty years. Porri evidently knew when to recede gracefully from the Venetian limelight and play the prima donna in less central locales.

Will we learn more of this singer who became such a familiar and, presumably, popular staple of the Venetian stage? Some tidbits may emerge from time to time from the Venetian archives, and certainly there are other morsels to be unearthed in Rome, Bologna, Pavia, and Milan. More importantly, however, our understanding of women singers such as Porri and their unique place in society will grow as we continue to further our knowledge of the workings of the opera industry, of the various ways that music served the people of the time, and, not least of all, of the richly patterned lives of all types of women of the seventeenth century.

Beatrice Bentivoglio; Cornelio Pepoli's son, Sicinio, became an influential impresario in the eighteenth century.

[96] Ricci, *I teatri di Bologna*, 44-46.

Chapter 10

Serf Actresses in the Tsarinas' Russia: Social Class Cross-Dressing in Russian Serf Theaters of the Eighteenth Century[1]

Inna Naroditskaya

A famous painting, *Portrait of a Woman in Russian Costume* by Ivan Argunov (1722-1804), hangs in Moscow's Tretyakov Gallery. The woman wears a tall ornamented *kokoshnik* (headdress) and a red garlanded *sarafan* (dress) – the traditional attire of a Russian peasant. The soft tone of the painting, the interplay of red and gold intensifying the dark softness of her eyes, and the woman's dignified posture made this art work one of the best known Russian paintings of the eighteenth century. The woman's smile, like the Mona Lisa's, stirred the imagination of artists and viewers. Who was she? A noble woman dressed as a peasant, or a village girl playing the part of an aristocrat? Since the painter himself was a serf in the Sheremetiev family, art historian Boris Brodsky suggests that "the unknown woman" may have been a serf actress in her stage costume.[2] The portrait was painted in the 1780s, when Count Sheremetiev's private serf theater, as well as other serf troupes, became prominent cultural institutions.

This study explores serf theater as a system of representation that transgressed and reinforced social norms, linking stage and society. Actresses in these theaters were both pioneers and victims in a gender "performance" caught between operatic plots and social realities. The dichotomy of transgression and reinforcement was especially tangled in Sheremetiev's theater, where a romantic operatic scenario

---

[1] Research in Moscow, supported by The University Research Grants Committee (URGC) at Northwestern University, enabled me to access sources in the Theater Library, State Historical Museum, Museums in Kuskovo and Ostankino Estates, the State Central Theatre Library the library at the Moscow Conservatory. In this research I was indebted to my colleagues in the USA and Russia. I am grateful to Roland John Wiley for his suggestions on bibliography and private sources he shared with me, and to Andrew Wachtel for his advice as I thought and wrote about the topic. I would also like to thank my colleagues in the Moscow Conservatory, Victor Varuntz and Svetlana Sigida,as well as art historians Lia Lepskaya (Museum Ostankino), Ludmila Rodneva (State Historical Museum,) and many others for their assistance and encouragement.

[2] Boris Ionovich Brodskii, *The Art Treasures from Moscow Museums* (Moscow: Izobrazitel'noe Iskusstvo, 1991), 192.

was replayed in real life by the count and his famous serf star – a love story that epitomizes the social and artistic paradigm of Russia in the second half of the eighteenth century.

Figure 10.1 Ivan Argunov. *Portrait of a Woman in Russian Costume*
Permission of Tretyakov Gallery, Moscow

The primary data on serf theater are scattered among diaries of contemporaries attending serf productions, as well as in records of theater owners.[3] Most of the scholarship on serf theater was produced during the Soviet period. Soviet scholars approached serf theater from an ideological platform, viewing it as a system of class exploitation and as evidence of the genius of the simple Russian folk, whom they considered forebears of the Soviet proletariat.[4] Though a number of creative and scholarly works[5] have been devoted to the study of serf theater, little has been written about serf theater in connection with Russian music.[6] Limited attention was also given to gender in Russian theater of this period until Catherine Schuler's article that

---

[3] The primary sources that I consulted in my research include, for example, the memoirs of Vigel, who visited serf theaters, the correspondence and financial records of Count Nikolai Sheremetiev, as well as *Elegia i teni grafini Praskovii Ivanovny Sheremetievoi* [The Eulogy and Shadow of Countess Praskovia Ivanovna Sheremetiev] (Moscow: Tipographia of Platon Beketov or Platon Beketov's Press, 1805.) Although Russian scholars produced extensive literature on the native theater of the nineteenth century, sources on theater of the eighteenth century and specifically serf theater are less substantial. Some works produced in the late nineteenth and early twentieth century do not specify sources or sometimes refer to sources no longer available, *Ostankino* (Author unknown, St. Petersburg: Tipographia M. M. Stasiulevicha, 1897), Drizen, Nv., Materialy k istorii russkogo teatra [Materials to the History of Russian Theater] (Moscow: Tipographia Bakhrushina, 1905). More primary sources may become available when the cataloguing system in the Ostankino and Koskovo archives is developed and completed.

[4] Soviet research on serf theater falls into three categories. One focuses on serf theater in general; for examples see Tatiana Dynnik, *Krepostnoi teater* [Serf Theater](Moscow: Academy, 1933); and Emmanuil Beskin, *Serf Theater* (Moscow: Kinopechat, 1927). Another explores the history of Russian theater and serf theater. See Nikolai Evreinov, *Istoriya russkogo theatra* [History of Russian Theater] (New York: Press after Chekhov, 1955); Vera Krasovskaya, *Russkii baletnii* teatr [Russian Ballet Theater] (Linengrad: Iskusstvo, 1958; Vsevolod Vsevolodsky-Geringross, *Russkii teatr* [Russian Theater] (Moscow: Academy of Science Press, 1957); and Borisoglebskii. The third focuses on specific serf troupes. See N. Kashin, *Teatr N.B. Usupova* [Theater of Count Yusupov] (Moscow: Krasnaya Presna, 1927) on Usupov's serf theater; and on Sheremetive's troupe see V. K. Staniukovich, *Domashnie krepostnye teatry XVIII veka* [Theater of archaic life in 18th century Moscow] (Moscow: Iscusstvo, 1988); Edward Sholok, *Ostankino I ego teatr* [Ostankino and its theater] (Moscow: Moscovskii rabochii, 1949); Nadezhda Alekseevna Elizarova, *Ostankino* (Moscow: Iskusstvo, 1966); and Lia Lepskaya, *Repertuare krepostnogo teatra Sheremetievyh* [The repertoire of the Sheremetiev's Serf Theater] (Moscow: State Central Theatrical Museum after A. Gachrushin Press, 1996).

[5] Along with scholarly research, literature on serf theater includes a number of novels, including Nikolai Leskov, *Tupeinyi hudozhnik* [Tupeinyi Artist] (Moscow: Gosudarstvennoe Isdatel'stvo hudozhestvennoi literatury, 1958); and Alexander Herzen, *Soroca-Vorovka* [The Thieving Magpie], *Razdumie* (Moscow: Tipographia Troian, 1870).

[6] Russian theater of the eighteenth century is synesthetic, encompassing dance, singing, and acting. The actresses of the serf troupes in most theaters were not specialized as operatic or dramatic performers. For example, even at the end of the century, the repertoire of Count Sheremetiev's serf theater, known for its operatic productions, also included the genre of opera-ballet (*Venetian Yarmarka, Beautiful Arsena, Atis*).

analyzed the status of serf actresses "doubly oppressed by class and a rigid set of largely unreconstructed medieval gender conventions."[7] While surveys of serf theater typically draw no clear distinction between the second half of the eighteenth century and the nineteenth century, my essay deals specifically with the eighteenth – an unprecedented period when Russia was ruled by several female monarchs.[8]

Background: the reformation of Russian society and the rise of serf theater

The emergence of serf theater, an important venue for musical production, coincided with the period of early modernity in Russia, which began considerably later than in Western Europe. Before the eighteenth century, Russia existed in relative isolation from the Western hemisphere. The cultural life of peasants and nobility alike consisted of pagan and semi-pagan rituals, plays known as *igrisha*, folk festivals, and religious celebrations connected with the Eastern Orthodox Church. The early seventeen hundreds brought drastic changes – the expansion of Russian borders to the West, the shift from Byzantine to European orientation, the introduction of Western fashions and life styles, and the education of young Russian aristocrats abroad. The emergence of professional theater, long present in Western Europe, was an artistic manifestation of the modernization/ Westernization of Russian society.

Throughout the eighteenth century, women were actively involved in theater.[9] Countesses and princesses appeared in private amateur productions, professional singers and actresses were employed in public and court theaters, and serf girls sang and danced in serf theaters. Peter the Great's (1772-1725) female relatives, including his sister Duchess Natalia and his niece Princess Catherine, were among early patrons of the theater. A reformer of Russian society, Peter the Great created a theatrical ambiance in his military, social, and cultural affairs. Expanding his empire westwards, he re-wrote the plot of Russian history, built a grand theatrical setting (the city of St. Petersburg), re-costumed his nobility,[10] and obliged his statesmen to bring their wives and daughters with them to attend his courtly events which included theatricals.[11]

---

[7] Catherine Schuler, "Gender of Russian serf theatre and performance," in: *Women, Theater, and Performance: New Histories, New Historiographies*, ed. Maggie B. Gale and Vivien Gardner (New York: Manchester University Press, 2000).

[8] Four women ruled Russia for the most of the eighteenth century: Catherine I (1725-1727), Anna (1730-1740), Elizabeth (1741-1761), and Catherine the Great (1762- 1796). Pushkareva writes that "traditionally, historians tended to play down the significance of female governance in Russia, asserting that these women rulers themselves played only a nominal role in the success and achievements of their reigns. Instead, all their accomplishments were attributed to the educated energetic statesmen who surrounded them. See Natalia Pushkareva, *Women in Russian History*, transl. Eve Levin (New York: M. E. Sharpe, 1997), 154.

[9] The appearance of women on the Russian stage from the beginning could be explained by the late advent of theater in Russia, which postdated the exclusion of women from the European stage, by foreign troupes that included women performers touring Russia

Under empresses Anna and Elizabeth, the royal successors of Peter the Great, foreign operatic and ballet troupes became permanent residents in both Russian capitals. The first native theaters and theatrical schools were founded, and acting classes were introduced in the new educational institutions for the native elite. The most distinguished families of Anna's and Elizabeth's Russia passed on their interest in theater to their heirs – the courtiers of Catherine the Great.[12] Count Usupov senior, for example, was in charge of the Corps of Schlachets – an elite military school famous for splendid spectacles attended by Empress Anna.[13] Usupov junior, a politician and courtier known for his serf ballet troupe, became director of imperial theaters in St. Petersburg (1791-1799). The post passed next to Count Nikolai Sheremetiev. Sheremetiev's father, a senator and *ober-kamerger* (house speaker), entertained both empresses, Elizabeth and Catherine, with his orchestra and choir. In his St. Petersburg palace, Sheremetiev senior indulged his guests with theatrical productions in which his children and other aristocrats acted together with professional actors and serfs.[14]

---

in the final decades of the seventeenth century, and by long-existing traditions of women acting in Russian folk drama. For the most part, women were limited to singing, dancing, and acting. Lists of school students and performers contain no names of female composers, directors, or instrumentalists in operatic orchestras. Among references to authors of popular songs one encounters the name of female composer M. V. Zubova. Tamara Livanova mentions that several poets used Zubova's melodies; see Tamara Livanova, *Russkaya muzikalnaya kultura XVIII veka* [Russian Musical Culture of the Eighteenth Century] (Moscow: Governmental Musical Press, 1952), 336. Gerasimov suggests that Zubova's romance "Ya v pustinu udalus" was performed in the ritualistic musical drama *Tsar Maximilian*. Iurri Konstantinovich Gerasimov, *Istoriia russkoi dramaturgii: XVII pervaia polovina XIX veka*. (Lreningrad: Nauka, 1982), 56.

[10] He radically changed the dress code of the Russian nobility and made them dance the minuet, allemande and other European dances. He cut the long beards of his noblemen, an act that echoed a hundred years later in Pushkin's *Ruslan and Ludmila*, where the Russian hero/liberator chops off the beard of an evil dwarf.

[11] Several times Peter, infatuated with the theater, attempted to create a public theater first in Moscow and later in St. Petersburg. In Moscow, between 1702-1707, Johann Kunst and later Otto Furst, leading a group of German actors and teaching Russian players, produced spectacles in both languages. Financial records of salaries of the groups and budgets of their performances show no female names either among members of the troupes or among actors' apprentices. In 1720 in St. Petersburg, Peter established a residence for a troupe of Czech actors led by German actor Johann Ekkenberg (Mann) See Vsevolodsky-Gergross, 398, 129.

[12] Counts Vorontsov and Apraksin acted on the stage during Anna's reign. Elizabethan nobility sang, danced, and, following a monarchial order, participated in cross-dressing during court masquerades.

[13] Anna included the study of "dance and music" in the curriculum of the Corps of Schlachets, one of the most prestigious native institutions. A choreographer from France, Jean-Baptiste Landé, became ballet master of the young pupils and future officers studying at the Corps of Schlachets, with whom he staged and performed several successful ballets attended by the Empress.

[14] See Elizarova, 18.

The mixing of serfs and masters on the stage raises issues related to political power in early modern Russia. In a hierarchical society where noblemen owed fealty to the tsar and where the peasants – their lives and their bodies – belonged to the nobility, cultural institutions such as the theater became an experimental arena that represented, defined, and altered social relations. "Every hegemony," Lizabeth Goodman suggests, discussing theater as a metaphor of power, "creates institutions which sustain a system of signification and representation."[15] One such institution in eighteenth century Russia, serf theater, embodied the society's social and patriarchal dynamics.

References to serfs appearing on stage date from the first decades of the century. Bernholdtz's 1722 memoir[16] tells how Princess Catherine, known for her love of the theater and her participation in all facets of theatrical production, ordered a male serf punished for his mistakes on the stage. The next day the serf appeared on the stage playing a king, with the queen enacted by the princess herself.[17] While serfs sometimes shared the stage with actors of different social classes, serf theater as a distinct institution emerged decades later. Significantly, the official birth of serf theater was associated with *The Ballet of the Flowers* of 1744, "given to mark the occasion of Peter II's betrothal to the German princess and future Tsar of Russia, Catherine II."[18] Under Catherine, who strongly encouraged the development of theater, serf troupes were founded in provincial cities and on country estates, some of them functioning as private theaters and others open to the public,[19] some of them hobbies of the self-indulgent owners and others a source of commercial profit.

Serf theater reached its zenith in the last quarter of the eighteenth century, when Catherine gave her nobility unlimited power over their serfs while liberating the aristocrats themselves from the mandatory service imposed by Tsar Peter.[20] Consequently, starting in the 1770s, the most affluent statesmen of the empire, such as counts Usupov, Sheremetiev, Apraksin, and Vorontsov, retired from imperial service, leaving St. Petersburg for their estates near Moscow or the Russian provinces, where they immersed themselves in art and theater.[21]

---

[15] Goodman, 7.

[16] Dynnik refers to Bernholdtz's memoir; Tatiana Dynnik, *Krepostnoi teater* [Serf theater] (Moscow: Academy, 1933), 39.

[17] Michail Ivanovich Semevsky, *Tsaritsa Praskovia, 1664-1723* (Moscow: Kniga, 1989), 172-173.

[18] Evreinov, 204.

[19] Among those were the theaters of Esipov, who lived near the city of Kazan; counts Shakhovsky, in Nizhnii Novgorod; and Kamensky, in Orel. See Dynnik, 87-88.

[20] Upon Peter's *ukaz* of 1720 Peter's "serf peasants and servants were assigned to serve 'aristocrats,' while the aristocrats themselves were to serve the empire until decease, death, the end." See K. N. Shepetov, *Krepostnoe pravo v votchinah Sheremet'evyh* [Serfdom in Sheremetiev's lands] (Moscow: Ostankino Museum Press, 1947), 8.

[21] Maya Dmitrievna Kurmacheva, *Krepostnaya intelligentsia Rossii* [Russian Serf Intelligence] (Moscow: Nauka, 1983), 17.

Significantly, all sources on serf theater identify men as the owners of serf theaters, even though female aristocrats took a strong interest in theater and frequently participated in productions.

Erecting magnificent palatial private theaters reminiscent of Versailles, creating their own courts composed of serfs who could magically turn into counts or peasants, Russian aristocrats competed with each other and with the monarch herself. The best serf troupes rivaled the theaters of St. Petersburg and the provinces. Maddox, the director of the Moscow Public Theater, repeatedly complained that Sheremetiev's productions were taking away the audience of public theaters.[22] Serf theater thus became an arena where aristocrats realized their personal and political ambitions.[23]

One area of competition among the most distinguished serf theater owners was musical theater, which required special training for singers, dancers, and musicians. Perhaps the best-known operatic troupes arising at the end of the eighteenth century belonged to Sheremetiev and Vorontzov.[24]

Operatic repertoire

The plots of operas staged in Sheremetiev's theater typified the spirit of French sentimentalism and showed the influence of *opera comique*, which was favored by eighteenth century Russian aristocrats.

In *La buona Figliuola Maritata* by Piccini, a poor young girl raised by a rich countess falls in love with the marquis, the countess's nephew. Learning about the romance between the two, the countess forces the girl to enter a convent. Finally discovering that the girl is the daughter of a colonel who had left his child in strangers' hands years ago, the countess happily blesses the young couple. This opera parallels the one-act *Laurette* by J. Mereaux, in which a count, falling in love with a peasant girl, asks her to follow him. When the heroine discovers that she is of noble descent, nothing prevents her from uniting with the count. In a similar Russian comic opera, *Anuta,,* by M. I. Fomin, a peasant girl, following the will of her father, is betrothed to a country bumpkin. However, the heroine and a local aristocrat Victor love each other. At a crucial moment, the news that Anuta is the daughter of noble parents allows the wedding of the heroine and her aristocratic suitor.

Operas about the unequal love between a low class girl and a nobleman became fashionable on the Russian stage in the last quarter of the century. The plots focused on two major motifs, the romance itself and the discovery of a girl's concealed noble identity. The first motif signified transgression of social

---

[22] Beskin, 13.

[23] Over forty serf theaters functioned in Russia at the end of the century, almost a half of them in Moscow, several in St Petersburg, and others in provincial cities and estates.

[24] Vorontsov's theater, existing between 1794-1805, was in the count's colossal estate in Vladimir province near the city of Tambov (Dynnik, 251.)

boundaries, while the second provided reassurance of social hierarchy. The juxtaposition of the two – which Amelia Jones defines as "disturbance and assertion," or the departure from and the return to societal norms – required the social class cross-dressing of a heroine."[25] How did serf theater disturb and assert the social structure of the Russian aristocracy? How did serf actresses, singing Italian arias and enacting sentimental French or Russian pastorals, navigate their liminal space between opera and society?

The operatic plots seldom disturbed the gender and social superiority of men. For instance, the romantic love between socially unequal protagonists rarely involved a man of low society and a heroine of the upper class. Only one of forty-nine operas staged in Sheremetiev's theater, *Azémia, ou Les sauvages* by D'Alayrac, exemplifies social class crossing by a central male character – Prospero. Beautiful Azémia and her father find themselves on a sparsely inhabited island after a shipwreck. Young Prospero, raised on the island among savages, falls in love with her. The heroine's father rejects Prospero as a suitor first because he sees him as a lowly savage and later, when a nobleman claims Prospero as his kidnapped son, because of Prospero's (newly elevated) social status. The nobleman and his son declare themselves above societal prejudice, however, and the union between the lovers is sanctioned.

At the beginning of *Azémia*, the father, attempting to prevent a romance between the young people, orders Azémia to dress as a boy. Such gender cross-dressing or transvestism is inseparable from the history of European theater, and according to Marjorie Garber, was "rather the norm" than "the simple aberration," and "came to mark and overdetermine this space of anxiety about fixed and changing identities." For Garber, transvestism was located at the juncture of "'class' and 'gender,' . . . for one kind of crossing, inevitably, crosses over the other."[26] Though there were examples of gender crossing on the Russian stage, it generally coincided with social (class) transgression. For example, in *L'infante de Zamora* by Paisiello, the princess, presenting a prize to the winner of a contest, falls in love with the brave knight. Though the games are finished, she initiates another contest to test the knight's character and feelings. In the course of her "theatrical" game, everything and everyone is transformed including the princess herself, who first plays the role of a poor girl and later the knight's page, returning at the end of the opera as her "true" self, a royal woman.

In several operas, the pattern of social crossing was extended and reiterated, at times confusing the identity of the main characters. In *Aline, reine de Golconde*, one of the most popular operas of Monsigny, the heroine, a milkmaid, loves a viscount, who leaves her to perform his duty. In the course of her adventures, the

---

    [25] Amelia Jones, "Acting Unnatural: Interpreting Body Art," *Decomposition* (Bloomington: Indiana University Press, 2000), 241.

    [26] Marjorie Garber, "Dress Codes, or the Theatricality of Difference," in: *Routledge Reader in Gender and Performance*, ed. Lizbeth Goodman (New York: Routledge, 1998), 177.

milkmaid becomes queen of a distant country. Learning that her beloved, now a diplomat, seeks an audience with her, she arranges to replay for him her initial role as a peasant girl. Mesmerized by the vision of his forgotten love, the viscount refuses the queen's offer of her heart, admitting his feelings for a simple milkmaid, at which point the queen reveals her identity. Consequently, in a dizzy succession of social crossings, the heroine of this opera, a peasant girl, turns into a queen, who enacts a peasant, while remaining a queen.

The frequent occurrence of the social class-crossing motif raises hypothetical/theatrical questions about the inversion of social norms and roles. Penny Gay, researching theater in early modern England, finds "danger" to an audience in being exposed to the "play of the possibilities" that could be transgressed in life.[27] What if the love story becomes a life story, with people traversing their social roles as an operatic plot spills offstage? It is intriguing to observe that the actress who played *all* the main heroines in the above operas staged at Sheremetiev's theater herself crossed social boundaries, born as a serf, dying a countess, and that her performances were overseen by one man, a count raised and nurtured on the ideals of French sentimentalism. Who was this actress who acquired in her short and extraordinary life a number of names – Gorbunova – Kovaleva – Kuznetzova – Kovalevsky – Zhemchugova – Sheremetieva? Nikolai Argunov, a son and apprentice of the painter of *A Woman in Peasant Costume*, made several portraits of the legendary singer and actress, best known by her stage name Praskovia Zhemchugova. In these paintings she wears on her bodice or necklace a sizable engraving of Count Nikolai Sheremetiev – a portrait within a portrait. What was the significance of this man? The image of the actress on the canvas reveals the complexity of social and gender issues inherent in the position of serf actresses.

---

[27] Penny Gay, "The History of Shakespeare's Unruly Women," in: *Routledge Reader*, 43.

Figure 10.2 Nikolay Argunov. *Portrait of P.I. Zhemchugova*
Permission of the State Historical Museum, Moscow

Figure 10.3 Nikolay Argunov, *Portrait of Kovaleva-Zhemchugova*
Permission of the Hermitage, St. Petersburg

Serfs on the theatrical stage

The performers in Sheremetiev's theaters were serfs. Though both male and female actors could have rigorous training, it was actresses who gave distinction to any troupe. These actresses were inherited, given as dowries, presented as gifts, borrowed, lost in card games, sold, and exchanged. Their commodity value and, consequently, their market prices were based on their abilities and professional skills: an ordinary young female serf in the provinces could be sold for two and a half rubles, while a singer in Moscow could cost eight hundred. The newspaper *Moscow Vedomosti* (1797) contained advertisements for serfs – for instance, a "'special bargain' on a sixteen-year-old maid with a nice voice, successful in singing and acting theatrical roles, also cleaning well and making delicious food." Count Kamenskii exchanged one of his villages with two hundred inhabitants for two musicians he desired.[28] In *Soroca-Vorovka*, Herzen recounts how, after the sudden death of the "kind owner" of one of the "best" Russian actresses, the troupe was sold wholesale on the public market.[29]

The girls selected for the theater ranged from children under ten to young women in their late teens.[30] They were the daughters of servants, *dvorovye* (working in a *dvor* – court-yard)[31] and peasants. The girls' families frequently opposed their recruitment, believing that theater deprived their daughters of their childhood, estranged them from their homes, and jeopardized their futures. Since the main criterion for selecting girls was their appearance, some parents hid their growing daughters from strangers and villagers.

Depending upon the owner, the theaters where these girls eventually performed could represent momentary whims, fashionable pastimes, or serious theatrical ventures. In some cases, actresses were "tried" in a theater for a short period, returned to their families and restored to their traditional serf occupations. When not on stage, they may have performed their regular agricultural or household duties. In more permanent troupes, actresses were placed in special

---

[28] Beskin, 6-7.

[29] Herzen, 281.

[30] Jacquetta Beth Fooks writes that, for example, in Vorontsov's theater, founded in 1776, "the age of female performers ranged between 11 and 19; fourteen was the minimum age for boys;" Jacquetta Fooks, "The Serf Theater in Imperial Russia," (Ph.D. Diss., University of Kansas, 1970), 40. While some data is available on actresses while they remained in the realm of aristocrat's theater, practically nothing is known about their post-theater life. For example, among twenty-five actresses in Usupov's troupe, twelve of the girls were under fourteen, ranging between five and twenty-nine year old. One may imagine that an actress could be a part of the troupe for as long as twenty years. What happened to these actresses when, after adapting to their marginal space and roles, they were recycled back to the domain of servants and serfs?

[31] In the hierarchical scale among serfs, *dvirovye* obtained a place below household servants whose closeness to their owners placed them at the "top" of serf society, and step above peasants who worked in the fields and were separated from landlord by a number of supervisors, mostly also serfs.

quarters where, caged in their cells, they were kept separate from fellow actors and from other serfs, including their families. Evreinov writes that actresses were supervised by matrons who accompanied them during rehearsals and performances, kept them in their dressing rooms, and prevented them from talking with male partners.[32] Lubov Onisimovna, the heroine of Leskov's novel *Tupeinyi Artist*, recalls that the landlord purposely chose matrons with children. The matrons were well aware that if any of the actresses were caught misbehaving, the matron's children would be tormented. Accordingly matrons acted as harsh *nadziratel* or jailers. Even the most liberal aristocrats, such as Sheremetiev, kept his actresses under tight surveillance in their quarters and under the supervision of matrons, the exception being their attendance at Sunday services at the count's own church.[33]

Physical punishment was a conventional method of training. After a spectacle, a serf actress could be sent back to the barn, flogged for her mistakes, or locked in her small cell. Old Count Kamenski, the owner of two theaters in Orlov, known even among his peers as a despot and a madman, usually attended performances of his troupe with a special notebook where he recorded inaccuracies and imperfections of his actors. During intermissions he used his whip, "punishing the 'guilty,' whose shouts and cries frequently reached the ears of audience."[34]

Among at least thirty serf troupes existing in the second half of the eighteenth century (fourteen at the verge of the nineteenth century), there was only one troupe whose owner, Count Vorontsov, abolished corporal punishment. Even moderates like Sheremetiev who did not generally beat their actresses did not rule out this measure completely. Because of their visibility on stage and their presence in the landlords' household, serf actresses were especially vulnerable to their owners. Moreover, because of their clothing and the special attention of their landlords, serf actresses were also exposed to the jealousy of fellow serfs and house servants. By becoming actresses, these women no longer fit the traditional roles of serfs.

Professional actresses?

Neither did they fit the image of professional actresses. Like the Tunisian-owned singing slave girls L. JaFran Jonce describes who were purchased along with "other cultural artifacts" during "shopping expeditions to Baghdad," Russian serf actresses were simply the property of a male owner. Like the singing slave girls, who "contributed significantly to the cultural brilliance of Cordova [and North Africa]," serf actresses were largely responsible for developing Russian artistic

---

[32] Evreinov, 229.

[33] Sholok wrote about the living conditions of Sheremetiev's actresses who were "kept under lock in humid cold cells, . . . were frequently ill, with the cases of tuberculosis were constantly increasing;" Sholok. 40.

[34] Beskin, 25. Even one of the most liberal of aristocrats, Nikolai Sheremetiev, ordered his assistant to punish young girls studying acting by keeping them standing on their knees and limiting their food to bread and water; see Staniukovech, 15.

traditions.[35] Nevertheless, serf performers cannot be equated with professional actresses. The level of education and training among serf performers varied greatly, depending on their intellect, temper, and the intentions of the owner.

Some serf girls were simply yanked from the field or collected from the barn or kitchen, and then made to memorize a couple of French sentences or a short song. They were powdered, dressed in hoopskirt, draped with jewelry costing many times the price of the girls themselves, and thrown on the stage to play the part of a countess, princess, or picturesque shepherdess. Beskin tells about the uneasy process of transforming two peasant daughters into actresses for Count Gruzinsdky's theater. For four weeks two serf girls, Dunyasha and Parasha, scared by the stage, could not memorize their lines, and finally were whipped to stimulate their learning. Following the flogging, the text was memorized quickly. In the spectacle, the girls played idyllic versions of themselves:

> As the curtain rose . . . , from one side of the back stage came the beautiful Dunyasha –
> a weaver's daughter, with made-up hair, decorated with flowers, a *mushka* [mole] on
> the cheek, dressed in a hoop-skirt (pompadour), a shepherdess with a stick with blue-
> pink ribbons. Next Parasha comes dressed as a shepherd. The two will begin talk
> about love and about their sheep, then sit next to each other and hug.[36]

In contrast, leading actresses in the private serf theaters of Sheremetiev, Vorontsov, Usupov, and Apraksin were trained by the best native and foreign theatrical pedagogues, who taught the girls to understand music and poetry, and to speak French and Italian. For example, from 1778 on, Italian Franz Morelli, a dancer of the [Moscow] Court Theater and an instructor at the Moscow University, began to work with Sheremetiev's troupe. Singing was taught by Italians, and acting was instructed by Russians. Count Sheremetiev himself frequently participated in rehearsals and practices.[37]   Similarly, Usupov's actresses were taught grammar, languages, vocal classes, and clavichord. The best instructors were engaged in the count's theater. Actresses were trained by native artists and foreigners, and studied with members of aristocratic families, from whom they were to learn genuine aristocratic manners. Some of them were taught together with free pupils in theatrical schools.

Nevertheless, even the ones who showed talent and received professional training differed significantly from their free counterparts – professional actresses, who to a certain degree chose their occupation, negotiated salaries, and supervised

---

[35] Especially considering that, at the end of the century, serf theaters constituted a main theatrical venue in proportion to imperial troupes and public theaters. "Several types of theater existed in Russia. The leading was St. Petersburg Imperial Court Theater, with regularly performing French, Italian, and German troupes. After 1780, urban public theaters were permanently established (Knipper in St. Petersburg., Medoks [Peter's Theater] in Moscow." See Lepskaya. 16-17.

[36] Beskin cites I. M. Pylaev, who himself recorded his recollection of a former *dvorovoi* serf of the Count Gruzinsky ("Staroe zhitie"), 11-12.

[37] Lepskaya, 19.

their training, placement, and repertoire – such possibilities were not feasible for serf actresses. While professional actresses in Russia as elsewhere were seen by male spectators as objects of sexual desire and sexuality was commonly associated with the trade of professional actress, serf actresses often found that sexual performance was a part of their duty.

Female sexuality and male empowerment

Chosen primarily for their youth and beauty, enacting princesses and shepherdesses, serf actresses stimulated the social and sexual imagination of their spectators, creating the same "circulation of erotic energy between actors and audience" that Gay finds in English Elizabethan theater.[38] Sexuality enacted on the stage commonly led to sexual performances afterwards demanded by the owner.

A Frenchman living in Russia described a landlord who surrounded himself with "serf actresses [who] were at the same time his maidens, servants, and seamstresses. They were also mistresses, wet-nurses, and the babysitters of the children they bore him."[39] Another nobleman, referred to as *barin* B., had a sort of seraglio which consisted of serf actresses, mistresses, dancers, and cooks. The master loved traveling with this company from one village of his estates to another. During frequent stops, two tents were set up, one for the nobleman with his "favorites" and the other for his musicians – about twenty people pleasing the master with singing while he occupied himself with his mistresses.[40]

Sexuality was seen as a part of the actress's act and as her serf's duty, and any departure from the master's sexual script could cause severe, even deadly corporeal retribution. The actress described by Leskov attempted to avoid her performance in the landlord's bedroom and was beaten unconsciousness. In Herzen's story, "the best Russian actress" was locked in her room for refusing sexual demands by her owner, and soon died in despair. Actresses' sexual performances fulfilled more than the erotic desire of their owner. Sex became a metaphor for the basis of the nobleman's social control.

While an aristocratic owner could sexually exploit his actresses and keep them for his sole use in his private space, outside his quarters he might impose a higher moral standard to control his serfs' sexuality. Actress Piunova recalled that in Count Shahovsky's theater, "female performers were ordered not to talk with any male member of the troupe." Vigel adds that in the same theater, touching actresses was prohibited even on the stage with "a precise distance prescribed between the male and female actors."[41] Matrimony was also controlled by the male owner. "When a woman reached the age of twenty five," writes Piunova,

---

[38] Gay, 45.
[39] Evreinov, 219.
[40] *Ibid.*, 220.
[41] Filipp Vigel, *Zapiski* [Notes] (Cambridge: Oriental Research Press, 1974).

"the owner gave her in marriage, which was a simple process. He called in all the unmarried male actors and asked who would wish to marry the available bride, after which he informed the actress of the groom and wedding arrangements, with the owner himself blessing the wedded couple, supplying them with a dowry and giving the man a raise."[42] (However, not many owners paid salaries to their serfs, including actors.)

Despite differences in treatment and professional training, serf actresses shared one common feature. These women – simultaneously serfs and performers – fit neither role, occupying a marginal space in which they were subjected to the unique institution of serfdom, the specific customs of the trade, and the gender bias of Russian society.

Traversing the theatrical and social spaces

When we discuss the "roles" of people in ordinary life "performing" daily tasks, we use a metaphor drawn from theater, acknowledging the function of theater as an arena for social construction. We may assume that for an ordinary actress, the role played on stage only occasionally gets confused with that performed outside. But the odd position of serf actresses created a strange dichotomy and at times an even stranger convergence between themselves and the heroines they enacted, revealing a paradigm of constructed social and gender roles in Russian society. A Russian serf actress, crossing the stage, turned into an elegant noble princess. Redressed Dunyasha and Parasha remind one of Shakespeare's disguised heroines – "boys pretending to be women pretending to be men."[43] The *gender* cross-dressing of Parasha, who appears as a young man, is secondary to her (and Dunyasha's) *social class* cross-dressing; each girl, rephrasing Kaplan and Rogers, can be seen as a "peasant pretending to be a noble(man/woman) pretending to be a shepherd(ess)."

Perhaps an aristocratic spectator in a serf theater would experience feelings similar to Goethe watching castrati singing: "the double pleasure is given, in that these persons are not women, but only represent women."[44] Here the observer would see elegant women on the stage, knowing them to be serf peasant girls. This process of "dual recognition" explicitly extended the drama beyond the theatrical space into a territory offstage. In his memoir, Vigel, recalling his visit to Esipov's estate in Kazan, describes how at dinner he was astonished by the appearance of a dozen attractive, elegantly dressed young women, who were rather too polite with a governor. These high society women, played by Esipov's serf actresses, sat at the table among the men, providing them with a wide range of services, accompanying the food and drink with passionate kisses, cuddles, and songs.

---

[42] Evreinov, 320.

[43] Gisela T. Kaplan and Lesley J. Rogers. "Scientific Constructions, Cultural Predictions: Scientific Narratives of Sexual Attraction," in: *Feminine masculine and Representation*, ed. Terry Threadgold and Anne Cranny-Francis (Sydney: Allen & Unwin, 1990), 221.

[44] *Ibid.*

In such cases, the distinction between theater and day-to-day life was blurred. Theatrical roles were displaced from the stage to the household, confusing the distinction between *theatrical role-playing* and *social role-playing*,[45] which together defined the liminal space occupied by serf actresses. For them, theatrical space and living space, though socially demarcated, were frequently one and the same thing – the master's estate or, literally, a palace including both the owner's living space and his theater (with actors inhabiting a quarter of the palace's wings attached to the theater).

Transformed into aristocratic matrons on the stage, the actresses excited the erotic energy and sexual appetite of their owners, who coerced the girls to continue or expand their theatrical act in the master's private quarter. Nikolai Leskov, in his novel *Tupeinyi Artist*, writes how, because of an accident involving the lead actress, the young singer and dancer Lubov Onisimovna volunteered to play a noble heroine – the countess de Burgland. The actress's daring initiative was noticed and encouraged by her owner, who sent her *kamarinovye* [mosquito] earrings, "a gift both gratifying and disgusting."[46] The earrings symbolized another re-dress, in which the actress, prepared for the role of immaculate Cecilia, all in white with a circlet on her head and a lily in her hands, herself a symbol of innocence, would be "delivered" to the master's apartment.

In this theatrical space beyond the stage, not only actresses but also their owners became involved in the act of re-dressing. The aristocrat who "played" an enlightened European in public "performed" the role in his private home of an "Asiatic" sultan surrounded by a harem of singing and dancing slave girls. Ivan Dmitrievich Shepelev, a nobleman living in the provincial city of Vyksa (Vladimir County), designed a music salon and a private quarter of his palace in the Turkish style. Conducting rehearsals of his female dancers and women's choir, the *barin*, surrounded by young attractive girls, wandered about wearing his Turkish robe, trousers, and a yarmulke woven with gold.[47] For an aristocrat impersonating a sultan served by harem girls or a "tsar sitting in his prefecture,"[48] the serf theater was his re-dressed court with subjects over whom he – a ruler with absolute power – exercised his own justice, punishment, and reward. Actresses, the glory of the theater/court and the owner's prize, were instrumental to his power.

What explains the obsession and enormous power drive of the male aristocrats with serf theater and actresses? Seeking the source of fascination with theater in early modern England, Gay writes that "one consistent feature of Shakespearian drama . . . is that it proceeds by way of *inversion* of the norms of behaviour"

---

[45] This distinction strikes me as substantially different from that drawn by Judith Butler between theatricality and performativity. (Butler, 282-287).

[46] N. S. Leskov, *Povesti i rasskazi* [Novels and Stories] (Moscow: Hudozestvennaia literatura, 1959), 225.

[47] Sakhnovskii, 21.

[48] That is how Beskin describes count Sheremetiev, whom his serfs referred to as "his majesty count-sovereign" (Beskin, 13).

providing "the exhilarating sense of freedom which transgression affords."[49]   In Russian serf theater, while the pleasure of transgression was triggered by the cross-dressing of a serf girl as a countess, the "exhilarating sense of freedom" was achieved when the theatrical "play-ground" was extended to a dreamland "in which people [aristocrats] did things that they could not or would never dare do."[50] Thus what they could not or would never dare do to real countesses, they were able to do to a *theatrical* countess impersonated by a serf actress. Theater thus offered owners the invigorating pleasure of exercising and exhibiting their power over (made-up) noblewomen.

Some serf theater owners not only slept with their actresses but viewed them as rudimentary material to be cut, carved, and shaped into works of art. Reversing the myth of Galateia, a statue coming to life, serf actresses were sometimes forced to imitate ancient statues, posing naked at noblemen's gatherings.[51] Some of these actresses, like Usupov's, were rewarded with "five rubles per month for tea with sugar,"[52] or with dresses and perfumes. One speculates that a Pygmalion syndrome inspired these noblemen, with much human material at their disposal,[53] not only to carve replicas of noble matrons, but to perfect the given model and by doing so to comment on their high-society women.

Whom did the nobleman, presumably an educated man of refined taste, see before him when he looked at a young serf actress in his theater? Unlike the singing slave girls documented by Jonce, Russian serf girls were of the same ethnicity as their owners.[54] Their physical features, figures, faces, hair, and eye color were no different from those of the countesses, patronesses, and princesses surrounding the nobleman in his social circle. These Russian girls also spoke the same language, perhaps (because of their training) even better than some noblewomen. Furthermore, selected for their youth and beauty,[55] the actress girls may have been more attractive than most countesses. The actresses, with their natural beauty, refined tastes, education, trained voices, movements, and their understanding of music and poetry, were expected to be submissive in an age when

---

[49] Gay, 43.

[50] *Ibid.*

[51] Evreinov suggests that these frozen statues became fashionable at the end of the eighteenth century (Evreinov, 217).

[51] Arguing that "people who sing and dance do not think about evil," Catherine called theater the "people's school" (*shkola narodnaya*) Schuler, 220.

[52] Kashin, 7.

[53] Sheremetiev, for example, owned 207,191 serfs by 1801, and Usupov possessed 21,421 *souls*; Shepetov, 25.

[54] It seems paradoxical that rise of nationalism coincided with the enactment of the most restrictive laws with regard to serfdom during the age of Russian enlightenment. Taruskin's revolutionary approach to the study of Russian nationalism in music has not yet been matched by a cultural study of nationalistic art in the context of slavery.

[55] Similarly, Howe remarks on English actresses of the late 1600s: "The heroine's important quality was her beauty." Elizabeth Howe, "English Actresses in Social Context: Sex and Violence," in: *Routledge Reader*, 61.

the traditionally patriarchal upper class Russian male elite was challenged by a chain of powerful tsarinas and by the emergence of noblewomen in the public arena.

Perhaps the obsessive fascination of noblemen with theater and actresses represented the dangerous possibility of reversing the theatrical and social scene and traversing social roles. Garber, investigating gender dress codes and social differences, sees theater as a generator of "deep-seated anxieties about the possibility that identity was not fixed, that there was no underlying 'self' at all."[56] The plot of *opera comique* to some degree probes this notion by making a peasant girl a concealed countess and by turning a milkmaid into a queen. By extension, the identity of the serf actress may be seen as non-fixed. Writing about this possible outcome of theatrical transgression, Gay states that "to get in touch with the fields of desire is fraught with danger. . ." Perhaps the most intriguing (and danger-fraught) example of the theatrical transgression is that of Shermetiev and Zhemchugova.

The settings

The story unfolds in two magnificent settings: Kuskovo and Ostankino. The first, Kuskovo, was a stunning park with artificial ponds, elegant fountains, canals with festive yachts and gondolas, and small ponds inhabited by fish and birds. A miniature zoo and a lion pavilion surrounded by water were built in the middle of the park, and ancient ruins rose in the romantic garden. The estate had a refuge for philosophers, a temple of silence, special guest houses in Italian and Dutch styles, as well as Chinese, Indian, and Persian gazebos. It was a place of endless masquerades, parades, fireworks, and theatre.

The second setting, Ostankino, had a palace-theater that contained crimson and green dining rooms, an Italian sculpture gallery, and an Egyptian banquet and concert hall.[57] The theater, known as *vokzal* (perhaps after England's Vauxhall Gardens), was an amazing construction whose rising amphitheater, spectator's balconies, wide stage, and columns could be dismantled in half an hour, transforming the theater into a royal audience or a large ball room for hundreds of people. During a visit of the Polish king to Ostankino, five hundred people attended an opera production, after which the theater was transformed into a ballroom.[58]

Catherine the Great's visit to Kuskovo was memorialized in the one-act opera *A Gardener from Kuskovo*,[59] performed after a two-act pastoral, *Useless Jealousy*

---

[56] Garber, 177.

[57] Sholok, 13.

[58] *Otgoloski stariny*, 47

[59] The opening recitative from *A Gardener from Kuskovo* refers to Tsarina Catherine's visit to Kuskovo in 1775, when a stage was constructed in the midst of a garden in which French actors performed a comic opera, Lepskaya, 18. Enjoying her visit to Kuskovo, the tsarina returned in 1785 and 1797; Elizarova, 21.

or The Coachman from Kuskovo[60] (1781). Staged in the open, the scenery of this production mirrored the real ponds, hills, and village. Both the opera and the estate displayed the wealth and generosity of the owner. The main character, a shepherd sings:

> Everybody is free and happy;
> All who want are entertained
> There is wealth and plentitude
> And countless delights
> Have you been there?
> Have you seen
> The owner and all of them?[61]

To what owner does it refer? Was it Peter Sheremetiev, who reconstructed Kuskovo in the early 1750s? Or was it his son, Nikolai, who remodeled the old theater and constructed the theatrical complex with indoor and outdoor theaters in 1787? In 1777, seeing Nikolai's strong interest in art, music, and theater, his father entrusted to him all the business related to the family serf theater. In the 1790s, in addition to the theater in Kuskovo and the family's Moscow palace, Sheremetiev junior erected the theater-palace in Ostankino (1792-1797). After the death of Catherine the Great in 1796, Ostankino hosted tsar Pavel during his 1797 coronation in Moscow[62] and entertained the next Russian tsar Alexander I at his accession in 1801. The Polish king Stanislav Ponatovsky also appreciated the hospitality of the owner, the beauty of his palace, theater, and its glorious star, Praskovia Zhemchugova, who gave her last performance for his visit in 1797.

The characters

Count Nikolai Sheremetiev, one of the wealthiest Russian aristocrats, refused court and military careers, devoting his life to the arts, music, and theater. Sheremetiev represented the thirteenth generation of a prominent Russian dynasty, which had emerged from the son of a Prussian king who assisted Alexander Nevsky in the thirteenth century and became the founder of several Russian families, including the monarchial Romanovs.[63] Nikolai Sheremetiev's grandfather, tsar Peter's favorite field marshal, was married to the widow of the tsar's uncle. Nikolai

---

[60] Text by Vasily Kolychev, music borrowed from popular French operas; Lepskaya, 23.

[61] *Ibid.*

[62] According to Jacquetta Beth Fooks, Zhemchugova, appearing "in medieval armor in The Samnitskie Marriages [*Les marriages Samnites* by Grétry], was applauded by the Austrian emperor Joseph II, by the Polish King Poniatowski, and later at Ostankino by Tsar Pavel I, who on a visit to this estate, and treated her graciously as if she were truly the mistress of the house." Fooks, 22-23.

[63] Aleksandra Barsukova, *Rodoslovie Sheremetevhkh* [Geanealogy of Sheremetiev] (St. Petersburg, 1899), 5.

Sheremetiev's father, named after tsar Peter, was among the most influential figures at the courts of both Elizabeth and Catherine. He was a close friend of Alexey Razumocsky, a singer from the Ukrainian chorus who became Tsarina Elizabeth's lover and companion. Following the fashion of "masquerades, choruses, orchestras and theaters inspired by Razumovsky,"[64] Peter Sheremetiev established his splendid *capel* (choir), horn ensemble, and later a serf theater. The star of the troupe was the operatic singer and actress Praskovia Zhemchugova.

Unlike the six hundred year genealogy of her owner, Zhemchugova's family history is barely known. The daughter of a serf, her family name was defined by her father's occupation and appearance. Thus Praskovia was known as Gorbunova (*gorbun* – hunchback) and Kuznetzova (*kuznetz* – blacksmith) or Kovaleva (from *koval*, blacksmith in Ukranian or Polish).[65] The Ukrainian/Polish rendition of the name could indicate either the ethnicity of the family or reflect, with regard to beautiful Praskovia's voice, a common belief that all the best voices were Ukrainians.[66]

A year after Praskovia was born, twenty-year-old Nikolai Sheremetiev left for four years of travel in Sweden, Holland, and France. He attended the University of Leiden and in Paris studied cello and absorbed the ideas and ideals of late eighteenth century Europe. He collected an enormous library, nearly half composed of books on music and theater. Driven by his passion for opera, in an age when most plays staged in serf theaters integrated dramatic, musical, and dance elements, he created a specialized operatic troupe on his return to Russia.

The song "Vechor posdno iz lesochku ya korov domoy gnala" tells a folk version of the first encounter between Sheremetiev and Zhemchugova. She was walking a cow and singing a song when she was knocked off her feet by a horseman. In the song, the count followed the girl to her hut, and, amazed by her song and her beautiful dark eyes, took the smith's daughter to his palace. In real life, the seven- or eight-year-old Parasha, like other serf girls and orphans annually selected for theater, was brought to Kuskovo to study in Sheremetiev's own theatrical school.[67] Under the patronage of the count's aunt, Parasha grew up in the count's house with ballerina Tat'yana Shlykova (Granatova); the singer and the ballerina became friends for life.[68] Along with acting, singing, and dancing, the girls studied French, Italian, music, grammar, and mathematics.[69] They were

---

[64] Elizarova, 300.

[65] *Ibid.*

[66] When Sheremetiev Theater ceased to exist, Count Dolgorukii wrote an epigram:
Teatr volshebnyi podlomilsa
Hohly v nem bol'she ne pout
[Magic theater ended its existence
Ukranians sing there no more.]

[67] Staniukovich, 13.

[68] Elizarova, 300.

[69] Staniukovich, 14.

coached by the best actors and musicians of Moscow and St. Petersburg.[70] Among Parasha's instructors were Sandunova, a singer, and Sinyavskaya, an outstanding performer of tragic characters. In addition, Parasha learned to play harpsichord and studied harp from the court musician Cordon.

According to various accounts, Sheremetiev was a meticulous entrepreneur involved in every detail of his projects, whether architectural designs, theatrical productions, choice of repertoire, the instruction of his actors, or living arrangements. He erected theatrical complexes modeled on the best architectural structures of Paris; in fact, Kuskovo was called a "little Versailles."[71] As he created a troupe that would be able to perform the repertoire of leading Parisian theaters, Sheremetiev paid great attention to the theatrical repertoire. His theater undertook Russian premiers of the most popular spectacles performed in France. For example, *Azémia, ou Les sauvages* by D'Alayrac was first staged in Fontainebleau, repeated by the Italian Comedy Theater of Paris, and then shown in Sheremetiev's theater. *L'infante de Zamora* by Paisiello was "borrowed" from the theater in Versailles; *Lucile* by Gretry, *Laurette* by J. Mereaux, and *Nina or La folle par amour* by Dalayrack were staged after their productions in the Italian Comedy Theater of Paris.

Many of the scores of French operas could be found only in Sheremetiev's possession. Like Catherine the Great, who frequently sought advice on theatrical repertoire from her correspondents Voltaire and Diderot, Nikolai Sheremetiev regularly wrote to Ivar, a cello player of the Paris Opera, whom he met during his European journey. The two corresponded for more than twenty years, during which time the count received every theatrical novelty from his Parisian agent – librettos and scores, sketches of theatrical buildings and their exteriors, costume and setting designs, and accessories for actresses.

The performer of all the main roles and the one for whom the most lavish royal dresses and jewelry were designed and made was Parasha Kovaleva, whom the count named Zhemchugova. She first appeared on the stage in the 1779 premier of *L'amitie à lepreuve* by Gretry, playing the small role of a maid. A year later, the eleven-year-old Praskovia performed the main character in *La Colonie* by Sacchini. In the summer of 1781, in the open-air theater in Kuskovo, Parasha played a shepherdess in *A Coachman from Kuskovo*, for the first time entertaining Catherine the Great. The career of the operatic singer, not yet in her teens, seems nearly impossible. At thirteen, Parasha played a dramatic role in the *opera comique Le Déserteur* by Monsigny. Her heroine, a farmer's daughter, reveals her willingness throughout the opera to sacrifice for her upper-class beloved one. Upon the demands of the soldier's relative, a countess, the girl refuses his love pretending to be engaged to someone else. Learning that in desperation, the soldier

---

[70] Cianfonel, a choreographer of the imperial theater in St. Petersburg, and Salomony, from Maddox Theater in Moscow, taught Sheremetiev's dancers.

[71] "Kuskovo not only corresponded to the type of French theater, but the plan of the auditorium was a copy of the opera theater in Versailles, built by the architect Gabrieli" (1753-1770). See Lepskaya, 32.

deserted the army, was caught, and was awaiting execution, the heroine seeks an audition with the king and saves her lover's life (as well as their romance). This and other similar characters became Zhemchugova's musical and artistic specialty as French *opera comique* became the most popular genre on the Russian stage.

Zhemchugova was the prize possession in Sheremetiev's jewel collection – his actresses, to whom the count gave the names of precious stones: singers Zhemchugova (pearl), Anna Izumrudova (emerald), Arina Yahontova (sapphire) Fekla Biruzova (turquoise), Avdot'ya Ametistova (amethyst), and ballerinas Tat'yana Granatova (ruby), Mavra Biruzova, and Arina Chrystaleva (crystal). Sheremetiev's human collections also included the best Russian artists, architects, and designers (the Argunovs, Muchin), the best Russian choirmasters (Deghtarev and Lopahin), and his own Russian Stradivarius – the best violin maker, Batov.[72] He likewise accumulated art galleries, rare scores, and books, spectacles that could not be seen in any other Russian theaters.

Though historical accounts, references of friends, visitors, and guests of Sheremetiev's wonderlands, as well as memoirs of family members and the count's own writing have left us with plentiful, sometimes contradictory material on count Sheremetiev, the image of Zhemchugova, whose fame and dramatic story continuously stirs the imagination of Russian musicians, historians, writers, and general audiences, remains unknown. Most literary accounts venerate her beauty, her voice, and acting; some also refer to her kindness and devotion to the count. Mythologized, the persona of the actress is hidden in the shadow of her theatrical roles as a noble shepherdess, disguised princess, and devoted lover. All of these roles were transferred from stage to life along with the dichotomy of social transgression and reassurance.

The romance

As in most operatic libretti, the beginning of the romance between the serf actress and the count remains unknown. Was it a handkerchief that brought Nikolai Sheremetiev to Zhemchugova's private apartment? (Bessonov suggested that the female troupe functioned as Count Sheremetiev's harem. According to the writer, the count, frequently passing through the actresses' quarter, used to "forget" his handkerchief in the girls' room, returning for it at night[73]). Or was it affection for a little girl "gifted with natural talents," whom he himself raised for "future great success," and to whom he grew "accustomed for twenty years."[74] Secrecy, inseparable from operatic transgression, characterized the real relations of the count and his beloved. While the count's father was alive, Nikolai's romances

---

[72] S. Golubov. "Ivan Batov-russian Stradivari," in: *Mastera Krepostnoi Rossii* [Russian Serf Artists], ed. B. Barhash (Moscow: Moodaya Gvardi Press, 1938), 161-195.

[73] Bessonov suggested that the young aristocrat, like many others, frequently visited actresses' quarters (Staniukovich, 41).

[74] Elizarova, 301-315.

were kept private. After his father's death in 1789, Nikolai Sheremetiev rebuilt an old bathhouse for his mistress in which the two lived together.

As the lead actresses of the troupe, Zhemchugova was marginalized among serfs. As the count's lover, on the other hand, she was marginalized among the actors. Serfs and actors began referring to her as *barskaya baryna* (literally translated as "nobleman's noblewoman" or a "made-up noblewoman").[75] This term was typically applied to a serf woman, peasant, or a maid who remained a landlord's mistress for an extended period of time and lived with him in his palace. In these cases, the woman, privileged by her owner, exercised power over her former equals. In response, serfs would designate her a *barskaya barynia*, expressing both their deference to and, at the same time, mockery of one who was elevated indefinitely. While the term itself signified the short-time transformation of a serf woman into a quasi patroness, in the case of Zhemchugova this title diminished the singer, actress, and star to the status of a temporary mistress. However, raised in the aristocrat's household, isolated from villagers, educated by the best pedagogues, and privileged by the special attention of the count's aunt and father, Zhemchugova was anything but a serf and a peasant. Though on stage the actress was seen as a marvel of aristocratic manners and refinement, in life she, in her role of *barskaya baryna*, was an imposter. Thus in her real-life *social role-playing*, the actress was engaged in an act of multiple transformation/transgression: from a peasant girl to an actress, to an operatic countess, and to a nobleman's mistress who in the eyes of others remained a serf enacting the role of "made up" *barskaya baryna*. In his attempt to detach his beloved from her past and at the same time pursue his own artistic ambitions, the count relocated the theater from Koskovo to Ostankino, where he built his monumental theater-palace. During this time, the public character of the actress's stage appearances increasingly contrasted with the privacy of her offstage life.   Compensating for her isolation, Zhemchugova surrounded herself with a few dedicated actress friends and family members. The count extended his favor and support to her companions. For example, in 1801 Sheremetiev ordered his *upravitel'* (manager) to find a nursemaid for Zhemchugova's sister, Matrena Kalmykova; clothes to be given to her husband and brothers; a wooden house to be presented to Ivan Kovalev; and the actress's mother be "given everything she wants for her hard work."[76] Continuously seeking ways of legitimizing his love for the actress and making her an equal among his associates, the count found an operatic resolution. He ordered a genealogical search of the actress's family of Kovalevs. Consequently his agents released the news that the name Kovalev was a Russian version of Kovaevsky and that the family descended from a noble but impoverished Polish dynasty.[77] In the best tradition of *opera comique*, the serf actress rediscovered her noble origin.

---

[75] Sholok, 9.

[76] *Stoletnie otgoloski*, 1801.

[77] Stanukovich, 57. The reference to Polish quasi-noble roots was not unusual at the time. Tsarina Elizabeth suggested that the actor Narikov change his name to Dmitrievsky, implying an association with the Polish nobility.

In the discussion of operatic librettos, in which a simple village girl suddenly discovers her noble identity, the questions remain: What inspires a noble hero to fall in love with a peasant or a milkmaid? Does this typical story imply that an aristocrat recognizes under the appearance of a beautiful peasant girl the true identity of a noble matron, or does the twist with the girl's recovered identity simply provide the happy ending of the love story? And accordingly, did Sheremetiev invent the actress's family story to justify his feelings for a serf actress, or was the count hoping for a formality that would advance his love affair to a happy ending?

In the operas produced in Sheremetiev's theater, the discovery of a heroine's noble identity led to a wedding. In real life too, the count sought and received the blessing of the patriarch of the Russian Church; the actress signed the matrimonial document with her ennobled Polish name of Kovalevsky. Nevertheless, the transgression and social crossing did not work in offstage Russian society nor did it prove effective at the rise of the nineteenth century. Tragic events for Sheremetiev's theater and the couple began to accelerate after the death of Tsarina Catherine the Great in 1796. Sheremetiev, along with other aristocrats, was called to the capital by the new ruler, Tsar Pavel. Though in 1797, Ostankino, the couple's home, hosted several royal guests, and Tsar Pavel and the Polish king S. Ponatovsky enjoyed the beauty of the theater and its star, the relocation of Sheremetiev's residence to St. Petersburg became inevitable. According to Lepskaya, spring 1797 was Ostankino's last theatrical season, and Zhemchugova's last public performance.

The marriage of the count and the actress, unsanctioned by the tsar, remained a secret. In addition, in the summer of 1801 both the actress and the count suffered tragic personal losses. Zhemhugova's sister Marfa died giving birth, and her mother died several months later. Sheremetiev lost his beloved niece from his half sister Remeteva, the daughter of his father and a serf woman.[78] These events accelerated the Sheremetievs' final departure from Moscow to St. Petersburg. There the actress faced tuberculosis, which had been developing for several years, perhaps resulting from Zhemchugova's extremely early singing career. In 1803, thirty-five-year old Countess Praskovia Sheremetieva died, twenty one days after giving birth to a heir of one of the most prominent Russian families. Although "St. Petersburg's aristocracy admired her [Zshemchugova's] acting in past years, they refused to participate in her funeral rites."[79] The funeral of one of the first and brightest stars of Russian theater, a woman praised by kings and tsars, was attended by only a few, including several servants, and the architect Gvarengi.[80]

---

[78] Remeteiva had been raised in the count's household and Nikolai Sheremetiev treated his father's granddaughter as his own daughter. (*Stoletnie otgoloski*, 1801.)

[79] Elizarova, 306.

[80] Staniukovich, 58. The son of the count and the actress, Count Dmitry Sheremetiev grew up indifferent to the theater, and though aware of the confession written by his father, revealed no interest in the persona of his mother.

Conclusion

The *opera comique* has a happy conclusion, usually culminating in a wedding. The *theatrical* ending leaves to the spectators' imagination the *social role-playing* that would result for the heroine if the play was re-enacted in the world outside the theater. The opera does not deal with personal and cultural issues – how a girl raised in a village would adapt to the environment of her aristocratic husband, or how the aristocratic society would perceive the actress in the role of countess and wife of the only heir of an eminent dynasty. The post-bridal roles of the "made-up" noblewomen were not staged, rehearsed, or written in eighteenth century Russia. While the romance of Zhemchugova and Sheremetiev mirrored the idyllic world of eighteenth century *opera comique*, the ending of their love story fell in a new century, during which operatic drama frequently unveiled the dramatic events following a wedding, as, for example, in the fairytale opera *Ruslan and Ludmila* (1842) by Mikhail Glinka. The wedding itself becomes a central episode in a number of Russian operas of the nineteenth century, leading to a dramatic shift in love stories and the portrayal of heroines, transformed, destroyed, or deconstructed, as in *Rusalka* by Dargomyzhsky, *Sadko* by Rimsky-Korsakov, and even *Eugene Onegin* by Tchaikovsky.[81] The destruction of women, dying of despair (and tuberculosis) became one of the main themes in European and Russian operas.

While the real life story of Zhemchugova ended in 1803, and the romantic count outlived her by six years, the interest in their romance endures. Entwined with the institution of early modern Russian serfdom, the story at the same time created a unique precedent that opposed or at least cast doubt upon this very system. Though one realizes that close, sometimes permanent, relations occurred between landlords and serf women, the marriage of the most prominent Russian bachelor to a serf actress star had great public visibility, and challenged the traditional hierarchy. Clearly mirroring the ideals of French-rooted Russian sentimentalism nourished in *opera comique*, this story became a part of native mythology, a social and artistic narrative that was retold, revisited, and re-estimated in the course of the following two centuries.

Largely forgotten or ignored by Sheremetiev's descendents, interest in the story was rekindled in the early twentieth century, when the romance between the actress and the count was scrutinized by socialistic writers. They explored the romance as a case study of social injustice providing substantial evidence of class demarcation manifested in "the unprecedented defiance of social norms,"[82] the secrecy of this marriage and in the count's refusal to openly defy social norms that:

> caused sufferings of the actress. She felt that her low origin burdened the count. With all his love for her. . . the marriage humiliated him. Not accidentally the count

---

[81] While in *Rusalka* and *Sadko*, weddings are actually staged, in *Eugene Onegin* the wedding is implied.

[82] Sholok, 9.

searched for examples of marriages between unequals among distinctive and famous men in the history of ancient Greece and Rome, as well as among Russian tsars.[83]

Some described Zhemchugova's fear, in her last days, of being separated from her child, the heir of a distinguished line.[84]

In post-Soviet work on the history and repertoire of Sheremetiev's serf theater, L. Lepskaya withdraws any social interpretation of the romance, laconically documenting that "the transformation of a poor girl into a countess occurred in real life. Happiness, nevertheless, was not long-lived."[85] Catherine Schuler, in her research on gender in Russian serf theater, briefly refers to Zhemchugova as "a sort of fairy-tale princess," "rescued from poverty and ignorance by the wealthy, urbane, thoroughly Europeanized Nikolai Sheremetiev."[86]

The story, mixing theater and reality, romantic love and social transgression, has inspired the production of musical plays, films, and fictional accounts. From the viewpoint of gender studies, the story deserves attention because of its context: the century of Russian reformation piloted by women rulers, all of them deeply engaged with theater, which served as a space for social experimentation, a space in which social roles and rules were probed and defined.

Postlude – masquerade: empresses and actresses

Two poor young women, living in different times, married royal men and became powerful tsarinas. Both of them changed their Germanic names to Catherine. Both were major players in Russian history: Catherine I as the wife of Peter the Great, and Catherine the Great as one of the most powerful Russian rulers.[87] The two Catherines marked the beginning and the end of women's rule over the Russian empire, which included four tsarinas following one another with only brief interruptions: Catherine I (1725-1727), Anna (1730-1740), Elizabeth (1741-1761), and Catherine the Great (1762-1796).

All of them were involved in acts of re-dress: social – from a poor laundry girl (Catherine I) and bankrupt princess (Catherine II) – and gender – both Elizabeth and Catherine appeared in men's military uniforms leading parades and conducting balls. The masquerade was to some extent the political and cultural engine of early modern Russia, in which social and gender roles were formulated, questioned, and reformed. The process reached its culmination under Catherine the Great, who ruled for more than a third of the century.

---

[83] Elizarova, 305.

[84] Beskin, 19.

[85] Lepskaya, 42.

[86] Schuler, 229.

[87] The maiden name of Catherine I, the daughter of a Lithuanian peasant, was Marta Skavronskaya. Catherine the Great, born in the German city of Stettin, came to Russia as Sophie Auguste Fredericke von Anhalt-Zerbst.

The librettos of operas written by Catherine the Great promoted the idea of a strong male ruler directed and supported by his mother. In *Novgorodskiy bogatir' Boyeslavich* (produced in Shereimetiv's theater in 1786-1787), the battle of the hero is followed by his wedding to his mother's choice of a bride. In *Fevey* (produced in Sheremetiev's theater in 1787), royal family disputes are concluded when Prince Fevey marries a princess found by his parents. According to Taruskin, these operas were "based on fairy-tales and meant as moral instruction for her grandsons, the future tsars Alexander I and Nicholas I."[88] In Catherine's other pursuits, legal, personal, and artistic, she was not limited by existing boundaries. Catherine's daring belongs to the world that also produced Zhemchugova.

One can picture an ornate theatrical auditorium. On one side, in a special balcony designed for royalty, sits Catherine the Great. Across from her, on a stage level with the royal balcony is Zhemchugova, leading a ballet staged for two hundred soldiers. In the finale she appears in a royal chariot.[89] Perhaps more than any other woman, Catherine could understand the transformation of a serf girl into a singer performing the role of the heroic Eliana, who against societal and gender rules declares her love and, when needed, cross-dresses as a soldier, defending her people, saving the commander, and winning the battle as a woman.

For a short moment, the paths of the two crossed, their life stories revealing paradoxical similarities.[90] Seven-year-old Parasha Kovaleva was taken away from her serf hut; the impoverished fourteen-year-old German princess was brought to Russia – both were separated from their families. The first was taught music and dance as well as French and Italian; the second assiduously studied Russian, dance, court manners, and Orthodox doctrines.[91] Zhemchugova, from an early age, appeared on the stage in a wide range of operatic roles. Catherine also enacted various roles during seventeen years of a miserable marriage with her ill husband

---

[88] Catherine herself wrote librettos for five operas: *Fevey* (1786, music by Pashkevich), *Novgorodskiy bogatir' Boyeslavich* ('Boyeslavich, Champion of Novgorod'; 1786, music by Fomin), *Khrabroy i smeloy vityaz' Akhrideich* ("The Brave and Bold Knight Akhrideich"; 1787, music by Vancura), *Gorebogatir Kosometovich* ("The Sorrowful Hero Kosometovich"; 1789, music by Martin y Soler) and *Fedul s det'mi* ("Fedul and his Children;" 1791, music by Pashkevich and Martin y Soler). In her literary works she was assisted by her literary secretaries, Ivan Yelagin and Alexander Khrapovitsky. Two of Catherine the Great's operas were produced in Sheremetiev's theater. In addition, the repertoire included Catherine's comedy *Mnimyi Mudretz* (False Wizard, 1785) which, unlike the tsarina's 'moral' operas, has a romantic plot: love between a maiden, Charming, and Count Lovely.

[89] The opera is *Les marriages Samnites* by Grétry. Today the carriage is still displayed in Ostankino museum (Staniukovich, 35).

[90] Catherine's literary secretary wrote about his search for jewelry and gifts that Catherine wanted to present to Zhemchugova; Elizarova, 303.

[91] Catherine recalled in her *Zapiski* [Notes] that, trying to win the sympathy of Tsarina Elizabeth and her courtiers, she secretly studied Russian at nights, which led her to severe exhaustion and pneumonia. *Sochinenia Ekateriny II*, 29.

and under the harsh observation of Elizabeth. Both women loved theater, one making the stage her empire, the other approaching her empire as a theatrical arena. One was an outstanding singer and actress, and an unsuccessful countess; the other an outstanding politician and a dramatist of relatively mediocre talent. Both came from a social background that provided no basis or preparation for the head-spinning traversing of roles and crossing the theatrical / social / political spaces that the two performed in their lives. Steven Greenblatt suggests in his writing on Shakespearian theater that "the boundaries between the theater and the world were not fixed, nor did they constitute a logically coherent set: rather they were a sustained collective improvisation."[92] The two women, Catherine II and Zhemchugova, represented opposite ends of a social spectrum in which social actors traversed territories of state and stage, testing, demarcating, and solidifying social, class, and gender roles.

---

[92] Stephen Greenblatt, *Shakespearian Negotiations* (Berkeley: University of California Press, 1988), 14.

WOMEN FROM THE CONVENTS

Chapter 11

The Good Mother, the Reluctant Daughter, and the Convent: A Case of Musical Persuasion

Colleen Reardon

The convent served diverse purposes in early modern Italy, many of them positive. Nevertheless, its most practical function was that of refuge for "superfluous" daughters. Cloistered religious institutions were especially useful to noble clans with abundant female offspring. In a number of Italian cities, girls from patrician families were more likely to take the veil than to marry.[1] Although it may indeed be reductionist to explain such a phenomenon in purely economic terms, it cannot be denied that many parents were unable or unwilling to pay the extraordinarily costly dowries required to make an honorable marriage for more than one daughter. Stated baldly, the convent provided a convenient and relatively inexpensive means of removing nubile but unmarried women from the secular world where they might stray or be forced into behavior that could bring dishonor to them and shame upon their family.[2]

The decision to take religious vows was, therefore, only sometimes prompted by individual vocation and probably more often spurred by a family's concern to keep its honor and patrimony intact. Understandably, not all girls destined for the

---

[1] The trend is evident, for example, in Florence, Bologna, Milan, and Venice; see Silvana Seidel Menchi, "Characteristics of Italian Anticlericalism," in: *Anticlericalism in Late Medieval and Early Modern Europe*, ed. Peter A. Dykema and Heiko A. Oberman (Leiden: E.J. Brill. 1993), 275; Craig A. Monson, *Disembodied Voices: Music and Culture in an Early Modern Italian Convent* (Berkeley and Los Angeles: University of California Press, 1995), 6; Robert L. Kendrick, *Celestial Sirens: Nuns and their Music in Early Modern Milan* (Oxford: Clarendon Press, 1996), 38-40; and Jutta Gisela Sperling, *Convents and the Body Politic in Late Renaissance Venice* (Chicago and London: University of Chicago Press, 1999), 18-19. I have no firm percentages on the number of noble Sienese girls who entered convents, but anecdotal evidence suggests that the situation was much the same there as in other urban centers. For example, Agostino Chigi and his wife Maria Virginia Borghese consigned ten of their eleven female children to nunneries; see Reardon, *Holy Concord within Sacred Walls: Nuns and Music in Siena, 1575-1700* (Oxford and New York: Oxford University Press, 2002), 19, 129-130.

[2] See, for example, Monson, *Disembodied Voices*, 21.

convent wanted such a life. Although both church officials and members of the lay community condemned the practice in writing, forced claustration was common during the sixteenth and seventeenth centuries.³ The most famous story of a woman compelled to take the veil against her will comes from the early modern period and served as fodder for two splendid chapters in Alessandro Manzoni's *I promessi sposi*. Inspired by the true story of Marianna de Leyva, the so-called "nun of Monza," Manzoni explores the psychology of Gertrude, a young woman who attempts to change her parents' plans for her.⁴ After eight years of education in a convent, Gertrude writes a letter to her father, declaring her unwillingness to become a nun. Some of Manzoni's most harrowing passages are dedicated to the process by which the family then proceeds to convince the young woman of her "vocation." They remove her from the nunnery, confine her to her room, and allow her no enjoyment and virtually no human contact. When Gertrude finally breaks, she is whisked back to the convent, presented to the nuns and, under the watchful eyes of her family, made to recite the formula her father has taught her:

> "I am here," began Gertrude, but on the point of offering the words that were to have almost irrevocably sealed her fate, she hesitated a moment and fixed her eyes on the crowd in front of her. She saw, in that moment, one of her companions, who was watching her with an air of compassion mixed with maliciousness and seemed to be saying, "Ah, the clever one has fallen into the trap!" That sight, reawakening with even more force in her soul all the old feelings, restored a little of her old courage and she was already searching for any answer other than the one dictated to her when, raising her eyes to her father's face, as if to test her strength, she saw such sinister anxiety, such threatening impatience that, prompted by fear, with the same readiness with which she would have taken flight before a dreadful object, she continued, " I am here asking to be admitted to take the habit in this convent where I was so lovingly raised."⁵

---

³ For an overview of attitudes in Milan on forced monachization, see Enrico Cattaneo, "Le monacazioni forzate fra Cinque e Seicento," in: *Vita e processo di suor Virginia Maria de Leyva, monaca di Monza*, ed. Umberto Colombo (Milan: Garzanti, 1985), 145-195. Giovanna Paolin looks at the effects of the practice inside the cloister in *Lo spazio del silenzio: Monacazioni forzate, clausura e proposte di vita religiosa femminile nell'età moderna* (Pordenone: Edizioni Biblioteca dell'Immagine, 1996).

⁴ Critical reactions to Manzoni's Gertrude are numerous and varied; see Umberto Colombo, "La Gertrude manzoniana," in: *Vita e processo*, 769-869.

⁵ – Son qui..., cominciò Gertrude ; ma, al punto di proferir le parole che dovevano decider quasi irrevocabilmente del suo destino, esitò un momento, e rimase con gli occhi fissi sulla folla che le stava davanti.   Vide, in quel momento, una di quelle sue note compagne, che la guardava con un'aria di compassione e di malizia insieme, e pareva che dicesse : ah ! la c'è cascata la brava. Quella vista, risvegliando più vivi nell'animo suo tutti gli antichi sentimenti, le restituì anche un po' di quel poco antico coraggio ; e già stava cercando una risposta qualunque, diversa da quella che le era stata dettata ; quando, alzato lo sguardo alla faccia del padre, quasi per esperimentar le sue forze, scorse su quella un'inquietudine così cupa, un'impazienza così minaccevole, che, risoluta per paura, con la stessa prontezza che avrebbe preso la fuga dinanzi un oggetto terribile, proseguì : – son qui a chiedere d'esser ammessa a vestir l'abito religioso, in questo monastero dove sono stata

That the real Marianna de Leyva was, to say the least, unsure of her commitment to the religious life was demonstrated by her subsequent actions: she took a lover and helped to murder a servant who threatened to expose her.[6] Historical accounts relate that other daughters also refused to go gently into the cloister or to remain peacefully within its walls. In mid seventeenth-century Milan, the young noblewoman Donna Maria Faustina Palomera left her convent in the company of two male admirers and did not return until the next day.[7] Venetian nuns, too, fled the cloister, often with the help of gentlemen or priests.[8] Other escape routes were more permanent: women sometimes killed themselves in despair.[9]

But what of the countless girls consigned to the cloister without vocation who somehow managed to accept their situation, become good nuns, and live out their lives with some kind of dignity? Exceptional women, famous or infamous, usually find their way into the documentary record, but the fate of the ordinary woman often disappears into what Francesca Medioli calls the "zone of silence."[10] One such woman was Laura Gori Pannilini. Born in 1656 to aristocratic Sienese parents, she was probably destined to the convent from birth and not overjoyed about the prospect at the beginning. We know only the barest details of her story, and in fact we lose track of her after she takes the veil at the Sienese convent of Il Refugio in 1673. But she appears to have professed willingly and her journey to that point can be reconstructed from letters that her mother, Olimpia Chigi Gori Pannilini, wrote to her own brother Cardinal Sigismondo Chigi and to her cousin Cardinal Flavio Chigi. These letters shed light on the relationship between mother and daughter as well as on the larger family dynamic; they reveal some of the strategies – one perhaps involving music – that the mother employed to ease her daughter's path into the convent. Clearly, what Olimpia says about Laura might not necessarily reflect Laura's thoughts. In the absence of Laura's voice, however, these frank and intimate letters from her mother to a well-loved brother and an esteemed cousin allow us to recover at least some echoes from the zone of monastic silence.

In the mid seventeenth century, Siena was home to twenty-one monastic or para-monastic institutions, in which about twelve percent of the city's female population lived as choir nuns, novices, or servant nuns.[11] As in other urban

---

allevata così amorevolmente – . Alessandro Manzoni, *I promessi sposi*, ed. Ferruccio Ulivi (Rome: Newton Compton editori, 1989), 173 (chapter ten). This and all translations of documents that follow are by the author, with invaluable help from Nello Barbieri.

   [6] See Ermanno Paccagnini, "La vita di suor Virginia Maria de Leyva," in: *Vita e processo*, 3-23.

   [7] Kendrick, *Celestial Sirens*, 96-97.

   [8] Francesca Medioli, ed., *"L'Inferno monacale" di Arcangela Tarabotti* (Turin: Rosenberg & Sellier, 1990), 121-122. See also Paolin, *Lo spazio del silenzio*, 52.

   [9] Luigi Fiorani, "Monache e monasteri romani nell'età del quietismo," *Ricerche per la storia religiosa di Roma* 1 (1977): 73.

   [10] "L'Inferno monacale" di Arcangela Tarabotti, 123.

   [11] Reardon, *Holy Concord*, 9-19.

centers, members of the patriciate sacrificed their sometimes unwilling daughters to the convent as part of a larger family strategy to conserve wealth, and non-aristocratic clans compelled their female offspring to enter religious houses either for the lack of a dowry or for the larger social good. In 1575, the apostolic visitor Francesco Bossi found the problem of forced monachization most severe at the house for reformed prostitutes, Le Convertite. During his interviews there, he heard (and his scribe recorded) the pitiful complaints of many women. One lament stands out for its striking tone of despair:

> It has been two years since I took the habit; I am not here willingly, and never was, because they put me here with blandishments and I came in tears. And I do not want to remain under any circumstances because I do not have the heart to observe the rule, and if I stay here I think it will be my damnation.[12]

Bossi's solution to the problem was to suggest that the abbess relax her harsh ways, but an institution whose mission was to convert prostitutes "by love or force"[13] was bound to have continuous and severe problems with discipline. Indeed, in 1629, three discontented nuns were blocked in their attempt to escape from Le Convertite.[14]

Nothing quite as dramatic emerges from the other Sienese houses with a more aristocratic clientele. Nevertheless, the problem does appear to lie just under the surface in records of some court cases officiated by the archbishop. In 1612, a certain Cecilia in the patrician convent of Ognissanti received a love letter from her brother-in-law Giovan Paolo, tucked into a book containing the Little Office of the Virgin Mary. The young man, who worked at the printing shop of Emilio Bonetti, tried to pass the entire incident off as a joke before the court, citing the strict ties of parentage between the two. It is, however, certainly possible to imagine an amorous bond between Giovan Paolo and a woman to whom he was related only through marriage, and we might suppose that Cecilia was not at all pleased to be consigned to the cloister while her sister savored the joys of carnal love.[15] The episcopal court also took up the matter of Alfonso Borghesi who, in 1632, kidnapped his niece Zemidea from the convent of S. Marta in order to

---

[12] "Sono due anni che sono vestita; non sto volentieri né mai so' stata, per che mi messero con lusinghe e venni piangendo et io non voglio star qui in modo veruno, per che non mi dà l'animo di servar la regola e stando qui credo saria la mia dannazione." Transcription from Giuliano Catoni, "Interni di conventi senesi del Cinquecento," *Ricerche storiche* 10 (1980): 180. Catoni's article provides both a useful summary of Bossi's 1575 visit and a complete transcription of the decrees he issued for Sienese nuns.

[13] Catoni, "Conventi senesi," 178.

[14] Franco Daniele Nardi, "Aspetti della vita dei religiosi a Siena nell'età della Controriforma (1600-1650), parte seconda," *Bullettino Senese di Storia Patria* 94 (1987): 163-168.

[15] Nardi, "Aspetti della vita dei religiosi," 158. Arcangela Tarabotti alludes more than once to the gnawing jealousy experienced by nuns with no vocation when they see their biological sisters, destined for secular marriage, "swimming in a sea of pleasure;" see Medioli, *"L'Inferno monacale" di Arcangela Tarabotti*, 43, 45.

"demonstrate publicly that her vocation was not forced upon her, as many people alleged."[16] In this case, the gentleman appears to protest too much; Zemidea was probably dissatisfied with her lot in life and the uncle was trying to terrify her into accepting it by means of humiliation.

One of the most interesting documents to speak to the issue of forced monachization in Siena is a discourse authored sometime in the late seventeenth century by a self-described Sienese priest who signed himself Thomas Borghi.[17] Borghi framed his story in the form of a dialogue between a mother and daughter. It appears that he took inspiration from an earlier dramatic work or play, for the prologue provides very specific details as background for the discourse.[18] The author informs the reader that a mother is attempting to impoverish her son Giovan Agnolo by depriving him of his rightful inheritance in order to enrich her favorite daughter, Fulvia. When her attempts with Giovan Agnolo fail, she begins a campaign to convince a younger daughter to renounce all claims to her maternal and paternal inheritance, as well as to money left her by an uncle, and to become a nun (50v).

After the prologue, Borghi summarizes (in indirect speech) all the arguments the mother trots out to persuade the daughter to such a course of action, most of them variations on a theme familiar from seventeenth century literature for or about nuns: the convent as an earthly Jerusalem and nuns as angels.[19] The mother contends that nuns are happiest among all women, for they do not have to suffer the hardships that wives must.[20] She states that nuns resemble angels, because they avoid all worldly traps and have the face of God always before their eyes. Finally, she declares that the convent is a paradise on earth, the sole place that a woman can live a life of perfect peace, tranquility, and love (50v-51r).

The daughter, who is home after living two years in a convent as an *educanda*, first sighs and then proceeds to relate all the ills that arise from forced monachization. Here Borghi switches to direct speech, lending these passages a forcefulness lacking in the mother's arguments. The daughter informs her mother that the most miserable women in the world are those who became nuns because they bowed to the violent exhortations of their relatives (51v). She describes one of

---

[16] Nardi, "Aspetti della vita dei religiosi," 169-170.

[17] I have been unable to find anything on Borghi's background or life. Certainly, however, Borghi was not the only priest to protest the practice of confining women in convents against their will; see Cattaneo, "Monacazioni forzate," 167-168; 174-179.

[18] Biblioteca Comunale, Siena, MS C.X.7., fols. 50r-58r, "Dell'impietà d'una madre in forzare una figliuola a farsi monaca contro la sua volontà, e de' cattivi effetti che da ciò seguono: discorso." Limitations of space forced the elimination of a complete transcription of the document. The original Italian is given in notes only for longer quotations from the manuscript; other passing references simply cite the appropriate folios in the text.

[19] Kendrick, *Celestial Sirens*, 161-163; Monson, *Disembodied Voices*, 89; Reardon, *Holy Concord*, 158.

[20] For more on the tactic of persuading girls to take the veil by comparing (happy) nuns to (unhappily) married women, see Cattaneo, "Monacazioni forzate," 182-183, and Reardon, *Holy Concord*, 82.

the ploys that families commonly exploited to induce their daughters to take the veil, the very one that Manzoni elaborated in such frightening detail in *I promessi sposi*:[21]

> Oh, how many thirteen or fourteen-year-old girls, raised with such terrible strictness by their relatives are seduced into thinking of nothing but getting away from the overly austere severity of their parents by choosing to enter a convent. They are lured by [the nuns'] celebrations without realizing the duties of everyday life. They do not dare to bat an eye to show their distaste, and they are even less able to say no. They believe (miserable ones) that they will taste ambrosia, but when they are eighteen or twenty years old, they realize that they have drunk a slow-acting poison that eats at their insides and kills their souls while they live in continuous torment. Then, they finally understand that the sole objective of all that austere treatment was to deprive them of their liberty.[22]

The daughter notes that most nuns would gladly abandon their "paradise" for a chance at marriage, even an unhappy marriage; she further observes that families place their daughters in convents not because they want them to serve God, but because they do not want to pay the dowries required for a secular matrimony (51v-52r).

Time and again during her long speech, the daughter rails against the cruelty of families who confine their female children to the cloister without the girls' freely given consent. She also severely criticizes the ecclesiastical authorities who allow this to happen and who do not examine the novices in the manner required by the Council of Trent. The church officials do nothing, states the daughter, because like their fellow citizens, they have the same interest in preserving family wealth (54v-55r).

The daughter proceeds to paint a stark portrait of the tormented thoughts and actions of women forced into the convent against their will. Nuns go to the grates and hear of the joys of worldly life and then return to their cells to weep uncontrollably and to curse all who had a part in imprisoning them (56r). Ambition, vanity, envy, and hate all flourish in the convent. The constitution goes unobserved, for the women violate the rules and scorn all commands (55v). Furthermore, they cannot control their unbridled passions. They read lascivious books, and are overcome by impure desires, which sometimes find vent, even in the cloister (56v).

---

[21]   See also Cattaneo, "Monacazioni forzate," 181.

[22]   Biblioteca Comunale, Siena, MS C.X.7, fol. 57r : "Oh quante giovanette di 13 o 14 anni, tenute ed allevate con sommo rigore da' parenti s'inducono senz'altra consideratione che di sottrarsi dalla severità tropp'austera de' lor genitori ad entrare nella relligione allettate da quelle gallorie senza cognitione de' pesi regolari e senz'ardire d'alzar pure un'occhio a mostrare la loro ripugnanza, non ché di poter contradire, e credendo (misere) d'assaggiare l'ambrosia quando poi arrivano all'età di diciotto o vint'anni, s'accorgono d'aver bevuto un veleno fabbricato a tempo che consuma loro le viscere o uccide loro l'anima mentre vivono in continuo tormento riconoscendo allora che 'l fine di quegli austeri trattamenti era solo per privarle di libertà."

The daughter compares the situation of women compelled to take the veil to that of the sacrificial victim; in her estimation, nuns have the worse deal:

> I have heard it said by the preacher that in ancient times they used to bleed the victims and then offer them to God in sacrifice, perhaps because blood is the principal seat of the bodily affections and it did not seem right to offer to His Divine Majesty a holocaust that was not purified of all earthly passions by bloodletting. But this is of no concern to the families, who sacrifice their miserable girls to God with all their affections and all their passions intact.[23]

According to the daughter, God does not want such offerings, and so the women are both "excluded from the world and unwanted by heaven" (54r). In one of her harshest judgments, the daughter implies that families who thrust their unwilling daughters into the cloister are the equals of Herod:

> Girls who are forced into a religious life are like those children [Herod killed] because they, too, are innocent and, under a pretense masked as religion, are separated from the living; the only difference between the innocents [of Herod's time] and the girls [compelled to take the veil] is that the former were killed and then buried, and the latter are buried behind walls before dying.[24]

The daughter's impassioned speech has no effect on the mother, who slaps her child and then tells her, "Ah, wicked girl, so these are meditations that you learned in the convent? Accept the fact that you will enter against your will, by force or by love, or you will die painfully by my hands." The discourse ends by grimly noting that the mother then took to beating her daughter every day (58r). The use of a "cruel mother" and the exclusion of a father figure in Borghi's discourse is striking and, as even Manzoni knew, not a realistic reflection of the dynamics of everyday

---

[23] Biblioteca Comunale, Siena, MS C.X.7, fol. 53v: "Ho inteso dire al Padre Predicatore che anticamente si solevano svenare le vittime e poi sacrificarle a Dio, perché forse consistendo nel sangue la principal sede degli affetti corporei non si stimava convenevole offerire a Sua Divina Maestà olocausto alcuno che non fosse stato prima depurato con l'effusione del sangue da ogni passione terrena, ma a questo non s'ha riguardo da parenti delle povere fanciulle che le sagrificano a Dio con tutt'i loro affetti e con tutte le loro passioni." This passage is very similar to an excerpt from Ferrante Pallavicino's *Le divorce céleste, causé per less dissolutions de l'Epouse Romaine* (1649), translated in Sperling, *Convents and the Body Politic*, 140. This might have been one of the earlier works that served as inspiration for Borghi's discourse.

[24] Biblioteca Comunale, Siena, MS C.X.7, fol. 55r: "Non fu già Cristo, no, ma fu l'impietà d'Erode quella che per l'occasione dell'humanato Salvatore diede morte a tanti fanciulli innocenti. Le fanciulle che involontarie entrano nella relligione sono in sorte eguali con essi poiché ancor loro innocenti per un pretesto mascherato di relligione son segregate dal concorso de' viventi non passando per avventura altra differenza tra quelli e queste se non che quelli furon fatti morire e poi sepolti, e queste fra quelle mura seppellite prima di morire." The image of women buried alive in convents was clearly a familiar one in seventeenth century Italy; see Medioli, *"L'inferno monacale" di Arcangela Tarabotti*, 34, 45; and Cattaneo, "Monacazioni forzate," 176.

life in early modern Italy. Arcangela Tarabotti, author of *L'Inferno monacale*, a ferocious critique of forced claustration, reserved her most vitriolic remarks for ruthless, tyrannical fathers who loved money above all things.[25] Mothers came in for only mild criticism concerning their lack of generosity towards daughters destined to be nuns, and Tarabotti noted that their actions were sometimes prompted by fear of their husbands.[26] Notwithstanding the sway husbands held over their wives, at least one case has come to light of a mother who fiercely protected her female offspring. The Venetian noblewoman Fiorenza Capello Grimani was so concerned that her daughters not be cloistered unwillingly that she made out her testament in such a way as to guarantee both that they would have dowries for secular marriages and that her husband could touch not a single *lira* of hers if he forced the girls to become nuns.[27] Although it seems that most mothers did not go to the lengths that Fiorenza Capello did, this does not mean that they were utterly heartless and that they consigned their female children to the convent without a care about their well-being or happiness. It is here that I wish to return to the case of Olimpia Chigi and her second oldest child, Laura, in order to explore how the mother might have approached the task of assuring her daughter the best life possible in the cloister.

Olimpia Chigi was born in 1635 to Augusto Chigi and Olimpia Della Ciaia. Only four of her siblings survived to adulthood: Verginia, Agostino, Laura, and Sigismondo, the last a child of her father's second marriage to Francesca Piccolomini.[28] Life changed for the men in this branch of the Chigi family after 1655, when their uncle Fabio became Pope Alexander VII. Two years after Fabio's ascension to the papal throne, Olimpia's cousin Flavio obtained the rank of cardinal; her half-brother Sigismondo was raised to the purple in 1667. The pope called Olimpia's brother Agostino to Rome and made him captain of Castel Sant'Angelo and of the papal guards, as well as governor of Benevento and Civitavecchia. In 1658, the pope arranged for the twenty-four-year-old Agostino to marry Maria Virginia Borghese, and disbursed enormous sums to acquire palaces, villas, and principalities for the couple in order to assure his nephew a social standing equal to that of his bride.[29]

Olimpia and her sisters experienced no such dramatic changes in their lives. All remained in Siena and followed the normal paths open to young aristocratic women: Verginia wed Giovanbattista Piccolomini in 1648, and in September 1653,

---

[25] Medioli, *"L'Inferno monacale" di Arcangela Tarabotti*, 31, 32, 34, 35, 36, 37, 38, 39, 43, 44, 50, 51, 52, 53, 55.

[26] *Ibid.*, 44, 46.

[27] Pa olin, *Lettere familiari della nobildonna veneziana Fiorenza Capello Grimani, 1592-1605* (Trieste: Edizioni LINT, 1996), 15-19; 79-80.

[28] All information on birth and marriage dates of the Chigi comes from Ugo Frittelli, *Albero genealogico della nobil famiglia Chigi, patrizia senese* (Siena: Arti Grafiche Lazzeri, 1922), 68-70; 133-35. For an abbreviated genealogical table of the Chigi family, see Reardon, *Holy Concord*, 124.

[29] See Reardon, *Holy Concord*, 123-125, 129.

at the age of eighteen, Olimpia Chigi married Giulio Gori Pannilini, a scion from another patrician Sienese family. The youngest surviving sister, Laura, entered the Franciscan convent of S. Girolamo in Campansi, where she took the religious name Suor Maria Pulcheria. Olimpia seems to have been fond of both her sisters; she and Verginia often wrote letters together to other family members, and many of Olimpia's letters mention Suor Maria Pulcheria. Unfortunately, none of the mail that passed among the sisters has yet surfaced; what does survive is the correspondence Olimpia sent to her relatives living in Rome, much of it to Sigismondo. Despite the difference in their ages, Olimpia was close to her younger half-brother, for her letters to him are intimate in tone and lively in style. Olimpia kept Sigismondo informed about local events, and up to date on the health and activities of immediate family members.

It was in 1669 that Olimpia first mentioned Laura in a letter to her half-brother. Olimpia and her husband Giulio had twelve children between 1655 and 1668. Five were daughters – Egeria, Laura, Leonora, Isifile, and Clarice – and every one of them survived babyhood.[30] By April 1671, the four oldest girls were living at the Sienese convent of Il Refugio as *educande*; Clarice joined her sisters in July of the same year.[31] The presence of all five sisters at a single house was, however, a relatively new development. In November 1663, Laura had been sent to S. Girolamo in Campansi with the clear intention of having her profess vows there. She remained at the convent as an *educanda* for five years, but in November 1668, her parents withdrew her from the institution before she had taken the habit.[32] Two months after her departure, a concerned Olimpia related to Sigismondo the problems she was experiencing with the child she affectionately nicknamed "Lala:"

> Your Eminence knows that I took Lala out [of Campansi] because she had a fever. After a month on the outside, the fever passed and she is well, but I am not sure that I am going to put her back in because it seems that the air is unhealthy for her. And I tell you this in confidence – Sister Maria Pulcheria is not to know – the girl is not really willing to stay up there [at Campansi] and so I think I shall tell Sister Maria Pulcheria that I will not put her back in [for that reason] because otherwise she will become angry with me. But as long as [Laura] must become a nun, I want her to be content and I believe that anyone to whom [Sister Maria Pulcheria] will voice her laments will

---

[30] Baptism dates for all the girls can be found in Archivio di Stato, Siena, MS A50: Galgano Bichi, "Raccolta di nomi di persone nobili battezzate in Siena, vol. 3," 74r-v. Egeria was baptized 12 September 1655; Laura, 21 August 1656; Leonora, 26 October 1661; Isifile, 31 August 1663; and Clarice, 22 November 1664.

[31] Archivio di Stato, Siena, Conventi soppressi 3866, "Memorie diverse 1671-1769," fol. 58v. Earlier records from the institution are spotty, so we have no way of determining precisely when Egeria, Laura, Leonora, and Isifile first entered its gates.

[32] Payments from Giulio Gori for Laura's room and board at Campansi may be found in Archivio di Stato, Siena, Conventi soppressi 1942, fols. 5v, 13r, 17r, 20v; and 1943, fols. 3v, 6r, 11r, 21r, and 24v.

think I am right, since I have tried to put her back in two times...Siena, 9 January 1669.[33]

In this letter, Olimpia reveals herself to be anything but a cruel mother. She takes her sick daughter out of the convent to recover at home, and she does not force the girl to return when she is disinclined. She is willing to risk both public criticism from (and the private wrath of) her sister, who is a nun at the institution. Finally, as she explains to her brother, she wants Laura to be happy, even if she is destined to live out her life in a cloister. Olimpia's predicament cannot have been unique. Certainly, other tender-hearted women in Siena (and in Italy, for that matter) must have been faced with a daughter reluctant to accept her fate as a nun. What was a mother to do?

The first thing an intelligent mother did was to choose very carefully the religious institution to which her daughter was bound. It was customary to place a girl in a house where sisters, cousins, and aunts were already enclosed in order to guarantee a cadre of concerned relatives to help ease the transition from the world to the cloister. Girls destined for the veil were also often sent to a convent for education when very young – usually around age seven – so that they grew up with the routines of religious life and had little chance to "learn about the other meager options life offered them."[34]

This strategy also worked to the advantage of professed nuns. In order to assure their own power base and prestige, they knew that they had to maintain a high number of relatives and members of allied families within the cloister. The choice of a religious institution was therefore subject to intense pressure by family and friends. An idea of the coercive forces at work is evident in the following letter that Suor Lutugarda Chigi – another of Olimpia's aunts, a nun at S. Margherita in Siena – wrote to either Flavio or Sigismondo Chigi. Her final statement expresses in harshest terms the reality of the situation for the young girl whose life was at stake:

The [wife?] of Signor Count Antonio D'Elci had promised me to send one of her daughters to this, our convent, to be a nun. Today, Signor Cavaliere Girolamo Ugurgieri does not want that to happen and is insinuating the idea that the mother should not satisfy the daughter's wishes and instead should persuade her to take the veil at Il Refugio. Now, this is what I desire of Your Eminence and why I am writing

---

[33] Biblioteca Apostolica Vaticana, Archivio Chigi 3871, fols. 32r-33r: "Vostra Eminenza sa che io cavai Lala che aveva la febre e dopo a un mese che è stata fuora gli è passata e sta bene, ma non so se io ce la rimetterò perché l'aria non mi pare che li si affacci niente e per dirla con confidenzia che Suor Maria Pulcheria non lo sappi, la citta ne meno ci sta volentieri su e così mi credo che come dirò a Suor Maria Pulcheria di non ce la rimettere che abbi a entrare in valigia bene con esso me. Ma mentre lei si à da far monaca voglio che lei si contenti e credo che ogni uno mi darà la ragione con chi lei si lamentarà mentre che ò provato a rimettercela due volte....Siena, il 9 gennaio 1669."

[34] Monson describes such tactics as "gentler, subtler forms of persuasion" for young girls fated to be nuns; see his *Disembodied Voices*, 21.

to bother you. Please write to said Signor Cavaliere [and tell him] that he should allow the one who must live perpetually in prison to content herself.[35]

It was rare that girls were able to choose their prison, and Laura is a case in point. Olimpia had named her second oldest daughter for her own sister, who had professed at Campansi. Laura's fate was thus sealed from birth: she had been promised to Suor Maria Pulcheria. The married sister had discharged a debt of honor, and the holy woman was guaranteed a family member to buttress her own position. The only problem was Laura, who was unhappy. It is at this point that Olimpia took matters into her own hands, placing her daughter's welfare above loyalty to her sister.[36] The second time around, she elected to send Laura to Il Refugio. Her decision was certainly motivated by familiarity: both Olimpia and her sister Verginia had lived at Il Refugio as *educande* before their respective marriages.[37] Furthermore, since Laura's sisters Egeria and Leonora were probably already in residence as boarders, and since Verginia had also sent her two daughters to Il Refugio for education, Laura could count on having both sisters and cousins as companions.[38] Just as important, the institution was under the aegis of the Chigi family.

Il Refugio began life in the 1580s as a sanctuary for poor, abandoned girls, and its founder, Domenico Billò, served as its leader until his death in 1593.[39] At that point, the Chigi assumed the guidance and protection of the institution. The new director, Aurelio Chigi, transformed the conservatory into something resembling a female monastery by writing up a rule and by insisting that the girls wear habits. Under Chigi's governance, Il Refugio also began to accept both aristocratic girls whose families had fallen into such poverty that they could not afford a normal convent dowry and rich noblewomen whose dowries helped finance the institution. Aristocrats and commoners were, however, kept strictly separated, and in the 1670s the "Abbandonate" (as the poor, non-aristocratic girls were called) were transferred to a new home. Il Refugio continued to take in

---

[35] Biblioteca Apostolica Vaticana, Archivio Chigi 3852, fol. 22r: "La [illegible] del Signore Conte Antonio d'Elci haveva promessa a me per monacarsi in questo nostro monastero una delle sue figlie. Oggi il Signor Cavaliere Girolamo Ugurgieri non vuole ed insinua la madre a non contentar la figlia persuadendole il monacarsi nel Refugio. Hora questo desidero dal Eminenza Vostra e che perciò mi fo scrivere per infastidirla e perché si compiaccia scrivere al detto Signor Cavaliere che voglia lassar sodisfarsi chi deve stare in una continua carcere vivendo...4 dicembre 1669...zia Suor Lutugarda Chigi."

[36] Suor Maria Pulcheria was doubtless appeased when her brother Agostino decided to send seven of his eleven daughters to Campansi; see Reardon, *Holy Concord*, 129-130.

[37] Verginia entered Il Refugio in 1640, at age seven, and Olimpia, in 1642, when she turned seven. Both sisters remained at the institution until at least 1650; see Archivio di Stato, Siena, Conventi soppressi 3888, pp. 91 left, 94 left-right, and fol. 97v.

[38] Archivio di Stato, Siena, Conventi soppressi 3866, fols. 57v-58r.

[39] Such protective institutions arose throughout Italy during the sixteenth century; see Sherrill Cohen, *The Evolution of Women's Asylums since 1500: From Refuges for Ex-Prostitutes to Shelters for Battered Women* (New York and Oxford: Oxford University Press, 1992), 19-21.

patrician girls, both rich and poor. The convent was medium-sized by Sienese standards, holding about forty-eight women. Girls wishing to join the community there had to undergo a probation of two years before taking the veil in a ritual ceremony. Afterwards, they lived a monastic life of prayer. The Sienese called these women nuns, but in point of fact, they neither took formal vows nor belonged to any established religious order. Furthermore, they had one privilege denied to every other nun in the city: with appropriate permission from their own chapter, they could exit the cloister for days at a time.[40] At a certain point – it is not clear just when – the individual privilege mutated into a requirement: the women were compelled to visit the outside world three times a year.

The liberty enjoyed by the women at Il Refugio must have been the most attractive feature of the house and the main reason Olimpia Chigi chose it for her daughters. It is therefore astonishing to read that in 1687, the convent's inhabitants tried to renounce that prerogative so that they might observe perpetual *clausura*. The male governing body opposed the move. The women appealed to the grand duchess of Tuscany, Vittoria della Rovere, asking her to intercede for them with her son, Cardinal Francesco Maria de' Medici, who also did not approve of their request.[41] In her response, Vittoria first complimented the women on their "unblameworthy shyness," then gently reminded them of the obedience they should show to their constitution, and finally suggested ways in which they could observe the rules without harm to their modesty or reputation:

> If it seems too much for you to go out of the cloister three times a year (as prescribed), then reduce the number to once a year. If it does not please you to go out all together, go out in small groups. And if you want not to be seen by a large number of people, go by turns to visit a church and obtain an indulgence early in the morning. We promise you that His Eminence will concede to grant these moderate changes. In conclusion, if our grace is dear to you (as you demonstrate) and with it the grace of the Most Serene House [of the Medici], who will never stop protecting you, carry out these orders, given to you for your good, without further delay. We ask for your prayers and we greet all of you with great affection. From Florence, 27 December 1687, your friend, Victoria, grand duchess.[42]

---

[40] This history of the institution is pieced together from the following sources: *Archivio di Stato di Siena: Guida-Inventario*, 2 vols., Pubblicazioni degli Archivi di Stato, 5-6 (Rome: Ministero dell'Interno, 1951), 1: 35; 2: 181; Girolamo Gigli, *Diario sanese*, 3 vols. (Lucca, 1723; 2nd ed., Siena, 1854; reprint ed., Bologna: Arnaldo Forni Editore, 1974), 1: 44, 2: 294-295; Alfredo Liberati, "Chiese, monasteri, oratori e spedali senesi: ricordi e notizie," *Bullettino Senese di Storia Patria* 48 (1941): 152-153.

[41] For the background to the letter, I have relied on Archivio di Stato, Siena, Conventi soppressi 3863, "Notizie della fondazione e stabilimento delle due Congregazioni del Soccorso oggi Refugio e delle Abbandonate," 52.

[42] Archivio di Stato, Siena, Conventi soppressi 3863, pp. 53-54: "Se troppe vi sembrano poi le tre volte che vi sono state prescritte di sortir fuori, riducetele a una semplice in capo all'anno. Se inoltre non gradirete di ciò praticare tutte congiuntamente, fatelo a una parte per volta. E se premete di non esser viste alla frequenza del popolo, andate di mano in mano a visitar qualche chiesa e a pigliarvi qualche stazione la mattina per tempo,

Olimpia's daughters thus had a freedom that other holy women in Siena could only dream of, and Olimpia made sure that they enjoyed it. This explains a casual remark in a letter to Sigismondo about taking the girls out of the convent for no other reason, it appears, than to enjoy a little vacation in the company of their relatives.[43] Neither Egeria (nor later, Isifile) appears to have raised a fuss about taking the veil, perhaps for this reason. However, even the transfer to a more "liberal" house might not have been sufficient to convince Laura, and it is probable that Olimpia had to deploy additional tactics. Here I enter in the realm of speculation, but I believe that the stratagem involved providing Laura with musical training.

Olimpia Chigi was passionate about music, and it is quite possible, considering her family background, that she was an amateur musician. In her letters to Sigismondo, she describes musical experiences with gusto and joy. In one letter, she reports enthusiastically to Sigismondo on a Sienese performance by the well-known operatic singer Giulia Masotti; in another, she recommends that he take the opportunity to hear the Sienese castrato Giacomo Campaluci; in another, she wonders why her brother did not go to see an opera more than one time since "music delights you so."[44] Olimpia's love of music is nowhere more evident than in the glowing description she gave Sigismondo of the first Sienese performance of Cesti's *L'Argia* in May 1669. Of utmost interest here, however, is the phrase in her letter where she reports that she took all her girls out of the convent and escorted them to a performance of the opera.[45]

It was in January 1669 that Olimpia had written to Sigismondo about her decision not to force Laura to return to Campansi. By May, the twelve-year-old girl was no doubt ensconced with her older sister Egeria and her younger sister Leonora at Il Refugio. Because of the rules allowing visits to the outside world, Laura was able to accompany her mother to the opera, and I suspect that this was a defining experience for the young girl. Olimpia must have seen that Laura had inherited her passion for music, and must have made arrangements for her to become a proficient musician. It would have been an easy proposition, given that Sienese archbishops possessed very liberal attitudes toward music-making by the nuns in their pastoral care. Lay musicians found abundant work in Siena's

---

promettendoci noi che a tutte queste moderazioni l'Eminenza Sua si degnerà condescendere. In somma, se vi è cara, come ci mostrate, la grazia nostra, e insieme di tutta la Serenissima Casa, che non lascierà mai di proteggervi, adempite senza maggiore indugio gli ordini che si son dati pel vostro meglio. E raccomandandoci alle vostre orazioni, vi salutiamo tutte quante con ogni affetto. Di Firenze, 27 dicembre 1687, Vostra Amica, Vettoria Gran Duchessa."

[43] Biblioteca Apostolica Vaticana, Archivio Chigi 3871, fol. 72r.

[44] *Ibid.*, fols. 16r, 26v, 45r. Olimpia's letter concerning Giulia Masotti is transcribed and translated in Reardon, *Holy Concord*, 126.

[45] The relevant portion of Olimpia's letter about *L'Argia* is transcribed and translated in Reardon, *Holy Concord*, 127. For more on the Sienese revival of Cesti's opera, see Reardon, "The 1669 Sienese Production of Cesti's *L'Argia*," in: *Music Observed: Studies in Memory of William C. Holmes* (Harmonie Park Press, forthcoming).

convents, teaching nuns, novices, and *educande* to sing and to play such instruments as lute, theorbo, violin, harpsichord, and organ.[46]

Laura Gori Pannilini learned to play the organ, and we can imagine that she had special advantages when it came to mastering the instrument. Most cloistered women in Siena had no problem obtaining access to music teachers, but they had to take their lessons from inside the parlor of their convent, with their teacher on the other side of a grated wall. Their contact with the musicians was necessarily limited to certain hours on certain days of certain seasons when they were not obligated to carry out their religious devotions.[47] With her ability to leave Il Refugio, Laura might have been able to take private lessons at home and thus might have received more intense training than was possible in a cloister. Among the talented organists living and working in Siena during these years, Giuseppe Fabbrini seems a good candidate as Laura's teacher. Fabbrini became organist at Siena Cathedral in 1672 and he assumed the direction of the *cappella* in 1685. During the last quarter of the seventeenth century, Fabbrini also taught music at no fewer than three Sienese convents: S. Abbondio, S. Maria degli Angeli, and S. Paolo.[48] Perhaps it was his experience with Laura that motivated him to take on so much convent teaching later in his career. That Laura was a model student is evident in a letter Olimpia wrote to Sigismondo in January 1671:

> Sunday was a feast day at Il Refugio and all Siena came and stayed right through Vespers because nothing was going on in the Piazza, and my Lala played the organ for the high Mass and all Vespers.[49]

Olimpia is clearly reveling in Laura's accomplishment. The fact that the nuns at Il Refugio entrusted Laura, then an *educanda*, to play the organ on a major feast for the two most important liturgical services of the day suggests that the mother's pride was justified: Laura was probably a remarkable performer, even at age fourteen and a half.

That particular holiday at Il Refugio appears to have been the critical turning point in Laura's life, for it marked her debut as a performer and her first taste of public acclaim. Afterwards, it might have dawned on her that she could pursue a "career" as an organist only within the walls of the cloister, and that realization

---

[46] Reardon, *Holy Concord*, 24, 38-42.

[47] *Ibid.*, 39.

[48] Fabbrini's tenure at S. Paolo is discussed in Reardon, *Holy Concord*, 40. A fuller record of his activities in Sienese convents is found in my "I monasteri femminili e la vita musicale a Siena, c. 1550-1700," *Quaderni di musica e storia* (Bologna: Il Mulino, forthcoming).

[49] Biblioteca Apostolica Vaticana, Archivio Chigi 3871, fols. 45r-46v: "Domenica fu festa alle monache del Refugio dove ci fu tutta Siena che per non essere niente in Piazza si ste a tutto il Vespero e la mia Lala suonò l'organo alla messa grande e a tutto il Vespero....Siena, il 21 Gennaio 1671...Olimpia Chigi Gori."

might have reconciled her to life as a nun.[50] In any case, from this time on, Olimpia's letters make no further references to problems with her daughter Laura. On the contrary, in January 1673, she informed Sigismondo that Laura and Egeria had finally made a decision that alleviated the family's preoccupations:

> I come with the news that my two oldest daughters want to enter into the novitiate at Lent in order to take the veil once Easter is over.[51] Believe me, I am truly delighted because if Lala did not become a nun, I do not know to whom I would marry her because here there is not a match of any worth...1 February 1673.[52]

Finding suitable husbands for marriageable girls was, in fact, problematic in Siena, plagued by a declining birthrate, the extinction of many noble families, and the impoverishment of others.[53] It is unclear if Olimpia meant what she said about trying to find Laura a husband, but the issue was clearly moot at this point in time: Laura was ready to embrace the religious life. The good mother did not, however, simply wipe her brow and wait for the day to arrive. She wanted to celebrate the occasion with a splendid investiture ceremony, and so she wrote the following request not to her young brother, but to her powerful cousin, Cardinal Flavio Chigi:

> Since my two oldest daughters have resolved to dedicate themselves to God and to take the veil at the convent of Il Refugio, I come with this letter appealing to the supreme kindness of Your Eminence [to ask] if on your passage here through town, you would be so good as to do a special favor for them and for me by clothing them...5 April 1673.[54]

Flavio Chigi did indeed come to town and officiate at the ceremony in which both Egeria and Laura took the veil.[55] A special *palio* was run in honor of the

---

[50] See Monson, *Disembodied Voices*, 2. Colleen Baade provides a different interpretation of the reasons some Spanish monastic women chose to practice music; see her "'Hired' Nun Musicians in Early Modern Castile," in this volume.

[51] The girls' "official" request to be admitted to the religious community is preserved in Archivio di Stato, Siena, Conventi soppressi 3862, fol. 3r-v.

[52] Biblioteca Apostolica Vaticana, Archivio Chigi 3888, fol. 88r-v: "Li do nuova che a Quaresima le mie due citte maggiori vogliono entrare in noviziato per vestirsi fatto Pasqua. Mi creda che ne ò un gusto grande perché se Lala non si facesse non saprei a chi darla perché qua non ci [sic] un partito che valghi niente....il primo febbraio 1673...Olimpia Chigi Gori."

[53] See George R. F. Baker, "Nobiltà in declino: Il caso di Siena sotto i Medici e gli Asburgo-Lorena," *Rivista storica italiana* 84 (1972): 584-616.

[54] Biblioteca Apostolica Vaticana, Archivio Chigi 3871, fol. 67r-v: "Essendosi le mie due figlie magiori risolute di dedicarsi a Dio e vestirsi monache nel monasterio del Refugio sono con questa a supplicare la somma bontà di Vostra Eminenza se nel passaggio che farà di qua voglia compiacersi di fare questa speciale gratia a loro et a me di vesterle....Siena, il 5 aprile 1673... Olimpia Chigi Gori."

[55] Archivio di Stato, Siena, Conventi soppressi 3866, fol. 58v: "E dì 18 giugno 1673 presero l'abito della nostra Congregatione dui delle sudette cioè la Signora Egeria et Laura e

cardinal, and I suspect that Olimpia took her daughters out of the convent to see the horse race as part of the festivities surrounding their investiture.[56] Laura and Egeria disappear into a documentary black hole at this point: their mother's letters all but cease, and the meager records from Il Refugio offer no clue as to either sister's subsequent activities.[57] The only thing we know for sure about Olimpia's daughters and Il Refugio is that Isifile took the veil there in 1680; it is hoped that her older sisters were alive and well and able to welcome her into the monastic fold.[58]

It is by now clear to the reader that, in reconstructing the story of Laura Gori Pannilini, I have relied on relatively few documents and leavened them with proportionately large doses of hopeful speculation. The sheer number of girls who entered the convent in the seventeenth century would lead to the conclusion that many went grudgingly, even in the absence of a correspondingly high number documented protests, escapes, and suicides. But many girls also learned to adapt to life in the cloister, and it stands to reason that their families helped them along in the process. If we still need more evidence of soft-hearted fathers to provide an antidote to the paternal monster so terrifyingly brought to life by Manzoni, Olimpia Chigi Gori Pannilini's letters intimate that not all mothers were as cruel as those portrayed by Thomas Borghi. Although Olimpia's role in encouraging and promoting her daughter's musical talent cannot be precisely determined, there is no doubt that she worried about her daughter, took the time to listen to her complaints, removed her from an unsuitable living situation, found ways to make her life more enjoyable, and ultimately rejoiced in her accomplishments. We also cannot be sure that love of performing convinced Laura to accept her fate, but ample evidence from Siena shows that musical prowess was rewarded inside the cloister and celebrated outside its walls, and that the convent was the only honorable forum for public music-making by female members of the patrician class. My story about Laura is quite possibly the story of a number of early modern women, and we can only hope that, sooner or later, their voices will resurface to enrich the burgeoning monastic choir.

---

furno vestite del habito monacale dal Eminentissimo et Reverendissimo Signore Cardinale Flavio Chigi."

[56] Judith Hook, *Siena: Una città e la sua storia* (Siena: Nuova immagine editrice, 1988), 181.

[57] Leonora's fate is not clear from the surviving documents, although I hypothesize that she, too, became a nun at Il Refugio. Olimpia and Giulio probably arranged a secular marriage for their youngest daughter, Clarice; see Archivio di Stato, Siena, Conventi soppressi 3866, fol. 81r.

[58] Archivio di Stato, Siena, Conventi soppressi 3866, fol. 80v.

Chapter 12

"Hired" Nun Musicians in Early Modern Castile

Colleen Baade

When María Ibáñez de Isaba entered the novitiate on 21 December 1698, she joined one of thirty-one houses of cloistered female religious then in existence in the Spanish capital.[1] The Franciscan Monasterio de Santa María de los Angeles – founded in 1564 by Doña Leonor Mascareñas, retired governess of Philip II – was, in fact, the first of twenty-three new female monasteries to have been established in Madrid since the king made his capital there in 1561.[2] Early modern Spain saw a proliferation of monastic endowments for both male and female religious; among the more prestigious houses for women were the respective foundations in Madrid of the Monasterio de las Descalzas Reales by Princess Juana of Austria in 1559 and the Monasterio de la Encarnación by Queen Margaret of Austria in 1611. For wealthy Spaniards concerned about their well-being in the hereafter, the foundation of a monastery ensured that Masses and intercessory prayers would be offered on behalf of the donor long after his or her death. In addition to the spiritual benefits to be gained by such charity, establishing a monastery for women could provide certain practical benefits for the donor's family, since at most houses a designated number of places were reserved for founders' relatives.

Documents outlining the terms of her acceptance into monastic life reveal that María Ibáñez was recruited by the nuns at Santa María de los Angeles because of her musical talent: in a petition to their religious superior, the sisters reported that María possessed "great abilities, such as playing harp, organ and *violón*, being excellent on all three instruments;" furthermore, María had demonstrated her musicianship with such "perfection and skill" that an examining official from the Royal Chapel affirmed that "in [good] conscience she should not be asked

---

[1] A list of Madrid's female monasteries with dates of their respective foundations is contained in an eighteenth century manuscript at Madrid, Biblioteca Nacional (hereafter Madrid, BN), MS 10923, *Noticia de todos los conventos que hay en Madrid*, fols. 47v-53r.

[2] On the founding of the Monasterio de Santa María de los Angeles, see Pedro de Salazar, O.F.M., *Corónica e historia de la fundación y progreso de la Provincia de Castilla de la orden del bienaventurado padre San Francisco* (Madrid: Imprenta Real, 1612), facsimile rep. ed. Antolín Abad Pérez, O.F.M. (Madrid: Editorial Cisneros, 1977), 383-384.

anything by way of dowry because of the superiority of her abilities." [3] In view of the examiner's recommendation, the dowry of five hundred *ducados* offered by María's parents was likely considered a good deal by both parties, since it represented a reduction by nearly seventy-five percent off the usual dowry price at Santa María de los Angeles.[4]

That nun musicians in early modern Europe sometimes received financial compensation in the form of dowry waivers is by now fairly common knowledge, though scholars are perhaps less informed about the regular stipends that monasteries sometimes paid to "hired" nun musicians.[5] And much remains to be understood about just what the opportunity for remuneration meant for girls who availed themselves of it, or what a monastery's willingness to offer compensation says about how female musicians and their music-making activities were regarded.

Dowry waivers for nun musicians may well have been granted already during the Middle Ages (the history of the practice remains to be explored). A relatively early reference to the practice in Spain is related in a chronicle of the Franciscan province of Granada: the chronicler tells of a Portuguese-born girl named Sor Ana de San Andrés (†1581), whose parents, "lacking the means to give her the necessary conveniences, taught her the art of music because she had an outstanding voice," thereby obtaining for her a place at the Monasterio de Santa Clara at Montilla.[6] Sor Ana's age at her death is unknown, but according to my

---

[3] Madrid, Archivo Histórico de Protocolos, Protocolo 13384, fol. 1256r: "...[tiene] grandes avilidades como es tocar arpa, órgano y violón, siendo exçelente en todos tres ynstrumentos [...] y abiendo ejecutado todo cuanto se le propuso con gran primor y destreça, y asegurando el dicho apuntador de la Capilla Real que en conçiencia no debía pedírsele nada por vía de dote por lo insigne que es en sus avilidades...." All English translations are mine.

[4] Madrid, BN, MS 7643, *Libro de quentas de este Real Convento de Nuestra Señora de los Angeles de Madrid...Año 1693* registers dowry payments of 1900 *ducados* for nuns professing during the 1690s.

[5] Recent studies of nuns' music in Italy discuss dowry waivers for nun musicians, but do not mention stipends; see Craig Monson, *Disembodied Voices: Music and Culture in an Early Modern Italian Convent* (Berkeley: University of California Press, 1995); Robert Kendrick, *Celestial Sirens: Nuns and their Music in Early Modern Milan* (Oxford: Clarendon Press, 1996); and Colleen Reardon, *Holy Concord Within Sacred Walls: Nuns and music in Siena, 1575-1700* (New York: Oxford University Press, 2002). Discussion of stipends for nun musicians in Spain appears in Matilde Olarte Martínez, "Las 'Monjas Músicas' en los conventos españoles del Barroco. Una aproximación etnohistórica," *Revista de Folklore*, 146 (1993): 56-63 and in Alfonso de Vicente Delgado "La actividad musical en los monasterios de monjas en Ávila durante la Edad Moderna: Reflexiones sobre la investigación musical en torno al Monasterio de Santa Ana," *Revista de Musicología* 23 (2000): 507-562. I wish here to thank Alfonso de Vicente Delgado for his kind and generous assistance throughout the course of my study of music in Spain's female monasteries.

[6] Alfonso de Torres, O.F.M., *Crónica de la provincia franciscana de Granada* (Madrid: Juan García Infançón, 1683), 662: "Sor Ana de San Andrés. Tuvo su nacimiento en Portugal, y faltándoles a los padres medios para darle conveniencias, le enseñaron el arte

calculations, the date of her profession must fall roughly around the middle of the sixteenth century: if she made her final vows at age sixteen and lived into her late sixties, her entrance into the novitiate could have been as early as 1530. If, however, she died before age forty, she might have entered the monastery as late as 1560. Sor Ana's situation – the concurrence of musical talent and economic necessity – likely corresponds to the circumstances of many of the nun musicians who received dowry waivers. A *vida* for two musicians at Avila's Monasterio de la Encarnación provides an example from the seventeenth century: the parents of Clara Eugenia and Eugenia Clara (it was not uncommon for biological sisters to become sisters in religion), described as "virtuous and poor" (so poor, in fact, that their names are not mentioned in the biography):

> wanted to give their two daughters to the Lord. [Since] they did not have the means to pay nuns' dowries, they – with the help of a brother who was a priest – taught the girls music. Doña Clara Eugenia, who was older, learned to play organ and harp, and the younger [girl], Doña Eugenia Clara, [learned] *bajón* [dulcian or curtal]. Because of [their abilities on] these instruments, the two were received free of charge.[7]

We know that throughout the sixteenth and seventeenth centuries, marriage dowries became increasingly unaffordable in Spain (as elsewhere in Europe), to the extent that various laws were enacted in an attempt to limit dowries to no more than five years' income of the parent.[8] As the cost of marriage dowries became

---

de la música, por tener sobresaliente voz; en que salió tan diestra, que la apetecían muchos monasterios, por su habilidad, y conocida virtud. Mas teniendo noticias de este sanctuario [Santa Clara de Montilla], rogó a su padres le traxera a él. Admitiéronla con gusto las Religiosas, ocupándola en el coro, luego que profesó. Fue tan devota en las divinas alabanças, que nunca mientras duraron se arrimó a las sillas, ni pared" ("Sor Ana de San Andrés. She was born in Portugal, and her parents, lacking the means to give her the [necessary] conveniences, taught her the art of music because she had an outstanding voice, in which [ability] she turned out to be so skilled that many monasteries found her appealing because of her ability and her recognized virtue. And having news of this sanctuary, she begged her parents to bring her to it. The nuns admitted her with pleasure, putting her to work in the choir soon after she professed. She was so devout in the divine praises [i.e., the Divine Office] that, regardless how long they lasted she never leaned against the chairs or the wall [to support herself]." Sor Ana de San Andrés belonged to the same monastery to whose abbess Juan Bermudo's *El arte tripharia* (Osuna, 1550) is dedicated. My thanks to Wolfgang Freis for bringing her to my attention.

[7] María Pinel, *Retablo de Carmelitas*, ed. Nicolás González (Madrid: Editorial de Espiritualidad, 1981), 200: "[Sus] padres virtuosos y pobres, que, deseosos de dar a nuestro Señor dos hijas que su Magestad les había dado, no teniendo dote que poder darlas para que entrasen religiosas, con la ayuda de un hermano que tenía en un curato, las enseñó música. Doña Clara Eugenia, que era la mayor aprendió órgano y arpa; y la menor, que era doña Eugenia Clara, bajón. Por estos instrumentos las recibieron de valde en el convento de la Encarnación."

[8] On dowries in early modern Spain, see Domínguez Ortíz, *La sociedad española en el siglo XVII*, vol. 2, *El estamento eclesiástico* (Madrid: C.S.I.C., 1970), 113-119 and James Casey, *Early Modern Spain: a Social History* (London: Routledge, 1999), 28-29 and 199-

increasingly prohibitive, religious life became the only solution for many of the daughters of both the Spanish nobility and the middle class, particularly for families with several daughters. Still, even a nun's dowry could easily amount to several years' earnings for a merchant or craftsman.[9] Thus, as Craig Monson has observed, the willingness of religious communities to grant dowry waivers to girls with musical talent made "the development of a daughter's musical gifts with an eye toward the nunnery...a very sound investment."[10] Indeed, the granting of dowry waivers to girls with musical talent was one of only two officially sanctioned exceptions to the dowry requirement.[11]

The present essay explores the circumstances of thirty-six nun musicians from sixteen different female monasteries in *Castilla la Vieja* during the late sixteenth through the eighteenth centuries, each of whom received some form of financial compensation in exchange for her musical services.[12] My study draws upon two principal types of sources: *protocolos* and *libros de cuenta*. The first of these sources is preserved in Spain's Archivos Históricos de Protocolos and Archivos Históricos Provinciales, which collectively house hundreds of thousands of legal

---

202. But see also Jutta Gisela Sperling, *Convents and the Body Politic in late Renaissance Venice*, (Chicago: University of Chicago Press, 1999), who contends that the drastic increase in female monachization that occurred in late sixteenth-century Venice owed more to a desire to preserve the integrity of noble bloodlines than to financial constraints.

[9] For income levels in early modern Madrid, see David R. Ringrose, *Madrid and the Spanish Economy, 1560-1850* (Berkeley: University of California Press, 1983), 66-81. According to the information in Table 4.6, *Distribution of Recipients and Income by Income Level, Madrid, ca. 1757*, about 83% of Madrid's wage earners made less 450 *ducados* per year, and another 7% made between 450 and 900 *ducados*; Madrid's median income was slightly under 140 *ducados* per year. Table 4.5, *Distribution of Income by Occupation Sectors in Madrid, 1757* shows that roughly 90% of craftsmen earned less than 650 *ducados* per year. Similar figures for the seventeenth century appear to be unavailable.

[10] Monson, *Disembodied Voices*, 2.

[11] Admission without dowry was also granted to a certain number of posts for girls who were relatives of the monastery's financial patron or patroness; see Fray Luis Lozano, *Claro espejo de religiosas*, (Madrid: Viuda de D. Juan del Barrio, 1699), 61; quoted in José L. Sánchez Lora, *Mujeres, conventos y formas de la religiosidad barroca* (Madrid: Fundación Universitaria Española, 1988), 115: "De ninguna otra forma, puedan las Monjas, aunque sean con consentimiento de todas: recibir Novicia alguna, a la profesión de Chorista, sin que traiga Dote; sino es, que entre en alguna plaza del Patrón, *ó se reciba por Cantora, Música u Organista*" ("In no way shall nuns, even if it be with the consent of all of them, receive any novice to profess as choir nun without her bringing a dowry, except that she enter one of the places [endowed] by the [monastery's] patron, *or that she be received as a singer, musician or organist*") (emphasis mine). But see also Mindy Nancarrow Taggard, "Art and Alienation in Early Modern Spanish Convents," *South Atlantic Review* 65 (2000): 24-40, on dowry waivers granted to two nun artists, one a sculptor, the other a painter. My thanks to the author for providing me a copy of her article.

[12] A list of the nun musicians considered in this essay and archival sources for each is contained in the Appendix below. One of the nuns included in the Appendix was a musician, though not a "hired" musician; hence the Appendix includes information for a total of thirty-seven nuns.

documents prepared by professional amanuenses (*escribanos*), bound together in volumes called *protocolos*.[13]   Among the various kinds of documents found in *protocolos* are copies of the legal agreements that were regularly drawn up between a monastery and the parents or guardians of a prospective nun. Conditions for payment of entry expenses and the eventual dowry were recorded in contracts variously labeled *obligación de dote*, *entrada de monja* or *recepción*. An accompanying letter of payment (*carta de pago*) verified the monastery's receipt of money for the food allowance (*alimentos*) paid during the novitiate, the novice's habit and various other expenses associated with entering a religious community. At the time of the nun's final vows, or *profesión*, a second set of documents was drawn up consisting of a *carta de pago* acknowledging the monastery's receipt of the dowry or *dote* (which, according to regulations set forth by the Council of Trent, was not to be paid until immediately before the novice made her final profession); a copy of the original *recepción* agreement; the *renunciación de legítimas*, or formal renunciation of inheritance rights; and a transcription of the *exploración* – the series of questions verifying the novice's age, the amount of time she has spent in the novitiate, and a statement that she is entering the monastery of her own volition.   Finally, the documents also include copies of the *licencias* authorizing the terms of the girl's entry into the novitiate and granting permission for her final profession.   The documents found in *protocolos* are tediously formulaic and repetitious, but they occasionally contain tidbits of information about the social and economic status of girls who became nun musicians, about their musical training and abilities and their obligations to the religious community. The other source of information for this study are monastery account books or *libros de cuenta*, thousands of which are now held at Madrid's Archivo Histórico Nacional. Account books record the receipt of dowry payments, and also register regular stipends – usually called *situados* – that were paid to nuns identified as musicians in the accounts. The information contained in *libros de cuenta* is generally less detailed than that recorded in *profesión* and *recepción* documents; account books usually include only a one or two-word identification of a nun's musical duties, but they can be useful for directing the researcher to the location of *profesión* and *recepción* agreements.

The costs associated with entering a monastery varied from one house to another, depending upon the monastery's relative prestige (which, of course, reflected the social status of the women who lived there). At the beginning of the seventeenth century, the dowry price at Madrid's Monasterio de Santa María de la Madre de Dios (commonly called "Constantinopla") was around one thousand *ducados* plus *alimentos* of fifty *ducados* per year during the novitiate and additional expenses amounting to another one hundred to two hundred *ducados*; around the same time, dowries at Valladolid's Monasterio de Santa Isabel cost seven hundred *ducados*, while Madrid's Monasterio de Santo Domingo el Real

---

[13] Although archives housing *protocolos* exist in many Spanish towns and cities, this study is limited to documents from Madrid's Archivo Histórico de Protocolos (AHPM) and Toledo's Archivo Histórico Provincial (AHPT).

commanded dowries of two thousand *ducados* as early as 1630.[14] Some "hired" nun musicians were exempted from the entire dowry and all related fees, but others who received dowry waivers were granted only a partial reduction of expenses. For example, Francisca de las Vírgenes was given a twenty percent reduction of her dowry at her entry into Madrid's Monasterio de Constantinopla in 1603, but paid all other expenses and brought a trousseau that included a clavichord and a *bajón* (dulcian or curtal). In 1605, her sister musician, Catalina del Castillo, was admitted without dowry, *alimentos*, *propinas* or trousseau.

At the Monasterio de Santa Clara in Madrid, *profesión* agreements show a gradual increase in the amount of compensation for dowry waivers granted during the seventeenth century to nuns who played the *bajón*; in 1608, Luisa de la Paz paid six hundred *ducados* (two-thirds the normal dowry of nine hundred *ducados*), twenty *ducados* for *alimentos*, twenty *ducados* for wax candles, and brought a trousseau of musical instruments and music books; in 1635, Mariana de Zabala paid a dowry of three hundred *ducados* with no additional expenses; in 1676, Catalina de Jubera was relieved of her entire dowry as well as "propinas, ajuar de sachristía, alimentos [y] los demás gastos que se acostumbran hacer" ("gratuities, trousseau for the sacristy, food allowance and the other customary expenses"). The differences in the amounts of these three dowry waivers might have been related to the economic circumstances of respective nuns' families, but the discrepancy may also reflect an increasing demand over the course of the century for players (and teachers) of the *bajón*.[15] In most cases, it remains uncertain to what extent the amount of a nun musician's dowry waiver depended upon her musical ability, her financial situation or the practice of a given monastery (though the case of María de Ibáñez suggests a direct correlation between skill and remuneration). Sources indicate that dowry reductions tended to be more generous toward the end of the seventeenth century than at the beginning, and by the eighteenth century it appears to have become fairly common for nun musicians to be exempted from the entire dowry and all related costs.[16]

The *situados* nun musicians received in exchange for their services as players and teachers also varied from house to house, ranging from as little as one or two *ducados* per year to as much as twenty. At the Monasterio de Santa Isabel at Valladolid, two musicians received regular stipends during the second half of the seventeenth century: for three decades organist Isabel de Guillamas and *bajón*-player Ana de Olea were paid eight and five *ducados*, respectively, until 1673,

---

[14] Dowries for Madrid's Constantinopla are recorded in Madrid, Archivo Histórico Nacional (AHN), Clero, libro 7446; for Valladolid's Santa Isabel, see AHN, Clero, libro 17501. For Madrid's Monasterio de Santo Domingo el Real, see "Consulta de la Cámara en 3 de noviembre de 1630..." transcribed in Antonio Domínguez Ortiz, *La sociedad española en el siglo XVII*, vol. 2, *El estamento eclesiástico* (Madrid: C.S.I.C., 1970), 261.

[15] On the incorporation of the *bajón* into nuns' music chapels in Castile, see Colleen R. Baade, "Music and Music-making in Female Monasteries in Early Modern Castile" (Ph.D. diss., Duke University, 2001), 98-104.

[16] Of fourteen contracts for nuns' dowry waivers from the eighteenth century, all but one granted a complete exemption from dowry and all other expenses.

when a visiting official's "reforms" mandated that their *situados* be reduced.[17] The provincial minister decreed that for the remainder of their respective musical tenures, the convent's two musicians should receive only enough money to cover instrument upkeep and repairs.[18] A closer examination of the accounts – beyond the scope of this study – would likely reveal that the Monasterio de Santa Isabel had fallen on hard times or was perhaps suffering from financial mismanagement. In either case, the "reforms" were probably the result of economic rather than spiritual concerns. The visiting provincial minister, Padre Fray Hernando de la Rua, presumably was assisted in his efforts by Doña María de la Rua (surely a relative of Fray Hernando), who began her first term as abbess of Santa Isabel in 1677.

Finances were a problem for many women's monasteries, and communities often struggled to balance their accounts at the end of each triennium. During the early decades of the seventeenth century, the Monasterio de Santa Isabel at Segovia was subject to several reprimands for spending more money than it took in, and in a case not unlike the one cited above, corrective measures imposed by the visiting official included a demand for a reduction in the *situado* of the convent organist. Antonia Bautista had begun her tenure as organist in 1614, and, like her sister organist at Valladolid, she received a stipend of eight *ducados* per year. In 1623, following a visit from the provincial minister, it was ordered that Doña Antonia's annual *situado* be reduced to four *ducados*. The monastery, however, complied only partially with the visiting minister's mandate. The accounts show that Doña Antonia Bautista's stipend was reduced to six *ducados*, which she continued to receive from 1624 through 1629. Another visit in 1630 prompted the following note in the account book:

Item. Six *ducados* are charged, which [the abbess] says she has given to Señora Doña Antonia Bautista, organist, for one entire year, which was completed at the end of 1629. Note: It was declared that this nun, so they say, entered the convent without dowry in the position of *tañedora* and *cantora*, [but] without any promise to be given a

---

[17] Account books for the Monasterio de Santa Isabel show that the two nuns' *situados* were paid consistently through the year 1673 (expenses recorded in 1674), but for the triennium 1674-1676, Doña Isabel received only half the usual amount, and Doña Ana was paid only two-thirds. These entries include annotations explaining that the monastery still owed the remainder of the *situados*, and the unpaid amounts were noted under the monastery's debts; see AHN, Clero, libro 17500, fol. 366r.

[18] AHN Clero, libro 17500, fols. 403v-404r: "...se mandó por Nuestro Muy Reverendísimo Padre Fray Hernando de la Rua, probincial que fue de esta santa probincia, no se pague el dicho situado y que tan solamente se dé lo que fuere nezesario para adrezar y componer el órgano y arpa...[y] tan solamente se diese lo que fuese menester para el adreço del instrumento que toca la dicha Señora Doña Ana" ("...it was ordered by Our Very Reverend Father Friar Hernando de la Rua, who was the provincial minister of this holy province, that said stipend not be paid and that [Doña Isabel] only be given whatever would be necessary for maintaining and repairing the organ and the harp...[and] [Doña Ana] only be given whatever would be necessary for the maintenance of the instrument that said Lady Doña Ana plays [i.e., *bajón*]").

situado. Therefore, said *situado* of six *ducados* shall not be given to her any longer without written permission from our Provincial Father. Until now there has not been [any such permission], nor has she had [any such permission], and any current or future abbess who acts contrary to this order will have to pay [the *situado*] out of her own funds and not those of the convent....[19]

One might imagine that such stern words would have produced compliance at last, but the accounts for 1633 show that once again Doña Antonia received the usual six *ducados* per year. She is identified in this entry, however, not as *organista* but simply as "monxa deste convento," and the payment to her is recorded not as a *situado* but rather as *renta*.[20] This bit of creative bookkeeping seems to have done the trick, for there is no mention of the organist's *situado* in the notes from the next visit. Unfortunately, the account book ends here, leaving us to wonder how long the abbesses at Santa Isabel managed to continue paying Antonia Bautista the stipend that they were clearly very determined she should receive.[21]

That nun musicians were paid at all is perhaps surprising, for one assumes that cloistered musicians would not have received monetary compensation the same way that musicians employed at secular churches and chapels did. We might wonder why a nun would need money and how she would have spent it inside the cloister. But the fact is that in early modern Spain (as elsewhere in Europe), cloistered nuns – who, upon entering a monastery, brought in revenues from various sources – often retained control of their own money, with which they were able to buy personal items, decorate private chapels, purchase furnishings for the

---

[19] AHN, Clero, libro 12583, fols. 247r-247v: "Yten sele descargan seis ducados que dice a dado a la señora Doña Antonia Bautista horganista de un año entero que cunplió en fin del de 629. *Nota*. Declárase questa señora religiosa según dicen entró en el convento sin dote a título de tañedora y cantora sin obligación de darle situado ninguno y así no se le a de dar de oy más el dicho situado de seis ducados sin licençia en escrito de Nuestro Padre Provinçial pues hasta aora no la avido ni la an tenido y la señora abadesa que es o fuere no contravenga a este horden so pena de que será por su quenta y no por la del convento...."

[20] *Ibid.*, fol. 281v. The word *renta* generally refers to income or revenue (from property, investment, money-lending, etc.), while *situado*, meaning "salary or allowance," designates money paid in exchange for services rendered and is the term used most commonly for the payments that monasteries made to nun musicians. However, account books employ a variety of terms including *situado*, *renta* and *legata* to register regular payments received by nuns and nun musicians, and it is not always certain what each particular term implies.

[21] Curiously, during this time no reduction was ordered for the yearly *situado* of five *ducados* paid since 1614 to the Santa Isabel's *bajonista*, Lorenza de Alemán. Receipt of Doña Lorenza's dowry of 187,000 *maravedís* (500 *ducados*) is recorded in the accounts from the year 1614 (*ibid.*, fol. 75v), followed not long after by record of purchase of a *bajón* and *bajón* lessons for Doña Lorenza (*ibid.*, fol. 112r). Although she received a *situado* of five *ducados* every year up to and including the accounts taken in 1633, Lorenza de Alemán is never identified as a musician in the entries that record payments made to her, which may explain why her *situado* was not targeted for a reduction.

sacristy or endow masses. In some houses, nuns even bought and sold their own cells.

The amount of a nun musician's *situado* was, of course, considerably les than the salary of any secular organist or *maestro de capilla*, but one post cannot be fairly compared with the other. The twenty *ducados* per year María Marzana received as *organista* at Guadalajara's Monasterio de Santa Clara at the end of the seventeenth century equals a little over one-tenth the salary of the organist at the Burgos cathedral around the same time; however, cathedral organists were not given room and board for life.[22] On the other hand, money paid to nun musicians was not necessarily theirs to keep. Account books indicate that at least part of the money allocated for *situados* was intended to be spent on supplies (i.e., strings, reeds) and instrument maintenance. We have already seen that the organist and *bajón*-player at Valladolid's Santa Isabel were expected to pay for instrument upkeep, which probably explains the absence of any such expenses in Santa Isabel's account books. A similar arrangement likely accounts for the fact that, at Segovia's Monasterio de Santa Isabel, payments to the salaried male *organista* (organ tuner and technician) disappear from the accounts the same year that organist Antonia Bautista began to receive her *situado*.

The existence of financial compensation in the form of dowry waivers and *situados* for nun musicians has occasioned speculation about society's valuation of nuns' music and the extent to which girls who possessed musical talent might actually have chosen convent life as a means of pursuing a "career" as a female musician. Craig Monson rightly observes that, "[f]or young women trained as musicians during the sixteenth and seventeenth centuries, the cloister was probably the most obvious milieu in which to practice that profession in its various respectable aspects."[23] Spanish musicologist Matilde Olarte Martínez proposes that the situation of remunerated nun musician was one of social privilege, since ordinarily, only the daughters of a monastery's aristocratic patrons were eligible to receive dowry waivers.[24] Olarte Martínez further asserts that for young women in

---

[22] Don Benito Belmonte, organist at the Burgos cathedral, was paid 1800 *reales* (about 164 *ducados*) per year, beginning in 1695. See José López-Calo, *La música en la Catedral de Burgos, La música en la Catedral de Burgos* (Burgos: Caja de Ahorros del Círculo Católico, 1996), 5: 349, item 4.106. A fairer comparison might be made with the salary of a parish church organist.

[23] Monson, *Disembodied Voices*, 2.

[24] Matilde Olarte Martínez, "Las 'Monjas Músicas'," 57: "El hecho de no tener que pagar la dote es un ejemplo muy claro: como aparece en todos los documentos de las fundaciones de los conventos, la dote era necesaria para la subsistencia del propio convento y solamente los fundadores o patrones de los conventos se reservaban el derecho a poder meter a familiares suyos sin tener que pagarla. Por tanto, la situación de la 'monja música' era socialmente privilegiada..." ("The fact of not having to pay a dowry is a very clear example: as appears in all the documents pertaining to the founding of convents, the dowry was necessary for the convent's very subsistence, and only the founders or patrons of convents reserved the right to place their family members [in convents] without having to

sixteenth and seventeenth century Spain, being a nun musician "represented the possibility of being able to work and of having economic independence from one's family."[25] These claims have their appeal, especially for scholars who favor a more positive assessment of women's roles in early modern society. We should be cautious, however, against an overly enthusiastic (and probably anachronistic) interpretation of the phenomenon of "hired" nun musician. Need does not necessarily preclude vocation, but it seems likely that for many young female musicians, acceptance of a dowry waiver had more to do with a family's economic circumstances than with anything that could be considered "career choice."[26]

It is, unfortunately, rather difficult to determine precisely what the abilities of nun musicians were worth in terms of family income, especially since *protocolos* seldom contain any information about the occupation of the girl's father, and income is not easily determined, even when the father's profession is known.[27] Other clues that might give an idea of the socio-economic status of girls who became nun musicians are equally hard to decipher. Several of the girls whose dowry waivers are studied here were orphaned of one parent or the other or relied upon financial assistance by persons other than their parents.[28] The names of some of the girls and the names of their parents appear in documents without the honorific *don* or *doña*. However, though these titles were once reserved for members of the upper nobility, already by the early sixteenth century their significance had become blurred, as their use was gradually appropriated by persons of lesser stations.[29] And, to be sure, nobility and wealth were not necessarily synonymous in early modern Spain. Furthermore, the fact that in many of Spain's female monasteries professed nuns were addressed as *doña* makes it

---

pay it. It follows, therefore, that the situation of the 'nun musician' was socially privileged...").

[25] *Ibid.*, 57: "Lo más destacado de este trabajo de dirección musical es el hecho de que representaba, para una mujer de los siglos XVI y XVII, la posibilidad de *poder trabajar* y de tener una *independencia económica* con respecto a su familia" (italics in original).

[26] But see Colleen Reardon's contribution to this volume for another view on the appeal a "career" as nun musician might have held for a daughter of Siena's patrician class.

[27] Only three of the dowry-waiver contracts studied here identify the father's occupation: the father of Francisca de las Vírgenes was a merchant; María Pacheco's father was the chief apothecary for Prince Ferdinand of Austria and the father of María Ibáñez de Isaba worked as a purveyor for the Spanish royalty ("proveedor de la Casa Real"); see also discussion below concerning Alfonsa González de Salazar, whose father was a goldsmith.

[28] The arrangements for the dowry waiver of Catalina del Castillo were made by her uncle; the brothers of Ana Paderlines paid off her dowry; the mother of Luisa de la Paz is identified as a widow, probably remarried; the dowry of Felipa de Aparicio was a charity paid by another nun from the convent at which she professed. Girls specifically identified as orphans of one parent or the other include Mariana de Zabala, Juana Ferrer, Margarita Limia and Catalina de la Fuente.

[29] See Casey, *Early Modern Spain*: "The Cortes of 1585 investigated the popularisation of the title 'don,' quietly usurped – over the last fifty years – by the upwardly mobile, tax farmers and ministers of the Crown, when in times past it had been reserved for the titled nobility" (144).

even more difficult to be sure just what the presence or absence of the titles in *recepción* and *profesión* documents implies.[30]

Class distinctions did not disappear inside the cloister, and the population of nuns of any female monastery in early modern Europe was divided into at least two categories.[31] In Spain, the terms *monja profesa* and *monja de coro* (professed nun, choir nun) designated a female religious who had paid a full dowry (unless exempted from it by virtue of her relationship to monastery's patron or patroness), had taken final vows, and whose primary occupation was the daily recitation of the Divine Office in the choir. *Monjas de coro* were also referred to as *monjas de coro y velo* or *monjas de velo negro* ("black-veiled nuns"), as distinguished from *monjas de velo blanco* ("white-veiled nuns"), also called *legas* or *freilas*, who were admitted with much smaller dowries. The *legas* or lay sisters were responsible for doing domestic chores and were usually exempt from reciting the Divine Office. "Hired" nun musicians, by virtue of their participation in the Divine Office, were admitted as *monjas de coro y velo* (and therefore were sometimes addressed as *doña*).[32] It appears unlikely, however, that these women would have been regarded as social equals with their sisters in religion whose parents were wealthy enough to pay a full dowry. In fact, because nun musicians worked in exchange for a dowry waiver their situation was in many ways comparable to that of the *legas*.[33]

If documents for dowry waivers are frustratingly vague about the economic circumstances of nun musicians' families, they are equally elusive about the duties of "hired" nun musicians. Stock phrases such as "she will play for the service of God and the divine office" or "she is received for the ministry of music and playing instruments in the praises of the divine offices" tell little about the daily obligations of a nun organist or *bajonista*.[34] Still, it is likely that being a nun

---

[30] On nuns' titles, see also n. 37 below.

[31] In addition to the *monjas profesas* and *legas* discussed above, the population of any female monastery also included novices, servants, slaves, and various other secular women and girls who made the convent their temporary or permanent home.

[32] Craig Monson notes that "[f]or a poor girl, musical talent offered the means to rise above the convent servant class...appropriate to a modest dowry, to the upper, governing class" (*Disembodied Voices*, 2). Monson's statement is true, at least in theory, but my contention is that "hired" nun musicians were nevertheless regarded as not possessing the same social status as those choir nuns who had paid full dowries, or who were otherwise exempted from a dowry on the basis of their parentage.

[33] See Nancarrow Taggard, "Art and Alienation": "[The] productive service activity [of nuns who worked as convent artists in exchange for a dowry waiver] lowered their prestige in the community...by likening them to the lay sisters who performed manual chores in the convent" (27). The contents of Taggard's article were first presented as a paper at the Second Annual Conference of the Mediterranean Studies Association, 26-29 May 1999, University of Coimbra, Portugal, at which session I also presented an earlier version of the material discussed here. See also n. 45 below.

[34] AHPM, Protocolo 7720, fol. 473r.: "...se obligó a tañer para el servicio de Dios y del Oficio Divino..."; AHPM, Protocolo 13384, fol. 1253r: "...se recivió...para el ministerio de música y tocar instrumentos en las alabanzas de los divinos oficios...." Similar examples are found in many of the documents consulted for this essay.

musician was a demanding job. Documents for dowry waivers emphasize that nun musicians were expected to serve – barring illness or incapacitation – their entire lives. Account books for the Monasterio de Santa Isabel at Valladolid show that the convent's two principal musicians received annual stipends for over a half-century: *bajón*-player Ana de Olea served fifty-five years, and the tenure of organist Isabel de Guillamas lasted sixty years. Both women must have lived and played well into their seventies.[35]

Contracts for dowry waivers give the impression that nun musicians were expected to play on demand, and their playing was not necessarily limited to the monastery's celebration of Mass and Divine Office. From the late seventeenth century onwards, many of the documents consulted for this essay contain a statement to the effect that the nun musician is "required to play for all of the divine offices and other occasions such as the abbess may require of her."[36] Those "other occasions" may well have included musical "entertainment" during the community's recreation hour, as was specified in the *profesión* agreement for Andrea María Theresa Soriano, a nun musician who played organ and also taught plainchant, polyphony and reading at Toledo's Cistercian Monasterio de San Clemente during the eighteenth century.

If a girl who entered a monastery with a dowry waiver decided for some reason that she did not want to continue serving as a musician, she was required to pay off her dowry in order to remain in the monastery. Such was the case with Ana Padrelines, who was relieved of her duties as singer and organist at the Monasterio de las Huelgas at Valladolid when her brothers paid back the two hundred *ducados* initially deducted from her dowry. Manuela García was required to sing and teach plainchant when she entered Madrid's Monasterio de Santa Clara, with the understanding that she would be released from the obligation as soon as she was able to pay off her dowry waiver of one thousand *ducados*; this she did six months after taking her final vows. Luisa de la Paz – who, at age forty-seven, after thirty-four years as *bajón*-player and assistant organist, was no longer able to play because of illness and indisposition – was required to pay back the three hundred *ducados* of her dowry waived at her entrance to Madrid's Monasterio de Santa Clara and to relinquish the revenues she received from *censos* in order to be relieved of her musical duties. (Incidentally, in the document laying out the terms of her retirement, Luisa is consistently identified as *Sor* Luisa de la Paz, while the

---

[35] Both women apparently continued to play until their respective deaths ca. 1700 and ca. 1703.

[36] See, for example, the documents for Catalina de Jubera, AHN, Clero, legajo 3937, unnumbered fol.: "Se a de obligar a cantar y tocar vaxón y bajonçillo en todos los ofiçios divinos que se ofrecieren hacer en la yglesia del dicho convento y en las demás ocasiones que se le ordenare y mandare por la señora avadesa..." ("She is obligated to sing and play *bajón* and *bajoncillo* at all the Divine Offices that are offered in the church of said convent and for the other occasions on which it is required and commanded of here by the abbess...").

abbess and nearly all of the *consiliarias* [nuns holding the various convent offices] who witnessed the agreement are identified with the title *Doña*.[37])

A novice whose musical abilities were found to be insufficient might also be required to reimburse a monastery for her dowry waiver before she would be allowed to take final vows. For example, Catalina de la Fuente, who sang and played organ, harp and violin at Toledo's Monasterio de Santo Domingo el Real, was deemed at the end of her novitiate to be only a "moderately skilled musician." In this case, the religious community was willing to accept her and to honor the dowry waiver that had been granted in the original agreement, but Doña Catalina decided to seek charitable donations that would enable her to pay off her dowry and to be released from her musical obligations. Paula de la Trinidad did not fare as well in her attempt to enter the Monasterio de la Concepción at Almonacid de Zurita as a singer: a note in the margin of an account book states that the novice was dismissed ("kicked out" might be a more accurate translation) "because she knew nothing" ("salió la comunidad en echarla porque no sabía nada").[38]

Perhaps the most telling case is that of Alfonsa González de Salazar, who entered Madrid's Monasterio de Constantinopla in 1609 at age fifteen. Although Alfonsa apparently possessed musical talent (she later would distinguish herself as a singer), Doña María de Salazar and Don Gonzalo González did not seek a dowry waiver for their daughter, but instead opted to pay the required dowry of one thousand *ducados* and all additional expenses. Perhaps because he was a goldsmith, Alfonsa's father could afford to pay his daughter's entry into one of Madrid's more prestigious female monasteries.[39] It is telling, however, that the

---

[37] I am unaware of any systemic study of the use of the titles *Sor* ("Sister") and *Doña* ("Lady") in monasteries in early modern Spain, though I have observed that its usage varies not only from one monastery to the next, but also among the various documents originating from a particular monastery. Generally speaking, *doña* is reserved for *monjas de coro*, and *sor* applies to *legas* (in Spain, this distinction applies not only in Benedictine houses but also in many Franciscan houses). However, in some monasteries (usually reformed houses such as the Discalced Carmelites) all of the nuns were called *sor*, regardless of their former social status. In most of the documents I have examined, *sor* accompanies religious names adopted at profession (i.e., Sor María Magdalena, Sor Juana Bautista; presumably the names of *legas*), while *doña* designates (presumably aristocratic) nuns who retained their secular names. However, as I have noted above, the appearance of the title *doña* does not necessarily guarantee that the bearer was the daughter of nobility. Interestingly, the signatures of the nuns at Madrid's Monasterio de Santa María de los Angeles who witnessed María de Ibáñez's *recepción* agreement all employ *doña*, while the same nuns, in what was doubtless in a show of humility, signed their secular names preceded by *sor* on the above-mentioned petition to their religious superior.

[38] AHN, Clero, libro 4148, fol. 21r.

[39] Gonzalo González is identified as a goldsmith in AHN, Clero, legajo 3954, unnumbered folio: "1628. Gonzalo González Platero de Oro y Doña María de Salazar su muger los quales mandaron azer un altar en este convento que le sirva ese de su entierro y encargaron a Doña Alfonsa de Salazar su hija relijiosa profesa en este convento lo pusiere en execución" ("1628. Gonzalo González, goldsmith, and Doña María de Salazar, his wife, ordered that an altar built in this convent that shall serve the former as his [place of] burial

documents pertaining to Alfonsa's *recepción* and *profesión* state emphatically: "She does *not* enter as a singer or player...*but she will sing and play and sweep* and will do the other things pertaining to her religion such as her superior may require of her, just as the other daughters of obedience do in said convent...(emphasis mine)."[40] (See Figure 12.1) The wording indicates – as I have already suggested above – that while a position as convent musician may have provided a welcome opportunity for some girls, for others it was viewed akin to that of a maid.

Alfonsa de Salazar went on to become a singer of apparent reputation, for she was the dedicatee of a collection of *villancicos* by poet Miguel de Toledano, in which volume Alfonsa's ability as a singer is praised in a sonnet by Miguel de Cervantes.[41] The book, entitled *Minerva sacra*, includes an illustration depicting the nineteen-year-old nun (she was actually twenty-two by the time of the volume's publication) dressed in a Franciscan habit, playing the harp and singing words from Psalm 137: "...in conspectu angelorum psallam tibi."[42] (See Figure 12.2) Toledanos's dedicatory also speaks of Alfonsa de Salazar's reknown as a singer; however, the actual extent of her "fame" remains uncertain, and one hesitates to construe Alfonsa's connection with Cervantes as evidence of her own celebrity. The dedication of Toledano's *villancicos* (or at least Cervantes's

---

and they charged Doña Alfonsa de Salazar, their daughter, professed nun in this convent, to see to it"). Victor Herrero Mediavilla, *Indice biográfico de España, Portugal e Iberoamérica*, 3d ed. (Munich: K.G.Saur, 2000) identifies as *plateros* Enrique and Gonzalo González (brothers?), who reportedly flourished in Madrid ca. 1613-15 (230). On the wealth and prestige of the Monasterio de Constantinopla, whose inhabitants included daughters of the Bracamonte, Luján, Mendoza and Zapata families, see Salazar, *Corónica*, 377 and Colleen R. Baade, "La 'música sutil' del Monasterio de la Madre de Dios de Constantinopla: aportaciones para la historia de la música en los monasterios femeninos de Madrid a finales del siglo XVI-siglo XVII," *Revista de Musicología* 20 (1997): 221.

[40] AHPM, Protocolo 2633, fol.1032r: "...no entra por cantora ni tañedora...pero tañerá y cantará y barrerá y ará las demás cosas tocantes a la religión que le mandare su perlada como lo haçen las demás hijas de la obediençia en el dicho convento...."

[41] Cervantes's sonnet, "En vuestra, sin igual, dulce armonía...," is published in modern edition in Angel Valbuena Prat, ed., *Miguel de Cervantes Saavedra. Obras completas*, 16th ed. (Madrid: Aguilar, 1970), 60-61. Miguel Toledano's *Minerva sacra* (Madrid: Juan de la Cuesta, 1616) is published in modern edition by Angel González Palencia, ed., (Madrid: C.S.I.C., Instituto Miguel de Cervantes, 1949).

[42] Ps. 137.1: "Confitebor tibi Domine in toto corde meo quoniam audisti verba oris mei in conspectu angelorum psallam tibi" ("I will praise thee, O Lord, with my whole heart, for thou hast heard the words of my mouth. I will sing praise to thee in the sight of his angels"; trans. Douary, revised Challoner).

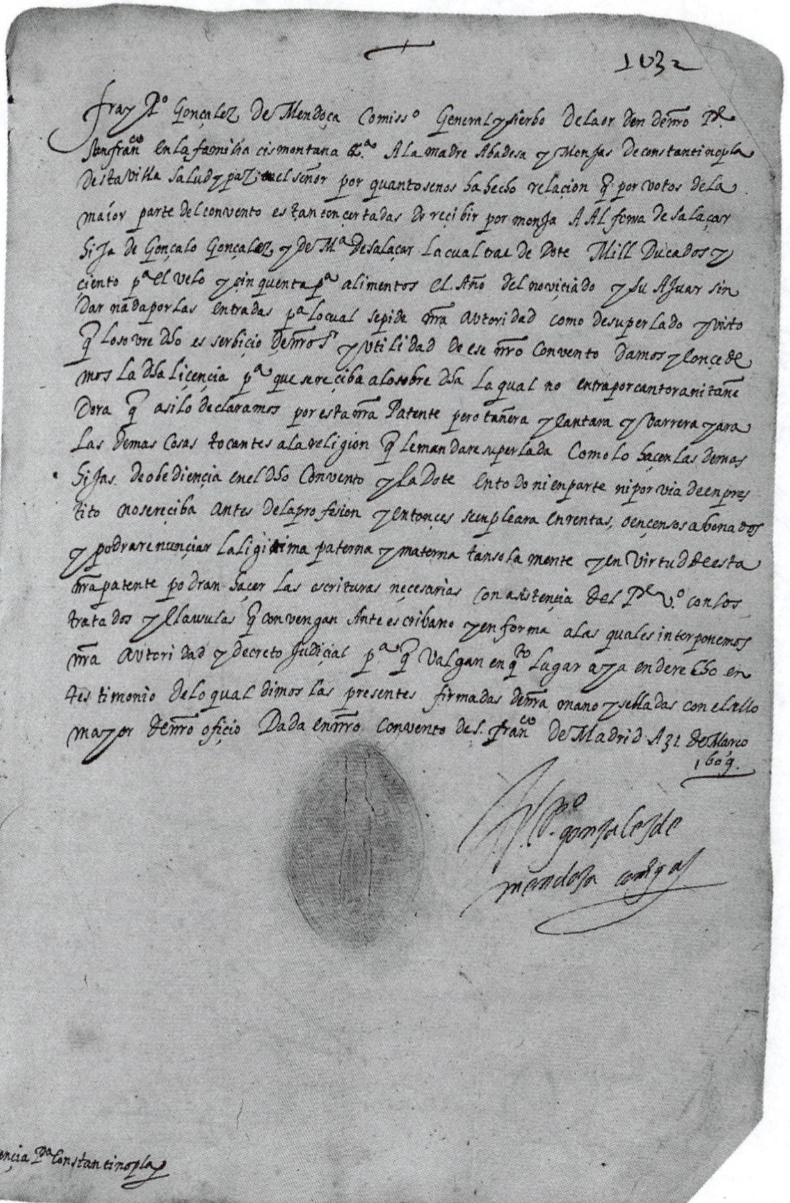

Figure 12.1 *Licencia* for entrance of Alfonsa González de Salazar into Madrid's Monasterio de la Madre de Dios de Constantinopla, 31 March 1609
Permission of the Archivo Histórico de Protocolos Notariales de Madrid, Comunidad de Madrid

A D. ALFONSA

GONZALEZ DE SALAZAR
Mõja en el Monasterio dela Madre deDios
de Constantinopla de Madrid.

Odas las cosas criadas las
dispuso Dios en su peso, y
medida de tal manera, q sa-
cllẽdo de su lugar por particular in-
tẽto q tienen, dessea volver a el;
como a su propio centro: yo quando
determiné dexar de una vez los
versos profanos, y aplicarme a los
diuinos, me resolui, en dirigirlos a
tã singular, y heroyco sugeto como
el de v. m. para q cantados por su
boca, fuessen cõ la de la fama jũta
mente cãtados. Pareciendome pues
q auiẽdo salido celebrados de voz,

Figure 12.2 First page of Miguel Toledano's dedicatory to *Minerva sacra*, Madrid, 1616, depicting Alfonsa González de Salazar
Permission of the Real Academia Española

association with the book) may owe to familial ties, as it has been suggested that Alfonsa González de Salazar was a relative of Cervantes's wife, Catalina de Salazar Palacios.[43]

It is difficult to know to what extent individual Spanish nuns actually enjoyed public recognition as singers or instrumentalists. Many of the nuns who were known as musicians among their sisters probably remained anonymous to outsiders who heard them perform from behind the grille. But whether or not Alfonsa achieved what could be considered fame for her musical talent, she surely was regarded differently from the sister musicians in her monastery who performed as a condition of a dowry waiver.[44] Despite her (cursory) promise to "sing and play and sweep," by virtue of having paid a full dowry, Doña Alfonsa González de Salazar would have been afforded a higher social status – both within her religious community and in the external community – than those (likely anonymous) nun musicians who "labored for a price."[45]

Still, if nun musicians whose presence in the monastery depended upon a dowry waiver were, in fact, regarded akin to servants, such an attitude clearly had to do with how professional musicians were regarded generally in early modern Spanish society. As Louise Stein notes, in seventeenth-century Spain:

> [c]omposers and performers were servants and artisans...Professional composers did not come from the upper reaches of society, and even the best could not rise to that level. The most fashionable and influential of the court composers lived as servants of the crown, with limited social and professional mobility. Generally excluded from high society, professional musicians were not welcomed in the *academias* of the aristocratic intelligentsia, with few exceptions.[46]

---

[43] The suggestion that Alfonsa González de Salazar could have been a relative of Catalina de Salazar Palacios was made by Federico Carlos Sáinz de Robles, *Ensayo de un diccionario de literatura*, 4th ed. (Madrid: Aguilar, 1973), s.v. "Toledano, Miguel." Catalina de Salazar also had familial ties to the Franciscan order, to which Alfonsa's monastery belonged: her brother Antonio de Salazar was a Franciscan friar, and Catalina herself became a Franciscan tertiary in 1609. Cervantes likewise entered the Order of Franciscan Tertiaries as a novice in 1613, taking his final vows on 2 April 1616.

[44] On nuns' music at the Constantinopla monastery, see Colleen R. Baade, "La 'música sutil'."

[45] I borrow the phrase from Nancarrow Taggard, "Art and Alienation:" "Privileged nuns who were free to paint or sculpt when they were not otherwise engaged in prayer because their dowries had been paid in full at the time of their profession were honored by their peers who interpreted their motive as love of God....*Obligated convent artists* María de la Santísima Trinidad and Estefanía de la Encarnación, on the other hand, *labored for a price equivalent to a dowry* [emphasis mine] at the time of their profession (about 2,000 ducats). Their art works expressed the collective will of the community they were pledged to serve, rather than the quality or condition of their souls. Their productive artistic labor with its finished art products reverted upon them, lowering their prestige by reconfirming their inferior class origins" (28).

[46] Louise Stein, "Spain," in: *The Early Baroque Era* (Engelwood Cliffs, New Jersey: Prentice Hall, 1993), 328-329.

"Hired" nun musicians in early modern Spain probably were held in no lesser esteem than their male counterparts.[47]

Questions remain about the identity and social status of Spanish nun musicians, despite my exploration of the topic here. Although the female monasteries whose music attracted public notice were often those that benefited from aristocratic patronage (examples include the Monasterio de San Blas at Lerma and the Monasterio de la Piedad at Guadalajara), it is not certain to what extent the musicians who performed in these houses were daughters of nobility.[48] (Indeed, at those most prestigious of female monasteries in seventeenth-century Madrid – the royal foundations of Las Descalzas and La Encarnación – public polyphony was performed by a chapel of salaried male musicians.) Neither is it clear whether dowry waivers were granted more frequently at larger and wealthier houses or at humbler ones, since documents for dowry waivers of nun musicians exist for affluent monasteries such as Madrid's Monasterio de Constantinopla and also for more modest houses such as Madrid's Santa Clara and Segovia's Santa Isabel.[49]

Such questions lead to the larger question of why monasteries were willing to offer monetary compensation to female musicians in the first place. Recent studies by Craig Monson, Robert Kendrick and Colleen Reardon have already gone a long way in making us aware of the "prestige represented by public polyphony" in women's monasteries in Bologna, Milan and Sienna.[50] The notion that nuns' polyphony held its own special status in early modern Spanish society may help to explain why the Duke of Lerma – when at the beginning of the seventeenth century he erected his court – built and financed the Dominican Monasterio de San Blas

---

[47] Kendrick makes a similar observation regarding nun musicians in Italy: "The questions of whether musical nuns should be considered professional musicians is somewhat misleading. On one hand, those novices who received dowry exemptions had to be good enough to justify the financial burdens; on the other, the social status of musicians in Seicento Milan was so low that, even if questions of gender had not been present, patrician nuns could never have considered the option" (*Celestial Sirens*, 185n.28).

[48] On nuns' music at Lerma's Monasterio de San Blas, see Alfonso de Vicente Delgado, "Referencias históricas," in: *El órgano de la colegiata de Lerma, historia y restauración*, ed. Alfonso de Vicente and Joaquín Lois (San Cristóbal: Junta de Castilla y León, 1996), 13-16; for Guadalajara's La Piedad, see Francisco Layna Serrano, *Los conventos antiguos de Guadalajara* (Madrid: C.S.I.C., 1943), 194-95; music and nun musicians at both institutions are also discussed in Baade, "Music and Music-making" 1-3, 9-10.

[49] Kendrick notes that in Milan, requests for dowry waivers initially came from "the less patrician and less famous Dominican and Franciscan institutions;" however, he goes on to say, "*dote* reductions were…permitted only when the monastery had enough financial resources to support its population, a factor that…tended to favor musical life in the more patrician institutions" (*Celestial Sirens*, 72).

[50] *Ibid.*, 184; see also *ibid.*, 415: "…nuns' music [in Milan] functioned as an emblem of prestige for the city as a whole, serving…to lure the important visitors, local and foreign, to the *chiese esteriori*. The frequency with which their music was mentioned underlines nun musicians' status as the most precious symbol of patrician pride and piety…."

with its chapel of nun musicians, whose talents were praised in a letter by Lope de Vega.[51]

Documents for nuns' *recepción* and *profesión* demonstrate that, inside the cloister, "hired" nun musicians were valued for their contributions both as players and as teachers of other nuns, especially (it appears) as the decrees of the Council of Trent concerning *clausura* were implemented. Teaching is an expressed obligation in the majority of dowry-waiver contracts for nun musicians from the end of the seventeenth century onwards, while contracts from earlier in the century contain no such requirement.[52] A ban against outside music teachers appearing in the constitutions of Avila's Carmelite Monasterio de la Encarnación as late as 1662 – more than a century after the final session of the Council of Trent – may be an indication of the extent to which Spanish nuns resisted compliance with Trent's decrees on nuns' enclosure.[53]

The monasteries that offered dowry waivers to nun musicians likely were concerned with maintaining a level of musical excellence even in their daily religious observances, and so they sought not only to please their public, but also befittingly to praise their God. Women's religious communities appear to have placed considerable importance on celebrating their liturgies "with customary

---

[51] Lope Félix de Vega Carpio, letter to the Duke of Sessa (12 October 1613), transcribed in *Lope de Vega en sus cartas. Introducción al epistolario de Lope de Vega Carpio*, ed. Agustín G. de Amezúa, 2d ed. (Madrid: Real Academia Española, 1989), 3: 127: "Lo nuevo de [Lerma] es excelente; los monesterios, de los mexores que he visto, y más bien servidos, y de notables ornamentos y plata, y alguno, con música que no tiene que envidiar a Constantinopla" ("All the new [construction in Lerma] is excellent; the monasteries are among the best I have seen, and most adequately furnished, with noteworthy ornaments and silver, and one, with music that has no [reason] to envy [the monastery of] Constantinopla").

[52] Kendrick also observes that petitions for dowry reductions "suggest that...musically talented novices were valued precisely for their abilities in coaching their companions" (*Celestial Sirens*, 184). Compare Colleen Reardon's study of nuns' music in Siena, where the availability and accessibility of lay music teachers well into the seventeenth century appears to account for an absence of requests for dowry waivers in that city (*Holy Concord*, 41). The relationship between dowry reductions, availability of outside teachers and enforcement of Tridentine decrees in seventeenth century Spain remains to be thoroughly investigated.

[53] *Constituciones y decretos para...el convento de la Encarnación de Monjas de N. Señora del Carmen de la Ciudad de Avila* (Salamanca: Ioseph Gómez de Cubos, 1662), 40: "Capítulo III. De la clausura, y de algunas cosas, que para conservarla son necesarias a las Religiosas....Yten ordenamos, que ninguna persona así hombre, como muger, Eclesiástico, Seglar pueda ir al Monasterio a enseñar canto llano, ni canto de órgano, y para que aprendan a cantar las que no lo supieren, podrá una Religiosa diestra, y antigua a una hora competente enseñar a las demás" ("Chapter 3. On enclosure and some things that are necessary for female religious to maintain it....We order that no person, neither man nor woman, cleric nor secular, shall go to the monastery to teach plainchant or polyphony. And in order that those who do not know may learn to sing, a skilled, veteran nun may teach the others at a convenient hour").

decorum and solemnity," as the nuns at Toledo's Monasterio de Santa Clara stated in their petition for the dowry waiver of a new organist to replace the ailing María Catalina Castel.[54] The testimony of the nuns at Madrid's Monasterio de Santa Clara indicates that (regardless of the attitudes of aristocratic nuns toward their "hired" sisters), the community placed a high value upon the work of musicians such as Luisa de la Paz. Indeed, the sisters at Santa Clara averred that Sor Luisa's thirty-five years of musical service were worth more to them than would have been an amount ten times her reduced dowry of six hundred *ducados*.[55]

There is much that remains to be understood about the social and spiritual ramifications of nuns' polyphony in Spain. What was the extent of nuns' contact with the public via music, both in liturgical and non-liturgical functions? On how many occasions per year did nuns' musical performances attract public notice? [56]

---

[54] AHP, Toledo, Protocolo 416, fol. 163r: "La abadesa y religiosas deste comvento...de Santa Clara desta ciudad de Toledo dizen que Sor María Cathalina Castel relijiosa del y organista a mucho tiempo está enferma e ympedida de una mano con muchos achaques por cuia razón a mucho tiempo no se zelebran los divinos ofizios con la asistenzia y solemnidad que se acostumbra con gran mortificazión y sentimiento de toda la comunidad..." ("The abbess and nuns of this convent...of Santa Clara of this city of Toledo say that Sor María Catalina Gastelu, [who is] a nun here and organist has for some time been ill and impaired in one hand with many pains for which reason for some time the Divine Offices have not been celebrated with customary decorum and solemnity, much to the great mortification and sorrow of the whole community...").

[55] AHP, Madrid, Protocolo 7720, fol. 4733r: "...la excluyen y apartan de la obligación de tocar el dicho órgano baxón y baxonçillo en consideración de lo mucho que asistió a ello en el discurso de más de treinta años y a que ya no puede acudir como solía al dicho exerçiçio por su mucha hedad y achaques. Y porque demás de lo susodicho en la aceptación desta escritura a de hacer renunçiaçión de los réditos de los dichos trescientos ducados en favor del dicho monasterio de que confiesan estarle muy agradecidas ansí por ello como por el cuydado y valor con que asta aquí a exercido la dicha música. Y se obligan a no reclamar sobre este caso para siempre xamás por que confiesan que aunque la dicha Sor Luisa de la Paz hubiera llevado seis mill ducados de dote a la dicha relixión no ubieran sido de tanto balor como su persona para la dicha música por que a sido de mucha utilidad y provecho" ("[The nuns at Santa Clara] exclude and remove her from the obligation to play organ, *bajón* and *bajoncillo* in consideration of how much she has devoted herself to it during the course of more than thirty years, and since she can no longer attend to said exercise as she used to, due to her advanced age and her [physical] indisposition....and they confess they are very grateful for the care and merit with which up until now she has performed said music. And they resolve not to bring any [further] claim in this case forever because they confess that even if said Luisa de la Paz were to have brought a dowry of six thousand *ducados* to said religion, it would not have been of as much value as her person for said music because it has been of much usefulness and benefit").

[56] See, for example, a letter from Inés de Párraga's letter of 13 October 1659 to chapelmaster Miguel Gómez Camargo, transcribed in Carmelo Caballero Fernández-Rufete, "Miguel Gómez Camargo: correspondencia inédita," *Anuario Musical* 45 (1990), in which a nun serving in the office of *vicaria del coro* states that she is in charge of procuring *villancicos* for Christmas and Corpus Christi (75). Were these the only occasions at which polyphony was performed at this particular (unidentified) monastery?

Were the possible benefits associated with public performance (greater prestige?, increased financial support from patrons?) sufficient to justify or to offset the expense of allowing nuns to enter without a dowry? Or do such questions place disproportionate focus upon the material gains that may have been associated with nuns' polyphony versus the spiritual gains nuns surely associated with "appropriate" worship?

There is also much that remains to be understood about the experiences of individual Spanish nun musicians. I have suggested that the majority of girls who received dowry waivers on the basis of their musical ability were likely prepared from early childhood to become nun musicians because their families had no other means of paying a nun's dowry, let alone any prospects for securing a suitable marriage. Still, I do not mean to imply that all "hired" nun musicians were forced vocations. In a society where women were effectively cloistered not only in the convent but also in the home, there were many reasons – the opportunity to play music being just one of them – why a young women might willingly become a nun. Furthermore, for a girl whose only option was the convent, it is easy to imagine that playing the organ was preferable to scrubbing floors. Still, one wonders to what extent even the daughter of an aristocrat might have aspired to convent life precisely because it was the only legitimate outlet for her musical talent. Three or four centuries after the fact, it is just as difficult to make a determination about a nun's musical vocation as it is to be certain of her spiritual vocation.

It is worth making a final note concerning two nun musicians who were also biological sisters: eleven-year-old organist María de Miranda entered Toledo's Monasterio de Santa Clara in 1700 with a complete waiver of her dowry and nearly all related expenses; her younger sister Juana, also an organist, entered Santa Clara twelve years later with a "half dowry."[57] Perhaps it is merely a coincidence that María and Juana share the surname of a prominent family of organ builders that flourished in Toledo around the turn of sixteenth century.[58] Still, it is intriguing to consider that a musical legacy might have been passed on to two Miranda daughters, who carried on the family trade as "hired" nun musicians.

---

[57] María de Miranda's impressive musical credentials, enumerated in the petition from the nuns at Santa Clara requesting her dowry waiver, are the subject of an anticipated future publication on the musical formation of Spanish nun musicians; see also Baade, "Music and music-making," 125-53.

[58] On the Miranda family of organ builders, see Louis Jambou, *Evolución del órgano español: siglos XVI – XVIII*, 2 vols. (Universidad de Oviedo, 1988), 1: 67-68.

Appendix: "Hired" Nun Musicians, ca. 1577-1772[59]

1) Francisca de Morales, Valladolid, Santa Isabel, 1577-1597. AHN, Clero, libro 17501, passim.

2) Phelipa de Santiago, Toledo, La Concepción, 1599. AHN, Clero, libro 15566, fol. 71r.

3) Agueda de Espinosa, Valladolid, Santa Isabel, 1600. AHN, Clero, libro 17501, fol. 291v.

4) Francisca de las Vírgenes, Madrid, Constantinopla, 1603-†1647. AHPM, Protocolos 2617, fols. 98r-200r and 2621, fols. 395r-398v; AHN, Clero, libro 7448, passim.

5) Catalina del Castillo, Madrid, Constantinopla, 1605. AHN, Clero, libro 7446, fol. 147v.

6) Luisa de la Paz, Madrid, Santa Clara, 1608-1642. AHPM, Protocolos 3073, fols. 205r-206v; 2643, fols. 1091r-1100r and 7720, fols. 471r-473v; AHN, legajo 3937, unnumbered folios.

7) Alfonsa González de Salazar, Madrid, Constantinopla, 1609-†ca. 1641. AHPM, Protocolos 2633, fols. 1029r-1032r and 2638, fols. 863r-867r; AHN, Clero, libro 7448, passim.

8) Lorenza (Laurencia, Lorenzia) de Alemán, Segovia, Santa Isabel, 1614-1628. AHN, Clero, libro 12583, passim.

9) Antonia Bautista, Segovia, Santa Isabel, 1617-1633. AHN, Clero, libro 12583, passim.

10) María Pacheco, Madrid, La Concepción Francisca, 1635. AHPM, Protocolo 5685, fols. 935r-947r.

11) Mariana de Zabala, Madrid, Santa Clara, 1635. Madrid, AHP, Protocolo 5683, fols. 163r-164v; AHN, legajo 3937, unnumbered folios.

12) Ana Padrelines, Valladolid, Nuestra Señora de las Huelgas, 1641. AHN, Clero, libro 16986, fol. 94r.

13) Isabel de Guillamas, Valladolid, Santa Isabel, 1643-†1703. AHN, Clero, libro 17500 and 17501, passim.

14) Ana de Olea, Valladolid, Santa Isabel, 1645-†1700. AHN, Clero, libro 17500 and 17501, passim.

15) María de la Presentación, Escariche, La Concepción, 1657-1684. AHN, Clero, libros 4241, 4242 and 4247, passim.

---

[59] The appendix is a chronological listing of "hired" nun musicians and their respective archival sources. The nuns listed here are those for whom I had encountered evidence of financial remuneration up to the preparation of this essay. Since that time, I have encountered documents for dozens more nun musicians whose circumstances could not be taken into account here. I can report, however, that further investigation shows that an astonishingly high percentage of nun musicians who received dowry waivers elected at some point or another to pay off their dowry and be relieved of their musical duties. For example, nearly fifty percent of "hired" nun organists who entered Toledo's Monasterio de San Clemente during the seventeenth and eighteenth centuries ended up paying a dowry.

16) Ana Conde, Toledo, San Pablo, 1669. AHN, Clero, libro 16001, unnumbered folio [36r].

17) Catalina de Jubera, Madrid, Santa Clara, 1676. AHN, Clero, legajo 3937, unnumbered folios.

18) María Catalina Castel, Toledo, Santa Clara, 1686-1715. AHN, Clero, libros 15814, passim and 15793, passim; AHPT, Protocolo 416, fol. 162v.

19) Paula de la Trinidad, Almonacid de Zurita, La Concepción, 1689. AHN, Clero, libro 4148, fol. 21r.

20) María Marzana, Guadalajara, Santa Clara, 1694-†1699. AHN, Clero, libro 4292, fol. 102v.

21) Felipa de Aparicio y Carrión, Madrid, Nuestra Señora de los Angeles, 1696. AHPM, Protocolos 13382, fols. 488r-497v and 13883, fols. 416r-425v.

22) María Ibáñez de Isaba, Madrid, Nuestra Señora de los Angeles, 1698. AHPM, Protocolos 13384, fols. 1252r-1261v and 13385, fols. 1296r-1300r.

23) Teresa Sancho, Guadalajara, Santa Clara, 1699-1719. AHN, Clero, libro 4292, passim.

24) María de Miranda, Toledo, Santa Clara, 1700-†1727. AHPT, Protocolo 416, fols. 162v-168v; see also AHN, Clero, libro 15817, fol. 218r.

25) Teresa de la Trinidad, Almonacid de Zurita, La Concepción, 1700. AHN, Clero, libro 4148, fol. 27r.

26) Isabel Galán de Montemayor, Toledo, San Pablo, 1704. AHN, Clero, libro 16001, unnumbered folio.

27) Juana Ferrer, Toledo, Santa Isabel, 1711-†1716. AHPT, Protocolos 3988, fols. 412r-414r and 3989, fols. 11r-14r; AHN, Clero, libro 15891.

28) Juana de Miranda, Toledo, Santa Clara, 1712-†1749. AHPT, Protocolos 623, fols. 179r-181r and fols. 228r-237r; see also AHN, Clero, libros 15817, fol. 220r and 15783, passim.

29) Josepha Manuela Pérez de Noriega, Toledo, Santa Clara, 1727. AHPT, Protocolo 627, fols. 189r-183v.

30) María Isidora de Artagoytia, Toledo, La Concepción, 1734. AHPT, Protocolos 628, fols. 192r-198v.

31) Cayetana Gertrudis de Perales, Madrid, Santa Clara, 1739. AHN, Clero, legajo 3937, unnumbered folios.

32) Manuela Baquero, Madrid, Santa Clara, 1740. AHN, Clero, legajo 3937, unnumbered folios.

33) Manuela García, Madrid, Santa Clara, 1740. AHN, Clero, legajo 3937, unnumbered folios.

34) María del Carmen Díaz Valentín, Toledo, Santo Domingo el Antiguo, 1761. AHPT, Protocolos 797, fols. 647r-648v and 4076, fols. 148r-153v.[60]

35) Margarita Limia, Toledo, Santo Domingo el Antiguo, 1762. AHPT, Protocolo 801, fols.741r-746v.

---

[60] I wish to express my thanks to Louis Jambou for informing me of the whereabouts of this document as well as the remaining documents below.

36) Andrea María Teresa Soriano, Toledo, San Clemente, 1767. AHPT, Protocolo 4077, fols. 608r-613v.
37) Catalina de la Fuente, Toledo, Santo Domingo el Real, 1772. AHPT, Protocolo 800, fols. 766r-768v.

Chapter 13

Sor Juana Inés de la Cruz and Music: Mexico's "Tenth Muse"

Enrique Alberto Arias

Although the life and works of Sor Juana Inés de la Cruz (1651-1695) have been much discussed, she remains one of the great enigmas in the intellectual history of the Hispanic Empire. The present study will reexamine her relationship to music but will also consider the ongoing impact she has had on the development of Hispanic creativity.

Edwin Williamson writes: "Sor Juana represents the creole culture and society of New Spain at its zenith towards the end of the seventeenth century. Hailed as the Tenth Muse during her lifetime, she became the greatest literary figure of the Hispanic World after the death of Pedro Calderón de la Barca in 1681."[1] Indeed her literary accomplishment has captured, and rightfully so, the greatest attention; but she was equally fascinated with music. Sophisticated theoretic concepts are given poetic expression and musical imagery is found frequently in her writings, suggesting a high level of musical expertise. In addition, there are indications that she participated in the daily musical life of the convent in which she lived and also, because of her talent, may have taught others the rudiments of music.

Biography

Sor Juana Inés de la Cruz was born in the village of San Miguel Nepantla in Mexico on 12 November 1651. This date is given by Diego Calleja, Sor Juana's first biographer. But, as Octavio Paz notes, "There is good reason to believe he was mistaken. No baptismal entry has been found recording her name and that of her parents."[2] He suggests instead that a certificate of baptism has been located at Chimalhuacán, the jurisdiction to which Nepantla belonged, that is dated 2 December 1648 for a girl named Inés. Her godparents are listed as being Miguel and Beatriz Ramírez, the brother and sister of Juana's mother, so this entry possibly refers to Juana Inés de la Cruz. Sor Juana was the illegitimate child of

---

[1] Edwin Williamson, *The Penguin History of Latin America* (London: Penguin Books, 1992), 160.

[2] Octavio Paz, *Sor Juana or, The Traps of Faith*, translated by Margaret Sayers Peden (Cambridge, MA: Harvard University Press, 1988), 65.

Pedro Manuel de Asbaje and Isabel Ramírez – a fact that would influence her life and perhaps her self-conception. She was possibly baptized as a "daughter of the Church" because of her illegitimacy. She was given the name Juana Inés, a name that she retained for the rest of her life.

During her early years she became a voracious reader, learning to read at the age of three, according to her own account, from an "amiga" of Amecameca.[3] By the age of seven, she had heard that there were schools in Mexico City and she wanted to attend them, but with a change of clothing (perhaps to disguise her age and sex since a small girl would hardly have been welcomed at a university). She also makes clear that she was entirely self-educated and that she punished herself by cutting her hair in order to learn more quickly. According to her account, study and reading were compulsions from a very early age.

Her grandfather's library in Nepantla was the source of her reading, and it provided books on a wide variety of subjects. In 1660, she went to live with her sister in Mexico City. It soon became evident that Sor Juana was a prodigy destined for a major intellectual career, but opportunities for women to advance in the Nueva España of the time were limited, so she remained largely self-taught. In 1662, she entered the court of the Viceroy's wife, Marquise de Mancera. She spent the next years of her life before entering the convent in this stimulating atmosphere, where she conversed with leading intellectuals of the day. By this time Sor Juana had already begun writing poetry, composing a loa (or hymn of praise) to the Blessed Sacrament at the age of eight.

On 14 August 1667 Sor Juana entered the San José convent of the order of the Discalced Carmelites (the same order that St. Theresa of Avila had entered in the sixteenth century and had helped to reform). Here she adopted the name by which she would subsequently be known, Sor Juana Inés de la Cruz. This name perhaps also had musical implications, for as Leonard writes, "Also musically gifted, her ecclesiastical name was possibly adopted in veneration of the instrument-playing hostess of Fray García Guerra and cofounder of the Carmelite convent, of which she was now a temporary inmate."[4] Sor Juana entered as a chorister, implying that music had already become an interest, but she soon found this order too austere and left the convent on 18 November of the same year. It is possible that she left because she believed she would not have the freedom to be creative.

On 21 February 1669 she entered the San Jerónimo convent of the order of St. Jerome. This order was considerably more liberal than the Carmelites and offered Sor Juana opportunities to write and conduct experiments. Her duties included teaching the other nuns music, which most certainly included the essentials necessary for singing Gregorian chant, and maintaining the financial records. She remained in this convent until the end of her life, where, in her final years, she

---

[3] Sor Juana Inés de la Cruz, *Obras Completas* (Mexico: Editorial Porrúa, 1975), *Respuesta de la Poetista a La muy Ilustre Sor Filotéa de La Cruz*, 830. All references are to this edition.

[4] Irving A. Leonard, *Baroque Times in Old Mexico: Seventeenth-Century Persons, Places, and Practices* (Ann Arbor: The University of Michigan Press, 1959), 271.

helped care for nuns dying of the plague. She herself succumbed to the disease on 17 April 1695.

Part of her responsibility while living in this convent was teaching the girls music and participating in the musical performances. It is also probable that she continued to teach herself music here. As Pamela Long notes, the convent of San Jerónimo was originally constructed from the home of one of the founders, Doña Isabel de Barrios, and the adjoining structure, the house of "Ortiz el músico," also known as "el tocador de bihuela."[5] Music was common in many Mexican convents, for, as Long also notes: "The practice and teaching of music in the convents was not the monopoly of the San Jerónimo convent, but rather a typical function of convents until the exclaustration of the nineteenth century."[6] In addition, the convent had a clavichord and was known for the nuns who accompanied the choir on musical instruments.[7]

In 1680, the Marquise de la Laguna and his wife, María succeeded to the viceroyalty. María and Sor Juana quickly became friends and evidenced similar interests, especially for literature. They unfortunately returned to Spain in 1688, resulting in a period of difficulty for Sor Juana. The Archbishop of Mexico, Francisco Aguiar y Seijas, was a fierce misogynist and opposed to secular drama,[8] although at first he seemed Sor Juana's friend. As can be imagined, he and Sor Juana eventually came into confrontation.

The source of this dispute was an essay entitled *Carta Atenagórica* that was penned, as she herself notes in the superscription, as a critique of a sermon given by a Portuguese Jesuit, P. Antonio de Vieira. His sermon was delivered in the College of Lisbon in 1650 (he would go on to be important as an early figure in the anti-slavery movement in Brazil). The *Carta Atenagórica*, written in 1690, is Sor Juana's most subtle theological statement, but it would ultimately end her career as a writer. The title can be translated as "a letter that evidences the wisdom of Athena." She had been invited by the Bishop of Puebla to compose this response to Vieira's sermon, not knowing that this was a trap. She offers a theological study of such points as whether Christ's death or absence is more profoundly felt. Each idea is presented and supported with appropriate quotations from scripture or a scholastic philosopher, with St. Thomas the favorite source. There is nothing controversial in the views Sor Juana presents, and she makes clear that she stands behind the orthodoxy of the Church. Probably what angered the archbishop was Sor Juana's extraordinary brilliance and the temerity of a simple nun to evidence such intellectual acumen.

In 1690, the Bishop of Puebla, Fernández de Santa Cruz, wrote a response to Sor Juana's *Carta* under the pen name Sor Filotea de la Cruz, an obvious reference to Sor Juana's own name. This essay criticized Sor Juana's interest in secular

---

[5] Pamela H. Long, "El Caracol: Music in the works of Sor Juana Inés de la Cruz" (Ph.D. Tulane University, 1990), 17.

[6] *Ibid.*.

[7] *Ibid.*, 18-19.

[8] Paz, 408.

literature. In 1691, Sor Juana penned a response titled *Repuesta a Sor Filotea de la Cruz*. This crucial treatise was an intellectual autobiography, but it also argued for the rights of women to attain knowledge. Throughout this powerful philosophical essay, Sor Juana quoted classical and scholastic authorities in the original Latin and demonstrated what was perhaps deemed an audacious virtuosity of thought. This led to the confrontation with the Archbishop of Mexico City. Sor Juana, now without the support of the viceroy and his wife, felt vulnerable. Listening to the advice of her Jesuit confessor, Pedro de Arellana y Sosa, Sor Juana abjured her creative life, and in 1693 she ceased writing. In 1694, she wrote a profession of faith in her own blood in which she defended Catholic orthodoxy.

Sor Juana entered the convent freely and perhaps because she felt this was a place that would allow her an intellectual life. Her choice of San Jerónimo was occasioned by its liberal atmosphere and easy access to other religious and cultural centers of Mexico City and environs. The nuns at San Jerónimo had private living quarters and servants.[9] They were allowed to receive visitors and to have personal libraries. This convent, which still stands in the center of Mexico City and is now a small college for the liberal arts, was pleasant and elegant. A positive organ, recently restored, was installed in the convent in 1670, perhaps coincidentally the year after Sor Juana's entrance, suggesting that music was intrinsic to the life of the residents.[10] At one point in the *Repuesta*, Sor Juana complains that the neighboring nuns were singing and playing instruments, implying that the nuns, including Sor Juana herself, probably had musical instruments in their rooms.[11] Music played an increasingly important role in her writings, and it was here that Sor Juana read and responded to some of the important musical treatises of the seventeenth century.

Sor Juana and music

Although Sor Juana is best known for her poetry, which has attracted the greatest critical attention, it was only a part of her intellectual interest. In fact, she used poetry to give voice to her views of science, music and philosophy. From her own statements and from the reports of others, Sor Juana read widely in philosophy and science and was interested in experimentation. She also evidenced an early musical ability. Her first biographer Padre Diego Calleja specifically praised her study of music and noted that she "estudió el arte muy de própósito."[12] From various references in her poetry it is obvious that she was interested in music theory, especially of the encyclopedic sort espoused by Pedro Cerone. These statements, scattered in several poems, form the basis of this article.

---

[9]   Paz, 120.

[10]   Michael Drewes, "The positive at San Jerónimo, Mexico City," *The Organ Yearbook* 19 (1988): 31-37.

[11]   *Obras*, 833.

[12]   Quoted in Long, 3.

Pedro Cerone (1566-1625) was perhaps the most important theorist of the Hispanic world during the seventeenth century. His *El Melopeo y Maestro* (1613) epitomized late Renaissance music theory. Although the principal source of his thought was Gioseffo Zarlino, Cerone alluded to or summarized many other theorists of the fifteenth and sixteenth centuries; thus his gargantuan and complex treatise encapsulated musical thought in late Renaissance Spain. Cerone discussed both the theoretic and practical sides of music, and it is for this reason that Sor Juana probably found his work attractive.

A copy of Cerone's treatise with annotations by Sor Juana was discovered in 1930 by the bookseller Demetrio García. Ermilio Abreu Gómez published these two pages in his biography of Sor Juana. Her copy of Cerone's treatise (several pages of which were missing) still existed in 1988 at the Biblioteca del Congreso in Mexico City, when it was examined by Octavio Paz while writing his study. Robert Stevenson included two pages with Sor Juana's annotations in his brilliant article on her connections to music.[13] The annotations included by Stevenson, found at the bottom of page 284 and running to the top of page 285 of Cerone's treatise, concern her reaction to a section in which Cerone considers the tuning of instruments.[14] According to Paz, these were the only annotations in this copy of Cerone's treatise, giving them considerable importance.[15] At the end of the annotation that comments on the acoustical topic of this portion of the treatise, she writes: "Esta Raçon de Ceron su discipula Juana Inés de la Cru," or, "For this reason, the disciple of Cerone Sor Juana Inés de la Cruz."

This is important for her thoughts on acoustics, but it also can be understood in a larger sense as well. Sor Juana was in every way a disciple of Cerone. His vision of music's place in the universe and his response to Pythagorean principles must have resonated with her. His treatise remained influential throughout the seventeenth and eighteenth centuries, and other theorists, such as Andrés Lorente and Padre Antonio Soler, borrowed from it liberally. Sor Juana may also have read Lorente's *El porqué de la música* (1672). It at first appears to be a replication of Cerone, but a more careful reading reveals that it is comprehensive and expands on Cerone much in the way that Cerone expanded on Zarlino. Its detail and constant probing of "why?" might have appealed strongly to Sor Juana, who perhaps saw Lorente, like herself, as an ardent student of Cerone.[16]

What other musical theorists was Sor Juana aware of? The Romance No. 50 alludes to Athanasius Kircher. One of the strophes reads:

Pues si la Combinatoria
En que veces *kirkerizo,*
En el cálcula no engaña
Y no yerra in el guarismo.

---

[13] Robert M. Stevenson, "Sor Juana Inés de la Cruz's Musical Rapports: A Tercentenary Remembrance," *Inter-American Music Review* 15 (1996): 1-21.

[14] *Ibid.,* 11.

[15] Paz, 239.

[16] Long, 35.

[If then in the art of combination
in which one follows (Athanasius) Kircher,
then in number there is no falsity
and the digit does not stray.]

This is a reference to the *Ars Combinatoria* by Athanasius Kircher, the Jesuit polymath of the seventeenth century. In addition to this treatise, Kircher is principally known for the *Musurgia universalis* (Rome, 1650) that may have influenced Sor Juana[17] (this German Jesuit's writings were influential throughout Nueva España). Like Cerone, Kircher proposed an encyclopedic view in which music is seen to reflect the divine order. But more so than Cerone, Kircher included various scientific experiments regarding acoustics and musical instruments. Throughout this testament to Jesuit science there are elaborate illustrations and symbolic representations. Kircher also sometimes alludes, although cautiously, to the Hermetic tradition that had found new energy in the Florentine Renaissance and the writings of Marsilio Ficino. These Hermetic allusions fascinated Sor Juana and inspired her own work as well.[18]

Sor Juana may have read other very influential treatises of the Hispanic world, such as Francisco de Montanos' *Arte del canto llano* (1648), a basic text at the time. The pious practicality of both this and Lorente's text would have appealed to her. They would have furthermore supported her work at the convent in teaching the nuns music (Montanos would have especially appropriate), as they would have affirmed many ideas found in her poetry.

Sor Juana's ideas regarding music are captured in the *Respuesta a Sor Filotea de la Cruz*. In it she defines music as one of the steps of the sciences and the humanities that leads to the summit of sacred theology.[19] The view of theology as the "queen of the sciences" is, of course, typical of scholastic philosophy during the later Middle Ages, but in this passage of the *Respuesta* theology becomes the reason for studying other subjects:

> How, unless one is very expert in music, can one understand those proportions and their beauty that are found in many spots, such as that where Abraham petitions God to save his cities if he can find fifty just men. Then this number is decreased to forty-five, which is the sesquinona (10:9) proportion as the interval from mi (understand ut) to re. This number is then decreased to forty and is the sequioctava (9:8) proportion and is the interval of re to mi. The number is further decreased to thirty that is the sesquitertia (4:3) that is the interval of the fourth. Then the number is decreased to twenty that is the proportion of the sesquialtera (3:2) and then to ten that is the dupa (2:1) and is the octave. And how can one understand that one cannot pass to other proportions? And how can one understand all of this without understanding music?[20]

---

[17] Paz, 143-144.

[18] *Ibid.*, 365.

[19] *Obras*, 832.

[20] Como Pues sin ser muy perito en la Música, ¿cómo se entenderán aquellas proporciones musicales y sus primores que hay en tantos lugares, especialmente en aquellas peticiones que hizo a Dios Abraham, por las Ciudades de que si perdonaría habiendo

This discussion clearly concerns the acoustical intervals and uses the Pythgorean system of measurement. How clever of Sor Juana to use the famous story about finding fifty just men as the basis for an acoustical presentation. Abraham is told by God that he will save the cities of Sodom and Gomorrah if he finds fifty just men. He cannot, and God then says he will save the cities if he can find forty-five. The proportion of 50:45 is the distance between Ut and Re. The next reduction is to forty that gives the distance between Re and Mi. Note that these distances are slightly different. The next reduction is to thirty that gives the distance of a fourth. The next is to twenty that gives the distance of the fifth. The last reduction is to ten that gives the distance of the octave, the last interval in music. Each interval results from the two numbers at each step of the reduction.

Another statement in the *Respuesta* reveals the tension between the theoretic and the practical so frequently found in Sor Juana's writings: " ...y mientras se toca el arpa sosiega el organo. " This quotation is interesting, partly because it is put enigmatically and partly because of its musical references. Sor Juana seems to be saying that habit and theory sometimes move in contrary directions "as when the harp plays, the organ is silent." But when does this occur? It happens in the realization of the basso continuo in Hispanic music of the period. The harp remained a favored instrument for accompaniment into the seventeenth century, except in liturgical circumstances, where the organ was the instrument of choice.

On a larger scale, Sor Juana apparently wrote a musical treatise, no longer extent, entitled *El Caracol*. The root meaning of the word *caracol* is "spiral." Paz maintained that the title was possibly derived from Athanasius Kircher's *Musurgia universalis* (1650), where various spiral musical instruments are discussed and illustrated; but I will suggest below that the title was actually used by Sor Juana in a quite different way.[21] The basic ideas of this treatise are summarized in Romance 21, *Después de estimar mi amor*. This short poem is divided into four parts: an introduction (lines 1-5), the musical discourse (lines 6-26), references to the treatise (lines 27-35), and conclusion (lines 36-43). Thus this Romance verifies the existence of the treatise and gives us some idea of its contents. (See the appendix for a complete translation of the Romance.)

The superscription indicates that this Romance is an excuse for not sending a book on music. I believe the unsent book was the treatise *El Caracol* mentioned within the poem. Clearly, Sor Juana intended to send the Condesa de Paredes this completed treatise, but at the time she did not consider it ready. The superscription also indicates that Sor Juana was *eminente*, or highly experienced in music, as evidenced by the poem with its specific references to music theory. Thus this poem

---

cincuenta justos, y de este número bajó a cuarenta y cinco, que es sesquinona y es como de ut a re; de aquí a cuarenta, que es sesquioctava y es como de re a mi: de aquí a trenta, que es sesquitertia, que es la del diatessarón; de aquí aveinte, que es la proporción sesquiáltera, que es la del diapente; de aquí a diez, que es la dupla, que es el diapasón; como no hay más proporciones armónicas no pasó de ahi? Pues ¿como se podrá entender esto sin Música?, 832.

[21] Paz, 243.

serves as both a microcosm of the treatise as well as a testament to Sor Juana's theoretic abilities. She says the treatise was written at the suggestion of the Condesa, and that this task was both important and trying. This Romance is an abstract of the treatise in poetic form.

Sor Juana indicates that music theory consists of notation and intervals and that the measurement of intervals is a difficult matter. She wonders if the Pythagorean semitone can be accurately sung and questions whether the fourth is a consonant or dissonant interval. She then makes a reference to Pope John (in 1324, Pope John XXII issued at Avignon the *Docta Sanctorum*, the famous bull in which he condemned many of the practices of the Ars Nova, especially the use of rhythmic complexity and the overloading of sacred melodies with intricate polyphony.) Sor Juana then ponders if the tuning of an instrument required the participation of a *coma*, or an interval smaller than a semi-step. This, of course, was a crucial question in the later Renaissance when the tuning of instruments in a group often resulted in unintended dissonance. It was a problem that ultimately led to the equal temperament system. It is also a question that was important for Cerone.

Sor Juana next turns to notation. The system that she described is essentially Renaissance mensural notation, and she could have learned it from Cerone's *El Melopeo*. She mentions geometric and harmonic divisions, demonstrating her expertise in mathematical acoustics. Is the distance from Ut to Re the same as from Re to Mi? It is in the equal temperament system, but it is not in the systems commonly used before the nineteenth century. Can these small intervals be perceived and what are their mathematical differences? All of this requires a greater capacity than was Sor Juana's, she claims.

The next two strophes are crucial and must be read carefully. Sor Juana began a treatise that would summarize the rules found in various sources, implying that she had read widely (but used Cerone as her guide). She began this, as indicated in the superscription, because of the request by the Condesa. She then says that if she remembers correctly, harmony is a spiral not a circle and that was the reason she called the treatise *El Caracol*. Harmony here must be understood to mean the essential elements of harmony, or intervals, and these intervals create a spiral not a circle. But she goes on to say that the question remains unformed and that the treatise is both unworthy of the hands of the Condesa and would be rejected by her in its present state. This implies that the treatise was either unfinished or, at least, not in the desired form at the time she wrote this Romance.

Was this treatise ever finished? This Romance is the only evidence of its existence and *El Caracol* may well have been left incomplete. But if heaven permits Sor Juana more time, she writes, she will complete and revise her promised treatise. The rest of the poem refers to her personal relationship to the Condesa, which was clearly based in some part on their mutual love of music. One can well imagine their conversation in which the musical matters alluded to in this poem were the subject of charming debates and delightful discussions.

Sor Juana makes clear in the Romance that *Caracol* refers to a system of harmony which is not circular but a spiral. But *Caracol* also means a snail, winding staircase, or cochlea of the ear. In addition, Stevenson notes that it was an Aztec signaling instrument.[22] Could the treatise have combined these meanings? Also, the title might have secondarily implied the convoluted nature of music theory as a whole (and given Sor Juana's brilliant sense of language it is easy to imagine her playing with the several senses of the word). Paz further suggests that *caracol* symbolized Sor Juana's need for protection and privacy ("to live in a shell"). Unfortunately we will never know, for what surely would have been a brilliant summary of musical thinking is lost to us.

Although other of her poems talk about music, the references are not as sustained as in the text just cited. For example, the Villancico 220 notes that only the song of the Virgin Mary is in perfect harmony with the eternal consonances, thus affirming the central idea of Romance 21. This villancico compares Mary to a divine mistress of a chapel, where each syllable of the hexachord reflects aspects of her glory, from the "ut" of the Annunciation to the "la" of her Exultation:

> Es especies musicales
> Tiene tanta intelligencia que el *contrapunto* de Dios
> Dio en el la más *Perfecta.*

> [She is best understood as compared with the aspects of music
> that the counterpoint of God gives her perfection.]

This villancico also notes the tension between those intervals that can be sung easily and those that are the result of precise acoustical measurement:

> Dividir las *cismas* sabe
> En tal *cuantidad*, que en Ella
> No hay *semitonio* incantable,
> Porque ninguno *disueña.*

> [She knows how to divide cismas (schisms or whole tones) in such a way
> as to not produce any unsingable semitones
> since no discord results.]

This strophe is crucial for an understanding of Sor Juana's thinking about music because it shows her awareness of the friction between those intervals that can be measured in a symmetric fashion, according to the Pythagorean scheme, and the practical necessities of music.

Sor Juana also wrote several loas. Originally these were monologues that served as preludes to comedies in which the royalty and audience were praised.[23] They became allegorical panegyrics either at the beginnings of operas or theater pieces, or self-sufficient short theatrical works for the court, and they involved music throughout. Sor Juana's loas were commissioned by the viceregal court, and

---

[22] *Ibid.,* 13.
[23] Paz, 140-141.

she received remuneration for their composition as well as protection from the court. The writing of these allegorical loas brought wealth and prestige to Sor Juana and her convent. Music would have been part of the performance, but since these were ephemera, the music has not been preserved. It is obvious from the performance indications of these works that music was integral. Could Sor Juana have made suggestions as to the kind of music that was appropriate? I believe she did and also that she may have worked closely with the composers during the realization of these projects. The loa at the opening of Tomás Torrejon y Velsaco's opera *La Púrpura de la Rosa* (1701), based on a text by Calderón de la Barca and premiered for the viceregal court at Lima in honor of the eighteenth birthday of King Philip V, is a glorious example. Choruses and solo sections alternate to praise the young king who is compared to the fifth planet. This introductory section creates an impressive musical beginning and established the theme and allegorical references for the opera that followed (much in the way that similar opening sections of the operas of Lully did in the later seventeenth century).

Self-sufficient loas also served to acclaim royalty or nobility, and music and dancing again were important. Sor Juana composed a number of these loas in which music participates as an allegorical figure. Long writes: "In Loa 376 dedicated to Carlos II, Sol, Cielo, Tiempo, Felicidad, Juvetud, Prudencia and three choirs discourse on the relationship between music, time, light and the virtues."[24] Loa 378 suggests the Copernican cosmology, with Sol as the center of the planetary system.[25] Loa 379, written for the birthday of the queen María Luisa de Borbón, celebrates the connections between music, will, understanding, and memory. All make use, as Sor Juana points out, of time, and music becomes in this poem the image of time that binds together the various faculties of the mind.

Loa 384 was written in celebration of the birthday of the Condesa de Galve and is cast in the form of musical comedy based on the syllables of the Guidonian hexachord. This loa comes closest to an actual musical work and could easily be set to music. It is in the tradition of works on the hexachord that originated in the Renaissance. The work begins with a prologue in which a chorus is heard singing behind a curtain, celebrating the harmonious nature of music (the chief musical image for Sor Juana). Music then enters, making several mythological references. Scene II begins with each note of the hexachord given a symbolic interpretation. A duet occurs for each note in which music presents the function of the note and the note itself expands on that function. Thus "ut" is seen to be the origin of music, while "re" creates the first interval. Although all of this is put in a charming and even humorous fashion, there is a more serious purpose evident here. Sor Juan wants to show that the hexachord system is based on each note having a function beyond the interval distances between the notes.

This is a musical discourse demonstrating Sor Juana's very professional knowledge of music theory but it also is didactic. Scene III makes clear that this is a celebration of the birthday of Elvira. Again the process of enumerating the

---

[24] Long, 131.

[25] *Ibid.*, 138.

syllables occurs, but this time each syllable is assonant with a key word; thus "re" becomes the first syllable of the word *regocijo*, or joy. This allows Sor Juana to expand on the virtues of the person being celebrated. The prologue to Scene IV notes that these are the pitches of the "Escala de Arentino" or the scale of Guido of Arezzo. This loa has several purposes: it demonstrates Sor Juana's knowledge of music theory, it explains the functions of each note of the Guidonian hexachord, and it presents the idea of music in the form of an allegory. It furthermore suggests that Sor Juana was perhaps familiar with the music of some of her important Mexican contemporaries.[26] It complements the Romance 21, but avoids the complex issues regarding tuning that were present in that poem.

The other loas do not emphasize music to the same degree; but all of these court works are structured like cantatas, with a choral section, solo episodes, and refrains. Sor Juana was influenced in their creation by the increasing prestige of the Italian style in Mexico at the time. Thus, for example, the Loa No. 373, written for the feast of the Conception of the Virgin Mary, begins with a double chorus in dialogue. This is followed by a long series of solo sections and duets. Loa 374, written for the birthday of Carlos II, likewise begins with a chorus. The first line "Hoy, al clarín de mi voz" sets the tone, sounding like a trumpet call. The second chorus answers with the lines "Hoy a la dulce armonía de mis bien templadas voces...," or "Today in the sweet harmony of my well tuned voices..." This implies that the various instruments' voices are in agreement, a concern central to Sor Juana's musical theories. Later in this loa, echoes occur between the longer lines and the answering solo voice of Music:

Aire: El Aire os rinda, de su Esfera, graves
Música: Aves
Aire: y, repetidos en los troncos huecos,
Música: Ecos

Many of these loas include precise directions as to how music was to be included, demonstrating that Sor Juana created these charming works with music in mind from the beginning. Loa 380, written for the birthday of Mariana of

---

[26] Francesco López Capillas (c. 1615-1673), one of Sor Juana's most distinguished Mexican musical contemporaries, composed a *Missa super Scalam Aretinam*. This Mass is admittedly old fashioned given the period in which it was written and demonstrates the composer's awareness of the hexachord tradition of Masses from Josquin through Palestrina. Another work form the earlier seventeenth century in Mexico, is both humorous and is based on the hexachord syllables: Gaspar Fernándes' villancico *La Sol Fa Mi Re*. This villancico is didactic in that the text instructs how to learn these syllables and their significance. Sor Juana may well have known the Mass by Capillas as well as the charming Francisco López Capillas (c. 1615-1673), one of Sor Juana's most distinguished villancico by Fernándes. Scene IV employs a technique found in some madrigals of the later sixteenth century and continued into the next century: that of using an echo to change the meaning of a word (a device also found in *The Divine Narcissus*). The final scene is a celebration of the birthday event in the form of a general chorus in which the syllables sing a solo answered by a choral refrain.

Austria, begins with a scene in which fame appears: "Aparece la FAMA en lo alto, y canta lo siguiente." ("Fame appears from above and sings the following.") There can be no doubt as to the implication for song, and. throughout the loa those portions that are to be sung are specifically indicated. In Scene V the following directive is given to Concordia: "Canta este y los demás cuatro versos." ("Sing this and the following four verses.") This implies, of course, that the previous section was declaimed, suggesting that these loas mixed speech and song. One of the strophes of this section reads:

> Y que unidos los Coros,
> Ordenadas se alternen
> Las cláusulas de Marte, de Adonis con los líricos motets.

> [And the united choruses alternate
> the phrases of Mars with those of Adonis in lyric motets.]

This strophe makes an important allusion to motets, highlighting the musical nature of this section of the Loa. Loa 381 begins with a duet between Venus and Belona "y cantan dentro," or "with singing from within." It continues with an extended double chorus; so this section was, or at least could have been sung throughout. Here Sor Juana fulfills the function of a librettist.

Loas are written in a complex, allegorical style that reflects the influence of Calderón de la Barca and other writers of the Spanish golden age. Sor Juana, however, was also aware of the popular poetic-musical styles of the time and she demonstrated this in her villancicos, which run the entire gamut of dialects and references to "common life." As Paz points out, villancicos became an important part of the celebration of matins in later seventeenth century Nueva España:

> Matins are divided into three nocturnes, each consisting of three psalms. *Villancicos* adopted the same division: three nocturnes of three lyrics each, although often the last lyric was replaced by the Te Deum. Thus, each of these *villancicos* was a set or series of eight or nine lyrics. In Mexico the custom of singing *villancicos* of three nocturnes to celebrate matins on liturgical holidays goes back to the second half of the aseventeenth century. The cathedrals of Mexico City, Puebla, Paxaca, and Valladolid (Morelia), among others, celebrated all important annual holy days with these songs. The frequency of the celebrations, the accompanying pomp, and the number of faithful who attended meant there had to be a permanent organization in charge of them. The *villancicos* were a spectacle—and spectacles, besides authors, actors, and audience, require stage directors, administrators, and managers: a bureaucracy.[27]

Matins with the inclusion of villancicos rivaled the Mass in musical importance, but there was an important difference. Mass was celebrated in Latin, musical settings were elaborate, and villancicos were sometimes included. But matins appealed to more popular sensibilities. Long writes: "The *villancico* was ordinarily performed during matins on feast days, and many times carried over to the mass

---

[27] Paz, 311.

itself. Sor Juana's San José 1690 set terminates with four *villancicos* "para la missa;" one set for the Epistola, Ofertorio, Alzar and 'Ite missa est'." [28] Sor Juana was commissioned to write sets of villancicos for the important cathedrals in Mexico. They were set to music, although the poetry alone often implies what kind of music she intended. They could also be metaphorical, as Long notes: "Music plays a wide range of symbolic and allegorical roles in the *villancicos*, especially those in praise of the Virgin Mary. The *villancicos* for the Mexico City cathedral celebration of the Assumption in 1676 involve the notes as a musical staircase of ascension to perfection which the Virgin makes use of in directing the choir." [29]

Some poems suggest Sor Juana's awareness of musical practice in Mexico and Spain. Villancicos 258 and 282 refer to "los sieses," or the Hispanic practice of choirboys. Villancico 6 from the 1680 set for the Nativity is an example of a *negro*. The piece ends the second nocturne of Matins for the nativity and forms a fitting climax. It is the sort of dialect villancico frequently set by Gaspar Fernándes and Antonio de Salazar.

Sor Juana's villancico begins with an invitation:

Alegres a competencia
En sus cánticos bozales,
Entraron con su capilla
Los Músicos de Azabache.

The estribillos continues with a description of the music:

1.—Canta, Flasquilla,
canta, canta;
toca sacanbuche.
2.— Vaya, vaya!

The reference to the sackbut clearly indicates that this instrument was included in the performance. Long notes that allusions to musical instruments appear in thirty-six of Sor Juana's works, from the classical lye to the indigenous calabazo. [30] She also points out that the San Pedro villancicos of 1691 show the wide range of instruments in use at the Mexico City cathedral at that time. Villancico 73 is a catalogue of fifteen instruments available to cathedral musicians of 1691. Long writes: "Just as all races of peoples are enlisted in her villancicos to lift up their voices in praise, so all instruments are summoned to accompany the worship ceremony: the Indian with his *calabazo*, the African with his *panderiyo*, the Spaniard with his *vihuela* and *violín*, and the creole with his *chirimía*." [31]

---

[28] Long, 74.
[29] *Ibid.*, 40.
[30] *Ibid.*, 166.
[31] *Ibid.*, 175.

These villancicos often imply performance practice by mentioning possible accompanying instruments, frequently by playing with the word sounds of the instrument names. In addition, many popular musical images appear in the sets of villancicos. In those villancicos that were commissioned by the Cathedral at Los Ángeles (the old name for Puebla) for the Christmas of 1680, musical effects, such as onomatopoeic phrases and sharply changing word rhythms abound. Villancico 8 contains a key line that can be summarized as "Tóquenle, cantenle," or "Sing and Play." This seemingly innocent line is interesting in that it again shows that instruments participated in the performances of villancicos..

The Villancico 1 from the 1686 set for the Assumption of the Virgin Mary for the Cathedral of Mexico ends with a strophe that includes the text:

Y con dulce armonía ,
En suave voz, en métricos concentos, por su Reina a María
Con sonoros la aclaman instrumentos,
Sin cesar armonioso el plectro de oro que sus glorias repite coro a coro.

[With sweet harmony,
In soft voice, in harmonious meter, for the reign of Mary,
Instruments acclaim without stopping,
The harmonious plectra of gold that is repeated choir to choir.]

This is not only a poetic image, but also a description of how this poem was sung and how it was to be accompanied by a string instrument using a golden plectrum. Choirs repeated the musical phrases, producing a climactic effect.

Stevenson notes that Sor Juana interacted with the major Mexican chapel masters of her day in creating these texts.[32] Antonio de Salazar, the distinguished chapel master at the Cathedral of Mexico, while at the Cathedral of Puebla (the second most important position at the time), composed Sor Juana's villancicos dated 29 June 1680 and 1684, 25 December 1680, 15 August 1681, and 29 June 1691 and 1692. José Agurto y Loaysa composed music for Sor Juana's 1676 set. Miguel Matheo de Dallo y Lana wrote music for three sets, and Matheo Vallados composed music for the 1691 set for Santa Catarina, Sor Juana's last set of villancicos. That her villancicos were commissioned not only demonstrates her fame and importance but also the awareness of her ability to create appropriate symbols and allusions.

Sor Juana's extraordinary ability to imitate a popular approach is also evident in the *Bailes y Tonos Provinciales*. These were performed in a festival at the San Jerónimo convent before the viceroy and his wife. The group of poems is like a suite of dances, with each dance representing a different region or style. There is even a *Panamá*, a dance that apparently had some association with that country. One could easily image a colorful spectacle, with dancers in gorgeous costumes and representatives from different tribes of the Americas. Another example from

---

[32] Stevenson, "Sor Juana Inés de la Cruz's Musical Rapports: A Tercentenary Remembrance."

this set, Endecha 71, is to be sung to the music and regional dance called the "cardador" (*El cardador* was apparently a well known song of the time). Similarly, No. 72 is based on the regional music called *San Juan de Lima*. Other references to dance types in the villancicos include the *Portorrico* (mentioned in the ensaladadilla of villancico 241), the *Calenda* (an African dance from Guinea common in the Americas at the end of the seventeenth century), and the *Tocotín* (an indigenous Mexican dance that appears in villancicos 224 and 141). In each instance the poem itself explains the designation and music. Performance practice treatises from the seventeenth century offer insights into the dances. Sebastián de Aguirre's *Método de cítarra* (c. 1650) and Lucas Ruiz de Ribayaz's *Luz y Norte Musical* (Madrid, 1677) refer and use as examples dances mentioned by Sor Juana. Ribayaz includes dances in tablature, some of which, like the *Chaconas* and *Zarabandas*, had New World origins. It is possible that Sor Juana could have known these widely disseminated treatises.

Other poems offer examples of the integration of Sor Juana's poetic ability and her knowledge of music. The Redondilla 87 has a caption that states it "paints the symmetric harmony that the eyes perceive in beauty and the other (ears) in music." Again Sor Juana's clever musical expertise is evident in the following image: " from the music stand of your eyes to the measure of your nose (compás is a musical term that designates the beat or measure) there sings re mi fa sol." Each part of the body is then described as a musical symbol.

All poets are musical, but Sor Juana was particularly so. Her knowledge of music is evident from the above discussion, but even in those poems that do not relate to music, there is an affirmation, as Paz points out, of the relationships between echoes and reflection. He writes:

> A major portion of her poetry revolves around these two motifs – or, more accurately, obsessions. Two magical objects, the mirror and conch shell that project two incorporeal progeny. In Sor Juana's symbolic system the echo, in the auditive mode, and the reflection, in the visual, are homologous; their values are interchangeable. Both are metaphors of the spirit: the echo is voice, word, music; the reflection is light, intelligence.[33]

This implies that the lost treatise *El Caracol* may have been more than a musical statement; it could have served as a summary of Sor Juana's poetic aesthetics as a whole.

Music in Mexican convents

Music played a powerful role in Mexican convents of the seventeenth century. Thomas Gage, the English Dominican priest who traveled in Mexico in the early seventeenth century wrote the following:

---

[33] Paz, 246.

It is ordinary for the Fryers to visit their devoted Nuns, and to spend whole days with them listening to their musick, feeding on their sweet-meets. And for this purpose they have many chambers, which they call Loquitorios, to talk in, with wooden bars between the Nuns and them, and in these chambers are tables for the Fryers to dine at; and while they dine, the Nuns recreate them with their voices.[34]

It would seem that many Mexican nuns were musical and perhaps entered the convent in part to allow their talent expression.

Although we do not know what sort of music was performed at Sor Juana's convent, another Mexican source from roughly the same period offers us a glimpse into the wealth and prestige of a convent that flourished in the seventeenth century, the Convento de la Encarnación. Founded in 1589 by Conceptionist nuns, it came to be one of the wealthiest in Mexico City and its close relationship to the Cathedral resulted in extensive musical resources. Originally in eight volumes, the present collection consists of six volumes containing Spanish sacred music as well as compositions by Mexican masters. Presently called the Newberry Choirbooks because they came to the Newberry library in Chicago in the late nineteenth century, this source is important not only for our understanding of Mexican music of the period but also for a better appreciation of convent life in the more liberal orders.[35]

Many compositions call for multiple choirs and are written in a grandiose manner. The works by Mexican composers range from a *Miserere* by Hernando Franco (c. 1520-1585) to an impressive *Dixit Dominus* by Don Juan de Lienas who flourished in the early part of the seventeenth century. The latter composition is written for two choirs and is a brilliant example of a style that was found in larger musical institutions in both Spain and Mexico. Its presence in this source demonstrates the musical capabilities of this convent. The variety of styles and the number of compositions found in the Newberry Choirbooks are impressive, and it is quite possible that Sor Juana heard several of these works.

The convent of Santa Paula (the original name of Sor Juana's convent, San Jerónimo) was founded in 1585, and it had a musical tradition from the beginning. (See the postscript for further information on this convent.) The nuns followed the conventual rule of St. Augustine, although they could not be properly called Augustinians. They lived "private" lives, which is to say that they were allowed a considerable amount of independence, and had servants. Some nuns owned property and amassed personal fortunes. The apartments they lived in were spacious and included kitchens, baths, and other small rooms. Sor Juana had a slave and an apartment that was on two floors. She received gifts from her admirers and was, by the end of her life, a relatively wealthy woman. Paz writes: "From the time she took the veil, Sor Juana participated in the theatrical and musical activities of the convent. Besides her *villancicos*, she composed many songs for *loas*, and the lyrics for several 'dances and provincial airs' written for an

---

[34] Thomas Gage, *A New Survey of the West Indies* (1648), quoted in Leonard, 12.
[35] Eliyahu Arieh Schleifer, "The Mexican Choirbooks at the Newberry Library, Case MS VM 2147 C36" (Ph.D. dissertation, University of Chicago, 1976).

entertainment held in San Jerónimo in honor of the Marquis and Marquise de la Laguyna."[36] Thus not all the music at the convent was sacred.

Although no music remains that was written specifically for Sor Juana's convent, there is good reason to imagine that sacred polyphony was composed for its services. Stevenson points out that the constitutions for the convent approved by the Archbishop of Mexico on 7 January 1673 included twenty pesos to be paid annually to the "maestro que compone la música." This suggests that the convent had a composer who wrote polyphony on a regular basis. The constitutions also ordain that six pesos be paid annually for players of strings and reeds, which would imply that the convent had a small orchestra.[37] This would not be surprising, for the Basilica of the Virgin of Guadalupe, just to mention one Mexican liturgical institution, could boast by the end of the eighteenth century an orchestra that rivaled those of Europe. One professed nun at San Jerónimo was the choral vicar for polyphony, while another was the corrector of plainsong. In addition, youthful singers were occasionally admitted to the convent without the requisite dowry. Strings and reeds were probably also used for special occasions, when concerted music would have been featured.

There is also evidence that Sor Juana herself owned musical instruments.[38] Diego Calleja, her first biographer, speaks of "her musical and mathematical instruments, of which she had many, precious and exquisite."[39] In addition, these instruments, which she probably received as gifts, may have been used in the musical performances at the convent. Paz suggests that these took the form of fantastic hybrids, but it is more probable that they were the kinds of instruments mentioned in her own villancicos. In addition to the singing of Gregorian chant, the presence of a portative organ installed in 1670 supports the idea that polyphony was intrinsic to the convent's musical life.[40]

The ongoing impact of Sor Juana

The first edition of Sor Juana's works was published in Madrid in 1689. A second edition, like the first dedicated to Doña María Luisa Gonçaga, Condesa de Paredes, was published in Madrid the following year, with the indication that the text was corrected by the author herself ("corregida y mejorada por su Authora"). The title of the Collection is *Poemas de la unica Poetisa Americana, Musa Decima*, thus giving the appellation of "Decima Musa" by which she has been known ever since. That this collection was published in Spain rather than Mexico is not surprising given the support of the Condesa who had by then returned to Spain. Also, the condemnation and the poetic silence of Sor Juana's later years would have made publication difficult in Mexico.

---

[36] Paz, 239.
[37] Stevenson, 9.
[38] *Ibid.*, 6-7. Many of these instruments were probably gifts.
[39] Paz, 246.
[40] Dreves, "The positive at San Jerónimo, Mexico City."

This second edition has an approbation by M. Fr. Luis Tiento de Morales, a member of the Dominican order. In it, he takes the opportunity to praise Sor Juana as "Ave rara, que solo en un Mundo nuevo pudiera hallarse" ("A rare bird that could only be found in the New World"). He continues by noting that women rarely evidence such poetic talent and concludes with the following statement allowing the publication of the document: "Por donde juzgo son muy dignos de salir a luz, para que todos vean, que cosas tan estupendas ay en el otro mundo, que ni tienen par, ni ay que compararlas." ("Thus I judge that they [the poems] are worthy to be published that all might see what marvels exist in the other world that there is nothing equal or can be compared to them").

Sor Juana's poetry was little appreciated in the eighteenth century. The increasing influence of French Rationalism in the Bourbon Hispanic Empire, beginning with King Philip V, changed reader tastes. As elsewhere in Europe, the complex conventions of Baroque poetry gave way to more direct expression and simpler vocabulary. During the seventeenth and eighteenth centuries she was forgotten and her vivid life became no more than a dim memory. It was the twentieth century that rediscovered Sor Juana, and this occurred precisely at the time when Mexico needed symbols of the past to support the future.

The development of interest in Sor Juana corresponds, quite incidentally but not for altogether different reasons, with the increasing veneration of the Virgin of Guadalupe. By the twentieth century, both had become twin symbols for Mexican women and indeed for Mexico as a whole. How could a country to whom the Virgin appeared and had given special consideration and a country that had produced such a genius as Sor Juana be a cultural and intellectual backwater? Both became mothers to Mexico (Sor Juana is often referred to as Madre Juana). Both were benevolent (Sor Juana cared for the other sisters of the convent in her last days during the terrible plague sweeping Mexico). And both serve as symbols for Mexican women of today. There are yet further parallels that intrigue. Both symbolized the development of society of Nueva España in the later colonial period, with its tensions and growing independence from the mother country. Both related Mexico to the rest of the world through a loving Catholic faith that transcended restrictions of dogma.

Octavio Paz's celebrated book on Sor Juana, frequently cited in this article, is as much about Mexico as it is about Sor Juana. Paz is considered one of Mexico's most distinguished authors and intellectuals of the twentieth century; thus in many ways his work parallels that of Sor Juana. Originally written in Spanish, this book appeared in 1988 in an English translation by Margaret Sayers Peden, bringing Sor Juana to the attention of the English-speaking world. But this book also served a national cause by showing that someone of Sor Juana's stature could exist in the Nueva España of the later seventeenth century. In the preface Paz writes:

In her lifetime, Sor Juana Inés de la Cruz was read and admired not only in Mexico but in Spain and all the countries where Spanish and Portuguese were spoken. Then for nearly two hundred years she and her works were forgotten. After the turn of the century taste changed again, and she began to be seen for what she really is: a universal poet. When I started writing, around 1930, her poetry was no longer a mere historical relic but had once again become a living text. What sparked the revival, in Mexico, was a small book by a poet, Amado Nervo; his *Juana de Asbaje*, 1910, dedicated "to all women of my country and my race," can still be read with pleasure. Between 1910 and 1930, numerous scholarly works appeared, devoted primarily to unearthing and establishing the texts.[41]

The revival of interest in Sor Juana coincided with the development of modern Mexico and its consciousness of a national past. In addition to reclaiming the glories of the pre-Colombian period, an examination began into the music and literature of the colonial period. Sor Juana came to symbolize the pride and accomplishment of Nueva España Pax, who had considerable musical knowledge, was among the first to show the importance of music to Sor Juana's thinking. It is his brilliant book that made Sor Juana an internationally recognized figure.

Paz's book led rather directly into an excellent film. María Luisa Bemberg, the Argentine director, created the film *Yo la Peor de Todas* (I, the worst of all) in 1990, starring Assumpta Serna and Dominique Sanda. The film was advertised as being based on Paz's book and it is a sensitive treatment of some of the implications of Paz's masterpiece. The cover for the video version of the film states: "When the Inquisition comes, the local Vicereine (*Dominique Sanda*) becomes Juana's protectress and erotic muse, and soon begins a thrilling romance of startling passion and intensity." A quote from the *Boston Globe* on the cover reads: "Lesbian Passion Seething Behind Convent Walls..." Of course, all of this has as much to do with the historical realities as *Amadeus* does with Mozart's last days; but Bemberg's film (which is tastefully done) had international distribution, and it brought Sor Juana to wide attention. It also affirmed Sor Juana's intellectual independence and her perilous relationships with the Mexican ecclesiastical authorities. The film portrays Sor Juana's musical activities at the convent and powerfully relates the sorrow of her last days.

The American composer John Eaton (1935-) has had much interest in the poetry of Sor Juana. In 1989, he composed a dramatic cantata *El Divino Narciso*, based on Sor Juana's play by this title and adapted by Nelda Nelson. This work, scored for coloratura soprano, mezzo-soprano, and tenor with a chamber group, including optional electronic enhancement, was premiered on 4 April 1990 by the Chicago Contemporary Chamber Players under the direction of Ralph Shapey. Eaton continued his series of Sor Juana compositions with the *Sor Juana Songs* for mezzo-soprano and piano premiered by La Decima Musa on 8 March 1998 in Chicago. *Tocotín* for mezzo-soprano and guitar was likewise premiered by Nelda Nelson and Paul Bowman at La Decima Musa. The most recent composition in this series, *Sor Juana's Dream*, is scored for mezzo-soprano, guitar, piano, and electronics and was premiered at the Mexican Fine Arts Musuem of Chicago on 23 October 1998 during the Sor Juana festival to be discussed presently. Eaton's compositions complement those of the seventeenth century that were written directly because of Sor Juana's poetry. He has responded to Sor Juana's innately

---

[41] Paz, v.

musical and powerfully dramatic texts. Eaton became aware of Sor Juana's poetry through his wife Nelda, as he wrote me on 28 June 2002:

> My wife introduced me to Sor Juana's poetry. Before seeking a doctorate in Spanish and Latin American literature at Indiana University, Nelda was a first-class opera singer, a soloist with the New York City, Houston, and San Francisco companies among others. I grew very excited about *El Divino Narciso* when she was studying it, and asked her to translate and shape it into a dramatic cantata with the possible inclusion of first and last choral-balletic movements. She did a brilliant job. I was inspired as seldom in my creative life by Sor Juana's incredible vision; and, it has become my favorite chamber composition, although it is seldom performed because of its difficulty. I simplified the action of the play in the inner movements to a confrontation between Human Nature, Narcissus, and Echo. You feel a poetic as well as very sympathetic mind at work in every phrase and in their continuity with each other.

Eaton went on to explain the origins of the other works of the Sor Juana series:

> I next wrote a song cycle for Nelda using three of Sor Juana's marvelous sonnets – again she helped me understand them. In the last song of the cycle, the singer calls Thisbe by singing into the strings of the piano and waiting for the echo of her voice. This cycle has profoundly moved audiences whenever it has been done. They also have been amused by my setting for guitar and mezzo of *Tocotín*, a Nahuatl poem of Sor Juana's. I chose the guitar because of Sor Juana's use of the vernacular language.

> Next to *El Divino Narciso*, my most ambitious work inspired by Sor Juana is my setting of much of *Dream* (or *First Dream*) for mezzo, piano (mostly played inside), guitar (with a plethora of unusual techniques), and electronics. It is called *Sor Juana's Dreams*. Again, I do not set the entire poem, but try to seize on a central dramatic line – or two attempts to scale the heights, so to speak, and the subsequent falls, hence the "s" in the title.

Thus Eaton continues the tradition of Mexican composers of the later seventeenth century, but he sets Sor Juana's philosophic rather than popular poetry.

Sor Juana Inés de la Cruz had become by the latter twentieth century a symbol of resolute integrity and was considered an advocate of feminine rights. The development of interest in Sor Juana coincided with the appearance of major Hispanic women writers, artists, and composers. Although I do not suggest a direct link between Sor Juana and Mexican women composers, she has provided a general model for creativity. Such composers as Gabriela Ortiz, (1964-), Marcela Rodríguez (1951-), and Mariana Villanueva (1964-) have written innovative music that is performed internationally. In general, Mexican women composers have become leading figures in contemporary Mexican musical life, frequently conquering the *machismo* attitude of Mexican culture.

Of the many festivals and celebratory events presently held in homage to Sor Juana, I cite the annual Sor Juana Festival held at the Mexican Fine Arts Museum in Chicago (already mentioned as the occasion for one of John Eaton's Sor Juana compositions). This festival has grown to be one of the most impressive of its kind in the world. Held annually in October, the festival includes films, concerts, roundtables, and a Sor Juana Achievement Award (the recipient in 2001 was Lois Weisberg, commissioner of the Chicago department of cultural affairs). This festival thus celebrates the accomplishments of women: "The Festival also commends Chicago Mexican women leaders with the Sor Juana Achievement Awards. And, as a testimony to the enduring spirit of women worldwide, the Festival honors a woman whose life reflects the spirit of Sor Juana."[42]

Sor Juana continues to inspire Hispanic intellectuals. Music was a major passion for Sor Juana, evident in the many musical allusions in her writings. She has the distinction of being the first and, up to her time, the only musical theorist who was a poet (if one discounts Plato). Did music console Sor Juana during those dark times in the later part of her life? Probably it did, but it also was ever an area of theoretic interest and experimentation. It gave Sor Juana a magnificent paradigm with which she could conceive of an orderly universe. Thus, ultimately, I do not see Sor Juana the poetess at her desk but Sor Juana the musician, with her beloved Cerone as a guide, writing about music and hearing the songs of the angelic spheres as she writes.

Appendix

Romance 21, translated by Manuel Blanco-González. This poem is an example of *conceptismo*, or the use of complex Baroque imagery common in the poetry of Góngora. In addition to being the outline of a treatise on music, it uses music as an image and as an occasion to honor Sor Juana's patroness.

(A romance) that she writes to the most Excellent Countess of Paredes, asking to be excused from sending a Book about Music; and she shows how eminent she was in this art, as she proves in the other arts.

After esteeming my love
Sublime, beautiful Mary,
That fact that in your divine one
You keep some memories of me;

After having admired
That in your sovereignty,
Not erased, of my love
The news are kept;

I pass to give you my reason
Which forces me to disobey
Your command, if there is

---

[42] *Sor Juana Festival 2001: A Tribute to Mexican Women.*

A good excuse for it.

A Book on Music
You ask, and of necessity
It creates in me a dissonance
That you ask me for harmonies.

Concerts from me, my lady,
When I throughout my whole life,
Have not done anything deserving
Of a good sound for myself?

I, the art of composing, staff-lines, characters, ciphers,
Proportions, quantities,
Intervals, points, lines,

Breaking my head about *sismas* and
If the *comas* are exact
To divide the tone?

If the semitone that is hard to sing
Has its secret in inequality
Pythagoras (worrying) about it
Turning to ashes

If the diatessaron must be
Held as a consonance,
Quoting an extravagance
In which Pope John affirms it;

If the tuning of an instrument
Needs the participation
Of a *coma* that is lost.

If the point of alteration
Inclines to the second note
More because it helps the text
Than because of the note it serves.

If the major perfect mode
In the maxima mode did or would consist,
And if the lesser perfect mode touches the long;
Which is two beats and which is three.

If the imperfection it causes

A smaller note is total or partial,
Essential or accidental.

If the voice which as we see
Is the successive quantity
Is worthy only of that consideration
From which one voice is separate from another

If the perfection of the diapason and diapente
Consists in that neither less nor more
In composition admits;

If the coloration is to the notes
That which takes away all their value,
Seeing thus that there are many
To which coloration gives value;

And how the harmonic means
Is distant from the two extremes,
And how the geometric
Is distinguished from the arithmetic.

If music is reduced
To two measures,
The one measuring the voice,
The other measuring time.

That the character of increasing
The number to its family,
I have in my soul impressed
If it does not come to the cheeks;

And if my misfortune
Deprives me to be at its feet,
I would serve it just by asking
From God your and its life.

Postscript

In 1863 Luis Alfonso y Piña wrote the *Relación Descriptiva de la Fundación, Dedicación, etc., de las Iglesias y Conventos de México* (Mexico: M. Villanueva, 1863). This book was inspired by the closing of many convents that occurred during the presidency of Benito Juárez and represents an invaluable source about the history of Mexican liturgical institutions. Alfonso y Piña clearly wanted to preserve important information about institutions that he was afraid would disappear. His book includes a short history of the San Jerónimo (spelled San Gerónimo in the book) as well as specifics regarding its finances. Sor Juana's convent is presently a College for the Liberal Arts in Mexico City.

El convento de relijiosas agustinas de S Gerónimo lo fundaron relijiosas de la Concepcion el año de 1585, siendo arzobispo el Illmo. Sr. D. Pedro Moya Contreras, y es uno de los mas grandes de la ciudad de México. La iglesia está situada de Poniente á Oriente, á ese viento el coro y á aquel el altar mayor: la puerta mira hacia el Norte. El número de relijiosas de este convento en 1861 era de 26.

Antes de ese año poeseia ese convento 89 fincas era de 682, 000 ps., sus capitales activos ascendian á 119,811 ps., pues producian un rédito de 5,991 ps,; sus capitales subian á...53,283 ps. 6 rs. En este convento tomó el velo, profesó la célebre poetista mexicana Sor Juana Inés de la Cruz.

Cuando fueron exclaustradas las relijiosas de este convento en Febrero de 1863, D. Francisco Gochicoa, nombrado inventor de este convento presentó con fecha 26 un inventario, en el que se ocupó de poner como de aumento muchos objetos inútiles y que en realidad no existian. Nada de vasos sagrados se apuntaron en el inventario y de las hermosas pinturas que allí existian, algunas de ellas se estraviaron.

[The convent of the Augustinian nuns of San Gerónimo was founded by Conceptionist nuns in 1585. The archbishop was than D. Pedro Moya de Contreras, and the convent was one of the grandest in Mexico City. The church is situated west-east, with the choir to the east and the major altar to the west. The entrance looks to the north. The number of nuns in this convent in 1861 was 26.

Before this year, the convent possessed 89 estates whose value was 682,000 ps. The assets were valued at 119,811 ps that produced interest of 5,991 ps. Sor Juana Inés de la Cruz, the famous Mexican poetess, took her veil, was professed, and lived many years in this convent.

When the nuns of this convent were exclaustrated in February 1863, Don Francisco Gochicoa was named to take the inventory of this convent. He presented an inventory dated 26 February 1863 that included many useless objects that in reality did not exist. None of the sacred vessels were noted in the inventory, and some of the beautiful pictures that existed there disappeared.]

The bibliography on Sor Juana is vast and has developed tremendously in the last ten years. www.dartmouth.edu/~sorjuana/ is a website sponsored by the Department of Spanish and Portuguese that is an ongoing bibliographic project with updates. Recent bibliography is listed as well as scholars who are Sor Juana specialists with their scholarly contributions. Links are listed to Sor Juana's Intellectual World, including a link, important from the perspective of this article, to Athanasius Kircher.

WOMEN, COLLECTIONS, AND PUBLISHING

Chapter 14

Patronage and Personal Narrative in a Music Manuscript: Marguerite of Austria, Katherine of Aragon, and London Royal 8 G.vii

Jennifer Thomas

During the years Marguerite of Austria served as regent of the Netherlands and as the patron of the Netherlands court chapel (1507-15; 1519-30), the Alamire scriptorium of the Netherlands court complex created a sumptuous presentation manuscript destined for the Tudor court of Henry VIII and Katherine of Aragon. (Appendix 1 contains an inventory of the manuscript's contents and full translations of key texts.) Virtually every aspect of that manuscript, London, British Library, Manuscript Royal 8 G.vii (hereafter LonBLR 8 G.vii),[1] has engaged the perplexed scrutiny of scholars with the following questions:[2]

---

* This essay further develops the ideas in a paper I presented at the American Musicological Society Annual Meeting in Atlanta, Georgia, November 2001. Data gathered from the database catalogue of sixteenth century motets that I created in conjunction with my dissertation research both impels and supports many of the arguments I make in this essay. For more information, please see Jennifer Thomas, "The Sixteenth-Century Motet: A Comprehensive Survey of the Repertory, and Case Studies of the Core Texts, Composers, and Repertory" (Ph.D. diss., University of Cincinnati, 1999). See the database catalogue online at www.arts.ufl.edu/motet/. I am grateful to Professor Robin Armstrong for many conversations about the manuscript and for her astute readings of drafts of this article and to Professor Karin Pendle for her critical reading and helpful suggestions.

[1] Herbert Kellman, Introduction to *London, British library, MS Royal 8 G.vii*, Renaissance Music in Facsimile (New York and London: Garland, 1987). Kellman succinctly reviews much of the published and unpublished research on the manuscript. Professor Kellman's pioneering work with the Alamire manuscript group and his expertise in interpreting these manuscripts and their contents have laid the foundation for all research in this area. I thank him for his rigorous questioning and constructive criticism of my approach to LonBLR 8 G.vii; his arguments influenced my thinking at every point.

[2] Certain themes and focal points recur in this body of scholarship, but each scholar, bringing a different point of view, has also brought a new interpretation of the manuscript. It

Who was the first recipient of the manuscript? [3]
What was the date of its creation and presentation? [4]
What was the occasion that prompted the gift? [5]
Why the recycling of motets originally dedicated to Anne of Brittany and Louis XII of France? [6]
Why the errors and corrections made in one of these recycled motets, *Adiutorium nostrum?* [7]
Why the irregularities in the Tudor coat of arms displayed in the illumination accompanying the opening motet, *Celeste beneficium?* [8]
Why the complete absence of composer attributions? [9]

---

is unlikely that conclusive evidence answering all the questions or proving one of these interpretations will ever emerge, but with each new approach, a more complete view of the work seems to be evolving.

[3] Frank Tirro argued, in "Strawberry Leaves, Single Arch, and Wrong-Way Lions," *Musical Quarterly* 67 (1981): 1-28, that Anne of Brittany was the original recipient of the manuscript. He points out the similarities between the lives of Anne and Katherine and links the *Dulces exuviae* and *Absalon fili mi* motets to Anne's failure to produce a male heir and to her many failed pregnancies. Tirro also thoroughly reviews the scholarship on the manuscript to the time of his article.

[4] Dating has revolved around suitable occasions for the giving of the gift and has assumed 1509, the year of Katherine and Henry's marriage as the earliest possible date with a *terminus* of 1528, when Henry formally began his divorce proceedings.

[5] Possible occasions include the wedding of Henry and Katherine in 1509, the engagement of Henry's sister, Mary Tudor to Charles V in 1513; the birth of Henry and Katherine's daughter Mary in 1516; the ceremonial meeting between Charles and Henry at Gravelines and Calais in 1520; a 1521 treaty between England and France that included the engagement of Princess Mary to Charles V; and Charles's only state visit to the Tudor court in 1520.

[6] The motets that open this manuscript, Mouton's *Celeste beneficium* and Févin's *Adiutorium nostrum*, were originally presented to Anne of Brittany and her second husband, Louis XII of France, for their wedding. The earliest surviving source for these motets is Petrucci's 1514 Fossombrone print, *Motetti de la Corona*. This anthology, published the same year that Anne of Brittany died, preserves motets by many composers of the French court.

[7] As many others have pointed out, the original names in the manuscript, Ludovicus, Anne, and Renatus (Anne's patron saint), are overwritten with the names of Henricus, Katherina, and Georgi (St. George). Several theories attempt to explain how and why this may have happened; see Tirro and Kellman. Calling it "the favorite second-hand motet of the Netherlands court," Kellman also points out the recycling of this motet in other sources: in VatP 1976-9 for Anne and Ferdinand of Bohemia and Hungary, and for Marguerite in OxfBLL a.8.

[8] Tirro, 12-15, 27. The lions within the crest are facing to the right rather than to the left, a symbol of cowardice, according to Tirro.

[9] Attribution practices in the Alamire scriptorium are spotty. Many manuscripts, including BrusBR 9126, BrusBR 15075, and FlorC 2439 contain complete or almost complete composer information. Others, such as BrusBR 215-16, may contain attributions for about half the works, and a few others, such as BrusBR 228 (Marguerite's *chansonniere*) and VatC 1976-79, are as uninformative as LonBLR 8 G.vii.

What about the authorship and notational irregularities of *Absalon fili mi?*[10] Why the unusual inclusion of five consecutive settings of *Dulces exuviae*, a passage from Virgil's *Aeneid*?[11]

Explanations for some of the mysteries involving the book and its contents fail to satisfy other concerns; none of the interpretations of the manuscript to this point resolves all of the questions. However, a new understanding of the five settings of *Dulces exuviae* and the motet that immediately follows them, *Absalon fili mi*, in the seventh of the manuscript's eight fascicles, may point to the purpose, donor, recipient, and dates of the manuscript as well as the meaning of its contents. This new interpretation, which plausibly reconciles many puzzling questions, takes into account the meanings the text brings from its original literary context, the meanings it acquires among the texts in the new context, and the significance these meanings may have had for the donor under this reading, Marguerite of Austria, and the recipient, Katherine of Aragon.

The text of the *Dulces exuviae* motets presents the principle and most striking challenge in decoding the manuscript. Most motet texts derive from scripture or liturgy; this one comes from classical epic poetry. At the end of Book IV of the *Aeneid*, Aeneas has abandoned Dido to establish his city on the Tiber. As his ship sails from Carthage, Dido climbs onto a funeral pyre, and, surrounded by mementos of her love affair with Aeneas, speaks the words set in these motets before killing herself with his sword:

Dulces exuviae, dum fata deusque sinebat,	Relics once dear, while fate and heaven allowed,
accipite hanc animam meque his exsolvite curis.	Take this my spirit, and loose me from these woes.
Vixi et quem dederat cursum fortuna peregi, et	My life is lived; I have fulfilled the course by fortune given, and now my shade
nunc magna mei sub terras ibit imago.	Passes majestic to the world below.

---

[10] Though Josquin was associated with this motet as a result of attributions in late sources, recent scholarship credibly proposes Pierre de la Rue as the actual composer. Opinion, however, is not unanimous. See Joshua Rifkin, "Problems of Authorship in Josquin; Some Impolitic Observations. With a Postscript on *Absalon, fili mi*," in: *Proceedings of the International Josquin Symposium Utrecht 1986*, ed. Willem Elders and Frits de Haen (Utrecht: Vereniging voor Nederlandse Muziekgeschiedenis, 1991), 45-52; Jaap van Benthem, "Lazarus Versus Absalon: About Fiction and Fact in the Netherlands Motet," *Tijdschrift van de Vereniging voor Nederlandse Muziekgeschiedenis* 39 (1989): 54-82; Nigel Davison, "*Absalon fili mi* Reconsidered," *Tijdschrift van de Koninklijke Vereniging voor Nederlandse Muziek Geschiedenis* 46 (1996): 42-56; and Honey Meconi, "Another Look at Absalon," *Tijdschrift van de Koninklijke Vereniging voor Nederlandse Muziek Geschiedenis* 48 (1998): 3-30.

[11] Other authors have discussed the possible reasons for the inclusion of this text: Tirro, 23-24 and Kellman, vii.

The troubling message of the text is intensified by its five-fold repetition. The reiteration sets it apart not only within this manuscript, in which no other text is repeated, but also because recurrence of a classical text falls outside normal practices. Repeated use of a particular text within a single musical source usually occurs in certain circumstances and normally for reasons clearly connected with the function of the source. For instance, manuscripts of intabulated music often contain multiple settings for individual pieces – presumably, to offer choices.[12] Many manuscripts collect motets on liturgically appropriate texts for practical use, thus the repetition of functional religious texts is not remarkable.[13] Among these sources are manuscripts that collect texts on a particular subject, most often Marian devotion. Such manuscripts present multiple settings of the most prominent Marian texts, such as *Salve regina*, *Regina caeli*, and the other major Marian items.[14] However, neither the text *Dulces exuviae* nor the manuscript LonBLR 8 G.vii falls into any of these categories. Why would a manuscript given to a royal couple contain multiple settings of this particular text, a text on the suicide of a queen? Might not the recipient interpret emphasis on this particular text as ill will, possibly even treasonous? Though one setting of the text would not call attention to itself, five settings definitely do. The multiple settings of this unusual text dictates that we regard it as an emblem of special significance to both the donor and the recipient of the manuscript.

Its significance lies in the message it conveyed to the donor and recipient. In his introduction to the Garland facsimile edition of LonBLR 8.G.vii, Herbert Kellman mentions the fact that one of the possible donors of the gift, Marguerite of Austria, may have found personal meaning in the *Dulces exuvaie* texts. Marguerite suffered many personal tragedies, and Martin Picker, in his edition of her *chansonnier*, Brussels 228, convincingly connects its many sorrowful texts to the specific tragedies of her life.[15] Among those texts are two settings of *Dulces*

---

[12] One example is WrocS 5, a manuscript of intabulated motets. Thirty-one of its 215 texts are repeated at least once; *Hodie Christus natus* appears ten times. A few individual motets receive more than one intabulation, for example, Josquin's *Praeter rerum* and Clemens's *Ab oriente venerunt* and *Angelus domini ad pastores*.

[13] For example, in AachS 2, a manuscript used by the Krönungsstift cathedral choir, several duplicated texts appear contiguously, perhaps for convenience in choosing a setting. *Angelus domini ad pastores*, *Delectare in domino*, *Ego sum panis*, and *O spes afflictis timor hostibus* are adjacent; *Misit me pater viven* and *Tu es Petrus* are within a few motets of each other.

[14] In fact, the Alamire scriptorium prepared just such a manuscript: MunBS 34, probably created for William IV of Bavaria, contains twenty-nine motets, all on the text *Salve regina*.

[15] Martin Picker, *The Chanson Albums of Marguerite of Austria. MSS. 228 and 11239 of the Bibliotheque royale de Belgique, Brussels* (Berkeley: University of California Press, 1965). Picker discusses Marguerite as patron, discussing at length her personal agenda and collection. Also see his essay, "Margaret of Austria," in: *Women Composers: Music Through the Ages*, ed. Martha Furman Schleifer and Sylvia Glickman (New York: G.K. Hall, 1996), 1: 88-92. Here Picker discusses a motet-chanson *Se je souspire/Ecce iterum*, possibly written by Margaret, in which the layered texts express Marguerite's personal, emotional response to the death of her brother, Philip the Fair. The text, as Picker points out, specifically refers to Marguerite as the author and to Philip as the deceased.

exuviae, one of them concordant with the second setting in LonBLR 8.G.vii. In the Brussels manuscript, *Dulces exuviae* is again the only repeated text, an indication that it had personal meaning for Marguerite – perhaps her response to the deaths of her two young husbands. In fact, though this text is not statistically significant in any other region of Europe, it has an unusually high profile in Netherlands sources generally, surpassed in use only by *Salve regina*. Its prominence may well be the result of Marguerite's attention to these verses.[16]

If indeed this text had particular meaning for Marguerite of Austria, she may have requested its inclusion in LonBLR 8.G.vii for personal reasons. Just as BrusBR 228 served as a vehicle for expressing Marguerite's state of mind, LonBLR 8.G.vii may well have served as the vehicle through which she conveyed a deeply personal message to Katherine of Aragon. That Marguerite had reasons and desires for significant communication with Katherine is not surprising: the two women shared a friendship and family ties as well as uncannily similar histories. The London and Brussels manuscripts commemorate many significant biographical events in the lives of the two women. In addition, the themes and ties so dominant in the lives of Marguerite and Katherine echo those of a third royal woman, Anne of Brittany.[17] Our knowledge of Anne's association with the opening motets of

---

[16] The text occurs only twenty-six times in the motet database catalogue. Eight of those occurrences are in the Netherlands court source group: five in LonBLR 8 G.vii, two in Marguerite of Austria's *chansonnier* BrusBR 228, and one in FlorC 2439. At least fourteen of the twenty-six total occurrences of *Dulces exuviae* are these settings or their concordances. For a more detailed study of text usage in the Netherlands sources, see Thomas, "The Sixteenth-Century Motet," 317-322.

Some have questioned whether women would have read a masculine book like the *Aeneid*. It is highly likely that Marguerite and Katherine, both learned and intelligent women, knew this book. Margaret King wrote about Katherine and her mother, Isabella of Castile: "In Spain the formidable Isabella guided religious reform and intellectual life, while in England, her learned daughter Katherine of Aragon . . . was surrounded by the leading humanists of the era," in *Women of the Renaissance* (Chicago: University of Chicago Press, 1991): 161. That women had an interest in such "masculine" stories is supported by a visual record: Marguerite's step grandmother, Margaret of York, is shown in an engraving receiving the two volume *Histories of Troy* (frontispiece MS R.B. 62222, Huntington Library, San Marino, CA, reproduced in Jean-Marie Cauchies, *A La Cour de Bourgogne: Le Duc, Son Entourage, Son Train* (Turnhout, Belgium: Brepols, 1998), 113.

In admonishing women to remain in their proper sphere, Gregorio Correr wrote, "Therefore, dismiss your beloved Virgil. . . . Take up instead the Psalter, instead of Cicero, the Gospel. . . ." (King, 176); this admonition, of course, would have been unnecessary had women not been reading Virgil in the first place. In addition, a venerable tradition of emulating Virgil and translating his poetry into English flourished from the time of Chaucer's *Troilus and Creseyde*. See *Virgil in English*, ed. K.W. Grandsden (London: Penguin Books, 1996), xix-xx.

[17] The standard biography for Katherine is Garrett Mattingly, *Catherine of Aragon* (Boston: Little, Brown, and Co., 1941); Alison Weir's *The Six Wives of Henry VIII* (New York, Ballantine Books, 1991), while covering a broader subject, offers details and dates not present in Mattingly. For Marguerite, a standard work in English is Jane de Iongh (translated by M. D. Herter Norton), *Marguerite of Austria, Regent of the Netherlands* (New

LonBLR 8.G.vii (see note 4) seems to cast her shadow upon the entire book, and, as Tirro has argued (see note 7), she would have been drawn to the *Dulces exuviae* text for the same reasons as Marguerite and Katherine. Given their own complicated family connections and near-connections, Marguerite was undoubtedly very familiar with Anne's story, and it is not hard to imagine that Katherine was as well; thus, Anne's story may have been part of the private communication. (See Appendix 2 for a synopsis of the similarities and connections among the three women's lives.)

The relationship between Katherine and Marguerite began when they were still in their teens. They became sisters-in-law in 1497 when Marguerite, at the age of seventeen, wed Katherine's brother, Juan, and came to live at the Spanish court. She and Katherine became good friends there, and Marguerite taught Katherine French.[18] Marguerite had learned French during her childhood spent at the French court, where she was groomed from the age of three to become the wife of Charles VIII. Charles later repudiated the betrothal for political reasons and dismissed her from court when she was eleven years old. In order to protect French territorial interests, he instead married Anne of Brittany, forcing her to renounce her proxy marriage to Marguerite's father, Maximilian I.[19]

Marguerite may have felt a sisterly sympathy for Katherine, whose childhood experiences paralleled her own in many respects. Though reared in her mother's court, Katherine was educated from the age of two to fulfill her parents' hope that she would eventually be the Queen of England. After many years of negotiations, her formal betrothal to Prince Arthur took place in 1497, when Katherine was eleven. She left her home for the English court in 1501, and she and Arthur were married when both were fifteen years of age and considered capable of consummating their marriage.[20]

The parallel continued: both young wives were widowed by their first husbands after very short marriages. Marguerite and Juan were married in April of 1497; he died in October, and their child was stillborn a few months later. Marguerite was seventeen years old. Katherine was married to Arthur, the son of Henry VII, by proxy in May of 1499 and again in May of 1501. They wed in person in November of that year; Arthur died 5 months later, in April of 1502. Katherine was sixteen years old. Both women also lost their young adult brothers to death. Katherine's brother Juan, who was also Marguerite's husband, died in 1497. Marguerite's brother Philip died in 1506.

York: Norton, 1953); Picker, *The Chanson Albums*, also contains biographical information, particularly with regard to Marguerite's patronage and taste in the arts. For Anne of Brittany, two helpful works are Philippe Tourault, *Anne de Bretagne* (Paris: Perrin, 1990), and Hervé Le Boterf, *Anne de Bretagne* (Paris: Éditions France-Empire, 1976).

[18] Weir, 22.

[19] This proxy marriage to Maximilian was contracted by Anne's father, François II, in order to enlist Maximilian's aid in his own territorial struggle. The move by Charles VIII simultaneously deprives Maximilian of his bride and rejects his daughter. Charles married Anne within two weeks of Marguerite's dismissal.

[20] Weir, 22-25.

In 1500, Katherine and Marguerite became the aunts of the future Charles V, whose parents were Katherine's sister Juana and Marguerite's brother Philip. This relationship was important to both women. Marguerite became Charles's guardian after his father's death. Though Katherine corresponded with Charles, they did not meet until his visit to the Tudor court in 1520. Anticipating this meeting Katherine said: "I thank God I shall see his face; it will be the greatest good that I can have on earth."[21] Years later, Katherine depended heavily, though in vain, on Charles's advocacy in her divorce proceedings.[22]

Both women remarried, and in these second marriages, both women participated in governing. Marguerite wed Philibert, Duke of Savoy, in 1501 and soon discovered her own political abilities and interests, exercising considerable authority at the court of Savoy in the vacuum left by her husband's lack of interest in government. After his early death in 1504 and that of her brother in 1506, she was appointed regent of the Netherlands, ruling in that capacity, with a brief interruption, until her death in 1530. In the early years of her second widowhood, she rejected the suggestion that she marry again; this time the prospective groom was the recently widowed Henry VII, Katherine's father-in-law. Katherine herself was also an early candidate to be Henry's second wife, as was her widowed sister, Juana.[23]

Katherine finally married Arthur's brother Henry VIII in 1509 after prolonged negotiations marked by many reversals, including Henry's secret repudiation of the betrothal in 1505 at the instigation of his father. Like Marguerite, Katherine gained governing experience, ruling in proxy for Henry during the summer and fall of his 1513 military campaign. Throughout her adult life, she remained politically active, representing not only her own interests at the English court, but those of Spain, in behalf of her parents, the Spanish monarchs Isabella and Ferdinand.

A significant connection between the sisters-in-law was the sorrow created by their unfulfilled pregnancies – one for Marguerite, five for Katherine – and it is this factor that points to the specific meaning of *Dulces exuviae* and its companion in fascicle seven, *Absalon fili mi*. Each woman experienced not only the physical demands of pregnancy, compounded by the emotional distress of any bereaved mother, but the failure of her first state duty: to produce an heir, preferably male. The lament near the end of the London manuscript, *Absalon fili mi*, not only commemorates the sorrow of the king and queen at the loss of five of Katherine and Henry's six children, but also creates a new context for the sorrowful words of the bereaved queen in *Dulces exuviae*. The motet draws its text from 2 Samuel 18:33 in the Old Testament:

> Absalom my son, my son Absalom,
> Would that I had died for thee,

---

[21] Weir, 129.

[22] Mattingly, 252-254.

[23] Mattingly, 59-60, 69, 93-95, 100-01; Weir, 42, 61.

My son Absalom.[24]
Let me live no longer, but
descend into hell, weeping.

Placed as it is immediately after the five *Dulces exuviae* motets, *Absalon fili mi* adds a new dimension to the original meaning of Dido's words. In Katherine's case, her abandonment by Henry results from the tragedies she has already experienced: the loss of her five infants.

These five consecutive texts on the death of a queen followed by one on the death of the king's son would seem to be in poor taste, if not treasonous, as a gift to monarchs who hoped to live long and establish their dynasty. However, considered as expressions of compassion and understanding to a queen failing to give her king an heir and mourning the loss of her children, these texts transform our understanding of the manuscript: it is not a perplexing state gift, but an extraordinarily sensitive and intimate personal gift. The five settings of *Dulces exuviae* followed by the lament *Absalon fili mi* mark Marguerite's compassionate response to Katherine's despair over her five dead infants.[25] Though mortality rates during the period were high and royal women were undoubtedly conditioned to regard their reproductive prospects in a political light, there is no reason to conclude that they did not experience deep maternal sorrow over the deaths of their children. Evidence shows that for Katherine, these losses were more than just a failure of her state duty.

A recent biographer, Alison Weir, writes that after the stillbirth of a daughter in 1510: Katherine suffered a strong sense of failure, compounded by guilt, because "she had desired to gladden the King and the people with a Prince . . . [She] was profoundly shaken by her loss and remained depressed for weeks . . . . When she wrote to break the news to her father, she begged him: Do not storm against me. It is not my fault, it is the will of God."[26]

In 1511 Katherine's 6-week old son, Henry, died after weeks of state rejoicing and ceremony. Weir reports: "A jubilant Henry ordered beacons to be lit in London and the distribution of free wine to the citizens. Churchmen went in procession through the streets, and in the churches the *Te Deum* was sung . . . . The celebrations for the birth of the prince continued for well over a month, culminating in the day when the palace doors were thrown open to the common people, so that

---

[24] Absalon fili mi, fili mi Absalon, quis det ut moriar pro te, fili mi Absalon. Non vivam ultra, sed descendam in infernum plorans.The Biblical text ends at this point.

[25] It is clear that throughout their lives, Katherine and Marguerite and their courts were in close communication. For instance, upon his father's death Henry VIII wrote to Marguerite announcing that he would finally marry Katherine; this personal letter is one of the most important documents chronicling his intentions (Mattingly, 120-121, cites *Letters and Papers of Henry VIII*). Persons seeking Katherine's favor at court sought Marguerite's intervention from afar (Mattingly, 145). During his military campaign of 1515, Henry spent a month at Marguerite's court. Mattingly writes that during that same time, "as one woman to another, [Katherine] begged her former sister-in-law . . . to send the best physician she could find to look after him." (158)

[26] Weir, 106. Weir embeds quotations from state documents in her descriptions.

they could watch the pageants." Upon the death of this child, Henry's concern "was mainly for Katherine, who, 'like a natural woman,' was devastated by the news and 'made much lamentation' . . . The King 'made no great mourning outwardly,'" but provided a lavish funeral for the baby, who was buried in Westminster Abbey.[27]   Garret Mattingly, in his authoritative biography of Katherine writes, "Henry was so grief-stricken that ambassadors dared not even offer their condolences . . . ."[28] More losses followed: in 1513 and 1514, infant sons died shortly after birth, and in 1518, a daughter also died shortly after her birth. Only one child of Katherine and Henry survived to adulthood: their daughter Mary, born in 1516. The despondent message of *Dulces exuviae,* then, recognizes and sympathizes with Katherine's despair at the deaths of her five infant children and the later despair at her abandonment by her husband.

Reading this pair of texts in this way suggests an explanation for the unusual aspects of the notation of *Absalon fili mi,* one of the most notable manifestations of the lament for this period. In LonBLR 8.G.vii, it appears in a version that has long caused consternation among scholars. Did the composer, whoever he may be,[29] really expect the basses of the period to produce a low Bb (however that pitch might have been realized at the time)? Might not this extreme rendering of this motet with its low regions and plethora of notated flats in all voices, rather, be another symbol of the depths of despair created by the loss of these five infants? This may have been a scribal choice, given the proficiency of the Alamire scriptorium, or, if the composer was Pierre de la Rue, as Honey Meconi convincingly argues, the composer himself may have been responsible for the unprecedented notational idiosyncrasies of the work and its visually and musically expressive qualities.[30]

Accepting the *Dulces exuviae* and *Absalon* texts as personal communication leads to a new interpretation of the significance of several other texts and motets shared between BrusBR 228 and LonBLR 8 G.vii. (see Appendix 1 indicates the shared texts and motets.) BrusBR 228 contains only ten motets on nine different texts. Most of these also appear in LonBLR 8.G.vii – four having both the same music and text, and three on the same texts but with different music. The concordant motets are:

- *Dulces exuviae* by Alexander Agricola

---

[27]   Weir, 110, 92.

[28]   Mattingly, 143.

[29]   See footnote 10.

[30]   Honey Meconi, "Another Look at Absalon." Meconi's stylistic arguments in favor of La Rue's authorship are powerful. If, however, Josquin did compose the work, Anne of Brittany's own vain attempts to raise a male heir would have provided Josquin with opportunities to compose such a work. Charles-Orland, the three-year-old son of Anne and Charles VIII died in December, 1495. This is a period for which no concrete evidence exists for Josquin's whereabouts. In the absence of evidence to the contrary, the French royal court should always be considered a strong possibility.

- *Doleo super te* by the most illustrious composer of the Habsburg/Burgundian court, Pierre de La Rue
- *Vexilla regis/Passio domini*, also by La Rue, and
- *Sancta Maria succurre*, set by Franciscus Strus

The concordant texts are:

- *Ave sanctissima Maria*
- *Anima mea liquefacta est*
- *Fama malum*
- four more settings of *Dulces exuviae*.

The intensely personal nature of Brussels 228, as described by Martin Picker, and the fact that it contains only a few motets endows each of their texts with special meaning. The shared motets underscore the suitability of viewing the London manuscript as a document conveying Marguerite's understanding of Katherine's life, particularly her sorrows, through motets that Marguerite marked as meaningful through her selection of them for her own *chansonnier*.

In Marguerite's *chansonnier*, La Rue's *Doleo super te*[31] expressed Marguerite's grief over the death of her brother, Philip; in the London manuscript, the same work conveys Marguerite's sympathy to Katherine over the death of her brother, Juan, who was also Marguerite's husband. In Marguerite's book, the Biblical text is paraphrased: "Doleo super te frater mi Philippe" (I grieve for thee, my brother Philippe). In Katherine's case the original Biblical name, Jonatha, is accurate for her brother Juan.

La Rue's *Vexilla regis/Passio domini*, echoes the theme of death in its closing lines of the contratenor on the *Passio domini* text:

> In that time, Jesus said to his disciples:
> My soul is sorrowful unto death.
> Jesus, when he had cried again with a loud voice, *yielded up* the ghost.

Like the *Dulces exuviae* texts, this text expresses the speaker's sorrow and also his choice in the impending death – "yielding up" his soul. M. Jennifer Bloxam, apropos the significance of the texts in polytextual motets, writes, "Polytextuality has served since the thirteenth century as a way for composers to create a network of textual and musical associations within a piece, and the texts were chosen primarily for their content, and only secondarily for their liturgical associations." [32]

---

[31] Like *Absalon fili mi*, *Doleo super te* is a lament of King David, this one on the deaths of Saul and Jonathan from 2 Samuel 1:26-27.

[32] M. Jennifer Bloxam, "On the Origins, Contexts, and Implications of Busnoys's "Plainsong Cantus Firmi: Some Preliminary Remarks," in: *Antoine Busnoys: Method, Meaning, and Context in Late Medieval Music*, ed. Paula Higgins (Oxford, Clarendon Press, 1999), 77. Bloxam is discussing the practice with regard to Antoine Busnoys's polytextual motet *Anima mea liquefacta/Stirps Jesse* in BrusBR 5557, a work and manuscript relevant

Bloxam points out the rarity of polytextual works in the fifteenth century and suggests that the practice suggests "an extra-musical reason for the marriage of these two texts." Since the practice is also rare in the sixteenth century, the attention to the meaning of the contratenor text seems equally pertinent in the present context.

In both the London and the Brussels manuscripts, *Vexilla regis* lies in close proximity to the other Virgil text, *Fama malum*. In BrusBR 228 they are separated by Marbriano De Orto's setting of *Dulces exuviae*; in LonBLR 8 G.vii, they are adjacent. The text of *Fama malum* describes the nature of rumor. The context of this verse within the *Aeneid* resonates with the doubts about the legitimacy of Henry and Katherine's marriage. These lines record Dido's desire to believe that she and Aeneas have participated in marriage rites, though she is deceived about this. The rumor that travels so swiftly spreads tales about this false marriage. The entire passage recalls the parallels between Katherine and Dido where rumor is concerned (from Line 166; motet text is in bold type; italics emphasize passages about rumor and marriage):[33]

speluncam Dido dux et Troianus eandem deveniunt. prima et Tellus et pronuba Iuno dant signum: fulsere ignes et *conscious aether*	Then Dido and the leader of the Trojans Arrive at the same cave. The Earth itself And nuptial Juno give the sign; lightning flashes And *heaven is awakened for the marriage*;
conubiis, summoque ulularunt vertice Nymphae ille dies primus leti primusque malorum causa fuit. Neque enim specie famave movetur,	The Nymphs shriek upon the mountain-top. That day was the first day of death, The first cause of all the ills that followed.
nec iam furtivum Dido meditatur amorem:	After that appearance and reputation Were nothing to Dido, and she thought no more
coniugium vocat; hoc praetexit nominee culpam	Of keeping her love secret. She called it marriage. And by the word sought to disguise her sin.
Extempo Libyae magnas it Fama per urbes	At once Rumour goes through the great cities Of Libya,
Fama, malum qua non aliud velocius ullum: mobilitate viget, viresque adquirit eundo; parva metu primo; mox sese attollit in	**Rumour—and no plague moves more quickly.** **She thrives on her ability to move**

---

to my discussion of the use of the *Anima mea liquefacta* text in LonBLR 8 G.vii. Also see footnote 15, which refers to Martin Picker's reading of a polytextual motet-chanson from Marguerite's *chansonniere.*

[33] Richard Sherr, arriving at an opposite conclusion from the one I present here, refers to specific language usage in Henry's divorce documents, comparing it with language in *The Aeneid*, in an unpublished paper he graciously shared with me.

auras,
ingrediturque solo,
et caput inter nubile condit.

And gathers strength as she goes along;
Little at first, through fear, soon she is
    big,
Walking on ground with head hidden
    in the clouds.

illam Terra parens, ira inritata deorum,

They say that Mother Earth gave birth to
    her

extremam, ut perhibent, Coeo Enceladoque
    sororem

When she was incensed against the gods
—Her last child, sister to Coeus and
    Enceladus;

progenuit, pedibus celerem et pernicibus
    alis,
monstrum horrendum, ingens, cui quot sunt
corpore plumae,
tot *vigils oculi* subter, mirabile dictu,
tot linguae, totidem ora sonant,
tot subrigit aures.

Rumour is swift of foot, quick on the
    wing,
A terrifying monster, huge: and see!
For each of the feathers on her body
There is a *watchful eye* underneath;
She has as many tongues and speaking
    mouths,
As many ears, and all pricked up to listen

nocte volat caeli medio terraeque per
    umbram

All night long she flied between heaven
    and earth,
Shrieking among the shadows, never
    closing

stridens, nec dulci declinat lumina somno.

luce sedet custos aut summi culmine tecti,
turribus aut altis, et magnas territat urbes,
tam ficti pravique tenax quam nuntia veri.

Her eyes in gentle sleep; and in the day-
    time
She perches on guard upon a roof-top
Or on high towers, in intimidating cities;
To what is false and wrong she sticks as
    fast
As to the true things that she announces.

haec tum multiplici populos sermone
    replebat
gaudens, et pariter facta atque infecta
    canebat:
venisse Aenean, Troiano sanguine cretum,
cui se pulchra viro dignetur iungere
    Dido...

Now her delight was through many
    tongues
To spread among the peoples of Africa
Stories both true and false without
    distinction:
Aeneas had come, a man of Trojan blood
Whom lovely Dido deigned now to
    marry[34]

Katherine, of course, became the victim of the false accusation by Henry that
she could not be his lawful wife since she was not a virgin when she married him,
but had in fact consummated her marriage with his brother Arthur. Katherine
vehemently denied that allegation her entire life. The issue of the legality of
Katherine and Henry's marriage had been present from the day of Arthur's death.
The Archbishop of Canterbury, William Warham thought the marriage of Henry
and Katherine "not only inconsistent with propriety, but the will of God Himself is

---

[34] Virgil, *The Aeneid*, transl. C.H. Sisson, (Manchester, England: Carcanet Press,
1986), 88-89.

against it. It is declared in His law that if a man shall take his brother's wife, it is an unclean thing. It is not lawful."[35] Some sources place as early as 1514 the rumors that Henry intended to dissolve his marriage with Katherine.[36]

The Song of Songs text *Anima mea liquefacta est*, placed near the end of the London manuscript after the *Dulces exuviae* settings and *Absalon fili mi*, refers to a lost or unresponsive love, a topic that certainly applied to Katherine at least by 1524, perhaps sooner.

> Anima mea liquefacta est ut dilectus meus locutus est:
> Que sivi ilum et non inveni: vocavi, et non respondit mihi.
> Invenerunt me custodes civitatis; et percusserunt me, et vulneraverunt me;
> tulerunt pallium meum custodies murorum.
> Filie Jherusalem nunciate dilecto meo, quia amore langeo.

> [My soul failed when he spoke; I sought him, but I could not find him;
> I called him, but he gave me no answer.
> The watchmen that went about the city found me, they beat me, they wounded me;
> the keepers of the walls took away my veil from me.
> Daughters of Jerusalem, tell my beloved that I languish with love.]

The meaning and position of this motet in the manuscript fits with Katherine's biographical chronology: her marriage failed after she failed to produce the desired heir. References to watchmen who found, beat, and wounded the speaker may refer to those at court who were hostile to Katherine, circulating rumors and encouraging Henry in his doubts about the legitimacy of his marriage. The last line, "Daughters of Jerusalem, tell my beloved that I languish with love," may reflect Katherine's isolation and estrangement from Henry and her lack of opportunities to express herself to him directly. Even before Katherine's banishment from court in 1531 she lived apart from Henry in a separate apartment, and Henry was having a serious affair with Mary Boleyn, Ann Boleyn's older sister, perhaps by 1519 or 1520.[37]

The *Anima mea* text may also convey a more complex message, however. Scholars have linked the text to other women named Margaret or Marguerite who were known to Marguerite of Austria. Mary Natvig has associated the text with the post-nuptial festivities of Marguerite's step grandmother (her mother's stepmother and the third wife of Charles the Bold), Margaret of York, with whom Marguerite had a close relationship.[38] Antoine Busnoys's polytextual setting with a tenor on the plainchant *Stirps Jesse* appears in a manuscript associated with their marriage and used by the Burgundian chapel, BrusBR 5557. Paula Higgins has linked the same motet to the story of Margaret of Scotland, or Marguerite d'Ecosse, whose story

---

[35] Weir, 40. Warham later staunchly opposed Henry's ecclesiastical policies.

[36] Mattingly, 451.

[37] Weir, 133-34.

[38] Mary Natvig, "The Latin-texted Works of Anthoine Busnois," (Ph.D. diss., Eastman School of Music, 1991), 279-301.

interlocks with those of both Marguerite and Katherine.[39] Both of these women figured in the life of Marguerite; she may have wished to allude to either or both of them by reference to this text.

Marguerite d'Ecosse arrived at the French court at the age of twelve to marry Louis XI, the predecessor of Marguerite of Austria's first betrothed, Charles VIII. She died there nine years later, some say as a result of the pernicious effects of rumors of her marital infidelity and the resulting persecution. Like Katherine, she repeatedly affirmed her chastity, and like Katherine, she failed to produce an heir. She died on 16 August 1445, the day before the Feast of the Assumption. Thus, her commemorative services (held daily for the first twelve months after her death, annually thereafter) may well have included the texts *Anima mea liquefacta est* and *Stirps Jesse*, both proper to that feast. Indeed, Paula Higgins suggests that Busnoys's motet may have been written for and performed in these services. Higgins makes a strong case for reading these texts as commentaries on the tragic circumstances of Marguerite d'Ecosse, citing the topics of fertility and abandonment, precisely the recurring themes of LonBLR 8 G.vii.[40] In addition to these specific themes, the manner of commenting on them – through a motet – applies to this discussion at several levels:[41]

- The original use of *Anima mea liquefacta/Stirps Jesse* to communicate a message about Marguerite d'Ecosse as an example of a motet resonating as a personal narrative;
- Marguerite's use of the same text to communicate with Katherine in the same manner;
- Marguerite's probable discernment of *Anima mea* as a commentary on Marguerite d'Ecosse and her possible allusion, then, to her life as well as to the text of the motet;
- Possible allusion to the absent text, *Stirps Jesse*, and its subject of fertility. Whether this could have been meaningful to Katherine is hard to say. In any case, Katherine may have known of the English tradition of *Anima mea* settings, and it is possible that Busnoys's use of the text may owe something to that tradition;

---

[39] Paula Higgins, "Love and Death in the Fifteenth-Century Motet," in: *Hearing the Motet* (Oxford: Oxford University Press, 1997), 147-151. Higgins reveals in detail her theory to which I here refer, associating Marguerite d'Ecosse with Busnoys's polytextual motet, *Anima mea/Stirps Jesse* and the significance of that association. She also discusses aspects of Song of Songs texts and the use of motets for their narrative qualities.

[40] The topics of Song of Songs literature and commentary, texts and musical settings, liturgical and secular interpretations, and associations with personal histories go far beyond the bounds of this paper. Higgins touches on many of the themes and sources in "Love and Death."

[41] Also see note 29 on Bloxam's discussion of the motet. The inclusion of this work in BrusBR 5557 does not rule out the possibility that it had been composed about twenty years earlier for a different occasion.

- Linking of Marian texts with the lives of other women (see discussion of Marian texts below).

Did Marguerite know of the history of Marguerite d'Ecosse? Undoubtedly; sharing her name as well as an intended (though unfulfilled) destiny in the French court, the story of Marguerite d'Ecosse and her sad end must have been a part of Marguerite's French education, formal or informal. Could she have known the Busnoys motet and its literary references? Certainly; Marguerite lived at the court of Charles the Bold under the care Margaret of York and may well have heard the work performed by the Burgundian chapel from BrusBR 5557. Later, her position as regent and patron of the Netherlands chapel along with her active interest in restoring, preserving, and furthering the artistic, historical, and familial aspects of the court may have brought her into closer contact with the manuscript.

Marguerite seems also to have had a strong affinity for the Virgin Mary. Her *chansonnier* was altered early on so that it would open with the motet *Ave sanctissima Maria* illustrated by an illumination of the virgin. The facing page displays Marguerite's arms and a miniature depicting her kneeling in devotion to the virgin on the preceding page. This motet, obviously of some significance to Marguerite, appears in the middle of LonBLR 8 G.vii, a portion of the manuscript containing many other Marian motets. It may have been meant to comfort Katherine and to recommend the Blessed Virgin as a source of comfort and faith.

Moreover, the emphasis in this manuscript on Marian items, ubiquitous in sources of Renaissance polyphony, subtly signals its feminine themes and texts – hiding, as it were, in plain sight. The contrast between Mary, the embodiment of motherhood, and the unsuccessful, mourning mothers, Marguerite and Katherine, may have somehow played into Marguerite's somewhat obsessive attention to tragic and sorrowful events and emotions. On the other hand, Mary also represented a sympathetic mother, one who also mourned the death of her son, also a king.

The Marian texts may have carried an additional, even more subtle message to Katherine, consoling her by reminding her of her own maternal success in bearing her own daughter, Mary, namesake of the Queen of Heaven. Marguerite may also have intended that the Marian texts remind Katherine that the Blessed Virgin herself was the daughter of an infertile mother, St. Anne, who, according to legend, conceived and bore her holy daughter after entering into a solemn covenant with God.

Mouton's *Celeste beneficium*, the manuscript's opening motet, addresses St. Anne, praising her as the mother of the mother of God and as one, who with her daughter, can reconcile mortals to Christ. Veneration of Anne was prominent in England during the sixteenth century and became controversial during the Reformation. References to St. Anne, then, might also impart a message of religious solidarity from the Catholic Habsburg realm to Katherine, daughter of the most Catholic Kings of Spain.

This motet also refers, of course, to Anne of Brittany, its assumed first dedicatee. *Celeste beneficium* and the following motet, Févin's *Adiutorium nostrum* were originally composed for Anne and her second husband, Louis XII, who was the successor to the French throne after the death of Anne's first husband, Charles VIII (he who was originally betrothed to Marguerite of Austria). Like Katherine, Anne suffered the death of her first son, Charles-Orland, in 1495. Three more infants were stillborn or died shortly after birth, thus after seven years of marriage with Charles and four pregnancies, she remained childless. These wedding motets for Anne and Louis, then, did not express typical well wishing that a newly married young couple would enjoy the blessings of children. *Celeste beneficium* is, rather, a plea from one childless woman to another who long was childless, St. Anne. *Adiutorium nostrum* conveys a sense of desperation around the issue of conception. The text reads: "Katherine prays, weeps, and pleads. Praying, we beg you, help us by your compassion. O blessed Georgi, Henry cries to you. Please hear our voice."

A few motets later, the text *Descendi in ortum meum*, from the Song of Songs, takes on a startling and pointed meaning as we continue to read the manuscript as a narrative of Katherine's life, keeping in mind that her device is the pomegranate, ironically a symbol of fertility.

> I went down into my garden to see the fruit of the valleys,
> to see if the vine was in bloom and the pomegranate in bud.
> Return, return, return, that we may look upon you.

In other words, "Are you pregnant?"

In closing this elaborate book of messages, Marguerite points Katherine's thoughts to her religious faith, reminding her in *Jesus autem transiens* that Christ overcame his own trials, and admonishing her in *Tribulatio et angustia* to find solace in the commandments and in prayer. These closing motets remind Katherine that ultimately, she must turn to her faith for consolation and perfect understanding.

What was Marguerite's intent in giving this gift? The London manuscript can be read as a retrospective meditation on Katherine's life as Queen of England. The motets originally dedicated to Anne and Louis acknowledge the parallel tragedies of the two queens, signaling to Katherine that Marguerite is fully aware of her circumstances at a time when the two women may have been unable to communicate directly. This motive could conceivably provide an explanation for the original inclusion of the names of Anne and Louis in the manuscript and the subsequent correction to Katherine and Henry. Is it possible that this copying error was a deliberate signal to Katherine? Could the corrections have been visible to Katherine?[42] If so, it would have been a veiled invitation to her to recognize in some episodes and events of her life an echo of Anne's. If no advice is intended, Marguerite at least communicates clearly her knowledge and understanding of Katherine's serious and sorrowful situation. By repeating texts from her own

---

[42] Herbert Kellman has examined the manuscript and attests that the corrections are not visible to the naked eye. I have seen only reproductions of the manuscript, but I also wonder whether the passage of time might have affected the look of the corrections – might it have obscured or revealed them?

chansonnier, Marguerite signals the personal nature of this collection. Perhaps the omission of composer attributions in this manuscript was a deliberate signal that the texts rather than the music or the status of the composers were to be the focus of this gift.

Given this interpretation, another anomaly of the manuscript may convey a meaningful message. Frank Tirro has pointed out that the lions in Henry's coat of arms face the wrong way – right instead of left. According to Tirro, "in English heraldry, lions facing *sinister* imply cowardice."[43] Richard Sherr has pointed out that another manuscript from the Alamire scriptorium, Jena 4, also contains this flawed version of Henry's arms, so perhaps the Alamire scriptorium simply misunderstood, but perhaps the unflattering symbol was deliberate – a further signal to Katherine of Marguerite's sympathy at Henry's treachery in his divorce proceedings. A more benign reading of the irregular heraldry is certainly possible: Flynn Warmington, who specializes in the interpretation of heraldry and other visual clues at a minute level, recently suggested that the direction of lions in crests may have been an aesthetic choice in many manuscripts and wonders if scribes simply preferred to have the lions facing in toward the music.[44]

Why would Marguerite have chosen an elaborate presentation manuscript as a vehicle for such personal messages? Why not a more intimate medium? The later date for the manuscript indicated by this interpretation (according to previous scholarship, the terminus would have been 1520; see footnotes 4 and 5), may place Katherine out of reach for normal channels of communication. The earliest possible date for creation of the manuscript would have to follow Katherine's sixth and last pregnancy, which ended in November of 1518. After this time, Katherine's standing began to wane, gradually at first, then accelerating over the next several years. The last bright spot occurred in 1519, when Charles V succeeded Maximilian as Holy Roman Emperor. Alison Weir writes:

> The election of Charles V had the immediate effect of improving Katherine of Aragon's status in England. She was his aunt, and could command greater respect as such than as Henry VIII's barren consort. In England, she now represented the combined might, and reflected glory, of Spain and the Empire, a formidable heritage. Yet, for all this, her life continued as quietly as before. The gulf between her and the King was widening all the time; her influence was still minimal, and her function now merely ceremonial. She had failed in every way that mattered, and beside this her considerable personal qualities paled into insignificance.[45]

From this time forward, Katherine's ability to communicate with her Habsburg family, her last source of power and prestige, came under attack. She openly opposed Henry's most powerful and trusted advisor, Cardinal Wolsey, on the matter of England's alliances – Katherine a natural advocate of her Spanish and

---

[43] Tirro, 12-15.
[44] Discussion following her paper delivered at the American Musicological Society Annual Meeting, Atlanta, Georgia, 2001.
[45] Weir, 125.

Habsburg family, Wolsey of France.[46] By 1524, Wolsey had aggressively begun to isolate Katherine from her natural alliances. Mattingly writes:

> He had his own spies among her ladies, and as she realized, he read her correspondence. He prevented her from ever seeing the Emperor's ambassador except when he, himself, was present . . . . She had a better brain and more experience of diplomacy that any of the pro-imperialist nobles on the council, and she was their chief link with the Emperor.[47]

Also in this year, any remaining sexual relationship between Henry and Katherine ceased; she was beyond the possibility of childbearing.

In the following year, 1525, Katherine's status suffered several more serious blows. The last official link between England and the Imperial Court was severed when Charles broke his engagement to Henry and Katherine's daughter, Mary. Marguerite had opposed the break and tried to foil it, but only succeeded in muddying the already poor communication on the matter.

In the same year, Henry openly acknowledged Henry Fitzroy, his illegitimate son by Elizabeth Blount, and bestowed upon him numerous titles, including Lord Admiral of England, Wales, and Ireland.[48] Katherine openly expressed her fury, and Wolsey, with Henry's consent, seized the opportunity to gain complete control over Katherine's retinue. The cruelest blow was her separation for the first time from her daughter Mary, aged 9, who was removed to Wales, to take up her duties as Princess there. Though Katherine wrote to Mary that her health was "meetly good," rumors that she was dying circulated, and she began to put her affairs in order. Perhaps because of this, Henry spent some time with her; the isolation was not complete.

After this time, Katherine's situation only deteriorates, especially since she persists in staying alive and acting as an encumbrance to Henry. A letter of comfort, acknowledgment, and solidarity would not have been permitted to permeate Katherine's isolation. However, a formal, public gift, especially from Marguerite, who was, after all, *not* the Emperor, stood a better chance of being received, especially if Katherine was believed to be approaching death. These may have been the years when the manuscript reached Katherine. The manuscript, then, may have been Marguerite's way of informing Katherine that she was fully aware of every detail of Katherine's circumstances, and thus, that Katherine was not entirely alone. The allusions to the *Aeneid* would have spoken volumes to Katherine and Marguerite, both well-educated women in the humanist tradition (see footnote 16). For Katherine, as for us, the significance of *Dulces exuviae* may have been the clue that guided her reading of the manuscript.

Henry could read the gift as a flattering, perhaps conciliatory gesture, from an out-of-favor branch of Katherine's family. He may have paid little attention to it as such, especially since it contains so many depressing texts. Katherine, on the other

---

[46] Mattingly, 208-214.

[47] *Ibid.*, 222-223.

[48] *Ibid.*, 229.

hand, may have had an intimate enough knowledge of her sister-in-law's artistic practices to glean from the manuscript its intended meanings.

The implications of reading this exceptionally fascinating manuscript as personal communication present it in a new light and may defuse many of the problematic issues surrounding it.

• The absence of composer attributions under this interpretation serves to focus attention on the words of the texts rather than the identity of the musical works or prestige of their composers.

• The wisdom of opening a presentation manuscript with second-hand motets might seem questionable if the book had been given for an important state occasion for the purpose of conferring honor on the recipient and garnering favor for the donor. Under this interpretation, however, the references to the life of Anne of Brittany fit perfectly the agenda of acknowledging sorrow and conveying sympathy to a bereaved queen. Even without an awareness of Anne's association with the motets, however, their messages resonate with Katherine's story.

• The mistakes in the text and in Henry's heraldry seem unfathomable in a manuscript created by a scriptorium as proficient as Alamire's and intended as a royal gift to a king whose self-importance is legendary. However, if the gift were intended for Katherine's private use, the alterations and aberrations are less alarming, no matter what their causes: the giver sought a personal connection, not status and favor.

• As a reference to Katherine's five disappointing pregnancies and the ensuing failure of her marriage, the five-fold repetition of *Dulces exuviae* becomes a necessity rather than a puzzling departure from typical practices.

• The low pitch level and numerous notated flats in *Absalon fili mi* underscore its mournful message and mark this motet as a metaphorical black crepe armband for the lost infants.

• The themes of the *Aeneid* speak to Katherine's marital situation, and the texts from Song of Songs layer further meanings upon the book as a whole – an evocation of Katherine's emotional and psychological state as well as recognition that other women have suffered similar indignity.

• The devotional texts take on a narrative rather than a structural purpose; they comfort, advise, and encourage.[49]

• The necessity of dating the manuscript relative to a state occasion vanishes. None of these works need have been created for this manuscript or for any particular occasion; indeed, the association of each of these motets with the life of some other person deepens and expands their meanings. It may have been Marguerite's intention to provide perspective along with sympathy.

Beyond its immediate application to this manuscript, such a reading also invites further application of the ideas suggested. It offers a concept of musical

---

[49] Kellman, vii, notes the pattern of the fascicle organization and contents.

works read for literary or narrative as well as for musical qualities; a view of patronage that transcends expressions of power, acquisition, or wealth; a glimpse of how royal women may have communicated and an idea of how they felt about their lives; and an example of applied humanistic education. Jennifer Bloxam's observations on the significance for composers of the literary or narrative content of their texts may also apply to this sixteenth century patron (see footnote 32). Marguerite was particularly well placed to carry out this sort of activity, and she may be one of the most visible women of this particular period to have engaged in such personal and deliberate acts of patronage. She may have imprinted other works emanating from the Alamire scriptorium with similar significance. [50]

Marguerite's personal concept of patronage served as an outlet for her own artistic impulses.[51] Picker has written of her interest in literature and the arts, but as regent of the Netherlands, she was not in a position to be an artist; her artistic proclivities could be no more than an avocation. These interests found their primary outlet in her patronage. Here, she uses her power as patron to create a manuscript that is more than the sum of its parts: this book functions as a work of personal communication, of emotional expression, of literary perception and interpretation, and of social commentary.

Marguerite's commentary on the lives of women is revealing. The royal women of the generations that created modern Europe were pawns in the games of political and territorial power. Marguerite revealed her distaste for the role typically assigned to women by choosing to rule the Netherlands rather than enter a third political marriage. The careful selection of texts for LonBLR 8 G.vii, sets the stories of Anne, Marguerite, Katherine, Juana, Margaret of Scotland, Margaret of York, and the Virgin Mary echoing through this manuscript in terms that attest to Marguerite's knowledge of the events of their lives and of her sympathies for their often trying, sometimes harrowing circumstances. Marguerite expresses concern for the burden of women in dynasty building, their exploitation as property to be used to gain power, the physical and emotional devastation of failing in the duty to bear offspring (especially male heirs), and the dangers of failing in this duty. To counterbalance these serious and heavy themes, Marguerite offers devotional comfort in the form of music and texts.

As significant as the themes she addresses is the demonstration of Marguerite's broad and detailed knowledge, her skill and artistry in assembling this collage of meanings, and her subtly nuanced communication. The many-layered,

---

[50] In fact, FlorC 2439, until now the only Alamire manuscript known to have been prepared for a woman, happens to contain De Orto's setting of *Dulces exuviae*, other musical and textual concordances with BrusBR 228, eight settings of *Fors seulement*, and several quirky features. Perhaps Margaret's hand was present here also, endowing this book with meanings not evident on the surface.

[51] Robin Armstrong, "Creator vs. Author: Redefining Creativity." Unpublished paper. In this essay focused on Isabella d'Este, Armstrong addresses issues surrounding creativity and patronage, especially among aristocratic women, the extent to which they controlled content of their commissions, and the use of patronage as an outlet for artistic, personal, and political expression.

multi-faceted meanings lying within these motets emerge like centuries old secrets, inviting us to venture further.

APPENDIX 1 – Contents of LonBLR 8 G.vii

& Motets concordant with BrusBR 228
# Texts concordant with BrusBR 228

TEXT	Composer	Comments
(Text of the motet)		

1 HONI SOIT QUI MAL Y PENSE   Morel
   Canon; later addition

2 CAELESTE BENEFICIUM   (Jean Mouton)

   Praises St. Anne; prayer for an heir;
   perhaps performed in 1503 for Anne's second coronation

   A heavenly gift entered into Anne, through whom the Blessed Virgin Mary
   was born for us.
   O Blessed woman, favorite of God, mother of the mother who gave birth by
   God the Father,
   Anne, with your daughter, reconcile us to Christ.

3 ADJUTORIUM NOSTRUM   (Antoine de Févin)

   Names altered from Anne, Ludovicus, and Renate to Henry, Katherine, and
   Georg

   Our help is in the name of the Lord. Who will not give thanks to you?
   Katherine prays, weeps, and pleads.
   Praying, we beg you, help us by your compassion,
   O blessed Georgi, Henry cries to you. Please hear our voice.

4 NESCIENS MATER (Anonymous here, this text is also set by Mouton and
   Févin)

   Innocent of man, the virgin mother without pain gave birth to the saviour of
   the world.
   The virgin alone suckled the King of angels, her breasts full from heaven

5 AVE REGINA CAELORUM   (Pierre de La Rue)

6   DESCENDI IN ORTUM 14.3   (doubtful attribution to Josquin Desprez)

I went down into my garden to see the fruit of the valleys,
  to see if the vine was in bloom and the pomegranate in bud.
Return, return, return that we may look upon you.

7   SANCTA TRINITAS 26.12   (Antoine de Févin)

8   & VEXILLA REGIS/PASSIO DOMINI   (Pierre de La Rue)

   CT text: Passio Domini

   Contratenor text:
In that time, Jesus said to his disciples: My soul is sorrowful unto death.
Jesus, when he had cried again with a loud voice, yielded up the ghost.

9   # FAMA MALUM   (Josquin Desprez)

Rumour—and no plague moves more quickly.
She thrives on her ability to move and gathers strength as she goes along;
Little at first, through fear, soon she is big,
Walking on the ground with head hidden in the clouds.

10   & DOLEO SUPER TE   (Pierre de La Rue)

I grieve for thee, my brother Jonathan: exceedingly beautiful, and amiable to
me, and above the love of women. As a mother loveth her only son, so did I
love thee. How are the mighty fallen, and the weapons of war perished?

11   O DOMINE JESU CHRISTE
       2. Et sanctissima mater

12   MAXSIMILLA CRISTO AMABILIS
     For Feast of St. Andrew, patron saint of Burgundy and the Order of the Golden
     Fleece

13   & SANCTA MARIA SUCURRE   (Franciscus Strus)

   Based on "O werder mondt" (T)

Holy Mary, succour the miserable, Help the frightened, refresh the
wretched
Pray for the people, Intervene for the clergy,
Intercede for the consecrated of the female sex.

14   SANCTA ET IMMACULATA

15   MISSUS EST GABRIEL 20.6   (Josquin Desprez)

16   DULCISSIMA VIRGO MARIA

17   TOTA PULCHRA

       S and CT canon on first 4 pitches of
       Salve regina chant/text: Salve

          2. O PULCHERRIMA MULIERUM
          B and T canon on first 4 pitches of
          Salve regina chant/text: Salve

18   O SANCTA MARIA VIRGO VIRGINUM

       Includes prayer for Charles,
       presumably Charles V elected in 1519

19   VERBUM BONUM   (Pierrequin de Therache)

20   RECORDAMINI QUOMODO

21   O BEATISSIME DOMINE JESU CHRISTE
          FAC ME TUA GRATIA

22   # AVE SANCTISSIMA MARIA

Hail most holy Mary, Mother of God, Queen of Heaven, gate of paradise,
Lady of the universe, You alone are a virgin pure.
You conceived the creator of the world in whom I have unwavering faith.
Pray for me to Jesus your beloved.

23   ECCE MARIA GENUIT   (Jean Mouton)

24   CONGRATULAMINI MIHI

25   EGREGIE CHRISTI MARTYR   (A. Fevin/ Mouton)
          2. ECCE ENIM FESTUS

26   ALMA REDEMPTORIS

27   # DULCES EXUVIAE

28   & DULCES EXUVIAE   (Alexander Agricola)

29   # DULCES EXUVIAE   (Josquin Desprez)

30   # DULCES EXUVIAE   (Jean Mouton)

31   # DULCES EXUVIAE   (Johannes Ghiselin)

Relics once dear, while fate and heaven allowed,
Take this my spirit, and loose me from these woes.
My life is lived; I have fulfilled the course by fortune given, and now my shade
Passes majestic to the world below.

32   ABSALON FILI MI 14.1   (La Rue/Josquin)

Absalom my son, my son Absalom, would that I had died for thee, my son
Absalom.
Let me live no longer, but descend into hell, weeping.

33   JESUS AUTEM TRANSIENS

Jesus also overcome (no more text)

34   # ANIMA MEA LIQUEFACTA   (Heinrich Isaac)
          2. Invenerunt me custodes
          3. Filiae Jerusalem

My soul failed when he spoke; I sought him, but I could not find him;
I called him, but he gave me no answer.
The watchmen that went about the city found me, they beat me, they
wounded me;
          the keepers of the walls took away my veil from me.
Daughters of Jerusalem, tell my beloved that I languish with love.

35   TRIBULATIO ET ANGUSTIA 18.11   (Josquin Desprez/ Verdelot)

Trouble and anguish have taken hold of me,
yet your commandments are my meditation.
Troubles and sorrow do I find, and I invoke the name of the Lord.

APPENDIX 2 – Biographical connections

KATHERINE (1485-1536) and **ANNE OF BRITTANY (1477-1514)**
MARGUERITE (1480-1530)

Family ties

1496 Marguerite's brother, Philip the Fair, married Katherine's sister, Juana.

1497 Sisters-in-law by virtue of Marguerite's marriage to Katherine's brother, Juan. Marguerite is Katherine's friend and French teacher during her time at the Spanish court.

1500, 24 February
Katherine and Marguerite are both aunts to Charles V (his mother is Katherine's sister Juana, his father is Marguerite's brother Philip).

1490 Proxy marriage, later repudiated, to Marguerite's father, Maximilian I.

1491 Marriage to Marguerite's former fiancé, Charles VIII.

Marriage and politics

1483 Marguerite is betrothed to Charles VIII and reared from the age of 13 at the French court as preparation for the marriage, which was designed to ensure the succession of the Habsburg line in the Netherlands according to the Treaty of Arras. Charles repudiates the betrothal in 1491 when it becomes more advantageous for him to marry Anne of Brittany to secure Brittany for France.

1502-9
After the death of Arthur, Katherine lives with littlesupport at the English court during the seven years

1490 Married by proxy to Maximilian in an attempt to preserve Brittany from French control; foiled by the aggression of Charles VIII.

1491 Charles VIII forces Anne to renounce her proxy to Maximilian and marry him; his goal is to prevent Habsburg control of

of negotiations for her marriage to Henry VIII. At one pointshe is considered as a bride for Henry VII.	Brittany.
1506 Marguerite rejects the suggestion that she marry the widowed Henry VII.	1499 Married to Louis XII, successor to Charles VIII.

The marriages of Katherine into the Tudor dynasty and Juan and Juana into the Habsburg family bind the Spanish family of Isabella of Castile and Ferdinand of Aragon to the major European dynastic lines. Charles V, the Holy Roman Emperor, is thus the grandson of both the Spanish kinds and the Habsburg Emperor.

A generation earlier, the lines of Burgundy and Habsburg were united by the marriage of Mary of Burgundy to the Archduke Maximilian. Isabel of Castile chose her own husband, Ferdinand of Aragon, unifying Castile and Aragon into modern Spain.

Motherhood

1498 Marguerite's only pregnancy, by Juan, ended in stillbirth.	1492-95 Anne and Charles have a son, Charles-Ormand, who lives a little over three years.
1510-18 Katherine suffered five pregnancies that resulted in stillbirth or children who died shortly after birth. Her daughter Mary, born in 1516, was the only child who survived to adulthood.	1492-15 Nine pregnancies result in one child who survives to adulthood, Claude, daughter of Louis XII. (Claude and Katherine met and became immediate friends at the Field of the Cloth of Gold in 1520).

Family deaths

1497 Katherine's brother

1504 Isabella of Castile, Katherine's mother

1505 Marguerite's brother, Philippe le Beau (husband of Katherine's sister Juana).

1509 Maximilian I, Marguerite's father

1498 Death of Charles VIII

Rumor

Katherine was plagued by rumors that her marriage was invalid. Earlier, rumor claimed that she had an improper relationship with her confessor, Fray Diego.

Beyond the well-known ramifications, the issue of the legality of Katherine's marriage was raised in 1527 in connection with the negotiations for the marriage of her daughter Mary and Francis I of France; the concern on the part of the French was whether Mary's birth was legitimate.

Anne was plagued by rumors that she was not a lawful wife of Charles, because she had previously been married (though only by proxy) to Maximilian. Her marriage to Louis was suspect and unpopular because she displaced his first wife, Jeanne.

Divorce

1533 Katherine's marriage to Henry declared invalid by Archbishop Cranmer.

1492 Louis XII annuls his marriage to "the saintly but misshapen Jeanne of France" (Brittanica) in order to Marry Anne of Brittany, preserving the alliance forged by Charles's marriage to Anne and enforcing the contract enacted at that first marriage.

Governing

1507-15; 1519-30 Marguerite: Regent of Netherlands.

1513 Katherine: Regent for Henry during military campaign of 1513.

1488 Anne succeeds her father in duchy of Brittany; Brittany's independence is the central focus of her life.

The arts and education

Marguerite inherited the Burgundian artistic tradition; her French education formed her tastes and developed her abilities in art, literature, and music. Her library was extensive, as was her art collection. Her court was a center of artistic patronage, supporting poets, composers, musicians, painters, sculptors, architects, illuminators. The great Alamire scriptorium and Burgundian chapel were under her control during most of her regency. Her *chansonnier*, BrusBR 228, is considered a reflection of her emotional life (Martin Picker, 1965).

Katherine's education at the court of Isabella of Castile exposed her to some of the most progressive thinking regarding the education of women. Isabella's court fostered humanism early and her daughters, Katherine, Juana, Isabella, and Mary received liberal educations.

Anne was the only heir of her parents, Duke Francis II of Brittany and Anne of Foix. She was a life-long patron of the arts, best known for the Book of Hours that she commissioned.

Chapter 15

Composing from the Throat: Madalena Casulana's *Primo libro de madrigali,* 1568

Thomasin LaMay

Every work written by an early modern woman seems to be, whatever else it is, a meditation on the fact that it is written by a woman.[1]

Prelude

In my role as college professor, I teach a class on prima donnas. We look together at the functions and cultural expectations of extraordinary female (or in some cases *castrati* and trans-gendered) singing voices – the high voice – and its empowering possibilities, across historical time and through multiple kinds of so-called "popular" and "classical" music. We begin with Madalena not only since she was a highly sought-after prima donna,[2] but also because she was the first woman we know in early modern Europe who was both an exceptional singer *and* a professional composer who chose to publish her works.[3] This was no mean feat for

---

[1] From Margaret L. King, "Women's Voices, the Early Modern, and the Civilization of the West," in: *Shakespeare Studies,* ed. Leeds Barroll (London: Associated University Presses, 1997), XXV: 23.

[2] The concept of the female prima donna was an emerging one, an identity not yet fully formed and one that developed more fully during the seventeenth century in operatic contexts. I make argument here, though, that Madalena was perhaps a formidable forerunner to the *bel canto* soprano of the next two centuries. For further discussion of the early prima donnas, particularly in Venice, see Beth L. Glixon, "Private Lives of Public Women: prima donnas in mid-seventeenth century Venice," *Music and Letters* 76 (1995): 509-532.

[3] There were a few other women just after Madalena who were known to publish their music. Vittoria and Raphaella Aleotti, probably the same person, published a collection of madrigals and also one of motets in 1593; and Cesarina Ricci's *Primo libro de madrigali* was published in 1597 (and survives only in the lower three voice parts). Neither of those women were singers, however. We also know that other singers did improvise their own pieces, though they did not publish. The seventeenth century saw a few more female composers, but no one until the remarkable Francesca Caccini exhibited the same forthright attitude about being a prima donna *and* a composer. As Suzanne Cusick points out in the

a woman in the mid-*cinquecento*. It was quite new that a woman's voice was heard outside private spaces as a singing voice. "She" had been silenced in all modes of public vocal production by the church and by a culture that saw such utterances as masculine prerogative. Casulana's absolute insistence on publishing, alongside her shameless self-promotion and popularity, added a healthy dose of early modern "attitude" to her singing persona.

Madalena was not the only extraordinary singer of her time, but because she demanded to be a performer who could write her *own* pieces I expected at least subliminally feminist things of her music. I wanted her to spell out for me in some fashion what it felt like to be a prima donna in her culture, and to offer correctives to the patriarchal penchant for poetically and musically fragmenting women's bodies into eyes, lips, "apples," and "bright suns." I was at first disappointed. As I scored out and thought about her *Primo libro*, I had hard questions for her. Most especially I wondered why she frequently picked texts similar to her male peers, who wrote about women in pieces, and as unfaithful, cold, far-away people who could never be had? If Margaret King's proclamation at the front of this essay rings true, what did Casulana want us to read in her scores?

Two pieces from my own background helped me re-tool this initial reaction. First was my long-done Ph.D. dissertation on Monteverdi's madrigals in which I compared his texts and music to concordant settings of the same poems to discern principles of imitation and emulation. While that work has found space on a back bookshelf, it did require me to look at literally hundreds of madrigals by composers known and unknown, all also working in Casulana's time frame (Monteverdi's predecessors). This allowed me to realize that Madalena's compositions were not in sync with things happening around her. They were not less-than or necessarily (though sometimes I think they were) more exceptional pieces, but they were different. During the 1550s and 1560s, when favored textures in printed collections were the three and four voiced, mainly homophonic canzonetta and villanella, or the more serious-minded but still largely homophonic madrigal, Casulana produced four-voice settings of exceptional polyphonic virtuosity and rhythmic complexity. While her poems reflected the tastes of the time, her method of vocal expression was quite different and her pieces looked out of place in collections such as *Il Desiderio*, where they were first published. During this time and well into the 1570s, she also had significant ties with composers such as Molino and Lassus, whose works showcased the burlesque local dialects of the *commedia dell'arte*. Molino even claimed her as his teacher, yet there is no evident relationship between their compositional styles and Casulana seemed to eschew this form of musical expression even as she availed herself of many friendships within the *commedia* community.[4]

By the 1570s and especially the 1580s, as *concerti delle donne* exploded onto the northern Italian cultural scene and madrigals were often composed to show off

---

Epilogue to this collection, Caccini's social circumstances were quite different than those of Casulana.

[4] Her relationship to Molino features significantly later on in this essay.

one, two or three *virtuose* above static lower voices,[5] Casulana's pieces had turned more reflective. She avoided not only the popular virtuoso style, but also many of the musical clichés embedded in the highly stylized late century madrigal. While her texts again reflected the standard repertoire (there are notable exceptions), her music was fluid and controlled, and her choice of harmonic textual representation was highly personal to her own compositions. It became clear to me that it was not the text itself, or the musical tropes she used to set them, which made her music different. It was rather how she chose to combine those tools, the words she elected to embellish, and importantly the words she chose to leave alone which gave her madrigals an integrity quite separate from that of her peers. While she wrote to showcase her virtuosity, she was also well-aware of how that virtuosity was heard and watched, and what it meant to her listeners.

Secondly to this story, I am also a singer – probably not of her caliber. But I do understand something of the narcissistic power of hearing your own voice soar over a space and body of people. I can marvel over the prima donna whose sounding body becomes, after all else, *the* voice, an ecstatic production of text, air, soul, spit and attitude that constructs meaning beyond itself. For early modern theorists, this sounding "body" was believed to be in the woman's throat. They contrived that the female vocal chords, or uvula, were simply an oral variation of her vulva, another entrance point for the phallus. Her throat was analogous to her uterus, and the clitoris was likened to the uvula since they both controlled entry to their respective and highly sexualized spaces.[6] When her uvula was undulating in the act of producing song she was considered especially "hot," her mouth open in an explicit invitation for sex, and her uvula in a rapturous state of "excessive *jouissance.*"[7]

It was this extraordinary flapping and caressing of the flesh in her throat that underlay the vocal production of early modern women singers. The action of her throat and the shape of her mouth around its expelled words were watched as well as listened to, with much anticipation and in close, intimate relational space to her viewers. While the voice of the modern diva is often extracted or separated in

---

[5] Rather suddenly during the 1560s and 1570s women began to emerge, curiously right along side *castrati* in Italy, as popular singing voices. If these ladies were especially good, they were paid enormous sums of money and courts would compete to have only the best women singers in their service. For a lengthy study of this phenomenon (minus the thoughts about *castrati*, which are my own and the subject of another paper) see Anthony Newcomb's well-known study, *The Madrigal at Ferrara 1579-1597* (Princeton: Princeton University Press, 1980). Ferrara was somewhat ahead of the rest of Italy in cultivating the *concerti delle donne*.

[6] For a more substantive discussion of this phenomenon, see Suzanne Cusick, "A Soprano Subjectivity: Vocality, Power, and the Compositional Voice of Francesca Caccini," in: *Crossing Boundaries: Attending to Early Modern Women*, ed. Jane Donawerth and Adele Seeff (Newark: University of Delaware Press, 2001), 87.

[7] I am indebted to Renata Salecl for this term, and for much more detailed description, in her essay "The Sirens and Feminine Jouissance," *differences: A Journal of Feminist Cultural Studies* 9 (1997): 14-28.

various imaginary ways from her body so that it can be internalized by her listeners (frequently, too, in highly-charged sexualized consumption), we are distanced from the physicality of vocal production.[8]   This was not so for Madalena or her peers, especially women singers, whose throats were the source of extraordinary aural pleasure, and whose opened mouths were tantalizing sites of *direct* access to the body.

Because of this connectedness, these soft-tongued mouths and undulating vocal chords were dangerous, whorish, needing containment and explanation even as they were cherished and admired. Casulana's remarkable counterpart during the *seicento*, Francesca Caccini, was thought for more than three centuries to have died of mouth cancer, a scenario projected through the summary of her life written in 1888 by Alessandro Ademollo.[9] Her current biographer Suzanne Cusick argues that Ademollo's agenda (and probably one also fostered during Caccini's lifetime) was to situate her death in her mouth – "the organ which brought her fame professional success and power" – in order effectively to silence her for history, to excise that which had flapped too much.[10]

Madalena herself was made poignantly aware of the punishment for over-undulating female throats. Her first patron and perhaps friend, Isabella Medici-Orsini, had aspirations to be heard both as singer and composer, unthinkable for a woman of her class. She used music as a means of pleasure in a marriage that was otherwise dismal. Both she and her husband Paolo Orsini had extra-marital affairs, but he was able legally to kill her because she sang – produced musical undulations from her throat – persuasively rendering her a whore in the cultural eyes of Rome in 1576. Thus, in the words of her biographer Donna Cardamone, "he took Isabella by the throat and degraded her there," perhaps even rolling over on her neck as a means of suffocation.[11]

It occurred to me that putting pen to paper for Madalena may have been an act not only of defiance and assertion, but also one of purposeful self-mapping.[12]

---

[8] This is especially true with opera. But even with the explicitly erotic performances of modern pop sirens, if we are close enough to see their vocal production we are watching on TV or movie screens, out of touching space; if we are at a live performance we are too far away to see the mouth. It is the body which enacts the mouth for us now. The means of vocal production does not need to convey the power behind the voice in the way that early modern women's singing tried to do.

[9] Alessandro Ademollo, *La bell'Adriana ed altre virtuose del suo tempo alla corte di Mantova* (Citta di Castello, 1888), 151.

[10] Suzanne Cusick, " Thinking from Women's Lives : Francesca Caccini after 1627," in: *Rediscovering the Muses, Women's Musical Traditions*, ed. Kimberly Marshall (Boston: Northeastern University Press, 1993), 206-226.

[11] Donna G. Cardamone, "Isabella Medici-Orsini : A Portrait of Self-Affirmation," in : *Gender, Sexuality and Early Music*, ed. Todd Borgerding (New York: Routledge, 2002), 19. Paolo Orsini suffered from a condition which rendered him exceptionally obese, making the deed all the more violent.

[12] Laurie Stras suggested, in a different context, that Ingegneri's *Hor che'l ciel e la terra s'el vento tace*, might actually be kind of scored out reportage of the famous Tarquinia

Since her music was not especially consistent with the products of her (male) peers, and because she had direct experience with the throat and its volatile relationship to her own power source, I wondered if her writing down was also a re-producing of herself as sounding body, or more particularly of her tremulous throat and how she chose to display it, or allow access to it via the workings of her mouth.   At this same time, the act of singing was also directly connected to courtesans, who were especially abundant in Venice.[13]   I have argued elsewhere that Casulana was not,[14] and I hope further to corroborate that here since it has become even clearer to me that she fashioned herself another kind of musical career altogether.   Courtesans thrived in the sphere of improvisatory song, and their virtuosity was, as suggested by Martha Feldman, of "metaphysical import because only beyond the reach of script could song attain that most esteemed, elusive, and mystical appellation of *aria*, an ineffable sensual power endowed with neoplatonic force."[15]   Casulana's insistence on writing down separated her from that tradition, even if perhaps her quality of singing did not. The things she wanted me to read were not just text (though occasionally that is exactly what she wanted), or just music, but the production itself. I imagine that she composed as she would have wanted to sing, but also as women needed to be seen in the physical act of producing *aria*, of exposing the tremulous throat in rapturous *jouissance*. It seemed likely that those two possibilities might be at cross purposes at least some of the time. My students howled as I diligently practiced flapping my vocal chords in public view, caressing Italian syllables within inches of their faces, spitting text, manipulating mouth and lips, and singing Madalena's songs as it had never occurred to me to do. So it is especially to the students in this class that I dedicate

---

Molza's performance style; Stras likened that composition to a description of the event, and not an attempt at re-creation. I would argue more directly here that since Madalena no doubt performed her own pieces, singing the soprano voice and accompanying herself on the lute with the lower parts, that she may have at least sometimes written that voice part with her own throat technique in mind. See Laurie Stras, "Recording Tarquinia: imitation, parody and reportage in Ingegneri's *Hor che 'l ciel e la terra e 'l vento tace*," *Early Music* 27 (1999): 358-377.

[13] I am also grateful for many conversations with Margaret Rosenthal at the conference *Courtesans and their Arts*, Newberry Library, Chicago, April, 2002. Her exemplary study of Casulana's contemporary, Veronica Franco, provided much of the initial enthusiasm for my work on Madalena, and I will always be curious as to whether Veronica and Madalena knew each other. See Margaret F. Rosenthal, *The Honest Courtesan: Veronica Franco, Citizen and Writer in Sixteenth-Century Venice* (Chicago: University of Chicago Press, 1992).

[14] Thomasin LaMay, "Madalena Casulana: my body knows unheard of songs," in: *Gender, Sexuality and Early Music*, 41-72.

[15] Martha Feldman, "Enacting Gender, Revising Class: The Courtesan's Voice in Renaissance Venice," paper read at University of Nevada at Reno (February 2002). See also Shawn Marie Keener's essay in this volume.

the following piece, my reading of Madalena Casulana – prima donna – from the throat.[16]

Behaving like a man, not a courtesan

Madalena Casulana claimed emphatically in the dedication to her *Primo Libro de madrigali a quattro voci*, published by Girolamo Scotto in 1568, that she expected to "show the world (as much as is allowed me in this musical profession) the conceited error of men. They believe so strongly to be the masters of the high intellect that, in their opinion, these gifts cannot likewise be shared by Women."[17] She boldly capitalized the "D" in *Donne*, while "gl'huomini" remained a lower-case non-entity. She further insisted that she would not *fail to publish* her madrigals, a remark which might seem insignificant except that it was issued by a woman and in 1568 this rhetorical gesture of claiming published voice was equivalent to behaving like, or being, male.[18] It distanced her significantly from the women singers of her time – courtesan and otherwise – who gained public space but never clamored for professional legitimacy. Casulana directed this dedication to Isabella Medici-Orsini, whose life featured prominently in Madalena's story, and who was also an aspiring composer and singer. Their shared musical connection contributed further to the direct challenge of the dedication on the part of both women. Casulana subsequently published at least two more collections – a second book for four voices in 1570, and a volume of five-voice madrigals in 1583. In this essay, however, I want to look specifically at this first volume because of its extraordinary claims for women, and also for the special relationship to Isabella that sustained its creation.

I suspect Madalena was well aware of the fact that her madrigals were the first published by a woman. While a very few others published later in the sixteenth century, she was remarkably alone as a female in this endeavor, and she seemed to

---

[16] Thanks go to all nineteen students in *Prima Donna: Images of the Fantasy Female in Performance*, Goucher College, fall, 2002, and especially to Ginnia Higgins and Audrey Ellis, who put in overtime.

[17] Signora, che queste mie primitie, per la debolezza loro, non possono partorir quell'effetto ch'io vorrei, che sarebbe oltre il dar qualche testimonio allEccellentia vostra della divotion mia, di mostrar anche al mondo(per quanto mi fosse concessi in questa profession della Musica) il vano error de gl'huomini, che de gli alti doni dell'intelletto tanto si credono patroni, che par loro, ch'alle Donne non possono medesimamente esser communi. Ma con tutto ciò non ho foluto mancar di mandarle in luce.... Madalena Casulana, Primo libro de madrigali a quattro voci, Novemente poste in luce, e con ogni diligentia corretti. Appresso Girolamo Scotto. MCLXVIII.

[18] Many recent studies have pointed to the notion that, during the sixteenth century, the classical one-sex model that defined sex differences and gender and allowed male and female to co-exist, in a sense, along one axis. To cite just one which most appropriately mirrors my argument: "to be a man or a woman was... to assume a cultural role, and not to be organically one or the other of the two sexes." See Thomas Laqueur, *Making Sex: Body and Gender from the Greeks to Freud* (Cambridge: Harvard University Press, 1990), 8.

make publishing a professional priority. She was the solitary woman among a large circle of composers working in and around Venice, and she evidently negotiated her way into this arena with little difficulty. Before her *Primo libro a Quattro* was published she was already a well-connected composer. Just prior to her 1568 edition, individual pieces by Madalena appeared in at least three different anthologies. In 1566, four of her madrigals were printed in *Il Desiderio I*, also published by Girolamo Scotto and compiled by Giulio Bonagiunta, who subsequently collected two further volumes, *Desiderio II* and *III*, printed in 1566 and 1567 respectively.[19] Casulana was featured in *Il Desiderio III*, as well as in a fourth Bonagiunta anthology, *Il Gaudio*, printed in 1567. That volume is lost, but the collection was re-issued in 1586 by the Scotto press[20] (until recently, the date of the original publication was unknown.)[21] Looking at the music and composers who collaborated in these anthologies is most helpful for situating Casulana in her compositional *milieu*, and also for recognizing those things in her music which were written, in King's words, from the point of view of a woman.

Bonagiunta, a singer, composer and music underwriter, was located briefly in Venice during the second half of the 1560s, where he quickly compiled no less than seventeen editions of music. He was one of the most successful musical underwriters of his time, and because he was looking at this as a for-profit venture, he clearly wanted to offer composers who would sell.[22] The *Il Desiderio* series took its name from the initial piece in the first collection, *Il desiderio e la speranz'amore*, by Cipriano Rore. The following three, as well as the final, pride-of-place madrigal in the collection are by Casulana; she subsequently re-printed all

---

[19] *Il Desiderio, Primo libro a Quattro voci.* In Venegia appresso Girolamo Scotto. M.D.LXVI;*Il Desiderio. Secondo libro de madrigali a cinque voci.* In Vinegia appresso Girolamo Scotto. M.D.LXVI; and *Terzo libro del Desiderio. Madrigali a Quattro voci.* In Vinegia apresso Girolamo Scotto. M.C.LXVII. Only a canto part survives for the third collection, but the first two have part books located in several libraries, and are housed on microfilm at the SUNY, Binghamton Library, Harry Lincoln collection. I am grateful to have been given copies of these films for research purposes. For further information on locations of surviving part books see Jane Bernstein, *Music Printing in Renaissance Venice. The Scotto Press (1539-1572)* (New York: Oxford University Press, 1998), 727-728.

[20] *Il Gaudio. Primo libro de madrigali a tre voci.* In Vinegia appresso Girolamo Scotto, M.D. LXVII. A microfilm of the 1586 reprint is also available in the SUNY Binghamton Harry Lincoln collection.

[21] I am much indebted here to Jane Bernstein's exemplary study, *Music Printing in Renaissance Venice.*

[22] Bernstein, 143-145. She suggests that the financing of Bonagiunta's volumes was more complicated than the usual contractual agreement between a composer and printer. All but three of the editions have printers' marks not associated with the Scotto press. Bonagiunta provided, edited, and proofread the music, and perhaps put up some of the money, Scotto printed it, and a different publisher financed the edition. The woodcut which appears on all three volumes of the *Il Desiderio* series is identified with the bookman Giacomo Anielli Sanvito.

four of those works in her *Primo libro*.[23] Giovan Leonardo Primavera, a composer who was often found in the vicinity of Madalena's undertakings, contributed a setting of *Amor quando m'invia*. A substantive six-part setting of the sestina *Si com'al chiaro giorno* by Lassus consumes much of the center of the volume. That Madalena's compositions should be offered and given special positioning alongside those of the elder, well-respected Rore, but especially Lassus, who was perhaps the most popular composer of that decade, speaks to the respect her compositions commanded.[24] Bonagiunta was also a primary editor for Lassus' Italian publications.

Madalena's connection with Lassus was lifelong, and he clearly thought highly of her work as both composer and singer. He had been employed since 1556 in Munich by the court of Duke Albrecht V, but was in Venice during 1567 to oversee the publication if his *Libro Quattro* for five voices, composed specifically for the Ferrarese Duke Alfonso's newly formed *concerto delle donne*.[25] It was probably during this visit that he became acquainted with Madalena, and in 1568 he invited her to come to Munich both to sing and to compose a motet for the wedding of Wilhelm V, the duke's son. The music does not survive, but the Latin text for the piece was included in a diary entry by Massimo Troiano, who attended the event. Troiano fancied himself a composer, and one of his madrigals was included in the aforementioned Primavera's *Primo Libro a quattro voci*, 1569. Troiano's extraordinary praise for Madalena reflects the esteem she enjoyed.[26]

It was also at this wedding that Lassus performed the Magnifico in *commedia* plays.[27] While Madalena never participated directly in the *commedia dell'arte*, she had significant connections to its early composers, especially Antonio Molino, whom she evidently taught to compose at the age of seventy[28] (her curious

---

[23] Those pieces are: *Vedesti amor giamai di si bel sole, Scolpio nell'alm'amore, Morir non puo il mio core*, and the final piece, *Se scior se ved'il laccio a cui dianz'io*.

[24] For further discussion of Lassus' print popularity, see James Haar, "Orlando di Lasso, Composer and Print Entrepreneur," in: *Music and the Cultures of Print*, ed. Kate Van Orden (New York: Garland Publishing, 2001), 125-151.

[25] *Di Orlando Lasso maestro di capella del serenissimo signor duca di Baviera, Libro Quarto de Madrigali a cinque voci...* In Venetiz appresso di Antonio Gardano. 1567.

[26] "Orlando Lasso fece cantare una opera a cinque della Signora Madalena Casulana, laquale fu udita con grandissima attentione, e poscia che non vi posso fare udire il concento, dell'alta armonia; voglio ch'udite I carmi, che son cherto (sic) che vi piaceranno. Volentieri l'ascoltarò che non posso se non credere che siano bellissimi, per mi, per pavervi fatto la musica quella virtuosissima signora, le cui alte virtù, qualità e costumi, sono note a tutti li spirti gentili di questa nosta felicissima Etade.'' *Dialoghi di Massimo Trioano, libro* terzo, in *Die Münchner Fürstenhochzeit von 1568* (München: Verlag Emil Katzbichler, 1980), 262.

[27] *Ibid.*

[28] Molino stated in the dedication to his first book of madrigals, published in 1568, that he was Casulana's composition pupil, and describes her as a teacher "whose ability is such that it would kindle in the hoariest intelligence a new desire for glory." The collection survives, minus the alto voice, in the Biblioteca Nazionale Marciana in Venice, Musica 345-

relationship to that gentleman will feature later in this story). Primavera's music, especially his *napolitane*, also evoked popular burlesque *commedia* traditions. Ferdinando Taviani, among others, suggests that the *commedia dell'arte* took shape when courtesans introduced their virtuoso musical and poetic gifts to the bawdy, sexually explicit all-male comedy surrounding *Il Magnifico* (later called Pantalone).[29] That Madalena decidedly negotiated around this entertainment despite the fact that it was primary compositional fodder for her close associates again serves to ground her in some professional, non-courtesan status of her own choosing.

Lassus shared a warm friendship with Andrea Gabrieli, who had been featured in the five-voice volume *Il Desiderio II*, and who was also connected to Molino and the *commedia*. Gabrieli, Merulo, and Rore were among several composers who set an entire volume of Molino's *greghesche* verses in 1564.[30] The volume, imbued with lewd texts and Venetian dialect so common to *commedia* pieces, was organized by Gabrieli and published by Claudio Merulo (both Gabrieli and Merulo later contributed to Bonagiunta's *Il Gaudio*). Gabrieli subsequently noted in a dedication to a 1571 collection, which also included Molino's burlesques, that this gentleman "had always been a father and patron to me by virtue of his unique qualities."[31] This was a relationship Casulana also enjoyed with Molino, as we shall soon see, and for all three the congenial rapport was important. Casulana moved comfortably amidst these men in what seems almost a familial relationship; she did so as the intellect she claimed to be, untouched, however, by their particular bent for the *commedia* and its musical representations.[32]

Casulana was not included in *Il Desiderio II*, the only one of the series for five voices (the composers included in this collection are also different from those in the other three Bonagiunta anthologies). *Il Desiderio III* , for which only a canto voice survives, contains one madrigal by Casulana, *Amorosetto fiore*. The

---

367.3, and I appreciate receiving a microfilm copy for study purposes. *Il dilettevoli madrigali a quattro voci di M. Antonio Molino* (Venice, Claudio da Correggio, 1568).

[29] Ferdinando Taviani, "Le fleur et le guerrier: les actrices de la Commedia dell'arte," *L'Energie de l'acteur: Anthropologie théâtrale. Bouffonneries*, 15/16 (1986): 61-93. I am grateful also to Martha Feldman, "Enacting Gender," and to conversations with Shawn Keener.

[30] *Greghesche, Libro I, 39 composizione di diversi autori su testi poetici di Manoli Blessi detto il Burchiella*, Claudio di Correggio [Merulo], 1564. All composers featured in the volume are Venetian, and the collection was compiled to commemorate the death of Willaert.

[31] Translated in Alfred Einstein, *The Italian Madrigal*, transl. Alexander H. Krappe, Roger H. Sessions, and Oliver Strunk (Princeton: Princeton University Press, 1949), II, 530.

[32] It would be fascinating to discuss in much further detail the relations and inter-actions among these composers, as doing so would add significantly to our understanding of the mid-*cinquecento* madrigal and the *commedia dell'arte*. What I hope to do here is to pull together enough connections around Casulana as to situate her in the midst of this activity; there are many other threads to this story which I do not have space for here.

volume opens with three madrigals by Lassus, and also includes settings by the theorist Zarlino, Constantio Porta, and Stefano Rossetto. The latter's long six part *Canzon, Ecco pur riede il sole*, is the centerpiece of this collection, just after his setting of *Stavasi il mio bel sol*, a text Casulana set that same year in *Il Gaudio*.[33]

Madalena's association with Rossetto was especially significant. He was in the service of Ferdinando de Medici and Isabella during the years 1565-1567, just as these anthologies were compiled, and as Casulana herself was no doubt working on the *Primo libro* she so forthrightly dedicated to Isabella. While he was in the Medici household, Rossetto published two books of madrigals. The *Musica Nova del Rossetto à 5* (1566) included a piece in honor of Isabella, and the *Primo libro de' madrigali à 6*, of the same year, was actually commissioned by her. It was also during this time that Isabella's affair with Troilo Orsini, cousin to her negligent husband Paolo, became publicly known. Paolo sent Troilo away on a series of diplomatic missions to be rid of him, and then refused to visit Isabella even when she nearly died of smallpox in 1567, claiming he had to take a cure for his obesity.[34] In poignant response to these circumstances Rossetto wrote an ambitious and lengthy cycle, *Il lamento di Olimpia*, which Cardamone suggests was commissioned directly by Isabella to draw attention to parallels between her own abandonment and that of Ariosto's exquisitely beautiful heroine in *Orlando furioso*.[35] Rossetto selected specific passages at Isabella's request, in a co-produced attempt to configure her as the loyal wife of an unworthy husband. The musical setting intensifies throughout the composition from four voices to six, and eventually ten parts.[36] Casulana must have known of this work and most likely visited Isabella's house herself during its unfolding, since it overlapped with the production of her *Primo libro*. Cast in this light, her dedication to Isabella rings out even more explicitly as an act of defiance not only for her own intellect, but for the very integrity of her patron. It was this particular relationship between Rossetto and Isabella which suggested to me that Casulana's collection might have also been interconnected in this endeavor to depict her patron in more favorable light (and to this we shall return).

Il Gaudio, also published in 1567, was the final Bonagiunta anthology to feature Casulana. She contributed only one piece, the previously mentioned *Stavasi il mio bel sol*, but the whole volume is fascinating in that it also offers two large six part *canzoni*. *S'io non v'amo & adoro*, which ends the volume, is an elaborate setting by Rossetto. *Mai non vo piu cantar com'io solea*, the center of the

---

[33] It is unfortunate that the canto voice only for Rossetto's piece survives, but there does not seem to be any compositional relationship between his piece and Casulana's if one can judge from the canto voices. Casulana did not engage in the kind of competitive imitation frequently used by her peers.

[34] Cardamone, 16.

[35] *Ibid.*

[36] Unfortunately there is no complete surviving edition of this formidable work, but some voices survive which indicate the extraordinary effort put into this story. I am grateful for a microfilm of the surviving parts from the Biblioteca Nazionale Marciana, Venice.

collection, was collaboratively composed by six different men, each providing one *parte*. The cycle's contributors included Merulo, Andrea Gabrieli, Francesco Bonardo, Antonio Grecco, Leandro Mira, and Danielle Grisonio, and again the music was rooted in the *commedia*. As noted by Bernstein, all of these composers had a personal connection with Bonagiunta, either as colleagues at the chapel of St. Mark's (where Bonagiunta was a singer), or as contributors to his other anthologies.[37] Bonardo was the *maestro di capella* at the Padua Cathedral from 1565 to 1571, and composed a full book of madrigals in 1565 which he dedicated to the Accademia dei Constanti, to which he belonged. He was also well-known in *commedia* circles.[38] Grecco and Grisonio were presumably singers, and Grisonio had earlier contributed to Gabrieli's *greghesche* collection on texts by Molino; connections among Merulo, Gabrieli and Bonagiunta and their cultivation of these texts have already been mentioned.

An interesting addition to this mix is Leandro Mira. Casulana included one of his madrigals as the final piece in her *Secondo libro de madrigali a quattro voci*, published in 1570, and I suspect that he may have contributed to the financing of the volume. In that same year, Mira published at his own expense Philippe de Monte's *Terzo libro di madrigali a cinque voci*. He wrote the dedication to the volume himself, suggesting that Monte's pieces had come into his hands and that "at the request of several gentlemen he had them printed."[39] The collection was offered to none other than Antonio Molino, "Casulana's pupil," and curiously Monte had connections both with Isabella and Madalena. Monte's first book of madrigals for six voices, composed around 1564, contains a piece celebrating Isabella's (unfortunate) marriage to Paolo Orsini. In 1575, shortly before her murder, Isabella commissioned Monte's sixth madrigal book for five voices. Cardamone also makes a persuasive case for Monte as a collaborative partner in constructing a six-voice version of the text *Lieta vivo e contenta*, originally designed by Isabella for her own performance as soloist with accompaniment.[40]

In 1583, Monte's only collection of three-voiced madrigals was published by Gardano and dedicated to Casulana, referring to her as the "Muse and Siren of our Age."[41] The dedication is fascinating for two reasons: the first is that it now refers to her as Madalena Mezari detta Casulana, imposing a new surname, and the second is that, as dedicatee, Casulana assumed the status of a patron. In her own *Libro primo de madrigali a cinque voci*, published that same year, she also refers to herself as Madalena Mezari detta Casulana Vicentina. Whether or not Madalena

---

[37] Bernstein, 728.

[38] From the dedication to his *Primo Libro di madrigalia quarto e cinque et a sei voci, Alla nobilissima et virtuosissima Compagnia delli signori Constanti. In Venetia appresso di Antonio Gardano.* 1565.

[39] For the complete dedication, see Bernstein, 816.

[40] Cardamone, 9-15.

[41] The entire dedication is given in Italian in Beatrice Pescerelli, *I madrigali di Maddalena Casulana*, Studi e Testi per La Storia della Musica 1 (Florence: Leo S. Olschki, 1979), 17.

contributed financially to the publication of Monte's volume (I cannot verify this either way) she had visibly arrived at the professional level of esteemed patron. She was by this time in her mid-forties, had pushed her way to the top in an intellectual arena which was exclusively male, and she was still a highly acclaimed singer. We know she sang with much *virtù* that same year for a production at the Accademia Olimpico in Vicenza.[42]   She was probably wealthy at this juncture, known in the business as an exceptional performer, composer, and at least in Molino's case also a teacher. She had forged for herself a career that negated any need for her to play the courtesan. She refused that role and secured her finances otherwise, "behaving like a man," and claiming an intellectual legitimacy. This perhaps also set her apart from associations of the "flesh," the female whorishness so very tied to the role of courtesan-*improvatrice*.

As Bernstein noted, composers during Madalena's time had become acutely aware of the possibility of addressing a larger audience by printing their music. They could use their publications as advertisements for positions, could augment their incomes by selling their works to printers, or by publishing and marketing their own works.[43] Casulana had seized this technology for herself with extraordinary vigor.   Also in 1583, her *Libro primo* of 1568 was re-issued simultaneously in Brescia by Vicenzo Sabbio, and in Milan by Simon Tini. This was the Tini establishment's very first publication, so in this market-driven endeavor they must have anticipated her volume to be in high demand.   Curiously the dedication to Isabella stands even though she had been dead for seven years and could have had no financial role in these later editions.

Casulana had constructed a formidable business around herself as an "entity," a prima donna in control of all aspects of her persona, and one who refused the traditional role as singing muse, singing courtesan, or even singing with a *concerto delle donne*. So what of the new surname? Others including myself have bandied about the notion that she married sometime during the 1570s and subsequently secured another name for herself. I now doubt this. No marriage documents survive in or around the places she worked to support such an assumption, and while that is in no way conclusive evidence, her high profile would have made it likely that such information might have been mentioned. The name *Casulana* has often been inferred to mean "from Casole," outside Sienna, and that she was "detta Casulana," or "called Casulana." As a rising young singer and composer of undistinguished background this sobriquet suited, or at least did her no harm. As

---

[42] Records for the Accademia Olimpica include four separate and highly complementary discussions of her virtuoso singing for a special event. *Atti dell'Accademia Olimpica*, li bri 10, 11, 12, 13; housed in the Biblioteca Civica Bertolinia in Vicenza, Prot.n.582/L-1. The performance was for a reading of a Pastorale at the Accademia, by Mr. Pace, and "there was also music of excellent quality while, in this time, it was flourishing a lot, and especially by women from Vicenza, in the Theater, where in that day the virtuosa "... Maddalena Casulana from Vicenza greatly excelled. Then there was a lavish banquet." I thank Nello Barbieri for assistance in transcribing this document.

[43] Bernstein, 139-140.

full-fledged composer, wealthy dedicatee, and established professional working right alongside men, she perhaps now claimed for herself the distinction of a proper surname rather than a "pet name." She asserted her right to the privilege of an intellectual identity. This is only conjecture, but I would not rule it out.

The trembling throat

It is fruitful now to return to Casulana's connection with Antonio Molino, a gentleman probably old enough to be her father, and one with whom she shared both affectionate and professional bonds. Also known as Manoli Blessi and La Burchiella, he was born around the beginning of the *cinquecento* and probably died in 1571. He spent his life in Venice and was educated in all the attributes of a gentleman, including dancing, singing and the playing of instruments. With his brother Armonio, organist of St Mark's, he founded an academy dedicated to reciting comedies in a variety of local dialects, and alongside Andrea Calmo and Angelo Beolco he was a seminal figure in the early *commedia dell'arte*.[44] It is unclear how or when Casulana came into his sphere, though clearly she had been a part of his circle sometime before her *Primo libro* was published. Also in 1568, Molino offered his *I dilettevoli Madrigali a Quattro voci* to her in recognition of her efforts to teach him composition.[45] In 1569 Madalena herself wrote the dedication to his *Secondo libro*, noting his important role as Magnifico.[46] Despite Molino's claims to have been taught by Casulana, his madrigals bear no resemblance to hers. Since the music for *commedia* was largely improvised, what Madalena may well have taught Molino was the practice of writing down, that "intellectual" aspect of music making which she so much associated with her own persona.[47]

Molino's *I dilettevoli madrigali*, published by Merulo, is unique to the madrigal repertoire of the period. Only a few of the poems treat the more traditional conceits while the others are all highly personal, in some cases autobiographical. Many of them describe Madalena by name and in remarkable

---

[44] See Paolo Fabbri, "Fatti e prodezze di manoli Blessi," *RIM*, xi (1976), 182.

[45] D M. Antonio Molino *I dilettevoli Madrigali a Quattro voci... In Venetia apresso Clausio Da Correggion,* 1568. The canto, tenore, and basso parts survive in the Venezia Biblioteca Nazionale Marciana, and I appreciate a microfilm copy from them for study purposes. I am grateful to Nello Barbieri for his thoughtful translations of the texts.

[46] Di M. Antonio Molino *Il Secondo Libro de Madrigali a quarto voci, con una Dialogo a ottl... Venetia appresso di Antonio Gardano,* 1569. The canto, tenore, and basso parts similarly survive for this collection in the Venezia Biblioteca Nazionale Marciana, and I appreciate a microfilm copy from them for study purposes. "Hora, perche il Magnifico Messer Antonio Molino, hoggimai di grande età, è dotato de la virtù della musica, mi ha fatto cono d'alcuni suoi madrigali composti novamente...."

[47] Molino's dedication even suggests that to be the case. He wrote that she "imflamed his cold mind to aspiration for glory, spreading in me the first lessons in this science." "Ma considerando, che dalla virtù vostra, atta ad accendere ogni fredda menta a disiderio di gloria, sieno stati in me sparsi li primi ammaestramenti di questa scientia..."

detail. They often talk of her *virtù*, a commonplace descriptor for talented people of both genders at the time; but Molino also made a point of discussing the chastity (*castità*) that elevated her above other women, further inscribing her as an intellect and not a courtesan.

Particularly interesting are the poems in which Molino wrote specifically about Madalena's act of singing, for they illuminate in suggestive detail the kind of vocal production, and its throaty associations, common to her time. The first text in the collection, titled *Signora Maddalena*, describes her "exceptional and divine" singing; he asks her thus to take up her lute, and with "its sweet, noble harmony deign to loosen [her] tongue in loving tones," in order to gratify the hearts of those who always burn with the desire of hearing her.[48] In order for the uvula to tremble in *jouissance*, a singer would have to loosen her tongue, most especially in the back of the mouth. The poem next suggests a direct connection between the loosened tongue and the gratification of a burning heart: the auditor pulls the sound into his mind and translates it into a (sexual) performance. In *Donna del mio cor chiave* he suggests that "my fire would be more pleasant if I could hear you singing, as I desire ... so [let your singing] be for me such."[49]

In another text, *Donna zendila*, Molino again addresses Madalena directly: "with the mellifluous singing of a siren, you create such a sweet harmony in the mind that everyone sheds tears and would like to listen to you forever, O dear Maddalena."[50] Her act of singing opens a metaphorical (sexual) space in the listener's mind, which is then filled with something rather slippery to translate due to the dialect. The potential for double meaning – something common in Molino's *greghesche* poems – is important, but either way one reads it, he captured her throat as the source of undulating pleasure. "Qual altra donna mai plio se la visto/Descazzar cul so gorza tremulande/Como fa vui dal cor la pensier tristo/nesuna" ·can mean something like: "What other woman was ever seen driving away sad thoughts from hearts with a tremolo in her throat, as you do? No one." He stresses how she was *"seen"* in this production. Or, the language may also imply a *direct* penetration of the phallus, aided by (in rather graphic terms) the tremolo in her throat.[51] This dual and highly erotic meaning in Molino's poem

---

[48] Signora Maddalena poi che sete/nel cantar cosi rara anzi divina/Ch'ogn'anima gentil v'ama & inchina/Il liuto prendete/E piacciavi al suo dolce alto concento/Snodar la lingua in amoros'accento/Perch'in tal guisa appagheret'il core/A chi sempre d'udirvi qrde d'amore.

[49] Donna del mio cor chiave/Qual foco piu soave/Saria del voco mio/s'vudissi cantar comio desio?/Siatemi dunque tale/ch'io goda (a pochi eguale)/De la vostra virtut'e del mio male.

[50] E col canto suave del Syrene/Vu feu si dulce in lapsicchi armonia/Chie ciascun buta lagrime e voria/Sempre ascultarte ò cara Maddalena.

[51] Every time I use this text in a presentation, I immediately get strong reactions from the Italian speakers in the crowd, who point to the obscene nature of the words. But my own translator, Nello Barbieri, as well as Giulio Ongaro, conclude that this is really a form of praise and the text does not imply any sexual act. I thank the several folks who have nodded heads with me over this poem. I am now convinced that both readings are valid, and not necessarily contradictory to the vocal production of the time.

mirrors the ambiguous power of female vocal production in Madalena's era. Her excited throat was a source of musical and sexual pleasure of the mind, a fantasy based in her flapping vocal chords and highlighted by her moving mouth. Molino's reportage may be only that, and not a summary of his own engagement with her throat in that manner. But the (imagined or real) potential for sexual intercourse with the female singer's throat as it trembled before the listener was vital to his appreciation of her art.

Another contemporary poem, written first in 1569 by Giambattista Maganza as an encomium for one of Madalena's performances (and re-issued in longer form in 1583 after she sang at the Accademia Olimpica) can further serve to underscore the sexualized undulating throat.[52] He first invokes his very physical presence in the act of her song: "Mistress, the day when I was near you to hear you singing [I would wish to become a bee so that with my buzzing] I could be the bass to your trilling (the Italian word is *sgorghezare*, which is almost a gushing out or overflow, an excess of trill), that kind of bass which a *piva sordina* (literally small bag pipe, but figurative for the male genitals) is wont to do in the back of the one who plays it."[53] The reference to her tremulous throat is explicit, as is his phallic response to her motions. He next describes her in typical fashion, as eyes, apples, hair net, and suggests that "it seems [those apples] want to pop out especially when you, Mistress, while singing, are used to taking a breath and sighing." Immediately he wants to "thrust my eyes and my face there, in the hole of that instrument" and asks Madalena to pretend that "in that place there was a nice lawn; and that I, who was listening to you, was a bee sucking the sweetness from your flower." Finally, as her song concludes, he also is spent: "No more, O song, because my throat is dry." His love making to her undulating throat, her very art of song, has become the substance for his own creative act of poetry, an ejaculation, in another sense, of

---

[52] The original poem appeared in *La terza parte de le rime di Magagnò, Menon e Begotto* (Venezia: Bolognino Zaltieri, 1569), 177-181. The longer version was noted in the entry for the Accadamia Olimpia in January, 1583, and was published in his *Rime rustiche, 3 parte* (Venezia: 1583), titled *L'ava de magagno alla S.Madalena Casulana Vicentina*.

[53] Maganza's text was originally published in *La tersa parte de le rime*, cited above, and is given here in its original dialect: Parona, el dì ch'a fu/lialondena da vu/per sentirve a cantare,/stagandove ascoltare/tutto pin de dolzore,/a disea in lo me cuore:/O sorte traitora,/perque drento e de fuora/non possegio muarme/Monben, parona, an mi/ co a fosse sto cosi/a gl'harae per me spasso/fatto quel contrabasso/con quel me sgronzolare/al vostro sgorghezare,/che na piva sordina/suol far de drio a la schina/de quelu che la sona/E po', parona cara, a serae na zolando/pur sempre sgronzolando/incima a quelle care/vostre drezze che pare/fior di pilincon/o ciribrustolon,/e tanto pi che vu/ghe tegnì da per su/na bella re' ingroppà/de sea verde indorà/Pumi che'l no s'in catta/du' altri de sta fatta/in sto roesso mondo,/agnon mostra esser tondo/e fatto col compasso,/ch'al despetto del casso/el par ver che dagn'hora/i vuoga saltar fuora,/massemamente quando/vu, parona, cantando/a solì repigiare/la ose, e suspirare/de quell argagno che,/per far piaser al me/dottor Cavra da ben,/a sonavi sì ben./E così vu, parona,/e bella e cara e bona,/fe conto che ivelò/serisi sta un bel prò./E mi ch'a v'ascoltava/a serave sto n'ava/che da le vostre fiore/g'harae zuzzà el dolzore./E'l buso on se ghe fa/le miele, serae sta/la panza del laùto./No pi,canzon, che'l gargatile è sutto.

his own *jouisssance*. It was precisely this sort of performative eroticism Casulana and her peers were trained to produce. Captured in these texts and others, it was this vocal technique which made these singers adored and whorish, excessive and exquisite, all aspects of which Madalena and Isabella would have been keenly aware. The ornamental undulations fashioned within musical lines were designed not only to delight the ears, but visibly to excite the erotic fantasies of men in close quarters who watched the mouth caress words as the throat produced tones, imagining themselves all the while "inside her."

Seizing the pen by the throat

Feminist writers throughout the twentieth and early twenty-first centuries have underscored the phallic fantasies of power inherent in seizing the pen.[54] This resonates particularly for early modern Italy, where the figurative words for pen (*penna*) and penis (*pene*) were jokingly inter-posed in popular literature. Maganza's poem to Madalena is but another exchange between (her) throat and (his) phallus which coerces his pen to compose, to bring forth seed even as his own throat becomes temporarily barren to her vocal power. So what is it Madalena would have us understand about her blatant appropriation of the metaphoric *penna*, particularly as she engaged that tool to construct her own throat in the undulating rapture of song? How might that pen have elected to depict and help refigure Isabella, whose tarnished public image needed sanctification (for she not only had been caught in an affair, but she had been heard and seen singing and composing, using the throat)?

The madrigal, whether in proper language or burlesque dialect, went hand in hand with the early modern Italian vision for sex and sexuality, and for how bodies could become visible within that paradigm. As noted by Laura Macy in her work about madrigal texts and sex, the madrigal's metaphors and musical gestures combined to mirror common sexual tropes, graphically describing physical intimacy in ways that were clearly understood by its auditors.[55] It was not only in the vocal technique, but also in the words expelled, that participants engaged in fantasy sex. In both the poetry and medicine of the period, "spirit" (referred to as both *spirito* and *alma)* resided in the heart, and represented not only the feelings but the semen of both the male and female ejaculated during intercourse.[56] It was widely believed that both partners needed to achieve orgasm in order for

---

[54] Of many examples, perhaps the most commanding directive was issued by Hélène Cioux in "Laugh of the Medusa," a title which resonates with our own book: "And why don't you write? Writing is for you, you are for you; your body is yours, take it." The article is included in *Feminisms: An Anthology of Literary Theory and Criticism*, ed. Robyn R. Warhol and Diane Price Herndl (New Brunswick, N.J.: Rutgers University Press, 1997), 348.

[55] Laura Macy, "Speaking of Sex: Metaphor and Performance in the Italian Madrigal," *The Journal of Musicology* 14 (1996): 1-34.

[56] Galenic medicinal theory was much in play during this time. For substantial discussion of this, see Laqueur, *Making Sex*.

conception to occur. Thus women, who were believed to be cold, had to be brought to the proper heat by men (thought to be warm) in order for her spirit to combine with the male semen. Body temperature was a primary marker of sexual difference in this culture. Life began with this co-joined semen and ended with the ejaculation of the spirit in one's dying, expelled breath. Sex and death had in common their shared emission of spirit, which explains much about the madrigal's fascination with death: *Io moro, il mio morire, morrò,* alongside *spirito* and *alma,* are the most common words in the madrigal literature.

How these conceits were played out in musical representations determined the impact on their listeners. The early madrigal, during the 1530s and 1540s, was replete with *implied* sex. The common tropes for death and emitted spirit were there, but generally placed early on in the musical setting. As Macy noted, these madrigals were most often sung by small groups of men, and the singers were their own audiences and auditors. It was a private male-bonding act, and most often the sexual tension in the musical setting was deflated at its conclusion with some form of humor.[57] It was genteel repartee, suitable for courtiers of Castiglione's polite world; while sex-filled, it was also "safe."

The advent of the virtuoso female singer during the 1560s changed the cultural role for the madrigal completely. The amateur (male) courtier-singers were replaced by women, *concerti delle donne* or women like Casulana, and hence the genre became "a spectator sport."[58] The audience changed from participants in sexual play to a group of noble voyeurs, and the women in these *concerti* were praised at least as often for their looks as for their voices. These women made the wanton words and musical friction for on-looking men. Their ecstatic throats expelled the words *spirito, moro,* and one can readily imagine the rounded, open (inviting) mouth as it encircled and exhaled the "o." This is the easiest vowel for singers to expose the throat most completely, their undulating vocal chords enacting the text with extraordinary *frisson.* For it was on these words that the vocal embellishments and roulades were placed, here where musical dissonance needed to rub and resolve in long-held notes over time, here where her vocal technique was most exposed, examined, watched, and imagined. In these madrigals humor was dispelled, "death's" piled up at the end of pieces and were repeated in rapturous forward motion until the final musical moment, where death finally meant, in Macy's words, "I'm coming."[59] As her mouth exhaled the last *moro,* the singer quite visibly climaxed with her viewer in a shared emission of spirit, enacted in her case by the throat.

It was into this rather new arena for women that Casulana emerged in 1568, claiming to compose from the intellect even as she participated in the bodily act of erotic singing. That she understood both sides of this proposition is evidenced in the re-configuration of musical and textual tropes that highlight her compositions.

---

[57] The piece Macy uses to describe this is Acradelt's *Il bianco e dolce cigno.* See Macy, 7-10.

[58] *Ibid.,* 17.

[59] *Ibid.,* 27.

For in this collection she denied neither her virtuoso technique nor the textual metaphors common to the repertoire; but she clearly chose where she would expose the caressing flesh of her throat and this had direct ramifications on Isabella's image as well. The *Primo libro a quattro* survives only in canto and tenor part books, with the exception of the four pieces she included from earlier *Il Desiderio* collections. This final stretch of this story will largely be told from the canto's point of view, since this is the voice she (and Isabella) would have sung.

The first piece is a blatant affirmation for Isabella. *Tant'alto s'erge la tua chiara luce... a Isabella de Medici Orsina*, written at the same time Isabella had commissioned Rossetto metaphorically to portray her as the abandoned wife of Paolo Orsini, offers Casulana's own vision for elevating her patron above the mire of public disdain. "Your bright splendor rises so high, O Lady, that you appear as a New Sun to our eyes; and so gracefully you shine that you inflame every soul to offer you sublime praise; therefore let the great, lovely name of Isabella proudly cleave the air all around."[60] Isabella, raised above the Sun who was traditionally the male god Apollo, becomes in his place the highest orb in the sky. The Virgin of the Assumption, a long-standing figure in Florentine culture for the Queen of Florence, was greeted in various offices of the day with a phrase "who is this woman who rises equal to the Sun?" So Casulana's poetic allusions invoke images of goodness and female power.[61] Casulana's setting of this moment is remarkable not only for its unique pitch but also for the positioning of the notes around the words. The music explodes with a high b on the words "gran nome d'Isabella," a pitch unheard of at this time. Even high g is somewhat unusual during the 1560s, the average canto range extending up only to an e or f in most cases (to my knowledge this is the only written use of a high b in the madrigal repertoire). This gesture is repeated twice. (See Music Example 15.1).

Not only did the pitch highlight what must have been an amazing vocal expulsion to its listeners, a musical moment which showcased Madalena as singer; and not only did this pitch literally raise up Isabella above all men, including the Sun. This note is also impossible to sing with the mouth opened in the back, or with undulating vocal chords. The vocal technique of Casulana's time, grounded in a mid-range which allowed for open mouths and undulating throats, did not envision this upper register, perhaps in part *because* it precluded that necessary visual aid. There was no caressing flesh enveloping the name Isabella, whose chastity had been called into question by her husband. The extraordinary musical word painting highlighted Isabella and the exceptional vocal range of the presumed singers (Isabella herself could have also performed it), while also shielding her from the very act of singing with a "uvulating" throat that invoked public reproach. The sex was taken out and the grand name of Isabella became cerebral,

---

[60] The Italian texts with English translations for pieces discussed in this section are given in Appendix III. I am grateful to Nello Barbieri for his diligent work on these texts, and for many discussions around their potential meanings and innuendo.

[61] I thank Suzanne Cusick for this thought, and for the reference to Mary Bergstein, "Marian Politics in Quattrocento Florence," *Renaissance Quarterly* 44 (1991), 673-719.

Musical Example 15.1 – "Tant' alto s'erge," Canto

apart from the flesh. The piece ends in a gentle and non-virtuosic semblance of propriety as the name Isabella "cleaves the air all around."

One of the most noticeable differences between Casulana's music and that of her peers is the fast paced rhythmic propulsion of the text. Eighth notes and off-beat accents abound, making the slower moving undulations of the throat even more noticeable. The word *morire* in its various permutations is also not common in Casulana's madrigals. The conceit appears in seven of the twenty-one texts, and there are no examples where the word is catapulted towards the end of the piece with "climactic" musical vigor. Rather it is internalized and often made impotent by use of vocal undulations on contrasting words which negate its erotic suggestiveness. The eighth piece, *Morir non può il mio cuore*, seems to embrace the typical metaphoric use of hearts pulling in and out of the other's breast in perpetual dying: "My heart cannot die: I would like to kill it, since that would please you, but it cannot be pulled out of your breast, where it has been dwelling for a long time; and if I killed it, as I wish, I know that you would die, and I would die too." This is one of the pieces printed first in *Il Desiderio*, and survives in all four voices.[62] In traditional fashion, the madrigal piles several deaths at the end, but the only vocal undulation in the whole piece comes very near the beginning, and emphases not death, but the text *ma trar non si puo fuori*, or my heart (sexual organ) can*not* be pulled out. The tremulous throat of the canto embraces *trar fuori* (especially *fuori*, or out), not death and orgasm. The many deaths which conclude the piece build up not in suspensions and resolved dissonance, but rather in rapid dialog which project his death in common chattering; hers comes at the end, almost an afterthought in the lower register of the canto voice and without ornamentation. The *jouissance* in this setting comes at the beginning, during "foreplay," and negates the typical male musical climax altogether. It is one of many deliberate re-settings in this collection of a poem designed for erotic meaning. But the fantasy goes "soft" at the end. (See Music Example 15.2).

Another of the four *Desiderio* texts in the *Primo libro* similarly treats the death conceit in non-masculine terms. *Sculpio n l'alm'amore* immediately follows *Morir non può* in the collection: "Love engraved your image on my soul and burns it constantly with such an ardent torch that it is dying: moreover, it regrets any delay of death. And while it feeds on the desire to die, it hides from death, and so do I." The canto voice opens as a voluptuous, embellished tease on the word *amore*, but again much of the piece proceeds in highly rhythmic dialog among all four voices, the embellishment of the throat coming on the word *desio*, or desire, but not on *morte*. The musical effect is to highlight her exposed throat around the perceived desire, but death itself is de-emphasized as she herself "hides from death" in harmonious musical concord at the end of the setting.[63]

Most of Casulana's texts had either very few or no prior concordant settings (or even later concordances), but there are two significant exceptions, *Là ver l'aurora*, a Petrarch text which had a long history and which had been put to music before Madalena by at least eight composers, including Lassus;[64] and Luigi

---

[62] The entire piece can be found in a transcription in Pescerelli, *I madrigali.*

[63] *Ibid.*

[64] Other settings include those by Palestrina, 1555; Vicentino, 1558; Menta and Striggio, both in 1560; Chamatero, 1561; Animuccia, 1565; and Vinci, 1567. I am grateful to the Harvard Loeb Music Library for permission to make copies of these settings from microfilm collections.

Musical Example 15.2 – "Morir non puo il mio core"

Tansillo's *Canzone A cas un giorno*, a four part piece first set by Casulana, Bonagiunta and Primavera (Gabrieli was among many others who later put it to music.) Its imitative history came after Casulana and forms another story.[65] But looking at *Là ver l'aurora* in this light is instructive. At this time composers often

---

[65] Einstein pointed to this text as one of the earliest dialogues in the madrigal repertoire, and one also favored by *commedia* writers. In listing the many composers who set it, he failed to mention Casulana's piece, one of the earliest. Einstein, II, 547.

quite literally competed with one another through settings of texts which made reference to other composers, suggesting that they knew someone else's work and could, in a sense, do it better. This sort of imitation was quite common, and has been documented by several modern scholars. What now seems completely unsurprising to me is that while other composers involved with this text clearly imitated one another, Casulana set her own course.

Là ver l'aurore was the first of several stanzas of Petrarch's longer *canzona* (Number 239 of his *Canzoniere*), and other composers including Lassus set the entire poem. Casulana set only this first part in the *Primo libro* (in 1570 she used the final stanza, *Ridon hor per le piaggie* as the opening piece of her *Secondo libro*). The text is as follows: "Towards dawn, when the breeze is wont to stir the flowers so sweetly in the new season, and the little birds begin singing their songs, I feel my thoughts inside my soul being stirred so sweetly that I must go back to my notes." The text plays with the name of Petrarch's imagined lover Laura in the form of *l'aura*, or breeze, and other settings make great ornamental fanfare around the breeze and the flowers. The canto in Lassus' version is typical, sitting right in the mid-voice preferred for its visible undulations and literally caresses the words. (See Music Example 15.3.)

Casulana's music for this piece is unique to her collection. The canto voice throughout is in an extremely low register, avoiding the mid-range and its vocal ambiguities almost completely. (See Music Example 15.4.) "Breeze stirring flowers" is a commonplace pastoral idiom which also implied sexual arousal. The lily and the rose, especially, were euphemisms for a woman's sexual organs. While the "wind" blowing through flowers could imply rape,[66] here it is a breeze, suggestively licking at the flowers, trying to get them involved. The voice speaking the text is the male, who is so stimulated by the thoughts of these "flowers" he must return to his notes (for Petrarch, the reference to Laura in interchange with *l'aura*, or breeze, was a particularly suggestive erotic conceit). This *frisson* was exploited by all other composers who set the text, but not by Casulana. The canto sings beneath the stirring up, under register, with only a very slight undulation on the word *dolcemente*. She is not engaged in the text's sentiment in the traditional way: her singing figuratively implies her abstention. The very fact that Madalena did not set the remaining verses, put to rapturous music by others and with an imitative musical history likely known to a contemporary audience, underscores even further Isabella's insistence on "stopping here" or retaining her vocal chastity. Lassus' version was written for his *Libro Quattro a cinque voci*, designated for the singing ladies of Ferrara and their explicit tradition for erotic singing. Casulana's recreation of this well-known text in an almost exaggeratedly non-sexualized manner for Isabella would not have been missed by listeners.

---

[66] Madalena used it in that sense and to great purpose in her *Libro primo di madrigali a cinque*, published in 1583, especially in the piece *Io o'odorate fronde*. I have discussed that piece in detail in "Madalena Casunala, my body knows un-heard of songs."

Là ver l'aurora seems also to lead towards a specific portrait of Isabella at the book's conclusion. It is the third to last piece in the collection, followed by *Occhi dolc'occhi car'occhi*. The piece is in common time and in much slower, simpler note values than others in the book. It is also in the lower register and there is no sense of virtuosity. The text imports a common trope – eyes – whose tears in many instances can emulate other bodily liquids such as semen. Here, however, they are the "only source of my well-being; since you are turning to me, grief will no longer remain in my heart to torment me." These eyes shed no tears and expel no dangerous fluid. It is as if the singer acknowledged her lover's glance, his coming back (as Paolo would not) and in simple, clean musical tones devoid of any undulating throat she looks expectantly for her Lord. (See Music Example 15.5).

The final text in the collection brings this point home. It is clearly spoken by a woman: "Alas, I feel my heart burning so in the fire of a new flame, that I can hope no more in any remedy for my deep sorrow; because it cannot express its desire, it languishes, caught in a sweet and endearing snare. Pray, Love, since you have caught me, warm the heart of my Lord, and let the blow be such that he might feel my great pain." These final three pieces form an interesting parallel to the opening song, which clearly elevated Isabella even as it underscored a remarkable vocal ability. In coming full circle, Casulana projects a contrite and lonely woman who longs only for her husband. This final poem tells of a woman unnoticed in love; because she is a woman, she "cannot express" her desire, so she asks Love to warm her *signor's* heart. Curiously in this setting it is the man, not the woman, who needs to be brought to proper heat. She hopes the blow, *colpo*, to his heart will cause pain (not death, not sex, but will force his attention). I can only surmise that this concluding text is a direct reference to Isabella and her absentee husband (and perhaps with reference to her lover, who had also been sent away from her).

Casulana once again charged the music with actions appropriate to a chaste patron. The opening *Ahi lasso* is a common madrigal conceit for (masculine) loss. The reminder of the piece is a truly beautiful, mournful lament in the canto part, remaining within a very limited number of pitches so as to avoid any thoughts of rhetorical outspokenness or inappropriateness.[67] While the woman does speak, she does so within the confines of real grief and a fixed vocal range, syllables set to each note and with no flirtatious embellishments from the throat save one: *colpo*, the blow she hopes Love will inflict, is given a mild yet clear throat articulation in the mid-register consistent with tremulous singing. But this undulation is not at all about sex. Instead it calls attention to the unjust pain of the woman speaking, and here the throat affects a well-deserved blow to the inattentive male lover. This articulation in a subtle but direct way seizes the pen by the throat and re-directs its motion towards a masculine subject deserving of its anger. In the same light it

---

[67] Laurie Stras wrote of the potential for wide moving melodic lines to convey excessive rhetorical, and therefore masculine musical content, whereas a very contained melodic line with few pitches or deviations from a mode suggest the "contained" and restrained female voice. Laurie Stras, *"Le nonne della ninfa:* Feminine Voices and Modal Rhetoric in the Generation before Monteverdi," in: *Gender and Sexuality*, 123-166.

Musical Example 15.3 – Lassus, "La Ver L'aurora," Canto

Musical Example 15.4 – "La ver l'aurora," Canto

Musical Example 15.5 – "Occhi, dolc' occhi," Canto

Oc - chi dolc' oc - chi car' oc - chi so - a -

vi, oc - chi che sol   ca-gion   oc - chi che sol ca-gion del   mio ben se -

te   oc - chi che poi   ch'a me vi ri-vol-ge - te vi-ri-vol-ge - te, Duol piu non

sia   duol piu non   sia che dent'   al   cor m'a-gra - vi,   duol piu non

sia   che   den - tro che   dentr'   al   cor   m'a-gra - vi.

looks with well-honed feminine modesty to exonerate Isabella from the throes of public shaming. (See Music Example 15.6.)

Isabella's life was not to be spared. In 1576 she was murdered at the throat, as described in humbling detail by Ercole Cortile, Ferrarese ambassador to Florence. He detailed how Isabella was summoned into her husband's room at midday; she seemed aware of what was in store and merely shrugged her shoulders as she was led away. Paolo threatened to kill the attending servants if they talked, and after he strangled her he had her body transported to Florence and placed in the church. The casket was left open despite the horrible disfigurement resulting from the heavy weight of Paolo's body.[68] Cortile especially noticed how people came to

---

[68] The document is given completely in Cardamone, 17. The summary of her disfigurement is enough to make one weep: "And it was said that a more ugly monster had never been seen: her head was enormous beyond measure, with huge black lips that looked like two swollen sausages.... And the stench from the body was so great that nobody could bear to be near it. It was completely black from the middle up and completely white from the middle down, according to [one gentleman] who lifted the cloths, like the others were doing, turning the body to see everything."

Musical Example 15.6 – "Ahi lasso io sent' il core," Canto

see her, lifted the cloths to look at her so, to see everything. In death, as in life, her throat had become a spectator sport. Her punishment for having used it was the object of this gruesome and curious gaze.

After Isabella's death, Casulana was not heard from again in writing until 1583. She was a different composer in the *Primo libro a cinque* 1583, one still well aware of the power of the throat but one who had much more confidence in speaking out in proto-feminist texts about matters concerning women.[69] In her 1568 collection, however, I believe her dedication to Isabella ran deeper than one typical of composer and patron. Embedded within were musical and textual references to traditional madrigal repertoire, chosen and manipulated to inform the public of her patron's chastity, abandonment, and obedience. Her absolute insistence on publishing, or reaching a wider audience, may have been motivated in part by her desire to offer those particular correctives. The music was virtuosic, but the undulating throat supported other than male sexual pleasure, even as the words often described it. The flapping flesh caressed desires, dreams, and blows to the hearts of unfaithful men, but never did it envelop the musical analogy to the penis. Madalena raised Isabella to beautiful heights, but bowed her patron's eyes to her absent Lord at the end of the story. Like Rossetto, she sought to paint Isabella as the victim, above reproach and deserving of sympathy. Madalena had not only seized the pen in defiance of male prerogative, but she seized it by the throat and in defense of *Donne* who might wish to use both instruments freely.

---

[69] I have dealt with this collection in the previously mentioned article, "Madalena Casulana, my body knows un-heard of songs."

Chapter 16

Princess Elizabeth Stuart as Musician and Muse

Janet Pollack

As the only surviving daughter of King James I of England (and the VI of Scotland), Elizabeth Stuart (1596-1662) was the beneficiary of the finest education England had to offer women at the time.[1] As a princess at court, she was exposed to some of the most magnificent artistic productions of the day. Although much is known about Elizabeth's life from court records, her diaries, and court commentators, and many fine books detail her role as Queen of Bohemia and her hardships living in exile following the outbreak of the War,[2] little has been said about her musical abilities and her impact on and relationship to the artistic world of early modern England. English women were not encouraged to be composers, and except for one piece, "O Deathe, rock me asleepe," attributed to Anne Boleyn, no compositions by women in England are known during this early period.[3] Nevertheless aristocratic English women did fashion varied connections to the

---

[1] Another daughter was born in 1598 to King James and Queen Anne, a princess Margaret, but she apparently lived for only two years. Mentioned in Alison Plowden, *The Stuart Princesses* (Gloucestershire: Alan Sutton Publishing Ltd., 1996), 3.

[2] The biographies of Elizabeth Stuart, many scholarly and others pure romance, are (listed alphabetically): Elizabeth Benger, *Memoirs of Elizabeth Stuart, Queen of Bohemia* (London, 1825); Alice Buchan, *A Stuart Portrait* (London: Peter Davies, 1934); Mary Anne Everett [Wood] Green, *Elizabeth Electress Palatine and Queen of Bohemia*, rev. S. C. Lomas (London: Methuen, 1901); George Hodges, *A Queen of hearts* (Ludlow: G. Woolley, 1902), a non-scholarly summary; Barbara Kiefer Lewalski, *Writing Women in Jacobean England* (Cambridge, Massachusetts and London, England: Harvard University Press, 1993), Ch. 2; Carola Oman, *Elizabeth of Bohemia* (London: Hodder & Stoughton, 1938); Alison Plowden, *The Stuart Princesses* (Stroud, Gloucestershire: Alan Sutton Publishing Ltd., 1996), Ch. 1; Josephine Ross, *The Winter Queen* (New York: St. Martin Press, 1979); Ida Woodward, *Five English Consorts of Foreign Princes* (London: Methuen and Company Ltd., 1911), 113-167. She is also treated at length in *Memoiren der Herzogin Sophie Nachmals Kurfurstin von Hannover*, ed. A. Kocher (Leipzig, 1879). An anonymous biography exists in the National Scottish Library in Edinburgh (shelfmark S. 122. f) by "a Lady," *The Life of Elizabeth Queen of Bohemia, A Scottish Princess* (London, 1857).

[3] Edith Borroff, "Anne Boleyn," in: *Historical Anthology of Music by Women*, ed. James R. Briscoe (Bloomington and Indianapolis: Indiana University Press, 1987), 14-17.

creative act. William Prizer and Robin Armstrong have recently shown that patronage was a means of empowerment for women who were generally denied the more accepted mode of musical recognition as composers.[4] This present chapter furthers the creative-patron argument while expanding its scope to include Princess Elizabeth Stuart, a woman whose personality and musical abilities impacted the development of English music in a novel way. For although Elizabeth defied neither the social boundaries prescribed by her station nor the conventional role as wife and mother, she nevertheless held a unique position in music history as the inspiration for and performer of the most important publication of early English music: *Parthenia, or the Maydenhead of the first musicke that ever was printed for the Virginalls* (1613).[5]   *Parthenia* was the first engraved book of English music, the first anthology of keyboard music anywhere, and a book of high-quality keyboard music that was destined to become the primer for keyboard study in England for more than a half century.   It was the benchmark by which all subsequent keyboard tutors were judged. At the time of *Parthenia's* publication the young sixteen year old Elizabeth was not widely recognized as a patron of artists, but she was already acknowledged as a musician of considerable skill.   It is this skill, its acquisition and its execution that is the focus of the present chapter.

Offered here is a different perspective on Elizabeth's Stuart's life, one that draws attention to those aspects that neither her diaries nor her other biographies adequately cover, namely, her ability as a keyboard player. Closely examined are the crucial years before her marriage beginning with her education in the care of Lord Harington and the time she was a pupil of the musician John Marchant, and later John Bull. Care is given to placing Elizabeth's musical accomplishments in the context of those skills advocated for women by educators, recommended by dramatists, described by poets, and visually represented by artists of the day.

The role of music in an aristocratic education

Music always seems to have been associated with gentility and found suitable for young maidens. By the early seventeenth century music was considered becoming

---

[4] See William Prizer, *Courtly Pastimes: the frottole of Marchetto Cara* (Ann Arbor, MI: UMI Research Press, 1980); Robin Armstrong, unpublished paper on Isabella d'Este.

[5] *Parthenia* (1613) is a relatively slim volume of twenty-one pieces for virginals by three of England's finest composers – William Byrd, John Bull, and Orlando Gibbons – all expertly engraved by William Hole. It was offered as a wedding gift to Princess Elizabeth Stuart and her betrothed the Elector Palatine of Heidelberg, Frederick V on or shortly before the marriage ceremony on Valentine's Day, February 14, 1613, at Whitehall Palace. The union had been in negotiation for more than six months, and Prince Henry, the bride's older brother, began preparations for an extravagant wedding celebration early in fall 1612. Fireworks, mock naval battles on the Thames, masques and stage plays, among other festivities surrounded the marriage ceremony, and were followed by numerous other entertainments as the couple progressed through major continental cities, a passage that climaxed with their triumphal entry into Heidelberg, the seat of the Palatinate.

to ladies and education in general was seen as a profitable means by which a socially ambitious young woman could snare a noble spouse. Young aristocratic women were encouraged to learn languages and dabble in the arts, though social conventions restricted where the young woman was permitted to study. The music tutor often lived with the family and instructed the young woman in private. In addition to teaching family members how to play an instrument, and to sing and dance, the music instructor was frequently called upon to teach rudiments of musical composition. Musical literacy, the ability to sing and play an instrument and talk about music in some knowing way, became firmly entrenched in the cultural model expounded by humanists.

This positive attitude to musical instruction was expressed by a number of influential educators and endorsed in the seventeenth century by playwrights; it became a requirement of employment for schoolmasters. Thomas Dekker, in *The Gull's Hornbook*, echoes many humanist sentiments when he stipulates that women should learn "to read and write; to play upon the virginals, lute and cittern; and to read prick-song."[6] The music master at Christ's Hospital was expected to teach children "to play upon an instrument, as upon the Virginalls or Violl, but especially upon the Virginalls." Robert Dow made this possible by buying "two pair of Virginalls and a Bass Violl" for the schoolhouse.[7]

While there were many other apologists for the inclusion of musical instruction in general education, not all who observed young women devoting so much time to musical practice saw its positive side. Thomas Elyot titled a section of *The book named the Governour* (1531): *In what wise music may be nobleman necessary, and what modest ought to be therein*, implying that educators feared virtuosity would appear immodest. Some criticized young women for devoting too much time to practice since they viewed other social graces as more important for attracting a husband. The differences in attitude may be explained in part by the clash between an earlier scholastic pedagogy and the move towards a more pragmatic form of humanism which emphasized teaching the "humanities," the arts in general, and promoting education for a wider segment of the population. Increasingly the middle class found they could better their social standing if they bought into the notion that social graces could be learned through education. Music instruction, as a result, became a thing that could be consumed and used to as a means to elevate oneself in society.

Richard Mulcaster, the highly distinguished schoolmaster of the largest school in London for 25 years – The Merchant-Taylors' School – and later St. Paul's, urged women to strive for a high level of proficiency and "excellencie" in language

---

[6] Q. William Chappell, *Old English Popular Music*, ed. H. Ellis Wooldridge (New York: Jack Brussel, 1961), 60f.

[7] F. G. Edwards, "A Visit to Christ's Hospital," *Musical Times* 46: 573-583; quoted in John Harley, *British Harpsichord Music* (Hants, England: Scholar Press, 1994) 2: 181.

and music[8] like "princesses" who when taught in the manner he prescribes have achieved an "ende more marvellous" than one could have hoped.[9] The instruments recommended by Mulcaster are the virginals and lute "because of the full music which is uttered by them." [10] By full music he means an instrument that is capable of playing both melody and harmony simultaneously. That Mulcaster encourages women to learn virginals in particular is in keeping with contemporary views about women and music. In the sixteenth and seventeenth centuries there were certain instruments considered fit for a woman, and many that were not. For instance, some found a woman playing the viol an abomination, for the viol, as Miss Mary Burwell's lute-master observed around 1670, "entangleth one in spreading the arms, and openeth the legs (which doth not become man, much less woman)."[11] However, playing the virginals appeared to be acceptable to most and Miss Burwell's Lute-master goes on to paint a more modest image of a musician who when playing the virginals turns her back to the company to convey her modesty; and he enthuses over the benefits of a shared love of music between husband and wife:

> And those that have the grace to lift up their mind to contemplations of heavenly things, this celestial harmony contributes much to raise our souls and make them melt in love of God. Nothing represents so well the consort of angelical choirs and gives more foretastes of heavenly joys and everlasting happiness. For the advantages of marriage, how many bachelors and maids have we seen advanced by this agreeing harmony, when persons of both sexes have neither considered wealth nor beauty of the person, but suffering themselves to be drawn by the charms of this sweet melody. Some hath believed that they should possess an angel incarnate, if they could unite themselves by a marriage to a person that enjoys this rare quality.[12]

Personal diaries from the early seventeenth century both support and occasionally contradict Miss Burwell's Teacher and his abhorrence of the viol for young women. Ann Clifford's 1603 diary tells something of the young lady's training and entertainment. It claims that a servant, Stephen, spent an entire month

---

[8] Richard Mulcaster, *Positions Concerning the Training Up of Children*, ed. William Barker (Toronto, Buffalo, and London: University of Toronto Press, 1994), 181. Education in grammar schools often included the teaching of elementary musical education. Since the two subjects shared the same physical space, teachers, and pupils, it is not surprising to see that their priorities frequently overlapped.

[9] Mulcaster, *Positions*, 182.

[10] Richard Mulcaster, *The First Part of the Elementarie* (London, 1582), 6. Mulcaster proposed a second part of the *Elementarie*, which was to include the teaching of virginals.

[11] Thurston Dart, "Miss Mary Burwell's Instruction Book for the Lute," *Galpin Society Journal* XI 1958): 48. Reference to this quote is also found in Thurston Dart's, "The History of *Mayden-Musicke*," *Bulletin of the New York Public Library* 65 (1961): 226-227.

[12] Dart, "Miss Mary Burwell's Instruction Book for the Lute," 49.

teaching her to dance, and that "virginal wires were purchased."[13] On the other hand, the same diary claims that Anne when visiting relatives often played the bass viol: "During our being there I used to wear my Hair color'd velvet everyday and learned to sing and play on the Bass viol of Jack Jenkins, my Aunt's Boy."[14] The diary also confirms that daughters of titled families, like royal children, were usually privately taught because attending a public school would have been improper.

Iconographic along with archival evidence further show that music making and the playing of virginals and various other types of keyboards were an important part of a young woman's life across the continent. Painters ranging from Venice (Jacopo Robusti Tintoretto 1518-1594), to Cremona and Palermo (Sofonisba Anguissola 1532-1625), to Brussels and Antwerp (Jan Brueghel 1568-1625), and beyond depicted women engaged in music-making with at least one of the women playing a keyboard.[15] Kristine K. Forney has recently uncovered an additional number of early paintings showing Antwerp women seated at virginals, demonstrating that in this city woman were indeed known as keyboard players early on.[16] Cornelius de Zeeuw's 1561 painting, for instance, shows the 12-year old daughter of Peter de Mucheron (in austere Calvinist clothing) seated at a hexagonal virginal along with her family. In another painting dated 1564, the same artist depicts a ten year old girl (the daughter of either the van Lier or van Doedenberg families of Antwerp represented in the painting) playing the virginals while a thirteen year old boy holds open a music book. Frans Pourbus the Elder paints the picture of a woman playing the spinet at the wedding (1577) of Joris Hoefnagel to Susanna van Onsen while two men accompany on lutes. In a 1561 portrait of the Van Berchem family, the artist Frans Floris depicts a woman at a hexagonal virginal while a man plays the lute nearby. All these scenes show that women playing virginals were a common sight in Antwerp, and women as keyboard players in domestic music making were generally accepted. Forney speculates that the Antwerp paintings were as much promotion of the city's instrument building as they were a careful documentation of social history. Additional archival evidence uncovered concerns the teaching of music at a private girl's school, The Laurel

---

[13] Ann Clifford, a contemporary of Elizabeth Stuart, was born at Skipton Castle in Yorkshire on January 30, 1590. She was the daughter of George and Margaret Russell. She was placed in the care of "Aunt Warwick," a lady at Queen Elizabeth's court, whose duty it was "to train the girl in country manners." D. J. H. Clifford, ed., *The Diaries of Lady Anne Clifford* (Gloucestershire, Phoenix Mill, Fair Thrupp, Stroud: Alan Sutton Publishing Ltd., 1990), 15, 27.

[14] *Ibid.*, 27.

[15] For information on Sonfonisha Anguissola as artist and musician, please see Linda Austern's chapter in this book.

[16] Kristine K. Fornay, "'Nymphes gayes en abry du Laurier': Music Instruction for the Bourgeois Woman," *Musica Disciplina*, 44 (1995): 151-187.

Tree (1576-1584), which makes it clear that music was an accepted part of a young girl's education in Antwerp.[17]

In England there is at least one famous painting linking an aristocratic woman, Lady Anne Clifford, with a musical instrument. The third panel of the famous triptych, the "Great Picture," shows Anne Clifford as a young woman surrounded by books and musical instruments. A lute stands upright on the floor leaning against a rectangular table upon which sits an open book. Above the neck of the lute is Anne's out-stretched left hand resting on the book's pages. All these clues suggest that Anne was highly educated and an accomplished musician at a young age. The middle panel depicts Lady Clifford standing next to a man and pointing towards two young children. In the panel on the right, Lady Clifford is shown only with a dog and cat at her feet, and again surrounded by books. Graham Parry views the painting as a political narrative stressing Lady Clifford's victory in securing her contested estates.[18] Kevin Sharpe, accepting Parry's interpretation for the most part, views the triptych as a representation of Lady Clifford's successful "assertion in a patriarchal world."[19]   What is important is that an English painting survives that shows a powerful aristocratic woman clearly associated with an instrument and music instruction at the time. The opened book near the lute may signify her musical literacy.

There are also a number of references to women playing virginals in English dramas, songs, diaries, and various court documents. Among literary references to English women and virginals is one familiar to many readers: Thomas Middleton's *Michaelmus Term*, where the woolen draper Ephestian Quomodo chases his daughter Susan out of the shop commanding her to "get you up to your virginals." Another is seen in the opening of Middleton's *A Chaste Maid in Cheapside* (1613) when Mistress Maudlin Yellowhammer, a goldsmith's wife, anxiously asks her daughter Moll: "Have you played over all your lessons o' the virginals?" We soon learn that the mother is anxious for her daughter to learn music and dance so that she can attract the attentions of the noble knight Sir Walter Whorehound.[20] That Middleton, one of the most popular playwrights in early seventeenth century London, designated virginals the appropriate instrument for the socially ambitious woman says much about the association between women and keyboards.

---

[17] Peter Heyns was the director (1555-1583) of the famed girls school situated at the sign of the Laurel Tree. Surviving records show the school to cater to approximately 464 middle-class girls ranging in age from 14-15 years. Kristine Fornay has found additional information about "The Laurel Tree's" clientele, textbooks, and type of music instruction.

[18] Graham Parry, "The Great Picture of Lady Anne Clifford," in: Howarth's *Art and Patronage*, 202-219. The "Great Picture" is reproduced in Kevin Sharpe's, *Remapping Early Modern England* (Cambridge, England: Cambridge University Press, 2000), 449.

[19] Sharpe, 448.

[20] Excerpts from Thomas Middleton are printed in Arthur Loesser, *Men, Women, and Pianos* (New York: Simon and Schuster, 1954), 190-192.

Yet other poetic references describe women playing keyboards in private, usually as a way to express sorrow over a lost or absent love. Edmund Spenser's heroine seeks solace by:

> Playing alone careless on hir heavenlie Virginals.
> ...If at hir Virginals, tell hir, I can heare no mirth.
> Asked why? say:...
> that lamenting Love marreth the Musicall.[21]

Such poetic scenes, as Regula Hohl Trillini points out, "fulfill the pattern of female display for male eyes and ears even when solitary playing is ostensibly described."[22] "Fair Annie," an old Scottish ballad, seeks comfort in her virginals when she is deserted by a man to whom she bore eight sons. The jilted Annie is left to serve at the wedding banquet of her lover and his new wife.

> When dinner was past, and supper was by,
> And a' were boun for bed,
> Fair Annie and her seven sons
> In a puir bye-chamber war laid.
> Fair Annie took out her virginals,
> And sadly did she play.[23]

From these and many other similar examples, it is evident a young woman's skill in music was considered a necessary accessory for achieving gentility and snagging a socially desirable husband. Robert Burton sums up the means for social climbing in *Anatomy of Melancholy* (1621):

> A thing nevertheless frequently done, and part of a gentlewoman's bringing up, to sing and dance, and play on the lute, or some such instrument, before she can say her paternoster, or ten commandments. 'Tis the next way their parents think to get them a husband, they are compelled to learn...'tis a great allurement as it is often used, and many are undone by it.[24]

Additional documentary evidence that music instruction was given at court and that royalty played virginals comes from Henry VIII's expense accounts. We

---

[21] Edmund Spenser, "Iambicum Trimetricum," *The Works of Edmund Spenser: A Varioeum Edition* (Baltimore: The John Hopkins Press, 1932-49), II: 267. I am thankful for Regula Hohl Trillini for bringing this to my attention.

[22] Regula Hohl Trillini, *The Gaze of the Listener: Another Look at Sonnet 128*. An unpublished manuscript, 5.

[23] "Fair Annie," in: *The English and Scottish Popular Ballads*, ed. F. J. Child (Boston and New York: Houghton Mifflin and Company, 1882-98), III: 77-79.

[24] Robert Burton, *Anatomy of Melancholy* (Oxford: Clarendon Press, 1989), III:ii:3, 1, 187.

know, for instance, that Henry owned virginals,[25] and from Melville's account that Queen Elizabeth, Henry's daughter, played the virginals "exceedingly well."[26] The humanist Roger Ascham, describing the education of his royal pupil Elizabeth I in a letter to Strum in April 1550, links the teaching of Latin and Greek with music and views her competence in all three as proof of her integrity and moral fiber:

> She has often talked to me readily and well in Latin, and moderately in Greek. When she writes in Greek and Latin, nothing is more beautiful than her handwriting. She is as much delighted with music as she is skilful in the art...She likes a style that grows out of the subject; chaste because it is suitable.[27]

Queen Elizabeth's excellence in languages along with her musical skill showed her to be an exemplary woman, a standard which carried over into Jacobean time. From similar accounts we also know that Mary Queen of Scots was an able player.

Further attesting to the instrument's use in teaching music to well-heeled young ladies in the late sixteenth and seventeenth centuries are a number of significant manuscripts consisting of virginals music written for, and sometimes copied by, women amateurs. *My Lady Nevells Booke, Suzanne van Soldt,*[28] *Lady Jean Campell's Virginal Book, Barbara Fletcher's Book, Ann Cromwell's Virginal Book,*[29] *Elizabeth Rogers Hir Virginall Book*[30] and *Priscilla Bunbury's Virginal Book* are ones generally listed, and there are doubtless others whose names are not inscribed on the covers and left anonymous. Only *My Lady Nevell* can compare favorably to *Parthenia* in the quality of music, care in assembling, and the technical requirements demanded of the performer. Both were conceived as lessons for women of high class and display careful selection of pieces, although *My Lady Nevell* is in manuscript and *Parthenia* is engraved and widely distributed. The remaining five virginals collections are clearly for beginning students. As John

---

[25] For prices of Henry VIII's virginals see Arthur Loesser, *Men, Women, and Pianos,* 192.

[26] For Melville's full account of Queen Elizabeth playing the virginals see J. E. Neale, *Queen Elizabeth* (London, 1937), 130-131; Melville's account is also mentioned in Lisa Jardine, *Still Harping on Daughters: Women and Drama in the Age of Shakespeare* (New Jersey: The Harvester Press, 1983), 172.

[27] T. W. Baldwin, *William Shakespere's Small Latine and Lesse Greeke* (Urbana, 1944) I: 259; quoted in *From Humanism to the Humanities,* 144.

[28] *GB-Lbl, Add. 29485.* The *van Soldt MS* is a collection of 33 keyboard pieces copied by a Flemish scribe. It contains psalm settings, dance tunes, and a teaching prelude by John Bull.

[29] *GB-Cromwell Museum, 46.78-748. Anne Cromwell's Virginal Book* (1638) is available in a modern edition edited by Howard Ferguson (London, 1974). It contains 50 keyboard pieces.

[30] *GB-Lbl, Add. 10337. Verso* of cover inscribed "Elizabeth: Rogers hir. virginall. booke. ffebruary ye 27: 1656." This manuscript contains 94 pieces of keyboard music. It is available in a modern edition titled *Elizabeth Rogers Hir Virginall Booke,* Charles Cofone, ed. (New York, 1975; second revised edition, 1982).

Harley points out, nearly all the volumes contain masque tunes illustrating "the spread of musical culture outwards from the court."[31]

That the first printed collection of keyboard music receives the title *Parthenia* – which refers to a young female virgin – contains the word "Maydenhead" in the title, is specifically intended to be played on virginals, is dedicated to a young woman, has the picture of a young woman playing a virginals as the frontispiece, and involves a number of women in the publication, all strongly suggest that the ability to play high level keyboard pieces like those in *Parthenia* was expected of aristocratic women in the early seventeenth century.[32]

Elizabeth's musical education (1596-1613)

Elizabeth was born on 16 (or 19) August 1596 at Falkland Palace.[33] Like her brother Prince Henry, Elizabeth was immediately placed in the care of Lord and Lady Livington at Linlithgow, in accordance with the usual practice of charging a trustworthy member of the aristocracy with the responsibility of raising the royal children. Elizabeth spent most of her first six years at Linlithgow, one of the

---

[31] Harley, *British Harpsichord Music*, vol. 2, 180.

[32] It has been suggested that the reason why virginals came to be associated with women may have to do with the amount of sound they created and the manner of playing them. Size, complexity, and loudness determined whether or not an instrument was feminine enough for women. Though considerably larger than lutes, sixteenth-seventeenth century harpsichords and virginals were not much louder and no more complex than plucked string instruments. Women could perform while seated demurely at the keyboard. Probably first used to accompany singing in a private domestic setting, it was found capable of rendering dances, songs, and contrapuntal pieces, and, as we will see, was often recommended as an aid in the teaching of music in general. See Lucy Greene, *Music, Gender, Education*, (Cambridge, England: Cambridge University Press, 1997), 59.

[33] The Palace is situated on a tongue of rock extending north from the foot of the East Lomond Hill, Scotland. The Royal Palace of Falkland was the residence of James II, James IV, James V, Mary Queen of Scots, James VI and I, and visited by Charles I. More than any other Scottish palace, Falkland witnessed the rise and fall of the fortunes of the Stewart dynasty until 1651: Charles II left Falkland to face defeat and exile. Like many royal buildings and churches, Falkland Palace was damaged by fire while occupied by Cromwell's troops. John Patrick Chrichton Stuart, the 3rd Marques of Bute, acquired the office of Keeper in 1887 and rebuilt and restored much of the Palace. In 1952, The National Trust for Scotland was appointed Deputy Keeper by Major Michael Crichton Stuart, grandson of John Patrick. and his wife Barbara,. Their son Ninian is the current Hereditary Keeper, although the Palace is now in the care of The National Trust of Scotland. A full-length portrait of Elizabeth as Queen of Bohemia (on loan from the Palace of Holyrodhouse) is in the dressing room of the palace. See Thomas Puttfarken, Christopher Hartley, Roger Grant, and Eric Robson, *Falkland Palace and Royal Burgh* (Edinburgh, Scotland: Howie & Seath Ltd., 1995).

grandest of Scotland's royal residences.[34]   After James was crowned King of England in 1603, he and his entire family moved to England, where Elizabeth was placed in the care of Sir John Harington and his wife of Exton, the Countess of Bedford's parents, on October 19, 1603 by an order under the privy seal.[35]   At the Harington's estate, Coombe Abbey in Warwickshire, she received her early education, and from all reports it was a happy time for the princess.   As the daughter of a king, she was instructed privately, which was the convention.   There is no evidence that she received the classical training (Latin and Greek) typical of noble women of an early generation, yet Harington took his duties seriously and provided for her tutors in French and Italian, writing (especially French composition), and dancing; letters indicate that she read "the Book of Martyrs, a great Bible, and divers other volumes of histories."[36]   In addition, James himself often urged his children "to practice music and dancing," and Elizabeth most likely became proficient in both at an early age.[37]

The court must have seemed exciting for the young princess.   James I's love for literature, theater and the arts in general, added to the splendor and provided the young Elizabeth with a rich diet of artistic experiences during her formative years. Masques, ballets, theater, and musical concerts were regular occurrences, and the court music scene provided numerous opportunities for Elizabeth to hear the finest music available in England at the time, including a number of foreign virtuosi. William Byrd, John Bull, and Orlando Gibbons, the finest English musicians of the day, were all members of the royal establishment and therefore active at court while Elizabeth was growing up. Prince Henry, Elizabeth's beloved older brother, recruited the best foreign musicians and artists for his court and in a short time his household included the keyboard virtuoso John Bull, composer and violist Alfonso Ferrabosco, the lutenists Robert Johnson and Thomas Cutting, Thomas Lupo, Thomas Ford, and the Italian composer Angelo Notari. Surely Elizabeth, given her deep attachment to her brother, would have shared in his enthusiasm for fashionable entertainments and taken advantage of the opportunity to hear Henry's musicians.   The acoustic world in which she lived appears to have been a smorgasbord of auditory delights that helped to shape her musical taste.

---

[34] Linlithgow occupied an important strategic position on the route between Stirling and Edinburgh. It is described as having a lush green countryside surrounded with gardens. See John Ferguson, *Linlithgow Palace, Its History and Traditions* (Edinburgh: Oliver and Boyd, 1910). An old print of Linlithgow Palace is found on page 252.

[35] For additional information on the Harington family see Ian Grimble, *The Harington Family* (London: Jonathan Cape, 1957).

[36] Lord Harington (of Exton) to Sir John Harington, January 6, 1607, in: *Nugae Antiquae: Being a Miscellaneous Collection of Original Papers... by Sir John Harington, Kent. and by others*, ed. Henry Harington, rev. Thomas Park (London, 1804) II: 375; Harington of Exton, *Accounts Book, Exchequer of Receipt, Miscellanea*, cited in Green, *Elizabeth Electress Palatine*, 24; quoted in Lewalski, *Writing Women in Jacobean England*, 47.

[37] *GB-LBl Harleian MS. 6989*, f. 24.

From 1608 on Elizabeth was a frequent resident at court. She had a suite of apartments at Hampton Court, with a fine view of the river and gardens, and another at Whitehall.[38] A third residence was established for her at Kew, where she could enjoy the proximity to the court while pursuing her studies. The court provided Elizabeth with the opportunity to see ballets, and to take part in masques. Apparently Elizabeth attended her first court ballet on January 14, 1609, and in the same year she attended one in early February along with *The Masque of Queenes Celebrated from the House of Fame* by Ben Jonson. Both entertainments were presented in celebration of the nuptials of Viscount Haddington and the Lady Elizabeth Ratcliffe.[39] For this masque a surprising number of musicians and dancers are mentioned in the text, including John Alleyn, singer, Hierome Herne, dancer, Thomas Giles, choreographer, and Alfonso Ferrabosco.[40] The masque songs were evidently popular since four dances appear in Robert Dowland's *Varietie of Lute Lessons* (1610), and at least one tune is found in a number of other English sources.[41]

During this same period Elizabeth had the opportunity to meet two influential Italian musicians and to hear the latest Italian monody, those expressive solo songs with simple instrumental accompaniment that were all the rage in Italy during the early seventeenth century. In 1607 Queen Anne appointed the Italian lutenist John Maria Lugario as groom of her privy chamber and documents show that his salary was exceptionally high for the time due to his musical skill. Before his arrival in England, Lugario was active at the court of Mantua, one of the centers of early opera and where at the time Monteverdi was *maestro di capella*. Confirming Lugario's interest in monody, records show that he corresponded with Ottavio Rinuccini (the librettist for Peri's and Caccini's *Euridice*, two of the earliest monodies).[42] Even more important was the lutenist/composer Angelo Notari (born in Padua in 1566) who was recruited by Prince Henry for his personal musical

---

[38] Mary Anne Everett [Wood] Green, *Elizabeth, Electress Palatine and Queen of Bohemia*, revised edition (London: Methuen and Co., 1909), 17.

[39] Green refers to "a ballet...and a masque by Ben Jonson." See *Elizabeth, Electress Palatine*, 19; the text of *The Masque of Queens* is GB-Lbl, MS Royal 18. A. xiv; reproduced in H & S, vii; mentioned in Peter Walls, *Music in the English Courtly Masque* (Oxford, England: Clarendon Press, 1996), 343. Walls refers to a dance "with geometric and alphabetic figures" contained in Jonson's masque (122).

[40] Walls remarks that performers and composers are rarely mentioned in masque texts. It is the nobility honored by the masque whose names are prominently displayed. Peter Walls, *Music in the English Courtly Masque*, 35.

[41] Two other English sources that contain tunes from *The Queens Masque* are GB-Lbl, *Add. MS 15117* and *GB-Ob, MS Tenbury 1018*. Walls, 100.

[42] See Ashbee, *Records of English Court Music* (Kent, England: Snodland, 1991), iv: 16. Mentioned in Walls, 100. Also see A. Bertolotti, *Musici alla Corte dei Gonzaga in Mantova* (1890; repr. Bologna, 1969), 80-81, and Ian Spink, *English Song, Dowland to Purcell* (London, 1974, rev. 1984), 42.

retinue sometime in 1610.[43] Notari is frequently credited with introducing the monodic style to England with his published 1613 collection of songs – *Prime musiche nuove*, engraved by William Hole. *Prime musiche nuove* contains various settings of songs from Italian poems and a portrait of the composer, perhaps after a design by Constantino de'Servi. The use of the affectation "*musiche*" rather than the more common "*musica*" in the title betrays a desire on the part of the composer to be associated with the new Italian vocal style then in vogue.[44] Hearing this "new" music may have predisposed the young princess towards the latest musical fashion. At least one piece in *Parthenia* (Gibbon's *Prelude PAR* XXI)[45] makes use of many of these idioms (e.g., sequential writing, tonally directed harmony, invertible counterpoint) and may have been devised to delight the young player.

Other accounts and court records show that Elizabeth danced the Nymph of the Thames in the masque *Tethys Festival,* written by Samuel Daniel, on 5 June 1610, celebrating Henry's investiture as Prince of Wales.[46] Though this appears to be the first masque in which Elizabeth actively participated, her association with the Thames Nymph stayed, and later wedding tributes describe her marriage as the marriage of Thames and Rhine.[47] During the performance the young princess's ears would have been filled with the sounds of "soft musique" made by "twelve Lutes and twelve voyces."[48] "Soft musique" did not necessarily pertain to dynamic levels but rather to degrees of sophistication, tone color, and quality. We also know, for instance, that on 5 June 1610 Samuel Daniel's masque *The Order and Solemnitie of the Creation of the High and mightie Prince Henry*, and on 1 January 1611 Ben Jonson's *Oberon, the Fairy Prince* were presented at court. During the performance of *Oberon*, Elizabeth heard a group of twenty lutes making the magical sound of "a thousand twangling instruments," as Shakespeare's Caliban would say. She would also have been treated to the nasal sound of oboes (shawms)

---

[43] *GB-Lbl-Sloane MS 1707* gives a contemporary biography of Notari within an astrological scheme.

[44] Ian Spink, "Angelo Notari and his 'Prime Musiche Nuove,'" *Monthly Musical Record*, vol. 87 (September-October 1957), 175. It is interesting to note that the term "monody" was not coined around 1630.

[45] *PAR* is the abbreviation for *Parthenia* and is used here when referring to specific pieces in the volume.

[46] Nicols, ii, 348; *Elizabeth, Electress Palatine*, 21; Walls, 151-153.

[47] George Wither, "Epithalamia, or Nuptial Poems," in: *The Poetry of George Wither*, ed. Frank Sidgwick (London: A. H. Bullen, 1902), I: 173. Wither composed two lengthy epithalamia for the Princess's marriage, both with anti-Catholic sentiments in the foreground. The second is the most overtly anti-Catholic with implications for a dynastic union fostering a pan-Prostestant alliance: "Make the Rhyne and Thame an Ocean / That it may with might and wonder, / Whelme the pride of Tyber under" (lines 372-374). The Tiber is the river that runs by Rome. In the first epithalamium, Wither writes: "We hope that this will the uniting prove / Of countries and of nations by your love, / And that from out your blessed loins shall come / Another terror to the whore of Rome" (lines 189-192).

[48] Samuel Daniel, *Tethys Festival*, 1: 303; cited in Walls, 152.

that announced the entrance of the royal party at the performance of *Oberon*. These oboes were part of "loud music" which typically functioned to announce the arrival of the king and/or the beginning of the masque. Elizabeth was treated to the high, bright yet somewhat mellow sound of the cornett played by satyrs in *Oberon* and again in Beaumont's 1613 *Masque of the Inner Temple and Gray's Inn*, one of the entertainments presented at Elizabeth's own wedding.[49] Two other masques were presented during her time at court: Jonson's *Love Freed from Ignorance and Folly* on 3 February 1611, and Jonson's *Love Restored* on 6 January 1612.

Not only can we imagine the young Elizabeth's acoustic world through such descriptions, a world made up of strange and wonderful sounds that helped to form her musical ear, but surviving financial records further provide insight into the nature of Elizabeth's formal education and information about the identity of her teachers. Particularly revealing records about Elizabeth survive from the office of the Exchequer providing detailed information on every aspect of her life: instruction, travel expenses, wardrobe, among other domestic activities. However, a major obstacle to an accurate assessment of Elizabeth's abilities is that a woman's intellectual and musical accomplishments, even for the daughter of the king, were often not well documented, and her musical establishment at Kew was far less impressive than her brother's.[50] Despite this fact, a number of records and account books do give us the names of some of her teachers and amounts they were paid, and a fair number of first-hand descriptions of the young princess's accomplishments survive. That there are any records and comments about her musicality *at all* speaks loudly to her talents and achievements.

From documents it is clear that John Marchant instructed the lady Elizabeth on the virginals and that in 1611 he died leaving the position vacant. William Frost, in a letter to the Earl of Salisbury dated 8 December 1611, asks for a recommendation for the position:

> Mr. Marchant is latelie deceased who taught the princess to play upon the virginals therefore it may stand in your honorable favour to recomend me into that place by the means of the lord Chamberlin and the lord Harington. With my industrie in my studies, my diligence in my service and my dutiful acknowledgement of your honors goodness towards me. I shall continually to the utmost of my abilities endeavor to merit it and even pray for your honors long life and hapiness.
> Your humble servant, William Frost[51]

Unfortunately for Mr. Frost, he did not obtain the requested position, but records show that he was made a Gentleman of the Chapel Royal in 1611. It was John Bull who obtained the envious position of royal music instructor. An account book stemming from the half-year before her marriage establishes John Bull as

---

[49] Walls, *The Courtly Masque*, 151.

[50] The Princess's establishment was formed in 1608 when she was eleven years old.

[51] *GB-LBl Lansdowne MS 91 Hick's Papers* (1608-1610), f. 130-131ʳ. The letter is written in secretary hand.

Elizabeth's keyboard teacher, [Thomas] Hazard as the tuner of her virginals, and Walter Tucker as the musician who provided music for her dancing:

> To Doctor Bull that teacheth her grace on the virginalls for the fee: 20 pounds
> To Walter Tucker that playeth to her gr when she dannceth for his fee: 10 pounds
> Paid to Hazard that keepth her graces virginalls in tune for his stipend for the qrter ending at xpemas 1612: 10s.[52]

From the amounts paid one can assume that either Bull was held in higher regard than Tucker or Hazard, or that Bull was called upon more often than either of the other two. Another court document dated December 1612 established Mr Thomas Cardell as Elizabeth's dance teacher.[53]

Although a contemporary description of Elizabeth Stuart actually playing her virginals may never be found, there are a number of accounts that do refer to the young princess's musical ability. The clearest indication that Elizabeth was an exceptional keyboard player is found in *Parthenia's* dedication where Hole states that "The virgin *Parthenia*...To you Gracious Lady...she was entended," and requests "Your Grace...to lend your white hands." Not only were these technically difficult pieces assembled and composed for the princess's personal use, but the suggestion that she play them may indicate musical activities of a fairly broad scope, perhaps even demonstrations for visiting dignitaries at the request of James I. This possibility is reinforced by comments made in the panegyric on King James and his family in 1608 by the Scottish dignitary, Thomas Rosa.[54] Here Rosa describes in hyperbolic terms Elizabeth's cultivation and proficiency in languages and music at age twelve:

> In her [Princess Elizabeth] mastery of a great variety of languages, she can be compared, or preferred to ZENOBIA, Queen of Palmyra, to ARETIA and Cornelia. She also diligently cultivates the art of music is a great proficient in this art. For from the beginning this peaceful and noble art suited the natural talents of this most serene and illustrious virgin. Add to these qualities the sweetness of her manners and the liberal pursuits of both mind and body, which are suited to a royal princess [virgo = parthenos], no vulgar abilities. And then whatever was excellent and lofty in Elizabeth, Queen of England, is all concentrated in this one Virgin Princess, as her years allow.[55]

---

[52] This account book covers the time from "Michaelmas 1612" to "Ladie Daie 1613." Exchequer, *E407 /57 /2*; listed in Andrew Ashbee, *Records of English Court Music* (1603-1625) (Kent, England: Andrew Ashbee, 1991), V: 207.

[53] Lord Chamberlain Records, *LC2 / 4 (6)*; Ashbee, 37.

[54] There is some question about the identity of Thomas Rosa.

[55] Thomas Rosa, *Idaea, Sive de Jacobi Magnae Britanniae, Galliae et Hyberniae* (London, 1608), 322-323. This is a small rectangular handbook having once belonged to W. Gray in 1757. The entire text is in Latin. The letter referred to above is found in the last chapter under the heading "Guilielmus Parkerus, Montis-Aquilarum Dominus." Rosa

Rosa's choice of words, such as "serene," "sweetness," and "virgin," demonstrates his familiarity with conduct writers who insist on chaste and modest behavior for women above all, while his mention of "pursuits for mind and body" shows that Rosa was also up on the latest educational trends and that the young princess was schooled in the most current liberal arts curriculum. Furthermore, the description of a young girl's musical abilities would have impressed and captivated the court and fit well within the guidelines for the accomplished woman. More importantly this description served to advertise her attractiveness to future suitors. It would have been unusual for a young noble woman to perform in front of a male visitor. Though music is recommended for study, musical performance by young women in front of men was strongly discouraged by conduct writers fearing that the women would appear wanton and unchaste. Linda Austern explains that these dual positions concerning music present a paradox: the musical art, while recommended for study by women of high class, was simultaneously considered dangerous for its ability to inflame passions and erotic desire.[56] On the other hand, taking pride in his daughter's artistic accomplishments to the point of having her perform for others would have been in keeping with James' habit of showcasing his artistic trophies.

Finally some thoughts on how Elizabeth actually learned to play the virginals. The primary method of teaching students the fundamentals of languages as well as music consisted in the memorizing and emulating so-called *exempla classica*, models by eminent masters. In this sense, learning of languages and music were closely interrelated, and both entailed copying down exemplary works of different kinds. This could explain in part why there are numerous hand-written versions of pieces from *Parthenia* in personal manuscripts. By copying, students would have learned the principles of harmony and counterpoint, rhythm and meter, form and structure. Thus it should be no surprise that *Parthenia* consists of a series of musical *exempla* intended for study in this fashion. One can presume that Elizabeth learned music and the virginals in the accepted fashion. It is regrettable that there are no manuscript versions or other actual documentation of Elizabeth having copied music for purposes of study in this way, or of her trying to compose, as we do have of her childish attempts at poetry.

Parthenia for the Princess Elizabeth's use

Parthenia's dedication, signed by the engraver William Hole, claims that the volume was compiled and intended for Elizabeth's personal use: "The virgin PARTHENIA...I offer up to your virgin / Highnesses. To you (Gracious Lady) even from the byrth she was entended;" and it claims that Dr. John Bull was

---

mentions Hermes Trismegistus on page 289. I am indebted to Diskin Clay for much of this translation.

[56] For a fuller discussion of the eroticized female musician, please see Linda Austern's chapter in the current volume.

Elizabeth's personal instructor in music. In all likelihood the contents of *Parthenia* reflect to a considerable extent the repertoire that Elizabeth was expected to master by age 16 years, her age at the time of marriage, and convey her personal tastes in music, her abilities, her concerns (both political and personal), and represent in certain cases even her name. An examination of the technical demands and styles of the 21 pieces not only provide information about Elizabeth's skills, but serve as indications of the high level of musical excellence she and aristocratic women in general were expected to obtain. The book consists primarily of high class English dances (fifteen pavans and galliards, four preludes, one regular set of variations, one fantasia) that show Elizabeth was familiar with all the significant forms an English pavan and galliard could take, and was acquainted with some of the finest and most instructive fantasia and preludes.

Parthenia also provides the means for seeing Elizabeth as a performer, how she *must* have moved, and how she must have appeared when playing *Parthenia's* twenty-one pieces. The numerous visual representations of young women seated at keyboards during the sixteenth and seventeenth centuries suggest a keen interest in a women's body, especially as it appears making music. Representations generally show the female musician as dignified, with a gaze directed away from the viewer, as if to proclaim her chaste and of good reputation.[57] A good example is the frontispiece on the title-page of *Parthenia* which makes play of these concerns by depicting a young woman with flowing hair (a sign of virginity) seated at the virginals and appearing transported by the sounds she is making. The young woman is richly dressed, and the multitude of folds in her garment disguises the shape of her torso. Her eyes are closed, her hands actively playing upon the keyboard with left-hand fingers curved inward away from the keys. The player's serene countenance and the activity of the hands serve to draw the viewer's eyes away from her body. Music is placed on a rack just above the keyboard, perhaps signifying that the contents of *Parthenia* are for study and the cultivation of musical literacy. The image conveys virginity, wealth, and refined taste.

Although various claims have been made about the identity of the woman on *Parthenia's* cover, ranging from Dorothie Evans to Princess Elizabeth and Parthenia herself, it is in fact an exact copy of an engraving by Jacob Matham (1571-1631) after a 1588 design by Henrick Goltzius (1558-1617).[58] In Hole's engraving the two angels found in the original picture behind St. Cecilia are omitted and the organ replaced with virginals, thus removing all obvious religious connotations. In all other respects the pictures are identical right down to the folds in her dress, hair, and position of hands.

---

[57] Please consult Linda Austern's chapter in this book for reproductions of women making music.
[58] Otto Erich Deutsch, "Cecilia and Parthenia," *Musical Times* 100 (1959), 591-592; also see *Hendrik Goltzius and the Printmakers of Harlem* (Connecticut: The University of Connecticut, Museum of Art, 1972).

In all likelihood Elizabeth and purchasers of *Parthenia* did not recognize the young woman on the cover as St. Cecilia, although recognition would have been possible among the well-bred.   There was a well-established literary and iconographic tradition associating Cecilia with music.[59] Certain current events may also have brought the saint to mind, and Cecilia's association with the idea of mourning-into-joy, "understood as a musical motion of the heart" would have made her the perfect emblem of a wedding gift for a musical princess who had recently lost her beloved brother.[60] Furthermore, nearly all sixteenth century representations of St. Cecilia are similar in portraying her as a noblewoman whose facial features betray an air of indifference to the physical world very like the image on the cover.

Writings in England and on the continent, while recommending the study of music for well-bred young women, also consistently emphasize that a woman must demonstrate modesty when performing, and must engage in limited physical motion. Both visual representations and conduct books repeat Baldassar Castiglione's insistence that a women's "sweet mildness" should be evident in all her deeds.[61] However, if one looks beyond conduct books with their prescriptions for womanly behavior and examines the pieces themselves, their technical demands and musical requirements, and considers what is actually involved in executing the passages, the picture that emerges is quite different from the prescribed one. Following the advice offered by the Spanish music theorist Santa María, Elizabeth would not have sat stiffly at the keyboard when playing rapid passages, but instead she would have inclined her hands a little towards the running part.[62] Traditionally studies in performance practice have been absorbed with reconstructing the musical text; however here it is suggested that it might be more fruitful to extend the notion of "practice" to include awareness of what Jane Bowers and Marcia Citron call "sociological nuances," those bodily movements required to perform *Parthenia's* pieces. An examination of this kind would be particularly important because it begins with a woman's actual experience with music rather than with a set of prescriptions that reflect male preferences, as do books on conduct and courtesy.[63] Did Elizabeth actually sit demurely at the keyboard with arms stretched wide at the opening of *The Queen's Command (PAR* XX)? How did she execute difficult turns

---

[59] See Thomas Connolly, *Mourning Into Joy* (New Haven and London: Yale University Press, 1994), and Peter Williams, *The Organ in Western Culture 750-1250* (Cambridge, England: Cambridge University Press, 1993), 3-7.

[60] Connolly, 4. Connolly points out that the word "motion" in earlier times carries the general sense of change without implying movement from place to place.

[61] Baldessar Castiglione, *The Courtyer of Count Baldessar*, transl. Thomas Hoby (London: Wyllyam Seres, 1561, sigs. Cci-Cci^v.

[62] *Libro llamado Arte de tañer fantasia* (Valladolid, 1565; facsimile Farnborough, 1972), fol. 38v.

[63] For a list of books on conduct and courtesy published in England between c. 1530-1640, see Frank Whigham, *Ambition and Privilege. The Social Tropes of Elizabethan Courtesy Theory* (Berkeley, Los Angeles, and London: University of California Press, 1984), 199. All books listed are by male authors.

and quick bass shifts in *Galiardo Mistress Mary Brownlow* (*PAR* V)? And how did she manage the incessant runs in the concluding *Prelude* (*PAR* XX1)? For if the young princess could play these pieces, then she would have had to have been an agile performer who could handle subtle metric ambiguity, able to make rapid movements with her arms, and a player who engaged in a wider range of physical gestures than generally acknowledged and prescribed by Castiglione and others.

A brief analysis of Orlando Gibbon's *The Queen's Command* (*PAR* XX) leaves little doubt that it was composed specifically for the princess on the occasion of her marriage. The piece is a series of short variations on a two-strain theme that varies the first section before the second section is played.[64] Gibbons (1583-1625), the youngest contributor to the volume,[65] was a member of the court establishment, appointed organist at the Chapel Royal sometime before 1615, virginalist to King James I in 1619, and later organist of Westminster Abbey in 1623.[66] It is in *The Queen's Command* that the emblematic significance of the pitches *E* (for Elizabeth) and *F* (for Frederick), musical tokens mentioned in the dedication, are fully realized. Not only does the soprano in each strain begin alternately on the pitch *E* or *F*, but also the first and second notes of nearly every strain are *E* and *F* (or *F* and *E*), as Musical Example 16.1 shows. That the two pitches are intended as a motto is made plain in the dedication when Hole speaks of learning "to twine together ... neighbor letters *E* and *F*, .. .that make so sweet a consonant ...[and when] wedded together seem lively hierogliphicks [sic]of the harmony of marriage." These metaphors are conventional since descriptions of Christian marriage are full of musical imagery often comparing wedded bliss to sweet harmony or the bride and groom to well-tuned musical instruments.[67] However, here we have not only the literary conventions in play but an example of them represented in music. These musical puns must have tickled the young bride-to-be. But how did Elizabeth perform this piece assuming that she recognized the musical puns? The very opening is unusual for the repertory: the two hands are set more than two octaves

---

[64] Gibbons varies the two sections the second time around. The variation of the repeat of the first strain, which itself is varied, employs a type of invertible counterpoint where the ground is now heard in the treble voice for the first measures of the variation; the running sixteenth-note figure of the of the first strain is now in the bass.

[65] For a recent, rigorously researched study of Gibbons's life, see John Harley, *Orlando Gibbons and the Gibbons Family of Musicians* (Aldershot, Brookfield, Singapore, and Sidney: Ashgate, 1999).

[66] The reason for his involvement in the publication of *Parthenia* is not clear other than he was one of the finest musicians at court at the time. Gibbons was not known to have had any close association with Princess Elizabeth or Prince Henry, nor was he involved with the wedding festivities other than contributing to the volume as far as can be determined. He did however, make a keyboard arrangement of a tune from Beaumont's masque for the wedding. It is assumed that Gibbons was part of the newly married couple's entourage that journeyed to Germany following the wedding in late April.

[67] Henry Smith, *A Preparation to Marriage* (London, 1591; reprint of first edition, Amsterdam: orbis Terrarum, 1975), 55.

Musical Example 16.1 – Orlando Gibbons, *The Queenes Command* (xx) mm. 1-14

mm.17-18

mm. 21-22

apart leaving the bosom of the performer in full view. Could this have meant to be enticing? Since Elizabeth and Frederick were only betrothed at the time, the music and prefatory material contain numerous puns on male and female virginity, and one suspects that, like the music, the performance enhanced the jokes. The dedication also declares that Elizabeth is to play the music for the pleasure of her "Great Frederike," her husband-to-be, thus keeping the music-making well within the bounds of expected propriety and marital fidelity.

To perform *The Queens Command* arms are spread wide and the right hand must continually and swiftly shift direction (in Strains V, VI, and VII) following the flow of ascending and descending groups of sixteenth-notes, the hand now inclined to the left and then to the right – coy, evasive movements. Similarly the left-hand impetuously rushes to-and-fro in Strain VIII. Only in Strain VI do the hands briefly come close, and only for a moment before rushing apart. The resulting visual image is one of an inviting (with arms open) yet flirtatious (fingers darting this way and that) woman.

The Queen's Command can also be heard as an ingeniously devised musical dialogue between the bride and groom. Not only can the pitches *E* and *F* be viewed as emblems, but they also serve as signals indicating who is "speaking" at any moment: the two-strain theme provides a convenient opportunity for a she-said / he-said structure, and where interplay within each strain is the rule. Elizabeth, signaled by the pitch *E* in the upper part, is the first to put forth her question playfully in dotted rhythms with a melody inflected upwards. Frederick represented by the pitch *F* briefly joins her in the second measure only to be cut-off in the third.   Strain II, beginning on *F*, could be thought Frederick's jocular response (to Elizabeth's Strain I) presented in nearly all quarter-notes, perhaps alluding to other early seventeenth - century dialogue songs where the bass singer's musical responses were often rhythmically rigid and characterized by leaps, the result of being tied to a functional bass line.   John Dowland's masque song, *Up Merry Mates* (from *A Pilgrimes Solace*) is a good example, especially measures 8-15.[68]   Strain III of *The Queen's Command* again beginning on *E* is a flurry of sixteenth-notes in the treble, maintained by the repeat of Strain I's bass line.   The reprise varies the bass in sixteenth-notes while the treble restates the opening four-measure tune.   Predictably, Strain IV begins on *F* and answers the exuberance of the last variation with its own flurry of sixteenth-notes. This interpretation suggests a very animated performance, one that would emphasize the highs (female) and lows (male) of the instrument.

Mary Brownlow Galliard (*PAR* V), the second of William Byrd's galliards in the *Parthenia*, is this composer's most splendid example of the galliard idiom. William Byrd (1539/40-1623), "a father of Musick," was the most prominent English composer of his time.[69]   Although he composed in most of the idioms of the day, it was his contribution to English keyboard music that is most astounding. In *Mary Brownlow Galliard,* rhythmic ambiguity and symmetrical balance are perfectly reconciled with virtuosity not encountered elsewhere in Byrd's keyboard dances, and even the leaping baseline is accommodated without awkwardness.

The Mary in question was one of the daughters of Richard Brownlow of Holborn, a lawyer of some prominence. She was born in 1591 and married in November 1613 to William Saunders.[70]   Inclusion of a galliard named in her honor was likely Byrd's wedding tribute to another young woman, possibly a former student.   Much of the galliard's interest comes from its shifting pulse, the constant ambiguity as to whether it is in 3/2 or 3/4 (or 6/4) meter. The rate of harmonic change in general is fast, and the wealth of sixteenth-note figures suggest a relatively slow, but jaunty performing tempo. Interesting is the way the rhythmic groups are articulated by changes in harmony, so that each stressed note in the melody (first of the new rhythmic groups) is accompanied by a significant chord change: the tonic is heard at the start of the first 3/2 group (beat 1, m. 1), the

---

[68] John Dowland, *A Pilgrimes Solace* (London, 1612); a portion is reproduced in Peter Walls, *Music in the English Courtly Masque*, 67. Not surprisingly, the "question" in Gibbons's piece is not put forth in speech rhythms as it is in the Dowland song.

[69] The epitaph is recorded in the Old Cheque Book of the Chapel Royal under the date 1623; quoted in John Harley, *William Byrd, Gentleman of The Chapel Royal* (Hants, England and Brookfield Vermont: Ashgate Publishing Ltd., 1999), 153. Harley provides the most detailed account of his Byrd's life to date. He has determined that Byrd was born between 1539-40, several years earlier than initially thought. See Alan Brown, "England," 36, for instance.

[70] See Lady Elizabeth Cust, *Records of the Cust Family*, 2nd Series (London: Wardour Press, 1909).

dominant signals the start of a 3/4 group (beat 1, m 2), the subdominant indicates a return to 3/2 (beat 1, m. 3), etc. Such subtly makes this the most intensely compelling of all Byrd's galliards, and perhaps the finest galliard of the entire repertory.   Though highly varied and complex, the planned symmetry of the rhythmic groupings (odd measures clearly in 3/2 and even measures generally in 3/4) contribute a sense of balance and dignity to what could be chaotic in a less agile composer, and could be rendered incoherent by an inapt performer. Playing some of the rapid turns and difficult hand shifts in conjunction with shifting metrical accents must have been a challenge both mentally and physically to the young princess.   Both require movements that are calculated, not delicate, and certainly not demure. "Sweetness" seems to have little to do with the execution of this most difficult piece.

The volume's final prelude (*PAR* XXI) is by Orlando Gibbons. Gibbons was widely recognized as a keyboard virtuoso, and his technical fluency is reflected in the rapid passages in many of his contributions to *Parthenia*. The "bell" passage (mm. 20-22) of the prelude is an example of such demanding writing, and one that would require great dexterity on the part of Elizabeth. It is characterized by sixteenth-note descending scales first as d^2 to d^1, then e^2 to e^1, f^2 to f^1, etc. This passage is particularly difficult for a number of reasons. The ingenious imitation between the bass and inner voice (namely, the bass begins on a weak beat and is answered a fifth above on a strong beat) must be brought out, and the doubling of key treble pitches by the inner voice which produces a marvelously novel effect by creating the sense of prolonging the pitches, requires considerable coordination.   When done correctly, this enhances the impression of bells, and suggests the "open" ringing of a peal (that is, bells without leather encased clappers) specifically associated with joyous celebrations such as victories, coronations and weddings.

Finally one must consider John Bull's contributions to the volume for it was he who instructed the young princess and would have known her abilities, weaknesses, and preferences better than any one else.   Bull's (1563-1628) involvement with the publication of *Parthenia* seems clear: he was appointed a Gentleman of the Chapel Royal in January 1585/6, associated with Prince Henry's establishment, as well as Princess Elizabeth's keyboard instructor. Shortly after Elizabeth and Frederick's wedding, he left England never to return.[71]

John Bull's contributions to *Parthenia* include two pavans in *G* major which differ in a number of telling ways. The *Pavana* (*PAR* XII) has three strains with decorated repeats, and F-natural is prominently placed (as second note in tenor);[72] whereas, the *Pavana: St. Thomas Wake* (*PAR* X) is actually a variation on a two-strain theme, where each 16-measure strain begins with an anacrusis, and F-sharp is

---

[71] The most thorough study of John Bull's keyboard music to date is Walker Cunningham, *The Keyboard Music of John Bull* (Ann Arbor: UMI Research Press, 1984).

[72] *PAR* followed by a Roman numeral stands for the number and position of the piece in *Parthenia*. Individual pieces are all given a Roman numeral in the original print.

prominently displayed (as the third tenor note). Bull appears to be concerned that his pupil distinguish between the different forms G major can take by either an initial emphasis on the natural-7th scale degree (which is perhaps an older, inflected style) or raised-7th scale degree (signaling the newer, decidedly major style). Bull's remaining contributions include four galliards also of markedly different character: in addition to one in three strains whose first is divided unequally (*PAR* XIV), Bull includes one in two strains of unequal length (*PAR* XV), one in three strains whose first is divided unequally (*PAR* XIII), and one which, like its paired pavan, is a set of variations of which the third and fourth strains feature a cantus firmus in the treble and the two-voice texture of bicinia. The galliards further display variety in metric accents, implied tempo, emphasis on florid writing, cadence structures, tonal proclivities, and other allusive features. Bull's G major galliards (*PAR* XI & XIII) introduce F-sharp/F-natural opposition, and require an active left hand capable of playing rapid eighth- and sixteenth-notes. Bull's final *D* minor galliards (*PAR* XIV & XV) make clear that the young Princess was expected to be able to handle both common and uncommon metric groupings, and symmetrical and asymmetrical cadences.[73] From all these one gets the sense that Elizabeth was an intelligent, capable musician aware of musical subtleties and with a quick hand-to-eye coordination.

Elizabeth as dedicatee

One final way to access the Elizabeth's relationship with the arts is through dedications, prefatory literature that adorns most music books of the period. Despite Elizabeth's musical accomplishments, dedications suggest that her primary duty was to be a model of (Protestant) Christian virtue. She attracted a large number of dedications over her life, particularly from religious writers and moralists like Thomas Cooper, Thomas Draxe, Daniel Dyke, and Francis Herring. Thomas Cooper's 1606 *The Romish Spider* was the first book to contain a dedication to the then ten year old princess, after which numerous other books and sermons began to appear with similar morally inspired dedications to her. Such books focused on *The Christian Armorie* needed to fight *Popish Pietie* and *The Romish Spider with his Web of Treason* and to sustain *The Christains Daily Sacrifice*.[74] More then likely these books were reactions to the shocking moment in 1605 when government authorities uncovered a secret plan to blow up the House of Parliament and King James along with it. The purpose of the Gunpowder Plot, as it

---

[73] The apposition of same genre pieces differing in some specific detail was nothing new; nearly all Venetian keyboard collections preceding *Parthenia* (Gabrieli, Merulo) were published according to genre (e.g., Toccatas in one book, Canzonas in another) and arranged to demonstrate the variety of invention possible for that given genre.

[74] Francis Herring, *Popish Pietie* (London, 1610); Thomas Cooper, *The Romish Spider with his Web of Treason* (London, 1606); Thomas Cooper, *The Christians Daily Sacrifice* (London, 1608).

was later called, was to reintroduce Catholicism as the state religion through the marriage of Princess Elizabeth Stuart to a Catholic. It is natural that authors dealing with the Protestant battle against Roman Catholicism would think to dedicate their books to the young princess who was nearly kidnapped and martyred.

The years 1610-1612 were also taken up with marriage negotiations for Elizabeth, and dedications frequently compare the young princess with the past Queen. Typically she is linked with Queen Elizabeth through association with the Queen's emblem of the phoenix. One dedication by Thomas Draxe (d. 1618), "Bachelar in Divinitie," who in 1611 published *The Christian Armorie*, calls her "the Phoenix...a glorious starre in our firmament" and wishes her to be "a conqueresse over sinne and satan." In 1611 the female poet Aemilia Lanyer praises the princess's "goodly wisdome" and refers to the dead Queen as "The Phoenix of her age."[75] The phoenix, a popular symbol of the Renaissance, stood for a variety of things including the sun, chastity, resurrection, immortality, eternal youth, self-sufficiency, and in Christian art, was "as much the bird of Christ as the nightingale was of Mary."[76] No doubt there was consensus that the lady Elizabeth embodied the spirit of the late, great Queen, a view encapsulated by Clement Cotton in his dedicatory epistle to her: "wherein your Grace shall walke in her Royall stepps, who though dead, yet now seemes to live in you."[77] There were many other dedications comparing the young princess to the former Queen. *Queene Elizabeth's Looking-glasse of Grace and Glory*, by James Maxwell, and *Queene Elizabeth Paraleld in Her Princely Vertues*, by William Leigh, are but two examples. The Scottish Maxwell further compares Elizabeth to her "most noble Grandmother Queene Marie of Scotland." A rare survivor from this period is by Barnaby Rich who marks Elizabeth as a good woman with the virtues of "modesty, bashfullness, silence, abstinence, sobrietie," all attributes that would make her the ideal spouse, at least in Jacobean England.[78]

During these same years Elizabeth is transformed into the icon of Protestant aspirations and identified with her brother Prince Henry and his internationalist Protestant policies. When Henry died suddenly in November of 1612 the country

---

[75] Aemilia Lanyer, *Salve deus rex Judaeorum* (London, 1611). This book also contains a dedication to Elizabeth's mother, Queen Anne, and one to "all virtuous ladies." The symbol of a phoenix was popular in the Renaissance and used by a number of women before Queen Elizabeth. Joan of Arc used a painted image of the phoenix in flames for her device; Mary Queen of Scots also used the phoenix in flames as her impress borrowed from her mother; and a phoenix in flames graced Jane Seymour's badge. See Douglas J. McMillan, "The Phoenix," in: *Mythical and Fabulous Creatures*, ed. Malcolm South (New York; Wesport, Connecticut; London: Greenwood Press, 1987), 59-71. Henry Peacham, the Younger, also refers to William Byrd as "our phoenix," in *The Compleat Gentleman* (London, 1622; reprint, New York: Cornell University Press, 1962), 112-113.

[76] Linda Austern, "Nature, Culture, Myth, and the Musician," *Journal of the American Musicological Society* 51 (1998): 1-47.

[77] Clement Cotton, *The Mirror of Martyrs* (London, 1613).

[78] Barnaby Rich, *The Excellency of Good Women* (London, 1613).

was plunged into mourning, and many books bemoaning or "bewailing" the prince's death were dedicated to Elizabeth: Robert Allyne dedicated his *Funerall Elegies* to her, and Thomas Campion included a dedication to her in his *Songs of Mourning Bewailing the Death of Prince Henry*. These tributes were balanced with others that celebrated Elizabeth's marriage, which took place only a few months after the Prince's death;[79] Henry Peacham, the Younger, even managed to combine mourning and nuptial hymns in one volume.[80]

The years 1614-18 were relatively happy times for the new couple. Accounts of her life in Heidelberg, the chief Palatinate city, were reported in detail to an England eager to hear. The English public learned of her hunting parties, her menagerie of monkeys and lapdogs, and read of the wondrous geometrical gardens with speaking statues, mechanical fountains, and musical grottoes devised by Salomon De Caus upon Frederick's command. News of Elizabeth's pregnancy almost immediately after arriving in Heidelberg gave rise to dedications in books such as *The Mothers Blessing*, by Dorothy Leigh, reflecting her new state.

Tragically this ideal life was not to continue. The Bohemian crisis of 1618-1620, which touched off the Thirty Years' War, was a time of serious struggle and hardship for Elizabeth and Frederick. They found themselves at the center of a religious war, their Protestantism pitted against the powerful Roman Catholic Habsburg league with no reinforcements forthcoming from James. Elizabeth and Frederick were forced to leave their Arcadian existence in Heidelberg and to seek refuge in Prague, where on 7 November 1619, Elizabeth was proclaimed a nursing mother of the church, and Queen of Bohemia. During this period there are only a few books with dedications to Elizabeth, perhaps reflecting James's pacifism and refusal to take any action in the proceedings.[81] William Lithgow, however, did include a dedication to her in his *The Pilgrimes Farewell. The Joyes and Miseries of Peregrination* (1618), and Francis Bacon included one in his *The Wisdom of the Ancients* (1619), published by John Bill. The years 1623-24 saw another wave of dedications to Elizabeth. John Wing, for instance, included a dedication to her in

---

[79] Three books published in London commemorating the wedding are: Joannes Maria de Franchis, *Of the Most Auspicious Marriage Betwixt Frederick, Count Palatine, and Elizabeth* (London, 1613); Abraham Scultetus, *A Sermon Preached Before Frederick the V* (London, 1613); and Robert Allyne, *Tears of Joy at the Happy Departure of Frederick and Elizabeth, Prince and Princesse Palatine* (London, 1613).

[80] Henry Peacham, the Younger, *The Period of Mourning; Disposed into Six Visions Together with Nuptiall Hymnes* (London, 1613).

[81] James is often condemned for not supporting his children in this affair, but the motivations for his refusal were complex. As Barbara Kiefer Lewalski points out, James "detested Protestant radicalism and the challenge to political absolutism, which it fostered." He preferred the role of mediator, not warrior; James hoped to strengthen ties with Hapsburg Spain, not sever them. See Barbara Kiefer Lewalski, *Writing Women in Jacobean England* (Cambridge, Massachusetts, and London, England: Harvard University Press, 1993), 56-57.

his *The Saints Advantage, A Sermon* (1623), an overtly religious book. All books dedicated to Elizabeth after 1630 are religious meditations on psalms, death, and Christian combat or pilgrimage.

From Elizabeth's association with noted Jacobean writers, visual artists, and musicians, one might expect a number of dedications to her in literary, musical, and other artistic works. Yet this does seem to be the case. No masque texts or romances are dedicated to her, and no song-books make mention of her. Evidently the public regarded Elizabeth more as a bastion of religious virtue than as an enthusiastic reader of novels and willing participant in revels. This may account in part for the overlooking of Elizabeth's musical significance in favor of a more political reading of her life. *Parthenia* is unique, for it is the only book that draws attention to Elizabeth's complex relationship with the arts, and the only musical work that firmly identifies Elizabeth as a musician capable of performing complex keyboard pieces. That this is the case does not diminish Elizabeth's importance in the history of music. It only emphasizes her achievements in a society where women's creative contributions were typically downplayed. *Parthenia,* and the woman to whom it was dedicated, offer us a fascinating glimpse inside a larger, untold female music making, of which Elizabeth was perhaps an exceptional example.

Chapter 17

Epilogue: Francesca Among Women, a '600 Gynecentric View

Suzanne G. Cusick

I want to begin this epilogue by affirming the metaphor invoked in this book's subtitle, and in Thomasin LaMay's introduction: where LaMay writes of many-headed melodies, the threatening proliferation of different paths through musical space, I read an echo of the multiplicity – the refusal to be One – long advocated by the complex and determinedly multivocal web of texts known as feminist theory that has been produced on both sides of the Atlantic since the early 1970s. I hear in my imagination Medusa's laugh, the virtuosic duet of *La jeune née*. In the many-headed melodies of these essays many pairs of lips speak together in their song. I hear the paradoxes of women's history and *ecriture feminine* that comes from listening closely to the traces of women's lives and voices as they rise and touch contrapuntally across cultures, across oceans, across intellectual frames of reference that allow both the sameness of "womanhood" and the many differences of culture and ethnicity to be, and to be clearly known.

I want, too, to affirm and to celebrate the ongoing (and necessarily multivocal, multidisciplinary, many-headed) work of feminist recuperation that these essays represent. For although it is sometimes shunned as if it were old-fashioned, "theoretically naïve," or in any case already done, the work of women recovering our own history has barely begun in our time. It is work that has been done before, work that has been shunned and then forgotten before. Like the similar knowledges "queer" scholarship has periodically recreated about the multiple forms and uses of human sexuality, women's knowledges about our individual and multiply, unpredictably collective pasts seem caught in an endless cycle of memory, forgetfulness, and re-membering. Perhaps the cycle of loss and recovery is simply true for all of us who are human; but the pain of loss is especially acute, the work of re-membering especially tiring for those of us who cannot bring ourselves to believe in the univocal world Athena crafted from Medusa's pain, that world that deliberately folded Difference so violently into One as to replicate the very theft of personhood and dignity and self that was the Gorgon's rape.

Toward the beginning of her introduction to this volume, Thomasin LaMay imagines for readers that such "exceptional" women musicians as Francesca Caccini and Barbara Strozzi might seem different to us if we knew them not through the documents, institutions and knowledges by which generations of androcentric music histories have defined the musical world that was important to men in early modern Europe, but instead through an understanding of a "larger musical culture which included women." How, she asks implicitly, would these well-known women seem if their lives and musicalities were understood from the vantage of a gynecentric music history focused firmly on re-membering early modern women's musical worlds? When I first read the challenge this book's introduction poses to music historians, I thought I knew part of the answer. For I had just been reading an extraordinary, twenty-three page manuscript sketch of Francesca Caccini's musical life, buried in a 161-page account of contemporary women's music-making as it could be known from the Granducato of Tuscany in the late 1620s. I had been reading, that is, an account of Francesca Caccini that situated her musical excellence firmly in a gynecentric vision of the musical world: and indeed, as LaMay's preface had predicted, both the woman and her work look different.

What is this source? What is its vision of a woman's musical world like? And how does Francesca Caccini look amid such a world? In homage to LaMay's vision and to the hard work of re-membering the authors in this volume have done, I offer here a preliminary account of Cristoforo Bronzini's 1620s portrayal of Caccini's gynecentric musical world.

The source: Cristoforo Bronzini's *Della dignità e nobiltà delle donne*

Commissioned by the two women who ruled Florence as Regents in the 1620s, Archduchess Maria Maddalena d'Austria and her mother-in-law Granduchess Christine de Lorraine, and published in four volumes between 1624 and 1632, Cristoforo Bronzini's *Della dignità e nobiltà delle donne* was part of an intensive cultural program to justify female rule.[1] Bronzini's arguments play out in the conventional form of a dialogue among leisured men and women. Seeking refuge from Rome's July heat in the garden of that city's Medici palace, their conversation was planned to fill twenty-four "days" in cooling contemplation of womanhood's capacity for excellence. Ably summarized by Constance Jordan and Letizia Panizza, Bronzini's dialogue has become relatively well-known to scholars of early modern womanhood as an important proto-feminist text, one of the last interventions in the centuries-long debate about gender sometimes called the "querelle des femmes."[2] Valorizing the

---

[1] Cristoforo Bronzini, *Della dignità e nobiltà delle donne* (Florence: Zanobi Pignoni, 1624-1632).

[2] Constance Jordan, *Renaissance Feminism. Literary texts and Political Models* (Ithaca and London: Cornell University Press, 1990), 266-269. See also Letizia Panizza's introduction to Lucretia Marinella, *The nobility and excellence of women, and the defects and vices of men* (*La nobiltà delle donne, co' difetti et mancamenti degli uomini*), ed. and trans. Anne Dunhill (Chicago: University of Chicago Press, 1999), and Ginevra Conti Odorisio, *Donne e società nel Seicento* (Rome: Bulzoni, 1979) for analyses of Bronzini's social and intellectual relationships with female proto–feminists of the early *seicento*.

feminine over the masculine at every conceivable turn, Bronzini asserted the equality of women and men as an absolute value, necessary to the welfare of the state. Sexual difference, for Bronzini, was irrelevant except insofar as "generation"– that is, what we call human reproduction – required that different body parts be put into play. In a still shocking adumbration of late twentieth-century constructionist views, he dismissed the hierarchies of gender as resulting from "the most insolent tyranny of men, usurped unjustly in every sphere of life."[3] Further, Bronzini envisioned an ideal political world in which courageous women would command with piety rather than violence, "victorious in a tranquil and loving peace..."[4] Like many Florentine apologists for Medici power, he grounded his notions of the state in classical references, especially those that used the well-ordered household as a metonym for the state, choosing his allusions carefully from sources that praised the equality of husbands and wives. Unusually for Florentine political theorists, Bronzini grounded his vision of an ideal state based on gender equality in Biblical exegesis, as well: he claimed that woman was first created "free," that she had been subjected to man as her punishment for sinning in Eden, and that she had been liberated from that subjection by the birth of Jesus. As Jordan quotes him "Woman herself (as Mary) has this advantage, regaining that legitimate lordship of the human race which she lost through diabolical wit."[5]

Although Bronzini's arguments were carefully couched in terms of the conventional counter-Reformation piety with which all his patrons' political behaviors were saturated, he soon ran afoul of the Inquisition's censors. Only four "days" of a projected twenty-four day dialogue were published.[6] But about ten years ago Kelley Harness discovered that the rest of the dialogue existed as a twenty-five volume manuscript among the Magliabecchiana in the Biblioteca nazionale centrale of Florence.[7] To my knowledge no one has attempted to engage the truly elephantine scope of this manuscript. Yet those twenty-five volumes, languishing ill-indexed, un-catalogued and all but impenetrable in Florence's Biblioteca nazionale, reveal the encyclopedic scope of the project the Medici women had assigned Bronzini. Most of

---

[3] Cristoforo Bronzini, *Della dignità e nobiltà delle donne. Settimana prima, Giornata prima* (Florence: Zanobi Pignoni, 1624), sig. H8v, as quoted in Jordan, *Renaissance Feminism*, 267.

[4] Bronzini, 1624, as quoted in Jordan, *Renaissance Feminism*, 266. See also her note 14, where she cites the original of this passage to sig. Bv.

[5] Bronzini, 1624, sig. A6v, as quoted in Jordan, *Renaissance Feminism*, 268.

[6] Two drafts of Bronzini's appeal to the Inquisition are bound together in I-Fn, Palat. 497.XIII, pp 190-195 and pp. 197-205.

[7] The manuscript, I-Fn, Magl. VIII. 1513-1538, includes the text of the four published volumes of Bronzini's *Della dignità e nobiltà delle donne*, along with eighteen volumes of fair-copy text (many with a second 'part' of draft material, and a draft index, and most between 300 and 500 pages long) that had been prepared for printing but never published, and three volumes of index. I am extremely grateful to Professor Harness for directing my attention to these volumes many years ago, in personal correspondence.

the volumes rehearse the central arguments about women's political authority that Jordan summarized, entwined with long lists and biographical sketches of "women worthies" whom he could claim to have made important contributions to some human enterprise. These claims usually adjoin a gynecentric exposition of the subject in question, whether it be philosophy, poetry, painting or politics. Almost always each woman's excellence is portrayed in terms of a narrowly circumscribed set of womanly virtues. Thus this gargantuan manuscript teems with the names and achievements of hundreds of women, mythical, allegorical and historical, whose almost infinitely proliferating individual accomplishments are made to demonstrate their shared modesty, industry, graciousness and devotion to the Virgin Mary in the figure through which she was most revered in Florentine culture, the Queen of Heaven.[8]

Bronzini's manuscript overwhelms a reader with its proliferating examples of women's excellence. The proliferating multiplicity can be easily linked to the early *seicento* literary fashion for almost infinitely elaborated texts, a fashion of which Giambattista Marino's massive romance *L'Adone* and Michelangelo Buonarroti il giovane's five day, twenty-five act dramatic work *La fiera* are perhaps the best-known examples.[9] But Bronzini's work also constitutes, I believe, an intellectual treasure that documents the Medici Regents' will to know (a will as indomitable as their better-known will to rule), their apparent conviction that a knowledge of women's history in all its multiplicity was necessary both as ground and elaboration of women's exercise of political authority, and the vastness of the women's history that was available to elite women in 1620s Florence. For these volumes show how much of the knowledge that some of us thought we had remembered only in the late twentieth century had been remembered before. Who among us would have imagined, for example, that Hildegard of Bingen's name would appear over and over in these pages, as a philosopher, theologian, physician, herbalist, poet, and, in the only allusion to what we

---

[8] On the importance of this figure of the Virgin to Florence's political mythologies, see Mary Bergstein, "Marian politics in Quattrocento Florence: the renewed dedication of Santa Maria del Fiore in 1412," *Renaissance Quarterly* 44 (1991): 673-719.

[9] The multiplicity of the manuscript's contents is matched by a multiplicity of copyists' hands so tricky as to invite intense paleographical examination. It is clear that Bronzini (or his principal copyist) had laid out frameworks for knowledge that was to be filled in later. Further, large chunks of the manuscript are in distinctive hands not his own. More often than not a single hand contributed a self-contained unit of the argument For example, the biographies of all the women singers at courts outside Florence are written in a single hand. Another hand takes up the discussion for the final biography of a singer active in Mantua, Settimia Caccini as a transition to the very long biography of her sister Francesca, and the brief mentions of such other Florentine singers as Arcangiola Palladina, Angelica Sciamerone Belli, Maria Botti, and Vittoria Archilei that follow. But even within this section there are two hands, one to copy in the texts of poetry praising these singers, and another to copy in the main narrative.) This multiplicity of hands suggests the possibility of multiple authorship, for the different hands may have belonged to research assistants, or to professional experts in various fields to whom he had in effect subcontracted the work of compiling coherently gynecentric narratives of various human activities in relation to women's virtues and achievements, as well as to copyists.

know as her compositional activity, as an inventive liturgist? Who among us would have supposed that perhaps Francesca Caccini, or Adriana Basile, or Vittoria Archilei, or Tarquinia Molza knew as much about Hildegard as do the ambitious women undergraduates some of us teach now?

Music in Bronzini's gynecentric world

On the fifteenth day of their imaginary dialogue, Bronzini's interlocutors turned the full force of their attention to the subject of music.[10] For 161 manuscript pages women's advocate Onofrio, their adversary Tolomeo, and the Mantuan matron Vittoria and the Florentine Leonora expound the state of musical knowledge as it might have circulated among the women of the Medici court. This was a population that ranged from their princess-class sisters, cousins, daughters and nieces through the paid members of their households (both noble and artisan classes) to the community of *gentildonne* the two granduchesses regularly convened in *veglie, collazione, balli,* pilgrimages to local and regional shrines, semi-religious processions through the streets of Florence for the public dowering of needy women, and hunting parties.[11] But fascinating as they are, these 161 pages are not the first time music was present in the fictional world of Bronzini's dialogue. For the whole of Bronzini's multi-volume text constructed women's world as regularly punctuated by music-making, a ground against which the conversation of his fifteenth "day" could seem to have constructed, as a complementary vision, a musical world populated almost entirely by women.

Music-making by women is present throughout Bronzini's fictional world in the dialogue genre's convention of ending each "day" with ceremonies that return the fictionally intellectualizing community to an embodied world. Bronzini's text marks that return mainly by describing communal meals – male interlocutors – and by the music-making of women. Thus the eleventh day concluded with the solo, self-accompanied song of a woman whose "magisterial notes not only astonished those who heard her with the sweetness of her voice, but made the meadows, springs and rivers respond with their own songs and murmurs," a clear effort to praise the soloist's musical power in Orphic terms.[12] The twelfth day, a Saturday that ended the dialogue's second week, ended with the group withdrawn to the *cappella* of the *palazzo* where "with infinite spiritual contentment to all, with select voices and instruments appropriate to worship they devotedly sang the litany and preces as they were sung at the Santa Casa di Loreto."[13] Here Bronzini's description resonated

---

[10] I-Fn, Magl. VIII, 1525, part 1, pp. 1-161.

[11] Many of these ceremonies of women's courtly life at Florence have been discussed by Kelley Harness in "Amazzoni di Dio: Florentine Musical Spectacle under Maria Maddalena d'Austria and Cristina di Lorena (1620-1630)," (Ph.D, diss, University of Illinois, 1996).

[12] I-Fn: Magl.VIII.1521/1, 554: "...così spiegò le maestrevole note, che non pur le genti attonite ascoltavano la dolcezza della sua voce, ma le domestiche selve d'intorno, le rispondevano; e le fonti, ed i rivoli più del suo solito, piacevolment mormorando..."

[13] I-Fn: Magl.VIII. 1522/1, 424: "...con infinite spirituale contentezza, con voci scelte ed

strongly with the musical practices of Archduchess Maria Maddalena's household, as they can be inferred from the very occasional comments by the official Tuscan court diarist Cesare Tinghi about evening offices sung by the Archduchess' *dama* under the leadership of Vittoria Archilei.[14]

Beginning with a whimsical description of the seven liberal arts as *donzelle* (maidens) and ending with a characteristic list of women worthies (scholars, poets and a few singers), that twelfth day's discussion of women's education had marked the first time Music emerged in the substance of the group's conversation. Bronzini's interlocutors had given remarkable prominence to Music as a subject worthy of women's study, and as a means of power grounded in Music's traditional position as a discipline of the mathematical arts known as the quadrivium.

While the figuring of the liberal arts as female was not at all unusual, some of the ways Bronzini characterized them in the discussions of the twelfth day would provide themes to be developed in subsequent days' descriptions of particular erudite women.[15] Grammar, for instance, was for Bronzini an invention of imperial necessity meant to allow speakers of different languages to speak through a common set of structures. But it was to his descriptions of the mathematical arts that he would allude most consistently in his subsequent discussion, three "days" later, of music and musicians. Arithmetic was a *donzella* who held miracles and marvelous secrets in her heart; among the results of her mastery of number were her understanding of the powers in the plant world (because she knew the numbers of leaves on all plants), as well mastery of time's many categories and mastery of infinite birth.[16] Geometry, by comparison, was less fecund, giving birth only to perspective; but because her special knowledge included motion, time, weight, line, surface, and depth, she had knowledge that was as important to agriculture as to painting, and mastery of instruments of that expanded human vision.[17]

The sixth liberal art was Music, figured in Bronzini's text as a girl seated on a blue sphere with a pen in her hand, her eyes fixed on a music book that rested on an anvil, a balance scale filled with iron hammers resting nearby, at her feet.[18] Bronzini's defender of women, Onofrio, interpreted the iconography of Music for his listeners: that she was seated represented music as giving rest to tired spirits; her seat on a blue sphere showed that the audible harmony of the world rested on the harmony of the heavens. Her book indicated the rule that everyone must participate in harmony, while the anvil was there to allow the possibility of writing new harmonies ("as Avicenna himself had allowed"), while the balance showed musical judgment to be based on the evidence of the ears, as justice was always based partly on the evidence of the senses.

---

instrumenti appropriati al culto Divino si cantarino devotissimamente le letanie e preci che goni sabbato e feste della Madonna si cantano nella Santa Casa di Loreto..."

[14] For one such description, see I-Fn: Ms. Gino Capponi 261, vol. II, f. 137v-138r.

[15] I-Fn: Magl. VIII, 1522/1, 12-22 covers the seven liberal arts.

[16] I-Fn: Magl. VIII, 1522/1, 17-19.

[17] I-Fn: Magl. VIII, 1522/1, 19-20.

[18] I-Fn: Magl. VIII, 1522/1, 20-22 describes Music.

More than any other maiden who embodied mathematical knowledge, the maiden who was Music seemed for Bronzini to be a figure whose mathematics could wield real-world power over others:

> By her are hearts awakened and excited in battle, and empowered to try difficult, even ferocious things. By her are spirits that have been made pensive by sadness relieved and liberated, so that they forget their usual troubles. By her, too, are devotion and a good inclination to praise and bless the sublime and glorious Creator of all awakened. By her the strength of the intellect is raised to think (knowing spiritual things) happy and higher thoughts.[19]

Music's power, for Bronzini, was exceeded only by that of Astrology, whom he described as inhabiting sublime realms where "wisdom, nature and reason" are in constant colloquy with heroic, intellectual and moral virtue, producing knowledge of great practical use to medicine, agriculture and navigation.[20]

Indeed, Bronzini's exposition of the seven liberal arts led seamlessly to a description of more practical ways to organize knowledge, in the still-female figures of ethics, politics and economics, the twelve virtues (only four of which he discusses), and finally to a fascinatingly eccentric discussion of the Muses.[21] For Bronzini the nine Muses were mediatrixes for knowledge, each representing a stage toward erudition. Clio, the Muse of history, represented the will to know, for example, while Terpsichore, the Muse of dance, was the ability to judge one's discoveries. Numerical relationships (best known to arithmeticians according to Bronzini) linked each Muse to an art form, and each particularly favored one ancient poet. For example, Calliope the Muse of voice was linked to heroic poetry, was the inventor of literature and writing, and inspired Orpheus. Erato, the inventor of Geometry, whose special gift was understanding the resemblances among knowledges, who found song delightful, and who was an inveterate transmitter of all she knew, was the muse of Sappho. Clio the historian with the will to know inspired Homer. Each Muse was, too, linked to a planet and to a virtue: Calliope was the sum of all stars, while Clio, who represented glory, fame, and the ability to learn, was linked to the moon; Terpsicore, who represented happiness and delight was linked to Mars, while Erato who represented love, likeability and the passion to invent was linked to Jupiter. Thus in Bronzini's world the nine Muses were each inventive figures through whom human arts, affects and

---

[19] I-Fn: Magl. VIII, 1522/1, 21-22: "... Per lei, sono eccitati, et svegliati i cuori nelle battaglie, et s'innaminiscano à cose difficili, e fiere. Per lei sono liberati, et rilevati gli Animi pensierosi dalla tristezza e si scordono delgi affanni consueti. Per lei, sono anco le divotione, e affettioni buone per lodate, e benedire il sublime, e glorioso Creatore del tutto. Per lei s'innalza il/22: ilvigore dell'intelletto a pensare (conoscendedno le cose spirituale) le felice, et corone."

[20] I-Fn: Magl. VIII, 1522/1, 22.

[21] I-Fn: Magl. VIII, 1522/1, 22-29 discusses the practical arts; 29-44 discusses the Muses.

cosmic forces were linked in a web of resemblances. He attributes to unnamed "ancients" the idea of conceiving these maidens' individual and collective relationships to the seven liberal arts through an image of their dancing, hand in hand – an image he said could be seen in a palace room adjacent to the garden in which his dialogue was set.

Bronzini quickly turned his discussion of the Muses to an eccentric, mythic account of the relationship between these variously gifted, benevolent, cosmically well-connected virgins and Music.[22] The nine virgin sisters, daughters of Jove and Memory, had been bought as servants by Megado, daughter of the ill-tempered, tyrannical King Macaro of Lesbos. The servant sisters had taught Megado and her long-suffering mother Music specifically how to play the *cetera* while telling stories of the ancients. Mother and daughter together by their music-making had placated Macaro's ire and restored harmony and balance to the Kingdom of Lesbos. Thereafter, Bronzini claims, the Argive word that had once meant "female servant," "musi," came to refer both to these female figures with power over the knowledges in the web of resemblance, and to the medium through which their gifts emerged as power in the world: that is, to Music. An astonishing tale of Music as a medium through which virtuous women of both servant and sovereign classes could engage successfully with patriarchal tyranny, Bronzini's account of the Muses is followed immediately by some of the most conventional Classical myths about musical power. In context, Bronzini could be taken to imply that women like the first muses and their patrons had access to the kinds of musical power to which the cited myths allude. While twenty-first century readers are most likely to recognize and focus on the familiar tale of Orpheus' song moving stones and fields to follow him, or of Hercules' tongue trailing gold and silver chains by which he led great crowds behind him by the ears, the myth to which Bronzini gave pride of place, and that would recur at least four times on the "day" devoted wholly to discussion of music, is the myth of Anfione, who:

> with his soft melody and music drew stones to him, and, mixing them together into form, built the walls of Thebes, which cannot mean other than that he, with his prudence and eloquence could lead men of this region who lived dispersed in fields and meadows toward living civilly together in the same city.[23]

Thus long before the fifteenth "day," Bronzini's text had envisioned music as a kind of knowledge embodied in female form that servant and sovereign women alike could use to intervene benevolently in human souls and political relationships.

On the fifteenth "day," the discussion in Bronzini's Medici Palace garden focused

---

[22] I-Fn: Magl. VIII, 1522/1, 43-44.

[23] I-Fn: Magl. VIII, 1522/1, 48: "...Anfione, con sua dolce melodia e Musica, tirava à se le pietre, e quelle fece in forma accozzare, siche fecero le mure di Tebe; il che altro non significa se non che egli con la sua prudenza, e soavissima eloquenza, potè condurre gli huomini di quella Religione, che habitavano sparsi pe' campi et per le selve ad habitare civilmente in una medesima città..."

entirely on music and painting as arts in which women, especially contemporary women, excelled.[24] As he had done in earlier volumes devoted to other human activities, Bronzini constructed a musical world made almost entirely of women: the only men mentioned are fathers, husbands, mythological figures or Classical authorities. Thus his narrative evokes a musical world as it might have been experienced by women who encountered everyday music-making primarily amid their gynecentric, "domestic" world. Populated exclusively by women musicians and their women patrons (most of them living) whose performances are either of chamber music, devotional music made at home among groups like those who populate the dialogue's fictional world, or in convents, the musical world of Bronzini's text is so pervasively strange as to make his narrative seem like a report from a parallel universe – a universe parallel to the world of "early modern music" most of us know from the standard histories, based on the standard sources.

Bronzini's story entirely fails to mention the sweeping revolution in musical style, aesthetics and taste we associate with early '600 Florence because of the self-promoting writings of Vincenzo Galilei, Giovanni Bardi, Giulio Caccini, Marco da Gagliano and Jacopo Peri, and the subsequently canonizing writings of Piero Bardi, Giovanni Battista Doni, Vincenzo Giustiniani, Severo Bonini and Pietro delle Valle. He all but entirely eliminates the emerging concept of the work (by which Caccini, Peri, Bonini and delle Valle had all made arguments that came eventually to construct part of the early music canon), and thus all but entirely eliminates the importance of musicians' engagement with print culture and with that familiar instrument late twentieth century feminists so convincingly linked to phallic fantasies of power, the *pen*.[25] A reader might reasonably infer that in the gynecentric, multi-vocal musical world Bronzini meant to describe music-making, musical excellence, and the exercise of musical power as primarily oral and somatic practices. Further, a reader might infer that neither the "new music/second practice" story nor the "birth of opera" story that were so important to the men whose writings have defined our knowledge of the era were important to contemporary women. For Bronzini not only fails entirely to mention the works and authors that constituted these stories, he also entirely fails so much as to mention the central aesthetic imperative that linked the two – humanistic debates over the proper relationship among words, tones, and rhythms in the most privileged kind of music (because the most rational), song. Indeed, Bronzini never once mentions the linguistic component of a woman's music-making, although he praises the multilingual virtuosity and literary acumen of certain women, notably the humanistically educated Tarquinia Molza and Francesca Caccini. Moreover, perhaps because he was so little interested in contemporary claims that music's power properly lay in its expression of a verbal text, Bronzini never mentions contemporary arguments about dissonance practice. Thus none of the women who formed part of his

---

[24] I-Fn: Magl. VIII, 1525/1, headed "Settimana Terza, Giornata Decimaquinta nella quale ragionano le medesime personae delle giornate antecendenti" is the fifteenth day.

[25] The exceptions are Maddalena Casulana, Vittoria Aleotti, and Francesca Caccini, whose printed collections of music Bronzini or his research assistants had clearly examined.

articulation of a gynecentric musical culture, no matter how powerful her music-making, could be caught in the rhetorical trap of the *sfacciata meretrice*, the image by which Giovanna Maria Artusi, at least, had dismissed dissonant, sonically disorderly song as like the socially disorderly, deceptive and illicit female sexuality of a painted whore.[26]

If Bronzini's gynecentric vision of music and musical behaviors in relation to the world avoids almost every trope familiar to us from several centuries of convention-ridden music histories, how is his gynecentric musical world constructed? Literally, the musical world of Bronzini's fifteenth "day" emerges as a fiction woven of diverse conversational threads. An opening claim that women's voices reveal the beauties of their souls more fully than could any art appealing to human eyes, a recurring affirmation that the first purpose of music-making is divine praise, and a conclusion that women's music-making is "the most welcome and perfect Harmony that can be heard" frame biographical sketches of sixty-three mostly living women who excelled at music: poems praising their performances, scraps of mythological, literary and philosophical debates about music's perils and powers drawn from Classical and Patristic sources, and brief explanations of musical modes as mechanisms of power. These heterogeneous bits seem as if patched into a fabric that continually returns to certain notions of praiseworthy womanhood that pervade the entire, twenty-four "day" dialogue. Like every other human activity to which Bronzini's text grants women full access, music-making enabled women to avoid the perils of idleness, to perform both modesty and social grace, and to focus the desires of their souls toward praise of the "Universal Creator," and of the Virgin as Queen of Heaven. Bronzini's rhetoric as he describes women musicians ensures that as a group they will be perceived to lead their listeners from lower to higher states of consciousness while they themselves seem to perform undeniable signs of the pre-eminent female virtue, modesty.

Given late twentieth-century notions of early modern women's musicalities, it is at first surprising that nearly half of the sixty-three biographical sketches begin by praising a woman's instrumental prowess, usually focusing on the delicacy and speed with which her hands touched the instruments she is known to have played. If she played more than one instrument, they are likely to be listed in an order that gradually becomes perceptible to the reader: keyboards (organ, cembalo, arpicordo) are followed by plucked-string instruments (lute, theorbo, chitarra), then by bowed strings (lira arciviolata, other viols, once a violin). The harp might come before this order of

---

[26] See Giovanni Maria Artusi, *Seconda parte dell'Artusi, overo delle imperfettioni della moderna musica* (Venice: Giacomo Vincenti, 1603), 38. For discussion of the gender rhetoric that pervades the exchange known as the Monteverdi-Artusi debate, see my "Gendering Modern Music: Thoughts on the Monteverdi-Artusi Controversy," *Journal of the American Musicological Society* 46 (1993): 1-25; Charles S. Brauner, "Communication," *Journal of the American Musicological Society* 47 (1994): 550-554 ; and my "New Musicology as a Second Practice: a reply to Charles S. Brauner," *Journal of the American Musicological Society*, 47 (1994): 554-563.

gender-appropriate instruments, or at the end of it; trombones and cornetti are mentioned only once, as among the instruments played by the women musicians at Ferrara. Descriptions of a woman's vocal performances follows as relevant. Bronzini's prose thus leads his reader's imagination over and over again from the virtuosity of a woman's hands toward the virtuosity of her throat and mouth. Following the path of neo-Platonist love theory from lower to higher beauties, Bronzini's descriptions also imply the movement of musically attentive ears from the harmonies (and formal structures) a woman's musical hands would produce as she played the gender-appropriate instruments of self-accompaniment toward the presumably texted melodies formed by her throat and mouth. Over and over, the trajectory of description leads from what he calls "the silent speech of the hand" toward the sung speech of the mouth, the privileged register of rational eloquence that much prescriptive culture made problematic for women.[27]

While Bronzini's text implies the conventional view that song, because linked to language, is a higher form of musical art than instrumental performance, his emphasis on the instrumental prowess even of such universally acclaimed singers as Adriana Basile and Francesca Caccini suggests that a remarkably subtle negotiation of the problem of women's eloquence characterized his gynecentric musical world. Because not all women performers whom Bronzini chose to praise were singers, while all apparently did perform on instruments, women's musicality was made to seem grounded in the wordless eloquence of bodily performance rather than in a word-dominated conception of music-making. Song seems, in his text, to rise from music, rather than to flow downward from language, an effect of Bronzini's rhetoric that simultaneously implies confirmation of women's supposedly greater entrapment in the materiality of embodiment and overturns the orderly hierarchy of words over music articulated by Plato in a passage from Book III of the *Republic* that circulated widely as a commonplace of early modern culture.[28] But for all that Bronzini's descriptions of women musicians' skills rework and challenge the hierarchies a twenty-first century reader might expect in early modern musical culture, the narrative trajectory of those descriptions also cleverly constructs the women's musicalities as grounded in handiwork. That is, over and over he describes women first as focused on the musical practices that an earlier writer on music-making in relation to womanhood, Annibale Guasco, had described as serving the same social function as that pastime recommended to women of all classes – the attention to needlework that kept a woman's eyes downcast, modestly avoiding the gaze of men.[29] Moreover, because

---

[27] Bronzini uses the phrase "col tacito parlar della mano" on p. 107 of I-Fn: Magl. VIII,1525/1.

[28] *The Republic of Plato*, transl. Francis M. Cornford (London: Oxford University Press, 1941), 3: 398-400, paragraphs 86-88, define *melodia* as consisting of words, tones and rhythm, of which the component that is to govern the others is the words.

[29] Annibale Guasco, *Ragionamento a d. Lavinia sua figliuola della maniera del*

Bronzini's descriptions have the effect of making song seem to emerge from a female musicality grounded in instrumental music's "silent speech," the women musicians he describes all seem to arrive at song as if from a reluctance to speak. As his biographical sketches of these women echo each other (creating something like a contrapuntal fabric of many-headed melodies), Bronzini constructs an ideal female musicality that embraces musical embodiment and overturns the usual mind-over-body, word-over-music hierarchies as strategies of modesty rather than as eruptions of sonic disorder.

A portrait of the artist as/among artistic women

At twenty-three pages, Francesca Caccini's biographical sketch is the longest Bronzini devoted to a woman musician.[30] Coming about two-fifths of the way through his discussion of Music, Bronzini's Francesca embodies synoptically, in a single *persona,* all the virtues he had elsewhere attributed to one or another of her music-making contemporaries. As a textual figure she pulls all those other descriptions into focus as contributing to a kind of composite portrait of "women musicians" built of information presented in distinct and predictable categories. Bronzini's relatively lavish attention to Caccini can be interpreted as the equivalent of his lavish attention to certain Medici princesses in the dialogue's volumes that are explicitly about politics: for Bronzini, Caccini's unusually detailed story functioned as the textual marker in his discussion of music of the Medicean greatness he had been charged by their common patrons to uphold. Even so, Bronzini's text includes biographical tidbits so personal, and so irrelevant to his book's overall project, as to lend an air of veracity to his story, as well as to have reminded courtly women readers in the late 1620s of a person they certainly knew as well as he did.[31] Perhaps the most striking such detail was Bronzini's surprisingly candid remark, overturning the usual tropes linking women's excellence to

---

governarsi ella in corte; andando per Dama (Turin: Eredi del Bevilacqua, 1586), f. 14v: "Finding yourself in the presence of your *padrona,* and also of the duke or other men of court, keep your head and your eyes on your needlework, or on your clavichord, or on your songbook...so that your eyes don't fly around the room, which would be taken as a sign of your availability as well as of flightiness..."

[30] I-Fn: Magl. VIII, 1525/1, 54-77

[31] Bronzini had known Francesca since 1616, when both served in Cardinal Carlo de'Medici's Roman household during the Cardinal's installation and possession – Bronzini as *caudatario,* or master of the Cardinal's ceremonial life, and Caccini as a chamber musician on detail from the court at Florence, along with her husband Giovanni Battista Signorini and Jacopo Peri. I-Fas: Carte Strozziane I, 13, ff. 137-150v lists the household at the time. They had served the Cardinal in Rome again in the 1623-24 winter season celebrating the election of Maffeo Barberini as Pope Urban VIII. During this second Roman sojourn, Bronzini twice mentioned Francesca's singing in letters to Dimurgo Lambardi in Florence. These letters are at I-Fas, Mediceo del Principato 3901, letter dated 28 October 1623; and I-Fas, Mediceo del Principato 3901, letter dated 24 November 1623. I am grateful to Janie Cole of the Medici Archive Project for leading me to these two letters.

physical beauty, that Francesca "was not well favored endowed by the gifts of nature." Not, then, a beautiful woman, she had not responded to her condition resentfully, but instead was "so likeable and miraculous...cheerful, gracious and sweet-mannered that everyone was drawn to her."[32] Equally interesting – indeed, tantalizing to a twenty-first century historian if not exactly relevant to the rhetorical agenda Bronzini needed her biography to serve – were his claims that Francesca had produced an exegesis of books three and four of the *Aeneid* by the age of twelve; that she had sung in Parma, Padua, Verona, Venice, and Bologna (in addition to her known performances in Paris, Rome, Turin, Milan, Genoa, and Modena); that she regularly wrote as many as twenty letters a week; that her passion for numbers extended to an extreme meticulousness in organizing her manuscripts; that as an intellectual she was most drawn to philosophy and "the occult sciences;" that she had meant to publish a second book of *musiche* but had been denied permission because the Granduchesses feared for her then-fragile health.

Most of Bronzini's account confirms "facts" about Caccini that music historians might already have known or inferred from the androcentric sources that fueled twentieth century historiography. Yet hardly any of Francesca's excellences seem, here, to be particular to her. Instead, portrayed amid a world of women musicians she seems exceptional only for her high achievement in the categories that defined contemporary norms of womanly musicality. Linguistic and mathematical erudition; spectacularly moving performances; prolific composition some of which she was able to make public through the medium of print; the ability to improvise odes and heroic verse in Latin to her own accompaniment; virtuosity on harp, harpsichord, lute, theorbo, guitar and "every sort of stringed instrument;" sensitive singing of sophisticated poetry in Latin, Italian, French, Spanish and German; skilled use of "difficult, sweet, artful *passaggi;*" the power of playing, singing, and conversation to astonish and transform the souls of her listeners; excellence in Geometry and Music ("without which nothing in the world is made"); the sharp intelligence she had shown as a girl, causing her father to ensure she was taught Latin, some Greek, literature, humanities, rhetoric, poetry, the *Poetics* of Aristotle, the arts of the quadrivium, a flawless chancellory hand; her passion for philosophy, for study of all sorts, for constantly industrious work to avoid idleness; even her "gleaming modesty and integrity;" Caccini shared each kind of achievement with several other women, each of them one parameter by which Bronzini's narrative had constructed the category of the virtuosic woman musician. Within those parameters, Bronzini's Caccini exceeds all other women he described, playing more instruments, singing in more languages, having studied a wider range of subjects with more uniform success and more intellectual passion. Indeed, Francesca is made to seem like a typical musical woman

---

[32] I-Fn, Magl. VIII, 1525/1, 56-57: "...ancorche poco venisse favorita de Doni di natura, fù ella nondimeno talmente amabile e mirabile, che non punto tediosa, non punto rincrescevole mà lieta, e graziosa, e piena di dolci e graziosissime maniere e modi à tutti si mostrava e tuttavia si mostra".

who exceeded conventional norms because she was lucky enough to have been born not beautiful, lucky enough to have born with a sharp and hungry intellect, lucky enough to have been born among the servants of a Granduchess who would channel the young polymath's intellectual energies toward musical work that served the interests of a (luckily for her) gynecentric political world. For Bronzini's account carefully reports that the young Francesca had first pursued music only as a pastime, "to please her father." Her evident musical gifts notwithstanding, in Bronzini's account Francesca seems not to have expected or intended to develop her abilities to virtuosic professional levels. She had instead emerged as a performer and composer whose work was "esteemed, sought and prized" by princes and professionals alike only after Grand Duke Ferdinand I and his wife Granduchess Christine de' Lorraine, "her most singular patron and benefactrix" had ordered her training in counterpoint.[33]

This particular construction of Francesca's professional formation emphasizes her resemblance to the courtly women who populated the fictional world of Bronzini's dialogue. The exemplary figure of a consummately skilled *virtuosa*, she thus could also serve as an exemplary figure for the erudite amateur, for Bronzini constructed Francesca as a latter-day embodiment of the aristocratic, humanistically educated lady whose gifts, when recognized, led others to grant her a social power she, in her innate modesty, would never have sought for herself. Thus Francesca's story echoed and reinforced the particular balance between high achievement and modestly invisible ambition for which Tarquinia Molza, whose biography hers most resembles, had been the exemplary figure in the discussions of the twelfth day.[34] Further, Bronzini ensured that Francesca be understood as exemplifying two kinds of social mobility. Just as her early signs of "sharp intelligence" had inspired her family to invest in her education, her servant-status dependence on the benevolence of an elite woman with political power had enabled her to move easily (and chastely) across the border that separated

---

[33] I-fn, Magl. VIII, 1525/1, 64-66: "...Il minor studio ch'ella facesse in così tenera età..era tuttavia minore quello della Musica, del Canto, e del suono, che se lo prendeva per passatempo, et per compiacerne il padre che per altro....Non fia maraviglia però, che la Cecchina riuscisse così eccellente nella Musica (poiche ordinariamente di buon seme ne suol venire/ buon frutto havendo alla dal ventre della madre recata quest'Arte, essendo che Lucia Gangoletti prima moglie dei suo padre..non meno che giulio suo Genitore, eccellentissima et veramente mirabile nel Canto...Cominciò poi questa giovane a compiacenza del Serenissimo Gran Duca Ferdinando Primo di felice ricordazione e di Madama Serenissima Gran Duchessa Cristina, ..sua signora e benefattrice singolarissima...ad applicar l'animo al contrapunto, et à passaggi, et in breve tempo essendosi impadronita dell'uno et degli altri, fece composizioni tali che da primi huomini della professione, e da Principi grandi furono poi sommamente stimate, richieste e pregiate." Bronzini's attribution of Francesca's musicality to her mother's seed is another instance of his determinedly gynecentric rhetoric. The textual closeness of that detail to his mention of the Granduchess agency in developing the fruit of that seed could be read as implying that Christine served the orphaned Francesca as a kind of substitute mother.

[34] I-Fn, Magl. VIII, 1522/1, 377-391. I am grateful to Richard Wistreich for reminding me, in conversation, that the trope of music as a pastime links both women to Castiglione's prescriptions about the role music should play in a courtier's life.

women for whom music was a pastime from women for whom music could be a technique of performative and political power. Indeed, Bronzini's construction of the relation that empowered Francesca, releasing her exceptional intellectual talent through musical work so that it became a means of wielding power, echoes his eccentric story of the Muses' relationship to patronage. For Francesca, like the muses, could be read as a hireling whose musical work in collaboration with her woman patrons changed the power relations of the state in which they found themselves.[35] Thus Bronzini ensured that the professional Francesca would be understood as a woman whose erudition, especially in mathematical arts and in their musical manifestation through the effective manipulation of the ancient modes, enabled her to do whatever she wanted with listeners, and to them:

> ...whether playing or singing or pleasantly telling stories, she worked such stupendous effect in the minds of her listeners/57 that she transformed them...we heard the marvelous lady accompany her Phrygian song with such grace, whether to the sound of the harpsichord or the lute or the theorbo and work such stupendous effects in the minds of listeners, making them seem pliant, pleasant, or wise at will that it was a wonder, and a thing in truth almost unbelievable. Whenever it suited her this same woman, no less than Anfione, and indeed, maybe even more than he, could by her singing and playing kindle astonishment and/58: boldness in the breasts of her listeners, so that they would agree to any undertaking no matter how burdensome. . .And by changing mode she changed her listeners.... she made.../59: Dorian music...with such sweetness lifting other minds to the contemplation of heavenly things, that she transformed (I almost dare say) men into gods....[while] the sound of her Lydian music took the mantle of joy away from hearts and These three *maniera* of Music (Phrygian, Dorian and Lydian), already much venerated in antiquity, were put to proper use by the excellence and good judgment of this rare woman. Our miraculous Cecchina knew not only these three *maniere* of song, but many others that created various effects/60: in human minds. Some of them pierced the rage of (listeners') hearts with the pleasure of meekness; and some moved the lascivious will of others to praiseworthy Temperance. With the soft sound of her playing and the sweetness of her song she invited every breast (even if opposed to chaste intentions) to pure self-containment and integrity, a skill for which her own modesty and integrity shone as equal to those most praised for this virtue. A few other *maniere* that she knew could bring the sick and weak of body to longed-for health and recovery of their strength.[36]

---

[35] This reading is especially salient in light of the importance Francesca herself gave to her work as a teacher, work she did amid the princesses as well as with their potential servants. Indeed, given the close parallels between the particular interests Bronzini attributes to them – geometry, song, resemblance, and pedagogy – the figure of Francesca resonates strongly with the figure of Erato, the Muse of Sappho.

[36] I-Fn, Magl. VIII, 1525/1, 56-60: "...E sempre sonando, ò cantando, ò piacevolmente favellando, oprava, ed oprà effetti di maniera stupenda negli animi degli ascoltanti/57: che gli trasmutava da quelli che erano....udimmò la maravigliosa donna accompagnare con tanta grazia, quando al suono d'un Arpicordo, quando d'un Liuto ò di una Tiorba, il suo Canto Frigio, ed operare effetti tanto stupendi agli animi degli ascoltanti, che hora pieghevoli et piacevoli, ed hora in tante altre guise gli disponeva, che era un stupore, e cosa nel vero quasi che incredibile. La stessa poi, ogni volta che à lei piaceva, cantando e sonando (non meno anzi

Echoing in its claims about her power to embolden listeners to great deeds, relieve their troubled spirits, and lift their souls toward the divine Bronzini's description of Music herself, this prolix account of Francesca's performative powers portrays her as exceeding even the art his rhetoric makes her seem to embody: for even Music did not invite her listeners to the paradigmatic female virtues of modesty and integrity. Only Francesca, of all the mythical, allegorical and historical women musicians whom Bronzini mentions, wielded such behaviorally transgendered power as to produce both masculine and feminine virtues in her listeners. Francesca's utter mastery over her listeners' minds, hearts and bodies through her apparent mastery of the ancient modes, rather than through a more conventionally praiseworthy mastery of symbolically feminine ornamentation, is quickly emphasized by Bronzini's grounding of her art in intellectual mastery of the quadrivium:

> ...it is enough to say that, being excellent in Geometry and Music she was
> excellent in all things, given that (as we have seen) nothing in the world is made
> without Geometry and Music...[37]

Bronzini's interlocutors bring up the powerful effects attributed to Dorian, Phyrgian, Lydian and other modes four more times in the course of the fifteenth day's discussion of music. Each time "the marvelous effects of these modes" are positioned in a slightly different relationship to certain other rhetorical themes: 1) the claim that Music's "first purpose" is to lead human minds and souls toward a praising relationship with the Divine;[38] 2) the claim that proper musical practices (including

---

vi è più che il famoso musico Anfione) accendeva in modo tale i petti delle genti di stupore/58: et di ardire, che ad ogni impresa (benche faticosa) si sarebbono poste...Altre volte..facendo ella sentire.../59: Musica che Dorica si noma...faceva con tal dolcezza salire le altrui menti alla contemplazione delle cose celesti, che trasformava (oso quasi per dire) gl'huomini in Dei. Della Musica Lidia...toglie in si fatta guisa i manti di letizia al cuore, et alla fronte, che solamente cinta del mesto delle malinconie, et del denso delle nubi oscure, piena rimane solamente del pianto...

Queste tre maniere di Musica (cioè Frigia, Dorica et Lidia), già molto dalla veneranda antichità poste (secondo l'occasioni) in uso, non pure da questa nostra rara donna si udivano apprese, mà in somma eccellenza, et con sommo giuditio à tempo usate. Ne solamente queste tre maniere di canti, ma molt'altre appresso eccellentissimamente la nostra mirabile Cecchina possedeva, le quali essendo varie, anco varii effetti/60: creavano nelle menti humane. Alcune delle quali piegavano l'iracondo del cuora alla piacevolezza della mansuetudine, et alcune il lascivo delle volontà d'altrui al lodato della Temperanza. Costei col soave suono de' stromenti, et col dolce del suo canto, invitava ogni petto (benche inimico di caste voglie) alla pura continenza ed honestà, per la cui virtù biancheggiava la di lei pudiciza ed honestà al pari delle più nominate in questa virtù. Alcune altre maniere ella ancora ne possedeva, che lo infermo, et il debole del languente corpo, al bramato della sanità et al fermo della gagliarda traevano..."

[37] I-Fn, Magl. VIII, 1525/1, 61: "...bastare a dirvi solamente, che essendo ella eccellentissima nella Musica, et nella Geometria, sia anco eccellentissima in ogni ocsa, posciache ... non è cosa al mondo fatta senza Geometria, et senza Musica..."

[38] I-Fn, Magl. VIII, 1525/1, 92, 135 and 161.

ubiquitous musical praises of the Divine) characterize well-ordered states;[39] 3) the story of Anfione, whose music-making drew stones together to build the city of Thebes, as the paradigmatic image of musical power;[40] and 4) the assertion that Geometry and Music, the mathematical arts of harmony and resemblance, were the means by which the world was made.[41] Although the order and density with which these strands of argument appear differs each time they cross, it is clear that each time they do they form a knot in the fabric of Bronzini's semi-fictional account of music in a gynecentric world. No matter what thread begins the knot, no matter what thread ties it up, each knot communicates clearly the idea that a musical performance grounded in the erudite and judicious use of the ancient modes could intervene powerfully in the very material of which the world was made. Intervening in other people's behaviors, preparing their souls for *virtù* and communal civic life, healing their bodies, if properly focused on directing the souls of all toward divine praise, these purely musical interventions (whether in instrumental sound or in song) would inevitably lead to civil and political order. Thus the effect of Bronzini's whole discussion of music is to claim the medium of music as a discourse of power for women which avoids the challenge to modesty that public verbal speech posed to them, and as a discourse available to both servants ("musi" in the Argive language) and to the royal women who bought their services. In this vision of a gynecentric musical world, any performer might serve her patron as the muses did the royal women of Lesbos, as Francesca Caccini did the royal women of Tuscany. Together, the women musicians and women patrons in Bronzini's gynecentric musical world could be imagined as collaborating in the establishment of a civil and political order.

Bronzini's vision of that order is best articulated in an image elaborated at almost the exact center of his discussion of music – at the point when the balance shifts from many individual women's stories toward abstract philosophical justifications of music's importance in any woman's life, drawn from both Classical and Patristic authorities. As if intending to mediate between a musical world of individually embodied women and one made of musical ideas, dialogue interlocutor Leonora comments that she and her husband had the habit of hiring musicians to come to their home to play and sing in praise of the Virgin, citing as one source of performance

---

[39] I-Fn, Magl. VIII, 1525/1, 9 and 135.

[40] I-Fn, Magl. VIII, 1525/1, 96 and 126. It is worth noting that on p. 126 the hostess in Bronzini's dialogue, Vittoria, insinuates that both Orpheus' misogyny and his sexuality might have made him an inappropriate model for musical power, for she interrupts the predictable rehearsal of his musical prowess to defend Orpheus' stoning by Thracian women "for having introduced that infamous abuse of which it is better to keep quiet than to remember it" ("...non per altro venne costui lapidato, et ucciso da quelle da Tracia se non per havere...dispregiato le Donne, nei I sagrifici di Lieo, et per haver introdotto quell'infame abuso, del quale meglio è il tacere, che il ramentarlo...")

[41] I-Fn, Magl. VIII, 1525/1, 96, which describes Geometry and Music as the means by which the harmony of the world soul is made, and 141, where Bronzini quotes almost exactly the language by which he had linked the two in Francesca's biographical sketch.

material Giovenale Ancina's 1599 collection *Tempio Armonico*.[42] A cleric among the discussants immediately praises her initiative as likely to lead to the sanctification of all in her household and predicts that:

> by such a singular and vivid example little by little other great titled ladies will be moved
> to do the same, or something similar according to their means, and thereby banish
> gambling and idleness, the plagues of Christian souls and nourishment of every evil,
> breaking away from every occasion of frivolity and vanity....thus, from this sovereign and
> princely city of Rome...[the practice] will spread to all states, from west to east and to all
> isolated lands and to cities across the sea...Such, Signora, are the rare and marvelous
> effects of the exciting sounds and song in Phrygian, and divine (sounds and song) of
> Dorian.[43]

Evoking one more time the power of the modes that was the basis for Francesca Caccini's singular music-making art, and a music-making occasion like those that characterized Archduchess Maria Maddalena's court, this passage affirms a vision of women's music-making that includes but does not privilege professionalism or virtuosity. A stirring vision of the power one elite woman's musical practice might have to organize others' behaviors toward virtue, at one level this passage shows how the activities of women patrons might replicate the power for the good that individual women musicians might wield over their listeners. These are the music-making practices in which even those of ordinary musical and intellectual gifts can share. At another level, Bronzini's vision that Leonora's private concerts in honor of the Queen of Heaven might be reproduced in other women's households throughout the known world was surely meant as an imperial vision – emblematic, perhaps, of Archduchess Maria Maddalena's literally Imperial sense of self, and her literal policy to use her

---

[42] Giovenale Ancina, *Tempio Armonico della Beatissima Virgine Maria N.S, fabricatoli per opere del R. P. Giovanela A.P. della Congregazione del Oratorio* (Rome: Mutij, 1599) [RISM 1599/6], published in partbooks, was one of the largest collection of *laude spirituali* for use by the followers of S Filippo Neri ever to be printed. It includes 128 titles in all, 35 unattributed and the rest by 38 named composers. Ancina himself composed only five of the *laude* included.

[43] I-Fn, Magl. VIII, 1525/1, 93: "...con tale singolare, e vivi esempio, si muoveranno di mano in mano altre donna grandi e titolati, inducendosi à far il medesimo, ed il simile à proporzione; e così daranno bando al gioco tanto detestato, et all'ozio peste dell'anima Christiana, e fomento d'ogni male, troncando l'occasione di molte leggerezze, e vanità, che per le case più licenziose, e larghe, communemente scorrere et in quelle finalmente annodar sogliono. Qunidi poi da questa Regia, e principal città di Roma, e capo nobilissimo di tutto l'universo si spanderà per tutti gli altri stati, e si stenderà dell'occidente all'oriente, ed a tutte l'isole terre, e città ultramarine, tal è tanta èla forza al bene de gli atti eroici, e dell'opre segnalate, che persona eminenti di facoltà, illustri di sangue, risplendenti d'honore, e di virtù maggiori, proceder si sentono, quali siete voi, e'l vostro consorte,. Eccovi, Sig.ra Leonora gli effetti rari e maravigliosi dell incitante suono, e canto della Musica Frigia, et il Divino della Dorica, citati di sopra.... "

Imperial family's connections to spread a notion of Catholicism that included a particularly Florentine cult of the Virgin as the Queen of Heaven.

From one perspective Bronzini's image is a horrifying congeries of evangelizing imperial ambition and wholly un-self-conscious elitism, representing all that makes twenty-first century people squeamish about the legacies of so-called "Western culture." Yet read in the context of the present book's many-headed melodies, it strikes me as also a pleasing image from early modern Europe of gynecentric music-making proliferating across the Mediterranean, gynecentric music-making that praises a gynecentric utopia in which women's musical and political power could be imagined to temper the harshness of masculine tyranny over both, and could be imagined as sending forth many-headed melodies of celebration and praise to heal the silencing wounds for which Medusa's many-headed sisters wept. However disturbing the image of many-headed melodies might be (reminding us, as it does, of the misogynist Orpheus' dismembered, singing body parts floating off Lesbos' shore), Bronzini's text makes his version of the image literally fabulous, linking the proliferation of women-sponsored sacred concerts to the multiplicity of women musicians whose tales he told, and to the multiplicity by which their foremothers, the Argive "musi," had managed the web of mathematically-constructed resemblances that made the world. Bronzini's is an image of cultural reproduction that gently evokes the idea of an empire born not of violence but of miraculously multiplying moments of woman-born song. Born as if parthenogenically of women's modest and pious desire to praise the creative power and sovereignty of the Queen of Heaven, these moments promise to bring order and stability to a troubled world; it is a vision that intentionally outshines even the performative power Bronzini attributed to Francesca Caccini's formidable erudition. In the context of Bronzini's whole, his spectacularly prolix twenty-five volume text praising women, it seems, too, is a vision of non-violent civic order born of women's desire to know each other's histories – a desire shared by the many readers and writers of this book. [44]

---

[44] Early versions of this essay were presented as a colloquia at Stony Brook University, and before the merged musicology seminars of the Åbo Akademie and the University of Turku in Turku, Finland. I am grateful for the very helpful comments on the substance of this essay offered by Amy Brosius, Janie Cole, Jessica Courtier, Bonnie Gordon, Sarah Fuller, Kelley Harness, Margaret McFadden, Pirkko Moisala, Martha Mockus, Anne Sivuoja-Gunaratnam, Annie Janeiro Randall, Richard Wistreich and Elizabeth Wood. I particularly thank Bridget Kelly Black for her characteristic wisdom and quiet patience toward me as I worked, and I dedicate the essay to her memory.

Index